INDUSTRIAL RELATIONS IN AUSTRALIA

INDUSTRIAL RELATIONS IN AUSTRALIA

DEVELOPMENT, LAW AND OPERATION

CAROL B. FOX
WILLIAM A. HOWARD
MARILYN J. PITTARD

Longman Australia Pty Ltd
Longman House
Kings Gardens
95 Coventry Street
Melbourne 3205 Australia

Offices in Sydney, Brisbane, Adelaide, Perth, and associated companies throughout the world.

Copyright © Longman Australia Pty Ltd
First published 1995

All rights reserved. Except under the conditions described in the Copyright Act 1968 of Australia and subsequent amendments, no part of this publication may be reproduced, stored in a retrieval system or transmitted in any form or by any means, electronic, mechanical, photocopying, recording or otherwise, without the prior permission of the copyright owner.

© Commonwealth of Australia 1995

All legislation herein is reproduced by permission but does not purport to be the official or authorised version. It is subject to Commonwealth of Australia copyright. The copyright Act 1968 permits certain reproduction and publication of Commonwealth legislation. In particular. s.182A of the Act enables a complete copy to be made by or on behalf of a particular person. For reproduction or publication beyond that permitted by the Act, permission should be sought in writing from the Australian Government Publishing Service. Requests in the first instance should be addressed to the Manager, Commonwealth Information Services, Australian Government Publishing Service, GPO Box 84, Canberra, ACT 2601.

Cover designed by Perdita Nance
Indexed by Russell Brooks
Typeset by Done To Perfection
Set in Palatino 10/12pt
Produced by Longman Australia Pty Ltd
Printed in Australia

National Library of Australia
Cataloguing-in-Publication data

Fox, Carol (Carol Browyn)
   Industrial Relations in Australia

   Includes index.
   ISBN 0582 871190

   1. Industrial relations — Australia. 2. Industrial relations — Law and legislation — Australia.
   I. Howard, W.A. (William Anthony), 1930– . II. Pittard, Marilyn J. (Marilyn Jane). III. Title.

331.0994

Contents

Figures	xi
Tables	xi
Abbreviations	xv
Foreword	xvii
Acknowledgements	xix
Preface	xx

Chapter 1 The nature of industrial/employee relations 1
What's in a name? 2
Analytical methods 3
The emergence of industrial relations 4
The contract of employment 6
Participants in the process 9

Chapter 2 Approaches to industrial relations 13
Dunlop 14
Walker 23
Flanders 23
Marx 24
Braverman 25
Kochan, Katz and McKersie 28

Chapter 3 Industrial conflict and industrial action 36
Manifestations of industrial conflict 37
Causes of industrial conflict 40
Unions and industrial conflict 44
Industrial action 46
• purposes of industrial action 47
• political strikes 49
Measures of industrial conflict 50
• Australian strike statistics 50
• the Australian Workplace Survey 59
• strike statistic: International comparisons 60
Functions of industrial conflict 62
Industrial conflict and absenteeism: comparative costs 64

Chapter 4 Major disputes: case studies 75
Broken Hill strike (1919-20) 76
Metal trades work value case (1967-68) 81

Mudginberri dispute (1985) 83
Victorian nurses' strike (1986) 86
Air pilots' dispute (1989) 90

Chapter 5 Conflict and control: industrial action and the law 96

The right to strike 97
- a matter of law 97
- a matter of practice 99
- sources of controls and sanctions 99

Control at common law of industrial action 100
- the individual worker: breach of the contract of employment 100
- liability in tort law 101

Secondary boycott legislation 108
- Trade Practices Act 108
- relationship between Industrial Relations Act and Trade Practices legislation 113
- reform 114
- state secondary boycott laws 114

Sanctions under industrial relations legislation 115
- breach of award 115
- cancellation of awards and stand-downs 116
- deregistration of unions 116
- statutory offenses 117

Other legislative controls 117

Chapter 6 Trade unions: objectives and strategies 124

Theories of unionism 125
Unions as institutions 136
Unions in Australia 137
- historical background 137
- objectives 142
- strategies 150
- contemporary behaviour 157

Chapter 7 Trade unions: membership and structure 169

Union growth 170
Union density 172
Patterns of organisation 177
Union mergers 181

Chapter 8 Trade union democracy 202

The case for democracy 203
The requirements for democracy 207
The feasibility of democracy 209

Legal regulation in Australia	215
• history	215
• current provisions	219
• amalgamation and rationalisation	224

Chapter 9 Management: theories and concepts   237

The functions of management	238
• management as 'co-ordination of bargains'	238
• management as 'control of the labour process'	240
Frames of reference (ideology)	242
• unitary frame of reference	243
• pluralist frame of reference	243
Management style	245
Management strategic choice	249
• stregic choice: a critique	253
• strategy: a conceptual refinement	255
Management strategy: alternative approaches	256
• strategy: an overview	258
Management structure	259
Employee participation in management	263
• theories of participation	263
• employee participation and industrial democracy	265
• employee participation: management motives	268

Chapter 10 Management in Australia   277

Ideology	278
Aspects of individualism and collectivism	282
• steel industry	284
Strategies	287
• metal and engineering industry	287
• mining industry	292
• communications industry	296
• small business survey	298
Structure	301
Recent developments: the North American influence	303
Employee participation in management	305
• management prerogatives and arbitration	305
• case studies	309

Chapter 11 Employer associations   321

Origins and development	323
Ideology	326
Functions	329
• collective bargaining	329
• specialised services	333

- relations with the state 340
- media and public relations 343
Membership and structure 344
Internal government 351

Chapter 12 Federal labour law 368

Constitutional power 369
Other constitutional heads of power 371
- trade and commerce power 371
- the corporations power 371
- the external affairs power 372
- the defence power 372
- the public service 372
- the Territories power 373
- the 'incidentals' power 373
Commonwealth law regulating industrial relations 373
Institutions 374
The power of the Australian Industrial Relations Commission 376
- industrial disputes 377
- the question of the matter in dispute 378
- the requirement that a dispute 'extend beyond the limits of any one state' 380
- the question of parties 381
- ambit of the award 383
Conciliation and arbitration: legal procedures 384
The award 385
Agreements 385
Enforcement of awards and agreements 388
Interaction of contract and award 388
Awards and collective bargaining 389
National wage cases 390
Registration of associations 391

Chapter 13 Legal Regulation of State systems 410

State industrial regulation 411
Institutions and jurisdictions 411
- New South Wales 411
- South Australia 415
- Tasmania 416
- Queensland 417
- Western Australia 418
Role of state tribunals in unfair dismissal 420
Union registration and legal status 422
- effect of registration and legal status 422
- the problem of dual registration 423

- possible solutions 425
- Awards and agreements 426
- workplace agreements in Western Australia 427
- unions and agreements 428
- Deregulation of labour law: the Victorian example 429
- employment agreements 430
- awards: voluntary arbitration 433
- award enforcement 434
- unfair dismissals 435
- institutions in Victorian industrial law 436
- industrial action 437
- secret ballots 438
- Victoria: concluding comments 438
- Dominance of the federal system and co-operation between federal and state systems 438

Chapter 14   Workplace safety and equity   444

- Workplace health and safety 446
- workplace safety: an industrial relations issue 446
- problems for federal jurisdiction and safety issues 447
- standard setting and the Australian Commission 448
- safety standards by legislative prescription 451
- Workplace Equity: discrimination and equal opportunity 456
- Industrial awards, agreements and equity 459
- wages 459
- parental leave 460
- discrimination and dismissals 460

Chapter 15   Conciliation and arbitration   473

- Development of the federal system 476
- The Australian Industrial Relations Commission: function and operation 477
- The process of conciliation and arbitration 482
- conciliation vs arbitration 482
- conciliation 483
- arbitration 485
- compulsion and compliance 488
- government intervention: formal and informal 492
- voluntary conciliation and arbitration 493
- relationship between conciliation, arbitration and collective bargaining 495
- Arbitrated awards: a critique 496
- 'floor' of rights 496
- coverage and structure 498
- centralism reconsidered 499

Chapter 16 Arbitration and economics   510

Equal pay   514
Wage determination   516
- basic wage and margin adjustments   517
- the total wage 1967   518
- work value inquiries   518
- productivity and wages: the *GMH* and *Oil Industry* cases   521
- wage indexation   523
The ALP-ACTU Prices and Incomes Accord   526
Progress of the Accords   529

Chapter 17 Collective bargaining   542

Nature of collective bargaining   543
- distinguishing features   543
- government involvement   544
- necessary conditions   545
- bargaining power   546
The technique of collective bargaining   551
The negotiation process: a behavioural approach   555
Collective bargaining in Australia   558
- hybrid processes   558
- distinguishing characteristics   560
- collective bargaining and public policy   564
- union purpose and collective bargaining   565
- grievance procedures   568
- bargaining and arbitration: consequences of co-existence   573
- recent developments: the Industrial Relations Reform Act 1993   575

Chapter 18 Enterprise bargaining: origins, techniques and applications   582

Enterprise bargaining and productivity   583
Origins of enterprise bargaining: a conventional model   584
- productivity bargaining: distinguishing characteristics   584
- necessary conditions   586
Productivity bargaining at enterprise level: a case study   589
- Fawley: the 1960 agreements   589
- Fawley: the 1960s to the 1980s   593
Enterprise bargaining in Australia   599
- early attempts   599
- wages policy and the evolution to enterprise bargaining   604
- the conventional model and the Australian case distinguished   624

Figures and Tables

Figures

2.1	General framework for analysing industrial relations issues	30
3.1	Causes of temporary on-approved work absence	67
3.2	Estimate of temporary non-approve work absence, Australia, 1977	68
3.3	Average rate of absenteeism (percentage of employees absent in one week), by employment size and by sector, 1989(AWIRS)	69
4.1	Percival Brookfield: radical rebel, improbable peacemaker	78
5.1	*Air Pilots'* case; interference with contractual relations	103
5.2	Mudginberri dispute; picket and breach of s. 45D Trade Practices Act	110
9.1	Management styles: the interconnections between individualism and collectivism	247
9.2	Employee participation and industrial democracy: a typology	267
15.1	The process of conciliation and arbitration: federal jurisdiction	486

Tables

3.1	APPM Burnie dispute 1992: picket line	39
3.2	Political strikes: issues	49
3.3	Industrial disputes: ABS definition	51
3.4	Industrial disputes by incidence, employees involved and working days lost, Australia, 1981-1992	52
3.5	Industrial disputes by duration, Australia, 1981-1992 (percentages)	53
3.6	Industrial disputes by cause, Australia, 1981-1992 (percentages)	55
3.7	Industrial disputes: working days lost by cause, Australia, 1981-1992 (percentages)	55
3.8	Working days lost per thousand employees by industry, Australia, 1981-1992	57
3.9	Industrial disputes by method of settlement, Australia, 1981-1992 (percentages)	58
3.10	Types of industrial action by sector (AWIRS)	59
3.11	Frequency of types of industrial action by employment size and by sector (AWIRS)	60
3.12	Combinations of industrial action (AWIRS)	61
3.13	Industrial disputes, working days lost per thousand employees, selected countries, 1980-1990	63
3.14	Absenteeism: Victorian Public Transport Corporation 1991	66
4.1	The last great conflict	79
4.2	Metal trades work value case: pronouncement by Conciliation and Arbitration Commission, 21 February 1968	84
4.3	Perspectives on nurses' industrial action: Victoria, 1986	88
4.4	Air Pilots' dispute (1989): major actions by employers, federal government and ACTU	92
5.1	Summary of main legal events in Mudginberri dispute	111
6.1	Union strategies: a model	131
6.2	Government policy toward trade unions	134

6.3	Government policy toward trade unions	134
6.4	Trade unions: institutional objectives	136
6.5	Union objects: Metals and Engineering Workers' Union	147
6.6	Union objects: Australian Nursing Federation	149
6.7	Metals and Engineering Workers' Union: policies (1992)	167
7.1	Union density Australia: 1971 to 1992 (Union collection) (percentages)	173
7.2	Union density Australia (ABS surveys) (percentages)	174
7.3	Union density Australia by occupation and gender, August 1992 (ABS survey) (percentages)	175
7.4	Union density Australia: public sector and private sector (ABS surveys) (percentages)	175
7.5	Union density Australia by size of location (ABS surveys) (percentages)	176
7.6	Union density Australia by State (ABS surveys) (percentages)	176
7.7	ACTU recruitment strategy for young employees	178
7.8	Trade unions Australia: number of unions by size of union, 1986 and 1992	181
7.9	Industrial unionism, ACTU Constitution May 1927	182
7.10	Some views on union mergers and industry unions, 1982	184
7.11	ACTU: proposed industry groupings 1987 (Draft program for amalgamation)	186
7.12	Union rationalisation: ACTU categories 1991	190
7.13	Number of unions, Australia 1986-1992	193
7.14	Union amalgamations Australia: federal jurisdiction, January 1992-June 1993	199
8.1	Rank and file legal challenge to disciplinary action: an illustration	217
8.2	Examples of union rules relating to election campaigns	222
8.3	Union staff appointments: external influences	229
8.4	Provisions of the *Industrial Relations Act* (Commonwealth) relevant to union democracy	234
9.1	Unitary ideology: the benefits for managers	244
9.2	Three levels of industrial relations activity	250
9.3	Advantages of the three-tier institutional framework	252
9.4	Management employee relations/industrial relations strategy: 'third order' critical choices	255
9.5	Alternative approaches to management industrial relations strategy	257
9.6	Theories of employee participation: categories	263
9.7	Theories of employee participation: core assertions	264
9.8	Forms of worker participation by level	267
10.1	Management frames of reference	278
10.2	Managers' attitudes to trade unions (percentages) n = 1383	279
10.3	Industrial relations vs. employee relations: Business Council of Australia perspective	281
10.4	Management approach to industrial relations/human resources management: ICI Australia Limited, 1992	283
10.5	Corporate strategy and industrial relations management: ICI Australia Limited, 1992	284
10.6	Management strategic choices: metal and engineering industry case studies	288
10.7	Plant (establishment) characteristics: metal and engineering industry case studies	289
10.8	Professionalisation of industrial relations management: metal and engineering industry case studies	290

10.9	Industrial relations strategies: Hamersley Iron Pty Ltd, 1981-1990	295
10.10	Award restructuring: Hamersley Iron Pty Ltd, 1986-1987	296
10.11	Interview with George Webster, Director, Human Resources, Optus Communications, 29 June 1994	297
10.12	Barriers to labour process changes: Small Business Survey (ACCIS), 1992	299
10.13	Award coverage preferred framework for determining wages and conditions: Small Business Survey (ACCIS), 1992	300
10.14	Who decides industrial relations issues (AWIRS)	300
10.15	Management rights and job control: federal tribunal views	308
10.16	Management views concerning joint consultation processes: Qantas and Telecom	313
11.1	Employer objectives in establishing organisations to represent their collective interests	323
11.2	Illustrations of industrial relations policy objectives: Confederation of Australian Industry, 1991	328
11.3	Functions of employer associations	330
11.4	Employer representation: *National Wage* case, April 1991	333
11.5	Interview with Roger Boland, Director, Industrial Relations, Metal Trades Industry Association, 3rd August 1993	337
11.6	Types of employer association services used (AWIRS)	341
11.7	Employer associations: organising principles	348
11.8	Employer associations: internal government structure	352
11.9	Extent to which member workplaces follow advice of employer associations on workplace issues (AWIRS)	357
11.10	Enterprise bargaining in the metal and engineering industry 1991-1993: the MTIA view	363
11.11	Business Council of Australia: Council Membership 1992	365
11.12	Australian Chamber of Commerce and Industry: Member Organisations 1992	366
11.13	Extract from ACM *Bulletin*	367
12	Appendix A Contents of Nurses (Victorian Health Services) Award 1992 (edited)	398
13.1	Coverage of workers by State awards, and also by breakdown of male/female workers	412
14.1	Conditions in the mines late 19th century	452
14.2	Employers' reactions to proposed safety legislation 1984, Victoria	457
14.3	New South Wales: employment complaints	463
14.4	Grounds of discrimination prohibited in legislation	464
14.5	Handling complaints of discrimination in New South Wales	466
14.6	Equal opportunity and affirmative action: ACTU policies	467
15.1	Australian Industrial Relations Commission: industry panels as at 30 June 1993	480
15.2	Characteristics of identified arbitration types	488
15.3	Government intervention: 1992 APPM (Burnie) dispute	493
15.4	Enterprise bargaining as proposed in Accord Mark 6	499
15.5	Government intervention: 1994 waterfront dispute	507
15.6	Major awards: Australia, May 1990	508
16.1	Overaward payments by occupational group and gender 1991	515
16.2	Percentage wage-differentials between female and male adult minimum legal total wages by occupation groups 1969	516
16.3	Extent of wage increases, 1971 to 1975	524
16.4	The Accord: before the 1993 election	527

16.5	Accord Mark 7: objectives concerning arbitration and bargaining	534
16.6	The Accord: ten years later	537
17.1	Factors affecting bargaining power	548
17.2	Bargaining power: the 1986 nurses' strike	549
17.3	Incidence of formal grievance/dispute settlement procedures by industry and employment size (AWIRS)	569
17.4	Reasons for introducing a formal grievance or dispute settlement procedure by industry (AWIRS)	570
17.5	Frequency of grievance procedure use by industry (AWIRS)	571
18.1	Main features of the 1960 Fawley productivity agreements: the 'craf' Blue Book and the 'TGWU' Blue Book	594
18.2	Management strategy: the influence of political factors	597
18.3	Federal tribunal exclusion of productivity bargaining, 1983	605
18.4	Federal tribunal policy objectives: March 1987 to October 1991	607
18.5	Restructuring and Efficiency Principle, March 1987	609
18.6	Internal labour market flexibility criteria	611
18.7	Structural Efficiency Principle, August 1988	612
18.8	Possible changes to working patterns and arrangements identified by the Australian Industrial Relations Commission, August 1989	614
18.9	Structural Efficiency Principle, April 1991	615
18.10	Award modernisation clause-an example	617
18.11	Enterprise Bargaining Principle, October 1991	619
18.12	Enterprise Awards Principle, October 1993	622
18.13	Differences between Enterprise Bargaining Principle (October 1991) and Enterprise Awards Principle (October 1993)	623
18.14	Restructuring and Efficiency Principle: a case of non-compliance?	627

Abbreviations

ABEU	Australian Bank Employees Union
AC	Appeal Cases
ACAC	Australian Conciliation and Arbitration Commission
ACM	Australian Chamber of Manufactures
ACOA	Administrative and Clerical Officers' Association Australian Government Employment
ACTU	Australian Council of Trade Unions
AEU	Amalgamated Engineering Union
AIEV	The Australian Insurance Employees' Union
AIRC	Australian Industrial Relations Commission
ALHMWU	Australian Liquor, Hospitality & Miscellaneous Workers Union
ALJR	Australian Law Journal Reports
ALR	Australian Law Reports
AMEU	Automotive, Metals and Engineering Union
AMFSU	Amalgamated Metalworkers, Foundry and Shipwrights' Union
AMIEU	Australasian Meat Industry Employees Union
AMWU	Amalgamated Metal Workers Union
APESA	Association of Professional Engineers and Scientists, Australia
APSA	The Association of Professional Scientists of Australia
APSF	Australian Public Service Federation
APTU	Australian Postal and Telecommunications Union
ARU	Australian Railways Union
ATEA	Australian Telecommunications Employees' Association
AWU	Australian Workers Union
BCA	Business Council of Australia
BWIU	The Building Workers' Industrial Union of Australia
CAI	Confederation of Australian Industry
CAR	Commonwealth Arbitration Reports
CBOA	Commonwealth Bank Officers' Association
CCCA	Commonwealth Court of Conciliation and Arbitration
CFMEU	Construction, Forestry and Mining Employees Union
Ch	Chancery (English reports)
CLJ	Cambridge Law Journal
CLR	Commonwealth Law Reports
EPU	Electrical, Electronics, Plumbing and Allied Workers Union
ER	English Reports
ETU	Electrical Trades Union
FCR	Federal Court Reports
FEDFA	Federated Engine Drivers and Firemen's Association
FIMEE	Federation of Industrial, Manufacturing and Engineering Employees
FLAIEU	Federated Liquor and Allied Industries Employees Union of Australia
FLR	Federal Law Reports
FMWU	Federated Miscellaneous Workers Union
FSPU	Federated Storemen and Packers' Union
HEF	The Hospital Employees Federation of Australia

HREA	The Health and Research Employees' Association of Australia
ILO	International Labour Organisation
IR	Industrial Reports
MEU	Municipal Employees' Union
MEWU	Metals and Engineering Workers Union
MLR	Modern Law Review
MOA	The Municipal Officers' Association of Australia
MTIA	Metal Trades Industry Association
NTR	Northern Territory Reports
NSWLR	New South Wales Law Reports
NUW	National Union of Workers
POA	Professional Officers Association, Australian Public Service
PPWFA	Pulp and Paper Workers Federation of Australia
QB	Queen's Bench (English reports)
RANF	Royal Australian Nursing Federation
SASR	South Australian State Reports
TGWU	Transport and General Workers' Union
TWU	Transport Workers' Union
VECCI	Victorian Employers' Chamber of Commerce and Industry
VR	Victorian Reports
VTHC	Victorian Trades Hall Council
WWF	Waterside Workers' Federation

Foreword

There can be little doubt that the past decade has witnessed some of the most significant changes in Australian industrial relations since the turn of the century. The changes were brought about by a number of factors including turbulence in the Australian economy, a reduction in long-established tariff protection, the decline of unionisation (especially in the private sector), decentralisation of the wage determination system, and a trend towards enterprise based bargaining. While high levels of unemployment have caused major social dislocation and weakened the bargaining power of unions, other changes have also altered the nature and organisation of work.

New technology has eliminated many former areas of employment and raised the levels of skills required both for those jobs which remain and new ones which have been created. Often there is a lag before sufficient workers are trained in new skills and many of those workers who have been displaced find it difficult to meet the new requirements. Award restructuring has sought to address some of these problems by giving high priority to skills development. However, changes in the industrial relations agenda have placed great pressure on the existing industrial relations institutions, such as the tribunals, which have found it difficult to adjust to the new environment.

The nature of employment has also been changing. While the numbers of part-time jobs have grown, partly in response to the new requirements by employers, full-time employment has declined. Although industrial disputation has fallen to record low levels, unions have been able to exercise little bargaining power and have tended to concentrate on preserving jobs rather than seeking higher pay and conditions.

Industrial relations has not only been a major focus of public policy and debate in recent times, but it has also come of age as an academic field of study. There has been a burgeoning literature on industrial relations with new journals being established and many more books being written as programs of studies at schools and universities have expanded. Related fields such as human resource management and organisational behaviour have also emerged as rivals to industrial relations, giving greater emphasis to behavioural aspects of work and organisational life. Some commentators have dismissed industrial relations as an old and declining paradigm while others, such as the authors of this book, have sought to define the field in a broader way.

This book reflects the growing diversity of issues which are of concern to scholars and practitioners in the industrial relations field. These include areas of perennial interest, such as the role of conciliation and arbitration, relationships between the unions and employers, strikes and conflict. However, the authors also examine newer issues such as enterprise bargaining and discrimination in employment. A major strength of the book is its thorough analysis of legal aspects of the employment relationship.

The authors have adopted a genuinely interdisciplinary approach, integrating aspects of economics, law, political science and sociology in their analysis of the field. They have also included several case studies from various industries to illustrate the dynamics of industrial relations. The authors are to be commended for developing an original and challenging approach to the subject. The book deserves to be widely read.

Russell Lansbury
Professor of Industrial Relations
University of Sydney

Acknowledgements

We are grateful to the following for permission to reproduce copyright material: AGPS, reproduced by permission of Commonwealth of Australia copyright:
Tables 13.1 (p. 412) and 15.6 (pp. 508-9) from ABS Cat No. 6315.0, May 1990; Tables 3.13 (p. 63), 15.6 (pp. 508-9), 16.1 (p. 515) and 16.3 (p. 524) from miscellaneous ABS Statistics; Table 15.1 (pp. 480-1) from *Australian Industrial Relations Commission Annual Report 1992-93*; Table 10.15 (p. 308-9) from 122 *CAR* 339 at 344-345; Tables 3.9 (p. 58), 3.3 (p. 51), 3.4 (p. 52), 3.5 (p. 53), 3.6 (p. 55), 3.7 (p. 55) and 3.8 (p. 57) from *Industrial Disputes Australia*, Cat No. 6322.0; Table 8.4 (pp. 234-6) from *Industrial Relations Act 1988*;
Figure 3.3 (p. 69), Tables 3.10 (p. 59), 3.11 (p. 60), 3.12 (p. 61) 10.14 (p. 300), 11.6 (p. 341), 11.9 (p. 357), 17.3 (p. 569), 17.4 (p. 570) and 17.5 (p. 571) from *Industrial Relations at Work: The Australian Workplace Industrial Relations Survey* by R.Callus, A. Morehead, M. Cully and J. Buchanon, Commonwealth Department of Industrial Relations, 1991; Table 4.2 (p. 84) from *Metal Trades Employers' Association vs The Amalgamated Engineering Union (Australian Section)*, 1968, 122 CAR 169 at 170-2; Table 18.3 (p. 605) from Australian Conciliation and Arbitration Commission, *National Wage* case, September 1983, 291 *CAR* at 53; Table 18.5 (p. 609) from Australian Conciliation and Arbitration Commission, *National Wage* case, March 1987, 17 *IR* 65 at 99-100; Table 18.7 (p. 612) from Australian Conciliation and Arbitration Commission, *National Wage* case, August 1988, 25 *IR* 170 at 179; Table 18.4 (p. 607) from recent *National Wage* cases; Table 18.10 (p. 619) from *Nurses (Victorian Health Services) Award 1992*, Part B Clause 36; Tables 10.12 (p. 299) and 10.13 (p. 300) from *A Survey of Small Business and Industrial Relations*, Department of Industrial Relations, Canberra, May 1993; Tables 7.6 (p. 176), 7.2 (p. 174), 7.3 (p. 175), 7.4 (p. 175) and 7.5 (p. 176) from *Trade Union Members Australia*, ABS Cat No. 6325.0, November 1976, Ref No. 6.65; Tables 7.8 (p. 181), 7.1 (p. 173) and 7.13 (p. 193) from *Trade Union Statistics*, ABS Cat No. 6323.0;
Australian Industrial Registry, Organisations Branch for table 7.14 (pp. 199-201);
BasicBooks, a division of HarperCollins Publishers Inc: Figure 2.1 (p. 30), Tables 9.2 and 9.3 from *The Transformation of American Industrial Relations* by Thomas A. Kochan, Harry Katz and Robert B. McKersie, 1986;
Blackwell Publishers for figures 3.1 (p. 67), 3.2 (p. 68), 9.1 (p. 247) and 9.4 (p. 255);
Butterworths for table 5.1 (pp. 111-2) from *Australian Journal of Labour Law*, eds. B. Creighton and R. Mitchell;
Chris Fisher for table 7.10 (pp. 184-5), Industrial Relations Papers, Research School of Social Sciences, Australian National University, 1983;
Fontana, an imprint of HarperCollins Publishers Limited for table 6.3 (p. 134);
Government Printer of the State of Victoria for the extract from *Nurses (Victorian Health Services) Award* (pp. 398-409) first published by The Law Printer, PO Box 292, South Melbourne, 3205. These documents are not an official copy of Crown Copyright material and the State of Victoria accepts no responsibility for their accuracy;
The Law Book Company (pp. 429-38) for the extract from *Australian Business Law Review*, Volume 21, 1993;
Macmillan Education Australia Pty Ltd for tables 6.2 (p. 131), 10.1 (p. 278) and 10.2 (p. 279);
Oxford University Press for tables 11.1 (p. 323), 11.3 (p. 330) and 11.8 (p. 352) from *Employers Association and Industrial Relations: A Comparative Study* by J P Windmuller and A Gladstone, 1984.

For permission to reproduce photographs we would like to thank the following: Andrew Chapman Photography for the photos in table 16.4 (p. 527); Barrier Daily Truth for figure 4.1 (p. 78); David Syme & Co. Limited for the photo in table 16.6 (p. 537) and the photo in table 18.14 (p. 627); Mirror Australian Telegraph Publications for the photo in table 7.7 (p. 178).

While every effort has been made to trace and acknowledge copyright, in some cases copyright proved untraceable. Should any infringement have occurred, the publishers tender their apologies and invite copyright owners to contact them.

Author Acknowledgements

The authors are indebted to many colleagues, students and teachers who have helped them form their views on employer-employee relations. They are indebted also to those whom they have met as colleagues or opponents in their practice of the art, for here their views have been tested and often modified. They are especially indebted to Dr John Hill and Professor Russell Lansbury for their kind permission to make use of material included in chapters 1, 2, 10, 11 and 12 of *Industrial Relations: An Australian Introduction*, John D. Hill, William A. Howard and Russell D. Lansbury, Melbourne, Longman Cheshire, 1982. They are indebted also to Helen Shaw and Nigel White for research assistance in relation to a number of chapters, and to Susan Collins, Linda Dunkley, Karolina Mosbauer and Audrey Paisley for expert and timely assistance in processing the manuscript.

Preface

This book was written during a period of considerable perceived change in industrial relations, but only time will show whether the changes are as great as is sometimes suggested. As with much of the national experience in this area it is difficult to discern whether or not the path that is being followed is a loop, so that we repeat the experiences of an earlier generation. It is clear that in the early 1990s, Australian industrial relations practice will experience some lessening of the authority of the arbitral authorities, an authority which grew greatly during the 1980s. Those who wish to believe that this is a change that takes us into unchartered waters would do well to remember that arbitral control and influence have waxed and waned constantly through the 20th century. In 1921, we find a Judge of the then Arbitration Court commending the parties before him on their constructive use of collective bargaining, and in 1936, the Arbitration Court struggled in vain to prevent the then Amalgamated Engineering Union from using collective bargaining to force over-award pay. Many unions struggled in the late 1960s, and eventually they succeeded in forcing the then Conciliation and Arbitration Commission to cease imposing sanctions on unions for use of the strike.

If the nation is about to enter on a period of relative decline in public involvement in the relations between employers, unions and employees, history suggests that it would be unwise to expect that some final equilibrium is being approached. Each successive episode may teach us more about the ways in which productive relationships may be built, and may show us more about the goals and tactics of those parties directly and indirectly involved, and it should be possible to gain from that knowledge. The authors hope that this book will help in the process.

The approach taken in this book is to introduce major theories and concepts. There is no attempt however to review the entire range of theories. Thus in dealing with theories of unionism for example, a total of six theories (three concerned with union origins, purpose and development, one with union growth and two with union strategy) are summarised in some detail. A similar approach is taken in dealing with theories of management in chapter 9, that is, to identify some influential ideas specific to the function of management rather than provide a comprehensive overview of theories. The intent is to acquaint the student with alternative perspectives and to provide sufficient information for the student to be able to apply a particular theory or concept to the Australian case without the need for recourse to primary sources. The *Further Reading* section of each chapter provides details of other important primary sources dealing with the issues covered in that chapter, in addition to the sources drawn upon directly.

In order to provide a cohesion and continuity to the study of this subject, some landmark disputes in Australia are referred to throughout the text. Thus for example, the 1989 Air Pilots' dispute is used to illustrate industrial conflict and industrial action (chapter 4), the legal position concerning the right to strike (chapter 5) and aspects of the operation of industrial tribunals (chapters 15 and 16). This approach is used with each of the disputes first discussed in chapter 4. These references indicate the importance of the disputes for analytical purposes. While each dispute is important to those directly influenced by it, the theoretical significance of these disputes does not imply that their direct impact was necessarily greater than some others.

A distinctive feature of the text is the inclusion of detailed introductory material relating to industrial law. Most introductory courses in this subject area endeavour to acquaint the student with a rudimentary understanding of the legal framework. In this book legal expertise gives precision and depth to the important aspect of regulation of the processes of industrial dispute resolution and their associated mechanisms at the federal level and in the States.

The study of employee relations is concerned with the ends and means by which the employer-employee relationship is structured. Some of those ends and means are pursued by governments as well as by the parties directly involved. Governments, however, may take action which impinges directly on the employer-employee relationship, but which is directed to ends other than that relationship itself. This category of government involvement includes legislation to ensure occupational health and safety, and legislation to prevent discrimination against particular groups, in employment and elsewhere. In determining conditions of employment, labour, management and the tribunals cannot agree on courses of action which breach legislation in the areas of occupational health and safety, or of equality of opportunity. In this respect they are restricted as completely as they are by their inability to breach laws governing PAYE taxation. Both these sets of legislation have profound effects on the workplace and the labour market These complex matters are discusse d in some detail in chapter 14 and the *Further Reading* section directs students to specialist publications in this area.

Employee relations, or industrial relations, is largely a matter of determining employment conditions within given limits. If the appropriate government authority should determine that, for example, certain materials cannot be used in industry, that certain personnel selection practices cannot be used, then employment conditions must be determined subject to those rules. Regulation of this type may restrict employee relations outcomes, but it is not generally part of the process. Those rules are important issues in the field of social and protective legislation. This book concentrates on employment conditions and their determination but also examines the boundaries or limitations themselves.

Carol B. Fox
William A. Howard
Marilyn J. Pittard

1
The Nature of Industrial/Employee Relations

Contents
What's in a name?
Analytical methods
The emergence of industrial relations
The contract of employment
Participants in the process

Employee relations, labour relations or industrial relations (the terms are used interchangeably in this book) may have a number of meanings, and each of these usually reflects particular interests. While a more precise definition is provided below, it may be noted here that to study labour or industrial relations is to study all those relationships that arise out of the employer-employee connection, and this includes relationships involving institutions as well as people. Like all complex fields, the study of industrial relations may involve a number of sub-specialisations.

What's in a name?

During the 1970s and 1980s both popular and specialist discussion increasingly found the terms industrial relations and labour relations being replaced by other terminology, employee relations and human resource management being the most popular. Something more than a change in style may have been involved here. The term human resource management was embraced by those who wished to emphasise that the function of management, in dealing with employees, was more than simply to respond to union-inspired encroachments onto its authority. Perhaps the most detailed and systematic articulation of this approach was that expounded by Thomas Kochan and his associates,[1] who sought to analyse managerial policy towards employees in terms of management's ability to make and execute strategic choices. This focus led writers in the human resource management field, together with those who describe the field as employee relations, to emphasise that there is a good deal of negotiation and interrelationship taking place between employer and employee which does not involve unions or other intermediaries.

Such an emphasis is timely, for many, perhaps the majority, of the commentators on labour management relations proceed as though all labour is organised, and as though the union always represents labour on all issues. Even in Australia, where union membership is a relatively high proportion of wage and salary earners, fifty-nine per cent remain outside union membership. The reach of the arbitral system is a good deal broader than union membership, and it is estimated some twenty per cent of wage and salary earners is award-free. The work of the human resource management writers does remind us that there are problems encountered in the relations of these employees with their managers, and that they are resolved in ways that do not involve any of the traditional mechanisms or institutions of industrial relations.

It is sometimes suggested that the terms employee relations, or human resource management imply an anti-union bias. There are undoubtedly instances in which that suggestion is justified, but those using the terms neutrally intend to emphasise that not every employer-employee transaction either provides for or involves union participation. Others who use the terms may do so to emphasise that their acceptance of union legitimacy does not entail their acceptance of union involvement as a joint participant in management.

Most of the earliest writers in the field would argue that there are some actions bearing on the employer-employee relationship which are not subject to challenge by the other party (there might well be wide divergence as to what those actions are). It was a view often left unexpressed, however, because much of the early work was directed to emphasising the legitimacy of, or the justification for unionism.[2] In addition to this, the industrial relations literature has often seemed to be disproportionately preoccupied with unions, and more concerned about their behaviour than it was with that of management. Usually this resulted from the fact that, while it could be assumed that the analysis provided by neo-classical economics, the concern with profit maximisation, would provide a rationale for the behaviour of managers, the neo-classical analysis could not explain union behaviour. If profit maximisation was the only feasible rationale for a business, a union could clearly have more than one feasible rationale. It would be as logical for a union to seek to maximise the wages of its members as it would be for it to seek to maximise the union's size, and these two policies are theoretically incompatible. Similarly it may be quite feasible for a union to seek to maximise some function entirely unrelated to the market place, it could seek to propagate a political ideology, for example.

A union, in short, is an exotic phenomenon in the world of business, and the pioneering writers, even if they were not concerned to justify it, at least were required to explain and interpret it more extensively than was necessary in the case of the firm and the employer. It can be argued that this tradition continued, and that understanding of union logic and objectives became increasingly sophisticated while analysis of management in its relations with unions remained, in the traditional industrial relations literature, either crude and simplistic, or was treated in isolation from the central concerns of business. The work of writers such as Ahlstrand, Purcell,[3] and Kochan, Katz and McKersie, who have concentrated on bringing employers' strategies towards employees under the general rubric of business strategy, has been a timely attempt to restore some analytical balance into what is a bipartite activity. If the observer is given a sophisticated guide to the methods and motivation of one party, but only a rudimentary idea about the other, a confused and inaccurate analysis is likely to result.

It is probably fair comment to suggest that the past generation of Australian industrial relations specialists was excessively concerned with the operations of tribunals and unions. As contemporary specialists seek to recover from the imbalance of the past, there may be some danger of their concentrating too closely on the unilateral goals of managers. It is to be noted that concern over these imbalances in examination is not a matter of political or class partiality (and in practice these are rarely involved, the imbalance normally resulting from the training and special interests of the writers). What is of concern is whether the interaction of labour and management can be analysed by those having a detailed understanding of one party, but only limited comprehension of the other.

Analytical methods

Popular discussion of employee relations has tended to centre on pay and related matters, but, important as these are, they are but part of industrial relations. Equally important are arguments over the proper way for supervisors to approach workers; over the extent of employer control over job content and methods, often described as the extent of managerial prerogative; over promotion systems; over the rights of unionists and union officers; over hiring and discharge procedures, and a multitude of other workplace activities. The fact is that if one person begins to work for another, the rate of pay is only one of the issues to be settled between them, and not every issue can be conveniently reduced to a monetary lowest common denominator.

Clearly, employee relations is complicated, and the few issues mentioned so far are sufficient to suggest that its analysis will not be achieved successfully by resort to any one discipline alone. Economics, perhaps the most analytically rich of the social sciences, is not suited to a complete analysis of industrial relations. Its central assumption is that the parties to economic activity maximise single dominant functions that is, the consumer maximises satisfaction through consumption, the entrepreneur maximises profits, and so forth. However, the trade union, an important feature of industrial relations, cannot reasonably be assumed to maximise any single function. One may ask whether it attempts to maximise employment or wage levels for its members, and the neo-classical theory would suggest that these cannot be pursued simultaneously. Similarly, the union's interest can be assumed to be in maximising or in minimising wage differentials. A union may reasonably be assumed to maximise either employment, wage levels or wage differentials, or it may have other goals. The assumption of economic theory that there may be only one goal for the rational entrepreneur to pursue, may be valid, but the rational leaders of unions cannot be assumed always to be concerned with only one dominant objective.

These sorts of considerations apply to the other disciplines by which one may wish to analyse industrial relations. It is impossible, for example, to understand the field without a grasp of industrial law, but, like economics, the knowledge it provides is necessary, but it is not sufficient. So it is with history, with politics, with sociology and the other fields which impinge on industrial relations; one simply cannot master the field without resort to them, but to rely on any one of these essential fields alone is to achieve a distorted view.

While this complexity makes the field of industrial relations fascinating, it also makes it difficult. It is a field in which prediction is rarely easy, and the problems in this are often worsened by the fact that essential facts are usually unavailable. It is one of the purposes of this book to attempt to alert readers to just what some of the facts essential for analysis and prediction might be.

The emergence of industrial relations

Labour problems exist in any kind of society where production is undertaken by applying labour to land or capital equipment. Obviously there are the problems of finding labour, of having it work effectively and of having it work continuously. But these are not necessarily industrial relations problems, for they need not involve the differences between employer and employee or between manager and managed which are essential to such problems. Military forces, prisons and family groups do not have industrial relations problems. They may have problems involving issues identical to those involved in labour relations, but the nature of the relationship between the manager and the managed is different from that in industrial work. In the family case, the linkages between labour and management are stronger and more complex than those existing in the employer-employee case, with each party relying on a mutual relationship for services that are based on a long-term set of expectations and dependencies. For example, the farmer's son or daughter may work virtually unpaid for years, in expectation that the farm eventually will be theirs and that their father will look to their interests in a way that an employer neither would nor could. In one respect the family example is also similar to the prison and military cases. A degree of freedom of choice, normally present in the traditional work relationship, is missing in these situations. Workers can, of their own volition, become ex-employees in a quicker and more direct way than they can become ex-sons or daughters, ex-prisoners, or ex-soldiers.

In societies of the Australian type, industrial relations problems are often rather crudely identified, and defined by the fact that one of the parties is a union which is representing employees. Unions, however, do not create either labour relations or labour relations problems. Rather, history has shown the reverse causality: that the existence of workplace problems has been the driving force in creating unionism, for the union is formed to articulate and institutionalise resolution of those problems. In fact, the hiring of labour is necessary to the existence of such problems and hence is an originating force in employee relations. If something more than labour is involved, as in the family case, or if the relationship is not based on hiring, as in the prison case, then the problems that exist between manager and managed are not employee relations problems.

What is it that creates industrial relations, and allows for the development of industrial relations mechanisms, and techniques for handling industrial relations problems? For most societies, this originating force has been industrialisation. The industrialising process has brought many changes, but most importantly it requires the introduction of a form of control, or industrial discipline, of employees. The very nature of specialisation, division of labour and mechanisation, so central to industrialisation, demands this. Industrial discipline is the creation of the attitude that induces people to work at tasks they find unpleasant or monotonous, at greater speeds and under more pressure than they desire; to use methods designed by someone else, and to produce goods of little or no interest to them. Of equal magnitude is the manner in which industrialism forces working people to change their whole way of life, as their working hours become geared to the demands of the production process. In the pre-industrial state it may have been tradition, superstition, climate or personal choice that ruled their lives. In the industrial world their lives are dominated by industrial logic.

In every newly-industrialised country, industrialism's greatest effect is that it creates a new class of people, those who depend solely on the sale of their labour for their livelihood. In earlier times, they may have been self-sufficient farmers, they may have been tenant farmers, or they may have lived in some form of obligatory bondage to social superiors. With the coming of industrialism there develops a wage-earning class whose only responsibility to its employer is that included in its contract of employment. This contract may replace a set of customary relationships or statutory obligations which had determined the rights and duties of employers and employees. In the early stages of industrial development the more sparse is the contract of employment, the fewer will be the responsibilities, and, probably, the rights, of the worker.[4] As industrialism produces a labouring class, or rather a class of wage earners, then some form of labour relations must emerge too. It may originate as merely a technique for the giving and receiving of orders, developing in complexity as industrialism proceeds and as institutions mature. As industrialism proceeds, a society will be wholly re-ordered on the entirely new basis of economic dependency. Pre-industrial societies may include a variety of social totems and codes of conduct, but it is only in an industrial society that labour relations begin to exist, or that labour relations problems influence the relationships between workers and employers.

The contract of employment

Most workers who supply their labour or services do so under a contract of employment. However, not every worker supplying labour for reward is an employee; some may be independent contractors.

The distinction between an employee and an independent contractor

The distinction between an employee (who works under a contract of service) and an independent contractor (who works under a contract for services) is an important one in labour relations law. Generally, industrial awards, federal or state, apply to employees rather than to independent contractors, so that entitlement to minimum terms and conditions in awards will depend on the category of legal relationship. Entitlement to workers' compensation benefits for industrial injuries under statutory compensation schemes applies to employees.[5] The legal character of the relationship between employer and worker is also important because it will determine the obligations which the courts at common law imply into such a relationship. For example, under a contract of employment an employee is under an obligation of fidelity (to serve the employer in good faith), and to obey the reasonable commands of the employer, and the employer is under an obligation to provide a safe system of work for employees. Such obligations are usually implied into the contract of employment regardless of the fact that they were never expressly agreed to by the parties at the time of entering into arrangement. Such obligations attach to the employer-employee relationship and not necessarily to that of employer-independent contractor.

The relationship of employer and employee not only has to be distinguished from that of independent contractor, but sometimes has to be distinguished from the relationship between partners of a business—are the two people working in a business regarded as being partners or is one employed as an employee by the other? Sometimes, too, the person will not be an employee but will be the holder of an office, such as a judicial office.

In many instances, there will be no problem in determining whether a worker is an employee or an independent contractor. For example, plumbers who run their own businesses, service their customers and in return are paid for services rendered, and who supply and maintain their own tools and equipment are regarded as independent contractors. On the other hand, clerical workers who are engaged to work specified hours per week, who attend their place of work and carry out their tasks under the direction of an employer or supervisor and who are paid a regular wage from which income tax is deducted are regarded as employees. However, in some instances it is difficult to ascertain whether the worker is an employee or an independent contractor. This might occur in the case of workers who largely do their work at home and are paid by results, for example, insurance agents, consultants and building contractors.[6] Over the years, the courts have grappled with this problem and have devised various tests to ascertain the legal nature of the relationships.

A number of considerations are relevant to the determination of the legal relationship. The degree of control or the right to exercise control by employers over their workers may indicate whether the relationship is that of employee or independent contractor. In the case of an employee, the degree of employer control will be considerable or, in the case of highly skilled persons in respect of whom an employer may not have the expertise to direct the manner of carrying out the tasks, the right to control will be considerable. By way of contrast, in the case of independent contractors, the person engaging the independent contractor will exercise little if any control over the manner in which the person exercises his or her tasks.

The degree of control test, although important, is not the only indicator. Other tests devised by courts include examining other factors such as:

a the mode of remuneration—if the person is paid on the basis of the job done, it tends to suggest the person is an independent contractor;
b who is responsible for providing and maintaining equipment—the independent contractor tends to supply his or her own equipment and to maintain that equipment; in the case of an employee, the employer usually supplies such equipment;
c the obligation to work;
d the hours of work—regular hours of work tend to suggest a contract of service;
e provisions for the taking of holidays—if paid holiday leave is part of the agreement, this supports the existence of an employer-employee relationship;
f the deduction of income-tax—the deduction of PAYE tax tends to suggest the person is an employee, although this is not conclusive, because the definition of 'employee' in taxation legislation includes some independent contractors; and
g the extent to which the worker can delegate work—an independent contractor can in turn subcontract whereas an employee is usually under an obligation to perform the task himself or herself.[7]

The 'organisation' test has often been used by the courts as a factor assisting categorisation of the relationship. Is the person carrying on business for himself or herself or for a superior? The fact that piece-work carried out by homeworkers in the clothing industry was part of the larger production process of clothing manufacturers was important, in the view of the industrial tribunal, in categorising the relationship of employer-employee.[8]

Sometimes the parties will make an agreement which contains an express term as to whether their relationship is that of employee or independent contractor. Usually this will be done where one or both of the parties wishes to avoid the consequences of the worker being regarded as an employee so that the expressed term includes a statement that the relationship is to be one of contract for services that is, employer-independent contractor. The courts, however, do not necessarily take such contracts on their face. In some instances, they will look behind the expressed intention of the parties and ascertain what is the 'real nature of that relationship'.[9]

Rights and duties of employers and employees

The contract of employment may be made orally or in writing or be a combination of written and other terms. These express terms are not the only source of an employee's rights and obligations: as indicated, the courts will imply some terms as a matter of law into the contract of employment[10] and some terms may be implied as a matter of fact depending on the surrounding circumstances.[11]

The contract of employment will determine rights and obligations between an individual employee and his or her employer. However, although the contract is fundamental to the relationship between employer and employee there may be other sources of employment duties and rights. These other sources include awards (federal or State), collective agreements, legislation and even the custom and practice in a particular industry.

Terms in an award made by industrial tribunals sometimes are regarded as being incorporated into the contract of employment.[12] Legislation which is increasingly another source of employer-employee rights and duties would not ordinarily form part of a contract.[13] Collective agreements which are registered pursuant to industrial legislation are enforceable in the same way as awards. If the agreements are not registered, they may be unenforceable at common law unless they can be regarded as being incorporated into each individual employee's contract of employment or as being a separate binding contract between employer and each individual employee. Matters of practice in the industry should form part of the contract in order to be strictly enforceable at law.

All of the sources should be examined to determine employment entitlements and obligations. For example, an employee in Australia today may look to the contract of employment (which may be evidenced by a letter of appointment) for a statement of the employee's job responsibilities and duties and length of employment, to an award for wages and other employment conditions, to legislation for entitlement to long service leave and to a collective agreement between union and employer for superannuation benefits.

Participants in the process

It is important for the student to distinguish the institutions of labour relations from its practice. The existence of familiar-sounding institutions, for example unions, in non-industrial states, does not necessarily imply that labour relations problems occur. On the other hand, the lack of these institutions does not mean that labour relations problems are not present. It may mean only that these problems may be prevented from surfacing in a particular way. For example, in totalitarian societies, the strike may not exist, yet this does not mean these societies have no labour relations disputes.

Once a system of industrial relations is established, then industrial relations problems may appear at a variety of levels. The problems of an individual worker, or of employees as a class, may constitute industrial relations issues. Usually however, the single worker can be brushed aside by the more economically powerful, and generally more resourceful, employer, while the problems of the working class as a whole are normally social or political rather than industrial, or at least social or political mechanisms are used to resolve them. The scope for industrial relations problems can vary, but normally some discernible group of workers is involved. An organisation of workers is usually required to pursue the workers' industrial interests, but a similar organisation of employers is not essential to industrial relations. The union is required because the workers' grievance is not likely to be prosecuted without a labour organisation, of which the union is a typical form. The employer, however, is usually in a position to prosecute his or her wishes and interests with respect to employees. The employer does not need an organisation for this; indeed, the employer may be viewed as representing an organisation of capital—that which is employed in the business.

The place of government in employee relations (other than in its capacity as an employer) is similar to that of employer associations—its participation is not essential to the practice. In some societies, governments determine totally the context of the employer-employee relationship, while in others they play no part at all. This indicates that the presence of government is far from essential in resolving industrial relations problems. There may be certain rules that governments need to enforce, but government involvement in the day-to-day workplace problem solving is not essential.

Conclusion

To reiterate, industrial relations and industrial relations problems are not created by the growth of institutions—unions, employer associations, government tribunals and departments of labour. Rather, industrial relations and its problems are brought about by industrialism. Problems that have the same fundamental causes may exist in pre-industrial, or non-industrial societies but in that earlier phase of economic development, they are handled by some process other than the methods of labour relations.

It may be that the critical factor in the development of industrial relations is that the only nexus between employer and employee is the contract of employment, or its equivalent. Societies or situations in which industrial relations problems and concepts are absent, such as peonage, slavery, military service, feudalism, extended families and the like, involve ties other than this employment relationship. It is, however, difficult to determine the precise limits to this notion, for the Japanese work relationship, for example, involves relationships other than the conventional industrial relations nexus.

One may conclude that the process of industrialism and the growth of the industrial society are critical factors in the development of industrial relations. To identify the originating force is not, however, to identify the appropriate means of analysing industrial relations problems. It is argued that one of the most useful ways that this can be done is by resorting to the concept of an industrial relations system, a method for the analysis and specification of industrial relations. The following chapter explains this concept together with some other useful theoretical approaches to the subject.

Notes

1 T.A. Kochan, H.C. Katz and R.B. McKersie, *The Transformation of American Industrial Relations*, Basic Books, New York, 1986.
2 A. Smith, *An Enquiry into the Nature and Causes of the Wealth of Nations*, Random House, Modern Library Edition, New York, 1937, Book 1, chapter 8.
3 See for example, J. Purcell and B. Ahlstrand, 'Corporate Management of Industrial Relations in the "Multi Divisional Company"', *British Journal of Industrial Relations 27*, September 1989, pp. 396-417. See also chapter 9, *Further Reading* section.
4 In contemporary times the courts imply terms into contracts of employment imposing rights and duties on the employee and the employer.
5 Many workers' compensation statutes however extend such benefits to independent contractors in order to avoid employers from escaping their obligations by organising their workers in such a way that they are classified as independent contractors rather than employees.
6 See, e.g., *Building Workers' Industrial Unions of Australia v Odco Pty Ltd* (1991) 9 ALR 735 where building workers were classified by the Federal Court of Australia as independent contractors and so not covered by a federal award.
7 See a recent High Court authority which discusses the various tests and indicia for determining whether the relationship is employee or independent contractor: *Stevens and Gray v Brodribb Sawmilling Co Pty Ltd* (1986) 160 CLR 16.
8 See decision of Riordan DP (Australian Conciliation and Arbitration Commission) in *Application of the Clothing and Allied Trade Unions of Australia to vary the Clothing Trades Award 1982 re Contract work* Print 4546 of 1985. The decision meant that clothing outworkers were entitled to the terms and conditions in the federal Clothing Trades Award. Previously they were paid very low rates based on quantity produced, were not eligible for paid holiday leave, sick leave etc.
9 See, for example, *Cam and Son Pty Ltd v Sargeant* (1940) 14 ALJR 162 and *Australian Mutual Provident Society v Chaplin* (1978) 18 ALR 385.
10 For example, the employer has an implied duty to pay wages in return for service of the employee; the employee has an implied duty to perform the work with reasonable competence or skill.
11 The courts may imply a term to give business efficacy to the contract.
12 See *Gregory v Philip Morris Ltd* (1988) 80 ALR 455 where the Federal Court of Australia held that a term in a federal award was automatically incorporated as a term in the

contract of employment. However, *Byrne v Australian Airlines Ltd.* (1994) 120 ALR 274 has overruled the decision in Gregory's case and held that award terms are not *automatically* part of the contract of employment.

13 See, e.g., *Employee Relations Act* 1992 (Vic), Part 5, Division 6 which sets out long service leave entitlements and *Industrial Relations Act* 1988, Part VIA, Division 3, which sets out minimum notice periods for, and rights in respect of, termination of employment.

Further Reading

What's in a name?

P.F. Boxall and P.J. Dowling, 'Human Resource Management and the Industrial Relations Tradition', *Labour and Industry 3*, June/October 1990, pp. 195-214.

D.H. Plowman, 'Personnel Management and the Industrial Relations Environment', in G. Palmer (ed.), *Australian Personnel Management: A Reader*, Macmillan, South Melbourne, 1988, pp. 222-246.

Analytical methods

D. Kelly (ed.), *Researching Industrial Relations : Methods and Methodology*, Australian Centre for Industrial Relations Research and Teaching, University of Sydney, Monograph No. 6, December 1991.

The emergence of industrial relations

A.L. Gitlow, *Labor and Industrial Society* (revised ed.), Irwin, Homewood, Illinois, 1963, pp. 3-18.

The contract of employment

A.S. Brooks, 'Myth and Muddle—An examination of contracts for the performance of work', 1988, *University of New South Wales Law Journal 48*.

W.B. Creighton, W.J. Ford and R.J. Mitchell, *Labour Law: Text and Materials* (2nd ed.), Law Book Co. Ltd, Melbourne, 1993, chapter 4.

B. Creighton and A. Stewart, *Labour Law: an Introduction* , The Federation Press, Sydney, 1990, pp. 95-115.

J.J. Macken, G.J. McCarry and C. Sappideen, *The Law of Employment* (3rd ed.), Law Book Co Ltd, Sydney, 1990, chapter 1.

R.C. McCallum, M.J. Pittard and G.F. Smith, *Australian Labour Law: Cases and Materials*, Butterworths, Sydney, 1990, pp. 15-44.

Questions

What's in a name?

1 How would you distinguish between (a) the study and (b) the practice of industrial relations and human resource management?

2 What activities of (a) unions and (b) managers, which are directly or indirectly connected to the employer-employee relationship, are generally agreed should not be challenged by the other party?

Analytical methods

3 It is sometimes argued that, however desirable and mutually satisfactory the employee relations of a particular nation might be, they cannot readily be transferred to a country which does not have those practices. What is the basis for this view? Do you agree with the argument?

The emergence of industrial relations

4 What are the main factors that result in the development of an industrial relations system as economies experience developmental change?

5 In some nations the armed services are organised in conventional trade unions, and in the Australian armed services a form of industrial organisation, the Armed Services Federation of Australia is present. Would you expect this to pose unusual difficulties for labour or management?

The contract of employment

6 What is the significance of the distinction between employee and independent contractor?

7 Can employers avoid award obligations by engaging workers and independent contractors rather than employees? (See Federal Court decision in *Building Workers Industrial Union v Odco Pty Ltd*, (1991) 99 ALR 735 involving workers supplied by Troubleshooters).

8 Does the power given to the Australian Industrial Relations Commission in sections 127A-C of the *Industrial Relations Act* 1988 (Cth) to review contracts with independent contractors on the grounds that the contract is unfair, harsh or against the public interest provide sufficient protection for independent contractors?

9 (a) Would you expect that the conditions of work and compensation for employees and for independent contractors would be similar or quite different?

   (b) What factors might lead to workers becoming independent contractors rather than employees?

10 (a) Would you expect Australian employers and independent contractors to have similar views about the specific nature of the implicit obligations on each party to an employment contract?

   (b) Would you expect this to be common to all sectors of industry?

Participants in the process

11 Try to identify the ways in which governments or government agencies are (a) involved directly in employer-employee relations and (b) indirectly influence the conduct of those relationships.

Exercise

1 (a) If you were to negotiate an employment agreement for yourself, which matters would you require to be included?

   (b) Compare your list with a current industry award of the Australian Industrial Relations Commission, and identify the main areas of difference.

   (c) Having seen the award covered material, in which areas, if any, would you now modify your original selection of issues?

2

Approaches to Industrial Relations

Contents
Dunlop
Walker
Flanders
Marx
Braverman
Kochan, Katz and McKersie

Introduction

The complexity of industrial relations has already been remarked upon, and this may result in an observer seeing only a formless mass of data, a mass which may be capable of description, perhaps, but not of analysis. One needs some means of marshalling the often confusing industrial relations data, a means of putting together the events and evidence so that it is possible to learn from them, and to achieve this, an appropriate theory, or a systematic account of the nature of industrial relations is needed.

There is probably no truly dominant industrial relations theory, and its development has not been a major interest for most scholars in the field. Many have made partial and specialised contributions to a theory of industrial relations, usually as by-products in the pursuit of larger topics.

In the late 1950s, John T. Dunlop published what was probably the most ambitious attempt yet to develop an entire theory of industrial relations. Dunlop's work, *Industrial Relations Systems*,[1] if it is not dominant, is at least the reference point for most industrial relations theorising. Dunlop's work is not without flaws, and some of these will be discussed below, but it is a useful means of ordering and classifying industrial relations information, of bringing some form to what would otherwise be a mass of confusing and sometimes contradictory information. Dunlop's view of industrial relations is important to this book, if for no other reason than that his model involves a useful taxonomy of the features of industrial relations. Whether or not his account of the interactions of these features is satisfactory is quite another matter.

Dunlop

The components of an industrial relations system are:

i   actors;
ii contexts (environments);
iii processes;
iv ideology—a body of beliefs and values that binds the system together; and
v the output of the system, workplace rules.

The interaction between the actors and their environments through various processes produces a web of rules which governs relationships at the workplace.[2] The output or dependent variable in the system is the body of workplace rules. For Dunlop, the central task of a theory of industrial relations was to explain why particular rules are established and how and why they change over time.

Dunlop began with the notion of a general social system, a concept developed by the distinguished sociologist Talcott Parsons.[3] This was comprised of a number of sub-systems which would include, among others, the economic system, the political system, the legal system, and of course, the industrial relations system. Each of these sub-systems was designed to produce a particular output for the society. Under capitalism, for example, the function of the economic system is to produce a system of prices, and these, subject to certain assumptions, serve to allocate resources within the society.

The function of the industrial relations sub-system of the general social system, Dunlop argued, was to produce what he termed the 'web of rules' which distributed rights and obligations among those at the workplace. The rules in question cover the entire employer-employee relationship, wages, hours and working conditions, worker-supervisor relationships, and the like, as well as the means by which those rules would be made. The industrial relations system was the mechanism for providing workplace government.

It is worth noting that in this system, the various social sub-systems were designed to produce quite particular outputs. In Australia we have often seen attempts to use the industrial relations system to produce some economic output, economic stabilisation or counter inflationary strategies have been common goals, and similarly there have been attempts to use the industrial relations system to produce political ends. Given that the system's essential purpose is to develop the web of workplace rules, it is unlikely that it will function effectively in striving to achieve these other ends, and to the extent that it is used to pursue goals other than workplace government, its performance in that central role will probably be less efficient than it might otherwise have been. This is not, of course to make a value judgement about such policies, it is simply to note that if society uses industrial relations as the means by which prices will be restrained, or labour demand varied, there may be problems in the government of workplaces.

Dunlop has defined the output of the industrial relations system as the web of rules, not because he wished to restrict the activity of any of the parties to industrial relations in any way, but because he sought to distinguish the industrial relations activity of those parties from other activities in which they might legitimately be involved. The Parsonian system did envisage that there would be overlap between the various social sub-systems, thus the parties involved in one sub-system might well play roles in others. Dunlop would not argue about the propriety of the action of any industrial relations party being involved in, for example, politics, but he would contend that any action it took that was not concerned with the making and application of workplace rules was not industrial relations.

The Dunlop version of the industrial relations system involved the interaction of three sets of quite different variables. The first of these was:

The actors

To Dunlop, the actors in the industrial relations system were those who took action, and he suggested there were three groups of these.[4]

Workers (non-managerial) and their representatives constituted the first actor. Workers' representatives are normally expected to be trade unions, but it is possible for them to take other forms. Identifying workers and their representatives as constituting two separate parties, Dunlop emphasises the often overlooked point that unions and their individual members do not always have identical sets of interests in industrial relations.

Managers and their representatives are the second of Dunlop's actors. Managers are, of course, the agents of the owners of capital, the stockholders who are not usually active in industrial relations. Managers too have their representatives in industrial relations, and they will include their internal employee relations or industrial relations and personnel departments, as well as retained external consultants, lawyers and negotiators. Clearly employers' representatives also include organised groups of employers, and in Australia, employers associations take a large role, probably larger than the norm, in industrial relations practice. Just as union officials are not employees, neither are employer association officials employers. It is also necessary to note that the interests of the individual employer will not always be identical to those of the employer association.

Government is the third of Dunlop's actors, and it is reasonable to assume here that he included under this heading both government proper and the specialised government agencies which are required to deal with labour matters. This is particularly important in Australia, since certain government agencies, notably the tribunals are, in theory at least, independent of government.

The arbitral tribunals do involve a greater degree of public intervention in industrial relations than Dunlop probably had in mind, and in Australia, government is involved in the practice of industrial relations, in relative terms, very considerably. Government's role may be in establishing dispute settling tribunals, as is the case in Australia, or it may involve no more than requiring that industrial relations parties obey the same laws as others, although more frequently it involves governments determining and administering required codes of conduct.

The unions too are the focus of more political activity than Dunlop may have expected, for their close and symbiotic relationship with the Australian Labor Party has facilitated a high level of political involvement in industrial relations. The federal industrial relations law, which regulates unions as well as industrial relations proper, has been amended approximately once per year since it was enacted in 1904. It is difficult to believe that each amendment has been a response to problems in industrial relations, for some amendments have certainly been intended to benefit or to hamper unions, and by extension their political allies, thereby extending political activity into the industrial relations system.

In Dunlop's system, these three parties, workers and their representatives, employers and their representatives and governments and their specialised agencies comprise the first of the system's three sets of variables. It is the interaction of these three actors which results in the web of rules being established, but the actors are not able to operate without regard to the world about them. Their actions are constrained in certain ways, and these constraints comprise Dunlop's second group of variables.

The environmental contexts

It is to be expected that workplace rules developed by the three actors will be influenced by the environment in which they function. Dunlop has identified three environmental factors he believed to be of critical importance in the development of workplace rules.

The technological context[5] was the first of these. Dunlop suggested that the state of technology has a considerable influence on the industrial relations outcomes. Quite clearly, the state of technological development has a considerable influence on the kinds of work that people do. In a technologically undeveloped society, one might expect the bulk of the workforce to be mainly agricultural workers, as well as a few fishermen and miners. Such a workforce might well be unionised, but a union of farm workers will usually be scattered, concentrated in very small groups, and, compared with factory workers, for example, will be more difficult and costly to organise, and will find it hard to develop a sense of unity simply because of the relative isolation in which members work. Similar influences will operate on managers. It might be noted in passing that the very effective unionisation of Australian shearers is one of few examples of successful organisation of a workforce that is both agricultural and itinerant.

The state of technology impinges in other ways. Dynamic, industrialised societies find it necessary to move constantly to new methods of production and of management, to seek constantly to find new markets and products. Such societies can exist, at least in part because their unions see that their members' welfare depends on their being able to prosper by sharing in the gains from industrial progress, and this of course influences profoundly the kinds of workplace rules that such unions pursue, and the forms that such unions will take.

Industrial relations balances can change considerably in consequence of changes in technology, and the experience of the Builders Labourers' Federation[6] is a case in point. Until at least the 1950s, the Builders Labourers' Federation had been a fairly minor player in the industrial relations of the construction industry, but in ensuing years it came to hold a critical position. In the years of its relative insignificance, major construction projects were dominated by the unions of the skilled construction workers, carpenters, plumbers, bricklayers and the like. These were the workers with the critical skills, these were the workers on whom managers depended to get projects completed on time. However as construction techniques changed, the skilled jobs tended to be done off-site, and prefabricated parts were brought to the sites to be fixed in place, and concrete applications became a more important part of construction, the role of the builders labourers who operated cranes and managed much of the concreting processes became critical to the industry, and the Builders Labourers' Federation assumed a central role in the industry. It was the change in the technology of construction which facilitated that change in the power balance of the construction unions.

Dunlop's point is that technology influences the functions, attitudes and the coercive capacity of each of the actors in the industrial relations system. Workers involved in the supply of electricity, such as the control room operators in Victoria's Latrobe Valley, enjoy considerable coercive capacity (or strategic power), by virtue of the nature of the work operations and their pivotal positions in those operations. This has been reflected in their relatively high rates of pay, and in competition between unions to enrol these workers as members. The technological context is the first of the three environmental contexts in Dunlop's system.

The market or budgetary context[7] is the second of them. It is almost axiomatic that industrial relations outcomes are influenced by the state of the economy.

A party that is dominant in periods of high employment and business prosperity may well be powerless in a depression. The ability of Australian unions to extract pay increases, or to reduce hours of work clearly declined in the late 1980s and early 1990s as depressed economic conditions saw unemployment rise. The market simply would not sustain ascendant unionism. While Dunlop's notion of the market context would include these fluctuations of the business cycle as being influential, his concern is directed to more fundamental economic aspects.

One of those aspects is the fact that the industrial sectors traditionally most vulnerable to unionism in the developed world, mainly in manufacturing, has experienced a slowdown, perhaps permanent, in growth, if not a secular decline. If the market environment has shifted in the last quarter of the twentieth century from an expansive and optimistic milieu to one of shrinkage and pessimism, the views and goals of unions, employers and governments will alter too, and that change will be reflected in their employee relations practices. The acceptance in February 1983 by one of Australia's more powerful unions, the then AMWU of wage restraints as part of a *quid pro quo* for ALP support for manufacturing industry[8] reflected the adverse labour market environment for many of that union's members at that time.

Other aggregative aspects are of relevance to the Dunlop view as well. Whether the economy is of the socialist, planned form, or is based on enterprise capitalism will be important in influencing the web of rules. So too will be the size of the dominant firms, and the degree of competition in industry. Of significance would be whether or not the country concerned was a colony or was independent, whether it was highly protected by tariffs, the extent and significance of the internal and external markets and similar aggregative and critical factors.

Both in the short term and over the long run, it is suggested that the workplace rules that the actors will produce will be shaped considerably by the latitude that is provided by the economic structure and performance of the economy. Dunlop's market context is the variable which is intended to capture this influence. It is the second of Dunlop's three environmental contexts.

The power context[9] is the third of them. Dunlop's treatment of the power context might have been more fully developed, but it is clear that his concern was in the distribution of power in the society as a whole. Power in this context is reflected in the political system, the public policy, the traditions and history of a country. Dunlop saw the power context as particularly important in defining the status of the actors and their mutual relationships. These would include, for example, rights which employers associations or unions may have, rather than microcosmic concepts of power at the level of collective bargaining. Bargaining power, where exercised, is expressed in industrial agreements and contracts. It is suggested by Dunlop that the distribution of power in the larger society will influence industrial relations outcomes. Perhaps the simplest illustration may be that a union allied with a labour party will appear to be more formidable when that party is in government than when it is not. The labour party may provide legislation of direct benefit to unions, for example by empowering industrial tribunals to award preference to unionists at various points in the employment relationship, or it may do no more than provide benign inertia in response to union wage claims. The labour party may in fact do nothing directly to assist the unions, but it could usually be expected to operate policies that incidentally create a favourable environment for unions. In those circumstances, they are likely to achieve their preferred workplace rules more easily. In 1992 the defeat of the Labor Party government in Victoria saw the incoming government move to change industrial relations laws to diminish what it believed to be an undue ability of unions to influence industrial relations outcomes and to reduce the influence of the State's industrial tribunal. The Victorian unions and their national affiliates reacted strongly to this, suggesting that the government sought by these changes to damage workers' interests. Whatever the long-term outcome may be, it is clear that the switch from a government allied to unions to one of a different outlook has certainly made it more difficult for unions to achieve their goals. In non-democratic states in which all power is monopolised by a particular segment of the population, unions are unlikely to exert influence in industrial relations unless they are allied with the ruling group, as indeed they were during the first regime of Juan Peron in Argentina. More usually, however, anti-democratic regimes leave small scope for union power.

Dunlop's argument is that if the power balance in society is tilted in favour of a particular set of interests in the society, it is likely that such a power bias will be reflected in industrial relations outcomes. Clearly this effect will be more profound if there are structural reinforcements which support the retention of the power imbalance than would be the case if the political process does, more or less routinely, produce shifts in political preference. Dunlop's notion of the power context is not so much directed to the case of the labour party that is, from time to time, elected democratically to office, as it is to the situation in which there is something that prevents a particular group achieving power, or which assures another of power. If, for example, all industrialised workers were of a particular racial group, and if that group were constitutionally denied political power, one would not expect the industrial workers' unions to achieve dominance over employers who were of other racial groups.

The environmental contexts which Dunlop argued were of significance in the development of the web of workplace rules are the technological, market and power contexts. When any or all of these change, it is reasonable to expect that the web of rules will alter to reflect this change in determining forces.

Ideology

The last of the three variables constituting Dunlop's system is ideology.[10] Dunlop was not concerned with the kinds of ideological issues that are often found in public discussion, whether or not a particular union is allied with the right or left of the Labor Party, for example. Dunlop's concern here was whether there was a sufficient degree of ideological compatibility to allow an enduring industrial relations system to evolve. He saw a minimal ideological compatibility as being necessary to bind the actors together. In the absence of such a compatibility, the actors could not cooperate sufficiently to pursue their separate interests within a framework designed to produce workplace rules. This aspect of the Dunlop model has attracted criticism on the ground that Dunlop fails to explain how the actors' ideologies interact with the other components of the system to produce order and stability, and that Dunlop merely asserts ideological compatibility between the actors, whereas the extent to which beliefs and values converge or diverge is a matter for empirical investigation.[11]

There have been stages of development in many countries in which governments, employers and unions have each declared that coexistence with one of the other parties is impossible, that one party will have to be eliminated if industry is to progress. In many countries, although not in Australia, there have been periods in which governments and employers have sought to eliminate unions from the making of workplace rules. Certain unions, in particular those influenced by the International Workers of the World (IWW), and by some communist parties, have stated their objective as being the destruction of private ownership, and consequently the elimination of employers from any part in workplace rulemaking. In Eastern Europe, the former Communist governments denied unions any role in the industrial relations process, and dominated the managers. In all of these situations, workplace rules were not produced by the kind of system which Dunlop evolved. Workplaces in those cases would be governed, but the process of government would not include the interactions of Dunlop's actors, nor would they be conditioned by the kinds of constraints which he outlined.

Dunlop has not argued that there needs to be an ideological uniformity in order for his system to operate, but he has suggested that there are ideological positions which any of the parties might adopt which would prevent their being able to function as elements in an industrial relations system. Because of that possibility, it was necessary for him to specify a degree of ideological compatibility as the third variable of his system, and fluctuations in the extent of that compatibility can, of course, cause systems to operate badly or otherwise from time to time. Kochan Katz and McKersie,[12] for example, have suggested that many American scholars have wrongly attributed to employers an ideological shift to explain their 'acceptance' of the New Deal industrial relations legislation which required their acceptance of the unionism they had previously rejected. The view of Kochan et al. is that employers made pragmatic, or strategic, decisions to cease opposing unionism because of the high costs that would be incurred, given the New Deal ethos, in repulsing or dislodging unions. This suggests that while the American manager's predilection remained one of distaste for unionism, he was prepared to do business with them where necessary. Such an attitude is probably compatible with Dunlop's notion of a minimal ideological consensus.

It is important to distinguish the role of ideology as a variable in Dunlop's model from the ideological implications of the model itself. It is all but axiomatic that every theorist in the social sciences has a doctrinal position to further,[13] and it is possible to read Dunlop's work as a conception rooted in the Cold War, justifying a rejection of socialism in favour of a society dominated by its middle classes and providing access to the institutions of electoral democracy. The implicit ideological orientation of the Dunlop model should be distinguished from the overt inclusion of ideological consistency as part of the model itself. The broader implications of Dunlop's work are not of concern in this book whose focus is the analysis and understanding of the operations of parties to industrial relations.

Dunlop's system envisaged his three actors interacting to achieve workplace rules that suited their interests, but their pursuit of these was conditioned by the environment in which they operated. In particular, Dunlop suggested that their output of rules would be influenced by the state of technology, by the market and by the power relationships in the larger society. The actors in the system, if it were to evolve, would need sufficiently compatible ideological outlooks to allow them to pursue their own needs without requiring the destruction or exclusion of one of the other actors.

The web of rules

The complex of workplace rules[14] is the output of this system, the reason for its existence. It is important to keep in mind that, without some means of devising rules for workplace government, there is no *prima facie* means by which rights and obligations might be identified, at least none that would not be challenged by some of the parties. The workplace rules that exist are of two kinds, *procedural rules* and *substantive rules*. Procedural rules are those which govern the processes by which the parties intend working. They would, for example, set out the processes by which agreed contracts of employment between worker and manager might be reached, but they would not specify any details of that contract. Procedural rules might set out the processes which would be followed to resolve conflict between the parties, but would not cover the terms on which any conflict would be settled. Many Australian industrial agreements and awards contain procedures which must be followed for the settlement of disputes which arise on the job. These do not attempt to determine outcomes, but they do prescribe methods that should be followed to resolve the matter. These are adopted because the parties find the processes concerned to be the most potentially useful method acceptable to all of them.

Procedural rules are concerned much more with how things are done than what in fact is done. Procedures adopted can influence not only the actual outcomes of the system, but they can profoundly influence the nature of the actors and institutions involved. The procedural rule requiring the settlement of industrial disputes by conciliation and arbitration tribunals has been very important in shaping the form, structure and behaviour of Australian unions, and in the industrial relations role of employer associations.

It is to be noted that procedural rules extend beyond the processes for making work rules and resolving conflicts with administration and interpretation of those rules. Procedural rules can also extend to rules controlling the internal governments of any of the actors. Some of those procedural rules are discussed below in the section dealing with union government and with employer associations.

The substantive rules are those rules which specify the rights and obligations of employers and employees. They may be contained in the contract of employment, which is frequently governed by an award, they may be contained in an industrial agreement, and they may be provided by some form of legislation. The rates of pay, the hours of work, the conditions of work are all substantive rules, and these are always contained in the formal awards and agreements, as are many other conditions. Substantive rules also include those practices that have been agreed informally over time, or have merely become accepted through longevity. These are the rules that are usually of the most direct concern to working people and their employers.

As a broad generalisation, it can be said that governments tend to be more interested in procedural than in substantive rules, while workers and employers tend to be more concerned with the substantive. Given the resources and expertise at the disposal of each actor, the range of interests and the constraints faced by each actor, it is probably reasonable to expect that the government will be the most effective party in the development of procedural rules, although the organisations of both workers and employers are also likely to have an interest in these.

Governments have, in several countries, including Australia, shown an interest in interfering with one aspect of substantive rules as they have attempted to curb inflation through the control of wage increases. (The matter of wage policy in Australia is further discussed in chapter 16.) There is little evidence to support the proposition that a successful policy of wage control would in fact reduce inflation, nor is there anything in economic theory to suggest that this process is the appropriate method of tackling a problem of inflation. While it is probably kind to assume that these wage control policies are an attempt to use the industrial relations system to achieve some increase in political popularity, of interest here is that they do indicate that governments can and do sometimes have an interest in substantive as well as procedural rules.

Dunlop has set out a systematic account of the way in which this network of workplace rules is determined. It has been argued generally that this does fall some way short of being a complete theory of industrial relations, a theory which will have predictive value, because it lacks an internal dynamic. There is no factor which explains the driving force of the system, and a complete theory must have this. However, as indicated above, to suggest that the theory lacks that dynamic is not to suggest that the Dunlop approach is without value to the student of industrial relations.

It does allow one to classify information, to understand the purpose of industrial relations activity. It can provide a useful means of testing whether or not an actor is taking part in industrial relations or some other activity, something which is useful in Australia where both unions and employer organisations are often interested in areas that go well beyond the making and administration of workplace rules, and where governments often seek to obtain political or economic ends from the industrial relations system. Dunlop's system may not explain exactly how various outcomes are reached, but it does enable the observer to comprehend something of the parties involved, and of the forces which bear on them. It is a useful way of identifying the differences and similarities between the industrial relations systems and outcomes of various nations, and of analysing changes over time in the industrial relations of any single country.

Walker

A variant on the Dunlop view provided by K.F. Walker[15] may have overcome some of the weaknesses, and certainly expanded on the original. Walker suggested that the processes of industrial relations were critical in developing the web of rules, thus the Australian tripartite arbitral processes might be expected to produce different outcomes to the closely regulated bipartite collective bargaining of the United States, and different again to the much less regulated form of collective bargaining that characterised England through the 1960s. Process, scarcely discussed in Dunlop's work, was a critical variable to Walker.

Perhaps of equal importance was Walker's extrapolation of the environmental contexts and of the ideological variable. His work alerts the reader to the importance of the process of evolution in industrial relations, that one cannot expect to install a new system, even if it should be inherently superior, without experiencing considerable turmoil, and without expecting that the results of such a newly installed system will be far from identical to those it produced elsewhere. The fact that enterprise unionism, for example, may be judged to have worked well in Japan, does not suggest that it will solve all the industrial relations problems of Australia, nor that the apparently successful conglomerate unions of the Federal Republic of Germany would be acceptable and workable in Australia. Walker suggests that institutional practices are developed out of a particular historical experience which has shaped not merely industrial relations, but the nature of society as a whole. The versions of the Australian arbitral system that have been adopted in certain Asian nations operate very differently to the Australian model, usually eliminating any scope for negotiation, and determining strictly enforced labour codes.

A very important lesson that can be drawn from Walker's work is that the industrial relations system must always be seen as a component of the general social system, thus it can only be varied within limits determined by that larger system. This does not mean of course, that industrial relations systems can never change. It does mean that major change, or seeking totally new directions can only be accomplished with difficulty and will meet resistance; it probably means too that outcomes may be different to those expected.

Flanders

Dunlop's approach to industrial relations is one of many. Not all analysts have elected to focus on the development of workplace rules, although this is at the heart of Allan Flanders' work.[16] His study, in many ways more insightful than Dunlop's, was developed independently, and is one of the few studies dealing with workplace rules (or job regulation, as Flanders called it) which is not a variation on the Dunlop theme.

One of the more valuable aspects of Flanders' work is that it emphasises that there are workplace rules, often unwritten, which may be developed quite independently by management or by labour. Workers and unions do not seek to influence every decision management makes, even though some such decisions may have some effect on them. Similarly, there are some elements of workers' behaviour on the job which employers do not attempt to influence or to control. Flanders' work points to the fact that every facet of workplace government is unlikely to be included in the web of rules that is created by the interaction of Dunlop's actors. There are some parts of the worker and managerial behaviour that are guided by rules that are known only to those directly involved. This custom and practice, or workplace culture, is usually highly individual and is often unwritten, but it may be at least as important as any formal regulation.

Industrial relations problems can arise when there is inconsistency between the formal rules, awards or agreements, and the accepted, or customary practices. Such inconsistencies can arise when the formal rule-makers do not involve people familiar with the practicalities of the workplace in question, or when either party seeks, unilaterally, to change the accepted practices. Attempts by either party to impose change is the exception rather than the rule, and usually these are caused by major changes in personnel, equipment or in trading conditions. While the past twenty years has seen an increasing awareness in Australia of the need for bipartite consultation in response to technical change and to economic performance, changes in personnel do result in disputes over departures from accepted standards. Where a manager or a union official has been newly appointed with a specific mandate to change the behaviour in question, conflict may be inevitable. On the other hand, as formal industrial relations rule-making becomes increasingly centred on the workplace, it should become easier for all to predict the extent of resistance to attempts to alter existing practices.

A good deal of industrial relations writing is concentrated exclusively on the broad dimensions and on the making, rather than the administration, of agreements. Flanders' work is an important starting point for those who wish to undertake the difficult, but essential, task of integrating behaviour in the workplace into an overall system of industrial relations.

Marx

An entirely different type of industrial relations theorising is that which is derived from Marx[17] and from Marxist writers. This branch of theory suggests basically that the most valuable insights can be gained from the study of the causes and areas of disagreement between labour and management, whereas the Dunlop focus on workplace rules is essentially concerned with how they reach agreement. In other words, the former is concerned primarily with the sources of industrial conflict, and the latter with its resolution.

The various Marxist approaches to industrial relations do not share the basic problem which arises in attempting to treat Dunlop's work as a theory, for the Marxist approach does incorporate a dynamic element. The fundamental clash of interest, which the Marxist interpretation of capitalism suggests must exist between worker and employer provides that element. On the other hand, it has been argued that the Marxist interpretation of the clash of interest between workers and employers is erroneous.

The alternative view is that the conflict exists, but it does not derive from the necessarily exploitative nature of capitalism, but from the clash between the progressive elements of industrial society and the conservatives.[18] Employers find their security depends on their being able to move to new methods of work and to new products, where the security of employees depends on their being able to prevent these from changing, for so long as work methods remain static, workers monopolise job content, thereby enhancing their security. Employers therefore represent a force for progress in industry, while workers seek to limit or prevent it. If that argument were accepted, it would suggest that the approach concentrating on workplace rules might be more productive than one which focused on conflict.

The conflict-based theories, probably always claiming a minority of adherents, have been displaced in the Marxist-derived literature over recent decades by the labour process theories. Marxist economic analysis depends heavily on the existence of a discrepancy between the amount of labour the employer purchases on the market and the amount applied to production. The discrepancy exists because of the employer's monopoly of access to employment in the competitive system. The capitalist is able, under the assumptions of the competitive system, to purchase labour at the competitive rate, i.e. subsistence wages, but can determine, given the monopoly of employment opportunity, the amount of time actually worked. Being required by the capitalist system to make a profit, the employer requires the worker to work for longer than would be needed to generate a subsistence wage, the rate the worker is paid. The discrepancy, or surplus value as Marx calls it, is the sole source of profit in the capitalist system.

Marx refers to the amount of labour for which the capitalist actually pays as labour power, and this is converted to what Marx refers to as labour, representing the quantity actually used in production and sold as part of final output of the employer. The calculations by which Marx identifies these quantities of labour power, labour, surplus value and the like, are based on the labour theory of value, a once-critical economic concept derived by David Ricardo, but long since abandoned by neo-classical economists. In Marx's terms, labour power is converted into labour by the labour process, a term which encapsulates the development of tasks by management, as well as the management, control and discipline of labour.

Braverman

Perhaps the major writer on the labour process is Braverman whose *Labor and Monopoly Capital*, published in 1974, generated a resurgent interest in the ideas of Marx. The focus of writers in the labour process school is the nature of work, with particular emphasis on the argument that the skill component is decreasing, and on the ways in which work is organised. Braverman applies Marx's theory to his study of the evolution of labour processes, that is the processes of production, in capitalist society, together with the evolution of management (see chapter 9), of technology and of the modern corporation.

The labour process comprises a number of aspects: labour power (the human capacity to perform work), the instruments of labour, the materials of labour and the products of labour. The starting point for Braverman's analysis is the transfer of control over the labour process from the worker to the capitalist and this major work is concerned primarily with the manner in which the labour process is dominated and shaped by the accumulation of capital.[19] Braverman explains that the *differentia specifica* of capitalist production is the purchase and sale of labour power which involves:

1 the separation of workers from the means with which production is carried on, access to those means being attained only by selling their labour power to others;
2 the freeing of workers from legal constraints such as serfdom or slavery that prevent them from disposing of their own labour power; and
3 the expansion of a unit of capital, belonging to the employer, becoming the purpose of the employment of the worker.

The labour process under industrial capitalism begins with a contract governing the conditions of the sale of labour power by the worker and its purchase by the employer. It is activated by two factors:

1 for the worker the contract represents the sole means of gaining a livelihood and
2 the employer, as the possessor of a unit of capital which he or she is endeavouring to enlarge, converting part of that capital into wages.

From this point on, Braverman argues, the labour process, which in general is a process for creating useful values becomes also, and especially in the mind and actions of the capitalist, a process of accumulation of capital.[20]

The acquisition and maintenance of employer control over the labour process is necessary because the employer is now responsible for it. In other words, the labour process becomes the responsibility of the capitalist when workers sell their labour power, that is, the power to labour over an agreed amount of time. Workers thereby surrender their interest in this process, which has now been alienated and the capitalist purchases something for which the outcome is neither certain nor definite, both the quality and quantity is undefined.[21]

Employer or management control derives from the manufacturing division of labour, that is the systematic division of the work of each productive specialty into limited operations. This division of labour destroys the craft, a process under the control of the worker and reconstitutes it as a process under the control of managers, that is those who are contracted to extract from labour power the maximum advantage for the capitalist.[22]

The gains derived from the manufacturing (to be distinguished from the social) division of labour, the creation of the life-long detail worker, are management control and productivity.[23] Braverman regards the Babbage principle[24] as fundamental to the evolution of the division of labour in capitalist society. The principle states that, in a society based upon the purchase and sale of labour power, dividing the craft cheapens its individual parts.[25]

Braverman derives a general law of the division of labour with the Babbage principle as a given: every step in the labour process is divorced from special knowledge and training, and reduced to simple labour. The capitalist method of production systematically destroys all-round skills where they exist and brings into being skills and occupations that meet its needs. Under feudal and guild handicraft, production work remained under the immediate control of the producers. Thus it was transformed from a capacity integrated in a single worker into dissociated elements.[26]

Importantly the shift of control from workers to employers, or their representatives, occurs in different occupations at different times and in varying degrees in different industries. Employers, argues Braverman, seek to displace labour as the subjective element in production and subordinate it as an objective element, to make it a factor of production in a production process conducted by management as the 'sole subjective element'.[27] They do not always achieve their objective and one reason for this is that the very pursuit of this objective brings into being new crafts, skills and technical specialties which are at first controlled by labour rather than management.[28] This was true initially for the occupation of engineering. By the 1970s this had become a new mass occupation in the United States, having grown from less than 100 000 in 1900 to about 1.25 million in 1970.[29] The large numbers, the emergence of duties which could be routinised and advances in solid-state technology[30] saw the separation of 'thinking' and 'doing' applied to this occupation. One example was the subjection of a major function of an engineer's job, namely design, to the traditional rules of the division of labour, including the transfer of part of the functions of an engineer to electronic equipment. Braverman observes that engineering thus began to exhibit features identified with other mass employment: 'rationalisation and division of labour, simplification of duties, application of mechanisation, a downward drift in relative pay, some unemployment and some unionisation'.[31]

Braverman also discusses office work which, in the last decades of the nineteenth century, began to change from something merely incidental to management into a labour process in its own right. He describes the conversion of the office routine into a factory-like process, in accordance with the precepts of modern management and available technology. A precipitating factor here was the need to maintain a shadow replica of the entire process of production in paper form. This brought into being large technical and office staffs. Braverman stresses that the proportion of this large group which holds the technical knowledge required to operate the various industries is very small and most of these jobs are closely linked to management.[32] In the case of the retail trade, the 'skills' of store operations are disassembled and in all decisive respects vested in management. Braverman's discussion in the early 1970s anticipates the revolution of computerised check-out systems which he predicts will bring retail workers close to factory operatives.[33]

Arguments that the component of skill in work is declining would be more convincing if supported by hard data, and the assertion that a diminution in skill is logically related to capitalism requires more logical support than it has been given. Labour process writers devote a great deal of attention to the control of workers by employers, and it is difficult for some, at least, not to interpret this as being based on the assumption that the major purpose of management is not to make profits, but to maximise its control of the workforce.

Littler[34] has provided an extensive review of the post-Braverman labour process literature. Littler's work reviews writing in the extensive field of industrial sociology in general. Bray and Taylor,[35] in the labour process tradition, direct their focus to Australian work and confine it to the bounds of what is more conventionally seen as industrial relations. Those interested in the area will find value in both these works.

Whatever may be its intrinsic strengths, this area of industrial relations theorising has not been widely influential. Perhaps its greatest value lies in its Marxist antecedents. Whether or not one accepts the Marxist analysis, it does make clear that the world cannot adequately be comprehended by reliance on a single discipline, and this is of critical importance in the study of industrial relations. One may reject the political, economic, psychological and sociological arguments that are implicit and explicit in the labour process writings, but the fact that they are made does remind the student of industrial relations that it is a complicated business.

Kochan, Katz and McKersie

The currently popular theoretical approach is that of Kochan, Katz and McKersie[36] and this is derived from the Dunlop and post-Dunlop literature. The work of a former Dunlop student, Kenneth Walker[37] (see above) in emphasising the importance of industrial relations processes, had done a good deal to overcome the major problem of Dunlop's work, the lack of an internal dynamic element. However, to the extent that Dunlop's work is now of diminished relevance, the major challenge to its supremacy has come not from the world of theory, but from the experience of American industrial relations in practice.

Dunlop's work was published in an era in which United States unionism seemed to have reached an enviable stage of power and authority. It had grown sufficiently in strength and influence to be seen to meet big business on equal terms. It had done much to reduce the insecurity of industrial employment, brought the rule of law to workplaces by requiring that managers show cause for actions against employees, unions had forced a high degree of acceptance in the councils of government, and they had gone a long way in the struggle to achieve dignified retirement for their members. The American unions had done this without challenging the capitalist system, and without sacrificing the interests of their members to those of employers. It is difficult to read Dunlop's *Industrial Relations Systems* without gaining the impression that he saw all of the capitalist world's unions as moving towards this model.

The experience of the 1970s and 1980s was that United States unionism declined enormously in relative terms, slipping from having thirty-three per cent of the workforce organised in 1956 to nineteen per cent in 1985.[38] Employers could be seen actively campaigning to drive unions from established workplaces, and relocating to areas in which unions could not easily gain representation. This was hardly the outcome that Dunlop's approach would have suggested. At the very least, the degree of ideological compatibility of management and labour may have lessened.

Thomas A. Kochan with his colleagues H.C. Katz and R.B. McKersie published in 1986 an account of American labour relations which incorporates extensive revisions to the Dunlop approach, and which seeks to account for significant changes in the practice of industrial relations. Kochan, Katz and McKersie have sought to analyse changes in American industrial relations rather than to develop a universal account, as did Dunlop, and their work, while not yet the dominant view, is certainly a central topic of discussion in the United States. Its American focus does not render it irrelevant to the rest of the world, for it deals with large themes which have some relevance for most of the developed capitalist world.

In large part Kochan, Katz and McKersie concentrate on the role of management in industrial relations. The Dunlop version paid little attention to the motives or practices of the actors, and the assumptions of entrepreneurial behaviour adopted by micro economists were implicit in Dunlop's treatment of management. The behaviour of unions is not explored in much depth by Kochan *et al*. nor is it treated extensively by Dunlop. A decade before Dunlop's work was published, Arthur M. Ross[39] published a most insightful account of the behaviour of unions in wage bargaining. Ross suggests that no simple maximisation assumption could be attributed to unions in this activity, but they have to be understood as economic agents operating according to a political rationality. Ross' valuable analysis, when read in conjunction with Perlman's[40] theory of the union probably provides a relatively complete theoretical account of the behaviour to be expected of unions in industrial relations.

In some senses, Kochan, Katz and McKersie have attempted to provide such a perspective on management. Through the 1970s and 1980s, the image of American management had altered from that of respondent in industrial relations to initiator. The stereotypical managerial role of respondency was never accurate, and probably resulted from the fact that the first overt step in collective bargaining was that the union served a demand on management which was subsequently rejected. The well publicised 'hard line' approach of General Electric Corporation[41] during the 1950s depended on managerial initiative, as did the 'work rules' issues (work practices, in Australian parlance) that arose regularly in collective bargaining throughout the years after the Second World War.

Kochan, Katz and McKersie have sought to explain the behaviour of managers in an era in which unions no longer seem to be the initiators in collective bargaining. There is no successful explanation of the process by which this role reversal in industrial relations took place, and these researchers have not sought to explain it, but to set out the behaviour of management in the changed circumstances. Their account covers the considerable change in labour management relations from the situation in which industrial relations managers sought agreement with unions on the rules which would govern labour to the current practice in which human resource managers assist in having managerial policy accepted by the employees, but examination of this transition is not the major thrust of their work. Their concern is not to explain why that change has taken place.

The central purpose of the Kochan, Katz and McKersie work is the explanation of how management operates in industrial relations. Although this explanation has emerged as management power in industrial relations generally has increased, the authors have not explained the means by which the ascendancy has passed to management. That has not been their intention, for their concern is to explain how goals are identified and pursued, something which, at least so far as management's role is concerned, has been lacking in the industrial relations literature.

Kochan, Katz and McKersie suggest that other actors in the industrial relations system, labour and government also make strategic choices which dominate their respective behaviours. Their approach is depicted in figure 2.1.

Figure 2.1 General Framework for Analysing Industrial Relations Issues

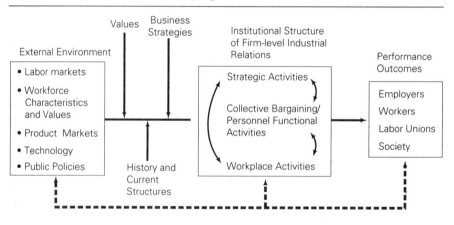

Source: T.A. Kochan, H.C. Katz and R.B. McKersie, *The Transformation of American Industrial Relations*, Basic Books, New York, 1986, p. 11.

While this is insightful, and is, at the very least a valuable expansion of the Dunlop model, it is not without its problems and critics. The concept of a strategic choice or decision is difficult. There is no doubt that businesses do have strategies, and that they make decisions based on those strategies, but the fact remains that it is easier to identify a strategic decision in retrospect than in advance, making it a concept of dubious theoretical value.

This framework draws attention to the asymmetry of management and union interests. Unions do have goals and concerns other than industrial relations, but this must be central to their activities and policies. Managers, on the other hand, are essentially focused on such business dimensions as meeting budget, achieving cost and production targets or expanding market share. Industrial relations can influence any of these but it is not always the central factor.

A gross over-simplification is that management behaviour may sometimes be driven by commercial goals which may make industrial relations seem unimportant. The unions with which managers deal will be mainly concerned with industrial relations outcomes, and will wish to treat commercial goals as relevant only to the extent that they impinge on industrial relations. This diversity can make both the practice and analysis of industrial relations very difficult. Under the arbitral system, to the extent that the tribunals too have policy objectives which are not identical to those of unions or managers, the complexity is increased.

Conclusion

The industrial relations world has not yet accepted the Kochan, Katz and McKersie analysis as the dominant approach. It has been analysed extensively, and the most prestigious of the specialist journals in the United States devoted an entire issue to such an analysis.[42] It has been criticised extensively, especially by David Lewin,[43] but it is a central topic for discussion. If it has done nothing else, it has forced analysts to direct their attention more closely to management behaviour, and to try to understand the needs and goals of managers in industrial relations. In the past there has been more attention paid to the process of bargaining and to contract administration than to the opposing goals which make bargaining necessary.

In the chapters that follow, the Dunlop account will be important, but it will be used as an organising device to assist in explanation, rather than as an analytical tool.

It is useful to keep in mind that Dunlop saw the rules that govern workplaces as the 'web' rather than as a code or some other form which may be more suggestive of orderly and logical development. Dunlop's term is appropriate to a body of regulation which is based more on fluctuation in balances of power than on adherence to any set of logical principles, or even on the long-term historical process which underlies more general legislation.

It may be noted that one lesson that Australians might learn from the Kochan, Katz and McKersie work is that if American analysts in the past have devoted excessive attention to union views and aspirations, many Australians have relegated to secondary importance both union and management goals, and have concentrated instead on government, as well as on the centralised organisations of both unions and management. These are relevant but by no means are they the totality of the actors.

Approaches to the study of relations may be classified as unitary, pluralist or radical. An influential work by Fox,[44] published in the mid-1960s, explains the first two concepts in terms of management values and a summary of his analytical framework is included in the chapter concerned with management concepts and theories (chapter 9). The writing of Dunlop, Walker, Flanders and Kochan, Katz and McKersie reflects a pluralist approach while that of Marx and Braverman reflects a radical approach.

Notes

1. John T. Dunlop, *Industrial Relations Systems*, Holt, New York, 1958, Reprint Arcturus Books, 1977.
2. *ibid.*, p. 7.
3. T. Parsons, *The Structure of Social Action*, McGraw-Hill, New York, 1937.
4. Dunlop, *op. cit.*, pp. 7-8.
5. *ibid.*, pp. 9-10 and pp. 33-61.
6. During the 1980s this union was removed from the formal industrial relations system in a number of jurisdictions by legislation (see chapter 6).
7. Dunlop, *op. cit.*, pp. 10-11 and pp. 62-93.
8. This agreement found formal expression as part of the *Statement of Accord by the Australian Labor Party and the Australian Council of Trade Unions Regarding Economic Policy*, February 1983.
9. Dunlop, *op. cit.*, pp. 11-12 and pp. 94-128.
10. *ibid.*, pp. 16-18 and pp. 21-23.
11. R. Hyman, *Strikes* (4th ed.), Macmillan, London, 1989, p. 71.
12. T.A. Kochan, H.C. Katz and R.B. McKersie, *The Transformation of American Industrial Relations*, Basic Books, New York, 1986, p. 14.
13. N. Arnold Tolles, *Origins of Modern Wage Theories*, Prentice Hall, Englewood Cliffs, 1964, pp. 5-7.
14. Dunlop, *op. cit.*, pp. 13-16 and pp. 383-387.
15. K.F. Walker 'The Comparative Study of Industrial Relations', *International Institute for Labour Studies Bulletin*, No. 3, November 1967, pp. 108-132.
16. A. Flanders, 'Industrial Relations: What is Wrong with the System?', in A. Flanders, *Management and Unions: The Theory and Reform of Industrial Relations*, Faber, London, 1975, pp. 83-128.
17. An accessible source of Marx's views on trade unionism is A. Lozovsky, *Marx and the Trade Unions*, International Publishers, New York, 1942.
18. C. Kerr, J.T. Dunlop, F.H. Harbison, and C.A. Myers, *Industrialism and Industrial Man*, Oxford University Press, New York, 1964.
19. H. Braverman, *Labor and Monopoly Capital*, Monthly Review Press, New York, 1974, p. 53.
20. *ibid.*, pp. 51-53.
21. *ibid.*, pp. 57-58.
22. *ibid.*, pp. 69-70 & 78.
23. *ibid.*, p. 78.
24. C. Babbage, *On the Economy of Machinery and Manufactures*, London, 1832, New York, reprint ed. 1963.
25. Braverman, *op. cit.*, pp. 80-81.
26. *ibid.*, pp. 81-83.
27. *ibid.*, p. 171.
28. *ibid.*, p. 172.
29. *ibid.*, p. 26.
30. *ibid.*, p. 245.
31. *ibid.*, p. 244.
32. *ibid.*, pp. 239-242.
33. *ibid.*, p. 371.
34. C. Littler, 'Labour Process Literature—A Review 1974-1986', in K. Hince and A. Williams (eds), *Contemporary Industrial Relations in Australia and New Zealand: Literature Surveys*, Proceedings of the Biennial Conference of the Association of Industrial Relations Academics of Australia and New Zealand, vol. 1, January 1987.
35. M. Bray and V. Taylor (eds), *Managing Labour? Essays in the Political Economy of Australian Industrial Relations*, McGraw Hill, Sydney, 1986.
36. Kochan, Katz & McKersie, *op. cit.*, chapter 1.
37. Walker, *op. cit.*
38. Kochan, Katz & McKersie, *op.cit.*, p. 8.

39 A.M. Ross, *Trade Union Wage Policy*, University of California Press, Berkeley, 1956.
40 S. Perlman, *A Theory of the Labor Movement*, Augustus Kelley, New York, 1928.
41 H.R. Northrup, 'The Case for Boulwarism', *Harvard Business Review*, October 1963, pp. 86-97.
42 Review Symposium, *Industrial and Labor Relations Review 41*, April 1988.
43 D. Lewin, 'Industrial Relations as a Strategic Variable', in M. Kleiner, *et. al.*, *Human Resource Management and the Performance of the Firm*, Industrial Relations Research Association, Wisconsin, 1988, chapter 1.
44 A. Fox, *Industrial Sociology and Industrial Relations*, Research Paper No. 3, Royal Commission on Employer Associations and Trade Unions, HMSO, London, 1966. Reprinted in A. Flanders (ed.), *Collective Bargaining*, Penguin, Harmondsworth, 1969, pp. 391-408.

Further Reading

Systems approach

A. Craig, 'A Framework for the Analysis of Industrial Relations Systems', in B. Barrett, E. Rhodes and J. Beishon (eds), *Industrial Relations and the Wider Society*, Collier Macmillan, London, 1975, pp. 8-20.

B. Dabscheck, 'Of Mountains and Routes Over Them: A Survey of Theories of Industrial Relations', *Journal of Industrial Relations 25*, December 1983, pp. 485-506.

J.T. Dunlop, *Industrial Relations Systems*, Holt, New York, 1958.

A. Flanders, *Industrial Relations: What is Wrong with the System*, Faber and Faber, London, 1965.

A.J. Geare, 'The Field of Study of Industrial Relations', *Journal of Industrial Relations 19*, September 1977, pp. 274-285.

K. Laffer, 'Is Industrial Relations an Academic Discipline?', *Journal of Industrial Relations 16*, March 1974, pp. 62-73.

G.G. Somers (ed.), *Essays in Industrial Relations Theory*, Iowa State University Press, Iowa, 1969.

K.F. Walker, 'The Comparative Study of Industrial Relations', *International Institute for Labour Studies Bulletin*, No. 3, November 1967, pp. 108-132.

Labour process approach

H. Braverman, *Labour and Monopoly Capital*, Monthly Review Press, 1974.

M. Bray and V. Taylor (eds), *Managing Labour? Essays in the Political Economy of Australian Industrial Relations*, McGraw-Hill, Sydney, 1986.

R. Hyman, *Industrial Relations: A Marxist Introduction*, Macmillan, London, 1975.

C. Littler, 'Labour Process Literature—A Review 1974-1986' in K. Hince and A. Williams (eds), *Contemporary Industrial Relations in Australia and New Zealand: Literature Surveys*, Proceedings of the Biennial Conference of the Association of Industrial Relations Academics of Australia and New Zealand, vol. 1, January 1987.

C. Littler, M. Quinlan, J. Kitay, 'Australian workplace industrial relations: towards a conceptual framework', in B. Dabscheck, G. Griffin and J. Teicher (eds), *Contemporary Australian Industrial Relations: Readings*, Longman Cheshire, Melbourne, 1992, pp. 37-63.

Strategic choice

T.A. Kochan, R.B. McKersie and P. Capelli, 'Strategic Choice and Industrial Relations Theory', *Industrial Relations 23*, Winter 1984, pp. 16-39.

T.A. Kochan, H.C. Katz and R.B. McKersie, *The Transformation of American Industrial Relations*, Basic Books, New York, 1986.

D. Lewin 'Industrial Relations as a Strategic Variable', in M. Kleiner, R.N. Block, M. Roomkin and S.W. Salsburg (eds), *Human Resources Management and the Performance of the Firm*, Industrial Relations Research Association, Madison, Wisconsin, 1988, chapter 1.

Questions

Dunlop

1 Explain Dunlop's concept of an industrial relations system and evaluate its contribution to the study of industrial relations.
2 Summarise the major criticisms of Dunlop's systems concept.

Flanders

3 Define the terms 'procedural rules' and 'substantive rules' introduced by Flanders.
4 Distinguish between the Dunlop and Flanders frameworks for analysing industrial relations.

Braverman

5 What are the major distinctions between the 'systems approach' and the 'labour process approach' to the study of industrial relations.

Kochan, Katz and McKersie

6 Explain the difference between the general framework developed by Kochan, Katz and Mckersie and Dunlop's systems framework.
7 Do you consider that 'strategic choice' is a useful concept for analysing industrial relations? (This question should be attempted after the relevant material in chapter 9 has been read).

Comparative approaches

8 How is a theory of industrial relations useful to students? Which of the theories do you find most useful?
9 It can be argued that each of the industrial relations theories, whatever its overall merits or defects, is of most use in analysing or understanding some particular aspects of the employer-employee relationship. In which areas do you find the following to be useful:
    Dunlop
    Flanders
    Marx
    Braverman
    Kochan, Katz and McKersie
In which areas are each of them most deficient?

10 The following are excerpts from speeches by two American participants in industrial relations of a past era.

> 'The rights of the laboring man will be protected and cared for—not by the labor agitators, but by the Christian men to whom God in his infinite wisdom has given control of the property interests of this country...'

(George F. Baer, spokesman for the coal industry employers in 1902.)

> 'I have never faltered or failed to present the cause or plead the case of the mine workers of this country. I have pleaded your case ... in the councils of the President's cabinet; and in the public press of this nation—not in the quavering tones of a feeble mendicant asking alms, but in the thundering voice of the captain of a mighty host, demanding the rights to which free men are entitled.'

(John L. Lewis, President, United Mine Workers of America, 1920-1960.)

If these statements reflected the values in employer-employee relations at the time, which of the theoretical approaches might have been the most useful analytical tool?

Exercises

1 Examine an industry award and identify the procedural and substantive rules. Identify the parties (unions, employees, managers, tribunals, governments) which you would expect to have the most interest in including each rule.

2 (a) Summarise Braverman's argument concerning the application of his theory to the work of engineers.

 (b) Examine the organisation of engineering work in a major statutory authority (for example, Telecom Australia; State Electricity Commission of Victoria) and evaluate Braverman's theory in this contemporary context.

 (c) Do you consider the research in (b) above to be a fair test of the theory?

3
Industrial Conflict and Industrial Action

Contents

Manifestations of industrial conflict
Causes of industrial conflict
Unions and industrial conflict
Industrial action
- purposes of industrial action
- political strikes

Measures of industrial conflict
- Australian strike statistics
- the Australian Workplace Survey
- strike statistics international comparisons

Functions of industrial conflict
Industrial conflict and absenteeism: comparative costs

Introduction

An important factor distinguishing some of the approaches to industrial relations discussed in chapter 2, was the differing characterisations of industrial conflict. This chapter considers various aspects of industrial conflict. The discussion on sources, or causes, of conflict necessarily has some commonality with arguments summarised in the previous chapter. Industrial action, which is a manifestation of conflict and can also be a catalyst for resolving it, is analysed here in detail. Further, industrial conflict as a source of lost time is placed in perspective. At the outset industrial conflict should be defined and Kerr[1] argues that industrial conflict exists in any of three possible situations. The most broad-ranging concept of conflict is simply a situation in which opposed interests intersect. Thus, for example, if unions are committed to increasing their members' wage rates, and employers to holding them constant, the existence of those two policies is itself a state of industrial conflict. A more restricted notion is that one or other of the parties holding these opposed policies may undertake some action to achieve its ends. That action may be no more than to make a demand on its opponent, but once the demand is made and refused, a state of conflict exists. The third, and most restrictive notion is that conflict exists only when some quite specific action is taken on the basis of opposed interests. Those who hold this view would argue that conflict does not exist until, for example, a union imposes work bans in support of its demands which have been refused by the employer.

Manifestations of industrial conflict

As the term conflict is used here, the second of the above meanings should be ascribed to it: conflict is some action taken to support the interests of one party which are opposed by another. This is a somewhat broader meaning than is often applied, and certainly it comprehends a much wider range of action than the strike. Clearly strikes and lock-outs are manifestations of industrial conflict, but they are one type, certainly not its totality. The manifestation, or symptom, may be diplomatic or coercive and it may be unorganised or organised. A log of claims submitted by a union or an employer is a diplomatic, organised manifestation of conflict. Some recent examples of coercive organised symptoms are the restrictions on flying hours imposed by members of the Australian Federation of Air Pilots in 1989 in relation to a union salary claim and the bans on so-called non-essential services by members of the Health Services Union in Victoria in 1991 in relation to an employer redundancy and redeployment claim. A century earlier, in 1891, a strike by shearers in Queensland was one of a number of strikes in response to employer attempts to re-establish freedom of contract, that is the right to negotiate directly with individual employees without regard to union-preferred rates or conditions.

It is obviously more difficult to cite empirical examples of unorganised conflict for they may not even be recognised as such by the employers involved. An in-principle example would be loss of co-operation in production: individual employees reducing their pace of work or wasting materials because of dissatisfaction with some aspect of their contract of employment, for example their relative rate of pay or the autocratic style of their supervisor. These actions could not be regarded as coercive but they do impose costs on the employer and are distinguishable from diplomatic unorganised action, such as a letter seeking a pay rise or lodging a complaint about a supervisor with senior management. It is important to appreciate that employer-employee conflict exists where employees are not organised. The above examples are only some of the various ways in which aggrieved employees can manifest their individual dissatisfactions. Employees may also damage equipment;[2] develop bad relations with supervisors and colleagues; absent themselves often from work; make excessive unjustified use of welfare facilities and generally try to provide as little as possible to the employer for the highest cost. These unorganised forms of conflict are often long-lasting, subtle and insidious; they are often not detected until they are well-established and habitual, and when detected they are often not even recognised as being symptoms of conflict. Clearly they can be extremely costly for employers.

An organised manifestation of conflict which is intended to be diplomatic is picketing. It may occur in conjunction with coercive action, by either employer or employees, or it may stand alone. Picketing usually involves attendance near the workplace with the object of persuading people not to conduct business (especially the delivery of supplies) with the enterprise or not to remain working for that enterprise. In addition to exhortation, picketing is one means of maintaining morale and group loyalty. It also provides a ready focus for electronic media coverage of a dispute and this is as likely to harm either party as much as it helps them. In the British common law tradition, a right to picketing exists, but it is essentially a right to do no more than to be physically present, although not to trespass on the employer's property, and to rely on argument and moral suasion to achieve the picketers' goals. Crouch argues[3] that the relevance of this right has diminished since the development of modern transport equipment and methods. On the other hand, situations do occur in which existing protection has been sufficient to enable picket lines to stop trucks. At the strike at APPM's Burnie mill in 1992, pickets did achieve that result and management took legal action in an attempt to break the picket line (see Table 3.1). It would probably be fair to say that picketing is an area where the spirit and intent of the activity is frequently transgressed by both sides in a conflict. It does need to be kept in mind that the law regarding picketing is complex. Pickets are rarely free of accusations of trespass, disrupting traffic or various forms of disorderly behaviour. When picket lines are removed by police, the action is rarely justified on the grounds that the picket line itself is unlawful. Usually it is argued that in the course of maintaining the picket line, the participants have transgressed in some other way.

The most dramatic symptom of conflict is the strike or lock-out. The former involves the total or partial withdrawal of labour by employees acting in combination to compel an employer to accept an employee demand or to withdraw an employer demand. A lock-out involves the employer

Table 3.1 APPM Burnie dispute 1992: picket line

Company awaits Supreme Court decision after breakdown of peace talks

APPM prepares to crash picket line

By BRUCE MONTGOMERY and BOB ENGLISH

Associated Pulp and Paper Mills last night signalled immediate action to break the picket line at its Burnie plant after the breakdown late last night of government-based peace talks in Hobart.

The timing of APPM's move on the picket hinges on the outcome perhaps today of the company's Supreme Court action to force Burnie police to assist the company to break the picket line to allow trucks out and workers in.

Mr Peter Wade, the managing director of APPM's parent company, North Broken Hill-Peko, said: "We will take workers through the picket line as soon as they can be assured free passage."

The talks, convened by the Premier of Tasmania, Mr Groom, and the federal Minister for Industrial Relations, Senator Cook, broke down after 5½ hours at 11pm when the company refused to give up its right to appeal against parts of a decision made on Friday by industrial relations commissioner Mr Paul Munro.

Mr Munro ordered employees to return to work at 4pm today but also ordered the company to give workers guarantees on safety and notice of dismissal.

The president of the ACTU, Mr Martin Ferguson, said workers would not return to work today because the company refused them fundamental rights included in the Munro decision.

"There is not a capacity to return to work," Mr Ferguson said.

"The company says return to work according to the Munro decision but it is not prepared to abide by the understanding (with the ACTU) reached earlier in the week with the union movement and it then says it wants the right to appeal the decision.

"That means it wants the right to appeal a requirement that it sit down and talk with the union movement, of workers being given warnings of dismissal, of the need for the company to ensure the workplace is safe.

"They are pretty fundamental issues to the workforce."

Mr Groom and Senator Cook attributed total blame to APPM for the breakdown, saying it appeared to be "lawyer-driven" in its handling of the dispute.

Senator Cook said that while it was possibliy unprecedented for a Labor and a Liberal government to come together to try to end a dispute, the company had chosen to reject the opportunity and there was nothing left for the governments to do but report that rejection today to the IRC.

The federal and Tasmanian governments had sought to achieve consensus last night when they presented both parties with a peace plan based on last week's short-lived agreement between APPM and the ACTU on workplace reform and the Munro decision.

In essence, the peace plan put by the two governments calls on the two parties to comply with the IRC order that there be a return to work after 4pm today and that the company and the unions negotiate during the next four months on new provisions in their award.

Mr Wade had entered the meeting in no mood to negotiate either with Mr Ferguson or with Mr Groom and Senator Cook.

"I don't know what there is to negotiate," he said. "Mr Munro has issued an order (to return to work at 4pm) and it is our belief that that order should be left."

Mr Wade said the only reason he and other executives of the company were attending the meetings was to gain a better understanding of the "various threats made on our business".

This was a reference to the Tasmanian Government's control of timber resources made available to APPM and the Federal Government's control of woodchip export licenses.

Mr Ferguson arrived for the meeting declaring that peace should be at hand, that a settlement was now "only a hair's breadth away".

He said that while the company was extolling Mr Munro's direction that workers return to the plant at 4pm today, in the same breath it was talking about appealing against parts of the decision.

Source: *The Australian*, 1 June 1992, p. 3.

temporarily closing down the business or refusing to provide work to compel employees to accept an employer demand or to withdraw an employee demand. The demand element is crucial here and, in the case of a lock-out, distinguishes the action from other employer motives, for example discontinuing an uneconomic enterprise. Whereas a strike necessarily involves collective action, a lock-out is usually the action of only one employer. A variation on the extreme employer action of a lock-out is an employer decision to 'take a strike'. This involves the employer holding firmly to an offer which the employer knows will be unacceptable to the union or employees concerned and is highly likely, if not certain, to result in strike action. Such a decision appeared to have been made by the Victorian government in 1986 in relation to conflict over the implementation of a new award for nurses. Government strategists estimated that a strike would last no more than one week and there was no substantive shift in the employer position in response to the threat of a strike by members of the then Royal Australian Nursing Federation.[4] The resulting strike lasted fifty days.

Industrial conflict could be regarded as extending to conflicts between the organisations representing employees or those representing employers. These are conflicts arising indirectly from the contract of employment and typically relate to jurisdiction or membership territory of unions or employer associations. The manifestation of such conflicts in Australia often takes the diplomatic form of argument before an industrial tribunal but in the case of unions may extend to coercive activity, a celebrated example being the conflict between the Builders Labourers' Federation and the then Federated Ironworkers' Association in the early 1980s over which union had constitutional coverage of employees undertaking the construction of the Omega navigation tower in South Gippsland.[5]

Causes of industrial conflict

The manifestations of industrial conflict must be clearly differentiated from the causes. The following discussion of possible sources of conflict includes the contrasting views that industrial conflict is avoidable and that conflict is endemic and ever-present in the workplace.

A view with considerable community support is that industrial conflict is fomented by agitators who disrupt what would otherwise be harmonious industrial relations. The agitators are invariably union officials: in Britain the most frequent target for the 'agitator' label is the shop steward, but in Australia full-time officials such as secretaries and organisers are more likely targets. The agitator thesis suggests employees are led into industrial action against their better judgement, if not against their will. This view is illustrated in a remark by the Victorian Health Minister David White at the outset of the 1986 nurses' strike: 'The nurses' decision to walk out … will cause bitterness and tension. It is clear the nurses are being ruthlessly manipulated by their federation's leadership.'[6] The decisions to strike were made at individual hospitals with voting by secret ballot; an influential local leader of the nurses' union later said. '… it was the first dispute the members ever ran. God could have been secretary and we still would have gone out'.[7] As was the case in this strike, union leaders are very often the instrument of conflict and rarely the cause. If they do seek to generate conflict in the absence of genuinely held grievances they are likely to be ignored, or in extreme cases to be removed from office via the electoral process. It is true that militant leaders will often be key players in articulating conflict and their tactical skills may be crucial in determining the effectiveness of a strike or other organised action. It is also true that they may be attracted to conflict and may derive job satisfaction from being at the centre of its expression. This is to be distinguished however from being the cause of conflict.

Another view, which regards workplace conflict as avoidable, is that industrial conflict is due to poor communications and poor social relations. This is associated with the human relations school, the leading exponent of which was an Australian, Elton Mayo. This perspective regards social needs as pre-eminent as a motivator of employee attitudes and behaviour. Conflict in the workplace can be eliminated by skilled people management, by treating employees as human beings and by adopting sensitive supervisory styles which facilitate employees' strong identification with the goals and interests of the enterprise. This was subsequently categorised by Fox[8] as the 'unitary approach' to industrial relations in which an identity of interests between employer and employees is assumed and conflict is seen as an aberration. The quality of human relations clearly has some relevance to the character of employer-employee relations given that the latter are also interpersonal relations and the actions and attitudes of individuals may generate conflict. Abrasive styles of supervision for example, are cited on occasions by employee representatives in counter-evidence both before industrial tribunals in disputes concerning disciplinary matters and in the context of the processing of in-house grievances. On the other hand, poor human relations might just as easily be a symptom of conflict as its cause and this factor is clearly not helpful in explaining the relatively high incidence of overt conflict in particular industries. Further, improved communications, at least on some issues, may trigger conflict. The transmission of information about profit levels or remuneration for company senior executives for example, may generate employee discontent over what is an enduring source of conflict: the distribution of income between wages and profits. What is income to employees is a cost to employers. Conflict is not inevitable if one or other party is interested only in absolute amounts of revenue. It is entirely possible, and not uncommon, for employees in profitable and growing enterprises to experience very large gains in their pay while obtaining a diminishing share of the total revenue. All that is needed is for total revenue to grow faster than the total wage share of revenue. The division of revenues, therefore, while being likely to lead to conflict in many cases, does not inevitably put the parties on conflicting courses, for it is possible, in some cases, simultaneously to satisfy the aspirations of each party. This source of conflict is enduring for two reasons. First, if the concern is with relative shares not absolute shares, the conflict will not dissipate even though national, or enterprise, income and standards of living are rising. The issue is one of proportions, or fair shares, not amounts and arguments of this kind are rooted in ideology rather than in money. Secondly, conflict persists where the balance of the distribution is constantly disturbed through changes in the cost of living and there is no law or custom which preserves a pre-determined distribution after shifts in income. Union claims based on changes in living costs, which in Australia are typically processed through national and State wage cases, reflect this conflict. During the period 1983 to 1989 the profit share of national income increased from 13.6 per cent to 16.6 per cent while the wages share decreased from 61.1 per cent to 57.5 per cent.[9] The capacity of unions to shift distributive shares in favour of wage and salary earners could be regarded as one indicator of the power of unions.[10] This source of conflict may be diluted by employee participation in profit-sharing schemes.

A source of conflict closely related to conflict over income shares is conflict over relative shares within the wages and salaries sector, that is, different occupational groups seeking to maintain or improve their relative position. This factor was an important motivation for claims lodged by teacher unions between 1988 and 1990: in addition to providing a career path for classroom teachers, the claims sought 'to provide remuneration comparable with that of comparably qualified employees—in other sections of the workforce.'[11]

Another important source of conflict relates to the conflicting nature of employer and employee security. Kerr, Dunlop, Harbison and Myers[12] argue that the conflict emanates from the fact that (capitalist) employers are tied to no industry, location or technique. Since the capitalists seek to maximise returns on their capital, then in the relatively short run, they will often seek to change locations and methods. In doing this they may enhance their own profitability and security, but will simultaneously damage the security and welfare of employees. It is possible to argue that the employees derive their security from preventing change and progress in industry, since their opportunity to apply their job skills is enhanced if work methods are unchanged. Employee opposition to changing techniques has persisted from the medieval era (although the Luddite riots in England in 1811-1812 may have been the first major organised episode to be recorded), and it remains a problem to which a satisfactory solution has yet to be found. The point, however, is that the employer, seeking to enhance employer security by progressing to new methods, techniques and locations, frequently does conflict with the goals of the employee who gains security by retaining the existing processes and locations. For these reasons, Kerr, et al. suggest that the Marxist interpretation of the clash of interests between capitalist and worker is misplaced. Marx[13] emphasises ownership and carefully develops the concept of the inevitable conflict between the owners of capital and the owners of labour. According to this view, the owners of capital can prosper only by ensuring that there is an imbalance, in the capitalist's favour, between the employee's input of labour and the monetary reward obtained from the capitalist; that is, the employee does not receive a wage equivalent to the increased value of production the employee has made possible. Marx believes this exploitative process provided the driving force of capitalism, and that it constituted an inevitable source of conflict. The interpretation of the labour-capital conflict by Kerr et al. denies this causality completely. They would argue that the employee and employer have basically opposing interests, not because of their ownership or otherwise of capital, but because the worker, being dependent on the sale of highly specific labour skills, is conservative and seeks to inhibit change, while the employer is progressive, seeking always to move to novel and improved techniques. In either of these quite fundamental senses, the economic exploitation argued by Marx, or the differing impact of technological progress outlined by Kerr et al., it is clear that the security and well-being of one group can be obtained only at the expense of the other. It could not be suggested that industrial society in the twentieth century has ever approximated a solution to the conflict that is generated from either of these sources. This is not to suggest that it has not been possible for the parties to agree on various redundancy schemes or other forms of compensation to displaced employees, or on schemes to retain employees. These ameliorating measures are susceptible to the resources of the industrial relations processes. A resolution of the underlying problem would involve a wider range of issues than those comprehended by industrial relations.

It was noted in chapter 2 that the focus of the labour process approach to the study of industrial relations is the establishment of control and this emphasis is illustrated in the foregoing discussion. Another illustration of the different emphasis of the pluralist approach, such as that of Kerr et al., and the Marxist approach to conflict, is evident in the analysis by a Marxist writer, Hyman. In addition to discussing job security in the Marxist terms described above, Hyman identifies 'power and control' or the exercise of managerial control as a separate, enduring and more general, source of conflict. This view emphasises that the worker has a lack of control, reflecting a lack of power. This follows from the status of labour as a commodity and the assertion that from the employer side, the labour contract is open-ended, thus: '... the employment relationship subordinates the worker to a structure of managerial control, designed to maximise the effort and application which he devotes in exchange for his wages'.[14] This continues the Marxist theme of exploitation. Examples of the exercise of managerial control cited by Hyman are a demand to perform a dangerous and demanding task, routine attempts to change work methods and speed up production and attempts to cut down on rest periods or tea breaks. The specific issues giving rise to conflict here could be categorised as the content, organisation and pace of work: what work is to be done, how it is to be done and how much is to be done, on any day or shift. Conflict over staffing levels is another example of conflict arising from this cause and a recent such dispute in Victoria was that between a government enterprise, MMBW (now Melbourne Water) and the AWU in the autumn of 1990 concerning the number of employees required for maintenance work. The industrial action included picketing and bans on the use of contractors and overtime availability.[15] The 'job control' category of conflict, whether viewed from a pluralist or radical perspective, includes conflict over work location and the extent of work specialisation; for example, employees may dissent from an employer decision to deploy employees to particular departments or work areas to meet variations in product or service demand.

In addition to change in work location, employer decisions may also involve a change in duties. Such changes may be readily accommodated within a job description or duty statement which contains a clause along the lines of 'other duties as required' but the changes may also precipitate conflict (overt or covert) in the absence of such a 'flexibility' clause or in the face of a strong commitment to custom and practice. It is in the context of conflict over job control that the term 'managerial prerogative' is most likely to arise and it refers to management's assumption of its right to unilateral control. In practice of course, control over work practices and the pace of work may rest with employees or with unions rather than with management and if management decides that it wishes to regain control, conflict may be generated. Hyman, while acknowledging that conflict can arise from workers attempting to extend the frontier of control, considers the more potent cause of conflict to be managerial resistance to the existing powers of workers at the point of production. He suggests that when the dominant social values endorse the legitimacy of those in control, the exercise of managerial control may only lead sporadically to direct questioning by workers or to overt conflict. However managerial legitimacy is vulnerable in four ways. First, social values may be ambivalent: society may value 'freedom' and 'democracy' as well as regarding 'respect for authority' as a virtue. Secondly, social values leave wide discretion for determining the appropriate degree of managerial authority and worker obedience. Thirdly, workers may not reject their employer's authority but may not believe in its legitimacy. Fourthly, the exercise of managerial control can generate resistance even from workers who do not ordinarily question its legitimacy and the seven week Pilkington (United Kingdom) strike in 1970 is claimed to have had this effect.[16]

Hyman argues that trade unionism has affected the impact of managerial prerogative on employees primarily in the sense of controlling its arbitrary exercise. Thus an employer may take disciplinary action against an employee provided the employer has a good reason, treats employees consistently and adheres to natural justice. Hyman contends that the achievement of unions in the United Kingdom is significant in this area, that 'trade unionism permits debate about the terms of the worker's obedience'.[17] In Australia, these restrictions on management disciplining employees are formalised in case law arising from industrial tribunal decisions and occasionally in statute law, although the stronger unions have often 'paved the way' through *de facto* incursions into this and other aspects of management control over work.

Consideration of these sources of industrial conflict suggests that unless society, industrial production and human nature are radically changed, conflict will remain central to industrial life. It is misleading and dangerous to suggest that conflict is unnecessary, that it is merely the result of mischievous forces, of self-interested agitation. To suggest to labour and management, the principal protagonists, that they should not be in conflict is to argue that one should surrender totally to the preferences of one's opponent, or that the dynamic elements of society should be eliminated.

Unions and industrial conflict

Industrial conflict, in any of the three senses described above, can and does emerge quite independently of the existence of unions. Popular discussion often infers that unions create industrial conflict, but it would be a more accurate reflection of the historical record to suggest that their central connection is precisely the reverse: unions have been created out of conflict between employer and employee. In the early stages of industrialisation in

England, sporadic and unorganised conflict occurred in industry, and, as employees formed unions to represent their interests, conflict continued, but took a new form. The essential quality which unions brought to industrial conflict was or organise it around some policy or objective to give it systematic character, and to direct the conflict into channels and render it more amenable to solutions. It is not, of course, intended to suggest that the union serves always to make conflict less costly or distasteful to the employer, but at times it certainly does have that effect. The union does collectivise individual grievances, and gives a clear and usually practical target for employees' dissatisfactions which might otherwise, through lack of any attention or articulation, persist as ill-defined discontent, defying solution simply because of its lack of direction and objective.

The union's influence on industrial conflict certainly gives it the unambiguous character which unorganised conflict often lacks, thus inhibiting its solutions. In processing conflict the union may very well change employee goals, and this can be productive when these are transformed from the unattainable ideal to the feasible. Such an effect is often present in cases of changing technology where new methods may result in groups of employees, who have hitherto been highly skilled and have undertaken critical functions in an enterprise, suddenly finding that their work has become simple, unskilled and routine. Employees in such positions want what they cannot have, for normally they want to stop, or to reverse, the trend of technical progress; to revert to a state in which they will again be valued and highly skilled employees. These wants, though acute and understandable, are rarely articulated. The union cannot, of course return such employees to past glories, but it can and unions frequently do, convert this diffused discontent into a more substantial and practical form. Unions can convince such employees that they do not want to return to the past, but rather they want monetary compensation for the obsolescence of their skills. While employers may not relish such demands, the union's influence on conflict here is to channel it into an area in which it can be resolved. Demands for money are susceptible to business logic, while non-specific dreams of reverting to a happier past are not.

In considering the relationship of unions to industrial conflict it is well to keep in mind that whatever else unions may do, they do translate and shape employee discontent into forms in which it is clearly recognisable, and place conflict on bases from which a settlement must be achieved. In so doing, unions do heighten the awareness of others to problems that might have otherwise gone unperceived, but, from the employer's viewpoint, this may have benefits as well as its obvious costs. Once a union organises and shapes the discontent of the workforce, the probability is increased that the underlying problem will be alleviated and resolved.

It has also been argued that union leaders (both head office officials and workplace leaders) may suppress employee grievances. This behaviour is manifest in unofficial or wildcat action. In discussing the functions of such action, Hyman rejects the argument that this phenomenon is a product of poor communication between members and officials. (He notes this may however apply to 'anti-official' action in response to an agreement signed in opposition to, or ignorance of, members' wishes.) Hyman contends that unofficial action reflects the role conflict between the union official and union members. The former's job centres on compromise and accommodation and leads the official to value protection of the permanent negotiating relationship with the employer. This contrasts with the spontaneous and volatile response of the shop-floor employees to their grievances and deprivations. Hyman regards the unofficial action as providing a counter-balance to leadership tendencies to institutionalise conflict. It prevents officials' behaviour diverging unduly from unionists' expectations and more positively, it can be an impetus for policy change. This is illustrated by the behavioural shift by a number of union executives in the United Kingdom, particularly in the public sector, in the early 1970s. In response to unwanted rank and file belligerence, they were compelled to discard their reputations for 'statesmanship' and 'responsibility' and to articulate membership demands by conducting major stoppages.[18]

Industrial action

Industrial action refers to organised coercive action undertaken in the context of the employer-employee relationship as a means of achieving, or assisting to achieve, the objectives of either party. It includes many of the organised manifestations of conflict identified above, with the strike or lock-out providing that most dramatic and visible example.

Industrial action may be initiated by either party, although in any particular case it may be difficult to ascertain which party is the principal antagonist since the origins of disputes are often highly complex. Employers may foment a dispute by laying-off or suspending employees, taking harsh disciplinary measures against them, or provoking union representatives into direct action by various forms of victimisation. They can also exercise their managerial prerogatives in an unduly harsh or dictatorial manner. Employers may also 'lock out' employees or 'stand down' employees, thus preventing them from getting on with their jobs. Unions, for their part, also engage in activities which may not precipitate a total strike yet have a significant and deleterious effect on an employer's operations. These activities include disruptions of work activities via go-slows; overtime restrictions; selective bans on equipment, and restrictions on an employer's access to labour. Recent technological advances, in particular, have provided some unions with numerous opportunities to hurt employers without resorting to the strike weapon. Examples of action in this category include employees in the telecommunications industry refusing to charge customers for calls and employees in the finance sector refusing to process cheques.

A form of industrial action which, until 1977, had been a traditional source of strength to Australian unions, is the secondary boycott. The commonly accepted meaning of a secondary boycott in the context of industrial relations is industrial action occurring outside a direct employer-employee relationship.[19]

The action is usually directed to causing economic harm by impeding the supply of goods or services to the company or organisation which is the primary employer directly involved in the industrial dispute. For example, a union representing retail shop employees in dispute with a particular retailer, may obtain the assistance of members of another union representing employees in distribution. The latter then take action (refusal to handle stock destined for the primary employer) against their employer who is the neutral or secondary employer. The objective here is to have the secondary employer put pressure on the primary employer. From 1977 to 1993, trade unions in Australia were liable to legal penalties for such action under legislation which is not concerned with industrial relations. The relevant statute, the *Trade Practices Act 1974*, is designed to ensure free competition by those engaged in trade and commerce, and to provide consumer protection. One activity prohibited is the secondary boycott.

A secondary boycott also occurs when a union and its members act in concert against the members' employer with the object of harming another employer. This occurred in NSW in 1980 when the TWU and its members put pressure on Amoco (the secondary employer) with a view to Amoco refusing to supply a bulk fuel distributor Leon Laidely (the primary employer) who wished to expand his fuel distribution 'market'. The union was concerned to protect its members' employment (and conditions) with the major fuel distributors. Trade practices law was invoked in this dispute but the dispute was eventually resolved through the federal industrial tribunal, the then Australian Conciliation and Arbitration Commission, acting without any formal powers.[20] In 1994 following passage of the *Industrial Relations Reform Act* 1993 restrictions on union secondary industrial action are now confined to the *Industrial Relations Act* 1988 (Cth).

Purposes of industrial action

It is evident that industrial action is heterogeneous in form. Similarly, at least in Australia, it is diverse in terms of purpose. In industrial relations systems where the process of collective bargaining is the legitimate process, industrial action over interest disputes is likely to have a 'trial of strength' quality. In other words, it is undertaken for the specific purpose of causing a fundamental and comprehensive shift in the substantive position of the other party. It is likely, but not inevitable, that bargaining will be suspended during the period of industrial action. Public regulation of industrial relations in Australia has typically eschewed the use of industrial action but there are nonetheless some disputes which have epitomised 'trial of strength' industrial action and others which have approximated it. They include the strikes of the 1890s (which predated the public regulation), the Broken Hill strike of 1919-1920, the SECV maintenance workers strike of 1977 and the Victorian nurses' strike of 1986. Some of these disputes will be discussed in chapter 4.

Industrial action may also be used for purposes other than directly enforcing or refusing a demand. It may for example be used in Australia to expedite an industrial tribunal hearing. Unionists may undertake a twenty-four hour strike or impose work bans for a few days as a tactic designed to ensure an early scheduling of tribunal proceedings and possibly also to convey a message of serious intent to the tribunal. This suggests a conviction that the tribunal may be influenced in some way by industrial action and such a view is associated with the term 'accommodative arbitration' (see chapter 15). In terms of union behaviour, it is reflected in the belief of many union leaders that the tribunal must be fully aware of the determination and militancy of the rank and file membership. R.D. Williams, federal secretary of the then Australian Bank Officers' Association in the 1960s and 1970s, frequently stated that 'only fools went to the Commission cold'.

Obviously, industrial action may be directed exclusively to employers as well as to tribunals and in both cases the action can form part of a comprehensive leadership strategy. This action, designed to soften up the employer or pressurise the tribunal in relation to union claims, can be classified as strategic industrial action. It is different from haphazard industrial action, usually confined to a single workplace, which is divorced from any overall plan for achieving particular objectives. The latter has traditionally been termed the grievance or protest strike (or industrial action). A widely accepted explanation for the high incidence of strikes of short duration (two days or less) in Australia has been the lack of effective grievance machinery, involving both the absence of grievance procedures and non-adherence to procedures. A brief, unscheduled and disruptive work stoppage may be seen by employees (or rank and file unionists) as the only way, or the most effective way of having a grievance brought to the notice of the aloof employer, the remote union hierarchy or the mysterious and seemingly slow-moving industrial tribunal. Here the rationale is to register dissatisfaction, the existence of an underlying conflict. Where the industrial action is a protest against a perceived injustice or even an appeal for help by employees, the employer is sometimes in the unenviable position of not knowing the underlying cause of the action. Isaac has pointed out that it is often difficult to separate the statistics relating to grievance-protest strikes from those strategically designed and located to soften up employer opposition to union claims.[21] The word 'grievance' has been used here without precision. In Canada and the United States, for example, it is used to describe conflicts arising during the period of operation of a collective agreement, usually over the interpretation or administration of the provisions of the agreement, and less commonly, conflicts arising from matters not covered by the agreement.[22]

An example of strategic industrial action was that undertaken by the Teachers Federation of Victoria in 1989-1990. This union umbrella organisation was pursuing a wages-career structure claim in the context of 'award restructuring', the colloquial term for the key element in industrial tribunal wage policy at that time, the Structural Efficiency Principle (see chapter 18). The major employer, the Education Department of Victoria, was seeking productivity improvements which included increased teaching hours. The dispute, which was resolved primarily through negotiation, supplemented with arbitration by the Victorian Industrial Relations Commission, saw the unions make skilful use of coercive pressure comprising a one day strike, rolling stop-work meetings and bans on work outside the classroom.[23]

Political strikes

Industrial action may be undertaken for reasons that are unrelated to issues arising from the employer-employee relationship, on issues termed 'political' or 'social'. In the case of politically- inspired industrial action, or action designed to protest against certain external actions, an employer may be unable to concede anything that might have prevented the dispute. Martin,[24] in seeking a comprehensive definition of political strikes, concludes that a strike or other form of industrial action may reasonably be judged political if it satisfies one or more of certain conditions relating to either the issue, the target or the dimensions. In the case of the issue, either the stated issue or the hidden issue (if any) must be political in character. Martin identifies five categories of political issue and these are set out in Table 3.2.

Table 3.2 Political strikes: issues

- issues unquestionably political in character, for example Indonesian policy in East Timor
- issues embodied in government social and economic policy, for example Medibank
- 'environmental' or 'social' issues involving some kind of community interest with at least some interest groups advocating active government intervention, for example bans on sandmining at Fraser Island
- issues of a distinctively economic or financial character, for example the 1971 ACTU ban directed against Dunlop's retail price maintenance policy
- issues relating to freedom of speech, for example the strikes in WA in 1979 which followed the arrest of some union officials for attempting to address a meeting of strikers in contravention of State legislation regulating public meetings

Source: Adapted from R. M. Martin, 'The problem of political strikes' in W.A. Howard (ed.), *Perspectives on Australian Industrial Relations*, Longman Cheshire, Melbourne, 1984, pp. 74-75.

The second sufficient condition for industrial action to be political is that the intended target is a government or public authority other than in its capacity as an employer. This means industrial action may be judged political even though it is about exclusively industrial issues. Martin regards industrial tribunals as industrial rather than political targets, first because they tend to fill a surrogate employer role in that those taking direct action are trying to compel tribunals to grant what they would otherwise have been pressing their employers to concede and secondly, because they are independent authorities with legislative or policy making powers. On this definition, the strike by federal public servants in 1985 against a decision[25] of the federal tribunal refusing to grant a wage increase was not a political strike. An alternative view would regard this action as political simply on the ground that the action was taken against one of the agencies of the state. Martin regards industrial tribunals as political targets if the decision activating action either was not about a clear-cut industrial issue or was pre-determined by a specific statutory direction. Thus action against a tribunal decision to deregister a union would be political. Similarly, the widespread strike action in the late 1960s against the enforcement by the then Industrial Court of federal law imposing penalties for industrial action was clearly political. The latter might also qualify as political in terms of issue, namely the right to strike, being comparable with industrial action concerning freedom of speech. Union opposition to what were generally known as the 'penal provisions' of the then Conciliation and Arbitration Act culminated in 1969 when 'Clarrie' O'Shea the Victorian secretary of the Australian Tramway and Motor Omnibus Employees' Union, was jailed for contempt of court after his union refused to pay fines imposed by the Industrial Court and he refused to meet the Court's request to provide information concerning the union's finances. This was very much a test case for the union movement, and it immediately declared total support for O'Shea by threatening an Australia-wide strike. Just as a general strike appeared imminent, a private citizen came forward to pay the fine and O'Shea was released. This was most fortuitous for the federal Liberal government, for they were in a 'no win' situation, detested by the unions, and deserted by most employers and the bemused public. The ACTU executive allowed further 'face-saving' by the government when it instructed its affiliates to refuse to pay any more fines imposed on them. The 'penal provisions' were thus tacitly abandoned. This ushered in a new era in which unions felt considerably less constrained by the industrial tribunals from engaging in industrial action.

The third sufficient condition identified by Martin concerns the dimensions of the action: that because of its scale, conduct or impact the action attracts open government intervention directly in its capacity as government. In this case both the issue and the target may be industrial and the motives of the strikers are irrelevant. Martin cites the reaction of the Victorian government to the eleven week industrial action of SECV maintenance workers in 1977. A more recent example is the intervention of the federal and Tasmanian governments in the 1992 APPM (Burnie) dispute (see Table 3.1 and Table 15). The industrial action which began in Victoria in November 1992 in response to the legislative reform of industrial relations by the Kennett government would qualify as political in terms of all three conditions: issue, target and dimensions.

The major processes for resolving industrial conflict are discussed in detail in chapters 15 and 17.

Measures of industrial conflict

Australian strike statistics

Official statistics on industrial conflict are limited to the most readily measurable symptom, the strike or lock-out, termed 'Industrial Disputes' by the Australian Bureau of Statistics (the Bureau). There is no continuing official record of other forms of industrial action such as work to rules, go-slows, overtime bans and sit-ins. Obviously no measurement is possible of unorganised covert symptoms of conflict. There are a number of indices of other sources of lost time, absenteeism for example, but unresolved industrial conflict is but one of a number of possible causes of these.

The Bureau has maintained records of industrial disputes since 1913 and its quarterly and annual reports provide the basis for much of the discussion concerning the level and nature of strike activity in Australia. The following discussion will identify some significant limitations to the official statistics and caution must be exercised when attempting to generalise from them. The Bureau for example, notes there may be non-sampling errors arising from the fact that it relies heavily upon information supplied by employers and unions involved in particular disputes. The Bureau statistics do, however, enable the pattern of industrial disputes to be analysed over time for discernible trends. These are considerably more meaningful than stark preliminary numbers. The statistics detail industrial disputes at aggregate, industry and State levels. The measures of strike statistics for the period 1981 to 1992 detailed here are: number of disputes; working days lost; duration of strikes; causes of strikes; strikes by industry and method of settlement of strikes. The Bureau's definition of industrial dispute in terms of type of action is set out in Table 3.3.

Table 3.3 Industrial disputes: ABS definition

The Bureau defines an industrial dispute as:

'a withdrawal from work by a group of employees, or a refusal by an employer or a number of employers to permit some or all of their employees to work, each withdrawal or refusal being made in order to enforce a demand, to resist a demand, or to express a grievance'.

The following types of disputes are included in the statistics:
- unauthorised stopwork meetings;
- unofficial strikes;
- sympathetic strikes (e.g. strikes in support of a group of workers already on strike);
- political or protest strikes;
- general strikes;
- work stoppages initiated by employers (e.g. lock-outs); and
- rotating or revolving strikes (i.e. strikes which occur when workers at different locations take turns to stop work).

The following types of disputes are excluded from the statistics:
- work-to-rules;
- go-slows;
- bans (e.g. overtime bans);
- sit-ins.

Industrial disputes in which employees resign are deemed to have been resolved. Statistics on those disputes will cease to be collected from the date of the employees' resignations.

Source: ABS *Industrial Disputes Australia*, 1992, Catalogue No. 6322.0, p. 16.

The Bureau statistics relate to disputes which involve stoppages of work of ten working days or more at the establishments where the stoppages occurred. This means that the impact of stoppages may be understated to the extent that they affect other establishments, for example a stoppage by transport employees, electricity supply employees or those involved in the manufacture of automotive parts, which causes interruption to production or service elsewhere. Table 3.4 provides some measures of strike activity for the period 1981 to 1992: the number of disputes, the number of employees directly and indirectly involved and working days lost per thousand employees. A strike is recorded as a single dispute if it is organised or directed by one person or organisation in each State or Territory in which it occurs, otherwise it is counted as a separate dispute at each establishment in which it occurs. The Bureau's method of counting the number of disputes has aligned with International Labour Office guidelines since December 1987. Prior to this date, where the causes of several disputes were the same, for example a national wage case, they were counted as one dispute in each State or Territory in which they occurred. In Table 3.4, the figures from 1985 to 1992 reflect the new definition. Employees indirectly involved are those who ceased work at the establishment where the stoppages occurred but who were not party to the dispute and are a small percentage of total employees involved, usually less than five per cent. The number of employees involved exceeded 1.2 million in 1981 and by 1983 had declined to just under 0.5 million. By 1992 it was 0.87 million employees. Working days lost per 1000 employees declined dramatically in 1982 and from 1983 to 1992 fluctuated in the range 158 to 265 working days lost. This figure can also be expressed as representing an average of just over a quarter of one day lost per year for each employee in Australia. The number of disputes in progress in 1992 continued the trend of annual decreases since 1984, representing a sharp decrease from 1991 and is the lowest number since 1942. The significant increase in working days lost in 1991 was due to industrial action in NSW which included one major general strike. This would be classified as a political strike as it concerned changes to industrial relations legislation. The number of working days lost per 1000 employees in 1992 was the lowest annual figure since this series was first recorded in 1967 although Victoria and Tasmania recorded high rates of 369 and 285 respectively.[26]

Table 3.4 Industrial disputes by incidence, employees involved and working days lost, Australia, 1981-1992

Year	Number of disputes (in progress)	Employees involved directly and indirectly ('000)	Working days lost per thousand employees
1981	2915	1247.2	797
1982	2060	706.1	358
1983	1787	470.2	249
1984	1965	560.3	248
1985	1895	570.5	228
1986	1754	691.7	242
1987	1517	608.8	223
1988	1508	894.4	269
1989	1402	709.8	190
1990	1193	729.9	217
1991	1036	1181.6	265
1992	728	871.5	158

Source: ABS *Industrial Disputes Australia*, Catalogue No. 6322.0.

The level of strike activity declined between 1981 and 1992 and also declined relative to the level of the previous decade when the average number of disputes from 1971 to 1980 was 2337 and the average working days lost per 1000 employees was 663. The two most significant explanations for this change can be found in changes in environmental variables, using Dunlop's terminology, the market context and the power context. In the case of the former, the economic recession and the high levels of unemployment, peaking at 10.6 per cent in 1992, acted as a deterrent to militancy. The power context was dominated by a trade union-political party alliance at federal level reflected in a written Prices and Incomes Accord (see chapter 16). This involved unions, through the union peak council, agreeing to forgo sectional claims in return, *inter alia*, for the prospect of wage increases keeping pace with living costs over time and being pursued through diplomatic channels namely, industrial tribunal proceedings.

This bias to diplomatic expression of industrial conflict was strongly reinforced by industrial tribunal policy, commencing in September 1983, which adopted the essence of the trade union-government agreement, and added a 'no-extra claims' component. (Tribunal wages policy is explained in chapter 16). This was a *quid pro quo* for unions obtaining national (or State) wage increases, requiring them to pursue all claims in accord with tribunal policy. It restricted the grounds upon which wages and other benefits could be sought and carried the implication that industrial action of any magnitude could precipitate abandonment of the policy. The dampening effect of this policy on the level of industrial action is widely acknowledged.

Table 3.5 shows the distribution of strikes by duration.

Table 3.5 Industrial disputes by duration, Australia, 1981-1992 (percentages)

Year	Up to and including 1 day	Over 1 to 2 days	Over 2 & less than 5 days	5 & less than 10 days	10 & less than 20 days	20 days & over	Total
1981	43.9	16.9	17.5	12.5	6.4	2.7	100
1982	49.3	20.1	15.6	9.3	4.0	1.7	100
1983	47.4	19.1	16.2	9.3	5.4	2.5	100
1984	48.6	20.5	16.4	8.9	4.2	1.5	100
1985	50.1	19.4	16.6	8.5	4.1	1.3	100
1986	53.0	19.5	15.6	7.9	2.8	1.3	100
1987	64.5	10.9	10.5	8.9	4.2	1.1	100
1988	62.7	12.8	10.7	9.7	3.3	0.8	100
1989	68.5	11.6	8.9	6.2	3.7	1.1	100
1990	67.2	14.7	9.4	6.1	1.9	0.8	100
1991	56.9	22.1	14.3	4.5	1.6	0.7	100
1992	58.4	21.1	15.2	3.4	1.2	0.7	100

Source: ABS, *Industrial Disputes Australia*, Catalogue No. 6322.0.

Throughout the twelve years, strikes of one day or less accounted for between forty-four per cent and sixty-nine per cent of all strikes. The latter half of the decade saw an increasing percentage of strikes of one day or less, with percentages fluctuating around a declining trend in other categories of duration. As noted above, Bureau statistics include stopwork meetings which are classified as strikes of less than one day's duration. Throughout the twelve years, strikes of short duration dominated, with those lasting less than five days accounting for at least eighty per cent of strikes. In 1992, strikes of less than five days duration accounted for ninety-five per cent of strikes continuing the trend of increases in short strikes. Strikes exceeding twenty days usually accounted for less than two per cent of strikes. This continues the long established pattern in Australia, the reasons for which were discussed above. The Bureau's definition of separate strikes is relevant to the figures on duration. The Bureau counts as single disputes all strikes over a single issue occurring within two calendar months of each other. Thus the four day strategic strike at APPM in Burnie, Tasmania in April 1992 and the more lengthy strike in May 1992[27] would be recorded as one strike.

Table 3.6 shows the number of strikes by cause and Table 3.7 shows working days lost by cause. The categories used by the Bureau can be related to the earlier discussion on causes of conflict. The categories of 'wages' and 'leave, pensions, compensation' relate to conflict over distribution of revenues between wages and profits and distribution of income within the wages and salaries sector. The categories 'hours of work', 'managerial policy' and 'physical working conditions' concern conflict over the issue of security or job control. In the category 'managerial policy', the Bureau includes both general and specific issues. It covers disputes concerning the exercise of managerial control (other than on wages or hours issues); new awards; award restructuring; work practices; principles of promotion or deployment of staff; disciplinary matters; employment of particular persons; and disagreement with managerial decisions. The category 'physical working conditions' includes safety issues but extends to 'new production methods and equipment' and 'arduous physical tasks'. It thus includes some of the matters covered by the cause of conflict identified above as 'the conflicting nature of employer and employee security' (pluralist) or 'power and control' (Marxist). The category 'trade unionism' covers union recognition and the employment of non-unionists as well as inter-union and intra-union disputes. Inter-union disputes are usually jurisdiction or demarcation disputes although demarcation disputes may also be symptoms of employer-union conflict over security (job control) for particular occupations or skill categories. The Bureau includes sympathy stoppages in support of employees in another industry. The primary cause of the dispute could be any one of those identified above but the sympathy stoppage may meet the legal definition of a secondary boycott. The Bureau's 'other' category covers political strikes, that is those involving an issue or target outside the bounds of the employer-employee relationship. The Bureau advises that the statistics of causes relate to the reported main cause of the strike and not necessarily all of the causes that may have been responsible. Thus the figures do not reflect the relative importance of all causes. In the case of the 1992 APPM dispute for example, an external observer would probably identify the dominant issue as 'managerial policy' and trade union recognition at workplace level as a (subsequent) significant cause. The principal parties in the dispute (if responding to the Bureau questionnaire) may differ in their assessment of the main cause.

Table 3.6 Industrial disputes by cause, Australia, 1981-1992 (percentages)

Year	Wages	Hours of work	Leave, pensions, compensation	Managerial policy	Physical working conditions	Trade unionism	Other	Total
1981	31.6	3.6	1.2	35.5	17.3	7.1	3.6	100
1982	17.6	5.7	*	40.4	20.8	9.5	6.0	100
1983	11.5	5.1	*	40.8	20.9	15.4	6.3	100
1984	10.5	3.8	*	39.1	23.6	15.8	7.2	100
1985	12.3	3.1	*	37.2	21.9	17.5	8.0	100
1986	14.0	1.6	*	41.7	20.7	12.2	9.8	100
1987	20.6	1.7	6.7	36.4	18.7	12.5	3.3	100
1988	18.4	1.5	4.5	38.6	21.9	12.3	2.9	100
1989	12.1	1.7	5.0	43.9	18.0	16.3	3.0	100
1990	9.0	1.5	3.7	49.7	18.4	14.5	3.2	100
1991	7.1	1.3	3.8	52.0	15.5	11.1	9.1	100
1992	8.3	n.p.	5.9	56.9	13.9	10.6	n.p.	100

*Included under 'Other' category.
n.p. not available for publication but included in totals where applicable, unless otherwise indicated.
Source: ABS, *Industrial Disputes Australia*, Catalogue. No. 6322.0.

Table 3.7 Industrial disputes: working days lost by cause, Australia, 1981-1992 (percentages)

Year	Wages	Hours of work	Leave, pensions, compensation	Managerial policy	Physical working conditions	Trade unionism	Other	Total
1981	46.7	24.8	6.3	15.5	4.0	2.0	0.7	100
1982	44.3	22.3	1.2	18.1	7.6	3.8	2.7	100
1983	12.3	5.0	4.0	43.4	31.5	3.3	0.6	100
1984	24.6	5.9	8.4	32.5	16.3	8.7	3.6	100
1985	23.1	3.8	3.2	24.8	14.9	16.5	13.7	100
1986	40.0	1.0	10.8	35.6	6.9	3.3	2.4	100
1987	43.0	1.7	16.1	27.4	7.3	3.0	1.5	100
1988	29.6	1.8	2.9	52.4	9.2	2.0	2.0	100
1989	14.8	0.5	7.4	54.6	5.4	6.4	10.9	100
1990	10.8	0.3	1.5	74.5	7.1	3.7	2.1	100
1991	2.3	0.2	1.4	53.6	3.7	1.9	36.8	100
1992	2.5	—	1.6	23.7	2.9	5.0	64.3	100

— nil or rounded to zero
Source: ABS, *Industrial Disputes Australia*, Catalogue No. 6322.0.

During the period 1981 to 1992, the broad-ranging category of 'managerial policy' accounted for the highest percentage of industrial disputes, followed by 'physical working conditions', 'wages' and then 'trade unionism'. The explanation for the importance of 'hours of work' as a cause of strikes in 1982 and 1983 is union campaigns for a standard working week of 38 hours which involved a number of agreements reached through direct, necessarily strike-prone, employer-union negotiation and minimal strike-averse tribunal involvement. The significance of the 'leave, pensions, compensation' category in 1986 and 1987 is attributable to union campaigns for improved superannuation provisions which, in contrast to the conflict over 'hours of work', was part of the agenda of industrial tribunal policy. A probable explanation for the atypically high figure for 'trade unionism' in 1985 is conflicts involving both private and public (Queensland government) employers over continued union recognition. The significantly higher figure of nine per cent of disputes or thirty-seven per cent of working days lost in the 'other' category in 1991 was probably attributable to conflict over industrial relations legislation in NSW. In 1992 the 'other' category accounted, atypically, for sixty-four per cent of working days lost. The political strikes in Victoria in relation to the introduction of the radical *Employee Relations Act* (see chapter 13 for discussion of this legislation) explain much of this increase. The relative importance of this 'other' category was accentuated by the general decline in working days lost.

During the 1970s, the 'wages' category was far more significant as a cause of strikes. As noted above, the continuation of the Prices and Incomes Accord, first negotiated in February 1983, channelled the determination of union claims over wages, and revenue distribution issues generally, into ACTU decision-making forums and subsequently into diplomatic conflict before industrial tribunals.

Certain major changes in the trend of causes of disputes can be brought about by tribunal policy shifts which may not necessarily reflect changes in employer or employee priorities. In the late 1980s tribunal policy, in a significant departure from past policies, integrated the 'reward for work' and 'work' components of the contract of employment. Its new concern with the 'work' component was reflected in prominent elements of the policy: these were the Restructuring and Efficiency Principle (1987) followed by the Structural Efficiency Principle (1988-1993). (For further details see chapter 18). The latter was known colloquially as 'award restructuring' which the Bureau includes under 'managerial policy'. In these tribunal policies, the wage outcome (for any given award classification) was usually pre-determined and the conflict, if any, concerned the consequential concessions to be made in terms of one or more aspects of work, for example, the content of jobs; roster patterns; demarcation between jobs; or wage criteria, for example, whether wages should be related to specified duties and responsibilities or to specified skill levels. This tribunal policy automatically increased the apparent significance of 'managerial policy' and reduced that of 'wages' as causes of dispute in the official statistics.

The Bureau's data on strikes by industry is detailed in Table 3.8. The average working days lost per thousand employees during the period 1981-1992 for all industries was 287. The comparable figure for mining was 4868. The strike-proneness of mining, especially coal mining, throughout the decade is consistent with the historical pattern for this industry although the 1992 figure of 2970 is the lowest rate since 1972. The high figures are due in good measure to the work environment, the dangerous and unnatural conditions. Additional factors include the high union density and participatory

Table 3.8 Working days lost per thousand employees by industry, Australia, 1981-1992

Year	Mining Coal	Mining Other	Manufacturing Metal products, machinery & equipment	Manufacturing Other	Construction	Transport & storage, communication	Other Industries*
1981	10 011	5 141	2 285	989	1423	1 104	239
1982	14 483	2 691	487	512	782	670	85
1983	3 223	3 375	353	186	1269	485	42
1984	3 543	3 286	327	387	427	346	94
1985	6 892	1 928	256	312	666	430	71
1986	10 741	3 328	445	328	458	135	72
1987	8 920	1 072	479	305	743	217	70
1988	15 543	1 777	750	183	725	177	85
1989	5 505	642	473	283	374	160	97
1990	4 879	1 643	1 293	210	203	300	62
1991	4 507	735	1 820	296	428	237	63
1992	2 970	997	352	275	151	214	235**

* Includes a miscellany of industries: agriculture, forestry, fishing and hunting; electricity, gas and water; wholesale and retail trade; finance, property and business services; public administration and defence; community services; and recreation, personal and other services.
** The Bureau published separate figures for Community Services in 1992 and the industry sector averaged 175 working days lost per 1000 employees.
Source: ABS, *Industrial Disputes Australia*, Catalogue No 6322.0.

democracy in the coal industry unions. Lee cites the importance of rank and file meetings in union decision making. Such meetings require 24 hour cessation of work to enable all shifts to attend and probably account for about four shifts per employee per year.[28] During the twelve year period, working days lost in coal mining ranged between 19 and 58 times the national average for all industry, while the figure for the metals fabrication component of the manufacturing sector ranged between 1.1 and 2.9 times the national average. The construction industry recorded an average of 637 working days lost per thousand employees from 1981 to 1992. During the 1980s the industrial action taken by the then major union, the Builders Labourers' Federation, led to the deregistration of this union by Labor governments at the federal level and in NSW and Victoria. The only years in which industries other than mining experienced strike levels in excess of one working day per employee were: 1981 (metals fabrication, construction and transport, storage and communication); 1983 (construction); and 1990 and 1992 (metals fabrication). The major tribunal award in the metals fabrication sub-sector is the *Metal Industry Award* which functions as a benchmark award for industry as a whole. During 1981 a major wages campaign was conducted through a broad sector of industry by the unions party to this award. The campaign included many strategic strikes and involved many employers and employees. The average working days lost per thousand employees in the metals sector from 1981 to 1992 was 776.

Table 3.9 shows the methods by which strikes have been settled between 1981 and 1992. The 'negotiation' category refers to bargaining between the principal parties or their representatives without intervention from the state. The 'settlement by legislation' categories refer to federal and State industrial tribunals providing settlement by the process of conciliation and/or arbitration. These two categories reflect aspects of the co-existence of bargaining and arbitration in Australia, a characteristic which is explained in chapter 17. The 'resumption without negotiations' category of settlement includes stop-work meetings and strikes about which no further information is provided. It may include some disputes which are settled subject to subsequent negotiation of a formal nature such as in tribunal hearings. The 'other methods' category covers: mediation; filling the places of employees on strike or locked out; closing establishments permanently; and dismissal or resignation of employees.

Table 3.9 Industrial disputes by method of settlement, Australia, 1981-1992 (percentages)

Year	Negotiation	State legislation	Federal & joint federal-State legislation	Resumption without negotiations	Other methods
1981	22.3	7.4	7.5	61.7	1.1
1982	22.8	5.9	6.2	64.7	0.4
1983	22.8	7.4	5.7	63.1	1.1
1984	21.1	6.8	5.9	65.0	1.2
1985	17.8	6.2	10.1	64.0	1.9
1986	19.2	7.6	10.0	62.4	0.8
1987	19.8	7.4	13.6	57.5	1.6
1988	19.7	9.6	12.8	56.1	1.8
1989	15.1	8.2	13.0	62.6	1.1
1990	15.2	9.0	11.4	62.9	1.4
1991	15.9	11.1	11.2	60.6	1.2
1992	15.7	5.2	9.9	67.4	1.8

Source: ABS, *Industrial Disputes Australia*, Catalogue No. 6322.0.

The most significant feature of the statistics is the dominance of the 'resumption without negotiations' category. This is consistently the method of settlement (*sic*) for more than fifty-five per cent of strikes and illustrates the importance in Australia of industrial action either as 'strategy in progress' or as non-strategic action to express a grievance. The relatively few strikes, approximately twenty per cent, settled by industrial tribunals may also be explained by the above factors. The tribunals were originally established to provide, in most jurisdictions, an alternative to strikes and lock-outs and they are involved in the settlement of many disputes where no form of industrial action is involved. Another measure of the significance of tribunal processes in strike settlement would be the percentage of total working days lost which is represented by strikes and lock-outs settled by industrial tribunals: in other words, industrial tribunals may be significant in the settlement of major strikes.

The Australian Workplace Survey

The Australian Workplace Industrial Relations Survey (hereafter AWIRS or Survey) conducted in 1989 provides a more realistic picture of industrial action than that provided by Bureau figures as it encompasses all forms of industrial action. A few examples of the comprehensive data on industrial action in the Survey Report are provided here. Table 3.10 shows the incidence of industrial action and the various types of action in the year preceding the Survey together with the percentage of employees involved in industrial action. Only twelve per cent of all workplaces in the survey population were found to have experienced industrial action and all forms of industrial action were significantly more prevalent in the public sector (see chapter 7 for details of union density in the public and private sectors). Further, the Survey found that seventy-two per cent of workplaces had never experienced any form of industrial action. These 88 000 workplaces represented 1.6 million or thirty-seven per cent of employees and the Report concluded that the overall absence of industrial action from Australian workplaces was perhaps the most dramatic finding from this part of the Survey.[29]

Table 3.10 Types of industrial action by sector (AWIRS)

Type of industrial action	% of workplaces with industrial action			% of employees at workplaces with industrial action		
	Private	*Public*	*All*	*Private*	*Public*	*All*
Strikes	4	20	6	15	38	22
Stop work meetings	4	29	8	21	53	32
Overtime bans	1	12	3	10	26	16
Go slow	0	2	1	3	8	5
Picketing	0	2	0	2	9	4
Work to rule	0	13	2	3	14	6
Other bans	1	10	2	4	21	10
No industrial action	93	57	88	75	34	62

Population: Australian workplaces with at least five employees. Figures are weighted and are based on responses from 2353 workplaces.

Note: Some workplaces had several types of action.

Source: R. Callus, A. Morehead, M. Cully and J. Buchanan, *Industrial Relations at Work: The Australian Workplace Industrial Relations Survey*, Commonwealth Department of Industrial Relations, Australian Government Publishing Service, Canberra, 1991, p. 63.

Table 3.11 shows that where industrial action did occur in the year prior to the Survey, stop work meetings were the most common form of industrial action followed by strikes and overtime bans.

Table 3.12 illustrates the extent of combinations of industrial action in workplaces where industrial action occurred in the year preceding the Survey. The Survey Report states that the reasons behind the choice of action are complex and include the likely effectiveness, cost and relative difficulty of undertaking a particular form of action.[30] One explanation for the combinations of different forms of action is that issues for decision at stop-work

Table 3.11 Frequency of types of industrial action by employment size and by sector (AWIRS)

	Strikes	Stop work Meetings	Over-Time Bans	Go Slow	Pickets	Work to Rule	Other Bans	Weighted Number of Workplaces
	%	%	%	%	%	%	%	'00s
All Workplaces (20 or more employees)	51	77	29	8	7	21	15	87
All Workplaces (5 or more employees)[a]	49	65	22	5	4	18	16	144
Employment Size								
5–19	(46)	(45)	(12)	(0)	(0)	(12)	(18)	(57)
20–49	49	71	22	2	6	22	16	28
50–99	54	77	27	14	4	30	12	23
100–199	44	80	27	6	8	17	10	18
200–499	51	83	39	11	6	13	13	12
500 or more	67	89	52	13	22	19	39	6
Sector								
Private	51	62	16	6	4	6	9	75
Public	46	67	29	4	4	31	24	69

Notes:
1. This table includes only those workplaces in which industrial action took place in the last year.
2. Estimates are based on management responses to the following question: 'Could you indicate which, if any, of these have taken place at this workplace in the last year?' (responses as per column headings).
[a] Unweighted N = 779 in this section.
Source: R. Callus, A. Morehead, M. Cully and J. Buchanan, *Industrial Relations at Work: The Australian Workplace Industrial Relations Survey*, Commonwealth Department of Industrial Relations, Australian Government Publishing Service, Canberra, 1991, p. 252.

meetings often include the taking of further action. Further, as discussed above, one of the functions of picketing is to encourage other unionists to take industrial action. Different forms of industrial action may also be used sequentially in the one dispute, in a series of escalations. This was evident in the Victorian nurses' dispute which is discussed in chapter 4.

The Survey Report also provides information on: industrial action by cause; duration; scope of action, that is whether the action was workplace specific or extended beyond the workplace to organisation or industry level; and workplaces where disruption in the supply of goods or services was experienced due to industrial action elsewhere. The data are disaggregated by industry in each case using the same industry classification used by the Bureau in its series on strike statistics, the Australian Standard Industrial Classification (ASIC).

Strike statistics: international comparisons

Australia's distinctive form of public regulation of industrial relations has meant that the performance of this 'system' is often compared with that of other

Table 3.12 Combinations of industrial action (AWIRS)

		Where Industrial Action Occurred in Last Year					
	No Industrial Action	Weighted Number of Workplaces	Strike and Stop Work Meetings	Strikes Only	Stop Work Meetings Only	Other Industrial Action Only	Weighted Number of Workplaces
	%	'00s	%	%	%	%	'00s
All Workplaces (20 or more employees)	71	305	37	12	27	25	87
All Workplaces (5 or more employees)[a]	88	1225	25	21	28	25	144
Employment Size							
5–19	94	920	(8)	(36)	(30)	(26)	(57)
20–49	81	147	29	17	33	21	28
50–99	72	83	42	8	17	33	23
100–199	60	44	31	12	35	22	18
200–499	44	22	41	7	27	24	12
500 or more	34	9	62	6	13	19	6

Notes:

1 Columns 1 to 2 include all workplaces. Columns 3 to 7 include only workplaces where industrial action occurred in the last year.

2 Estimates are based on management responses to the following question: 'Could you indicate which, if any, of these forms of industrial action have taken place at this workplace in the last year?' (responses as per column headings).

[a] Unweighted Ns are 2353 in columns 1 to 2 and 781 in columns 3 to 7.

Source: R. Callus, A. Morehead, M. Cully and J. Buchanan, *Industrial Relations at Work: The Australian Workplace Industrial Relations Survey*, Commonwealth Department of Industrial Relations, Australian Government Publishing Service, Canberra, 1991, p. 254.

forms of public regulation in democratic states. A popular basis for comparison between countries is the strike record. The various official publications which present international statistics invariably detail a number of caveats attaching to the use of the data for comparative purposes. These relate to

1 differing definitions or inclusion criteria; and
2 differing methodologies concerning collection and compilation.

Table 3.13 provides a comparison of working days lost per 1000 employees for selected countries during the period 1980 to 1990. This data, published by the Bureau in 1991, draws on a number of official sources.

The threshold for inclusion of strikes varies between countries and may include one or more of the following: the number of workers involved; the length of the dispute; the number of working days lost. Australia has a relatively low threshold for inclusion: ten working days, which is equivalent to the amount of ordinary time worked by ten people in one day, regardless of the length of the stoppage. Japan excludes strikes lasting less than half a day while the threshold for inclusion in the United Kingdom is that a strike either lasts one full working day or involves at least 100 working days lost. In the United States a strike must last at least one full day or shift and involve at least 1000 workers. Not all countries include workers indirectly involved. The countries in Table 3.13 which do include this category of worker are: Australia; United States; United Kingdom; and New Zealand. Another criterion for inclusion which varies between countries is political strikes. The countries in Table 3.13 which do include this category of dispute are: Australia; Federal Republic of Germany; Italy; Canada; and Sweden.[31] The sources of strike data also vary and include compilation both individually and severally by government agencies, employers, employer organisations and unions.[32] Of the countries in the table only the Federal Republic of Germany has compulsory reporting and Australian statistics are compiled mainly from data obtained from employers (both public and private sector), trade unions and reports of government authorities.[33] It is evident that the inclusion criteria and collection methods in Australia have the effect of inflating the statistics relative to most of the other countries. Nonetheless, Australia is the only country whose public dispute-settlement machinery has traditionally sought to offer an alternative to strikes.

Functions of industrial conflict

It is commonplace to encounter discussion of the destructive and negative aspects of conflict, of the fact that it may be uncomfortable and unpleasant for a wider group than the direct participants. While it is undeniable that conflict does have its negative characteristics, it is possible to argue that it may also have some positive characteristics. To pursue this argument is not, of course, to contend that the benefits outweigh the costs but rather to suggest that as well as the costs, there may be lessons to be learned, or gains to be had from the experience.

The industrial relations system is society's instrument for transforming the diverse goals of labour, management and government into a network of workplace rules. One of the forms taken by the diverse interests in industrial relations is, of course, conflict, and the industrial relations system must accommodate this. Continuing and persistent industrial conflict may well result in a restructuring of, or in changes to, all or any of the parties to the system and to the processes which it uses. The general social interest however, is served by the evolution of acceptable workplace rules, and is largely unaffected by the survival, or demands of, any particular process or structure of parties. As a preliminary to examining the functional aspect of industrial conflict therefore, it is worth noting that although some processes and interests in industrial relations may be destroyed by conflict, the industrial relations system itself will survive all but the most comprehensive of social upheavals.

Perhaps the most obvious area in which a positive aspect to industrial conflict can be discerned is in its capacity of testing the relevance and suitability of workplace rules. Unless conflict is tolerated and allowed to emerge, no such test will exist. The needs and attitudes of managers and employees in industrial life may be so diverse, and their objectives so different, that it is possible to

Table 3.13 Industrial disputes, working days lost per thousand employees, selected countries, 1980-1990

Year	Australia (a)	USA (b)	Japan (c)	Federal Republic of Germany (d)	Italy	UK (d)	France (e) (f)	France (g)	Canada (a)	Sweden	New Zealand (h)
1980	649	232	25	5	1,135	520	..	95	930	1,150	362
1981	797	86	14	2	726	195	..	85	894	54	n.a.
1982	348	101	13	1	1,283	248	..	131	607	–	n.a.
1983	249	92	12	2	975	178	..	84	465	9	n.a.
1984	248	89	8	246	611	1,278	..	77	396	8	n.a.
1985	228	73	6	1	266	299	..	50	(i)134	126	n.a.
1986	242	19	6	1	390	90	..	59	546	171	1,057
1987	223	44	6	1	319	164	..	55	225	4	290
1988	269	42	4	2	226	166	..	69	(i)307	199	315
1989	190	55	5	4	300	181	..	50	182	101	165
1990	217	54	n.a.	15	n.a.	83	..	n.a.	299	188	n.a.

(a) Excludes disputes in which time lost is less than 10 staff days. (b) Excludes disputes lasting less than a full day or shift, and disputes involving less than 1,000 workers. (c) Excludes disputes lasting less than half a day. (d) Includes disputes lasting less than one day only if more than 100 working days lost. (e) Excludes Agriculture and Public administration. (f) Localised disputes. (g) Comprises localised and generalised disputes. (h) Excludes public sector conflicts. (i) New series. Stoppages involving 500 employees or more. Excludes workers indirectly affected.

Source: *ILO Year Book of Labour Statistics*, 1989-90, 1991; *Industrial Disputes, Australia*, February 1992 (6321.0); *Department of Employment Gazette, Great Britain*, December 1990; *Key Statistics, New Zealand*, March 1992. Published in ABS, *Labour Statistics Australia*, 1991, Catalogue No. 6101.0.

imagine managements inadvertently creating rules quite intolerable to employees. The conflict that would follow the installation of such rules would cause management to re-evaluate its need for the rules in question, and to determine whether it wished to retain the rules in the face of employee opposition. It is to be noted that this testing function is most effective when the conflict involved takes an overt form—the imposition of bans, demands for negotiation and so forth. Where union weakness or institutional practice has the effect of stifling the overt form of conflict, employee dissatisfaction may well be vented in other, unorganised, ways as discussed above. Where the less overt and not fully organised manifestations of conflict take such forms as absenteeism, low productivity or even sabotage, because of their very diffuseness they may not always be recognised as specific employee protests.

There will be certain issues which will resist resolution by all means other than direct conflict between the parties to the matter in question. There may not be many such issues, and the solutions that are provided may be far from ideal when tested against any normative scale, but the alternative to resolution by the test of strength is to allow unresolved issues to fester and to poison relationships between labour and management. While there can be no general rule concerning the circumstances in which issues of this kind arise, factors which would be consistent with their development would be an irrational attachment of the leaders of one or other group to some issue. Union recognition disputes have historically often had this character, as have changes in historical balances of power between two parties. Even though the parties concerned may be fully aware of the costs of a struggle, in certain cases, they may simply be unwilling to compromise until forced to do so. In such circumstances, the issue will only be resolved after the conflict has run its course.

Industrial conflict and absenteeism: comparative costs

Studies of industrial conflict tend to focus on strikes which, although the most obvious and spectacular example of conflict, often assume therefore an exaggerated significance. Other important and often more costly manifestations of industrial conflict such as sabotage, accidents, labour turnover and absenteeism, attract far less attention than strikes. Furthermore, considerable effort is expended by governments and statutory authorities in attempting to place limitations or restraints on strike activity without examining the underlying causes of industrial conflict. A balanced assessment of the costs of strikes requires that they be considered in relative terms as well as absolute terms. The bases of comparison with the costs of strikes are the costs of other forms or manifestations of industrial conflict and the costs of other causes of lost working time. Costs can be measured in economic, political or social terms. The political costs relate to the impact of industrial conflict (as measured by strikes) on the electoral success/failure of governments. The 1980s saw an increasing societal consciousness of the costs of other causes of lost production but there is no evidence to date of these indices competing with the strike index as an issue, in terms of either promise or performance, in election campaigns.

The total economic costs of strikes is not easily measured. The number of working days lost or even the value of wages foregone do not indicate the total economic cost. A short strike in the power or telecommunications industries, for example, may disrupt the nation because of its effect on the economy. By contrast, a short strike by city garbage collectors may inconvenience ratepayers but will not usually bring the city to a standstill. An employer-induced strike in an enterprise with excess stocks may represent a net saving to the company and a net loss to those on strike. It is possible, in tight labour markets, that some employees may obtain work elsewhere while a strike is in progress.[34] Further, some or all of the working days lost may be made up through either working longer hours or increasing the workforce upon resumption of work. This does not occur however where perishable commodities such as newspapers or air travel are involved. As already noted, wages lost is an imprecise and only partial measure of the cost of strikes. Indeed, a strike of railway workers may even result in a saving to the government since the annual deficit incurred by the railways is reduced by the non-payment of wages. This also represents a saving to taxpayers. Yet it would be inferred from the official statistics that there was a considerable monetary cost to society. This is not to deny that the inconvenience of having no trains imposes considerable social and economic costs on members of the community who are dependent upon rail transport. Thus strikes vary in their social and economic costs to the community according to their breadth of impact, length and timing, and the industry in which they occur, but calculation of those costs is often likely to be difficult and imprecise.

Organised industrial action other than strike action may have significant economic or social costs: during 1984, nurses in Victoria imposed bans on non-nursing duties for ten weeks in a dispute over workloads. These bans, together with a crucial decision not to cross the bans by the then Hospital Employees' Federation, the union whose members had formal responsibility for many of the duties which nurses were banning, severely disrupted patient services in about twelve major public hospitals.[35]

The costs of other forms of industrial conflict and lost time unrelated to industrial conflict, may outweigh those of strikes. Until the 1980s scant attention was given to this, one reason being that time lost due to strikes is relatively easy to identify. Other sources of lost time, which may include industrial conflict as the precipitating cause, such as labour turnover, wastage, sabotage, absenteeism and industrial accidents are more difficult to isolate and quantify. Strikes are often dramatic, newsworthy and telegenic. They involve sometimes colourful characters, hyperbolic oratory and apocalyptic prophesies. For these reasons alone they attract a good deal of attention, more, perhaps, than their measurable effect on productivity might suggest is warranted. Australian politicians and political parties have long tended to attach themselves, like succubi, to industrial conflict and this too ensures that strikes are in the forefront of public attention. Historically, the Australian public, assailed from all sides by an insistence on the high cost and alarming frequency of strikes, is largely denied alternative interpretations and has little choice but to accept the proposition. The position changed somewhat during the 1980s, due in good measure to legislative initiatives in relation to occupa-

Table 3.14 Absenteeism: Victorian Public Transport Corporation 1991

> # Spyker to act on 'sickies'
> BY DAVID BALHAM
>
> Giving workers more authority could be the answer to the Public Transport Corporation's huge absenteeism problem, the Transport Minister, Mr Peter Spyker, said yesterday.
>
> Mr Spyker told 'The Sunday Age' that the Government was also considering giving prizes to depots with the lowest absenteeism, but would not offer workers cash incentives for not taking sick leave.
>
> The Auditor-General's report released this week found the corporation's 2000 workshop staff took an average 20 days sick leave last year, costing 34.5 million. The Australian average is around 10 days a year.
>
> My Spyker said absenteeism in the corporation was far too high and had to be reduced, but he would not say that sick leave was being abused until he had seen a breakdown of figures to establish which workshops, sections and age-groups were the worst offenders.
>
> Several private companies have reduced 'sickie' rates by up to 50 per cent by using management techniques that rely on worker peer-group pressure to control absenteeism.
>
> As part of an enterprise-bargaining agreement, the chemical giant ICI has granted employees unlimited paid sick leave at its Yarraville and Deer Park plants, while retaining the right to request a doctor's certificate after long absences.
>
> Workers have been placed on salary, and overtime has been abolished. Management has encouraged workers to take greater responsibility for reaching production targets. The company claims that this has reduced sick leave because workers realise that if they are sick their colleagues have to work harder.
>
> ICI's employee relations manager, Mr Jim Grant, said absenteeism was now down to below two per cent of man-hours, compared with an average 4.2 per cent in private industry and 6.6 per cent in the public sector.
>
> Mr Spyker said that as part of an enterprise-bargaining agreement now being worked out he wanted to decentralise authority in the corporation and give workers greater responsibility, along the lines of the ICI initiatives.
>
> 'The workforce responds well if it has some say in changes,' he said. 'It doesn't respond well to someone on the 17th floor of Transport House giving orders.'

Source: *The Sunday Age*, 10 May 1992, p. 2.

tional health and safety by Labor governments in a number of jurisdictions. The expanding research in this area confirms that production losses due to strikes are relatively low when compared with other sources of lost production.

As noted above, during the 1970s the annual average time lost per employee due to strike activity was 0.67 days and between 1981 and 1992 the average was 0.29 days. A survey by the Australian government on the level of temporary non-approved absence from work in all sectors of the workforce conducted in 1973 and 1976 found on the average, in any one year, four per cent of the workforce were absent on any working day as a result of sickness and accident.[36] More recently, the Auditor-General's report on the Victorian Public Transport Corporation found that the Corporation's workshop staff took an average of twenty days sick leave during 1991 (see Table 3.14).

Crawford and Volard estimate the relative importance of the different causes of lost working time in Australia in 1977. The researchers distinguish avoidable and non-avoidable non-approved work absences as shown in Figure 3.1. They regard 'the sickie' reflecting an employee's conscious decision not to go to work, as the only completely avoidable type of absence.[37]

Their estimates of causes of working time lost, shown in Figure 3.2, draw on the above-mentioned Australian government survey, together with ABS data on industrial disputes and published and non-published data from the Australian Health Survey, September quarter 1977, conducted by the ABS.

Figure 3.1 Causes of temporary non-approved work absence

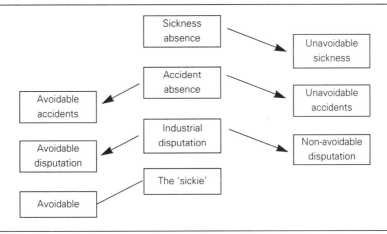

Source: B. Crawford and S. Volard, 'Work absence in industrialised societies: the Australian case', *Industrial Relations Journal*, vol. 12, no 3, 1981, p. 51.

The estimates show almost forty per cent of absence as due to various specifiable and clearly medically verifiable sicknesses. Substance abuse, which Crawford and Volard note is increasingly being classified as sickness but is not as clearly medically verifiable,[38] accounts for a further eighteen per cent of total absences. Thus total sickness is estimated to account for fifty-one per cent of all non-approved absences. Three types of accidents are identified: industrial, traffic and other 'off the job' accidents due to sporting, recreational and domestic causes. Crawford and Volard explain the comparatively low figure for traffic accidents as due to, *inter alia*, accidents caused by alcohol and drug abuse being included elsewhere and exclusion of people not in the workforce.[39] The percentage of total estimated working days lost which could not be accounted for by any identifiable causes was 18.9 per cent, leading Crawford and Volard to conclude that for every five days taken off work by employees in Australia, it could be expected that one day would be due to employees consciously deciding not to go to work.[40] A 1990 report to the federal Minister for Industrial Relations refers to published and unpublished data which indicate that in 1986-1987 lost working time in Australia due to occupational injury, was at least ten times greater than time lost due to industrial disputes.[41] The fact that strikes may be less costly than other sources of lost time does not diminish the level of public concern with the former. Howard[42] argues that the reason the Australian public has a strong aversion to strikes is the widespread perception that the arbitration 'system' provides a fair and legitimate alternative to strikes for employees. The attention strikes continue to attract may be compounded by the fact that they are seen as a challenge to the authority of management as well as to the authority of industrial tribunals.

Recent data on absenteeism includes that provided by the Workplace Survey conducted in 1989. The average rates of absenteeism presented in Figure 3.3 show significant variation in absenteeism rates by employment size. In the Survey sample only one workplace with more than 500 employees

Figure 3.2 Estimate of temporary non-approved work absence, Australia, 1977

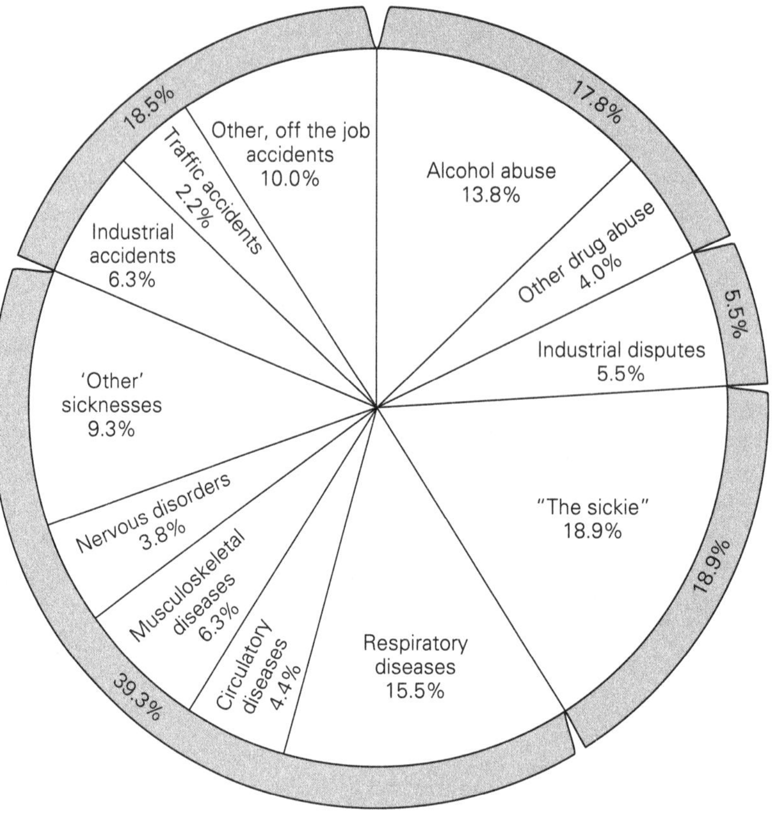

- Other, off the job accidents 10.0%
- Traffic accidents 2.2%
- Industrial accidents 6.3%
- 'Other' sicknesses 9.3%
- Nervous disorders 3.8%
- Musculoskeletal diseases 6.3%
- Circulatory diseases 4.4%
- Respiratory diseases 15.5%
- "The sickie" 18.9%
- Industrial disputes 5.5%
- Other drug abuse 4.0%
- Alcohol abuse 13.8%

Source: B. Crawford and S. Volard, 'Work absence in industrialised societies: the Australian case', *Industrial Relations Journal*, vol. 12, no 3, 1981, p. 53.

had no absentees. In terms of industry the average rates were: mining (6.6 per cent); manufacturing (5.3 per cent); electricity, gas and water (6.4 per cent); construction (4.0 per cent); wholesale and retail trade (4.4 per cent); transport and storage (7.6 per cent); communication (6.3 per cent); finance, property and business services (5.1 per cent); public administration (5.4 per cent); community services (5.5 per cent); recreational, personal and other services (0.8 per cent).

It is assumed that all absences recorded here were unauthorised. The Survey does not distinguish causes of absence but the Report refers to the literature, noting that sickness that is not directly work induced is perhaps the most common form of absenteeism and the odd day off work (equating to Crawford and Volard's category 'the sickie') is a phenomenon of industrial societies. Social scientists regard this as a form of withdrawal caused by boredom and frustration with work or even a more general social alienation.[43] The Report mentions a reason for absence not included in the Crawford and Volard work, namely family and personal commitments.[44] In the period

Figure 3.3 Average rate of absenteeism (percentage of employees absent in one week), by employment size and by sector, 1989 (AWIRS)

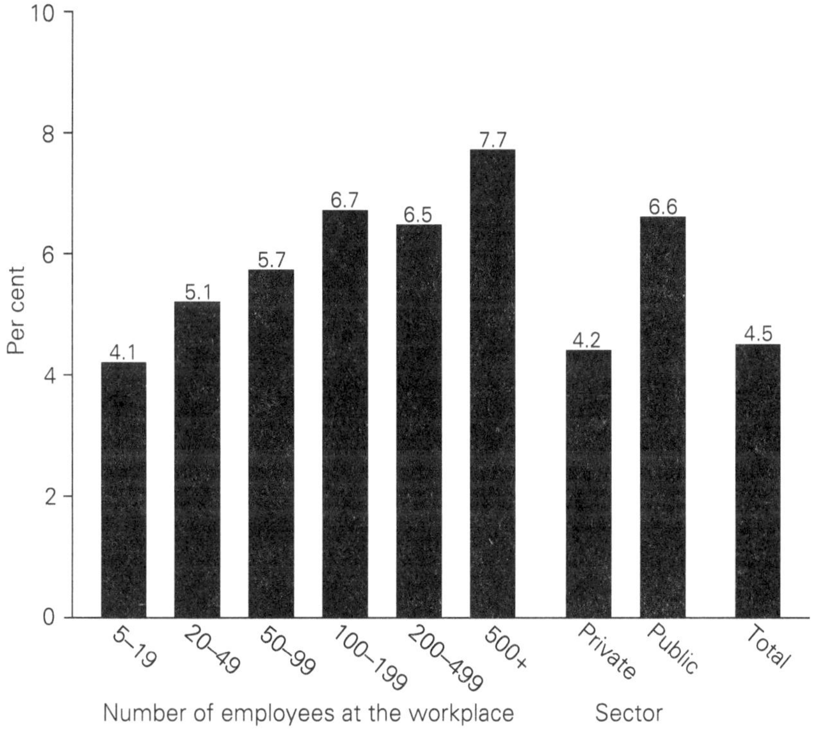

Number of employees at the workplace	Per cent
5–19	4.1
20–49	5.1
50–99	5.7
100–199	6.7
200–499	6.5
500+	7.7

Sector	Per cent
Private	4.2
Public	6.6
Total	4.5

Population: Australian workplaces with at least five employees. Based on responses from 1948 workplaces. All estimates are weighted.

Notes:

1. This figure includes only workplaces which responded to the Employee Profile Questionnaire or the phone survey.

2. Estimates are based on management responses to the following question: 'Over one week, what percentage of all employees here were absent from work?'

Source: R. Callus, A. Morehead, M. Cully and J. Buchanan, *Industrial Relations At Work: The Australian Workplace Industrial Relations Survey*, Commonwealth Department of Industrial Relations, AGPS, Canberra, 1991, p. 60.

between these two studies there has been growing recognition of the need for working patterns to accommodate family responsibilities. This has been formalised in the creation of rights to special forms of leave such as maternity and paternity leave. In 1994, the ACTU lodged a claim with the Australian Industrial Relations Commission for five days' paid family leave per year. In terms of the central issue here, the relative importance of organised expressions of industrial conflict as a cause of lost working time, workplace rule changes which broaden the categories of leave entitlements may have the effect of diminishing the relative importance of 'the sickie' as some of the component of 'family commitments' within this broad category shifts to authorised absences. To the extent these entitlements are for unpaid leave, then the costs to the employer may diminish, although administrative and (possible) operational costs would need to be offset against any savings in wages. The other dimension here which is relevant to costs of lost working time is employee motivation and effort. This may improve if commitments outside the workplace are acknowledged.

Conclusion

Given its sources, it seems that unless human nature changes, conflict will always be an element of industrial relations. This suggests that communities would profit by developing institutional means which ensure that the process of conflict is not permitted to damage the community at large, even though it may harm the direct participants. It is the function of labour law to institutionalise conflict in the ways which meet community needs, and the various forms of labour laws that exist reflect varying views of these needs. There is, of course, a great danger that the institutional means provided may become, in some sense, ends in themselves, and that attempts to force resolution of labour-management conflict by particular means may develop as a discrete and new source of conflict. It is to be noted too that most institutional forms of directing or resolving conflict in the community interest, centre on the conflict itself. For the most part it is rarely the conflict which is the concern of the community at large, but the service which may be reduced or withdrawn as a result of it. It is considerably more difficult to imagine ways in which service can be maintained during a conflict than it is to imagine methods of seeking to inhibit or delay particular forms of conflict, especially the strike. In the long run, however, it may be that only this more difficult route can resolve the conflicting preferences of the parties to industrial relations and the citizens affected by their disputes.

No one could deny that industrial conflict may often impose a considerable cost on the participants and on their communities. In accepting this, one should not lose sight of the fact that there are positive aspects to the process. The fact is that if one is willing to learn from conflict, one can do so, and conflict may be an important force for progress in an industrial society. While conflict may be unpleasant, even wasteful, attempts to suppress it may be dangerous and even destructive. The sources of industrial conflict are pervasive and ever-present; thus, suppression of one manifestation of conflict will lead to its surfacing in another form, and suppression of all its forms may well lead to an eruption of conflict that in its bitterness and intensity may be out of all proportion to the events which triggered it. It must be accepted that industrial societies will be marked by industrial conflict. These societies should seek means of accommodating conflict, and of learning from it.

Notes

1. See, for example, C. Kerr, 'Industrial Conflict and its Mediation', in C. Kerr (ed.), *Labour and Management in Industrial Society*, Anchor Books, Garden City, 1964, pp. 167-168.
2. It has been suggested that the incidence of employee sabotage is considerably higher than is often thought. See P. Dubois, *Sabotage in Industry*, Penguin Books, Ringwood, 1979.
3. C. Crouch, *The Politics of Industrial Relations* (2nd ed.), Croom Helm, London, 1982, pp. 160-161. The legal aspects of picketing are discussed in chapter 5.

4 C. Fox, 'Tribunal Policy and Dispute Settlement: The Nurses' Case 1986-87', *Journal of Industrial Relations 35*, June 1993, p. 294.
5 For some details of this conflict see *R v Marks and Federated Ironworkers' Association; Ex parte Australian Building Construction Employees' and Builders Labourers' Federation* (1981) 35 ALR 241.
6 *The Age*, 5 November 1986, p. 1.
7 I. Collins, Interview with R. Curlewis, *Oral History Journal*, no. 10, 1988.
8 A. Fox, 'Industrial Sociology and Industrial Relations' Research Paper 3, HMSO, London, 1966, reprinted in A. Flanders (ed.), *Collective Bargaining*, Penguin, London, 1971, pp. 390-409.
9 *The Age*, 14 March 1990.
10 C. Kerr,'Trade unionism and distributive shares' in R.L. Rowan (ed.), *Readings in Labor Economics and Labor Relations*, Richard Irwin, Homewood, 1972, pp. 444-453.
11 ACTU, *Blueprint for Changing Awards and Agreements*, Submission to *National Wage* case, February 1989, p. 131.
12 C. Kerr, J.T. Dunlop, F.H. Harbison and C.A. Myers, *Industrialism and Industrial Man*, Oxford University Press, New York, 1964, pp. 14-139.
13 See A. Losovsky, *Marx and the Trade Unions*, Martin Lawrence, London, 1935, chapter 1.
14 R. Hyman, *Strikes* (4th ed.), Macmillan, London, 1989, p. 95.
15 For details of the dispute see Australian Industrial Relations Commission, Melbourne Metropolitan Board of Works and Australian Workers' Union CNo 30706 & 30707 of 1990, *Transcript of Proceedings*, 25 March, 9,11, & 20 April, 1990.
16 Hyman, *op. cit.*, pp. 96-98.
17 *ibid.*, pp. 99-100.
18 *ibid.*, pp. 50-54.
19 See also chapter 5 and E.I. Sykes, *Strike Law in Australia* (2nd ed.), Law Book Co., Sydney, 1980, p. 56.
20 For an account of the dispute see B. Creighton, 'Law and the Control of Industrial Conflict', in K. Cole (ed.), *Power, Conflict and Control in Australian Trade Unions*, Penguin, Melbourne, 1982, pp. 137-141.
21 J.E. Isaac, 'Professor Niland on Collective Bargaining and Compulsory Arbitration in Australia', *Journal of Industrial Relations 21*, December 1979, p. 474.
22 The operation of grievance procedures is discussed in chapter 17.
23 *The Age*, 27 October 1989, p. 1, 21 February 1990, p. 3, 23 October 1990, p. 3.
24 R.M. Martin, 'The problem of 'political' strikes', in W.A. Howard (ed.), *Perspectives on Australian Industrial Relations*, Longman Cheshire, Melbourne, 1984, pp. 68-81.
25 In the matter of applications by the Administrative and Clerical Officers' Association, Australian Government Employees and others to vary Determinations and Awards in relation to rates of pay (1985) 297 CAR 404.
26 ABS, *Industrial Disputes Australia* 1991 and 1992, Catalogue No. 6322.0, pp. 1-2.
27 For details of the dispute see H. Thompson, 'The APPM Dispute: The Dinosaur and Turtles vs the ACTU', *The Economic and Labour Relations Review 3*, December 1992, pp. 148-164.
28 M. Lee, 'The Coal Industry Tribunal: The Case for its Retention', *Australian Bulletin of Labour 15*, December 1988, p. 14.
29 R. Callus, A. Morehead, M. Cully and J. Buchanan, *Industrial Relations At Work: The Australian Workplace Industrial Relations Survey*, Commonwealth Department of Industrial Relations, AGPS, Canberra, 1991, p. 62.
30 *ibid.*, p. 61.
31 United Kingdom, *Employment Gazette*, vol. 97, no. 6, June 1989, p. 312.
32 *ibid*.
33 ABS, *Industrial Disputes Australia*, 1992, Catalogue No. 6322.0, p. 14.
34 J. Benson, K. Hince, G. Griffin, 'Industrial Relations Policy: A Case Study of Organisational Change', Paper presented to the Australian and New Zealand Association for the Advancement of Science, Perth, W.A., 1983, Mimeo, p. 11.

35 This dispute is analysed in C. Fox, *Industrial Relations in Nursing: Victoria 1982 to 1985*, Australian Studies in Health Service Administration, No. 68, School of Health Services Management, UNSW, 1989, chapter 4.
36 For a discussion of the survey see R. Harkness and B. Krupinski, 'A Survey of Absence Rates', *Work and People*, vol. 3, no. 2, Winter 1977, pp. 3-9.
37 B. Crawford and S. Volard, 'Work absence in industrialised societies: the Australian case', *Industrial Relations Journal 12*, May/June 1981, p. 51.
38 ibid., p. 52.
39 ibid.
40 ibid., p. 53.
41 Report by the Review Committee to the Minister for Industrial Relations, *Review of Occupational Health and Safety in Australia*, AGPS, Canberra, November 1990, p. 18.
42 W. Howard, 'Centralism and Perceptions of Australian Industrial Relations', *Journal of Industrial Relations 25*, March 1983, pp. 1-18.
43 Callus *et. al.*, *op. cit.*, pp. 59-60.
44 ibid., p. 60.

Further Reading

Manifestations and causes of industrial conflict

R. Drago and M. Wooden, 'The Determinants of Strikes in Australia', *Journal of Industrial Relations 32*, March 1990, pp. 32-52.

R. Hyman, *Industrial Relations: A Marxist Introduction*, Macmillan, London, 1975, chapter 7.

R. Hyman, *Strikes* (4th ed.), Macmillan, London, 1989, chapters 1-5.

C. Kerr, J.T. Dunlop, F.H. Harbison, and C.A. Myers, *Industrialism and Industrial Man*, Oxford University Press, New York, 1964, pp. 14-139.

Industrial action

S. Frenkel, *Industrial Action*, Allen and Unwin, Sydney, 1980.

P.R. Hay, 'Political Strikes: Three Burning Questions', *Journal of Industrial Relations 20*, March 1978, pp. 22-40.

R.M. Martin, 'Political strikes and public attitudes in Australia', *Australian Journal of Politics and History 31*, No. 2, 1985, pp. 269-281.

R. M. Martin, 'The problem of political strikes' in W.A. Howard (ed.), *Perspectives on Australian Industrial Relations*, Longman Cheshire, Melbourne, 1984, pp. 68-81.

Report of the Committee of Review of Australian Industrial Relations Law and Systems, vol. 2, AGPS, Canberra, 1985, chapter 3, Part III.

S. Silverman, 'Political strikes in Australia', in J.E. Isaac and G.W. Ford (eds), *Australian Labour Relations: Readings* (2nd ed.), Sun Books, Melbourne, 1971, pp. 79-92.

Measures of industrial conflict

Australian Bureau of Statistics, *Industrial Disputes Australia*, Catalogue No. 6322.0.

Australian Bureau of Statistics, *Labour Statistics*, Catalogue No. 6101.0.

G.J. Bamber and R.D. Lansbury, *International and Comparative Industrial Relations* (2nd ed.), Allen and Unwin, Sydney, 1993, pp. 309–317.

J.J. Beggs and B.J. Chapman, 'Australian strike activity in an international context: 1964-85', *Journal of Industrial Relations 29*, June 1987, pp. 137-149.

P. Bentley and B. Hughes, 'Australian Cyclical Strike Patterns', *Journal of Industrial Relations 13*, December 1971, pp. 352-367.

R. Callus, A. Morehead, M. Cully and J. Buchanan, *Industrial Relations At Work: The Australian Workplace Industrial Relations Survey*, Commonwealth Department of Industrial Relations, AGPS, Canberra, 1991, pp. 61-66 & 251-256.

S.W. Creigh, 'Australia's Strike Record: the International Perspective', in R. Blandy and J. Niland (eds), *Alternatives to Arbitration*, Allen and Unwin, Sydney, 1986, pp. 29-51.

L. Perry, 'Trends in Australian strike activity, 1913-78', *Australian Bulletin of Labour 6*, December 1979, pp. 31-51.

United Kingdom, *Employment Gazette*, vol. 97, no. 6, June 1989, pp. 309-313.

Functions of industrial conflict; industrial conflict and absenteeism: comparative costs

R. Callus, A. Morehead, M. Cully and J. Buchanan, *Industrial Relations At Work: The Australian Workplace Industrial Relations Survey*, Commonwealth Department of Industrial Relations, AGPS, Canberra, 1991, pp. 53-61 & 248-250.

B. Crawford and S. Volard, 'Work Absence in Industrialised Societies: the Australian Case', *Industrial Relations Journal 12*, May/June 1981, pp. 50-57.

R. Dubin, 'Constructive aspects of industrial conflict', in A. Kornhauser, R. Dubin and A. Ross (eds), *Industrial Conflict*, McGraw-Hill, New York, 1954, chapter 3.

W. A. Howard, 'Centralism and Perceptions of Australian Industrial Relations', *Journal of Industrial Relations 25*, March 1983, pp. 1-18.

Report by the Review Committee to the Minister for Industrial Relations, *Review of Occupational Health and Safety in Australia*, AGPS, Canberra, November 1990.

M. Wooden, 'The "sickie": a public sector phenomenon?', *Journal of Industrial Relations 32*, December 1990, pp. 560–576.

Questions

Industrial conflict: manifestations; causes; functions

1 Explain the positive or constructive aspects of industrial conflict.
2 Identify the major causes of industrial conflict and provide a recent illustration of each.
3 What is the relationship between trade unions and industrial conflict?

Industrial action and measures of industrial conflict

4 Explain Martin's concept of political strikes.
5 Critically evaluate the following statement: 'Strikes are a major economic problem in Australia and the major cause of strikes is the fact that trade unions have too much power.'

6 Discuss strikes in Australia in the 1980s in relation to:
   i incidence
   ii duration
   iii causes
   iv method of settlement
7 (a) Obtain information from the Workplace Survey on the causes of industrial action and summarise the results.
  (b) Explain how the categories of causes of industrial action in the Workplace Survey differ from the categories of causes of dispute used by the Australian Bureau of Statistics in its statistical series on strikes in Australia.
8 Identify the limitations of the strike statistics published by the Australian Bureau of Statistics.
9 What are the qualifications which need to be made in considering comparative levels of strike activity between countries?

Exercises

Measures of industrial conflict

1 Locate the primary source for strike statistics for a country other than Australia appearing in Table 3.13.
   i   Prepare a summary of the factors affecting the figures in that country during the 1980s.
   ii Identify and discuss the similarities and differences in the explanatory variables between Australia and the selected country for the decade of the 1980s.

Industrial conflict and absenteeism: comparative costs

2 An estimation of work absences from various causes in Australia in 1977 was made by Crawford and Volard. Research relevant Australian publications for any comparable or similar data from official sources relating to the 1980s and prepare a summary of the similarities and differences between the various data sets. Discuss the differences in
   i   methodology;
   ii conclusions.

4

Major Disputes: Case Studies

Contents
Broken Hill strike (1919-1920)
Metal Trades Work Value case (1967-1968)
Mudginberri dispute (1985)
Victorian Nurses' strike (1986)
Air Pilots' dispute (1989)

Introduction

In this chapter a number of major Australian disputes are analysed in terms of the concepts discussed in chapter 3, drawing on published accounts in each case. These disputes will be referred to in later chapters to illustrate other concepts and practices in industrial relations and in chapter 5, two of the disputes, Mudginberri and the Air Pilots' dispute, will be analysed specifically in terms of the law relating to industrial action in Australia.

Broken Hill strike (1919-1920) (Howard)

This strike, in a single industry desert town, was a quintessential 'trial of strength' strike and the longest in Australia's industrial history, from 20 May 1919 to 10 November 1920. The major actors in the dispute were the then Amalgamated Miners Association, the Mining Managers Association, the State member of parliament for Broken Hill, the President of the NSW Industrial Commission, acting in an extra-jurisdictional capacity, and the NSW Premier. The dispute began when the mining companies did not re-open the mines following settlement of a union demarcation dispute, thus effectively locking the miners out. A federal consent award between the miners' union and the managers' association was due for renegotiation in June. Perceiving their members to be locked out, the miners' union served its log of claims on employers on 19 May 1919 and it was rejected by the managers' association the following day.

The log of claims included: a six-hour day; a five-day week and two shifts with night shift being abolished, abolition of contract mining; compensation on full pay for those made unable to work by accident or disease; each drilling machine to be crewed by two men. The main items in contention were the compensation and hours claims. The causes of the dispute thus involved the intermingling of health and safety issues with pay and conditions of work. In terms of the current Bureau categories of causes of industrial disputes the strike would not readily be allocated to a single category as the major issues in dispute covered the categories 'hours of work', 'leave, pensions, compensation' and 'physical working conditions'. In the conditions on the mines in 1919 there was a clear connection between the hours claim and health: the miners wanted shorter periods of exposure to dust and lead particles, they wanted a shift roster which would permit an evacuation of the mine during and after firing the explosive charges to loosen the ore. The miners had two demands not directed at employers. They were the implementation of the recommendations of the 1914 Royal Commission on working conditions in the mines (these had not been acted on due to the pressures of the First World War) and an inquiry into the incidence of occupational disease (tuberculosis, pneumoconiosis and lead poisoning).

Howard[1] describes how the strike was settled by a process of voluntary arbitration with an overlay of intrigue, political lobbying and hints of blackmail. It would thus be classified under 'Other Methods' in the Bureau statistics. Early attempts by the employers to settle by negotiation were unsuccessful. The miners conceded nothing, although some of the unions would have been willing to accept an employer offer of two weeks annual leave made early in the strike. As noted, the parties were covered by an award of the then CCCA. The miners however had no confidence in the Court and refused to return to it. They were convinced that legal chicanery would be used to force them back to work with little benefit. The employers made no attempt to exercise their right of unilateral reference to arbitration, realising that the miners would be unlikely to accede to any return to work order from the tribunal. The mine managers, like most employers at that time, also regarded the Court as an encroachment on management rights and exhibiting a bias toward labour. The Court did not have the powers its successors acquired unilaterally to bring the parties before it.

The impasse was broken by a significant concession to the miners from an agency of government, the NSW Board of Trade, which ordered the establishment of a scientific enquiry into the occupational health problems of the miners. The inquiry into occupational disease was undertaken by a Technical Health Commission established on 19 December 1919. This decision followed a conference in Broken Hill between the miners' union and the Board's President, Judge Edmunds, who was also President of the NSW Industrial Commission. He was in Broken Hill to deal with claims by two breakaway unions which had sought awards from the Commission. The establishment of the enquiry followed disturbing information from a report undertaken by a medical officer at the Broken Hill Hospital. This suggested that, on average, each miner shortened his working life by thirty per cent and that many of those on the job suffered severe wasting. Further, the earlier Royal Commission had found that one-third of the labour force suffered accidents in a period of eighteen months, that deaths on the job and from industrial disease occurred in numbers that would now be regarded as disastrous if they applied to the nation's entire workforce.

Acceptance of a process of voluntary arbitration as the method of settlement was made possible by the appointment of Judge Edmunds as arbitrator by the NSW and federal governments and by the first interim report of the Technical Health Commission. The findings caused both protagonists to shift their positions in relation to method of settlement. The findings were sobering and upset the strongly held beliefs of the mine managers that the mines were healthy. The Commission found, for example, that 215 miners had died of pulmonary complaints (which might reasonably be largely attributed to their employment) in the three years ending June 1920. The evidence also was probably sufficient for the miners to abandon their in-principle objection to arbitration, although the appointment of Judge Edmunds also diminished their aversion to this process.

The voluntary arbitration award was announced after proceedings lasting five weeks. Contrary to expectations Judge Edmunds awarded very little of the miners' claim. The union leaders had been alerted to this outcome by Percy Brookfield, the member of State Parliament for Broken Hill (see figure 4.1). He was a radical and militant leader of the Miners' Association, expelled from the Labor Party in 1920 for his refusal to repudiate the revolutionary Industrial Workers of the World. Brookfield held the balance of power in the NSW Parliament and used this position to persuade the Premier to convince Judge Edmunds that it would be appropriate for the matter to be returned to him.

The arguments or inducements the Premier offered the judge are unknown but they were sufficiently persuasive to lead the judge to explain that he had intended his award to apply at some later stage but that in the interim, conditions would be prescribed which met the needs of the circumstances of the industry at the time. The interim award was sufficiently favourable for the miners to vote to end their strike on 10 November. It provided for a thirty-five hour week, abolition of night shift, control of firing and increased wages.

Figure 4.1 Percival Brookfield: radical rebel, improbable peacemaker

Source: *Barrier Daily Truth*, Centenary Souvenir Edition, Broken Hill Centenary 1883-1983, p. 22.

Although the final award provisions were to be fixed on the report of the Technical Health Commission, the interim provisions were retained as the base and when negotiations on the Edmunds award were resumed in 1925, mine managers made no attack on either hours or the night shift. These negotiations marked the beginning of a commitment to collective bargaining which served both sides well for over fifty years. The strike had shown both parties that the involvement of governments and third parties did not always provide a satisfactory basis for settlement. Table 4.1 contains an extract from the Centenary Souvenir Edition of the *Barrier Daily Truth*, the union newspaper to which all union members were required to subscribe. This short extract of events during August and September 1920 conveys some of the atmosphere and issues in dispute during what the newspaper calls 'the last great confict'.

Table 4.1 The last great conflict

The tribunal

Proceedings commenced in Sydney on August 11, 1920, with Baddeley and Willis (Miners' Federation), G. Kerr, J. J. O'Reilly and P. Lamb representing the strikers.

The companies were represented by C. J. Emery, G. D. Delprat, G. Wier, G. King, C. Klug and C. Fraser.

It was a difficult situation for the workers' representatives — the thought of the depleted coffers that provided the spuds and onions, and little else, for the miners and their families — the desire to bring an end to this struggle, and to return home with the winning of a five day week of seven hours a day, compensation for the diseased victims, the abolition of night shift a reality, improved health conditions and an increase in pay their continuing aim.

As the case continued, Edmunds gave all the indication that he favored the strikers' claims, and as Wetherall writes: "In the middle of all was promoted the speculation: 'Just how far will he go?'"

Wetherall said that the bad news was conveyed to him by Brookfield in a telegram which read: "Colt broken down. No chance in seven furlongs race. Amazed. Letter following."

He said that this was telling them in Broken Hill, that those in Sydney felt that a change had occurred in the judge's attitude, though he had done nothing to warrant such a feeling.

Letters from O'Reilly and Brookfield convinced them that their confidence had been misplaced.

"It was the end of a tragic drama," said Wetherall.

Any hopes that remained were shattered when Edmunds gave his decision on August 31.

It ruled that hours remained at 44 a week, the only change being that the crib time was increased by 10 minutes to 30 minutes, the night shift claim was rejected but stoping work was abolished, but this didn't affect the biggest mine, the BHP, that did not work night shift.

Holidays were changed only to conform with Edmunds' decision in the claims of the BWA and the Trades and Labor Council.

Regarding compensation, this was held over to be dealt with at an early date, though the decision did declare that compensation would be paid to all withdrawn from the industry.

The ominous paragraph in the decision revealed the hard attitude of the tribunal:

"All previous conditions, except insofar as they are not altered in this decision, are to continue unchanged upon the resumption of work". There was no alteration to the 44 hours of $5\frac{1}{2}$ days.

The Tribunal decision had dashed all the hopes of those who were sure that a favorable decision was forthcoming, and all the suffering and privation of the previous 16 months had been worthwhile.

The cold facts were that the grim story of the conditions in the industry and the diseases brought on by those conditions had not won the sympathy of the Tribunal.

The next day the decision was given to the Premier, who had himself worked on the line of lode, and to the representatives on the Tribunal, but was not made public.

What to do?

The union representatives and Brookfield were now faced with a momentous decision — Should they accept the findings, or should they work to have it changed?

It was agreed that something should be done to reverse the decision and to have the original claims granted.

It was the general consensus that the Tribunal had contradicted his pointed observations on hours during the hearings.

Wetherall writes that, "it was here the ever-fertile brain of J. J. O'Reilly played yet another masterly feat. The alert and restless industrial whirlwind declared from the blue that to get Edmunds back to the road there was but one plan and it may work. He had to be faced with these facts; The Government's confidence had been broken. The Government and State, by his verdict, had been plunged into most serious dangers, chief of which was the grave threat of industrial action by the seamen and railwaymen, and particularly the Miners' Federation. There was still a higher place in the judiciary for Edmunds and this was in contemplation. There was the appointment of a Royal Commissioner to inquire into the railway strike. Surely it could be assured that the Government planned to hand this important commission to his honor. It should be conveyed to this judge that as it stood such plans could not be carried out.

"... Let us make no mistake here of the position of Brookfield. He held the balance of power in the State Parliament. He applied the pressure. He never once threatened to cross the floor of the House but very definitely did threaten to leave it to tour the country to solicit finance for the workers' fight and that would have exposed the Government to defeat — a big matter for the Government itself. This — unless."

Brookfield and McKell quickly acquainted Storey with how the union representatives saw the decision could be reversed by Edmunds giving a more "definitive" interpretation of his finding. Storey saw the wisdom of this advice, and intimated, in private discussion, that Edmunds would miss out on a job he coveted, the Royal Commission into the 1917 railway strike, if his original decision stood.

This was sufficient to convince Edmunds that there was merit on the Broken Hill unionists' 35-hour week claim for underground workers.

Industrial history

At this point Edmunds' interim award, although it had been given to the Premier, and the mining and union representatives, had not been made public, although, as always, in such circumstances there had been leaks in the press.

There had to be a complete volte-face by Edmunds if he was to give a decision favorable to the unions.

But, man is a fickle creature, and the original interim award was altered to, what is now, the most famous award handed down in the Australian mining industry.

The companies' representatives on Tuesday, July 13, at a conference in Sydney, had locked themselves into the situation that they would accept the decision of an independent tribunal, and Edmunds was fully aware of this.

Barrier Daily Truth, August 14 wrote:

"Sydney, August 13: At the compulsory conference today the companies' representatives stated that they had considered the positions, and in view of the Technical Commission findings did not intend to better the previous offer, which was rejected. They were perfectly willing to submit the whole matter to an independent tribunal, consisting of a judge, mutually acceptable to both parties, each side to be represented by three representatives. They were prepared to bind themselves to abide the decision of the tribunal, provided the AMA representatives gave a similar undertaking.

Edmunds called the Tribunal together in a special hearing, with the mining companies thinking that he sought some discussion and clarification of his interim decision, especially regarding compensation.

The discussions continued for some days, with the mining companies challenging his actions, contending that only one decision was necessary, and he had already given it.

Finally Edmunds challenged the companies' representatives on the ground of their "lack of legal knowledge." ... "They are no doubt capable mine managers but know nothing of the law."

This brought a retort from BHP manager G. D. Delprat, that "We thought your Honor's first decision, which we received in writing, was your final decision. We thought the language was so clear that even we could understand it."

It was sufficient excuse for Delprat to pack up and leave.

Emery was unhappy with the situation asserting that; "... if the demands of the miners were conceded the output of three-shift mines would be reduced by 77.5 per cent. A reduction in hours, in the proprietors' views, meant a corresponding reduction in output."

(It is interesting to note that this claim was shot to pieces by the WIU of A president, R. E. "Dick" Quintrell in the 1924 conference in Melbourne, at which the lead bonus came into being. He produced figures that conclusively proved that production had immeasurably improved since 1920, under the 35-hour week).

After going through the motions, Edmunds gave his final decision on Thursday, September 30, 1920.

In it underground hours were to be 44 hours per week, whistle to whistle, including a crib period of 30 minutes. Surface shift workers 44 hours, with 30 minutes for crib, and day shift workers 46 hours, with 30 minutes for crib. Monday to Friday 8am to 5pm; Saturday 8am to 12noon.

But,

Until the Technical Commission had been carried out the hours shall be:

Underground, five shifts of seven hours, Monday to Friday, including 30 minutes for crib. One winding in the employer's time and one in the employee's time.

Night shift to continue underground and on the surface, night shift stoping to be abolished.

Holidays: New Year's Day, Easter Monday, Good Friday, Eight Hours Day, Christmas Day, Boxing Day.

Wages were to be based on a minimum of 15/- a day — 90/- a week.

The amount payable per week for compensation for occupational diseases:

Single man with no dependents, 40/-; single man, including widower with dependent child, mother, father, sister or brother, 60/-; with addition in respect to each child under 14 years, 8/6 per week.

The award was to be subject to the Technical Commission Inquiry.

Source: *Barrier Daily Truth*, Centenary Souvenir Edition, Broken Hill Centenary 1883–1983, pp. 30–31.

In the ensuing years, Broken Hill was by no means strike-free and the characteristics of many of the union leaders did much to ensure that the strikes which did occur came to public attention. In an industry which was, historically, a major source of industrial disputation, Broken Hill in fact contributed very little to that record. Its strikes were, on the whole, predictable, usually being confined to contract negotiation, as might be expected in a mature bargaining system, and such disputes were rarely of as much as a week in duration. There is a public perception that the Broken Hill mines have been characterised by poor industrial relations, but this is far from the actuality. The novelty of parties working entirely by collective bargaining, and the occasional robust rejections of arbitration by union spokesmen may have confused observers conditioned to the belief that industrial relations belonged in tribunals and involved intermediaries more genteel than did the Broken Hill experience. The unions have tended, over most of their history, to place entirely local concerns ahead of national issues, thus the miners did not hesitate to strike during the Second World War emergency conditions. This insularity of purpose, coupled with the close involvement of the unions with the governance of the City of Broken Hill, has helped to colour the external perception of Broken Hill industrial relations. In fact, while union attitudes, rhetoric and scope of interest may be unusual, the industrial relations of the mines has been more orderly and productive than that of the industry as a whole.

Metal trades work value case (1967-1968) (Hutson)

The key actors in this conflict were: the twelve unions party to the *Metal Trades Award*, the Metal Trades Employer Association and the Australian Conciliation and Arbitration Commission. This case illustrates well the use of strategic strikes by Australian unions over both industrial and political issues and directed at both employers and industrial tribunals. From the outset, the conflict had a contrived or ritualistic quality: a log of wage claims, presented by a group of seven unions which had carriage of the union case for all the unions party to the *Metal Trades Award*, was served in response to a federal tribunal initiative. The ensuing coercive conflict was related to the distribution of revenues but it was triggered only when employers sought to implement a recommendation contained in the tribunal's wages decision. The tribunal had proposed conducting a work value case because classifications in the *Metal Trades Award* were used as benchmarks in adjusting other awards. There had been no work value case since 1930 thus the Commission was concerned to re-examine this standard-setting award following significant changes in its key wages (see chapter 16). The tribunal was also concerned that wage rates in this award were lagging, by a growing margin, behind market-rates, a fact which diminished the authority and status of tribunal awards. The tribunal decision of December 1967[2] awarded the full union claim for the majority of tradesmen positions, including the key benchmark classification of 'fitter' which was awarded an increase of sixteen per cent. Hutson[3] notes that the increases approximated average over-award rates for tradesmen. Much lower increases were awarded for classifications involving lesser skill levels, thereby altering long-standing intra-award relativities.

The majority decision explicitly encouraged employers to absorb over-award rates, that is to pay the new legal minimum rates out of existing over-award rates, thereby leaving actual pay rates unchanged. The minority decision recommended lower wage increases and did not consider absorption feasible. In response to the unexpectedly large increases, the employer association recommended to member companies that they absorb over-award rates. The unions, with ACTU support, strongly opposed the employer association position. The most common effect of the case, had the majority view of the bench been realised, would have been to increase the award component of wages and to decrease the over-award component, with a shift from profits to wages resulting only where over-award rates were less than the award rates increase. The strikes, and Hutson[4] records that there were 400 stoppages during January and February 1968, concerned the distribution of revenues. They also were related to a political issue, the right to strike, or more precisely, the enforcement of laws which enabled an award to contain a clause prohibiting all industrial action and which provided for substantial financial penalties for contravention of such clauses, known as bans clauses. The *Metal Trades Award* had contained a bans clause since 1952. The employers tried unsuccessfully to have the Commission order that industrial action to enforce over-award rates was a breach of the award. Nevertheless the Commission said that in response to industrial action, the employers and the community would be entitled to the protection of the Commission, intimating that the benefits of the decision could be taken away.[5] The employer association advised members it would take action under the *Conciliation and Arbitration Act* which enabled employers to obtain restraining orders from the Industrial Court. If the industrial action continued, contempt of court charges and substantial fines would follow.[6]

On 22 January 1968, a meeting of shop stewards under the auspices of the Metal Trades Federation, supported a twenty-four hour national strike which took place on 6 February involving 180,000 employees in five states. The Bureau's statistics for the March quarter 1968 record working days lost nearly four times the figure for the March quarter 1967. During February, there were seventy restraining order applications and 135 summonses for contempt, with fines totalling $58,160 for the two month period. The employer association also sought a blanket restraining order of twelve months against seven unions to cover all metal factories in NSW. The secretary of the NSW Branch of the Metal Trades Federation responded that union members would switch to work-to-regulation so as to cut production and that they had 'rocked the boss with stoppages and were now going to roll him with regulations.'[7] On 8 February, the ACTU executive recommended a national stoppage of all affiliates in opposition to absorption and the use of the penalties provisions in the *Conciliation and Arbitration Act* unless the dispute was settled within a week. Also during February, an employer application to delete the new award rates and substitute the old rates was referred to a five member full bench, which included the three members from the work value case bench. On 21 February, the Commission, by majority decision, awarded seventy per cent of the earlier increases, operative from 22 January, divorced from any expectation or requirement for absorption, with the remaining thirty per cent deferred to the *National Wage* case in August. The bench noted that because of a situation where industrial disputes abounded, an essentially practical decision had been made. This was a formal acknowledgment by the tribunal that strategic industrial action had forced a reversal of a tribunal recommendation in relation to conflict over revenue distribution. The method of settlement of this conflict would have appeared in the Bureau statistics in the category 'Federal legislation'. The text of the pronouncement issued by the Commission is set out in Table 4.2.

The major union in this dispute, the Amalgamated Engineering Union, merged with two smaller craft unions in January 1973 to form the Amalgamated Metal Workers' Union. This union continued to occupy a prominent position among Australian unions and to feature in 'watershed' decisions during the 1970s and 1980s. The AMWU, which in 1993 became part of the Automotive, Metals and Engineering Union, is further discussed in chapter 6 while the policies and strategies of the major employer association in the metal trades sector, the Metal Trades Industry Association are considered in chapter 11.

Mudginberri dispute (1985) (Kitay and Powe)

The key actors in this conflict in the meat processing industry were the Australasian Meat Industry Employees Union (AMIEU), Mudginberri Station Pty Limited, the National Farmers Federation, the Meat and Allied Trades Federation of Australia and the Federal Court of Australia. The dispute occurred in the Northern Territory and the major industrial action, which had dramatic consequences, was the establishment of a picket line by the AMIEU over a four month period from 10 May to 8 September 1985. The impact of the picket line on the financial position of the employer, Mudginberri Station Pty Limited, became an important part of the evidence presented to the Federal Court in proceedings alleging the union action constituted a secondary boycott under section 45D of the *Trade Practices Act*. The applicant, Mudginberri Station Pty Limited, sought an injunction and subsequently an award of damages against the AMIEU. As with the 1967-1968 metal trades case, a precipitating factor in this conflict was a decision by the federal tribunal.

Kitay and Powe[8] identify the origins of the conflict in claims by the AMIEU to extend federal award coverage to the many, usually small, award-free sheds in the Territory and thereby eliminate contract labour systems. These systems allowed management to offer workers high wages while keeping labour costs low, especially through limiting the number of workers. In mid-1984 the AMIEU placed pickets at several abattoirs, receiving backing from the ACTU and practical support from the TWU and WWF. The Federal Court granted a permanent injunction against the unions. In an agreement reached in August 1984 before the Commission, the unions lifted all bans and the employers withdrew their legal action. The AMIEU gave a commitment to accept and work to any award made by the tribunal in resolution of the dispute.[9]

Table 4.2 Metal trades work value case: pronouncement by the Conciliation and Arbitration Commission, 21 February, 1968

'A situation having developed where industrial disputes and stoppages abound in the metal trades industry it falls to this bench to attempt to find a solution.
2. We are unanimous that the parties and the community should know what we have decided at the earliest moment and also that the solution must be a practical one.
3. It appears to all of us that substantial absorption in over-award payments of the wage increases recently granted has not in this industry except in special cases been practicable in the existing circumstances.
4. We all agree that this is a changed circumstance which has developed since the decision of 11 December 1967.
5. We all consider that this changed circumstance requires positive action by this bench.
6. We all agree that the work value decision of the Commission as to its amounts should stand. There can be no question of substitution of different amounts than those prescribed by the majority.
7. However, we all consider that, had it been known at the time of the decision that there would be neither complete nor partial absorption, the burden of the increased rates decided by the majority should not then have been imposed without deferment of some portion of the increases.
8. Although different weights may have been given to different factors in arriving at our estimate, we have been able to reach common ground.
9. (a) We reject the employers' application to include in the award a specific provision permitting absorption but we recognise the possibility of the odd case where some absorption is inescapable. Subject to this the rates which follow are based on an assessment which in the words of Mr Robinson, for the Employers, 'is divorced from assumptions that absorption should and would take place' (transcript page 17. Mr Robinson was then supporting an alternative submission that the Commission should reduce the rates prescribed by the majority).
   (b) We have decided that 70 per cent of the prescribed increases under clause 4 of the award shall be payable in accordance with the decision of 11 December and that 30 per cent shall be deferred as decided in paragraph 10 with the exception that where the increase was $1.60 or less the full amount shall be paid without deferment and where the increase was more than $1.60 the increase payable without deferment shall be at least $1.60. This decision applies to adult males and females with some consequential effects in the case of apprentices.
10. We are all of the view that the bench which will deal with the economic case anticipated to commence on 6 August this year should also decide when the deferred portion of the increases shall be payable.
11. We all consider that with the total wage system now prevailing the task of deciding when the deferred portion of the increases shall be payable will fall appropriately to that bench without suggestions from this bench as to how it should undertake its task.
12. We all agree that this is not a case in which increases in wage rates in the metal trades award set a pattern for wages in other awards. It will be for those who constitute benches dealing with work value cases in other awards to arrive at their decisions without being bound in any way to follow what has happened in the metal trades award.
13. Because of what has just been stated and because this is an essentially practical decision in which we have striven to reach common ground in a practical way we will not follow the usual practice of publishing detailed reasons for arriving at this common decision.
14. We order the Metal Trades Award as varied up to and including the variation of 11 December last be further varied in accordance with this decision. The form of the order will be settled by the Industrial Registrar with recourse to the Senior Commissioner. Any adjustments shall be in multiples of 5 cents.
15. We have found what we all consider to be a solution of the situation mentioned in our opening paragraph. We appeal to all in industry to co-operate with each other and the Commission to make this solution work and to end the industrial disputes and stoppages which called us to our present task.'
Kirby, C.J., President, Moore, J., Deputy President, Senior Commissioner Taylor and Commissioner Winter.

Source: *Metal Trades Employers' Association and others v. The Amalgamated Engineering Union (Australian Section) and others* (1968) 122 CAR 169 at 170-172.

In September 1984, a full bench (Moore P, Keogh DP and McKenzie C)[10] held that a contract system did not provide adequate award coverage but it would allow a contract for payment of wages only (the most satisfactory being a method which was essentially a piecework system for work actually done); all other substantive rules, for example, annual leave and sick leave, would be determined by the award.[11] In April 1985, Commissioner McKenzie, who the AMIEU had sought unsuccessfully to have removed from the case in 1983, handed down details of the new award. The Meat and Allied Trades Federation had sought a clause allowing negotiation of payment rates by contract at establishment level between the employer and the majority of employees. It argued for exclusion of both union and employer association from negotiations on practical grounds. The arbitrated clause allowed for possible exclusion of the union. It read: 'The terms of any system of payment by results ... shall be established by negotiation and agreement between the employer and the majority of employees concerned, or their nominated representatives'.[12] Kitay and Powe note that allowing the exclusion of a union from negotiations over a fundamental aspect of an award, wages, set a remarkable precedent for an industrial tribunal.[13]

The next point of conflict was between the union and the employees at this particular workplace, the Mudginberri abattoir: the union wanted a unit tally payment system[14] and the employees did not. Further, the employer wanted to negotiate piecework rates directly with the employees and they agreed. The AMIEU then established a picket line outside the abattoir. None of the picketers was an employee of the company. Meat inspectors from the Commonwealth Department of Primary Industry who were members of the Meat Inspectors' Association, refused to cross the picket line. This resulted in the suspension of the company's export licence. Production for the domestic market later continued using Northern Territory inspectors. The financial loss to the business became an issue in the subsequent proceedings for damages before the Federal Court, as did the fact that none of the picketers was an employee of the company. The features of this dispute provide a clear example of a secondary boycott.

The Court issued injunctions requiring the union to withdraw the picket, which it refused to do. The AMIEU was fined and its property and income sequestrated for defiance of Court orders. In July 1986 the Court awarded damages of $1.76 million against the AMIEU (see Table 5.1). This was the first occasion on which action against a trade union under section 45D had proceeded to this stage (for a discussion of the legal proceedings see chapter 5). Kitay and Powe conclude that the union position was weak due to: the isolated site; the high wages which encouraged an 'individualism' ethic; the antagonistic union-employee relations at Mudginberri and limited assistance from other unions. On the other hand, the employer position was strong with the backing of a militant employer association, the National Farmers Federation, against whose member companies the union had no leverage, and financial support from the Queensland and Northern Territory governments.[15]

This dispute began as a purely industrial conflict but became political if Martin's 'dimensions' criterion is accepted. In terms of the causes of conflict discussed in chapter 3, this was foremost a dispute about trade unionism, specifically the exclusive representation rights accorded trade unions in the negotiation process. The (original) dispute demonstrated that the costs of a particular form of industrial action, the secondary boycott, could be prohibitive for Australian unions. (For a discussion of the nature of the costs incurred see chapter 5.)

The dispute was settled by the federal tribunal in March 1986 following an AMIEU application for an award variation. The Commission rejected the union's application for a union right of representation to negotiate substantive rules but granted the union a consultative role, with the decision on employee representation remaining the prerogative of employees at a particular workplace.[16] In terms of the Bureau of Statistics' categorisation, the method of settlement here would be classified in the category 'Federal and joint federal-State legislation'. The only aspect of this dispute which would appear in the ABS industrial dispute statistics is the series of twenty-four hour stoppages in the meat processing industry in August and September 1985 as no official statistics are collected on the major form of industrial action relevant to this dispute, namely, the picket line.

Victorian nurses' strike (1986) (Fox)

The key actors in this conflict were: the Victorian branch of the then Royal Australian Nursing Federation with a membership of about 20 000; the Victorian government; the Industrial Relations Commission of Victoria and the ACTU. Private employers, mainly private hospitals, were party to the dispute but had a secondary role as the public sector was traditionally the lead sector in negotiations in the health services industry. The fifty day strike, from 31 October to 19 December 1986, was precipitated by a tribunal award, unacceptable to the nurses, handed down on 20 June 1986 and by the response of the major employer, the Health Department of Victoria, in implementing that award. The award had been completely restructured by agreement with only a few aspects of structure, albeit important aspects, arbitrated. Wage rates and qualification allowances were also arbitrated, for the most part between demand and offer.

The dispute was lengthy. Its origins lay in the submission of a union log of claims to government as early as January 1985. The log was an extensive one but the major items were: claims for significant wage rises for all award classifications from student nurse to director of nursing positions; the creation of new classifications to ensure a clinical career path; and increases in a range of allowances. In the ensuing months the union was distracted by the demands of implementing a work practices (non-nursing duties) agreement negotiated in August 1984 and it did not focus on the log of claims until around August 1985. It then launched a campaign of graduated industrial action around the log, together with new claims relating to parking, security and child care. The industrial action in August and September included stop-work meetings, marches and bans on agency (casual) staff. In October there was a five day strike, the first state-wide strike by nurses in Victoria, in which the union sought, in vain, to induce the government to improve an offer it had made on 30 September in response to the escalating coercive pressure. The strike occurred after full bench proceedings on the union's claim had commenced. Nursing Federation members voted by a small majority and amidst confusion to return to work. The failed strike left many nurses harbouring righteous anger, directed both at their union and government.[17] The tribunal hearing, by a full bench of the Victorian Commission (Garlick DP, Eggington & Williams CC), commenced on 9 October 1985 and concluded on 21 May 1986, with fifty-eight sitting days, seventy-seven witnesses and 3105 pages of transcript. Leave to intervene was granted to the ACTU, CAI and the Commonwealth Department of Employment and Industrial Relations. An unusual feature of the case was the coexistence of negotiations relating to a new award structure and occurring outside the tribunal, with lengthy submissions to the tribunal concerning wage rates.[18] In other words, the case for and against particular wage increases was being argued before the parties had agreed on the classification structure of a proposed new award.

During May 1986, while the tribunal was deliberating upon submissions, Nursing Federation members elected a new secretary, Irene Bolger, who had campaigned on a militant platform, rejecting the new award structure agreed between the union leadership and the government. There had been negligible consultation with constituencies by either principal party in relation to the acceptability of the new award structure they had negotiated. Following the tribunal decision on 20 June, a four month battle ensued over the implementation of a badly crafted award. This culminated in a decision to strike by a general meeting of union members on 30 October. Between July and October, the union employed other forms of industrial action including stop-work meetings and protest action such as working out of uniform and the wearing of badges which read: 'Don't ask me, I'm only a Grade 1 nurse'.

These various industrial actions were all part of the one dispute but would not be recorded as such by the Bureau which records strikes as separate disputes when the return to work is for two or more calendar months. Arguably the major symptom of conflict, the fifty day strike, would fit the Bureau category of 'work stoppages initiated by employers'. During the period of implementation of the new award there was evidence of major dissatisfaction with it by both hospital managements and nurses. By early October 1986, amid widespread dissension in the field, government strategists assessed that, at their current offer, a strike was likely but would not last long, no more than one week. There was no shift in the employer position toward union claims on the basis of this analysis and the employer decision thus represented a decision to 'take a strike'. Employer assessments appear to have been influenced by the union's unsuccessful five day strike in October 1985.

There are several ways to view the cause of the conflict manifest in late 1986. First, the conflict can be viewed as a response to unacceptable decisions by the representatives of the principal parties and by an industrial tribunal. The award structure, with some significant exceptions, was an agreed matter. Thus the constituency of one of the principal parties was rebelling against the joint decisions of its previous leadership and the employer. The wage rates, the important qualification allowances and a few aspects of structure affecting classification of positions, were the product of arbitration; to this extent the conflict arose from a tribunal decision. Secondly, the conflict can be seen as deriving from conflicting objectives concerning methods of settlement. This is how the government portrayed the cause during the course of the strike: as a conflict about wage fixation processes and the importance of adherence to tribunal policy (the 'guidelines'). The union persisted with its demand for the government to negotiate directly with the union and for its members to remain on strike until agreement was reached on major items. Thirdly, and this was the primary cause, the conflict was over revenue distribution: the appropriate wages and allowances for nurses *vis-à-vis* the wages of a range of other occupations (inter-occupational wage relativities) and the distribution of wage levels within the award (intra-occupational wage relativities). The issue here was not the wages-profits conflict but rather the issue of what proportion of the state's health budget was to be allocated for (increased) wages for nurses. In the Bureau's statistics on causes of industrial disputes, this strike would probably be classified under 'wages' as the reported main cause, although aspects of the category 'managerial policy' namely, principles of promotion and disagreement with management (in this case, Health Department) decisions on classification, were significant contributing factors. The strike in fact reflected conflict over both interests and rights.

The duration of the strike, fifty days, was exceptional. During 1986, just over one per cent of strikes in Australia exceeded twenty days and throughout the 1980s strikes of this duration never exceeded three per cent of strikes. The conflict represented a true 'trial of strength' in that the union members did not vote to return to work until after the government had made a substantial offer, albeit in the form of a submission to the tribunal rather than directly to the union. Table 4.3 provides a collage of perspectives on the industrial action by nurses during 1986.

Table 4.3 Perspectives on nurses' industrial action: Victoria, 1986

If industrial action does occur, the outcome can be at best only a resumption of that case. If the federation wishes to contemplate industrial action, the only appropriate time for it to consider such a course is at the end of the proceedings before the full bench.

David White
Minister for Health
Victoria, *Parliamentary Debates*, 379:307
16 October, 1985

Mr White said the nurses' decision to walk out (at Western General) would cause bitterness and tension.... It was clear nurses were being 'ruthlessly manipulated' by their federation's leadership he said.

Age 5 November, 1986, p. 1.

Are we to believe nurses will take strike action at the drop of a hat, that they are normally a militant group, that they are not committed to their task? Nurses would much rather be back working and they find striking to be foreign to their normal objectives. We know that. It is plain on its face that that is the truth. However, the Government, by its tactics of deception and half-truths, has turned RANF into a rogue union.

Mark Birrell MLC
Opposition Health Spokesman
Victoria, *Parliamentary Debates*, 384:1100
19 November, 1986

> I doubt we would ever recover to the state we were. It is going to take a long time to repair the damage that has been done and rebuild the relationships and rebuild the service that was here. The whole thing is dreadful. It is very depressing.
>
> Dr. Geoffrey Dreher
Chief Executive
Royal Melbourne Hospital
Age, 15 November 1986, p. 1.
>
> ......it was the first dispute that the members ever ran. God could have been secretary and we still would have gone out.
>
> Isabell Collins RN
RANF Job Representative
Western General Hospital
Interview with Richard Curlewis
Oral History Journal No. 10, 1988
>
> It is up to the nurses to make up their minds, They will be told the Commission has ordered them back to work. But as I walk around the picket lines the nurses are saying they will not go back.
>
> Irene Bolger RN
RANF Secretary (Vic Branch)
Age, 10 November, 1986, p. 1.
>
> ...The nurses' union has put itself outside the industrial system and unnecessarily allowed its members to lose two weeks' pay and a considerable amount of public support. It is not good enough for the union's secretary, Ms. Irene Bolger, to argue that the union is responding to an irresistible swell of feeling from the members. A good union official leads. There is an all-too-familiar flavour to this dispute and the rhetoric about the members not going back until they get what they want. It is reminiscent of the behaviour of the Builders' Labourers Federation...
>
> Editorial Opinion,
Age, 12 November, 1986
>
> If I knew 6 weeks ago what I know now and I knew the way the Government would treat us, I suspect I probably would have supported a full walkout from the first day of every nurse from every area...They have played on our charity and they have played on our—what used to be—dedication, that is now worn out. I really do not know where this will end. It will end for most of our colleagues very soon.
>
> Margaret Nuttall RN
Charge Nurse
Royal Melbourne Hospital
Age, 9 December, 1986, p. 4.
>
> It should now be clear that the strike and any earlier industrial action directed to matters before the Board or the Commission was at all times unnecessary and futile.
>
> Industrial Relations Commission of Victoria
Registered Nurses (Salaries and Career Structure) Reference [No 2]
2 VIR (1987) 296 at 298

The settlement of the conflict was formally achieved by the Bureau category 'state legislation' which means 'intervention or assistance of an industrial authority—created under state legislation'. However the settlement cannot be attributed entirely to this method because of the significance of informal, private negotiations between the ACTU and the government. An attempt by the tribunal, the Industrial Relations Commission of Victoria, to preside over more formal negotiations in early December was aborted when the union intensified its industrial action. The prominent role for the ACTU in the settlement of a State dispute was the product of two factors: (1)

acquiescence by the federal office of the RANF in ACTU management of the union's wages policy and strategy and (2) the support of the Victorian tribunal. Formally, the dispute was settled by an arbitration process but in fact the new award structure, modelled on the major nurses' award in NSW, and the final demand and offer wage rates, which produced narrow ranges within which arbitration occurred, were the product of private negotiation.[19]

Air pilots' dispute (1989) (Smith)

The key actors in this dispute were the Australian Federation of Air Pilots (hereafter Pilots' Federation); Ansett Transport Industries; Australian Airlines; the federal Government and the Australian Industrial Relations Commission (hereafter the Commission). The primary source of conflict was conflict over distribution of revenues. The concern of the pilots' union was with both the absolute and relative wages of pilots. The Commission's *National Wage* case decisions in recent years had involved some plateau indexation and the occupational groups which pilots had traditionally used as a basis of comparison, namely self-employed professionals and business executives, had received increases well in excess of employees covered by the tribunal Principles. On 17 July 1989 for example, federal judges were awarded wage rises of between fifteen and twenty per cent and in 1989 the salary of the chief executive of Australian Airlines was doubled.[20] On 26 July, the Pilots' Federation submitted a claim for a 29.47 per cent wage increase to four companies: Ansett Transport Industries, Australian Airlines, East-West Airlines and IPEC Aviation. In terms of the Bureau of Statistics' categories of 'cause of dispute' this conflict would be classified under 'wages', distinguishing it from the disputes summarised above, each of which arguably had more than one primary cause.

Early in the dispute however another source of conflict emerged, which came to dominate and which determined the (final) outcome. The issue was the methods available in Australia for resolving industrial conflict. The dispute established that a union which asserted the right to bargain directly with the employers of the union's members (outside the wage fixing principles of the tribunal) and to use direct industrial action in support of its claim, could incur massive penalties, both in financial terms and in terms of its right to retain legal status as an actor in the industrial relations 'system' created by the federal industrial relations statute. The Pilots' Federation had a distinctive history reflected in its origins in 1959 as an association operating outside the conciliation and arbitration system. Pilots, dissatisfied with arbitration, had left their then registered association and formed a new union. The union had negotiated directly with the airlines until 1967 when a special tribunal was established by legislation. The Federation acquired the right to represent pilots before this tribunal which operated until the *Industrial Relations Act* of 1988, after which time the Federation appeared before the Commission.

The industrial action undertaken by the pilots in August 1989 took the form of a restriction on hours of work, specifically a union directive to fly only between the hours of 9 a.m. and 5 p.m. This action would not be recorded in the ABS catalogue of industrial disputes because it did not represent a total withdrawal from work. However the stop-work meetings, at which pilots received reports from the leadership and made decisions on objectives and tactics, would be included. The industrial action followed a resolution carried at stop-work meetings, held in defiance of a directive from the federal tribunal, which authorised the Federation President to take whatever action was necessary, including a national stoppage, to 'restore the true value of pilots in Australia'.[21]

The Federation's claim was perceived as excessive, and the pilots portrayed as 'greedy' by the then Prime Minister, because under the wage fixing Principles then operative there was provision for a six per cent wage increase. The vehicle for this was the Structural Efficiency Principle which provided for a form of productivity bargaining (see chapter 18). There was however provision for special cases enabling higher increases to be granted. The Pilots' Federation expressed the view that the wage fixing principles were derived from the ACTU-Government Accord (see chapter 16) and as a non-affiliate of the ACTU the union had not been party to that agreement. Further and more significantly, the Federation had indicated it did not wish to participate in 'the system' as represented by tribunal wages policy. In return for a national wage increase unions agreed, for the duration of the relevant award, not to pursue any claims, either award or over-award, except in accordance with the Principles.[22] The federal tribunal national wage bench in the 1986 national wage decision had explained that any industrial action was unnecessary and contrary to the spirit and intent of the Principles.[23]

The pilots' direct action commenced on 17 August. Four days later the tribunal granted an employer application to cancel the awards and agreements to which the Federation was respondent. This meant the pilots and their employers were operating in an award-free environment. The pilots maintained impressive solidarity, resisting employer attempts to have them cease the industrial action. The solidarity was further tested on 24 August when the employers, with the public approval of the federal Government, sought redress via the common law. The airlines, again with public support from the federal Government, began filing writs claiming damages against pilots. This prompted the immediate resignation of the pilots en masse, an action permitted under their contracts of employment.[24] The common law action initiated by the airline companies invoked a number of grounds for an award of damages which are known collectively as the economic or industrial torts. (The application of this aspect of the law to industrial relations is explained in chapter 5.)

The tactical decision to resign terminated the employer-employee relationship. Smith explains this decision proved wise in hindsight given the subsequent success of the common law proceedings, namely the awarding of damages of $6.5 million against the Federation.[25] If the pilots' work bans had been incorporated in the Bureau of Statistics figures on industrial action (in fact these are confined to strikes and lockouts as discussed above) then the pilots' action would have meant the dispute was recorded as settled. This is because the 'other methods' category in the Bureau's categories of methods of settlement includes 'dismissal or resignation of employees' and the Bureau ceases to collect statistics on a dispute from the date of the resignations: a dispute in which employees resign is deemed to have been resolved.[26]

In fact of course the dispute was far from over. From the date of the resignations (24 August) until the Supreme Court decision (23 November) which held the defendants, the Federation and a number of officials, liable in tort, there was a trial of strength conflict in which the airlines operated in an informal alliance with the federal Government and the ACTU. This fact is reflected in the observation by Smith that '... the airlines were not satisfied with their victories thus far, and seemed to be bent on the total destruction of the Federation'.[27] Table 4.4 lists the major actions taken by the employers, the Government and the union peak council which reduced dramatically the relative bargaining power (see chapter 17 for a discussion of this concept) of the Federation. This listing does not include the important ACTU inaction and absence of criticism of employer and government actions at crucial stages of the conflict. Smith's analysis of the dispute discusses these factors and explains the complementary and significant roles of both the law, including the absence of certain legal rights, and the actions of the other major parties. Smith demonstrates how the dispute highlighted the absence of laws guaranteeing freedom of association, free collective bargaining and the right to strike and the breakdown of the convention which hitherto constrained employers from exercising their legal rights at common law in relation to industrial action. Smith notes that the dispute has reinforced *inter alia* perceptions that Australian labour law and industrial relations have become highly corporatist and dispelled the idea that if a union does not give the required commitment under the guidelines it is free to pursue its claims outside the system.[28]

Table 4.4 Air pilots' dispute (1989): major actions by employers, federal Government and ACTU

Ansett Transport Industries and Australian Airlines
- Application to cancel awards and agreements covering pilots' employment.
- Filing of writs claiming damages against pilots (24 August).
- Recruitment of former pilots and foreign pilots on individual contracts.

Federal Government
- Declaration of 'war' on the Federation by the Prime Minister (20 August).
- Authorisation for Royal Australian Air Force and international airlines to carry domestic passengers (23 August).
- Compensation to airlines for paying wages to staff such as flight attendants and maintenance employees in respect of whom a stand down order had been issued by the tribunal. The compensation took the form of a waiver of future landing charges conditional on the tribunal orders not being enforced against any flight attendant who declared themselves available to work (12 September).
- Expediting the entry into Australia of leased foreign passenger aircraft and foreign pilots.

ACTU
- Congress resolution (September 1989) which criticised the actions of the Pilots' Federation as well as those of government and the employers.

Source: Adapted from G. Smith, 'From Consensus to Coercion: the Australian Air Pilots Dispute', *Journal of Industrial Relations 32*, June 1990, pp. 241-243 & 250-251.

Conclusion

The disputes summarised here have been the subject of detailed study because of their significance. They are however significant for diverse reasons, the most notable being: duration of strike action (Broken Hill and Nurses' Strikes); the use of statute and common law in relation to industrial action (Mudginberri and Air Pilots); the challenge to wage control by industrial tribunals (*Metal Trades Work Value* case and Air Pilots). The case studies illuminate many of the issues discussed in chapter 3 such as: the distinctions between symptoms and causes of conflict and between industrial and political strikes; the functions and costs of conflict; and the alternative methods of settlement. Other aspects of importance or interest are the response of industrial tribunals to industrial action, the diversity of types of action covered by these five disputes, union strategies, employer strategies and the perennial tensions between the dispute settlement and wages policy objectives of industrial tribunals. A number of these matters are discussed in detail in later chapters.

Notes

1. W.A. Howard, *Barrier Bulwark: the life and times of Shorty O'Neil*, Willry Pty Ltd, Melbourne, 1990, chapter 3.
2. *Metal Trades Employers' Association and others v The Amalgamated Engineering Union (Australian Section) and others* (1967) 121 CAR 587.
3. J. Hutson, *Six Wage Concepts*, Amalgamated Engineering Union, Sydney, 1971, p. 195.
4. ibid., p. 199.
5. ibid., p. 198.
6. *Conciliation and Arbitration Act* 1904, ss 109 and 111.
7. Hutson, *op. cit.*, p. 201.
8. J. Kitay and R. Powe, 'Exploitation at $1000 per week? The Mudginberri Dispute', *Journal of Industrial Relations 29*, September 1987, pp. 365-400.
9. ibid., p. 375.
10. (1984) 294 CAR 424.
11. Kitay and Powe, *op. cit.*, p. 377.
12. Australian Conciliation and Arbitration Commission *The Northern Territory Meat Processing Award*, 1984, clause 33(c), Print F8207.
13. Kitay and Powe, *op. cit.*, p. 396.
14. For an explanation of this distinctive form of piecework payment see *ibid.*, p. 367.
15. Kitay and Powe *op. cit.*, pp. 394 & 396.
16. ibid., pp. 390-392.
17. For an account of the October 1985 strike, see C. Fox, *Industrial Relations in Nursing Victoria: 1982 to 1985*, Australian Studies in Health Service Administration 68, School of Health Services Management, University of New South Wales, 1989, chapters 4 & 5.
18. C. Fox, 'Antecedents of the 1986 Victorian nurses' strike', *Journal of Industrial Relations 32*, December 1990, p. 470.
19. For a detailed account of the management and settlement of the strike see C. Fox, 'Tribunal policy and dispute settlement: the nurses' case 1986-87', *Journal of Industrial Relations 35*, June 1993, pp. 292-315.
20. G. Smith, 'From Consensus to Coercion: the Australian Air Pilots Dispute', *Journal of Industrial Relations 32*, June 1990, p. 241.
21. ibid.

22 Australian Industrial Relations Commission, *National Wage* case, (1988) 25 IR 170 at 178.
23 Australian Conciliation and Arbitration Commission, *National Wage* case (1986) 14 IR 187 at 212.
24 Smith, *op. cit.*, p. 242.
25 *ibid.*, p. 246.
26 ABS, *Industrial Disputes Australia,* 1992, Catalogue No. 6322.0, p. 17.
27 Smith, *op. cit.*, p. 243.
28 *ibid.*, pp. 252-253.

Further Reading

C. Fox, 'Antecedents of the 1986 Victorian Nurses' Strike', *Journal of Industrial Relations 32*, December 1990, pp. 465-487.

C. Fox, 'Tribunal policy and dispute settlement: the nurses' case 1986-87', *Journal of Industrial Relations 35*, June 1993, pp. 292-315.

B. Howard, 'The toughest nut? Work practices at the Broken Hill mines', *Work and People*, vol. 13, no. 3, Department of Industrial Relations, AGPS, Canberra, undated.

W.A. Howard, 'The Rise and Decline of the Broken Hill Industrial Relations System', in K. Tenfelde (Hrsg), *Sozialgeschicte des Bergbaus*, Beck, Munich, 1992, pp. 715-736.

W.A. Howard, *Barrier Bulwark: The life and times of Shorty O'Neil*, Willry Pty Ltd., Melbourne, 1990.

J. Hutson, *Six Wage Concepts*, Amalgamated Engineering Union, Sydney, 1971.

J. Kitay and R. Powe, 'Exploitation at $1000 per week? The Mudginberri Dispute', *Journal of Industrial Relations 29*, September 1987, pp. 365-400.

K. McEvoy and R. Owens, 'The Flight of Icarus: Legal Aspects of the Pilots' Dispute', *Australian Journal of Labour Law 3*, August 1990, pp. 87-129.

J. McDonald, 'Industrial Relations Strategies in the Air Pilots' Dispute 1989', *The Economic and Labour Relations Review 1*, June 1990, pp. 121-144.

M. Pittard, 'Trade Practices Law and the Mudginberri Dispute', *Australian Journal of Labour Law 1*, May 1988, pp. 23-58.

T. Sheridan, *Mindful Militants: The Amalgamated Engineering Union in Australia 1920-72*, Cambridge University Press, Melbourne, 1975, chapter 10.

G. Smith, 'From Consensus to Coercion: the Australian Air Pilots Dispute', *Journal of Industrial Relations 32*, June 1990, pp. 238-253.

Questions

1 Distinguish between the symptoms of conflict and the causes of conflict for each of the disputes discussed in this chapter.
2 Assume a hypothetical situation in which (a) the five disputes discussed in this chapter are the only disputes occurring in a particular calendar year and (b) that the ABS records data on industrial disputes in accord with current practice. In what ways will the picture provided by the ABS statistics fail to reflect the reality of industrial conflict?
3 Summarise the method of settlement for the 1919-1920 Broken Hill strike.

4 Discuss the responses of the various parties to the industrial action undertaken by nurses in Victoria in 1986.
5 Were any of the disputes considered in this chapter 'political' disputes in terms of Martin's definition? (see chapter 3). Give reasons for your answer.
6 In chapter 3 it was suggested that industrial tribunals may be significant (in the context of alternative methods of settlement) in the settlement of major strikes. Evaluate this proposition in relation to any two of the disputes summarised in this chapter.
7 Discuss the similarities and differences in the method of settlement of the disputes considered in this chapter.

Exercise

1 Assume you are engaged as a consultant by either the Australian Nursing Federation or the Australian Federation of Air Pilots to provide an *ex post facto* analysis of (i) union objectives and (ii) strategy in either the 1986 strike or the 1989 dispute respectively. What advice would you provide. (This exercise should be undertaken after union objectives and strategies (chapter 6) and the concept of bargaining power (chapter 17) have been studied.)

5

Conflict and Control: Industrial Action and the Law

Contents

The right to strike
- a matter of law
- a matter of practice
- sources of controls and sanctions

Control at common law of industrial action
- the individual worker: breach of the contract of employment
- liability in tort law

Secondary boycott legislation
- Trade Practices Act
- relationship between Industrial Relations Act and Trade Practices legislation
- reform
- state secondary boycott laws

Sanctions under industrial relations legislation
- breach of award
- cancellation of awards and stand-downs
- deregistration of unions
- statutory offences

Other legislative controls

The right to strike

How far should workers be permitted to engage in industrial action without liability or sanction? What right or freedom to strike should workers have? Such questions have troubled workers, employers, governments and the public in most western countries in our industralised society. These questions are often focused upon from one vantage point—either that of union, the employer, the affected public and so on—thereby giving rise to partisan considerations about strikers' rights.

The right to strike has sometimes been likened to a proprietary right which can be negotiated—diminished or enlarged—by agreement between employer and employee. Under this view of the right to strike, workers can agree that they will forego strike action in return for certain gains. Others argue that the right to strike is a basic human right, a civil liberty, in an industralised society[1] and that such a right is akin to that of the right to vote or citizenship rights which are not subject to negotiation.[2] But the question remains whether that 'right' should be exercised freely in all circumstances. This in turn gives rise to many policy issues. To what extent should the right to strike exist in industries vital to the community such as health? To what extent should the 'innocent' public have to bear the burden of strikes? Should small businesses have any right to be compensated for the impact of secondary boycotts? Should the right be exercised only during negotiations for new terms and conditions of work? To what extent should our society tolerate political strikes? These questions necessitate balancing competing interests and claims of worker, employer, other businesses, the state and the community (or sections of it). Although the International Labour Organisation Conventions[3] do not specifically refer to the right to strike, the view has been taken by the Committee on Freedom of Association and the Committee of Experts that the right to strike is 'essential',[4] but the precise nature of that right is not spelt out. Article 8, United Nations International Covenant on Economic, Social and Cultural Rights provides for a right to strike, but it seems it is not an absolute right to strike freely in all circumstances because the Covenant refers to the right so long as it is exercised in conformity with the laws of the particular country. The clear implication is that the right should not be completely curtailed.[5]

Whilst we speak of the right to strike, strikes are not the only form of industrial action and similar policy considerations apply to these other forms of industrial action.[6]

A matter of law

In Australia there has never been an unlimited right to strike on the part of trade unions or employees. A 'right to strike' has not been guaranteed or enshrined in the Constitution of the Commonwealth Parliament or the Constitutions of state Parliaments. Until recently, it was not granted in any legislation governing industrial relations at federal or state levels.[7] Rather than protecting the right to strike in certain circumstances, the law as developed by the courts has curtailed this right by the adoption of principles of liability in tort law for industrial action on the part of trade unions, union officials and employees and in contract law for breaching the employment contract by the striking worker. Further, parliaments, both Commonwealth and at state levels, have enacted legislation from time to time which restricts the freedom to strike by either prohibiting some forms of industrial action or imposing liability, either civil or criminal, in some circumstances for industrial action.

In many countries, the method or process of resolution of industrial disputes and the right to take industrial action go hand in hand. For example, it is a feature of many collective bargaining systems that there is a right to strike whilst negotiations are under way for any new agreement but once the agreement is concluded there are usually restrictions on the ability of workers to undertake industrial action.[8] The original philosophy behind the implementation of the Australian system of conciliation and arbitration at federal level was that as there was a formal system set up by which industrial disputes of an interstate nature could be resolved by an independent tribunal, there was no need for the parties to resort to coercive industrial pressure in the form of either a lock-out on the part of employers or some form of industrial action or strikes by employees. In the original *Conciliation and Arbitration Act* 1904 (Cth) there were provisions which prevented industrial action (either strikes or lock-outs) being undertaken in relation to industrial disputes.[9] The philosophy was that the Court of Conciliation and Arbitration was established to prevent and settle industrial disputes thus making unnecessary direct recourse to industrial action. These provisions were repealed by the early 1930s by a Labour government. Since then in the federal legislation there operated until recently various provisions which curtailed strike action in certain circumstances or which made it an offence for union officers to incite strikes, but there is no longer any direct, absolute prohibition on strikes under the *Industrial Relations Act* 1988 (Cth). In addition, there are other controls on industrial action in Australia—there are prohibitions in some state systems on industrial action, sanctions against strikes have existed under the federal *Trade Practices Act* 1974 (Cth) and, as already indicated, there can be liability at common law under the law of contract and torts imposed on employees engaging in industrial action, on union officials and on unions.

When there was no guaranteed right to strike set down in any legislation, it was misleading to speak of the 'right' to strike in Australia. It was more appropriate to speak of the 'freedom' to strike which can be defined as that area which remains after taking into account the restrictions on strike action which exist under statute and at common law. Since the enactment of the *Industrial Relations Reform Act* 1993 (Cth), there is a right to strike laid down in some circumstances. Certain conditions as to either notification to the Commission of an industrial dispute or involvement in negotiations during a declared bargaining period must be met and then a certain immunity is thereby conferred on striking workers.[10] However, whilst the right to strike without liability exists in certain circumstances it is generally true to say that the legislation operates by the granting of a freedom to strike—the common law torts have not been abolished but are restricted in use.

In Australia generally there has been no immunity or protection given from civil suit in respect of industrial action in furtherance of a trade dispute so that the freedom to strike is theoretically quite limited.[11]

A matter of practice

Whilst as a matter of strict law there is not unlimited freedom to strike in Australia, in practice strikes have been and are undertaken without civil liability actually being imposed on the striking workers or their union officials or any other form of legal action being taken against them. However, the point is that the potential for liability is always present and in some notable instances has occurred—for example when the air pilots took industrial action in 1989 they found that their union and some individuals and trade union officials were sued in the industrial torts and damages of over $6.1m were assessed to be paid by the defendants to the airline companies to compensate them for economic loss suffered.[12] Although for the large part, in Australia, the law and the practice of the parties in industrial relations diverge in the sense that it is only rarely that an employer will be prepared to pursue to finality legal action against unions, the potential for liability is great.[13] As a matter of practice, it may be thought that there is a reasonable freedom to strike but this could change at any time depending on a number of factors. When liability is imposed, the burden may be heavy on union officials and unions and almost ruinous for individual workers.

Sources of controls and sanctions

What are the limits or potential limits on the freedom to strike in Australia today? First, there are the controls which are creatures of the courts. At common law, an employee who goes on strike may be in breach of his or her employment contract. The employee and/or union or union officials may be liable in the industrial or economic torts which include civil conspiracy, intimidation and interference with contractual relations. In both instances of actions for breaches of contract and tort, the courts may order that the industrial action complained of cease and, if damages are claimed, order that damages are paid.[14]

Secondly, the legislatures of some jurisdictions have enacted prohibitions on conduct which can loosely be described as secondary boycotts. At federal level, s. 45D of the *Trade Practices Act* 1974 (Cth) enabled remedies in the form of injunction and/or damages to be imposed on those taking part in the action but also enabled a monetary penalty to be imposed. This liability (but not the monetary penalty) is now contained in the *Industrial Relations Act* 1988 (Cth). Equivalent prohibitions exist in some of the states.[15] Thirdly, there are sanctions imposed under industrial relations legislation, federal and state, which can be used against strikers, the union and unionists. Finally, other sanctions exist in a wide range of legislative schemes, not just legislation confined to industrial relations—for example, Victorian essential services legislation and the Commonwealth *Crimes Act*.

These restrictions on the freedom to strike will be discussed below.

Control at common law of industrial action

'The common law is strangely equivocal about the employment relationship. On the one hand, the employer and employee are seen as two individuals of equal bargaining power who freely enter a contract. On the other hand, the common law, through the device of implied terms, loads the employee with obligations derived in part from the traditional master and servant relationship. This reinforces the inequality which the law pretends does not exist. Efforts by employees to establish a "countervailing power"[16] to that of the employer by combining together have been traditionally viewed with suspicion by the judges, who tend to see industrial action as a challenge to the legitimate authority of the employer as embodied in the contract of employment. The employer's capacity to coerce through his economic power is recognised not as problematic but as a legitimate property right.'[17]

Use of this 'countervailing power' could result in liability on the worker for breach of contract or on employee and/or the union and its officials in the industrial torts.

The individual worker: breach of the contract of employment

It is fundamental to every contract of employment that the worker performs work as directed by the employer in return for remuneration by the employer. It would be a rare contract of employment that would expressly grant a right to strike to the employee. It would also be unusual for the courts to imply a term in the contract that the employee could go lawfully on strike. Courts may imply in the employment contract terms based on custom and practice or the need to give business efficacy to the particular contract. In the *Ansett Airlines v Australian Federation of Airline Pilots*[18] Brooking J rejected an argument that there was an implied term in the pilots' contracts of employment that they could undertake industrial action without being regarded as breaking their contracts of employment.[19] Thus, in the case of the usual contract where there is no express or implied term giving a right to strike, if the worker undertakes industrial action by going on strike, then that worker is not performing an essential condition of the contract of employment.

The view which prevails today in Britain seems to be that the contract of employment will be breached by the worker undertaking strike action and that such breach will amount to repudiation of the contract allowing an employer to terminate it.[20] There has been a surprising lack of judicial authority in Australia on this question as a matter of contract law, but judicial opinion tends to support the British approach[21] although there have been some doubts and contrary views expressed.[22] This means that the employer could ignore the breach altogether (and treat the contract as remaining on foot) or the employer could elect to treat the contract as having been terminated and dismiss the employee without notice (summary dismissal) and the employer could institute proceedings against the employee to obtain damages which might flow from that breach of contract. As a matter of practice, summary dismissal or seeking damages for breach of contract by an employer in Australia would be most unusual[23] but the point is that it is legally possible—each time employees go on strike they may be putting in jeopardy their continued employment.[24]

The courts have grappled with the notion that if appropriate notice were given that strike action was proposed then the contract of employment is simply suspended rather than breached,[25] but this has not received judicial support in Australia.[26] Industrial action short of total withdrawal of labour could also result in similar legal consequences to that of total withdrawal of labour as the employee would not be performing the essential terms of the employment.[27]

Major reform has taken place at federal level to eliminate the possibility of breach of contract actions against employees in some circumstances. The *Industrial Relations Reform Act* 1993 (Cth) amended the *Industrial Relations Act* 1988 (Cth) to give some measure of protection to striking workers from breach of contract where the industrial action is 'protected action'[28] and an employer cannot dismiss an employee who engages in industrial action in relation to an industrial dispute which has either been notified to the Australian Industrial Relations Commission or which the Commission has found to exist.[29]

Liability in tort law

Employers in Australia seem more willing to institute proceedings against trade unions and their officials for civil actions which have become known as the 'industrial torts' rather than proceeding against the individual employee for breach of contract. Even so, actions in the industrial torts are not common and, when initiated, rarely proceed to final judgment and a court order. It seems that proceedings may be initiated which ultimately provoke a resolution of the dispute, but it may be queried whether the underlying industrial relations problem is resolved because it is not the function of the courts to adjudicate upon the merits of the dispute. Indeed in most instances the actions are initiated as part of the bargaining or negotiating tactics used by employers for resolution of the dispute. Claims which proceed to hearing and judgment usually involve the employer seeking injunctive relief (in the form of restraining orders), and an award of damages is unusual.

This use and the potential use of tort law against unions has been facilitated in Australia by the development of the law in relation to the legal status of trade unions. At federal level the *Industrial Relations Act* 1988 (Cth) grants a trade union, which is registered as an organisation under that Act, corporate legal status—it can hold property in its own name, can lease or mortgage property and is a corporation[30] thus having a legal existence separate and distinct from the members which comprise it from time to time. However, this brings with it the correlative disadvantage that the union as an organisation can be sued as a defendant.[31] Most state jurisdictions, except Tasmania and Victoria, confer corporate legal status on registered unions. This overcomes many legal difficulties which would otherwise exist when suing an unincorporated association or suing individually the members of the trade union.[32] Corporate status enables employers to seek damages from the union itself and to keep the proceedings at a greater distance from the immediate employer-employee relationship—the employer is not seen as suing its employees but the union to which many belong.

Such litigation has been reasonably frequent in the United Kingdom and the Australian courts have adopted the law as developed by the courts in the United Kingdom. This adoption has occurred even though the main processes for the resolution of industrial disputes differ markedly between the two countries and even though the English law has operated since the early part of the twentieth century in the context of immunities in some circumstances from civil action. Practically no judicial attention has been given in Australia to the applicability of the industrial torts in the Australian context.[33]

The 'sanction' imposed on the employees, the union officials and/or the union is liability in damages and/or an injunction to discontinue the conduct or to refrain from certain types of conduct. If the court injunction is disobeyed, a contempt of court is committed and this may be punished by fines or gaol.

Interference with contractual relations

The tort of inducing breach of contract or, as it is known in its modern form, interference with contractual relations, involves, generally, deliberate interference with a contract by a person who is not a party to the contract, such interference causing economic loss to a person who is a party to the contract. Whilst its origins can be traced back to the case where a third party persuaded an opera singer not to perform her contract with a theatre manager,[34] the tort was soon applied to industrial action. Most forms of industrial action today will involve the commission of the tort of interference with contractual relations. Union officials who persuade or induce employees to go on strike in breach of their contracts of employment with their employers will commit the tort. Thus employers may be able to sue the union officials and probably the union in tort as well as the employees for breach of contract. The scope of liability, then, is not limited to the striking workers in contract but is extended to those 'initiating' the strike in tort. This form of the tort involves direct interference in the contract leading to economic loss.

The tort of direct interference with contractual relations will be committed where a person (or persons) prevents a party in a contractual relation with an employer from performing that contract by direct action on that party which includes persuading or procuring that party to break or not fulfil the contract with the employer. As the tort has developed in modern times, the conduct is not required to cause an actual breach of contract.[35] It is sufficient if the conduct interferes with the performance of that contract causing economic loss.[36] It is therefore relatively easy to make out the requirement of interference with contractual relations. Certain other legal requirements must be met however—the defendants must know of the existence of the contract which is being interfered with (they need not know its precise terms but may need to know generally the nature of the contract) and they must intend to interfere with that contract. These conditions are usually easily proved in industrial disputes. The intention to interfere is usually an integral part of the reason for taking the industrial action; the very reason for going on strike is to exert industrial pressure on the employer. In any event, some of the stricter requirements of the tort have been loosened in the modern evolution of the cause of action thereby facilitating the imposition of liability.[37]

The form of interference does not have to operate directly on one of the contracting parties as an indirect form of the tort has developed, again expanding the scope of liability in industrial disputes. For example, trade union officials may induce members of a union to go on strike in breach of their contracts of employment with a supplier which in turn prevents the supplier who has contracted with the plaintiff (with whom the union has the industrial 'quarrel') from fulfilling the contractual obligations thereby causing the plaintiff financial loss. Although the union officials (who would be the defendants in this case) have not acted directly towards the supplier but have acted via the members of their union who are the suppliers' employees, this is regarded as giving rise to civil liability because the defendants have used unlawful means to so interfere with the plaintiff's contract—the unlawful means in this case being the breach of the employees' contracts of employment—and the causal connection between the conduct and the loss has been made out.

Unlawful means is an essential element in the indirect form of interference with contractual relations. The unlawful means need not be confined to breach of the employment contract and are fairly easily established in Australia where often a breach of award may be committed or some other contravention of industrial legislation in the context of virtually any form of industrial action. In the *Airline Pilot's* case,[38] s.312 of the *Industrial Relations Act* 1988 (Cth) was breached when the air pilots were persuaded by the union officials to undertake industrial action by working between the hours of 9.00 am to 5.00 pm only[39]—this was sufficient unlawful means to found an action in interference in contractual relations. The airline companies in turn could not fulfil contracts of carriage etc. leading to financial loss (see Figure 5.1). The commission of other torts, such as trespass or assault, may provide the element of unlawful means.[40] In Victoria, the array of unlawful forms of industrial action set out in s.36(1) of the *Employee Relations Act* 1992 (Vic) will ensure easy fulfilment of this ingredient of the tort.

Proceedings alleging the commission of this tort were successfully instituted in recent times in disputes which attracted much publicity—the airline dispute,[41] picketing by members of the Federated Confectioners Association in support of wages claims[42] and the attempt by the Building Workers Industrial Union to stop labour hire arrangements of building workers[43]—and two notable cases in South Australia in the 1970s.[44]

Figure 5.1: *Air Pilots* case: interference with contractual relations

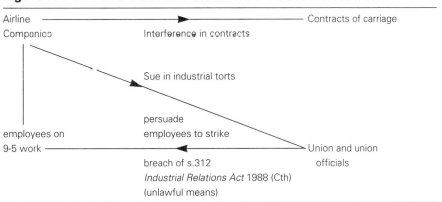

Interference with trade

Another tort which may owe its origins to interference with contractual relations is the tort of interference with trade by unlawful means. This tort was made out in the *Air Pilots* case and is committed when 'one person interferes with the trade or business of another and does so by unlawful means ...'[45] The precise scope of this tort remains uncertain today and the question whether it is necessary to establish an intention or predominant intention to interfere with trade remains unresolved. If the plaintiff must establish a predominant intention to interfere with trade, then the motives or reasons for taking the industrial action must be examined. If the predominant motive is not to cause harm, but to further trade union goals or protect industrial award conditions, the necessary element will not be made out.[46]

Intimidation

Even where industrial pressure does not give rise to an interference with contractual relations, there may be liability in the tort of intimidation. This tort is regarded as being committed where a person (A) threatens to commit an unlawful act which puts pressure on another person (B) to act in a detrimental way to a third person (C) (the plaintiff) and which does not cause any breach of contract between B and C but inflicts C with some economic loss. The classic situation in which this occurs is where the union (A) threatens to undertake industrial action on the part of its members which would be a breach of their contracts of employment in order to 'persuade' the employer (B) to dismiss a particular employee (C). Usually this threat is in the context of some dispute between the union and that employee. The employer may quite lawfully dismiss the employee in the sense that the employer gives the employee adequate notice to terminate that employee's contract of employment, so that, unfair dismissal laws aside, the employee will not have a cause of action against the employer. However, the threat of unlawful action causing the employer to act in this way gives the dismissed employee a right of action against the union officials in the tort of intimidation.

This tort, adopted from the United Kingdom,[47] has been used successfully in Australia: in *Latham v Singleton*[48] seventy-one defendants (union members) in NSW were sued (approximately forty of them successfully) by an individual employee, Mr Latham, whose employment had been terminated lawfully by his employer, the Broken Hill City Council, as a result of union pressure. The employees (the defendants) acted in combination by walking off the job every time they were rostered to work with Latham, thereby breaching their contracts of employment and constituting a threat to the employer to act to Latham's detriment by dismissing him.[49] The Supreme Court of New South Wales found that conspiracy to intimidate Latham had been committed and awarded Latham the sum of $100 000 plus $10 000 interest in damages. This tort, like the indirect form of interference with contractual relations, relies on establishing the threat of an unlawful act, which could be a crime, tort, breach of contract or breach of statute. Again, this element is relatively easy to establish in Australian industrial disputes. This tort is by no means always the province of a disaffected unionist (or ex-unionist) towards his or her union, but may be claimed by an employer as in the *Air Pilots* case where the airlines (unsuccessfully) sued the union and some of its officials in intimidation in respect of threats made to prevent 'strike breakers' signing on with the airline companies.[50]

Civil conspiracy

In industrial relations disputes where two or more employees act together by going on strike thereby placing pressure on the employer to grant wage rises or other demands, there is the potential for the employer to sue the individual employees for civil conspiracy.

i Conspiracy to injure

Conspiracy to injure, one form of civil conspiracy, is committed where two or more persons act together to carry out a certain course of conduct with the predominant intention of causing injury to a third party. Conspiracy to injure is usually not available today in the industrial relations context because employers must establish that there is a predominant intention on the part of the employees to injure the employer. If the main motivating factor of the employees is to pursue, for example, some economic gain to themselves (e.g. a wage increase or improvement in working conditions) by placing pressure or inflicting damage (causing loss of production etc.) on the employer, then conspiracy to injure will not be available because the predominant motive is not to harm the employer. This cause of action did not succeed in the *Air Pilots* case when the pilots resigned en masse because the court considered that the defendants had not acted with the predominant purpose of injuring the employers. If there is such predominant intention to harm the employer the action will be made out but such circumstances would involve some element of overriding spite or ill will which will not be present in the usual industrial dispute. It is a question of establishing the main, the sole or the true purpose of the conspiracy.[51]

ii Conspiracy by unlawful means

However, another form of civil conspiracy is quite readily available for use by employers against employees in industrial relations disputes. Conspiracy by unlawful means will be made out where two or more employees act in concert to take industrial action which injures their employer and use unlawful means to carry out this action. As with unlawful means for interference with contractual relations, it is relatively easy to establish the relevant unlawful means—this can be done by breach of the employee's contract of employment, tortious acts (e.g. assaults which might occur on a picket line)[52] or contravention of some industrial legislation. This was once again illustrated in the *Air Pilots* case where the pilots who engaged in industrial action were liable in civil conspiracy by unlawful means, the unlawful means being supplied by contravention of the *Industrial Relations Act* 1988 (Cth).[53]

An issue unresolved for some time was whether *predominant* intention to injure was required in this form of conspiracy. If so, the tort would be rendered largely irrelevant in the industrial relations context as has occurred with conspiracy to injure. However, recent English authority has decided that only intention to injure is required[54] and in Australia, the matter has not been discussed at High Court level in recent times. However, the court in *Williams v Hursey* (in 1959) regarded intention, but not predominant intention, as a necessary element, as did the Supreme Court of Victoria in the *Air Pilots* case.[55]

Causing loss by unlawful means

The limits of the tort of causing loss by unlawful means are still being resolved and defined by the courts. 'Causing loss by unlawful means' is sometimes regarded as a general name for the torts which have been previously discussed in this section, as they generally have those elements of unlawful means being used to cause loss to the employer. However, there has been a suggestion by the High Court of Australia in *Beaudesert Shire Council v Smith*[56] that where one party does an act which is unlawful, intentional and positive and which results in harm or loss as an inevitable consequence, this gives rise to a right of civil action for the 'victim' and the ensuing loss suffered as a consequence of this action will be able to be recovered in damages. Whilst this tort has been restricted severely in Australia and has not been adopted generally in the context of industrial relations,[57] the *Beaudesert* case has not been overruled by the High Court, so the potential remains for its revival, and use in industrial disputes.

Justification

Are there any defences to these torts? Can action giving rise to these industrial torts be excused or justified in law? Apart from conspiracy to injure where the sole or true purpose of the conduct is taken into account, there is little scope for defences to these industrial torts. The courts have always been troubled by the notion that the civil claims which rely on unlawful means can be justified—the judicial attitude is how can action involving unlawful means ever be justified? In addition, there has been a reluctance to acknowledge that legitimate trade union goals or aims may relieve the unions or unionists of liability. In rare cases where some practice is egregious the courts have allowed the defence.[58] However, the defence has not succeeded in other cases, for example, where it was argued that the union was defending conduct by the employer designed to eliminate the union itself[59] and where it was argued that industrial action was taken in order to eliminate the practice of employers of engaging independent contractors instead of employees thereby undermining award conditions.[60] The precise scope of the defence has not been tested. For example, if health and safety of workers is at risk and the industrial action is engaged in for the purpose of avoiding work practices which might cause injury to workers will the defence be available?[61]

In Australia, where, generally speaking, there has not been protection from civil suit given to workers who engage in industrial action, it might have been thought that the defence of justification would have developed. However, the narrow approach to justification taken by the British courts has been adopted here, yet those torts developed in Britain in a quite different legislative context.

The merits of the dispute and the industrial torts

Whilst, as indicated above, the courts have not been keen to permit defences to the commission of the industrial torts, the relevance of the industrial context in which litigation occurs has not been irrelevant. The courts in exercising their discretion to grant injunctive relief will take into account such matters as whether there is an appropriate industrial tribunal to settle the dispute[62] and whether the parties have attempted resolution of the matter.[63]

Litigation in the industrial torts may impose a settlement of the immediate matter—either by court order to restrain the conduct and/or an award of damages—but the underlying industrial relations problem of the dispute may be quite unresolved. An attempt has been made in South Australia in s.143a of the *Industrial Relations Act* (SA) 1972 to prohibit litigation at common law until the parties have endeavoured to settle the dispute.

In Victoria, civil proceedings may now only be brought in respect of industrial action which is not unlawful. However, this protection under the *Employee Relations Act* 1992 (Vic) is limited. First, many strikes or forms of industrial action would be regarded as unlawful under the Act[64] and secondly, the protection does not apply at all to industrial action arising out of picketing, a common form of action.

The Commonwealth Industrial Relations Bill 1987 attempted to limit the operation of the torts and strengthen sanctions within the federal system, but the Bill was withdrawn from federal Parliament when employer groups indicated their opposition to aspects of the Bill. Since 30 March 1994, the *Industrial Relations Act* 1988 (Cth), as amended by the *Industrial Relations Reform Act* 1993 (Cth), provides a measure of protection from civil action where the industrial action is protected action. In essence, this means that where the parties have properly notified their intention to bargain and negotiations are taking place during the bargaining period, there is an immunity on civil action.[65] There is also a three-day limitation on instituting proceedings against organisations or their members, employees or officers, in respect of industrial action taken to support claims that are the subject of an industrial dispute.[66]

Surprisingly little debate has taken place about the policy issues concerning the availability of the industrial torts, or actions for breach of contracts against striking workers.

The whole philosophy of the use or potential use of common law actions against strikers should be addressed in the context of the Australian system for dispute resolution. This is particularly vital at a time when there are moves to deregulate labour relations and move to a system of bargaining where the right to strike should at least be acknowledged as a matter of law and practice where workers are negotiating terms of the industrial agreement. This 'right to strike' has been acknowledged at federal level in some circumstances, but many states are moving to enterprise bargaining where the strike weapon may be used as part of the bargaining process and consideration should be given to similar mechanisms to provide a measure of protection to striking workers during this process. In Queensland, the *Industrial Relations Act* 1990 now mirrors the provisions at federal level in relation to bargaining and 'right to strike'.

Secondary boycott legislation

One of the most frequently used provisions against trade unions and officials were those set out in sections 45D and 45E of the *Trade Practices Act* 1974 (Cth). When the *Trade Practices Act* 1974 (Cth) was first enacted to prevent certain restrictive practices by corporations and those engaged in trade and commerce, trade unions were specifically exempt from the scope of the legislation. In 1977 following the establishment of the Trade Practices Review Committee (the Swanson Committee), recommendations were made that businesses which were affected by industrial action but which were not the ultimate or main target of the industrial action should be protected and that they should be able to seek either relief by way of damages or injunctions against unions and officials. The industrial torts were regarded as 'dead letters in practice'.[67] The aim was to prevent secondary boycott conduct—that is where for example, a union puts pressure on a person who is in a contractual relationship with the employer in order to force the employer to improve wages and conditions. Hence, in a secondary boycott, industrial action is not taken directly against employer but by members of the union against a person who has a dealing with the employer. (See chapter 3 and chapter 4 for further discussion.)

In 1977 the *Trade Practices Act* 1974 was amended by the addition of s.45D (which has been amended over the years) prohibiting such secondary boycotts. This section has been used frequently by employers and the most often sought remedy under these provisions is an injunction to restrain the conduct. However, in some notable instances the provisions and full range of remedies have been extensively used—the main example being the Mudginberri dispute, where the Australasian Meat Industry Union was ordered to pay $1.76m in damages.

These provisions involved complex drafting in large part caused by reliance on the trade and commerce power and the corporations power, s.51(1) and s.51(20) respectively in the federal Constitution. The amendments to s.45D since its enactment in 1977 added to the complexity of drafting. After the enactment of the *Industrial Relations Reform Act* 1993 (Cth) to amend the *Industrial Relations Act* 1988 (Cth) the provisions relating to secondary boycotts in the *Trade Practices Act* have been transferred to the *Industrial Relations Act* 1988 (Cth), leaving s.45D of the *Trade Practices Act* to apply to commercial, non-industrial situations. The provisions in the *Trade Practices Act* which could be used and were used from 1977 to 1994 are examined below, and the new provisions are then analysed.

Trade Practices Act

Scope of s.45D(1) and (1A)

Several elements had to be established to maintain an action for breach of s.45D(1):-

a There had to be a person (A) who engaged in conduct in concert with another person (B). Thus, like civil conspiracy, the provision relied on persons combining together to act.

b The conduct must have hindered or prevented the supply of goods or services by a third person (C) to a fourth person (D) or the conduct must have hindered or prevented the acquisition of goods or services by a third person (C) from a fourth person (D). In each of these cases, D must not have been the employer of A.
c The purpose of the conduct must have been to cause either substantial loss or damage to D's business or a substantial lessening of competition in any market in which D dealt. If the purpose of the conduct included one of these relevant purposes, under s.45D(2) the person was deemed to engage in conduct for the relevant purpose. Unlike conspiracy to injure, there was no inquiry to determine the true, sole or predominant purpose of the conduct. This considerably widened the scope of s.45D.
d The effect of the conduct must have been to cause, or have been likely to cause, either substantial loss or damage to D's business or a substantial lessening of competition in a market in which D dealt. Where D was a corporation, these elements would have established breach of s.45D(1)(b). If D were not not a corporation but C were a corporation, to establish liability under s.45D(1)(a), the applicant would need to have made out the four elements (a) to (d) above and to have established in addition a fifth element:
e The relevant conduct must have had or be likely to have had the effect of causing either substantial loss or damage to the business of the corporation C,[68] or the conduct must have had or be likely to have had the effect of causing a substantial lessening of competition in any market in which C (or a body corporate that was related to C) supplied or acquired goods or services.[69] This element relied on effect or likely effect but required no proof of the purpose of causing loss or damage to the corporation.

In addition, relying on the trade and commerce power, s.45D(1A) was enacted. This provision was contravened if two persons, A and B, acted in concert with each other and engaged in conduct having the purpose of preventing or substantially preventing a third party, (not the employer of A) from engaging in either interstate trade, overseas trade with or from Australia and trade within a territory, or between a territory or State, or between two territories.

Section 45D of *Trade Practices Act* was introduced after curiously little debate on the applicability of such laws to trade unions. Most of the discussion was about the scope of the section and the concern that an early draft of the provision applied to primary, as well as to secondary, boycotts. The section survived challenges to its constitutional validity[70] although the High Court held that one subsection (s.45D(5)), designed to attach liability clearly and easily to unions by deeming a union to be involved in contravention of the section unless the union established that 'it took all reasonable steps to prevent the participants from engaging in that conduct', was invalid as it was not within the corporations power.[71]

The scheme of the legislation contained a defence (s.45D(3)) but it was generally very narrowly interpreted and applied basically to prevent primary industrial action being covered by the section. Thus, where employees of the employer took action directly against the employer, this would not normally be caught by s.45(D). In addition, the defence applied to a limited range of employment matters being pursued by those engaging in the industrial action.

Section 45(E) of the Act was introduced in 1981 in the *Trade Practices Act* to prevent deals or understandings being concluded between the union and the parties upon which the union was bringing pressure.[72]

The Mudginberri dispute is a significant example of the use of s.45D of the *Trade Practices Act* and the extent to which such legislation could be used against unions and unionists. The Australasian Meat Industry Employees Union (the AMIEU) was in dispute with Mudginberri Station Pty Ltd (Mudginberri) which operated an abattoir and export meat processing works in the Northern Territory. The issue between the AMIEU and Mudginberri was the union's wish to introduce a unit tally system of payment for Mudginberri workers who, in the main, did not want such a system. In order to place pressure on Mudginberri, pickets were established at the road leading to the Mudginberri plant. The picket affected Mudginberri's ability to export cattle and buffalo which it slaughtered, as the approval of inspectors appointed by the Commonwealth Department of Primary Industry was required before the carcasses could be exported. The inspectors could not cross the picket line and goods could also not be transported to the abattoir.[73]

Figure 5.2: Mudginberri dispute: picket and breach of s.45D Trade Practices Act

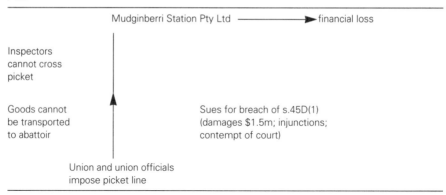

Mudginberri initiated proceedings in the Federal Court of Australia seeking injunctions and damages in respect of AMIEU's industrial action in breach of s.45D(1) of the *Trade Practices Act*. Various injunctions of an interim, interlocutory and permanent nature were granted against the AMIEU and four officers of the union engaged in the picket (the union's federal secretary, the union organiser who was based in the Northern Territory, the federal president and secretary of the Queensland Branch of the AMIEU and the AMIEU's national organiser). For the summary of the main legal events in chronological order associated with the action, see Table 5.1.

The end result of the numerous proceedings and appeals before the Federal Court was the award of nearly $1.8m damages against the AMIEU for contravention of the section, and orders of interim and permanent injunctions.

Table 5.1 Summary of main legal events in Mudginberri dispute

12 June 1985	Beaumont J of the Federal Court of Australia granted interim injunction for breach of s45D(1) of Trade Practices Act 1974 (Cth) (1985) 27 AILR para 245.
21 June 1985	Fine of $10 000 plus $2000 per day was imposed by Bowen CJ for contempt of the court's order granting the interim injunction (1985) 27 AILR para 311; [1985] ATPR 40-580.
12 July 1985	Morling J granted permanent injunctions to restrain conduct in breach of s45D(1) (1985) 61 ALR 280.
18 July 1985	Order to sequestrate the AMIEU's property to enforce payment of the fine was made by Bowen CJ (1985) 61 ALR 291.
14 August 1985	Application by Mudginberri, to review decisions made by Commonwealth Department of Primary Industry in respect of provision of meat inspectors to Mudginberri, dismissed by Neaves J of Federal Court (No NT G16 of 1985).*
16 August 1985	AMIEU was found by Lockhart J to be in breach of the order of Morling J (1985) 94 FCR 398.
10 September 1985	Full bench of the Federal Court upheld the decision of Morling J granting permanent injunctions (1985) 61 ALR 417.
11 September 1985	Fine of $100 000 on the AMIEU was imposed by Lockhart J for contempt of the permanent injunction plus a sequestration order (1985) 28 AILR para 21.
17 September 1985	Appeal by the AMIEU against the fines and sequestration orders made by Bowen CJ was dismissed by the full bench of the Federal Court (1985) 61 ALR 635.
19 December 1985	Appeal by Mudginberri against order of Neaves J in respect of whether there was an obligation to the Department of Primary Industry to provide meat inspection services. Full Court of Federal Court held there was such an obligation (1985) 68 ALR 613.*
21 February 1986	High Court refused leave to appeal from decision of Full Court of Federal Court in relation to decision about provision of meat inspectors to Mudginberri (noted in (1986) 28 AILR para 100).*
14 April 1986	Application by Mudginberri to Gray J of the Federal Court to dismiss application by AMIEU that orders of the court had been procured by fraud or false evidence of the Managing Director of Mudginberri, on the basis that the AMIEU's application was frivolous or vexatious. This was dismissed by Gray J (1986) 65 ALR 683.
21 July 1986	Application by AMIEU to challenge the grant of the permanent injunction on the basis that it had been procured by fraud or false evidence, was dismissed by Morling J (No VG36 of 1986) (1986) 28 AILR para 444.
21 July 1986	Morling J ordered that the AMIEU pay Mudginberri damages in the sum of $1 759 444 for engaging in conduct in breach of s 45D(1) of the Trade Practices Act 1975 (Cth) (1986) 8 ATPR 40-708 (noted in (1986) 28 AILR para 283).

13 August 1986	The High Court of Australia upheld the power of the Federal Court of Australia to fine the AMIEU for contempt of court (1986) 161 CLR 98; 60 ALJR 608; 66 ALR 577.
15 December 1986	Full Bench of the Federal Court of Australia dismissed an appeal by the AMIEU against the decision of Lockhart J to fine the AMIEU $100 000 for breach of its order (NSW G244 of 1985; NSW G294 of 1985) noted (1987) 29 AILR para 203.
16 June 1987	Full Bench of the Federal Court dismissed an appeal by AMIEU against the award of damages by Morling J in respect of breach of s45D of the Trade Practices Act but varying the quantum of damages to $1458810 (1987) 74 ALR 7.

*These were proceedings in administrative law: Mudginberri sought (unsuccessfully) a court ruling that the government department was obliged to provide the services of meat inspectors.

Reprinted from M. Pittard, 'The Trade Practices Act and the Mudginberri Dispute', 1988, *Australian Journal of Labour Law 1*, p. 23.

Contempt of court proceedings were also instituted in respect of AMIEU's failure to obey court injunctions, and fines of over $100 000 were imposed by the Federal Court in respect of these breaches of the injunctive orders. Further, orders were made to sequestrate the AMIEU's property in order to enforce payment of the fines. It can be seen then that the full potential use of s.45D of the *Trade Practices Act* against an organisation of employees was realised.

Liability could attach fairly readily under s.45D because the requisite purpose was satisfied easily. The provision which applies to conduct elsewhere in the Trade Practices Act is that the purpose of the conduct, although one of a number of purposes, must be a substantial purpose.[74] However, s.45D(2) eliminated the requirement of substantial purpose in relation to s.45D(1) or (1A) thereby avoiding any enquiry as to the true purpose of the conduct (unlike conspiracy to injure).[75] In the Mudginberri dispute, s.45D(2) meant that as one purpose of the respondents' conduct was the purpose of damaging Mudginberri's business, the relevant purpose was established with ease.

Even where the union may have what was regarded as a union purpose, there was frequently an accompanying purpose of causing substantial loss or damage to a corporation's business as the industrial pressure would be meaningless if this were not involved.

The defence

Section 45D(3) contained a defence to a contravention of s.45D(1). The defence sub-section was drafted in a complex manner but in essence enabled industrial action to take place without incurring any liability under s.45D where two conditions were met. First, conduct had to be undertaken by an organisation and/or its officers, and an employee or employees who were employed by the same employer who acted in concert (and not in concert with any other person) and secondly, the dominant purpose of that conduct had to be substantially related to specified matters—remuneration, working conditions, conditions of employment and hours of work of the employees or termination of employment. The Federal Court held in the *Mudginberri* case the defence was not made out because the picket line was not related to the matters enumerated in the sub-section but rather to the general policy of the AMIEU in respect of the adoption of the unit tally system in the Northern Territory.[76] On appeal, the Full Court of the Federal Court was not prepared to find that the defence was made out.[77]

The narrow defence saved primary strikes over some issues contravening s.45D but from 1977 to 1994 s.45D(3) was generally not interpreted broadly or applied generously by the courts.[78]

Relationship between Industrial Relations Act and Trade Practices Legislation

The philosophy differed between the *Industrial Relations Act* 1988 (Cth) on the one hand, and the *Trade Practices Act* 1974 (Cth) on the other hand. The former Act endeavours to resolve industrial disputes by conciliation and, if that fails, by arbitration and contains some sanction provisions which are directed towards ensuring compliance by unions with awards and orders and procedures of the Commission. The *Trade Practices Act* regulates the conduct of businesses to promote competition and attempts to limit or eliminate restrictive trade practices. It can be queried whether regulation of trade union behaviour was ever appropriate through the mechanism of trade practices legislation which suffered the same drawback as the common law remedies— the inability to resolve the industrial relations issues. Historically, of course, it was concern about the impact of trade union action on small businesses which prompted this method of regulation but the control went beyond the protection of small businesses.

An attempt to bridge these philosophical differences was made when the interrelationship between the two Acts was altered by amendment in 1980. The Australian Industrial Relations Commission was given power to settle disputes which were the subject of proceedings in the Federal Court.[79] A procedure could be invoked whereby a party might notify the President of the Commission or the Registrar when there was an application to the Federal Court for an injunction to restrain conduct which would breach s.45D of the *Trade Practices Act*. The Commission had power to settle the dispute by conciliation but did not have the power to arbitrate on the matter. There was also a procedure for the operation of an injunction to be stayed when there was a proceeding pending before the Australian Commission if staying the injunction would facilitate the settlement of the dispute.

Following the Mudginberri dispute, 'questions arose as to the appropriateness of such sanctions and legal procedures against unions, or the ability of the employer to claim damages from unions in respect of industrial action. The Labor government itself regretted the use of s.45D of the *Trade Practices Act* in relation to the dispute[80] and favoured the approach of using the processes of conciliation and arbitration to resolve the matter.[81] Undoubtedly, the answer to these questions will vary according to the value judgements and philosophies of individuals and interest groups within the Australian community.'[82]

Reform

In 1984, the federal Labor government attempted to repeal both ss 45D and 45E.[83] The attempt was unsuccessful. More recently, the government established a committee to review s.45D and sanctions and debate began to emerge on the appropriateness of sanctions for industrial disputes to be found in trade practices legislation.

The major reform was brought about on 30 March 1994 by the *Industrial Relations Reform Act* 1993 (Cth) which has effected the following changes in secondary boycott sanctions:

a the provisions relating to secondary boycotts are now in redrafted form in the *Industrial Relations Act* 1988 (Cth), leaving s.45D in the *Trade Practices Act* 1994 (Cth) applying to commercial situations;
b the provisions are more simply drafted and rely on the trade and commerce power and the corporations power in the Constitution;
c the provisions still retain the notion of two (or more) persons acting in concert;
d the provisions retain concepts of 'purpose' and 'effect' of conduct, but purpose is now confined to main purpose so that it is less easily established;
e the defence sub-section to avoid attaching liability is maintained;
f the Australian Industrial Relations Court, instead of the Federal Court, now has jurisdiction to hear these cases.

Peaceful picketing is exempt from these provisions.

A major change, however, concerns the procedure. A person wishing to institute proceedings for breach of the boycott provisions cannot do so unless the Australian Industrial Relations Commission has attempted to resolve the matter by conciliation and issued a certificate to that effect. The Commission is under an obligation to issue the certificate in any event if the boycott conduct has continued for seventy-two hours. There is, in effect, a prohibition on institution of formal proceedings in the court for three days.[84]

These reforms have acknowledged more fully the industrial relations aspects of boycott disputes and set in place a procedure designed to resolve the dispute itself rather than to compensate those affected by the dispute. The remedies of injunction and/or damages remain, but it is no longer possible for a fine to be imposed on the parties.[85]

Between 1977 and 1992, approximately 181 actions for breach of sections 45D and 45E of the *Trade Practices Act* 1974 (Cth) were instituted. Applications for injunctions were refused in 18 of the cases and a large number (67) were withdrawn or discontinued without order. In about 52 cases, interim injunctions were granted.[86] These figures show that there was a willingness to use these statutory procedures, but a considerable number were settled ultimately or at least withdrawn. The provisions introduced by the *Industrial Relations Reform Act* 1993 (Cth) will probably result in fewer proceedings being initiated, due to the necessity for the Commission to attempt to settle the matter first.

State secondary boycott laws

For a time Queensland had the equivalent of s.45D in its *Industrial (Commercial Practices) Act* 1984 (Qld) (now repealed) and New South Wales has made s.45D applicable in its *Industrial Relations Act* 1991 (NSW). In the *Employee Relations Act* 1992 (Vic) it is unlawful (and so a quasi-criminal, or even a criminal, offence) under s.36(1) for employees to engage in secondary boycotts. Secondary boycotts laws, therefore, exist at state level too.

Sanctions under industrial relations legislation

Industrial relations legislation, both at federal and state levels, contain a variety of sanctions aimed at ensuring compliance with the system of dispute settlements and awards. These provisions which range from fines for breaches of awards to cancelling the registration of a union, thereby affecting its legal status, are analysed below.

There are also some indirect controls—for example, the Australian Industrial Relations Commission has the power to direct parties to cease industrial action before it exercises any of its powers in respect of conciliation and arbitration.[87]

Breach of award

Industrial action which is taken in contravention of an award or agreement containing a bans clause will be in breach of that award or agreement. A typical bans clause is as follows:

> 'No organisation or party bound by this award shall in any way, whether directly or indirectly, be a party to or be concerned in any ban, limitation or restriction upon work in accordance with the provisions of this award.'

A bans clause can only be included in a federal award or agreement (certified agreement or enterprise flexibility agreement) by order of the Full Bench of the Commission and by following a procedure laid down in s.125 of the *Industrial Relations Act* which is designed to provide a check on such clauses being 'automatically' included in awards. When a bans clause is in an award and there is conduct which breaches it, the employer cannot institute enforcement proceedings directly against the person who is breaching the award. Notice of the breach must be given to the Registrar and a Presidential member of the Commission must try to effect a settlement of the dispute using the Commission's powers. If conciliation does not succeed, the Presidential member shall record that attempts have been made to end the conduct and the employer may apply for a certificate for enforcement proceedings to be brought. It is only when a certificate has been issued that proceedings for breach of an award or agreement can be brought under s.178.[88] Monetary penalties are the sanctions for breaches of award: the maximum penalty for breach of award is $1000.[89] The maximum penalties for breach of certified or enterprise flexibility agreements are higher—generally $5000 plus $2500 per day whilst the breach continues. Bans clause procedures and court restraining orders for breach of award were used extensively under former legislation[90] until amendments were made to the Act providing for some safeguards in the use of these sanctions.[91] Although sanctions are available today the emphasis has shifted to procedures designed to achieve a settlement of the matter.[92]

State industrial relations legislation contains enforcement mechanisms for awards but usually without the same emphasis on settlement procedures as contained at federal level. The Victorian *Employee Relations Act* 1992, for example, makes it a quasi-criminal, or arguably criminal offence to breach an award for which proceedings may be instituted in the Industrial Division of the Magistrates' Courts.[93]

Cancellation of awards and stand-downs

An award can be cancelled if the parties, either union or workers, do not abide by its terms. One of the steps in the air pilots dispute was to cancel the Air Pilots' award because the pilots had not given a commitment to the central system of wage fixation.[94]

Most awards today will contain clauses giving employers the right to stand-down employees who cannot usefully be employed because of industrial action in another part of the plant. In Victoria, all awards and employment agreements must contain such provisions.[95]

Deregistration of unions

Another sanction directed to the legal status of trade unions is deregistration. In jurisdictions where legal status is conferred on trade unions, it is simple to place conditions on the continuing legal status and recognition of such unions: if the unions fail to comply with the relevant union law, they can lose that status.

Under the *Industrial Relations Act* 1988 (Cth) the registration of organisations can be cancelled for various grounds laid out in s.294 of the Act. These grounds are as follows: where the organisation continues breaching an award or an order of the Commission (or such breach occurs through the action of a substantial number of members of the organisation) and there has been a prevention or hindering of the achievement of an object of the Act; where the organisation (or a substantial number of its members or a section or class of members) have engaged in industrial action which has prevented, hindered or interfered with interstate or overseas trade and commerce; or where the same persons have been or are engaged in industrial action which has an impact on the safety, health or welfare of the community or a part of the community.[96]

The Federal Court was the body which made a determination about deregistration, but this function has now been transferred to the Australian Industrial Relations Court. Applications for deregistration are not only the province of employers as any person interested, an organisation or the relevant Minister may apply for cancellation of the registration.

Once the registration has been cancelled the organisation is no longer a body corporate under the *Industrial Relations Act*.[97] It does however exist as an association and the members of the association are no longer entitled to the benefit of any award or order of the Commission. As an alternative to deregistration the court may order an alteration in the eligibility rules of a union to exclude a section or class of members.[98] The court may also make orders as to suspension of rights and privileges and use of union funds and property.[99]

It has often been said that deregistration is a 'double-edged sword' because, whilst there are obvious disadvantages for the union, the union is placed outside the operation and controls of the federal system. The sanction of deregistration has been used infrequently—in 1974 the Builders Labourers' Federation was deregistered[100] under former deregistration procedures[101] and successfully sought re-registration two years later.[102] Later, specific legislation was enacted by federal and state governments to deregister the Builders Labourers' Federation and its state counterparts.[103] This legislation did not rely on using the procedures in industrial relations legislation to cancel the unions' registration but relied on direct government legislative intervention. Such action is unusual in Australia (and indeed was without precedent). It may be questioned whether it is a desirable procedure for governments to invoke when industrial relations decisions in Australia are usually made by industrial tribunals and the courts and there is a specific statutory procedure for consideration by the court of applications for deregistration.

Some states have separate procedures for deregistration contained in their industrial legislation.

Statutory offences

Industrial relations legislation has traditionally provided other statutory offences for ensuring compliance with awards and orders. Under s.311 of the *Industrial Relations Act* 1988 (Cth) where a person wilfully contravened an award or order of the Commission that person would be liable to a maximum fine of $500 (in the case of a natural person) or $1000 (in the case of a body corporate). It was an offence under s.312 of the Act for officers or agents of an organisation, or a branch of an organisation to incite members not to work in accordance with awards or agreements. This section was used to provide the unlawful means in respect of the industrial torts in the *Air Pilots* case. However, both ss 311 and 312 were repealed folowing the reforms introduced by the *Industrial Relations Reform Act* 1993 (Cth) so that there will not be additional liability for union officers who encourage conduct in breach of awards. There still remain other offences directed at organisations endeavouring to coerce an employer to prejudice a member who has not complied with an organisation's direction etc.[104]

In Victoria, the *Employee Relations Act* 1992 has made certain conduct unlawful which exposes the employees to liability for an offence under the Act for which fines may be imposed. Section 36(1) lists unlawful industrial action and includes industrial action taken without secret ballot, secondary boycotts and industrial action where awards or agreements are in force.

Other legislative controls

Essential Services legislation, in existence at State and Federal levels, contains provisions to invoke emergency procedures where industrial action in essential services is involved. These procedures vary from state to state but in Victoria the *Vital Industries Act* 1992 (Vic), recently enacted extensive controls in respect of vital industries.

Provisions in the Commonwealth *Crimes Act* 1901 can also be invoked and used against unions.[105] Whilst this would be unusual the potential remains for use.

Conclusion

The cumulative effect of the controls at common law and by legislation imposes severe restrictions on the freedom to strike. In many instances, such controls will not be used, but the potential impact is enormous. An award of common law damages on an individual employee would be ruinous for that employee and also expose the family of the worker to devasting consequences. The range of sanctions is damages, injunction, and contempt of court for which there may be pecuniary penalties or gaol. To a certain extent, these have been ameliorated under federal law where there is a measure of protection given against civil action.

The precise scope of any freedom to strike in Australia today has been examined recently at federal level and a policy decision made to give effect to the right to strike. It remains to be seen whether the 'correct' balance has been achieved in terms of the competing interests of parties and the public. In some other jurisdictions there still needs to be consideration of the precise scope of the freedom of workers to engage in industrial action without liability. The question remains: To what extent should workers have freedom to strike in our industrial relations system?

Notes

1. See R. Ben-Israel, *International Labour Standards—The Case of Freedom to Strike*, (Kluwer, Deventer, 1988) who states that, through the ILO, freedom of association was recognised as a fundamental human right and that 'freedom to strike has emerged as an essential tool for the implementation of such a freedom as freedom of association' (p. 1). K.D. Ewing, *The Right to Strike*, Clarendon Press, Oxford, 1991, refers to the right to strike as a basic right so regarded by the man in the street.
2. See, e.g., B. Dabscheck and J. Niland, *Industrial Relations in Australia*, Allen and Unwin, Sydney, 1982, p. 40.
3. See Convention No. 87, Freedom of Association and Protection of the Right to Organise, 1948; Convention 98, Right to Organise and Collective Bargaining.
4. See ILO, *General Survey of the Committee of Experts on the Application of Conventions and Recommendations: Freedom of Association and Collective Bargaining* (ILO Geneva, 1983), para 200.
5. See *Industrial Relations Act* 1988 (Cth) as amended by the *Industrial Relations Reform Act* 1993 (Cth) which provides in s.170PA that the object of the Division 'is to give effect, in particular situations, to Australia's international obligation to provide for a right to strike'. The obligation is stated in the section as arising from the ILO convention, the Internal Covenant of Economic, Social and Cultural Rights, the constitution of the ILO and customary international law relating to freedom of association and the right to strike.
6. See discussion at pp. 36–38 chapter 3 of forms of industrial action.
7. The developments under the *Industrial Relations Reform Act* 1993 (Cth) and the *Employee Relations Act* 1992 (Vic) are discussed later in this chapter.

8   See Lord Wright in *Crofter Harris Tweed Co. Ltd v Veitch* [1942] AC 435 at p. 463 who said 'The right of workmen to strike is an essential element in the principle of collective bargaining'.
9   See ss 6 and 6A.
10 These provisions are explained more fully at pp. 102–103 and 115–116.
11 Compare UK *Trade Disputes Act* where such immunity has been given. Note Queensland had a similar system of protection until 1976 and the Victorian *Employee Relations Act* 1992 has provided since January 1993 a form of protection in some limited circumstances against civil action. The *Industrial Relations Act* 1972 (SA) provides a 'filtering' mechanism in s.143a: settlement of disputes must first be attempted before civil proceedings can be instituted. The amendments to the *Industrial Relations Act* 1988 (Cth) (made by the *Industrial Relations Reform Act* 1993 (Cth)) in effect (and speaking generally) provide a three-day immunity on bringing action in tort against unions, officers and unionists who engage in industrial action but the limited protection will not apply where there is personal injury or damage to property.
12 See chapter 4. It is understood that the plaintiff airline companies have not enforced this judgement debt against the defendants.
13 Brooking J in *Ansett Transport Industries (Operations) Pty Ltd v Australian Federation of Airline Pilots* (1989) 95 ALR 211 notes the distinction between law and practice.
14 The usual remedy is the court's injunction to cease the form of conduct the subject of complaint; e.g. in *Dollar Sweets Pty Ltd v Federated Confectioners Association of Australia* [1986] VR 383, the Supreme Court of Victoria granted injunctions to restrain the picketing of the employer's premises which was disrupting the employer's business. Employers rarely pursue claims for damages but $175,000 was paid in settlement of the damages claim by the defendants in the *Dollar Sweets* case.
15 See *Industrial Relations Act* 1991 (NSW).
16 O. Kahn–Freund, *Labour and the Law* (3rd ed.), Stevens, London, 1983, p. 20.
17 J. Mesher and F. Sutcliffe, 'Industrial Action and the Individual', in R. Lewis (ed.), *Labour Law in Britain*, Blackwell, Oxford, 1986, chapter 9 at p. 243.
18 (1989) 95 ALR 419.
19 Brooking J took the view that a term could not be imported into the contract which relieved one of the parties from his/her obligations to work as required under the contract.
20 See discussion in K.D. Ewing, *The Right to Strike, supra*.
21 See generally *Adami v Maison De Luxe Ltd* (1924) 35 CLR 143 and *Ansett Transport Industries (Operations) Pty Ltd v Australian Federation of Air Pilots* (1989) 95 ALR 211, where Brooking J considered that unlawful means for the industrial torts were provided by breach of the employees' contracts of employment. For a lucid analysis, see K.D. Ewing, "The Right to Strike in Australia" (1989) 2 *Australian Journal of Labour Law* 18.
22 See Griffith CJ in *R v Commonwealth Court of Conciliation and Arbitration; Ex parte BHP Co Ltd* (1909) 8 CLR 419 at 437–8; Keely J in *Hall v General Motors Holden Ltd* (1979) 45 FLR 272 at 278 9; Macken J of NSW Industrial Commission in *Re Federated Storemen & Packers Union of Australia, NSW Branch* (1987) 22 IR 198.
23 K.D. Ewing, *The Right to Strike supra* argues that as a matter of practice the contract is suspended during a strike.
24 In the air pilots' strike, the airline companies instituted legal proceedings against the pilots for breach of contract but did not pursue that aspect of the claim. Since the *Industrial Relations Reform Act* 1993 (Cth), at federal level there may be some protection to workers from suit for breach of contract or dismissal on account of being involved in industrial action—see *Industrial Relations Act* 1988 (Cth), ss 170PM(3) and 334A.
25 See, e.g., *Morgan v Fry* [1968] 2 QB 710 where Lord Denning said at p. 728 that where proper strike notice was given and a strike takes place 'the contract of employment is not terminated. It is suspended during the strike: and revives again when the strike is over'.

26 See *Latham v Singleton* [1981] 2 NSWLR 843 for comments by Nagle CJ on *Morgan v Fry*.
27 See, e.g., *Secretary of State for Employment v Associated Society of Locomotive Engineers and Firemen* (No.2) [1972] 2 QB 455.
28 See s.170 PM(2).
29 See *Industrial Relations Act* 1988 (Cth) s.334A(1).
30 See s.192 *Industrial Relations Act* 1988 (Cth).
31 This ability to be sued is expressly stated in s.192 *Industrial Relations Act* 1992 (Cth). There has never been federal legislation conferring on *trade unions* an immunity from suit in the industrial torts, but the *Industrial Relations Reform Act* 1993 (Cth) has provided a measure of protection for unions and striking workers if the industrial action is 'protected industrial action'.
32 See chapter 13.
33 For legislative restriction on the ability to bring civil action in the industrial torts, see discussion 'The Merits of the Dispute and the Industrial Torts' p. 107.
34 *Lumley v Gye* (1853) 2 E&B 216; 118 ER 749.
35 For a statement of the elements of the tort, see *Woolley v Dunford* (1972) 3 SASR 243.
36 See *Torquay Hotel Co v Cousins* [1969] 2 Ch 106 where the tort was made out even though an exemption clause meant there was not a breach of contract.
37 See P. Elias and K. Ewing, 'Economic Torts and Labour Law: Old Principles and New Liabilities' (1982) 41 CLJ 321.
38 *Ansett Transport Industries (Operations) Pty Ltd v Australian Federation of Air Pilots* (1989) 95 ALR 211.
39 See discussion of dispute at pp. 90–92.
40 See, e.g., *Williams v Hursey* (1959) 103 CLR 30 where, in the view of some judges of the High Court of Australia, the torts of assault and nuisance provided unlawful means for conspiracy by unlawful means.
41 The *Air Pilots* case, *supra*.
42 *Dollar Sweets* case, *supra*.
43 *Building Workers Industrial Union v Odco Pty Ltd* (1991) 29 FCR 104.
44 *Woolley v Dunford* (1972) 3 SASR 243; *Davies v Nyland* (1975) 10 SASR 75.
45 Lord Denning in *Daily Mirror Newspapers Ltd v Gardner* (1968) 2 QB 762.
46 Brooking J in the *Air Pilots* case found that the sole purpose of the defendants' conduct was to bring pressure on the airline companies to cause them economic loss. But see *Lonrho PLC v Fayed* [1991] 3 WLR 188; [1991] 3 All ER 303, decided after *Air Pilots* case where Lord Templeman stated that the precise ambit of the tort required analysis and reconsideration by the courts.
47 See *Rookes v Barnard* [1964] AC 1129. For criticism of the judicial basis of the tort, see Lord Wedderburn, 'Intimidation and the Right to Strike' (1964) 27 MLR 527.
48 [1981] 2 NSWLR 843.
49 The precise cause of action was conspiracy to intimidate but workers could have been sued individually in intimidation.
50 See also *Dollar Sweets* case.
51 See *McKernan v Fraser* (1931) 46 CLR 343.
52 See *Williams v Hursey* (1959) 103 CLR 30 and *Dollar Sweets Pty Ltd supra*.
53 Section 312. Note that s.312 has been repealed by the *Industrial Relations Reform Act* 1993 (Cth).
54 See *Lonrho PLC v Fayed* [1991] 3A11 ER 303.
55 In the *Air Pilots* case counsel for the defendants conceded that predominant intention to injure need not be established. In *Williams v Hursey* (1959) 103 CLR 30, the High Court decided conspiracy by unlawful means was established in a situation where predominant intention could not be proved.
56 (1966) 120 CLR 145.

57 It was alleged in the *Air Pilots* case but was not decided on this basis. See R.C. McCallum and M. Pittard, *Australian Labour Law: Cases and Materials*, Butterworths, Sydney, 1994, chapter 14.
58 See, e.g., *Brimelow v Casson* [1924] 1 Ch. 302 where industrial action was taken to try to improve wages of chorus girls who, because they were paid so little by their employer, had to resort to prostitution.
59 See *Air Pilots* case where Brooking J of the Supreme Court of Victoria referred to this as a 'novel' defence.
60 See *Building Workers Industrial Union v Odco Pty Ltd* (1991) 29 FCR 104 where the Federal Court held that the employees had not breached award conditions because the workers were independent contractors; the court left open the question whether the defence would succeed if the federal award had indeed been breached.
61 This was not resolved in *Ranger Uranium Mines Pty Ltd v Federated Miscellaneous Workers Union of Australia* (1987) 54 NTR 6. Note that some state legislation permits work stoppage or some instances over health and safety issues (see *Occupational Health and Safety Act* 1985) (Vic), s.26) but the interaction between this and any possible common law defence is not certain.
62 See, e.g., Street J in *Henry M. Miller Attractions v Actors and Announcers Equity* [1970] 1 NSWR 614 who said at 615 'But in point of discretion, it is a well-settled approach in this court that injunctive relief will not ordinarily be granted where it can be seen that there is another tribunal particularly suited to deal with the matter in issue and having the exquisite authority to resolve the issues between the parties'.
63 See, e.g., Wells J in *Woolley v Dunford* who granted an injunction only after he was satisfied 'that a real, prolonged and strenuous attempt [had] been made to compose those differences' (1972) 3 SASR 243 at 295.
64 See s.36(1).
65 See s.170PM. It should be noted that the immunity also applies to employers who engaged in a lock-out.
66 See s.166A.
67 Report of the Trade Practices Review Committee, AGPS, 1976, p. 86.
68 See para (i)(A).
69 See para (i)(B).
70 See *Seamen's Union of Australia v Utah Development Co* (1978) 144 CLR 120 and *Actors and Announcers Equity Association of Australia v Fontana Films Pty Ltd* (1982) 150 CLR 169.
71 *Actors and Announcers Equity Association of Australia v Fontana Films Pty Ltd* (1982) 150 CLR 169.
72 See, e.g., *Gibbins v Australasian Meat Industry Employees' Union* (1986) 77 ALR 355.
73 For an analysis of the dispute and its industrial relations aspects, see pp. 83–86.
74 See: Para 4F(b) provided:

'(b) a person shall be deemed to have engaged or to engage in conduct for a particular purpose, for a particular reason if —
(i) the person engaged or engages in the conduct for purposes that included or include that purpose or for reasons that included or include that reason, as the case may be; and
(ii) that purpose or reason was with a substantial purpose or reason'.

75 Section 45D(2) provided:

'Para 4F(b) does not apply in relation to sub-section (1) or (1A) of this section but a person shall be deemed to engage in conduct for the purpose mentioned in that sub-section if he engages in that conduct for purposes that include that purpose'.

76 See *Mudginberri Station Pty Ltd v Australasian Meat Industry Employees Union* (1985) 61 ALR 280.
77 See (1985) 61 ALR 417.
78 See *Ascot Cartage Contractors v Transport Workers Union of Australia* (1978) 32 FLR 148. The only case in which the defence was successfully made out is *GTS Freight Management v TWU* (1990) 95 ALR 195.
79 See Division 5A *Industrial Relations Act* 1988 (Cth), before amendment by *Industrial Relations Reform Act* 1993 (Cth).
80 See Hansard, 20 August 1985, House of Representatives, p. 53.
81 See Hansard, 12 September 1985, House of Representatives, p. 846.
82 M. Pittard 'Trade Practices Law and the *Mudginberri* Dispute' (1988) 1 *Australian Journal of Labour Law* 23 at p. 58.
83 See *The Trade Practices Act*, Proposals for Change, 1984, Commonwealth Government Printer, Canberra 77-115.
84 See s.163A-D, *Industrial Relations Act* 1988 (Cth).
85 This was the case under s.45D of the *Trade Practices Act* 1974 (Cth) but to the knowledge of the authors, no fines were ever imposed for contravention of s.45D. There were, however, fines imposed on the union in the *Mudginberri* case for contempt of court.
86 See Table 37.1 in W.B. Creighton, W.J. Ford and R.J. Mitchell, *Labour Law: Text and Materials* (2nd ed.), Law Book Co. Ltd, 1993, p. 1269, based on figures made available by the Commonwealth Department of Industrial Relations.
87 See s.111(1)(g)(iv),(v) and s.92. See further R. Hamilton, 'Strikes and the Australian Industrial Relations Commission', 1991, *Journal of Industrial Relations 31*, p. 340.
88 See s.181 (Commission's powers and obligations in respect of breach of bans clause) and ss 182 and 183 (certificate requirements).
89 For further discussion of the history and operation of bans clauses see R.C. McCallum and M.J. Pittard, *Australian Labour Law; Cases and Materials*, 1994, Butterworths, Sydney, chapter 16.
90 See C.P. Mills, 'The Application and Enforcement of Strike Penalties and Sanctions', 1960, *Journal of Industrial Relations 2*, p. 31.
91 See McCallum and Pittard, *supra*, chapter 16.
92 See also s.170PM (2) *Industrial Relations Act* 1988 (Cth) (amended by *Industrial Relations Reform Act* 1993 (Cth)) which effectively means that breach of award proceedings cannot take place where a union is engaging in negotiations for a certified agreement during a bargaining period, i.e. protected action.
93 See M.J. Pittard, 'Industrial Conflict and Constraints: Sanctions on Industrial Action in Victoria', 1993, *Australian Journal of Labour Law 6*, p. 159.
94 See *Applications by East-West Airlines (Operations) Ltd; Re Cancellation of Pilots Awards*, Print H9340, Australian Commission, 19 August 1989.
95 See *Employee Relations Act* 1992 (Vic) s.10.
96 See *Industrial Relations Act* 1988 (Cth) s.294.
97 See s.298 for consequences of cancellation of registration.
98 See s.294(4).
99 See s.295.
100 *Master Builders Association of NSW v Australian Building Construction and Builders Labourers Federation* (1974) 23 FLR 356.
101 See *Conciliation and Arbitration Act* 1904 (Cth).
102 See (1976) Industrial Arbitration Service—Current Review X77. For analysis of this deregistration and later re–registration, see G.H. Sorrell, *Law in Labour Relations: An Australian Essay*, Law Book Co 1979, pp. 82–90.
103 See *Building Industry Act* 1985 (Cth), *BLF (De-recognition Act* 1985 (Vic)), *Industrial Arbitration (Special Provisions) Act* 1984 (NSW).
104 See s.335 *Industrial Relations Act* 1988 (Cth).
105 See McCallum and Pittard, *Australian Labour Law: Cases and Materials*, Butterworths, 1994, chapter 16.

Further Reading

W.B. Creighton, 'Enforcement in the Federal Industrial Relations System: An Australian Paradox', 1991, *Australian Journal of Labour Law 4*, p. 197.

W.B. Creighton, W.J. Ford and R.J. Mitchell, *Labour Law: Text and Materials* (2nd ed.), Law Book Co. Ltd, 1993, Part IV.

W.B. Creighton and A. Stewart, *Labour Law—An Introduction*, The Federation Press, 1990.

K.D. Ewing, 'The Right to Strike in Australia', 1989, *Australian Journal of Labour Law 2*, p. 18.

J.J. Macken, G.J. McCarry and C. Sappideen, *The Law of Employment*, (3rd ed.), Law Book Co., Sydney, 1990, chapter 12.

R.C. McCallum and M.J. Pittard, *Australian Labour Law: Cases and Materials*, Butterworths, 1994, chapters 14, 15 and 16.

G.J. McCarry, 'Amicable Agreement, Equitable Awards and Industrial Disorder', *Sydney Law Review 13*, 1991, p. 299.

K. McEvoy and R. Owens 'The Flight of Icarus: Legal Aspects of the Pilots' Dispute', 1990, *Australian Journal of Labour Law 3*, p. 87.

M.J. Pittard, 'Trade Practices Law and the Mudginberri Dispute', *Australian Journal of Labour Law 1*, 1988, p. 23.

M.J. Pittard, 'Industrial Conflict and Constraints: Sanctions on Industrial Action in Victoria', *Australian Journal of Labour Law 6*, 1993, p. 159.

Questions

1. To what extent should Australian workers have a right to strike?
2. Should the freedom to strike by employees depend on the type of system for the resolution of industrial disputes? If deregulation of wages is accomplished in Australia, should there be greater or fewer sanctions on industrial action?
3. Why do you think the common law has been willing to apply the laws of tort and contract to workers who engage in industrial action?
4. What are the arguments for and against trade practices legislation being used to control union conduct?
5. In 1987, the federal government proposed to establish a Labour Court to deal, amongst other matters, with enforcement of awards. As part of the proposed package of reforms, common law liability was to be eliminated? Although these proposals did not become law, do you think they have any advantages or disadvantages? See R. Lansbury and E. Davis, 'Australia' in G.J. Bamber and R.D. Lansbury, *International and Comparative Industrial Relations* (2nd ed.), Allan and Unwin, Sydney, 1993, chapter 5.
    Do you think that the immunity provisions in the *Industrial Relations Reform Act 1993* (Cth) have provided a sensible and workable solution to the question of the right to strike for workers during negotiations in respect of enterprise bargaining?
6. What liability might be incurred for unions and their officials and/or workers if they organise and/or participate in a picket at an employer's premises?

6

Trade Unions: Objectives and Strategies

Contents

Theories of unionism
Unions as institutions
Unions in Australia
- historical background
- objectives
- strategies
- contemporary behaviour

Introduction

Industrial relations problems in democratic states are often rather crudely identified and defined by the fact that one of the parties is a union which is representing employees. As noted in previous chapters however, unions are not necessary for the practice of industrial relations, that not every employer-employee transaction either provides for, or involves, union participation. Nonetheless an organisation of workers is usually required to pursue workers' industrial interests and this chapter, together with chapters 7 and 8, is concerned with aspects of the typical form of workers' representative organisation, the trade union. In terms of Dunlop's systems framework, trade unions are the dominant organisational form for one of three groups of actors, namely workers and their representatives. The discussion below concerning union objectives and strategies will provide illustrations of the interaction of these actors with the environmental context identified by Dunlop, in particular the power context. Some of the theories and behaviours considered however provide views concerning the purpose and functions of unions which are different from those implicit in the Dunlop framework.

Theories of unionism

There are many theories which seek to conceptualise the complex phenomenon of trade unions. They include attempts to answer the question why trade unions in particular countries at particular times have particular characteristics. Theories seek to explain the origins, structure and behaviour of unions and some seek to provide a basis for predicting future behaviour or other characteristics. Some examples are provided here.

Union purpose and development

There have been many theories concerning the emergence and development of trade unions in capitalist economic systems. Some contrasting, well-known theories are now considered. The first is that provided by Karl Marx whose seminal ideas concerning the relationship between economics, political and industrial relations were outlined in chapter 2 in the context of alternative approaches to industrial relations. Marx, writing during the middle decades of the nineteenth century, sees the important role of unions as one integral to the process of social revolution. The consequences Marx predicts for capitalist systems of production are well-known: a falling rate of profit, intensification of competition, increasing exploitation of wage earners and ultimately a revolution when workers' tolerance of their continued degradation reached its limits. In this predicted transformation of the social order, trade unions were the means by which the working class would gain political power. This was the long-run or political purpose of these 'schools of socialism' or 'schools of solidarity' as Marx terms them: organising centres which would provide workers with an elementary class training. Trade unions also had a short-run or economic purpose: waging the day-to-day struggle against capital.[1] This quest for improvements in wages and conditions could be explained in terms of the origins of unions, as spontaneous attempts by workers to restrict competition among themselves. Marx argues that any gains would be recouped by the capitalists, so this economic purpose was less important than unions' political purpose: to promote the abolition of the very system of wage labour. Union reformism could not alleviate the problems that exploitation forced on workers; only socialism could do that. Political activity was not an objective in itself but a means to the end of economic emancipation.

Marx defines the (prescriptive) relationship between trade unions and the political party of the proletariat in the interaction of the economic struggle and the political struggle as one in which the party dominates. As Lozovsky explains, this did not mean the trade unions turning into a political party or the removal of all differences between the unions and the party but rather that 'the political class tasks of the trade unions were more important than the private corporative tasks of the trade unions and that the political party of the proletariat must define the economic tasks and lead the trade union organisation itself'.[2] The unionism developing in Britain in the middle of the nineteenth century was very different from the revolutionary unionism predicted in works such as *Capital* and the *Communist Manifesto*. Hyman contrasts the optimism in the early works of Marx (and Engels) with the pessimism in their later published correspondence. The dominance of job-centred craft unionism and the absence of revolutionary initiative was explained in terms of

1. existing unions not representing all of the working class, only a privileged minority;
2. the corruption (material or ideological) of treacherous leaders enabled by rank and file passivity (a charge based on the British General Election of 1868); and,
3. 'the embourgeoisment of the British working class, a consequence of the monopoly position of British capitalism in the world economy'.[3]

Hyman points to some evidence in the writings of Marx of support for a natural tendency for union activities to be restricted to those presenting no serious threat to capitalist stability but concludes that at the level of general theory his early revolutionary interpretation of trade unions remains unquestioned.[4] The implication of Marx's theory is that the structure of unions would evolve from exclusionary (craft) to industrial or general unionism, and that with this evolution would develop worker awareness of the necessity for political action.

The most concisely stated of the communist union theories is Lenin's work in his *Iskra* period.[5] Lenin's theory is more detailed and didactic than Marx. He is also more pessimistic. Lenin's analysis concentrates on aspects of trade unionism which inhibited any overt challenge to capitalism. He argues that the bargaining activities of trade unions pose no threat to the stability of the capitalist order. Oppressed workers in capitalist societies formed unions to shield them from employer power but this stage of 'trade-union consciousness', as Lenin terms it, was self-defeating: to counter-balance employer power was both illusory and counter-productive in terms of the ultimate salvation of the workers. Lenin argues, as does Marx, that the capitalist class, forced by the system relentlessly to pursue surplus value, would inevitably retake any concessions unions won. Lenin, as a disciple of Marx, continues with the argument that the real power of unions lies in the political arena but this was an insight not shared by the ordinary worker. For trade unions to be transformed into instruments of revolutionary change, a higher stage of understanding, a 'political consciousness', would have to be developed. A revolutionary movement required a revolutionary ideology and this would be provided by revolutionary intellectuals (the bourgeois intelligentsia). They would lead the unions, using the economic struggle only to demonstrate its limitations, into the political struggle for a socialist system.[6]

Placing Lenin's work in context, Hyman states that the most influential currents of twentieth century socialist theory have focused on aspects of trade unionism which appear to inhibit any overt challenge to capitalism. Lenin's theory is termed a theory of integration, with two other strands of analysis being Michel's theory of oligarchy (see chapter 8) and Trotsky's theory of incorporation.[7]

An influential view of union emergence and behaviour was that developed by John Commons[8] who links the emergence of trade unions to the separation of workers from the ownership of the means of production. His thesis is that the most significant determinant of the development of a labour movement in the United States in the nineteenth century was the historical process of a geographical widening of product-markets which enabled mass production. This changed the collegiate, mutual interest relationship between master and journeymen (skilled workers); their mutual support for product prices at 'reasonable' levels was lost. The master workmen, producers turned merchants, developed a primary interest in mutual association to hold down wages against the concerted protest of the journeymen whose special status was being eliminated by the industrial re-organisation. Their response was to seek their own protection through trade unions.[9]

The ideas of Commons were formalised by Selig Perlman[10] who, writing in the United States in the late 1920s, built his theory on an examination of the emergence of trade unions in Britain, Germany, Russia and the United States. For Perlman, the union should not be the agent of the working class, the union rather should be the agent of its dues-paying members. He argues that the shape and character of the labour movement in any country would be determined by the interaction between, and the relative strength of, three groups within society, each with its own social and economic philosophy:

1 the business class with its opportunity consciousness;
2 the manualist class with its scarcity consciousness; and
3 the intellectuals with their revolutionary/reformist tendencies wanting to change fundamentally the social and economic order.[11]

Scarcity consciousness reflected the mentality of wage earners. Perlman argues that for workers, jobs were the key to scarce resources and that they perceived workers as always more plentiful than jobs. Their response to these perceptions of scarcity was to seek control over job opportunities. They would do this by seeking to assert proprietary control over the production process, to negotiate a rate for the job and to control the allocation of work amongst the work group. If left to its own devices 'organic labor', to use Perlman's term, would develop job-conscious unionism. The dominant behavioural pattern of organised labour would be combating competitive menaces and bargaining for control of the job.[12]

Workers had a desire for collective control of their employment opportunities and to restrict managers in this area of management but they had no desire to take the reins of management generally. Perlman acknowledges that unions may become interested in efficiency but only in pursuit of their primary interest in jobs. He argues that if unions are given the opportunity to exist legally and to develop a leadership from among their own ranks, the trade union's mentality will eventually come to dominate, that is the home-grown mentality of scarcity consciousness.[13]

As a supreme example of job-conscious unionism, Perlman cites a number of the workplace rules developed and applied unilaterally by the oldest trade union in the United States and Canada, the International Typographical Union. There was for example, union control of hiring and firing: the foreman had control of this function and he had to be a member of the union. If there was any conflict arising out of his decisions it was resolved internally through the union judicial machinery, the employer had no say in the matter. The union also had a code of 'rules of occupancy and tenure' which included compulsory sharing of job opportunities: overtime was prohibited when a union printer was out of work; during slack times there was a compulsory reduction from a six day to a five day week. A closed shop rule was designed as much to conserve jobs as it was to make bargaining solidarity with the employer 'treason-proof'. Supply was controlled by strict regulation of apprenticeships. Perlman argues these rules demonstrated the group psychology of the wage earner, the vigorous pursuit of common 'ownership' of the totality of economic opportunity open to the group.[14]

Perlman believes that job-conscious unionism could exist in any structural form but that in a craft union there would be stronger bonds tying members together, a spontaneous solidarity. Further, job-conscious unionism could be involved in a common class action, a sympathy strike or joint political action. However there would only be strong support from members for this if the purpose of the common action was kept sufficiently close to the core of union aspiration that shop floor unionists could not fail to identify it as such.

By 'intellectuals', the third of the social groupings he identifies, Perlman means the educated non-manualists who were either leaders of labour in their own right or exerted influence over trade unions through contacts with the labour movement. For Perlman, the involvement of intellectuals was typically a negative influence. They perceived labour not in terms of individuals with tangible aspirations but in an abstract way, as 'an abstract mass in the grip of an abstract force'.[15] They had not experienced life as workers themselves and they neither knew nor understood the philosophy of these people. Perlman believes that intellectuals could have a positive influence if they simply articulated labour's home-grown philosophy, for example worked to encourage or create favourable public opinion or undertook research which had a concrete impact on the workers' welfare. Perlman identifies three types of intellectuals, distinguished by the nature of the 'abstract force': revolutionary intellectuals, ethical intellectuals and efficiency intellectuals. Characteristics of each type are detailed in Table 6.1.

Table 6.1 Perlman's theory: types of 'intellectuals'

Revolutionary intellectuals
- see the 'abstract force' as material production embodied in technology and work processes.
- in seeking to break through the 'strait-jacket' of capitalism this abstract force was projected against the political and legal system controlled by the capitalist class.
- individual worker a class-conscious proletarian who will risk material benefits wrung from the employer to advance the interests of the working class.
- include Marx and Lenin.

Ethical intellectuals
- see the 'abstract force' as labour's 'own awakened ethical perception' which leads to the pursuit of 'ethical self-realisation'.
- individual worker seeks the freedom to elect managers and regards industrial freedom as the removal of all authority from above and the opportunity for all workers to 'participate in the total creative planning of industry' that is, the highest levels of management.
- include Christian Socialists, advocating self-governing workshops; Anarchists advocating labour communes.

Efficiency intellectuals
- see the 'abstract force' as an 'awakened burning interest' in a planned economic order in which technical efficiency and social efficiency will be maximised.
- envisage society moving from 'a state of disorganisation to a state of order', with waste and deprivation being progressively removed.
- individual worker indifferent as to who gets a particular job or jobs; workers will pursue employer observance of union standards on wages and hours but will leave the employer free to choose the fittest worker for the job in the interests of maximising efficiency.
- include the English Fabians, in particular the Webbs.

Source: Adapted from S. Perlman, *A Theory of the Labor Movement*, Augustus Kelley, New York, 1949, (1st ed. 1928), chapter 8.

From his study of the development of the labour movement in Britain, Germany, Russia and the United States during the period 1917 to 1927, Perlman identifies three factors which operated to mould the direction of any labour movement:

1. the resistance power of capitalism;
2. the extent of influence of the mentality of the intellectuals (who overestimated labour's will to radical change and underestimated capitalism's resistance power) and
3. the degree of maturity of a trade union mentality.

In the United States for example, the strong resistance of capitalism produced a protracted struggle for the right of unionism to be recognised but the intellectuals had very little influence on worker attitudes. In Great Britain, a class war culminated in the general strike of 1926 in which the capitalist order won.[16]

A different kind of theorizing, and one which influenced the methodology of John R. Commons and his followers, was that of the British scholars, Beatrice and Sidney Webb. No less than Marx, they are concerned for fairness and justice for the wage earner, concerned that labour should not be treated as a commodity in economic transactions. One of many major differences between the prescriptions of Marx and the Webbs is that Marx sees revolutionary change as necessary and inevitable, while the Webbs favour gradualism; those who saw Marx as a bloody revolutionary, saw the Webbs as bloodless revolutionaries.

The Webbs see as entirely proper the unions' pursuit of economic gains for members, where Marx sees it as folly. For the Webbs, the problem lies in the means by which the unions could secure and spread those gains. They were among the earliest and most influential scholars to argue that unions were legitimate elements in systems of market capitalism. It was the accepted wisdom that unions were merely monopolies whose actions would distort and restrain trade. The Webbs argue that unionists could do a good deal to improve their lot through collective bargaining which would ease pressure on wages, hours and working conditions. Collective bargaining power of unions would need to be enhanced, in the short term, by unions restricting the numbers of workers to be admitted to particular trades and occupations. The Webbs concede that monopolistic tactics of this kind would eventually reduce national welfare and productivity, thus workers would, in the longer term, need to abandon the restrictive policy, but in the short term, it was an important tool in gaining bargaining power.

As that bargaining power grew and the condition of labour improved through collective bargaining, organised labour would be able to press for the common rule, the establishment of legislated minima in wages, hours and working conditions. Drawing on their monopoly power, the bargaining unions would lead the way, and in their wake, all workers would benefit by the establishment of national minima. These activities were to be supplemented by what the Webbs call mutual insurance, and this would provide, through the unions, some security against accidents and loss of income during unemployment, as well as death cover. These proposals for the common rule and mutual insurance were almost certainly the source of the legislation in later years to establish minimum and protective labour standards through the twentieth century.

An important part of the Webbs' work was their influence on the methodology of industrial relations and labour studies. Analysis of the labour market by economists had rarely been adulterated by close observation of the institutions and individuals comprising those markets. In skilled hands, this abstract application of economic theory can lead to quite startling results: an influential and celebrated study in economics[17] once showed that people unemployed were, in fact taking voluntary leisure (and presumably enjoying it). It is improbable that the unemployed people covered in the study saw it exactly that way, but in the methodology of economics, their opinions, even on matters so fundamental as this, are irrelevant.

The Webbs were important pioneers of the late nineteenth century of what later became institutional economics, and Commons and his followers were certainly influenced by the Webbs. In the late nineteenth century, mainstream economics was not concerned with social reform, but proceeded in a quite mechanistic way from a simple set of assumptions about markets, assumptions which made it unnecessary to treat labour differently in the market to the treatment of corn. Institutionalists like the Webbs preferred to deal with the real, rather than the hypothetical world. In the labour market, in reality, the critical decisions are those involving groups of workers and their employers, not individuals. They judged it more productive therefore to study the behaviour of those groups of workers (usually unions) and to understand the markets characterised by the institution of unionism.

Perhaps the enduring legacy of the Webbs is less in their two major works[18] than their effect on methodology. It is difficult indeed to be an industrial relations student without understanding unions, tribunals, employee relations departments and industrial law. If the need to understand the nature of the institutions which interact in the labour market is now properly understood, the Webbs may be the persons most responsible for bringing that about.

The above theories concerning union purpose and development provide one important context for analysing the emergence and development of Australian unions. The Webbs' concern with union methods provides a link with another context—theories concerning union strategy.

Union strategies

The above theories were primarily concerned with union purpose and union development. Union behaviour can also be distinguished in terms of how unions implement policies and programs. Gardner,[19] writing in Australia in the 1980s, has developed a union strategy model which seeks to define the areas where union practice varies and where unions decide among alternatives. The focus is on union action in policy implementation and on union choice. Gardner's concept of strategy draws on literature relating to unions and public policy decision-making literature, such as Lindblom's[20]

Table 6.2 Union strategies: a model

i	Policy Arena	Industrial	Political
ii	Level of Negotiations	Centralised	Decentralised
iii	Membership and Leadership Involvement	Concentrated	Diffused
iv	Union Method	Autonomous Collective Bargaining	Arbitration Political
v	Range of Industrial Tactics Used	Narrow	Broad
vi	Relationship to Other Unions	Isolated Conflictual	Integrated Co-operative
vii	Sequence of Activity	Follower	Leader
viii	Union Values	Leadership Discretion Autonomous Action	United Action

Source: M. Gardner, 'Union Strategy: a Gap in Union Theory' in B. Ford and D. Plowman (eds), *Australian Unions: An Industrial Relations Perspective*, (2nd ed.), Macmillan, Melbourne, 1989, p. 56.

notion of elites 'muddling through'. It also draws on empirical observation of regular and common patterns in the way unions pursue policies. Gardner defines a union's strategy as 'the characteristic means by which a union attempts to implement policy and achieve its goals. These means need not be consciously or explicitly selected but will be, in general, the result of accretion of experience; an unconscious but customary process'.[21] A union's characteristic strategy is a sum of a series of decisions occurring within eight discrete areas, each with a range of options as identified in Table 6.2.

The choice in terms of policy arena is between the industrial arena (action undertaken against employers) and the political arena (action pertaining to the state, especially government). The choice in terms of level of negotiations is between centralised (national or state level) and decentralised (company or plant) negotiations. Level of negotiations is distinguished from the third area of choice, the degree of membership involvement in policy implementation: a trend to decentralisation in negotiations is not necessarily accompanied by an increase in the involvement of rank and file members. Thus Gardner argues, political lobbying (centralised negotiations) could be confined to a small group of full-time officials or involve mass membership demonstrations.

In the case of union method, autonomous job regulation involves unions setting wage rates by controlling the labour supply through control of training and the closed shop, a characteristic of nineteenth century craft unionism. Political action involves reliance on the government and the political arm of the labour movement for legislative regulation or other state action. The other methods are collective bargaining and arbitration: in the case of Australian unions there have been many time periods in which a choice between these 'methods' have been available to them. The range of industrial tactics used is regarded as the common proxy for union militancy. An examination of industrial campaigns will identify the variety of tactics used by a union and whether the range is broad or narrow.

The nature of the relationships among unions may affect the type of policies able to be pursued and the possibilities for successful union campaigns. Gardner cites campaigns for legislative change as frequently requiring a broad and co-operative relationship between unions. One choice here is affiliation with union peak councils or other federations, indicating some preparedness to be part of a 'union movement' but Gardner notes this decision is compatible with minimal involvement with other unions. Inter-union shop committees, either *ad hoc* or permanent, are an example of integrated relationships at a decentralised level. As the categories in the model indicate, integrated relationships may be conflictual or co-operative. The sequence of activity refers to the union as leader or follower *vis-à-vis* other unions.

The final area of union choice is termed union values or ideology and is the most complex. Gardner argues that the political factional alliance (ideology) of a union is not necessarily congruent with industrial strategy, for example that unions associated with the 'left' may be distinguished in terms of their choice of strategy and similarly with unions of the 'right'. Thus the notion of factional position, which may be important for union policy and inter-union alliances, needs refinement to capture values relevant to industrial strategy. The tentative scale of values suggested by Gardner, leadership discretion, united action and autonomous action, implies that the area of union values important to industrial strategy is support given to leadership control versus rank and file control. The ideological distinction here is between support for:

1 leadership serving membership demands, and
2 leadership affirming the importance of membership demands in terms of active participation.

The choice of leadership discretion is based on leadership expertise and experience justifying leadership control of industrial campaigns, with membership the passive recipient of services. The united action choice represents a call from the leadership for rank and file action and solidarity. Rank and file action is important but operates on a military model. Gardner regards this category as consistent with the rhetoric and approach of traditional left politics. The autonomous action category emphasises rank and file action almost to the exclusion of leadership direction. It supports independent action by groups of members, whereas the united action strategic choice emphasises broad campaigns which may play down the demands of particular groups for the good of all.[22]

This theory argues that a strategy operates irrespective of the particular objective being pursued, rejecting the notion of a strategy formulated to achieve a particular set of goals. Nonetheless it admits the possibility of interaction between goals and strategies, for example in the case of an arbitration dependent strategy, arbitral precedent and practice will not only affect outcomes (union achievements) but will indicate possible goals and objectives. From the perspective of union behaviour, this model complements the detailed development of environmental variables and their impact on the power and behaviour of the actors which is characteristic of Dunlop's systems model. The union strategy model is most useful for considering the behaviour of individual unions over time, but the distinctions developed by Gardner could be applied to the general case of the behaviour of Australian unions.

Crouch,[23] writing in Great Britain in the early 1980s, has built upon an eighteenth century theory of the state, corporatism, to explain the behaviour of unions in the latter part of the twentieth century. The development of a theoretical literature, including the work by Crouch, occurred as a consequence of the adoption of incomes policies in Great Britain and Western Europe in the 1960s and 1970s. There are many definitions within the substantial body of literature on corporatism but two features common to most analyses are a central role for one or more agencies of the state in economic regulation and an ideology emphasising social consensus. The ideology argues that society cannot afford the luxury of competition and conflict between the various organisations which constitute society and this extends to the practice of industrial relations. Competition and conflict must be replaced by co-operation and consensus in pursuit of the common good.

Corporatism requires organisations, including trade unions, to put aside sectional interests and concentrate on the so-called needs of the nation as a whole. As Palmer expresses it:

> 'The ideological support for corporatist structures is that the national interest requires government regulation of the economy, and the active involvement of union and business groups in the administration of the necessary controls. Social contracts or accords are presented as the legitimatory base for government involvement in the regulation of market activities.'[24]

Palmer points out that distinctions drawn between different forms of corporatism are usually on the basis of degrees of coercion and autonomy thought to exist between the state and the other parties, that is, the nature of the relationships between the state, unions and employer associations varies.[25] These distinctions are reflected in the concepts of 'pure corporatism' and 'bargained corporatism' introduced by Crouch. The context of his analysis is policy choices available to governments in Great Britain, especially since the Second World War and with particular reference to the relationship between trade unions and government. He also distinguishes between liberalism and corporatism. The options Crouch identifies are set out in Table 6.3.

Table 6.3 Government policy towards trade unions

Nature of System	Position of Trade Unions			
	Strong		Weak	
Liberal	1.	Free collective bargaining	2.	Neo-*laissez faire*
Corporatist	4.	Bargained corporatism	3.	Corporatism

Source: C. Crouch, *The Politics of Industrial Relations*, (2nd ed.), Fontana, London, 1982, p. 201.

Neo-*laissez faire* and corporatism constitute the pure models and in both cases labour is weak: under *laissez faire*, or classic economic liberalism, labour is weak because it is unorganised and under corporatism because trade unions are controlled from above and outside. In contrast, free collective bargaining and bargained corporatism involve compromises with workers' rights to form and control their own powerful organisations.[26]

Pure corporatism is defined as a system of politico-economic organisation in which:

> 'The economy remains capitalist in the sense of being privately owned, but the stability of the system is ensured through the close *integration* of political, economic and moral forces, rather than through their separation. And workers (and others) are subordinated, not through individualism, but through the very fact of belonging to collectivities, organisations; the organisations which represent them also regulate them.'[27]

Crouch distinguishes this ideology from pure liberalism which also subordinated labour. Pure, or economic, liberalism refers historically to the emergence of the modern world out of feudalism and the accompanying process of the separation of the political, economic and moral spheres of life. This meant freedom from interference by the state in the economy, allowing market forces to work unhindered. For individuals it meant liberation from the traditional feudal obligations binding them to 'groups and loyalties' but also being forced to remain as individuals and not combine with others in unions. This ideology, prevalent from the late 1700s to the late 1800s, gradually accommodated collective liberalism that is, the acceptance of trade unions and the right of unions to define themselves autonomously without state interference.[28]

Under full or pure corporatism, power within trade unions is concentrated in a small elite rather than autonomous trade unions where power is with the members. Union leaders accept the priorities determined by government and employers and then impose the required restraint on their members.[29] Crouch argues this is untenable in a free society. In fascist or communist states, non-co-operative unions may be liquidated and membership of co-operative unions made compulsory. However in a free society, union consent to corporatist relations can only be gained by continuous bargaining. Union leaders will be unable to deliver the consent of the members to restraint if they never offer them anything to make acceptance of co-ordination by the leadership worthwhile.[30]

In terms of Gardner's strategy model, when unions voluntarily participate in corporatist structures and processes they are choosing the political arena of activity. Union objectives however may be diverse or narrow; they may be concerned with a wide range of economic and social issues as well as industrial relations issues or confined to industrial relations issues. Corporatism does nonetheless have one connotation in terms of union objectives: union participation in the process implies union acceptance of some measure of union responsibility toward interests extending beyond the interests of the dues-paying members. The concern for membership interests may be reflected in the dynamics of bargained corporatism: for example the union leaders may seek concessions from government which compensate the rank and file members directly. The concessions may also include some which compensate the leaders for the difficult time they may have with a membership less than enthusiastic about an ideology requiring worker sacrifice and restraint for the common good.[31]

Crouch views bargained corporatism very positively. He believes a genuine bargained corporatism is possible in situations when labour is strongly organised, when the state does not have the power to be coercive and when capital interests are themselves divided. He argues that the support many trade unionists have given to corporatist policies is based on the belief that the state can aid the working classes even in a predominantly capitalist economic system and that such intervention by the state is preferable to more radical social change. Crouch explains union participation in bargained corporatism thus:

> 'It involves acceptance by unions of several strategies which, compared with liberal collectivism [free collective bargaining], constitute a set-back for [workers'] interests. But it also holds out the chance of advances. Unions are tempted—and frightened—by corporatist developments to sacrifice some of their entrenched but

narrow and unambitious achievements in exchange for the possibility of greater political influence and more and broader power for their members in the workplace, but at the same time to accept more restraint, a more obvious role for the unions in restraining their members, more state interference and fuller acceptance of the industrial order and its priorities.'[32]

Korpi[33] has pointed out that the beneficiaries of societal bargains or exchanges, of which Crouch's bargained corporatism is one example, need to be empirically determined, not set as *a priori* theoretical assumptions. The balance of advantage and cost to the parties concerned, in this case trade unions, will depend on the power resources available to such groups at the time. It will also depend of course on their capacity and willingness to exploit those resources.

Unions as institutions

The function of a union, or at least of a union as envisaged by Selig Perlman, is to act as agent or representative for its members. The union is however also an institution with needs of its own, and these, as well as those of its members, must be served. In many countries the immediate precursors of unions were united worker groups which arose around particular issues, and dissolved when that issue was resolved. A modern union, however, is an organisation of some permanence; it remains in existence between crises, as it must do if it is to have the capacity to protect workers in times of difficulty.

The institutional objectives of trade unions are reflected in activities such as those detailed in Table 6.4.

Table 6.4 Trade unions: institutional objectives

- the pursuit of various forms of union security arrangements such as closed shop and union preference provisions and payroll deductions of union dues;
- the expansion and protection of membership territory to establish sovereign rights to represent particular categories of worker, job or employer activity;
- cultivating and cementing inter-union and political alliances;
- removing restraints on union organising;
- disciplinary action against members for behaviour considered contrary to the union's best interest; and
- opposition to secession and the formation of new unions by dissident members.

Source: Adapted from N.W. Chamberlain and D.E. Cullen, *The Labor Sector* (2nd ed.), McGraw-Hill, New York, 1971, p. 80.

The phenomenon of institutional interests is of course not unique to unions but is rather a characteristic of institutionalised society. There are two reasons why the union as an organisation needs to pursue matters which do not reflect the immediate interests of the current membership. First, there is the responsibility upon leaders which derives from the continuity of benefits flowing from past struggles. The present membership benefits from the past achievements of the union and current leaders arguably have a responsibility to pass on the organisation to their successors in as good shape as it was when they assumed office. This may require current sacrifice to keep the union vital and alive for future members. The task of the union leader is, in one sense, not unlike that of an executive of a public company who must ensure that the needs of shareholders are met, whilst also ensuring that the company is managed so as to be able to continue to meet shareholders' needs. The company director will therefore ensure that not all of the operating surplus is distributed in dividends, but that some is retained for expansion and other purposes. In similar fashion, the union leader will not devote all the unions' staff and resources to the welfare of members; some of that effort will be devoted to the maintenance of the union itself.

Secondly, membership needs and aspirations can only be enforced through union power, industrial or political or both. Leaders must be concerned with means as well as ends and in pursuing power for the organisation, or institutional objectives, the leaders are creating an instrument for the pursuit of members' objectives.[34] Clearly, it is difficult for union leaders to balance institutional needs against the requirements of their current membership. Electoral democracy has been the instrument selected to enable union members to monitor this balance, and to express their support, opposition or disinterest. This aspect of unionism is considered in chapter 8.

Unions in Australia

Historical background

Unionism exists in most countries of the world, and it has usually been established with the intention of bettering the working lives of union members. The nature of the betterment sought and the means used to achieve it, are likely to vary among countries and over time, as will unions' success in attaining their goals.

In Great Britain, most of Europe and in Canada and the United States, the regions to which many Australians look for precedent, unions have usually emerged after struggles with the law and with property owners. In most of those regions, the employee who joined in the formative years of unionism became an outlaw, or, if joining the union happened not to be unlawful, taking action against employers to secure union goals would almost certainly have been. The unions which have grown from these beginnings were required to develop the strength which would enable them to resist the opposition of employers from whom they sought concessions, and of the state which denied their legitimacy.

A consequence of this history is that, inevitably, the unions which survived this hostile environment and eventually achieved legitimacy, had learned, through conflict and struggle, to survive hostility, thus, from their beginnings as legitimate entities, they emerged as organisations with a good deal of power. It is often difficult to define exactly what power means in the context of trade unionism, but in considering the qualities which allowed unions to shed their dubious status, obviously union power would include the capacity to win concessions from employers, to retain the loyalty of members and to influence the social and legislative climates. Without those qualities, unions would not have won social and legal acceptance.

The unions which followed this route entered legitimate industrial society as mature and durable organisations which had survived and grown in periods of vicissitude. They understood how to win struggles with employers and with the state, and how to lose those struggles without being destroyed. To such organisations, the removal of state opposition and illegality would not have been an end in itself, but simply the minimisation of a major impediment, and to the extent that there is such an entity as institutional memory, it would probably have left the unions with the same wariness toward the state and the courts as they feel in dealing with employers.

This pattern of evolution was not followed in Australia. It is difficult to identify the birth date of Australian unionism, but certainly there was some union activity as early as the 1830s.[35] Quite obviously, Sydney in that era was not a hospitable climate for the assertion of the rights of the working person, for the origins of the colony as a British prison were still apparent in the powers of the governor. The fact that British law applied in the colony of New South Wales meant that, had working people been able to have the law applied, their right to unionism would have been protected by British law. In these early years, of course, even in Great Britain, the law merely permitted union membership, and certainly did not protect the unions' right to organise opposition to employer wishes.

Nevertheless, the repeals of the British Combination Acts did ensure that union membership was lawful from the time that the first vestiges of union activity had appeared in Sydney. The application of British law until self-government was achieved, and its powerful persuasive effect subsequently, meant that the legal status of unionism was enhanced in Australia far more quickly than would have been the case had domestic influence been the only force at work. These beginnings for Australian unionism have left it with at least one important characteristic not shared by British and American unions. In the early phases of Australian union development, the only influence of the law was benign. The growth of union legitimacy in Great Britain through the nineteenth century was a good deal more rapid than the growth of union organisation in Australia, with the consequence that Australian unions enjoyed legal conditions far more favourable than any which could have been forced from Australian society. The British *Trade Union Acts* of 1871 and 1876 and the *Conspiracy and Protection of Property Act* 1875, were intended to legitimise fully British unions. In fact they failed to do that, but they probably did so in the Australian case. The importance of the British laws in the history of Australian unionism was that in the relatively class-free Australia of the nineteenth century, they created a presumption, or an expectation, that unionism was not unlawful. Australian unions developed in this environment, and their growth to significance probably began in the 1880s, although, as mentioned previously, their origin was perhaps half a century earlier, and they had progressed in response to various stimuli through the intervening years.

The unions began the decade of the 1890s with strikes that eventually involved almost all of the unions. The strikes began on the Melbourne waterfront, but were best known for the shearers strikes of 1890–1891.[36] Australia in the 1890s had entered a major depression, and this was scarcely the time for unions to begin a campaign. The union leaders, however, perhaps best exemplified by W.G. Spence who led the Shearers Union, were organisers rather than strategists. Their experience had been of tight labour markets and feeble opposition, they had no experience of survival through lean years.

The unions were soundly defeated in 1890-1891, their first major confrontation with employers. They were, in some industries, and notably in shearing, refused recognition by employers; employees either contracted individually and directly with employers, or they did not work, and the unions emerged from the fray industrially irrelevant. The unions, or their members, were not, however, politically irrelevant. The ideologue of early organised Australian labour, William Lane, had always counselled against the political involvement of unions, for he feared it would tarnish the purity of the labour ideal. But Lane had gone, he left with a band of true believers to found a Utopian colony in Paraguay, and his departure removed the major ideological impediment to the remnants of union leadership pursuing, by political means, the gains which had eluded them industrially.

The first step was to form labour electoral leagues to send to the colonial parliaments representatives sympathetic to the union cause, and in the first attempt, in 1891, labour electoral league candidates captured the parliamentary balance of power in New South Wales. From these beginnings grew the Australian Labor Party. A major union interest in such a party was to ensure that governments did not support the employer cause, which they arguably had done in the 1890-1891 disputes, and, more importantly, to provide mechanisms to overcome the unions' industrial weakness. The chosen mechanism was conciliation and arbitration, and through the 1890s, organisations to provide these were established by the separate colonial legislatures. All but two of the colonies, or states as they became after 1900, established courts as their tribunals for conciliation and arbitration, as did the Commonwealth in 1904. The two dissenters, Tasmania and Victoria, persisted with a system of tripartite industry boards until 1975 and 1981 respectively, when they were substantially recast in the likeness of the compulsory arbitration systems.

The use of courts for this purpose conferred particular advantages on unions, but one might speculate that at similar stages of their development, neither the American nor the British unionists would have accepted that courts would provide support to unions; their experience had been such as to lead them to expect quite the reverse of this behaviour from courts. The Australian unions, however, saw that legislation requiring compulsory conciliation and arbitration of disputes immediately overcame the two problems on which the collective bargaining of the early unions had foundered. First, the system resolved the problem of union recognition. Provided that the court, or tribunal, would recognise the legitimacy of the union as the workers' representative, it did not matter whether the employer did so or not, for the employer was bound to observe the orders of the tribunal. The old tactic of employers insisting on freedom of contract would no longer be available.

The second immediate advantage of the tribunal system for the unions was that it took dispute resolution out of the trial by strength mode. Under a system of entirely free collective bargaining, which the unions had used successfully in the years before 1890, outcomes were decided entirely on the basis of coercive capacity. If the union could force the employer to submit, it achieved its goal. If the employer did not concede, and held out through a long stoppage, the union would have to concede with no gains. Under this system, the extent to which unions could succeed was entirely a function of their bargaining power. The strikes of the 1890s had convinced many unionists that they were unlikely to gain at all by that method. To progress, they needed a mechanism which would not be swayed by relative strengths and weaknesses.

The ideal mechanism from the union viewpoint, was a court. All parties are equal before the law, and success in the courts is dependent on being right, legally, rather than being strong. It presumably seemed to the survivors of the 1890s defeat that if disputes could be resolved in favour of the right and the deserving, this would be ideal, and establishing a system to secure that was the prize for which their political allies should strive. No doubt the early unionists felt far more confident of their ability to compete with employers through the quality of argument rather than through the trial of economic strength, the method which had failed them in 1890-1891.

As Rawson[37] and others have pointed out, unions were neither the originators nor the prime movers for these court systems. The architects were lawyers turned politicians: Wise (NSW); Pember Reeves (New Zealand); Kingston (South Australia); Deakin and Higgins (Victoria). Rawson argues that the basic attitudes of the liberal politicians and the unions towards the function of this state intervention were in conflict. The scheme's architects had an optimistic belief in the power of the state to suppress the anti-social and self-interested demands of both employers and unions. They appeared to view employers and unions as possessing equal power and the law would suppress 'the private wars between great employers and great unions' as Higgins[38] later describes them. It followed that to suppress both strikes and lock-outs would be just and impartial. Most unions however viewed the arbitration systems as reducing the partiality of the entire economic system. They were an attempt to provide a balance to what the unions saw as the greater 'long-run' power of employers which derived from employer control over the processes of production. This fundamental assumption made by the unions has survived and is important in understanding and explaining union responses to tribunal decisions over the decades. As Rawson says, the belief in the need for institutional biases to moderate dominant employer power meant:

> 'There was thus from the beginning an implicit ambiguity in the unions' endorsement of arbitration. They did not really want arbitration systems that would be 'impartial' if the cost of this was the total suppression of strikes. Not only did they not want this; they were not prepared to tolerate it. Their objective was not an 'impartial' system in itself but one that would give greater 'impartiality' to the overall conduct of industrial relations by strengthening their own position relative to that of the employers.'[39]

In the federal sphere, the *Conciliation and Arbitration Act* was passed in 1904, and it provided unions with the protection and success they had previously lacked. One might expect that, in the absence of this protection, it would have taken many years of struggle for the unions to have rebuilt the strength they would need to represent members effectively to employers. Their growth would have been slow and painful, obstructed at every step by employers, and an eventually victorious union would be one that was a fighting organisation, one most likely to consist of a series of distinct centres of power, allied by common policies, industry or craft. The necessity of overcoming the individual employers at each site at which the union was represented would have necessitated such a structure, and it would evolve over years of contest with employers.

The experience of the Australian unions led them to develop structures of a different kind. The unions did not have to win and retain recognition from employers, a process which would have required the development of coercive strength, but instead they had to be recognised by the arbitral tribunal, or the Court as it was in its early days. The legislation provided its own processes for union recognition, and these required unions to satisfy bureaucratic tests rather than the test of strength. The legislation has required that the union be registered as the legitimate representative of employees, and it must be so registered (or recognised) with the relevant tribunal. In the federal jurisdiction in the years since 1904, the registration process has become increasingly complex, but in the first two decades of the twentieth century, the major test that seemed to be applied was that of exclusivity. A union would be registered if there was not one already established to which the employees concerned could 'conveniently belong'.[40] In the earliest years of the tribunal, it was an easy matter to satisfy this test[41] and it can be hypothesised that the tribunal, in those years, did a good deal to encourage the development and registration of unions—indeed, the encouragement of trade unionism was stated as a principal objective of the Act:

> 'To facilitate and encourage the organisation of representative bodies of employers and of employees and the submission of industrial disputes to the Court by organisations, and to permit representative bodies of employers and of employees to be declared organisations for the purposes of this Act.'[42]

A union, therefore, came into being by obtaining registration, and it survived by retaining it. It mattered not that it had few members, that it could recruit none, and that the union had insufficient influence over its members to insist that they take particular actions. The union was relevant for the purposes of conciliation and arbitration if it was registered, and no matter how weak it might be, relative to an employer, it could still prevail industrially over that employer, for the tribunal did not award on the basis of strength, but on the basis of certain principles. An Australian union survived, therefore, by doing what was necessary to retain registration, and it would not be required to undertake extensive organising campaigns, nor to worst employers through conflict. Such unions are required only to conduct their affairs as required by the arbitral law. These requirements do not make any organisational form essential, but they have certainly facilitated a centralisation of power. A bargaining union would need to develop pockets of power, with organisational resources distributed at strategic locations in industry. The existence of a huge manufacturing plant, in a climate of collective bargaining, would require a very large branch of the relevant union at that site, and officials of that particular branch would, necessarily, be persons of considerable power within the union's organisation.

The Australian systems of regulation facilitate the concentration of power at union headquarters, and this is the typical pattern. While some unions do have pockets of local power there is no need for a strong organisation at each worksite, for issues that arise at such sites may, if necessary, be resolved at arbitration. In Australian practice, conciliation and arbitration is a centralised process; from inception the tribunals have tried to keep decisions consistent and this supports the central management of the unions' tribunal business. It is almost a truism that in collective bargaining, the union officers who have access to the actual bargaining process are those who have all the power within the union organisation. It might be similarly argued that those officials within Australian unions whose positions and knowledge give them control of access to the tribunals are those who hold the power in the unions.

The origin of the unions has given them the characteristics of organisations designed to coexist with the political and industrial systems, rather than fighting them. Their centralism facilitates the rise to power in the unions of the persons who have technical and bureaucratic skills, rather than those with the popular appeal, leadership and the power to inspire the rank and file. Obviously, through the history of Australian unions, there have been organisations and officials who have had other characteristics, but they have not been the norm. Of recent times, some of the officials with strong populist tendencies have found organised support of other union officials hard to come by. The solidarity that other union leaders have been able to count on was denied Norm Gallagher of the Builders Labourers Federation, and Irene Bolger of the Nursing Federation.[43] No doubt there were many reasons for this, but it seems possible to argue that among those reasons were concerns that either of them was more likely to respond to demands from the rank and file than to appeals to reason from colleagues in other unions or union peak councils.

Objectives

This section applies the theories summarised above to the objectives and strategies of Australian unions. The internal behaviour of trade unions, that is the relationship between the union leadership and the rank and file members is considered in chapter 8. The ideology of Australian unions in terms of union objectives is now considered.

The support of Australian unions for revolutionary ideologies has been isolated and short-lived. A revolutionary ideology did find institutional expression in the Australian labour movement in 1919 and in 1920. In 1919, an industrial wing was created, the short-lived Workers Industrial Union of Australia, an antipodean version of the One Big Union.[44] This unsuccessful attempt to form One Big Union reflected the objectives of the syndicalist Industrial Workers of the World, a class-oriented organisation whose aim was the overthrow of capitalism via a general strike and the substitution of social ownership of industry.

A year later, in 1920, a revolutionary political wing of the labour movement was created with the establishment of the Communist Party of Australia.

During the 1960s this organisation fragmented, resulting in three separate communist parties and the mid-1980s saw the virtual demise of a revolutionary party. The influence of the Communist Party in unions was less a product of the political sympathies of the masses than of the Party's sponsoring and assisting selected members to gain office within the unions. An organisation such as the Communist Party, with a good understanding of the electoral and political processes of unionism could easily overcome the typically unsophisticated bids for office of most candidates. Between the mid-1930s and late 1940s the Party was highly influential in unions, and its members held key positions in many unions, and notably those in the maritime, stevedoring, mining, metals and engineering, building and public transport areas. Communist Party union officials attracted opposition and challenges from candidates backed by ALP Industrial Groups. Like the Communist officials, the Groupers, as they became known, functioned within unions but received support from an external source, the Catholic Social Movement (later the National Civic Council). Both the Communist Party and the Groups represented, in the terminology of Selig Perlman, intellectual attempts to divert unionism from its natural, or organic purposes. While neither group represented mainstream political preferences of the time, Communism was certainly the least popular, and the Industrial Group challengers were able to lobby successfully for legislative reforms designed to alter some of the undemocratic aspects of union government that had assisted the incumbent Communist minority to achieve office. The historically subordinate status of a revolutionary ideology in Australian unions is reflected in the widespread view that the success of Communist Party members as union leaders has been due to their industrial policies and skills not their political philosophies. In other words, they have been elected and re-elected due to their capacity to 'bring home the bacon'. Dufty and Fells note that the Communist Party always required its members to be professionally competent union officials who were therefore likely to be elected to office.[45]

In contrast to the revolutionary ideology, the ideology of social reform in Australian trade union objectives has had a long and pervasive history. This ideology is reflected in the pursuit of a gradual improvement in society through the two wings of the labour movement. The trade unions' (the industrial wing) objective is to protect and advance workers' terms and conditions of employment. The Labor Party (the political wing), whose membership includes many trade unions, has responsibility for reducing social and economic inequality. Rawson says that at the time of the emergence of the ALP, Australian unions were not concerned only with the disadvantaged status of labour in the workplace; there was also a widespread belief that trade unionists represented a deprived and disadvantaged section of the community which was also unfairly treated in social life generally. As a logical consequence, union objectives extended beyond better conditions of employment to include the extensive reform of the whole society, to remedy the disadvantages suffered by unionists in virtually every aspect of their lives.[46]

Rawson argues that the formation of political parties (initially in the various colonies) by Australian unions was only possible because there were unions with a wide range of social objectives. He says it was because unions had policies concerning 'the whole ordering of society', on matters such as social services, education and foreign policy as well as employment issues that they could form and maintain labour parties. A political party could not have survived if the concern of unions had been limited to improvement in conditions of employment by political means.[47] Thus in terms of objectives, Australian unions have had a superficial relevance to the Marxist theory except that typically, the revolutionary aspects have been absent. Further, while they have reflected the job consciousness identified by Perlman, their commitment to other objectives dilutes this characteristic.

In 1959 the High Court held that a registered organisation could make payments for political objectives and could impose levies on members for expenditure on such objectives, provided this was authorised by its rules.[48] The case arose from a refusal by two members of the Tasmanian Branch of the Waterside Workers' Federation to pay a levy struck to provide funds to the ALP. Generally union activity within political parties is not visible and even if identified, it would be difficult to distinguish the time union officials spent pursuing industrial relations issues (in the sense defined by Dunlop) from the time spent pursuing other issues. The area of non-industrial union activity which is usually highly visible is direct action and a number of illustrations of such activity were provided in the discussion of political strikes in chapter 3. A small number of unions have a record of continuous involvement in the pursuit of non-industrial objectives through the use of direct action. The best known of these are the Waterside Workers' Federation and the Seamen's Union who have often used their industrial power in relation to issues of foreign policy, human rights and the environment. During the 1970s the Builders Labourers' Federation in New South Wales was active in environmental issues, such as the protection of historic sites. It has been pointed out that this activity coincided with a period of excess demand for the labour of the union members concerned. This meant the union did not have to choose between protection of jobs and the pursuit of social objectives. Many union leaders engage more in rhetoric over non-industrial issues than in action, thus a distinction needs to be made between symbolic or non-operational expressions of interest in non-industrial issues and the commitment of organisational resources to such objectives.

Those unions most active on non-industrial issues are usually regarded as part of the radical stream within the reformist ideology. The radical ideology subscribes to socialism as an ultimate aim. Proponents seek to introduce union members to socialist ideas at the same time as they seek to maintain the commitment and support of rank and file members by protecting and advancing their interests at work. Traditionally they have advocated the formation of industry-based unions reflecting a working-class, or wage and salary earning class, consciousness. During the 1980s, the pursuit of industry-based unions became associated with a more conservative objective: the efficiency of capitalist industry (see chapter 7 for further discussion). Rawson discusses the marginalisation of radical objectives within the labour movement beginning around the mid-1950s. He suggests the changing composition and character of unionism, especially since the late 1970s, has weakened the perception within unions of a rough correspondence between union members and the socially disadvantaged.[49]

The changes include first, the extension of unionism among the relatively well-off and secure sections of the workforce. As the figures on union density in chapter 7 will show, union members are increasingly non-manual workers and employees of government, both departments of state and statutory authorities. This results in a relative decline in the numbers of those who fare badly under capitalism and it widens the range of income levels among unionists which might be expected to be associated with a diversity of opinions and attitudes. Secondly, increasingly the most disadvantaged sections of society, such as the long-term unemployed and others dependent on social security payments are outside trade unions.[50] Thirdly, the proportion of total unionists who belong to unions affiliated with the ALP is declining. Rawson concludes that these changes have meant the virtual disappearance of revolutionary ideas or leaders.[51] The unions' move away from any serious concern for socialist objectives has been matched by the ALP. Rawson concludes that there has been a *de facto* endorsement of capitalism and:

> 'Both the Party and the unions are in practice committed to seeking a more efficient, though also a more equitable, capitalist society; and to do so in collaboration with the owners and managers of industry.'[52]

In contrast to Rawson, Howard suggests that what he terms the 'class orientation' of Australian unions, together with their interest in issues extending beyond the industrial relations system, for example, environmental issues and social equity, has never been a real priority of unions. Rather it has been a product of particular methods available to unions which frees union leaders for these activities. The essence of the Howard thesis is that Australian unions have been able readily to discharge their (minimal) obligations in relation to their primary purpose, namely obtaining improvements in workplace rules, and are thereby able to 'indulge' in other, class-oriented activities directed to social reform. The facilitating factors are those discussed above in the section on historical development: the easing of union officials' workload by regulatory systems which obviate union organising battles and maximise the spread of workplace rules arising from tribunal decisions. Thus, Howard's argument is that with the workplace interests of members being safeguarded by the tribunals and with the mechanism of the tribunals being such that considerable economies of participant effort are effected, it has been possible for union leaders to attend to needs which in other circumstances they would probably have found impossible.[53]

Notwithstanding the concern of most Australian unions with issues extending beyond industrial relations as defined by Dunlop, they have always been concerned to gain improvements in the terms and conditions of employment of their members. The extent to which rank and file unionists consider any pursuit of broad social objectives appropriate is unknown. However, if unions were to offer two levels of membership dues, one for the pursuit of improved conditions at work and a higher level of dues for the additional function of pursuit of social equity goals, it would be interesting to see how unionists would choose. The formal objectives of two Australian unions are set out in Table 6.5 and 6.6. The Metals and Engineering Workers' Union (MEWU) with a membership of 167,360 in 1992 is a multi-occupational union which is a product of

1 a series of amalgamations of various craft unions with the Amalgamated Engineering Union over two decades beginning in 1973; and
2 an amalgamation between the then Amalgamated Metal Workers' Union and the Association of Draughting, Supervisory and Technical Employees in 1991.

The MEWU is affiliated with the ALP in all States and Territories. (In February 1993 the MEWU amalgamated with the Vehicle Builders Employees Federation to form the Automotive, Metals and Engineering Union). The diverse objects contained in the union's registered rules reflect a social reform ideology, job conscious concerns and a self-sufficiency ethos, that is, provision of direct benefits to members, like craft unions in the Perlman mould. They also reflect the institutional interests which are a feature of all organisations. The female membership was only four per cent of total membership in 1992, and the gender bias in the language of the rules reflects the traditional dominance of males in the areas of employment covered by this union.

The single occupation union, the Australian Nursing Federation, provides a contrast, with females representing ninety-three per cent of its 1992 membership of 92,300. An estimated seventy per cent of this union's membership is employed in the public sector, contrasting with the private sector concentration of the MEWU, with less than twenty per cent of the membership working in the public sector. The formal objects of the Nursing Federation are less diverse than those of the MEWU. They are distinguished by the concern with notions of professionalism, reflected in the object 'To foster high standards of nursing practice' and by the absence of any explicit object extending beyond the interests and obligations of the membership in the context of employment, other than those concerning the institutional interests of the union. None of the branches of the Nursing Federation has ever been affiliated with the ALP although during the 1980s, for the first time, a number of elected officials were members of the ALP, establishing a measure of informal affiliation which is a characteristic of many 'white-collar' unions. Both unions are ACTU affiliates, the MEWU and its predecessors being affiliated since the establishment of the ACTU in 1927 and the Nursing Federation since 1977. It is important to appreciate that the union objects, which appear in the registered rules as a requirement of the *Industrial Relations Act* 1988, provide no indication of the relative importance of the various objects in practice. This is also true of union policies although these do provide a partial guide to the range of concerns and specific positions of the unions. The wide range of policies of the MEWU in 1992 are listed in Table 6.7 (see appendix). This list does not include extant policies not amended in 1992.

There are isolated examples in Australia of unions which have approximated the Perlman model in terms of objectives. The Australian Federation of Air Pilots, which was decimated in a 1989 dispute with the airlines and the federal government (see chapter 4), was a prominent exception to the political and class orientation of the majority of Australian unions. It remained ideologically aloof and single-minded in its concern with workplace rules. The union confined itself to a narrow range of objectives focused exclusively on advancing the interests of its members in their occupation as air pilots, and rejected both industrial and political affiliations. The membership of this union was of course among the most well-off unionists, a status protected and enhanced by the successful pursuit of favourable employment conditions by the union. A similar behavioural focus has characterised a group of unions representing workers from an income range very different from that of air pilots. They are the affiliates of the Barrier Industrial Council at Broken Hill, including the Miners Federation (known incongruously in Broken Hill as the Workers Industrial Union of Australia). These unions, like the Pilots' Federation, have devoted themselves to influencing all facets of the employer-employee relationship. Despite the fact that they have been involved in local, state and federal politics, the evidence is that such activity is subordinated to local and job related needs.[54]

Table 6.5 Union objects: Metals and Engineering Workers' Union

The objects of the Union shall be:-

The control of industry in the interests of the community.

The organisation of all workers qualified for membership, the development of the most cordial relations with other unions in the industry with a view to the bringing into existence of one union for the foundry, engineering, ship-building and kindred trades, and the obtaining and maintaining of just and proper hours of work, rates of wages, and conditions of labour.

The negotiation and settlement of differences and disputes between the members of the Union and employers by collective bargaining and agreement, withdrawal of labour or otherwise.

To provide superannuation and long service leave and like benefits for the paid officers and or employees of the Union.

Generally to promote the welfare of the members of the Union.

The provision of benefits to members as follows:-

Assistance to members when out of employment or in distressed circumstances, assistance in cases of sickness, accident and disablement, superannuation, assistance for funeral expenses, and for compensation for loss of tools and such other assistance as may from time to time be decided by the Union, together with all such forms of assistance as are already provided for by these rules.

The provision of legal advice and assistance to members where necessary or expedient.

The provision of grants for rest and convalescent treatment and grants and endowment to colleges and institutions having for their object independent working-class education.

The futherance of political objects as provided by these rules.

The transaction of insurance business.

The extension of co-operative production to assist in altering the competitive system of society for a co-operative system.

> The establishment of carrying on or participation, financial or otherwise, directly or otherwise, in the business of printing or publishing of a general newspaper or newspapers, or of books, pamphlets, or publications of any kind whatsoever in the interests of and with the main purposes of furthering the objects of this Trade Union or of Trade Unionism generally, namely:-
>
> The furthering of, or participation, financial or otherwise, directly or indirectly, in the work or purpose of any association or federal body having for its objects the furthering of the interests of Labour, Trade Unionism, or Trade Unionists.
>
> The furthering of any other purpose, or the participation, financial or otherwise, directly or indirectly, in any other purpose, so far as may be lawful, which is calculated in the opinion of the Union to further the interests of Labour, Trade Unionism, or Trade Unionists.
>
> The holding, purchase, or leasing, or mortgaging, or other dealing with land, including the assistance of members in acquiring houses and real property.
>
> In order to achieve the above objects the Union shall have power, in addition to any other powers conferred by law or by these rules to impose such restraints upon the labour of its members or generally to interfere whether such interference is in restraint of trade or not but so far only as may be lawful, with the trade or conduct of such industries, businesses and occupations as may be deemed expedient.
>
> In particular the Union shall have in relation to the investment of the funds of the Union the legal capacity of a natural person and power to provide funds for maintaining all or some of the benefits from time to time authorised in pursuance of these rules, and for the establishment or maintenance of any undertaking of any kind, financial or otherwise authorised by the Union, and for any action, including collective bargaining, striking, withholding of labour, taking action under the Australian and State Industrial Acts or other statutes, either severally or jointly or in conference, securing agreements concerning wages or other conditions of the contract of service, whether in defence of its own members or in support of other workers of allied or other industries, which may in the opinion of the Union or of its National Council be deemed to be calculated to further the interests of the Union or of the Trade Union Movement generally.
>
> Source: Metals and Engineering Workers' Union, Federal Registered Rules, 1992, Rule 3-Objects, pp. 9-11.

The institutional objectives of Australian unions are reflected in an objective which is standard in union rule books, namely: 'To obtain and secure for members preference in employment'. The preference may be qualified (requiring the employer to give preference to the union member if all other things are equal) or absolute (requiring the employer to give preference unconditionally to the union member). The preference may relate to any aspect of the employment contract, for example promotion or retrenchment, although hiring is the aspect most often subject to preference provisions in practice. Unions may also seek and obtain compulsory unionism or the closed shop. This may be pre-entry, where an applicant for a position must be a union member, or post-entry, where union membership is required only after hiring has taken place. Pressure on employees to join unions may result from direct pressure by unions, or from unions aided by employer or tribunal assistance.

The extent to which Australian unions have become reliant on various forms of compulsion for their institutional security is not known because of the difficulty of isolating the percentage of unwilling conscripts to unionism.

Table 6.6 Union objects: Australian Nursing Federation

(1) To promote and protect the interests of members and in particular to provide professional and industrial leadership for the nursing industry and the health sector.
(2) To improve the industrial and statutory rights and benefits of members.
(3) To represent members in industrial disputes and in relation to industrial matters.
(4) To improve the conditions of employment of members.
(5) To obtain and secure for members preference in employment.
(6) To foster high standards of nursing practice.
(7) To promote the educational, industrial and professional advancement of nurses.
(8) To assist the formation, establishment and maintenance of Branches, Sub-Branches, Sections and/or units of the Federation.
(9) To establish and maintain publications, journals and other literature.
(10) To affiliate, amalgamate, enter into any agreement with or otherwise co-operate with or assist any other Organisation, Association, Institution or Group in pursuit of these objects.
(11) To grant or make contributions for the purpose of financing superannuation benefits, pensions, retiring allowances, endowment, long service leave and general benefits to employees, members or officers (past and present) of the Federation by grants of moneys, insurance or other aid to them or their dependants and connections and establishing and subsidising funds and trusts and medical, educational, housing, recreational and other amenities.
(12) To do any things incidental to or conducive to the carrying out of any of the objects as are necessary, expedient, desirable, or advisable.

Source: Australian Nursing Federation, Federal Registered Rules, 1992, Rule 3—Objects, p. 1.

It is evident, however, that the closed shop is a widespread and significant phenomenon in Australia. Zappala, using data from a secondary analysis of the Workplace Survey, estimates that closed shop arrangements cover fifty-seven per cent of all employees in unionised workplaces.[55] The data show the major source of the closed shop to be a union-management agreement at industry, enterprise or workplace level (forty-nine per cent of workplaces), followed by custom and practice (thirty-five per cent), preference clause (eleven per cent) and other sources (five per cent of workplaces).[56]

It is assumed that unions typically initiate moves for various forms of union security, but it is possible for them to have a degree of management support. The two most publicised union-management agreements are:

1 the industry level agreement between the Australian Bank Employees' Union and the banks which required new employees to join the union and which operated from 1973 to 1984 when it was terminated by employers, and
2 the industry level agreement between the Shop, Distributive and Allied Employees' Association and the major retail companies, operative since 1968.

Both these agreements provided for post-entry compulsory unionism, that is the union did not control the labour supply to the banks and retail companies respectively but employers ensured that all recruits joined. Another common form of union security provision in Australia is the 'check-off' system, whereby the employer automatically deducts union dues from the employee's wage or salary and sends this directly to the union concerned. Employers may charge fees for this service. Its widespread use eliminates the minimal contact which may occur between union members and their organisation in discharging this basic element of their contract. The security for unions in this practice arises from guaranteeing the continuing financial status of the members and the associated flow of funds. It also simplifies an administrative function but in so doing may reduce membership-leadership interaction, especially where previously the collection of dues was undertaken by workplace representatives. Where union workplace organisation is weak, the 'check-off' is an important financial asset whose benefits may encourage officials to disregard, even to tolerate, the industrial weakness it conceals.

The pursuit of institutional objectives is also reflected in competition between unions for members. This may take the form of applications to the industrial registrars to expand the union's organising territory, which is determined by the 'conditions of eligibility' provision in union rule books. It may also take the form of recruiting drives before, after, or in conjunction with, a tribunal application. An example of a long-standing inter-union conflict concerning an institutional objective has been the contested membership territory of the enrolled nurse[57] between the Australian Nursing Federation and the Health Services Union of Australia. From time to time, unions will reach agreements over membership territory which may involve trading particular territory, a practice reminiscent of the reallocation of national boundaries associated with peace settlements in international relations. Trade union support, via the ACTU, for legislative amendments in 1991 which increased entry barriers for new unions by making registration requirements more stringent at federal level, represents union institutional objects in another form. Opposition by trade unions in Victoria in 1992 to legislation which, *inter alia*, removed unions' exclusive representation rights[58] is another example of activity directed to institutional interests.

Strategies

In this section, three of the areas of union strategic choice in Gardner's model—union method, relationship to other unions and union values—provide a framework for illustrating Australian union action in implementing objectives, in both the general case and individual cases.

Studies by Bray and Rimmer and Rimmer and Sheldon have demonstrated examples of autonomous or unilateral job regulation by Australian unions covering transport workers and labourers in the latter part of the nineteenth century.[59] This method is usually associated with craft unions, in the Perlman mould, who control the supply of particular skills through control of training as did the International Typographical Union in North America in the nineteenth century. Studies by Buckley and Hagan, of engineering tradesmen and printers respectively, illustrate Australian craft union methods in that era.[60]

The co-existence of a hybrid form of bargaining with arbitration in the legal frameworks in Australia (see chapters 12, 13 & 15) complicates identification of union choices between bargaining and arbitration. Because particular unions may exhibit a strong preference for negotiation within the arbitration 'system' this is discernible only by detailed investigation of union behaviour. The final product (the new workplace rules) when it emerges in the form of an award or other instrument of one of the industrial tribunals, usually fails to reveal the extent to which alternative methods, bargaining, for example, have prevailed over arbitration in making the new rules. It is clear however that a union choice to rely exclusively or overwhelmingly on collective bargaining has been rare in Australia. The well-known examples are: the group of unions at Broken Hill operating as a coalition in the form of the Barrier Industrial Council from 1920 to the mid-1980s; newspaper printing industry unions in Melbourne; the Australian Federation of Air Pilots during the 1960s. In the case of the Pilots' Federation, union choice was eventually proscribed by special legislation seeking to bring the union within the legal framework of arbitration.

Most unions have chosen to retain access to compulsory arbitration. Favourable decisions for unions by the federal tribunal in the early decades may have generated sufficient goodwill to retain union support for arbitration in the face of unpalatable decisions. In January 1931, the then Court reduced the basic wage by ten per cent, thereby destroying the belief that this represented an irreducible standard. In 1934, at the first ACTU Congress after the economic recovery had begun, affiliated unions voted seventy-two to forty-eight to stay with the 'Arbitration Courts' despite what happened in 1931.[61] There was a significant shift toward greater reliance on (unregulated) collective bargaining by a number of major unions in the manufacturing sector during the period of the mid-1950s to the early 1970s. Union density in this sector was high, above the national figure of about sixty per cent, and the market context was favourable for unions, in particular there was a persistent shortage of skilled tradesmen. Further, in 1953, the federal industrial tribunal abolished the automatic adjustment of the basic wage in response to changes in a price index. Many unions, the most prominent being the then Amalgamated Engineering Union, successfully exploited their greater bargaining power by negotiating directly with employers for over-award wages and in some cases other benefits. It is also pertinent that this occurred during a period when Labor governments were conspicuous by their absence. This episode of union independence, in the form of departure from overwhelming reliance on Labor governments and industrial tribunals, was not sustained. The re-establishment of tribunal pre-eminence in the making of substantive rules occurred in April 1975 (see chapter 16). In the post-1975 period, unions have chosen from time to time to negotiate with employers as some have always done. Typically, however, this choice has involved negotiation in the context of tribunal management of industrial relations processes.

Gardner provides an illustration of a conglomerate union, the Australian Workers' Union, choosing different methods for different industries: a sustained preference for arbitration in many areas, but a bias to bargaining on behalf of its building industry membership.[62] Unions representing nurses have traditionally placed heavy reliance on arbitration. An example of the forfeiture of some measure of autonomous job regulation and of a strong preference for arbitration is provided by the actions of the Victorian Branch of the then Royal Australian Nursing Federation in 1985-1986 in relation to a major wages and career structure claim.[63] The union participated in a tripartite career structure working party charged with rewriting the nurses' award, but ironically this process was ultimately controlled, both operationally and intellectually, by employers, through union neglect. The union had foregone an opportunity to exercise some autonomy on award structure, something a union which encompasses technical knowledge and managerial authority is well placed to do. Further, the union did not engage in any political action: none of the key officials had any influence within the ALP, then in government, and there was no political lobbying attempted.

Union preference for arbitration was strong beginning with the lodging of a claim in April 1985 before it was clear on what it wanted. Arbitration proceedings coincided with complex multi-party negotiations concerning award structure. The tribunal heard lengthy argument about pay rates before a clear award structure existed, much less bipartite agreement on it. The union over-invested in showcase advocacy work and tragically under-invested in negotiations. In practical terms the voluminous transcript was 'froth and bubble': 3105 pages of expensive transcript but not one document formally recording crucial agreements and understandings arising from negotiations. This imbalance contributed to a badly crafted award and post-award conflict which culminated in a fifty day strike (see chapter 4).

Changes in some legal and policy frameworks in Australia in the early 1990s have reduced union choice in relation to method of policy implementation. In the federal jurisdiction, a combination of tribunal policy in 1991 and legislation in 1992 proscribed arbitration in relation to most substantive rules until October 1993 (see chapters 12 and 18 for details). In the Victorian jurisdiction in 1992, legislation[64] made individual bargaining the automatic method in the absence of a bipartite preference for either access to arbitration or collective bargaining (see chapter 13 for details).

The continued affiliation of a significant number of Australian unions with the Australian Labor Party reflects the strategic choice of heavy reliance on the political wing of the labour movement. This choice is designed to bring benefits for unions in relation to both political and industrial objectives when Labor parties attain government. Predictably, during the 1980s Australian unions gave pre-eminence to the political method in pursuit of diverse objectives. Elements of corporatism are present in the Accords negotiated between the industrial and political wings of the labour movement at a national level. The initial Prices and Incomes Accord was negotiated between the ALP and the ACTU just prior to a federal election. The agreement promised mutual support once the ALP achieved government. It also championed tripartite consensus as the path to economic recovery. The initial agreement and those subsequently negotiated (Accords Mark 2-7) are bipartite: employer associations were not party to the agreements although they were participants in a number of tripartite structures concerned with economic policy established under the provision of the Accords. The Accords embodied both union objectives and strategies. The range of issues in Accord

Mark 1 reflected the unions' political orientation discussed above, while the industrial relations issues in all of these agreements represented both the use of a political method and class-oriented union behaviour.

Rawson[65] says the original Accord, which ran to some 5000 words, was a combination of general propositions and highly specific assurances to particular unions and their members. These unions represented significant power blocs in the ACTU constituency. Examples of general propositions included the virtues of prices and incomes policies and government support for maintenance of real wages over time. Examples of specific assurances included the undertaking to public sector unions to maintain wage relativities with the private sector and to repeal anti-union legislation specific to government employees. Unions in the manufacturing sector received a number of undertakings based around a tripartite consensus approach to manufacturing industry policy. Consultative structures included the Economic Planning Advisory Council and the Australian Manufacturing Council. Specific projects included industry plans in relation to motor vehicles, steel and heavy engineering. These actions reflected a government commitment to a diversified manufacturing sector and (according to Rawson) a transition of the economy into a planned framework. Singleton observes that the Economic Planning Advisory Council has emerged as a medium for mobilising consent for government policy generally.[66] It thus serves an important symbolic function but does not involve making decisions about investment or prices.

For the unions generally, the benefits of the initial Accord included ALP support before the federal industrial tribunal for real wage maintenance over time together with legislation or other support for a range of industrial relations, economic and social welfare policies. Some of the economic policies have already been mentioned. Others included: restrictions on the employer's capacity to dismiss labour; various non-wage concessions, embodied in the term social-wage, in the areas of taxation, education and health; establishment of a Prices Surveillance Authority to set standards of reasonable and fair behaviour in relation to product pricing; indirect measures for restraints on other incomes. From the government's perspective, the major benefit was union commitment to a centralised wage fixing system. This was later expressed as a formal commitment to industrial tribunals that they would not pursue claims for wages or other benefits outside the guidelines established by the federal tribunal. An implied term of the commitment was they would not use industrial action in pursuit of claims. The government thus benefited from a public perception that it was controlling the unions or alternatively from its close association with a trade union movement seen to be acting responsibly. A further positive consequence was the reduction in the overt symptoms of conflict or industrial action, which is often taken as a proxy for good industrial relations. Five of the six subsequent agreements, negotiated between 1985 and 1990, were considerably less detailed than the 1983 agreement, with the issues of wage fixation and income taxation dominant.

The fact that the original Accord was largely a reflection of pre-existing ALP policy and ACTU policy, prompts the question of the rationality of union support given the union concessions. The collective union response was rational if the assessment was that the existence of the Accord was a necessary condition for the ALP to win government and that the benefits this offered to unions were both desired and could not be obtained by other methods without comparable concessions. Discussion earlier in this chapter drew attention to the need to distinguish the interests of the union as an organisation, the union leaders and the rank and file union members. An assessment of the costs and benefits for unions of these government-union agreements would need to isolate these categories. The government-union relationship since the early 1980s is considered in detail below.

Another aspect of the Accord process which can be assessed in terms of the corporatism concept is the method of decision making and the locus of control among and within the unions. The negotiating team representing the unions comprised full-time ACTU officials who engaged in some measure of intra-organisational bargaining with the ACTU executive. The latter comprised 30-40 delegates representing industry groups (affiliated unions grouped by industry) and officials of the state trades and labour councils. The affiliates' ratification of the agreements took place at either the ACTU biennial congress or a special unions' conference attended by delegates from all affiliates. The initial Accord was ratified by a special conference in February 1983 after drafts of the agreement were distributed to affiliates at federal office level. The special conference of over 500 delegates was carefully organised (as any comparable event, a shareholders meeting for example, would be) but dissent was negligible. The only delegate to vote against the Accord was the recently elected secretary of the New South Wales Nurses' Association who considered the agreement was not in the interests of the members of the Association. At the time there was a severe and widespread shortage of nurses, and the Accord's wage policies could have prevented the Association from exploiting the opportunity for wage gains.

The delegates may have voted as directed by the governing bodies of their unions at federal level, or, in some cases, on the basis of decisions of general meetings of the rank and file. Anecdotal evidence suggests however that the involvement of the rank and file in the individual union's decision on the Accord was rare. Nonetheless, decision making by the elected governing body of the union, even on matters as fundamental as those raised in these agreements, does meet a necessary condition of representative democracy (see chapter 8). Further, the fact that rank and file unionists did not, in most cases, have the opportunity to vote directly on the Accord does not establish that the agreements lacked rank and file support. If democracy exists in unions the views of the majority will be manifest during elections. Changes in union leadership may signal disaffection with the methods, and perhaps also the prioritising of objectives, inherent in the Accord. Conversely, leadership stability may signal majority support for the *status quo.*

Another indicator of the support of trade unions for the class-orientation of the Accord, would be the incidence of defections or attempted defections from the agreement or from the tribunal guidelines based on the Accord. Defections were negligible, largely because the build-up of pressure points of likely defection within the ACTU constituency was dealt with by a combination of skilful intra-organisational bargaining and the use of safety valves in tribunal wage policies. These safety valves allowed for special case treatment for the unions with political or market power: the awarding of preferred treatment for those affiliates for whom the costs of the Accord agreement were likely to have outweighed the benefits. Affiliates of the ACTU which received support for special case status during the period 1983 to 1990 included unions representing nurses, transport workers, telecommunications technicians and teachers. As discussed in chapter 4, a group which paid a high price for their dissent from the constraints of the Accord were airline pilots. Their union, the Australian Federation of Air Pilots, was not an ACTU affiliate and therefore not a party to the agreement. In seeking collective bargaining with the airlines outside tribunal guidelines, and using industrial action to coerce the employers to bargain, the union encountered comprehensive opposition from an employer-government alliance supported by the ACTU. Their choice of a method unacceptable to the Accord parties for obtaining preferential treatment produced a disastrous outcome, in stark contrast to the results for unions which pursued sectional objectives through the channels advocated by the ACTU. The dominant value of equal treatment for all employees within wage-fixing guidelines established with the initial Accord was nullified with Accord Mark 6 which endorsed (differential) supplementary wage increases based on enterprise profitability and productivity (see chapters 16 and 18).

Writing in the mid-1980s, Rawson observes that the Accord reflected and reinforced the increasing influence and power of the ACTU, and a corresponding weakening of the autonomy of individual unions. It also marked a closer relationship between the ALP and the ACTU despite the growing gap between the two in terms of union affiliations with the ALP: in 1983 about forty per cent of unionists were in unions affiliated to the ACTU, but not affiliated with the ALP. In other words about sixty per cent of unionists belong to ALP affiliated unions. This compares with an estimated sixty-seven per cent in the late 1960s. The increasing gap is due to the growth of non-manual unions which have never been affiliated. Rawson discusses the pre-conditions for the Accord including one crucial pre-condition, the changed position of the then AMFSU (later MEWU), which had a membership of 165 000 in 1983. The AMFSU and other unions in the metal products and machinery section of manufacturing industry, experienced considerable membership losses during 1982 as a result of sharp increases in unemployment in late 1981 and 1982. As Rawson explains:

> 'These were circumstances which strengthened the hand of those within the unions who sought more orderly and consensual relations with employers and with governments. Specifically, it significantly altered the stance of the AMFSU, which had a long tradition of decentralised militancy. The threat which the new circumstances presented to its members and to the size and strength of the union itself led to it becoming one of the most important advocates of collaboration with a prospective Labor government and the pursuit of traditional union objectives by political means.'[67]

On this reading, the union whose history suggested it was the least likely to embrace tribunal determination of its disputes and collaboration with government, had found adversity necessitated a pragmatic reassessment of its long-standing philosophic and strategic positions. The then AMFSU took its unaccustomed place on the side of the angels to preserve the standing and membership it still retained.

In implementing objectives, unions have choices concerning their relationships with other unions. The degree of isolation/integration may vary between objectives, for example political objectives versus industrial (relations) objectives and between different levels or areas of industrial relations activity, for example award issues versus non-award workplace issues. Anecdotal evidence suggests a strong tradition of integrated co-operative relationships among Australian unions, at least in the private sector, in support of other union industrial campaigns. This tradition has been tested and understandably found wanting in recent years with the advent of stringent legal barriers to secondary industrial action.

The inter-union co-operation which has characterised Australian unions can also be regarded as reflecting a (wage and salary earning) class-orientation. Fraternal support, that is a union involved in a dispute receiving assistance from other unions, was evident in the 1890 maritime strike: members of the Waterside Workers Federation refused to handle wool shorn by non-union labour and in fact the strike began when other seafaring and waterfront unions supported the ships' officers. The ten week strike by Latrobe Valley maintenance workers in 1977 involving eleven unions saw evidence of fraternal support for the strikers by rank and file unionists around the state although they were not supported, at least in terms of their chosen method, by the (state) branch officials of their unions or union peak council officials.[68]

Unions in the metal trades and in the oil industry have for many years maintained integrated co-operative relationships in relation to award negotiations, with only spasmodic conflicts within these coalitions. The nature of inter-union relations in the building industry has varied, with conflictual relations dominating in the 1980s. In the health sector, relations have typically been isolated, with coalition bargaining or advocacy the exception to normal behaviour. A major source of inter-union conflict has been the institutional objective of organisational territory, and this has accounted for most of the conflict in the health sector, and for a good deal of the conflict in building and construction. Inter-union co-operation is reflected in the formation of peak councils. At the federal level in Australia this means the ACTU (although a 'David' to the ACTU 'Goliath' of peak councils, the Australian Council of Professional Associations with eight affiliates has survived an era of peak council mergers).[69] Affiliation with the ACTU is a choice made by almost all unions in Australia. As an affiliate, the individual union traditionally has had considerable choice concerning the nature of the relationship: for example, the extent to which it follows ACTU policy, the extent of involvement in campaigns over political issues and the extent of support or guidance it seeks in industrial campaigns but affiliates' autonomy in practice may have declined over the Accord period. Inter-union relationships at workplace level may parallel or diverge from the nature of the relationship of the same unions at 'head-office' level or peak council level.

As explained above, the major area of union values identified in the Gardner model as important to industrial strategy, was support given to leadership discretion versus rank and file control. Gardner cites the Federated Ironworkers' Association in the post-war period and the Federated Clerks' Union as unions which relied on the rhetoric of leadership discretion and the AMWU, BWIU and NSW Teachers' Federation as advocates of united action. She observes that few unions have been associated with the value of autonomous action, that is, support for independent action by groups of members, and those that have been, such as the Builders Labourers' Federation and the Food Preservers' Union tend to be regarded as mavericks by other unions.[70] Gardner's observations probably relate to the 1980s. In earlier decades however, autonomous action was a feature of unions such as the WWF, the AEU and the Miners' Federation.[71]

The 1985-1986 wages/career structure claim by the nurses' union in Victoria also provided an example of the choice of leadership discretion. Membership involvement in the crafting and negotiation of the new award was minimal, confined to inconsequential, limited participation in formulating benchmark job descriptions. Action was concentrated in the hands of a very small group of officials, particularly full-time officials. This was apparently accepted by the elected governing body, the committee of management, whose role was also passive. There was no evidence of membership education concerning the possibility of accommodative arbitration (see chapter 15) and membership ratification of the negotiated elements of the new award was not sought. At one stage in the lengthy campaign the value of united action was evident. This was during the five day October 1985 strike and other industrial action preceding it, but the strike was hampered by poor timing and leadership equivocation about purpose.[72]

Chapter 8 (below) makes it clear that the extensive legal framework relating to the internal government of trade unions does not constrain union choice significantly in the area of union values as defined by Gardner.

Contemporary behaviour

The relationship of the unions to the Australian Labor Party (ALP) is interesting, and has given the unions particular character. In the 1950s, it was not uncommon to find that the textbook definition of a union was something like 'A continuous association of wage earners, designed to maintain and improve the conditions of their working lives'. While this remains relevant to some part of the behaviour of all workers, it would be idle to suggest that it now defines unions. If they seek to maintain and improve the conditions of members' working lives, this is by no means all that they do: in contemporary Australia, they often show a concern with the working conditions of non-members, and they are often involved in matters that go well beyond the working lives of members. If there is anything in the definition to suggest that the union members comprise an industrial proletariat, or even that the membership is confined to manual workers, that would not apply to contemporary Australia where the majority of unionists follow white-collar occupations.

In the early 1990s, it is difficult to identify specifically the objectives and strategies of unions, for these have become intertwined with those of the federal government. Since the formation of the forerunners to the ALP, there has always been a close relationship between the Party and the trade unions, but for most of their history, it has been difficult to argue that either has been clearly dominant. With the arrival of the Hawke-led ALP government, there developed a far closer relationship between the Party and its affiliated unions than seems ever to have existed previously. Whether or not the Party has been dominant, it would be fair to say that through this period, the trade unions have been rather more attentive to the needs of government than has been government to what might be expected to be the needs of union members. The Party's economic policy, for example, has required a declining real wage through this period, and that policy has been accepted by union spokespersons. Whatever the merits of such a policy might be, it is scarcely something which union leaders would have adopted in response to a groundswell of rank and file opinion.

Trade union officials generally have taken the view that there is more to be gained by working closely with government than by opposing its views, and unions which have attempted to pursue goals independent of, or in contradiction to, government policy, have been attacked by government, and abandoned by other unions. In 1985 and 1986, the Australian Building Construction Employees and Builders Labourers' Federation was subjected to a range of hostile tactics by the federal and Victorian governments,[73] some of which were of dubious legality, as were employers who attempted to continue dealing with the organisation. The union's members were coerced into joining other organisations and the governments attempted, vainly, to take control of the union's funds. This unprecedented assault on the union was brought about by its refusal to refrain from using the strike and other coercive tactics to support claims for increases in wages and allowances.

A similar assault was undertaken by the federal government against the Australian Federation of Air Pilots in 1989-1990. As noted above, this organisation, unaffiliated to either the ALP or to the ACTU, also attempted to continue to use collective bargaining to force a wage increase. The federal government used Defence force personnel and aircraft to enable the companies to continue to offer some flights, it facilitated rapid licensing and immigration procedures for strike-breaking foreign pilots and facilitated the use of charter aircraft. The unaffiliated status of the Pilots' Federation is relevant in that government's wage policy was based around an agreement with the ACTU and this included a policy of wage restraint. This agreement, the Accord, is discussed further in chapter 16. Its relevance to the Pilots' dispute, however, is that as the government lacks the constitutional capacity to regulate wages directly, its capacity for wage control rested entirely on its agreement with the vast majority of unions.

The Pilots' Federation, being unaffiliated, was not a party to the Accord, so it is difficult indeed to understand arguments that it should be bound by that agreement. Under the spell of Parliamentary hyperbole, the accord had, by 1989, become the Accord, and in some quarters had attained an almost mystical quality and associated with that status, its dimensions had acquired the imprecision appropriate to mysticism, so that it could accommodate almost anything.

The experience of these disputes supports the suggestion that Australian unions in the early 1990s were very much the junior partners in the alliance with the ALP. They have, it would appear, accepted that any union which flouts the Party's wishes inevitably will be punished, and that they will accept treatment from the ALP government which they would not tolerate from any other party. If Australian union officials have given thought to the nature of Party-union relations, they have not spoken much about it. Notwithstanding the precedents which the Builders Labourers' and Air Pilots' cases have set, it seems that the Party has not yet taken any actions in industrial relations which unions have been prepared directly to resist.

The strength of the union-government alliance was further demonstrated in April 1991 when the Industrial Relations Commission (Maddern P, Keogh & Hancock DP, Connell & Oldmeadow CC) brought down a decision in the *National Wage* case which was at variance with submissions made by the government and the ACTU. After many years of strong attachment to the central control of wages, the ACTU and government submitted that the Commission should award a flat increase of $12 per week to all covered employees, plus further increases to be determined on the basis of what was termed 'enterprise negotiations'. The Commission instead opted for an award of a 2.5 per cent increase to all covered employees. Perhaps self-preservation was some part of the Commission's motive, since logic would suggest that it would have only a slight role in enterprise-based industrial relations, and in part too, it may have been concerned at the flattening of the wage structure which follows across the board flat monetary wage increases. Whatever the tribunal's motives, these were of slight concern to the Accord parties. If the Commission was not prepared to accept the Accord, they thundered, then it was no longer relevant to Australian wage determination. As the Builders Labourers and the Pilots had argued, much to the concern of the ACTU and government, the Accord parties decided that if the Commission would not help them, they would desert it.

The episode is discussed in more detail in chapter 16, but it may be remarked here that it suggests that government interests may have been considered ahead of those of union members. The Commission awarded 2.5 per cent increase to all workers, and the Accord claim was for $12. All workers with annual wages of more than $25,000 would obtain less than 2.5 per cent if they took the $12. It is difficult to know how wage levels are distributed among union members, but at the time of the decision, male average weekly earnings were $585.60 and female average weekly earnings were $385.70.[74] It must be noted that the $12 was to be followed by collective bargaining, but in the rapidly deteriorating labour market of the time, many workers may have had little reason for optimism regarding bargaining outcomes. The government, on the other hand, was under considerable questioning regarding the wisdom of its economic policy, and an overt flat rate increase of $12 might have promoted better public relations than an across the board 2.5 per cent which would have entailed large increases for high salary earners. While there are obviously many other forces to consider, this episode has done little to refute a hypothesis that the ALP is the dominant party in its coalition with the unions.

Trade unionism in every country has unique aspects, as well as common threads and aspirations. It is not easy to find a close parallel to the Australian unions, but in some respects they have come to resemble those of the Soviet Union in the era before *glasnost*. Unions in the USSR were huge, covering in excess of ninety per cent of the workforce, and it could be argued that a very important source of their large membership was their involvement in the social security system. Only union members were eligible for benefits, and, while from time to time there were probably other inducements to join, access to social security benefits would be a powerful and enduring reason for belonging. Australian unions, of course, looked to other means to secure large memberships.

Apart from their size, the unions of the USSR shared other characteristics with Australia. They made few demands of their members, and certainly did not call on them to strike for extended periods. Mr N.S. Kruschev once pointed out to Vice-President Richard Nixon that one would not expect strikes in a socialist state, since the workers had no-one to strike against but themselves. That is an explanation as remarkable as was the fact that Mr Nixon raised the matter as an implicit criticism that the Soviet Union was somehow deficient in that it recorded no strikes, a position at odds with his usual view of industrial relations. The closest similarity between the old Soviet unions and at least the highest levels of modern Australian unionism lies in their attitudes to productivity. The Soviet trade unions of the past era not only recorded no strikes, but they acted as agents to enhance productivity among workers: it is not to be forgotten that A.G. Stakhanov, a coal miner who habitually exceeded production quotas, was created a hero of the Soviet Union. In Great Britain, the United States, or even Australia he might have been regarded with some suspicion by his colleagues. On the other hand, in 1991, an ACTU officer noted:

> 'Industrial relations in Australia is undergoing a period of fundamental change. The need for such change has grown out of a general recognition that our industrial relations system, its award and union structures have hindered the ability of Australian enterprises to respond quickly and efficiently to changing economic circumstances....'[75]

Admirable as such sentiments might be, they have not often reflected the views of trade unionists. If the essential characteristics of the pre-*glasnost* Soviet trade unions were large membership, peaceful co-existence with the employer, attention to bureaucratic tasks and sensitivity to the will of the Party, they may seem not to be philosophically alien to the Australian unions of the 1980s and 1990s.

Conclusion

Two of the influential theories concerning union purpose and development considered here, those of Marx and Perlman, see the origins of unions as spontaneous attempts by workers to restrict competition among themselves. They then diverge dramatically concerning the continuing purpose of unions in democratic capitalist states. One offers a vision of unions as agents for the working class and facilitators of social revolution, the other, a vision of unions as job-centred agents of dues-paying members. The theories also highlight the phenomenon of intellectuals and their influence on union objectives.

One set of objectives common to all unions, as organisations of some permanence, are institutional objectives. Membership needs and aspirations, whether broadly or narrowly defined, can only be enforced through union power, industrial or political or both and this means leaders will devote some of the union's resources to the maintenance and strengthening of the union itself.

The means by which unions pursue their objectives have been characterised here as union strategies. The model of union strategic choice can be applied to longitudinal studies of particular unions but it is also useful in considering the general case of Australian unions. The concepts of 'pure corporatism' and 'bargained corporatism' provide a possible (partial) explanation for union behaviour in recent decades, primarily in terms of strategy, but also in terms of objectives. Some possible interdependence between strategy and objectives has been considered, especially in the Australian context, where it has been argued that pursuit of a diversity of objectives by many unions is a product of their heavy reliance on both the political method and arbitration for achieving at least minimal improvements in the job-based needs, that is workplace rules, of their members. These methods yield economies of participant effort thereby providing time for a concern with matters such as social equity and the environment. An alternative view sees a concern for social reform as a perennial feature of Australian unions and that the unions which created a political party following their industrial devastation in the strikes of the 1890s were in many cases unions with a wide range of social objectives. Thus, the reasons for the heterogeneous objectives of many Australian unions is a contested issue as is the matter of the priority given to job-conscious objectives. Aspects of twentieth century Australian unionism which appear to be universally agreed among writers are: the prevalence of reformist ideology and the transient and marginal role of revolutionary ideology; the stimulus and support provided to unions by the regulatory systems of conciliation and arbitration and the overwhelming preference for arbitration over collective bargaining.

The prevalence of Labor governments during the 1980s provided a distinctive environment, or in Dunlop terms, power context, in which to study the behaviour of Australian unions. Their character has been shaped by their relationship to the Labor Party and it has been argued here that unions, for most of whom the chosen voice has been the ACTU, appear to be the junior partners in an alliance with the political party which a number of those unions created in the final years of the nineteenth-century. This assessment will undoubtedly be contested and it is desirable that this should be so. A comprehensive assessment of the union-political party relationship would include a consideration of all contemporary legislation specific to trade unions. The objects of recent legislation by Labor governments relevant to union status and union amalgamations is one of the issues considered in the following chapter.

Notes

1 A. Lozovsky, *Marx and the Trade Unions*, Martin Lawrence, 1935, in W.E.J. McCarthy (ed.), *Trade Unions*, Penguin, Ringwood, 1972, pp. 47-48.
2 *ibid.*, pp. 56-57.

3 R. Hyman, *Marxism and the Sociology of Trade Unionism*, Pluto Press, London, 1971, pp. 8-10.
4 *ibid.*, pp. 10-11.
5 V.I. Lenin, *What Is To Be Done?* International Publishers, New York, 1928 (written in 1902). Hyman, *op cit.*, p. 12, has pointed out that Lenin's arguments here are widely cited as of more general relevance than Lenin intended, that he was concerned with the status of unions in Czarist Russia rather than within capitalism generally.
6 W.A. Howard, 'Australian Trade Unions in the Context of Union Theory', *Journal of Industrial Relations 20*, September 1977, pp. 257-258.
7 Hyman, *op. cit.*, p. 12.
8 The most relevant of his many works is *Labor and Administration*, Macmillan, New York, 1913.
9 N.W. Chamberlain and D.E. Cullen, *The Labor Sector* (2nd ed.), McGraw-Hill, New York, 1971, pp. 272-276.
10 S. Perlman, *A Theory of the Labor Movement*, Augustus Kelley, New York, 1949, (1st ed. 1928).
11 Chamberlain and Cullen, *op. cit*, pp. 278-279.
12 Perlman, *op. cit.*, pp. 241–243.
13 *ibid.*, pp. 277-278.
14 *ibid.*, pp. 262-272.
15 *ibid.*, p. 280.
16 Chamberlain and Cullen, *op.cit.*, p. 280. For a critique of the Perlman theory see C.A. Gulick and M.K. Bers, 'Insight and Illusion in Perlman's Theory of the Labor Movement', *Industrial and Labor Relations Review 6*, July 1953, pp. 510-531.
17 R.E. Lucas Jr. and I.A. Rapping, 'Real Wages, Employment and Inflation', *Journal of Political Economy 77*, September 1969, pp. 721-754.
18 B. and S. Webb, *History of Trade Unionism*, Longmans Green and Co., New York, 1894; *ibid.*, *Industrial Democracy*, Longmans Green and Co., New York, 1897.
19 M. Gardner, 'Union Strategy: A Gap in Union Theory' in B. Ford and D. Plowman, *Australian Unions: An Industrial Relations Perspective* (2nd ed.), Macmillan, Melbourne, 1989, pp. 49-72.
20 C. Lindblom, 'The Science of 'Muddling Through' in F. Kramer (ed.) *Perspectives on Public Bureaucracy* (3rd ed.), Winthrop Publishers, Cambridge, 1981.
21 Gardner, *op. cit.*, p. 55.
22 *ibid.*, pp. 62-64.
23 C. Crouch, *The Politics of Industrial Relations*, (2nd ed.), Fontana, London, 1982.
24 G. Palmer, 'Corporatism and Australian arbitration' in S. Macintyre and R. Mitchell (eds), *Foundations of Arbitration*, Oxford University Press, Melbourne, 1989, p. 315.
25 *ibid.*, p. 316.
26 Crouch, *op, cit.*, p. 201.
27 *ibid.*, p. 145.
28 *ibid.*, pp. 142-144.
29 *ibid.*, p. 153.
30 *ibid.*, p. 212.
31 *ibid.*
32 C. Crouch, *Class Conflict and the Industrial Relations Crisis*, Heinemann, London, 1977, p. 263.
33 W. Korpi and M. Shalev, 'Strikes, industrial relations and class conflict in capitalist societies', *British Journal of Sociology 30*, June 1979, pp. 164-187 cited in Palmer, *op. cit.*, p. 318.
34 Chamberlain and Cullen, *op. cit.*, pp. 80-81.
35 J.T. Sutcliffe, *A History of Trade Unionism in Australia*, Macmillan, Melbourne, 1967 (Reissue), pp. 28-29.
36 *ibid.*, chapter 4.

37 D. Rawson, 'Law and Politics in Industrial Relations', in G.W. Ford, J.M. Hearn and R.D. Lansbury (eds.), *Australian Labour Relations: Readings* (4th ed.), Macmillan, Melbourne, 1987, pp. 53-54.
38 H. Higgins, *A New Province for Law and Order*, WEA, Sydney, 1922, p. 150.
39 Rawson 1987, *op. cit.*, p. 55.
40 *Conciliation and Arbitration Act* 1904, s.59. The language of the original section gave the Registrar discretion to refuse to register an applicant association and this discretion was retained in a 1909 amendment. The section then read: 'The Registrar shall, unless in all the circumstances he thinks it undesirable so to do, refuse to register any association as an organisation if an organisation, to which the members of the association might conveniently belong, has already been registered'.
41 Howard, *op. cit.*, p. 86. For further analysis of registration decisions see G. Griffin and V. Scarcebrook, 'The Dependency Theory of Trade Unionism and the Role of the Industrial Registrar', *Australian Bulletin of Labour 16*, March 1990, pp. 21-31.
42 *Conciliation and Arbitration Act*, 1904, s.2 (VI).
43 For a discussion of the isolation of the Nursing Federation in Victoria under Irene Bolger's leadership, see C. Fox, *Enough is Enough: The 1986 Victorian Nurses' Strike*, Australian Studies in Health Service Administration, No. 73, School of Health Services Management, University of New South Wales, 1991.
44 For a detailed account see J. Hagan, *The History of the ACTU*, Longman Cheshire, Melbourne, 1981, chapter 1.
45 N.F. Dufty and R.E. Fells, *Dynamics of Industrial Relations in Australia*, Prentice-Hall, Sydney, 1989, p. 121.
46 D. Rawson, *Unions and Unionists in Australia*, (2nd ed.), Allen & Unwin, Sydney, 1986, p. 114.
47 *ibid.*, p. 17.
48 *Williams v. Hursey* (1959) 103 CLR 30.
49 Rawson 1986, *op. cit.*, p. 4.
50 *ibid.*, p. 16.
51 *ibid.*, pp. 113-114.
52 *ibid.*, p. 115.
53 Howard, *op. cit.*, pp. 88-89.
54 For a detailed account of this job-conscious unionism see W.A. Howard, *Barrier Bulwark*, Willry Pty Ltd, Melbourne, 1990.
55 G. Zappala, 'The Closed Shop in Australia', *The Journal of Industrial Relations 34*, March 1992, p. 11.
56 *ibid.*, pp. 15 & 28.
57 This category of nurse is known in the industry as the second level nurse who undertakes 12 months training for registration in contrast to the more numerous registered general nurse classification for which three years training is required.
58 *Employee Relations Act* 1992 (Victoria), ss 8 and 9.
59 See for example M. Bray and M. Rimmer, 'Compulsory Arbitration vs Managerial Control: Industrial Relations in Sydney Road Transport, 1888-1908', *Historical Studies 22*, October 1986, pp. 214-231; M. Rimmer and P. Sheldon, '"Union Control" Against Management Power: Labourers' Unions in New South Wales Before the 1890 Maritime Strike', *Historical Studies 23*, April 1989, pp. 274-292.
60 K.D. Buckley, *The Amalgamated Engineers in Australia, 1852-1920*, Research School of Social Sciences, ANU, Canberra, 1970; J. Hagan, *Printers and Politics: A History of the Australian Printing Unions, 1850-1950*, ANU Press, Canberra, 1966.
61 J. Hagan, *The History of the ACTU*, Longman Cheshire, Melbourne, 1981, pp. 100-101.
62 Gardner, *op. cit.*, p. 60.
63 C. Fox, 'Antecedents of the 1986 Victorian Nurses' Strike', *Journal of Industrial Relations 32*, December 1990, p. 466.
64 *Employee Relations Act* 1992 (Victoria); ss 8, 9, and 92.

65 Rawson, 1986, *op. cit.*, p. 69.
66 G. Singleton, 'The Economic Planning Advisory Council: the Reality of Consensus', *Politics*, May 1985, cited in B. Dabscheck, *Australian Industrial Relations in the 1980s*, Oxford University Press, Melbourne, 1989, p. 58.
67 Rawson, 1986, *op. cit.*, p. 67. For a history of the AMFSU (the Amalgamated Engineering Union until 1973) from 1920 to 1972 see T. Sheridan, *Mindful Militants*, Cambridge University Press, Melbourne, 1975.
68 J.W. Benson and D.J. Goff, 'The 1977 Latrobe Valley SECV Maintenance Workers' Strike', *Journal of Industrial Relations 21*, June 1979, pp. 217-228.
69 See G. Griffin and V. Giuca, 'One union peak council: the merger of ACSPA and CAGEO with the ACTU', *Journal of Industrial Relations 28*, December 1986, pp. 483-503.
70 Gardner, *op. cit.*, p. 60.
71 See for example K. Hince, *Conflict and Coal*, University of Queensland Press, St. Lucia, 1982, p. 41.
72 Fox 1990, *op. cit.*, p. 469.
73 The relevant statutes were, 1. Commonwealth: *Building Industry Act* (1985); *Builders Labourers' Federation (Cancellation of Registration) Act* 1986; *Builders Labourers' Federation (Cancellation of Registration) Consequent Provisions Act* 1986, 2. New South Wales: *Industrial Arbitration (Special Provisions) Act* 1985; *Builders Labourers' Federation (Special Provisions) Act* 1986, 3. Victoria: *BLF (De-Recognition) Act*, 1985.
74 Australian Bureau of Statistics, *Average Weekly Earnings, States and Australia*, August 1991, Catalogue No. 6302.0. Figures quoted are for February 1991.
75 I. Ross, 'Restructuring Made Easier', *Workplace*, Autumn 1991, p. 28.

Further Reading

Theories of unionism

C. Crouch, *The Politics of Industrial Relations*, (2nd ed.), Fontana, London, 1982.

A. Flanders, 'What are Trade Unions for?' in A. Flanders, *Management and Unions*, Faber, London, 1970, pp. 38-47.

M. Gardner, 'Union Strategy: A Gap in Union Theory', in B. Ford and D. Plowman, *Australian Unions : An Industrial Relations Perspective*, (2nd ed.), Macmillan, Melbourne, 1989, pp. 49-72.

R. Hoxie, *Trade Unionism in the United States*, (2nd ed.) Appleton, New York, 1926.

R. Hyman, *Marxism and the Sociology of Trade Unionism*, Pluto Press, London, 1971.

A. Lozovsky, *Marx and the Trade Unions*, Martin Lawrence, 1935.

R.M. Martin, *Trade Unionism: Purposes and Forms*, Clarendon Press, Oxford, 1989.

S. Perlman, *A Theory of the Labor Movement*, Augustus Kelley, New York, 1949 (1st ed. 1928).

M. Poole, *Theories of Trade Unionism: A Sociology of Industrial Relations*, Routledge & Kegan Paul, London, 1981.

S. and B. Webb, *History of Trade Unionism*, Longmans Green and Co., New York, 1894.

S. and B. Webb, *Industrial Democracy*, Longmans Green and Co., New York, 1897.

Unions in Australia

ACTU, *Future Strategies for the Trade Union Movement*, September 1987.

B. Dabscheck, *Australian Industrial Relations in the 1980s*, Oxford University Press, Melbourne, 1989.

J. Child, *Unionism and the Labour Movement*, Macmillan, Melbourne, 1971.

K. Cole, 'Unions and the Labor Party' in K. Cole (ed.), *Power, Conflict and Control in Australian Unions*, Pelican, Ringwood, 1982, pp. 85-101.

L. Cupper and J.M. Hearn, 'Australian Union Involvement in 'Non-Industrial' Issues: the Newport Dispute 1971-78', G.W. Ford, J.M. Hearn & R.D. Lansbury (eds), *Australian Labour Relations: Readings* (3rd ed.), Macmillan, Melbourne, 1980, pp. 50-75.

S. Deery, 'Union Aims and Methods', in B. Ford and D. Plowman (eds), *Australian Unions: An Industrial Relations Perspective* (2nd ed.), Macmillan, Melbourne, 1989, pp. 74-103.

N. Dufty and C. Mulvey, *The Sources of Union Power*, Australian Institute for Public Policy, Perth, 1987.

G. Griffin and V. Scarcebrook, 'The Dependency Theory of Trade Unionism and the Role of the Industrial Registrar', *Australian Bulletin of Labour 16*, March 1990, pp. 21-31.

J. Hagan, *Australian Trade Unionism in Documents*, Longman Cheshire, Melbourne, 1986.

J. Hearn, 'Corporatism Australian Style: The Prices and Incomes Accord', in G.W. Ford, J.M. Hearn & R.D. Lansbury (eds), *Australian Labour Relations: Readings*, (4th ed.), Macmillan, Melbourne, 1987, pp. 424-437.

W.A. Howard, 'Australian Trade Unions in the Context of Union Theory', *Journal of Industrial Relations 20*, September 1977, pp. 255-273.

R.M. Martin, *Trade Unions in Australia*, Penguin, Harmondsworth, 1975.

G. Palmer, 'Corporatism and Australian arbitration', in S. Macintyre and R. Mitchell (eds), *Foundations of Arbitration*, Oxford University Press, Melbourne, 1989, pp. 313-333.

D. Rawson, *Unions and Unionists in Australia* (2nd ed.), Allen & Unwin, Sydney, 1986.

L. Sharkey, *The Trade Unions*, Current Book Distributors, Sydney, 1942.

J.T. Sutcliffe, *A History of Trade Unionism in Australia*, Macmillan, Melbourne, 1967.

G. Zappala, 'The Closed Shop in Australia', *Journal of Industrial Relations 34*, March 1992, pp. 3-30.

Questions

Theories of unionism

1 Explain the theories concerning union purpose and development presented by Marx and Perlman and highlight the essential differences between them.
2 Discuss the Webbs' contribution to the literature relating to union objectives and strategies.
3 How did Lenin's vision of trade union purpose differ from that of Marx?

4 Explain
  (a) the purposes of Gardner's union strategy model and
  (b) the 'union method' and 'union values' areas of strategic choice.
5 Distinguish the concepts of 'pure corporatism and 'bargained corporatism' in the context of union behaviour, introduced by Crouch.
6 What is meant by the term 'the institutional objectives' of trade unions? Provide some examples.

Unions in Australia

7 Identify the advantages for unions which followed from legislation providing for the regulation of industrial relations by compulsory conciliation and arbitration.
8 Do you consider that the Marxist theory of union purpose and development has any relevance to Australian unions? Give reasons for your answer.
9 What are the differences between the objects of the Metals and Engineering Workers' Union and the objects of the Australian Nursing Federation? What additional information would you need in order to assess whether either of these unions approximated the Perlman model?
10 Discuss the choices made by Australian unions in relation to 'union method'.
11 Discuss the following statement indicating whether you agree or disagree:

   'The political and class-oriented behaviour of Australian unions in the 1980s represents a continuation of their traditional behaviour in relation to union objectives'.

12 In what ways was the Prices and Incomes Accord (Mark I) between the Australian Labor Party and the ACTU an exercise in corporatism?
13 What do you believe to be the most important sources of power for Australian unions. Explain your answer.
14 Consider the quotation from John L. Lewis in chapter 2, question 8. Aside from the terminology, to what extent do you think that the statement reflects the current values of Australian unions?

Exercises

1 Form two debating teams and debate the following: 'During the 1980s and early 1990s in Australia the trade unions have been the junior partner in the relationship between the two wings of the labour movement'.
2 Locate the objects of any two federal unions and compare and contrast them with the objects of the MEWU and the ANF.

Appendix

Table 6.7 Metals and Engineering Workers' Union : policies (1992)

- **Wages, Hours of Work, Working Conditions**

    Bonus systems; Merit/performance pay; Employee share ownership plans; Skill based pay systems; Hay point systems; Time off in lieu of overtime; Gainsharing; Annualised hours and pay; Leave — portability of leave entitlements; Leave — long service; Leave — paternity leave; Trade Union education leave; Leave — sick leave; Overtime; Shop committees; Shiftwork; Right of entry; Termination, change and redundancy; Penalty rates; Tools; Shop stewards; Wage and tax strategy policy; Reduced working hours; Employment — casual; Bankruptcy of companies; Disputes benefit; Contract labour; Stand down clauses; Contracting out; Superannuation.

- **Occupational Health and Safety**

    National Occupational Health and Safety Commission; Research and education; Job action organisation; Union rights; Union Occupational Health & Safety Committee; Joint Union and Employer Occupational Health & Safety Committees; Agreements; Legislation; Levy on wages bill; Employment-based medical services; Asbestos; Workers' Health Centres; Discomfort rates; Migrant workers; Training of workers in OH&S; Chemical confidentiality; Noise-induced hearing loss; Welding; Synthetic mineral fibres; Hand injuries from power presses; Hazardous substances; Heat; Seasonal (transient) heat; Heat: stress areas; Manual handling; Statistics; Rehabilitation; Publications: Public transport drivers; Behavioural accident prevention; workers' compensation; Drug & alcohol.

- **Skills Development, Training and Appprenticeships**

    Training: Award rights and training contracts; Training leave; Entry level youth training and wages; Equality of access; Electrical licensing; Current apprenticeship training; Standards; Government funding of training; Retraining allowance; Australian centre for best practice.

- **Industrial Democracy, Work Organisation, Youth and Women**

    Industrial democracy; Youth employment and training; Equal Employment Opportunities Act; Affirmative action plan for women; Youth (W.A. Acts).

- **Political, Economic, Social Wage Issues**

    Uranium and Nuclear Industry; Taxation; Socialist objective; Social security; Privacy; Prices Surveillance Authority; Pensions; Retiree concessions; Early retirement problems; Multinationals; Medicare; Human rights; Health care system; Health—public health, Health and prescribed drugs; Hearing aids; Construction sites; Forestry industry; Identification cards; Financial deregulation; Balance of payments; Insurance; Pensioner loans; Petroleum prices; Pharmaceutical companies; Takeover; Aboriginal land rights; Conservation; Alpine National Park; Disarmament; Immigration; Trade unions and migrants; Discrimination; Sport; Social wage; Accord; Centres of excellence; Republic of Australia; Housing; Consumer protection; A.L.P.; Banking; Child minding centres; Liberal Party's 'Fightback' package; Social justice; APPM dispute; Black deaths in custody; Environment; Program for the Social welfare sector; Inquiry into wealth; Public sector—contracting out; Commitment to public sector; Corporation Act—amendment; Aussie bonds.

- **The Australian Economy and Industry Development**
- **Union Structure, Research, Rules**
- **Union Education**

    Art in Working Life Policy

- **International**

    Israeli/Arab conflict; South Africa; Moses Mayekiso; NUMSA; Zimbabwe; Indonesia; Asia/Pacific; Eastern Europe; Cuba; Tibet; World poverty; Foreign aid; French colonialism in the Pacific; Asian and Pacific Region; South Korea; Political prisoners; Trade unionism, international; Ozone depletion—Greenpeace Du Pont campaign; Environmental Protection Agency; A sustainable and livable environment; Agriculture and primary industry; Nature conservation; Energy and industry; Waste, pollution and hazardous materials; Science, research and design; Work; International strategies; Political and legal; Economic.

- **Publicity**

    Media cover; Education.

Source: *Addresses, Reports and Decisions*, Metals and Engineering Workers' Union, 11th Biennial National Conference, Surry Hills, NSW, 26-31 July, 1992.

7

Trade Unions: Membership and Structure

Contents
Union growth
Union density
Patterns of organisation
Union mergers

Introduction

The aspects of trade unionism considered in this chapter have become central to union peak council policies and also to public policy in industrial relations in Australia in the early 1990s. One impetus for this has been a decline in levels of unionisation during the 1980s. This decline in union density is an international phenomenon however, with a number of countries experiencing a greater decline than Australia. Another impetus for the prominence of issues relating to union structure has been the public policy of award restructuring which is discussed in chapter 18. This policy has been a central feature of the wages policy of the federal industrial tribunal, the Australian Industrial Relations Commission. It includes concepts based on the restructuring of work processes and organisation to improve efficiency and productivity and support for an increasingly workplace oriented focus for industrial relations practice. Union restructuring is relevant to wages policy because it is seen by a number of actors, particularly some employer associations and the federal government, as a means to both facilitate and accommodate these other changes.

This chapter is concerned with an historical perspective on union growth and patterns of organisation as well as recent developments. In the previous chapter, union growth was considered in the context of various consequences of the adoption of systems of compulsory conciliation and arbitration in Australia. The focus here shifts to the full range of factors affecting union growth in Australia and prior to this, an early theory of union growth is summarised.

Union growth

There is a substantial literature concerned with theories of union growth. One influential model is that developed by Shister,[1] writing in the United States in the 1950s. A theory of union growth seeks to explain what factors enable unions to grow or cause them to decline, why they grow or decline at particular times and at particular rates. Shister's model comprised three determinants:

1   the work environment,
2   the socio-legal framework, and
3   the quality of union leadership.

His hypothesis is that union growth requires a favourable work environment and socio-legal framework, but that, given these circumstances, astute and competent leaders are needed to capitalise on them. Without such leaders these factors are not fully exploited. On the other hand, in the absence of a favourable work environment and socio-legal framework, there is little even an outstanding leader can do to achieve union growth.

The work environment variable has many aspects which Shister discusses under the headings of the rate and pattern of economic change; the structure of the relevant industry and the proximity influence. The economic change factor includes the rate of occupational mobility which is inversely related to union growth in the long run: growth is encouraged by the crystallisation and maintenance of a 'working class consciousness' by which Shister means employees who are members of a working class and who see little opportunity for moving out of that class. The other aspect of economic change is cyclical change in employment levels. Cyclical expansion in areas where unionism is strong is an important source of increases in membership but Shister argues a cyclical decline in employment is likely to cause a proportionately smaller membership decline because workers who have lost their jobs often see advantages in retaining membership.

Shister disaggregates the industry structure variable into

i   the technical and market contexts, and
ii the composition of the workforce.

In relation to the former, the factors include the size of firms; the rate of labour turnover and union bargaining power deriving from technical and market factors. Shister predicts a lower propensity to unionise in small firms due to company loyalty and higher union costs of organising and maintaining membership. The rate of labour turnover dampens workers' propensity to unionise and increases the costs of organisation to the union while union bargaining power affects the union's utility and attractiveness to current and potential members. Workforce composition is relevant because propensity to unionise varies with gender, age, race and ethnicity. (It does need to be noted, of course, that Shister's observations were drawn from the 1950s.) Females are less prone to unionise than males, seeing themselves as less permanently tied to their employment. Shister argues younger workers have a higher propensity to unionise than older workers because they are typically less subject to the constraint of feelings of company loyalty, more inclined to militancy, having less to lose if their union activities result in dismissal. Further, better educational opportunities make them more resentful of the arbitrary exercise of management power and more aware of their legal rights. Shister regards ethnic diversity in the workforce as an initial obstacle to unionisation, becoming less significant over time. The final aspect of the work environment categorised by Shister is the proximity influence on growth, meaning that growth in one sector can promote growth in another sector where there is physical or institutional (same industry or union) proximity. Here the increase in unionisation arises from the changing attitudes of workers, unions or management. Thus for example, workers may be less fearful of an adverse employer response when a successful lead sector is established and may observe the utility of union membership. In the case of management, resistance to unionisation may diminish where competing businesses are unionised, thus removing a fear of labour-cost disadvantage or a fear of criticism from other employers for failure to resist unions.

The second, and major, determinant of growth trends is the socio-legal framework comprising public opinion and legislation. Shister explains that union growth requires a favourable climate of public opinion which will be reflected, albeit slowly, in favourable trade union law. He argues the law is shaped by public opinion but reacts very slowly to changes in this, even more slowly in the case of the judiciary than the legislature. In the short run, the law can depart from public opinion but in the long run the legal framework reacts to and reflects the changes in the social climate.

The third determinant is the quality of trade union leadership: astute and competent leadership is regarded as necessary to capitalise on favourable conditions in the other determinants. Shister suggests differences in particular growth patterns are related to a considerable extent to the different abilities of particular leaderships in terms of organising techniques, the internal operation of the union and collective bargaining relationships with the relevant employing or governmental unit. Further, once the union is organised, its survival and growth will be largely conditioned by leadership ability to adapt the constituency to changing socio-economic conditions. Leadership aptitude here covers recognising new conditions, developing policies to meet such conditions and persuading the rank and file to pursue them. There may also be a proximity influence operating with lead sectors emerging due to leadership skill influencing the followers in other sectors.

The discussion on proximity influence and other aspects of Shister's model reflects in part distinctive features of the then industrial relations system in the United States and its history.

Union density

Among advanced capitalist societies, Australia has consistently maintained a high union density, that is the proportion of employees who are trade union members. Union density is one important factor influencing union power. Most of the statistical information on unions published by the Australian Bureau of Statistics since 1912 is derived from questionnaires completed annually by individual trade unions although since 1976 periodic workforce surveys by the ABS have provided both more diverse data and some alternative (conflicting) data. In respect of the annual information from trade unions, consideration of changes in density rates is complicated by the revision of figures by both academic researchers (Bain and Price for the years 1911 to 1976) and by the ABS (for the years 1968 to 1979). The Bain and Price series,[2] based on revised estimates of the labour force, produces significantly lower densities, up to 11 per cent, until the mid-1940s. Thereafter the ABS figures remain consistently higher but the differences do not exceed 5 per cent. According to Bain and Price, Australia had a union density of 42 per cent in 1920. By 1927 it had risen to 47 per cent but fell to 35 per cent in 1933 during the Depression. From the mid-1930s density levels rose steadily to a peak of 59 per cent in 1954 and declined steadily to 51 per cent in 1970. Table 7.1 shows ABS density rates from 1971 to 1991 and for 1971 to 1979 includes the revised figures.

Many of the variables usually identified as affecting union growth in Australia were included in the Shister model, although the nature of the socio-legal framework in this country differs markedly from that in the United States. The variables are: the establishment and operation of the conciliation and arbitration systems; workforce composition including manual versus non-manual occupation and gender distribution; industrial structure including significance of different sectors (type of industry and public vs private sector) and the size of firms; the nature of employment contracts (full-time vs

Table 7.1 Union Density Australia: 1971 to 1992 (Union collection) (percentages)

	All employees	Male	Female
1971	51	58	38
1972	52	58	42
1973	53	59	42
1974	55	61	44
1975	56	62	46
1976	55	61	45
1977	55	61	46
1978	56	62	46
1979	56	61	47
1980	56	61	47
1981	56	60	48
1982	57	62	49
1983	55	59	48
1984	55	61	44
1985	57 (51)	65 (57)	46 (43)
1986	55 (50)	63 (56)	44 (41)
1987	55 (49)	63 (55)	44 (41)
1988	54 (48)	62 (54)	43 (40)
1989	54 (47)	62 (52)	44 (41)
1990	54 (48)	62 (54)	43 (40)
1991	56 (50)	63 (55)	47 (44)
1992	53 (47)	59 (51)	45 (43)

Figures in brackets denote financial membership. Prior to 1985, the ABS questionnaire did not distinguish financial and non-financial membership.
Source: Australian Bureau of Statistics *Trade Union Statistics Australia*, Catalogue No. 6323.0.

part-time, casual vs permanent; self-employed vs employee status); the level of unemployment; the political party in office; statutory provisions relating to union security; employer attitudes to union security; employee perceptions of union achievement; union recruitment activity and the public image or popularity of unionism. There is universal acceptance of the stimulating effect on union growth of the introduction of conciliation and arbitration in the early decades (as discussed in chapter 6) while there is a good deal of equivocation concerning the significance and nature of the net impact of variables such as the public standing of unions, and at least during the 1980s, the presence of Labor governments.[3]

In relation to the figures in Table 7.1, the most frequently cited explanations for the increasing density during the early 1970s have been the union security arrangements achieved by negotiation in the retail, banking and insurance industries and the increase in public sector employment, especially at Commonwealth level. This set of data shows the density to be stable from the mid-1970s to 1991, fluctuating within a narrow range of 54 to 57 per cent and in the case of the financial membership figures available since 1985, within the range 47 to 51 per cent. A different picture is provided by the data compiled from the ABS' periodic sample surveys of the Australian workforce and shown in

Table 7.2. The significantly higher figures obtained from the union questionnaires can be explained by double counting resulting from multiple union membership and by an understandable union preference for higher rather than lower figures, especially where uncertain financial status or employment status makes membership status ambiguous. Thus the figures in Table 7.2 probably provide the more reliable estimate of union density.

Table 7.2 Union Density Australia (ABS Surveys) (percentages)

	All employees	Male	Female
1976	51	56	43
1982	49	53	43
1986	46	50	39
1988	42	46	35
1990	41	45	35
1992	40	43	35

Source: Australian Bureau of Statistics, *Trade Union Members Australia*, Catalogue No. 6325.0; *Trade Union Members*, November 1976, Ref. No. 6.65.

The factors frequently identified to account for the steady decline in union density from the mid-1970s until the late 1980s are: changes in the occupational and gender composition of the workforce; the nature of employment contracts and the size of firms or workplaces as measured by number of employees. The workforce has expanded in areas with a lower propensity to unionise while contracting in areas with a higher propensity to unionise: growth in non-manual occupations in service industries in the private sector and a relative decline in employment in manufacturing and in the public sector.[4] The impact of the gender difference in propensity to unionise, in conjunction with the growth of female employment in industries and sectors with relatively low union density, is another generally accepted contributor to the decline of unionism. The gender-based difference remains, although the ABS workforce survey figures suggest a lesser gap than indicated from union questionnaire figures and both show a trend of a diminishing differential.[5] Another factor likely to have a negative effect on density levels is the high level of unemployment, peaking in 1983 at 10 per cent and again in 1992 at 10.5 per cent and fluctuating between 5 and 10 per cent during the period 1976 to 1992.[6]

The wide variations in density rates between occupational groups and between the public and private sectors are evident from Table 7.3 and Table 7.4 respectively.

The proportional increase in self-employed workers and in casual and part-time contracts[7] since the mid-1970s has had a negative impact on union density. ABS survey figures show density levels in the latter two categories to be significantly lower than for full-time employees: in August 1992 for example, the density level for casual employees was seventeen per cent and for part-time employees the level was twenty-five per cent.[8] This is due to both a presumed lesser interest in unions for employees under these contracts

Table 7.3 Union Density Australia by occupation and gender, August 1992 (ABS Survey) (percentages)

Occupation	All employees	Males	Females
Managers and administrators	18	18	20
Professionals	44	38	51
Para-professionals	54	57	52
Tradespersons	46	48	22
Clerks	32	48	26
Salespersons and personal service workers	27	21	31
Plant and machine operators and drivers	65	68	47
Labourers and related workers	44	46	39
All occupations	40	43	35

Source: Australian Bureau of Statistics, *Trade Union Members Australia*, Catalogue No. 6325.0.

Table 7.4 Union Density Australia: public sector and private sector (ABS Surveys) (percentages)

	Public sector	Private sector
1982	72.9	38.6
1986	70.6	34.5
1988	67.7	31.5
1990	66.8	30.8
1992	67.1	29.4

Source: Australian Bureau of Statistics, *Trade Union Members Australia*, Catalogue No. 6325.0.

and greater recruitment difficulties for unions. Barriers to organising (and perhaps a disinclination to organise) may also explain in part the negative effect on union density of the relative growth in recent decades of firms employing fewer employees.[9] Recent ABS surveys show a strong positive correlation between union density and the number of employees per firm as set out in Table 7.5. Employer resistance to unionism may be greater in smaller firms although this factor was not mentioned in the Shister growth model. Recruiting costs relative to returns will be greater for unions in the small business sector and employee loyalty to the firm is likely to be greater here than in large corporations.

Union density by state is shown in Table 7.6. The union security provision factor, or the significance of 'conscripts to unionism' to use Rawson's term, may account for the significant decline in union density in Western Australia where the power of the State's Industrial Commission to award union preference was removed in 1979. The reverse impact (not shown in table) occurred in South Australia following the legislature's granting of power to

Table 7.5 Union Density Australia by size of location (ABS Survey) (percentages)

Size of location (employees)	1990	1992
Less than 10	16.4	16.3
10—19	30.3	29.8
20—99	46.0	46.1
100 or more	58.2	57.6
Don't know	42.1	38.0

Source: Australian Bureau of Statistics, *Trade Union Members Australia*, Catalogue No. 6325.0.

award preference to the Industrial Conciliation and Arbitration Commission in 1971. Another important factor affecting the variation between states is industry composition.

Table 7.6 Union Density Australia by State (ABS Surveys) (percentages)

State	1976	1982	1986	1988	1990	1992
New South Wales	51	51	46	42	41	38
Victoria	50	48	46	42	41	41
Queensland	53	50	45	39	39	38
South Australia	50	50	47	46	45	44
Western Australia	50	46	41	37	35	37
Tasmania	60	58	55	52	52	51
Northern Territory	51	41	43	35	42	37
Australian Capital Territory	60	44	42	39	38	40

Source: Australian Bureau of Statistics, *Trade Union Members Australia*, Catalogue No. 6325.0; *Trade Union Members*, November 1976, Ref. No. 6.65.

A factor not mentioned above is the relationship between union density and the age distribution of employees. Australian unions are concerned about the level of union membership among young employees and, in recent years, the ACTU has launched a campaign to increase union membership among young people. The peak council has determined that the appropriate way to achieve this is to use union organisers from the same age group as the employees it is seeking to recruit to unions (see Table 7.7).

The decline in union density is all but universal in advanced capitalist societies. Australian unions have fared reasonably well by international standards, except for the Scandinavian countries.[10] Nonetheless the loss of union membership in Australia became part of the rationale for a union peak council policy designed to expedite a dramatic reduction in the number of unions. This is further considered below after a discussion of the historical patterns of organisation of Australian unions.

Patterns of organisation

The membership coverage or organising base of each Australian union is defined in its constitution, framed initially by the founders of the association but subject to approval by the industrial registrar, or the (now) Industrial Relations Court, as the case may be, at the time of registration. A registered union wishing to alter the conditions of eligibility for membership, or organising base, has been subject to the same legislative criteria and case law as that applying to the registration process (see chapter 12). For most of this century the court, at least in the federal jurisdiction, has been sympathetic to unionists wishing to create new organisations, granting registration to separate associations on a variety of grounds including: distinctive philosophy or ideology; preventing the swamping or neglect of particular (usually occupational) interests; ensuring unionists were brought 'within the system' given their preference to otherwise remain unrepresented; and the supervisory status of unionists. The decisions reflected judicial interpretation of, and judicial discretion permitted by, the 'conveniently belong' provision.[11]

The special factors in the origins of Australian unions have not, to date, conferred unusual characteristics on their organisational basis. The unions have fallen into three broad organisational categories: craft unions, industrial unions and general unions. Craft unions were the original form of union. They sought to enrol only workers of one particular skill, and, in the earliest times, they were concentrated in occupations with a relatively high level of skills. In the formative years of British unionism, the craft unionists, being the only people capable of training others in their skills, were able to control entry to the occupations they organised. By ensuring that there was rarely, if ever, a surplus of the skilled labour they organised, craft unionists could bid up wages, in effect profiting by using their monopoly power, rather than by using force to extract concessions from their employers. Originally most Australian unions were craft unions, but very few conform to the strict craft union form today. Most of the original craft unions have accepted members who work at similar or related occupations, and in instances in which a particular occupation dominates some industry, craft unions have often recruited in that industry without regard to the crafts of the workers concerned. Obviously, however, some, like the Association of Professional Engineers, the Seamen's Union and the Electrical Trades Union have retained something close to the single occupational basis of craft unions.

Industrial unions are the other major form of union. These seek to organise the workforces of entire industries, and do so without regard to occupational differences. Industrial unions were later to emerge than craft unions, and they developed in response to the growth of large mass production industries. The majority of factory workers in those industries did not have scarce skills which required long training periods and which were understood only by the craftsmen themselves. In these circumstances, they could not prosper by using the monopolistic tactic of restricting entry to the craft, thereby forcing up wages. If industrial unions were to benefit their members, they had to do so by direct confrontation with employers rather than by manipulation of the labour market. The strike was therefore an essential part of the industrial

Table 7.7 ACTU recruitment strategy for young employees

Youth seek union of relevance, reform

BY STEVE DOW

On the job... union recruiter Kelli Leach, 22, drums up support in a Melbourne supermarket – Picture: LYNDON MECHIELSEN

In the ACTU's fight to remain relevant in the rapidly changing industrial relations landscape and to reverse a sharp decline in membership, Kelli Leach represents new, young hope.

At 22, the union recruiter and former supermarket worker from rural Victoria believes unions will not only survive but also strengthen because of the cultural shift to enterprise bargaining, which the Government plans to open to non-unionists.

Such youthful enthusiasm is being taken very seriously by a trade union movement under pressure to face up to radical workplace reform. Early next month the ACTU congress is likely to adopt a proposal to form 'flying squads' of up to 200 young union recruiters aged 20 to 25 over the next two years.

It is a bid to bolster its flagging younger membership through peer pressure and may help dilute the Government's controversial plan to allow most of the workforce, which is not unionised, to strike workplace deals.

The 'flying squad' proposal was put by a group of Australian unionists after seeing a similar scheme in the United States on a study tour. But despite the fanfare, the idea is not new and has successfully been the province for several years of one union across Australia in department stores.

Ms Leach is a casual union organiser employed for the past six months by the Shop, Distributive and Allied Employees Association, which pioneered the scheme in Victoria about 13 years ago. She spends her Thursday and Friday nights and Saturday mornings liaising with members in shops and signing up new recruits.

The ACTU president, Mr Martin Ferguson, said when announcing the plan recently that unions in the past had made the 'bad practice' of waiting for people to join the movement.

Yesterday he predicted unions would remain strong in traditional areas such as the public sector, and in hospitality and mining, 'but in the growth industries, we have got to get in there'.

'We are not as strong as we should be in hospitality and clerical,' he said.

The new 'army' of union recruiters would be drawn from a wide variety of sources, with emphasis on hiring women and those from multicultural backgrounds, he said.

The plan has been criticised by the Victorian Employers Chamber of Commerce and Industry as a 'last ditch' attempt to recruit young workers who see no relevance in joining a union.

The chief executive officer of the VECCI, Mr David Edwards, said this type of recruitment tactic suggested 'union muscle' could be used on young workers, rather than educating them on the relevance of unions.

'Given the long-term decline in unionism, then the ACTU has a long road ahead of it to justify its relevance,' he said.

In the book What Should Unions Do?, edited by Michael Crosby and Michael Easson and published last year, the problems of measuring the fall in union membership are pinpointed by Don Rawson, an associate director of the Research School of Social Sciences at Australian National University.

He says that if the 'trade union statistics' series compiled by the Australian Bureau of Statistics and based on the unions' figures is used, during the past 15 years there has been a very small decline — from 55 per cent of the workforce in unions in 1976 to 5 per cent in 1990.

However, if the ABS 'trade union members' series is used, from a labour force sample, it charts consistent decline from 51 per cent in 1976 to 41 per cent in 1990 with a particularly steep fall from 46 to 42 per cent between 1986 and 1988.

Most people, he contends, find the members series more valid and accurate.

Ms Leach said the shop assistants' unions had remained strong because of the program of employing young union recruiters and she predicted more young people would elect to have unions represent them.

'I feel with the changes in industrial relations, that the trade unions will strengthen,' she said. 'People realise they deserve their entitlements and are willing to fight for those entitlements, and to maintain and improve their conditions.'

But the real task of the baby-faced recruiters is yet to come. The SDAEA has served a federal log of claims on the McDonald's food store chain, which has so far strongly resisted unionisation of its vast and growing workforce. The strength of peer pressure is about to be put to the test.

Source: *Weekend Australian*, 21-22 August, 1993, p. 4.

union's armoury, whereas craft unions had, in the nineteenth century, far less resort to it. The industrial union in pressing for concessions could apply pressure only by threatening to withdraw all labour from the employer. In the formative years of unionism in both Great Britain and the United States, the industrial unions which posed overt threats to managers and relied on direct coercive pressure, were generally seen as constituting a greater challenge to established authority than did the equally effective craft unions which used less visible tactics.

The third of the common forms of union is the general union. Its organising base is defined by neither occupation nor industry, but only by pragmatism. The general union will organise whatever is available to it, and usually comes into being as the consequence of the merging of other existing unions. Typically, general unions are large, as are the Australian Workers' Union and the Federated Miscellaneous Workers' Union, and their history often shows that they have been put together by the efforts of an outstanding unionist.[12] General unions often contain concentrations of particular occupations or industries, and these will reflect the interests of the founding organisations.

Enterprise unions have not been part of the traditional typology of union organising base, at least in Australia. This is due presumably to their rarity. Two examples of enterprise unions are the Commonwealth Bank Officers' Association and the Australian Broadcasting Corporation Staff Union. The latter union merged with a major public sector union, the then Administrative and Clerical Officers' Association, in 1988.

In Australia, the distinctions between craft, industrial and general unions have become blurred. Craft unions have tended to organise several occupations, and to show signs of organising industries. This was true for the Amalgamated Engineering Union which expanded its organising base beyond a limited number of skilled trades to cover most employees in the metals fabrication sector of manufacturing industry. As noted in chapter 6, in April 1991, as the AMWU, it amalgamated with the Association of Draughting, Supervisory and Technical Employees (ADSTE) to form the Metals and Engineering Workers' Union (MEWU). Similarly, the Vehicle Builders Employees Union (VBEU), an industry union, began as a craft union representing coach builders. Industrial unions have tended not to be confined to single industries, and it needs to be kept in mind that the boundaries of industries are far from precise. That is, the automobile industry may be defined by one observer as being the industry which manufactures automobiles. Another may feel it includes also the industries which manufacture automobile components, and another may argue that it includes as well the manufacture of trucks and other similar products. As there are many ways to define any industry, it is possible that industrial unions may want to define their sphere of operations broadly or narrowly. It is to be noted too that there are concepts of industry which are based not on the output of the industry, but on its inputs or processes. Concepts such as a 'Metals Industry', or a 'Food and Beverage Industry' clearly embrace very large sectors of industry. Unions which attempt to cover industries defined in this way have at least as much in common with general unions as they do with the industrial form. These problems are necessarily ignored in the 1987 ACTU policy on union amalgamations which groups affiliated unions in twenty 'industry' categories with diverse criteria for determining boundaries, for example: Road Transport; Local Government and Services; Building, Construction and Timber Products; Retail and Clerical; Banking and Insurance (see Table 7.11). These groupings reflected the governmental structure of the ACTU at that time.

The organising base of unions has very little effect on its behaviour. A union may be militant or otherwise in response to many factors, but its status as a craft, industrial or general union does not appear to be critical to that. General unions tend to be large, but they are not always bigger than industrial unions. The industrial relations tactics that are applied do sometimes owe something to union type. Craft unions often represent a minority of unionists at particular workplaces, and they may seek concessions that are distinct from those sought by unions representing the majority of workers. In some instances, small numbers of workers in strategic locations will seek to exploit that situation, and craft unions often have expertise in such tactics. The Federated Engine Drivers and Firemen's Association (FEDFA) was an example.

A proliferation of craft unions in Australia often means that there is more than one union in any workplace. It is commonly argued that this makes for particular difficulties in industrial relations negotiations and in changing work organisation. Some of these problems can be overcome if unions will agree to use forms of coalition bargaining, but the fact is that if more than one union is present, the likelihood exists that there will be inter-union quarrels over rights to particular kinds of work. These demarcation disputes[13] as they are called, can be particularly difficult to resolve, and often result in managements accepting undesirable staffing and work allocation to settle the disputes. These issues can sometimes expose a fundamental difference in philosophy and tactics between craft unions and the other forms.

While the differences between unions of differing forms have decreased over time, and are certainly much less than they were in the nineteenth century, it is still likely that craft unions see their members' prosperity as depending on different factors than do the industrial or general unions. Craft unions will usually see the survival of a particular skill or occupation as critical to survival and prosperity. Such unions will therefore often oppose changes in production methods or in products where such changes have the effect of reducing or making redundant the skills of their members. The well-being of the industrial union, on the other hand, is much more closely related to the well-being of the industry. The industrial unionist may not be too much concerned about the methods that an employer uses; that unionist will be concerned only to retain a job, and to ensure that the workforce shares in the prosperity of the industry resulting from any changes that are made. The craft unionist is more concerned with the production methods that are used than with the enhanced prosperity of the industry.

To the extent that union organising base does influence union industrial relations behaviour, craft unions are more likely to retard changes in methods and technology than other types. Either, of course, will resist changes that lead to reductions in the numbers of their members required on the job, and each will seek increased rewards for work that is more complex or unpleasant than it has been. The behavioural differences that have been apparent in the evolution of these union types have grown less over time.

Union mergers

Since the early 1980s a prevailing view among union and employer peak councils and the federal industrial tribunal has been that Australia has too many unions. The number of unions in Australia (see Table 7.8) and the complex patterns of organisation are the product of a permissive legal framework and the preferences of groups of workers for a separate organisational identity. The existence of separate state systems of industrial relations regulation has also contributed significantly to the number of unions: in 1986, for example, 187 of Australia's then 326 unions operated in only one state. This section provides an historical perspective on the issue of number of unions and union organising base as well as detailing recent developments in union policy and in legislation relating to union structure at the federal level.

Table 7.8 Trade Unions Australia: number of unions by size of union, 1986 and 1992

Size of Union (number of members)	June 1986 Number of unions	June 1986 Per cent total unions	June 1992 Number of unions	June 1992 Per cent total unions
Under 100	40	12.3	32	14.1
100 and under 250	40	12.3	26	11.5
250 and under 500	32	9.8	18	7.9
500 and under 1000	43	13.2	28	12.3
1000 and under 2000	45	13.8	21	9.3
2000 and under 3000	}39	}11.9	14	6.2
3000 and under 5000			16	7.0
5000 and under 10 000	23	7.0	19	8.4
10 000 and under 20 000	19	5.8	15	6.6
20 000 and under 30 000	12	3.7	7	3.1
30 000 and under 40 000	7	2.1	6	2.6
40 000 and under 50 000	10	3.1	5	2.2
50 000 and under 80 000	8	2.4	5	2.2
80 000 and over	8	2.4	7	3.1
100 000 and over	*	*	8	3.5
TOTAL	326	100.0	227	100.0

*Category not included in 1986 survey
Source: Australian Bureau of Statistics, *Trade Union Statistics, Australia*, Catalogue No. 6323.0.

Industrial unions, radical ideology and the formation of the ACTU

In the early decades of this century industrial unionism was seen by some union leaders as the means for realising the revolutionary objective of overthrowing the capitalist system via a general strike and replacing it with a system of worker control of industry. The unions which had supporters of this ideology and strategy included those representing miners, waterside workers and seamen. The organisational basis for the direct action strategy was to be a One Big Union. The internal structure of this union was to comprise six departments and thirty sub-departments each representing one major branch of production. Fisher discusses the intellectual origins of this strategy and the influence on Australian unions of the establishment of the International Workers of the World (the Wobblies) in Chicago in 1907.[14] Australia's One Big Union, the Workers' Industrial Union of Australia, was short-lived. Established in 1918, it failed to attract widespread support and only one department was established, the Mining Department comprising the Miners' Federation and the Barrier Miners. The latter were the unions at Broken Hill (see chapter 4 for an account of the 1919-1920 strike). Fisher identifies a number of reasons for the demise of the Workers Industrial Union of Australia within two years of its formation. First, there was resistance from established unions. The Australian Workers' Union was opposed to the existence of an alternative general union and there was opposition from craft unions for the reasons discussed above: the desire to retain their craft traditions and control through monopoly power. Secondly, there was resistance from those who benefited from the power and influence associated with the existing structural relationship between the industrial and political wings of the labour movement. Of relevance here was the intention of the supporters of the One Big Union concept to deny the importance of Labor parliamentarians. Thirdly, there were groups within the heterogeneous labour movement who found the explicit revolutionary objective unpalatable for religious or other reasons. Finally, and in Fisher's view perhaps decisively, for those vigorously supporting the radical industrial strategy there was a major diversion of energy into developing strategies for the Communist Party of Australia which was formed in 1920.[15]

Despite the failure of the One Big Union concept to materialise, support for industrial unionism as the sole organising principle for unions remained an influential school of thought within the labour movement. Hagan[16] argues the concept formed part of the inspiration for the creation of the ACTU in 1927. The establishment of the ACTU represented a compromise between the radical and reformist ideologies: for some groups, the ACTU was seen as facilitating a strategy with a focus on parliament and the arbitration system. In terms of Gardner's union strategy model, this meant the choice of the political arena for the pursuit of objectives and the choice of arbitration as a method of action. For other groups, it was seen as the means of developing the One Big Union. The constitution of the ACTU in 1927 included an objective of a gradual move to industry unionism (see Table 7.9). An expanded version of this objective became a priority goal of the union peak council in the late 1980s.

Table 7.9 Industrial unionism, ACTU Constitution May 1927

3. Methods
(a) The closer organisation of the workers by the transformation of the trade union movement from the craft to an industrial basis, by the establishment of one union in each industry.
(b) The consolidation of the Australian labour movement with the object of unified control, administration and action.
(c) The centralised control of industrial disputes.

Source: J. Hagan, *The History of the ACTU*, Longman Cheshire, Melbourne, 1981, Appendix.

Union mergers and public policy, 1972 and 1982

The matter of union amalgamations has been a public policy issue in Australia on two previous occasions, the early 1970s and the early 1980s, when the impetus came not from the ACTU but from non-Labor governments. Until 1972 the process of union mergers was not subject to public regulation. It was simply a private matter between unions and possibly union peak councils. At some point a merger would have required an application for deregistration of an existing organisation or an application for registration of a new association and this of course meant third party involvement, the Industrial Registrar or possibly the Court. External control of the union merger process began in the federal jurisdiction in 1972 when a Liberal-National government legislated what were generally regarded as exacting voting requirements for amalgamation: that more than half of the eligible memberships vote and that a majority of voters in each union vote in favour. These, and associated barriers, have been progressively lowered by Labor governments with amendments in 1974, 1983, 1988 and 1990. The 1972 legislation has been seen as a response to a then imminent amalgamation between the Amalgamated Engineering Union, the Boilermakers' and Blacksmiths' Society and the Sheet Metal Working and Agricultural Implement and Stove Making Industrial Union to form the Amalgamated Metal Workers' Union. These were each militant and effective unions and for those opposing the amalgamation it raised the spectre of excessive union power where power is presumed to correlate strongly with union size.[17]

In 1982, there was an abortive attempt by a Liberal-National government to legislate to encourage the restructuring of unions away from a craft or occupational base towards an industry base. The Bills,[18] promoted by a radical Minister for Industrial Relations, Ian Viner, also sought to remove the union preference power and strengthen tribunal powers in relation to stand-downs. The attempt to change organising bases followed a proposal to encourage company (enterprise) unionism which was shelved after strong union opposition. A Senate select committee, to which the Bill was referred, recommended against proceeding. The Bill had been intended to deal with perceived major problems allegedly caused by a large number of unions organised mainly on an occupational basis, including:

1. jurisdiction and demarcation disputes;
2. difficulties for employers in negotiations at either enterprise or industry level;
3. the inefficient use of the finite resources of unions;
4. union insensitivity to the needs of particular industries; and
5. encouragement of wage 'flow-ons' across industries without due regard for the appropriateness of this.

These perceived problems were cited in a number of submissions to the Senate committee.[19] A notable dissenting voice at this time was BHP (see Table 7.10). Many of the arguments presented in the early 1980s re-emerged in the late 1980s, when the vigorous promotion of a radical change in union structure by the ACTU began (see below). Fisher places the early 1980s debate about industrial unionism in ideological and historical context. By the 1980s industrial unionism reflected an 'industrial relations' school of thought, external to the labour movement, and embracing a commitment to 'harmony' in industry. Fisher links this with a 'social engineering' ethos, an assumption that:

> '... the existing economic and social arrangements are more or less right except for various `problems' which are there to be solved in the same way as an engineer might solve a problem in the design of a bridge or a piece of machinery. Industrial relations `problems' are often thought of in managerial terms concerning the efficiencies and inefficiencies of different ways of handling people as factors of production ... the behaviours, policies and forms of trade unionism then are assessed according to whether they promote `good' industrial relations or represent 'problems' for the social engineer to solve.[20]

Table 7.10 Some views on union mergers and industry unions, 1982

Department of Employment and Industrial Relations

The Government's policy on the formation of industry based unions is expressed in the Liberal Party and the National Country Party 1975 Employment and Industrial Relations Policy in the following terms:

> 'The Liberal and National Country Parties believe that industry–based unions would reduce the frequency and likelihood of industrial disputes. The multiplicity of unions in some industry fields made (sic) the task of negotiation and consultation more difficult. Industry unions would be better placed to communicate with employer organizations and Government departments and we would seek to discuss this matter with the union movement.' (p.37)

Difficulties arising within Australian industry as a result of the present Australian trade union structure, include:

- demarcation disputes between unions with overlapping eligibility for membership rules;
- inefficient use of the finite resources available to Australian trade unions from what are presently often small and fragmented memberships;
- problems in negotiations between employers and trade unions as to terms and conditions of employment arising from the multiplicity of trade unions not only within an industry but often a particular enterprise;
- lack of identification by trade unions which have a membership in several industries with the interests of a given industry;
- rigidity in the structure of an industry's workforce arising from the understandable reluctance of unions to accept workers moving from their area of coverage to that of other unions within the industry;
- the possibility of flow-on of wage levels appropriate to one industry to another industry without proper consideration of their appropriateness in the context of the second industry; and
- the possibility of wage leap–frogging within an industry resulting from the multiplicity of trade unions. (pp.38–39)

Australian Council of Trade Unions

It is sometimes claimed that the present structure of trade union organisation in Australia contributes to a number of problems including

- problems in negotiations where an employer has to deal with several or many different unions representing employees;
- the limited resources of small unions restricts the range of services offered to members

> and, in some cases, hinders the effective representation of workers in the conciliation and arbitration system; and
> - competition between unions for membership leading to demarcation and jurisdictional disputes. (pp. 87–88)
>
> Although there is some support in Australia for the concept of 'industry union', there are enormous definitional problems as well as practical problems in the way of any general re-organisation of trade union structures in this country along industry lines. Indeed *the main objection to the proposed legislation designed to encourage the creation of industry based unions in Australia is a practical one.* A move toward industrial unionism (that is, one union for all employees in the same industry regardless of occupation) would involve a drastic change in trade union organisation given the present craft or occupational basis of most unions. To achieve genuine industry unions it would be necessary to slice off sections of existing unions and to put them into new unions. Such actions would be strongly resisted by unions and their members and would be impossible to achieve without massive coercion. (pp. 96–97)
>
> ### *Amalgamated Metal Workers' and Shipwrights' Union*
>
> The general policy of the A.M.W.S.U. has been aimed at achieving a single metal industry union and to that end the union has actively pursued its policy by endeavouring to seek and encourage amalgamation with unions having a majority of members employed in what can loosely be defined as the metal industry.
>
> This policy has been singularly successful in creating the A.M.W.S.U. and currently an amalgamation ballot will be held in September of members of the Moulders' Union. Proposals for amalgamation with the Federated Engine Drivers and Firemen's Association have also been agreed to. However, these have not proceeded to ballot because of the restrictive nature of the provisions of the Act relating to union amalgamations, particularly the requirement that 50% plus one of the union's members must vote in order for any result to be obtained. (pp. 110–111)
>
> The A.M.W.S.U. believes that existing unions have eligibility and industry provisions broad enough to cover all classes of employees in either a craft, occupational or industry basis and that no further registration of unions should be facilitated except where it is a result of an amalgamation of existing organisations. (p. 111)
>
> Source: C. Fisher, *Industrial Unionism: Some Documents*, Research School of Social Sciences, ANU, Canberra, 1983.

Table 7.10 provides a sample of extracts from the submissions to the Senate select committee in 1982. These supplement Fisher's analysis and, in the case of the ACTU, foreshadow the position adopted in 1987. The extracts need to be read in context, that is, as extracts from submissions or views concerning 1982 proposals for changes in the federal law relating to union structure by the then Liberal-National government.

1987: a policy offensive

In September 1987 the ACTU, under the intellectual leadership of secretary Bill Kelty, launched a publication entitled *Future Strategies for the Trade Union Movement*. A centrepiece of this document is a program for union amalgamations, specifically, a proposal for discussion emanating from an ACTU Executive suggestion in March 1987 that the union movement plan the establishment of about twenty union groupings. These would then act as a catalyst for union amalgamation and co-operation.[21] The proposed groupings are listed in Table 7.11.

Table 7.11 ACTU: proposed industry groupings 1987 (Draft program for amalgamation)

1   Textile, Clothing, Footwear

    To formally establish a TCF Federation.
    To assist in the processes of amalgamation between the TCF unions.

2   Shipping and Stevedoring

    Formally to establish a Stevedoring and Maritime Industry Federation.

3   Rail and Tramway

    To consider the possibilities of amalgamation between the Rail and Tramway Unions.

4   Road Transport

    To assist in the amalgamation of unions within the transport sector, to forge an alliance of all Road, Rail and Air Transport Workers.

5   Food and Transport

    To assist in the amalgamation of the FSPU/Rubber Workers.
    To assist amalgamation between the Millers/Manufacturing Grocers.
    To promote the amalgamation further between the Food Unions, including the FSPU.

6   Airline Industry

    Establish an Airline Industry Federation.

7   A.P.S.F.

    To continue recognition of A.P.S.F. To have further discussion between the A.P.S.F. and other unions.

8   Education

    To establish an Education Federation consisting of all unions in the Education sector as a forum for discussing amalgamation.

9   Post and Telecommunications

    To assist in the process of amalgamation between:
    ATEA
    Telephonists
    APTU
    Other Postal/Technical Grades

10 Printing and Publishing

    To assist in the process of amalgamation of Printing Unions.

11 Local Government and Services

    To assist in the process of amalgamation between:
    MOA
    Technical and Service Guild
    MEU
    Other State or Local Unions

12 Large Union Amalgamation

    Discussions of the possibility of large unions amalgamating such as the AWU, FLAIEU and FMWU. These unions are also considering a range of further amalgamation options.

13 *Australian Government*

To promote amalgamtion between:
ACOA
APSA
POA
Other unions in APS

14 *Building, Construction and Timber Products*

Immediate objectives:

(a) Formally establish a Building Trades Federation consisting of all unions currently in Building Group.
(b) Cement amalgamations being discussed:

— BWIU/FEDFA
— Carpenters & Joiners, PPWFA and Timber Workers

(c) Seeking to organise through the Building Trades Group further discussion on amalgamation.

15 *Retail and Clerical*

The unions with members in the Retail and Clerical industries further to consider amalgamation within those industries and other sectors.

16 *Banking and Insurance*

Establish a Finance Union Council with membership from CBOA, AIEU, ABEU, Trustee Company Officers.

17 *Health Industry*

Immediate objectives:

1 To assist HEF/HREA in their endeavours to amalgamate.
2 To consider the possibility of futher developing a federation of health unions.
3 Through regular meetings of the Health Industry Group to consider means of promoting greater co-operation between the unions representing nurses.

18 *Metal Industry*

1 Formally to recognise the Metal Trades Federation.
2 To establish a Vehicle Industry Federation.
3 To assist in amalgamation discussions between all the unions in the industry.

Source: ACTU, *Future Strategies for the Trade Union Movement*, September 1987, pp. 50-54.

In the Strategies document, a reduction in the number of unions is held to be a necessary condition for the provision of improved, and more diverse, services to union members. The improved services, together with improvements in recruitment practices and the marketing of unions, will contribute both to the retention of existing members and the attraction of new members. The objective is to arrest and reverse the decline in union density. The report analyses the adverse trends in union density and expresses particular concern with the decline in the unionisation of young workers, reinforced by ACTU research findings that many young people are fearful of unions and critical of their priorities. The report asserts that most Australian unions provide an inadequate level of service. This claim would be more persuasive had it been substantiated by research and particularly by obtaining the views of members. A consideration of the distribution of Australia's then 326 unions by number of members (see Table 7.8) led the ACTU to conclude that it was obvious that Australia had too many unions.

The report advocates the provision of a high level of service both industrially and in a broader social context. In respect of the former, there is support for a concern with a broader range of 'quality-of-working life' issues. These include job security; family leave; participation in decision-making processes; occupational health and safety and investment decisions.[22] The 'broader social context' presumably refers to other union objectives, included in the following statement of purpose:

> 'The basic philosophy of the trade union movement has always involved a combination of the pragmatic and the ideal. It supports peace as an international objective, the pursuit of membership claims for improvements in wages and working conditions, greater job security, more satisfying employment, and the capacity to retire with an acceptable level of income security. In summary, the union movement is about reducing inequalities in society with the aim of reducing and eventually eliminating poverty. At the same time it seeks to make a major contribution to the creation of wealth through development of the economy'.[23]

The ACTU rationale for its 1987 policy relies heavily on an efficiency argument, supplemented by a less strongly articulated premise concerning union purpose. The notion of efficiency relates to the quality of services to members and presumes that small unions are invariably inefficient. The argument is that unions are under-resourced for two reasons, the large number of small unions and the low levels of union subscriptions, which should be increased to one per cent of the relevant award rate. It is asserted, for there is no supporting evidence, resources are wasted because of the inefficient structure of the union movement and resources could 'be put to much better use through the economies of scale possible with larger, better resourced unions.'[24] The improved funding base would facilitate the establishment of fighting funds to provide membership support during major disputes and enable provision of training services to members.[25]

The ACTU argues that an adequate level of industrial representation has not been possible because there are insufficient full-time officials. There is too much reliance on unpaid, untrained and over-worked lay officials and very few unions have adequate research staff. No exceptions are acknowledged in this anecdotal evidence and no optimum size (or range) is identified. An uncomplicated and universal relationship between union size and union effectiveness is assumed. There were clearly noteworthy exceptions here, Australian unions of less than 10 000 members or even less than 5000 members, which have been eminently successful in 'bringing home the bacon' for their members, some operating as quiet achievers in the process. They include the Waterside Workers' Federation of Australia (7000 members), the Food Preservers Union (about 8500 members), the Seamen's Union of Australia (5331 members), the Ambulance Employees' Association of Victoria (1640 members).[26] Table 7.8 (see above) shows that in June 1986 there were 61 unions in Australia with a membership between 5000 and 40 000 so there may have been others where membership satisfaction with union services and achievement was high. A comparative analysis of the performance of unions of varying size or surveys of membership views have not been part of any published material advocating fewer unions.

The union peak council argument begs the question of union purpose. The ACTU view concerning union purpose can be found in the concept of 'strategic unionism', discussed in *Australia Reconstructed*,[27] on which its union structure policy is predicated. In behavioural terms, strategic unionism means *inter alia* trade union acceptance of a high degree of responsibility for national economic performance and pursuit of the social wage and social equity. The former objective means trade union participation in planning of both economic policy and industry policy. The objectives also illustrate the labourist, or social reform, tradition of Australian unions (see chapter 6). The diverse characteristics of 'strategic unionism' extend to other dimensions, for example 'extensive delivery of research and education services' and 'strong local and workplace organisation'. It is argued 'strategic unionism' is not effective without an increase in central co-ordination and a reduction in the number of unions.[28]

It is noteworthy that there is great diversity in the number of unions in countries with whom Australia is usually compared. The former West Germany had about twenty but this structure was not a natural development: it was imposed by a post-war military government and one objective of the structure was to create a countervailing power to business with the object of preventing a resurgence of Nazism. Japan has thousands of unions (73 000) with enterprise unions the dominant structural form. Levine argues that given the strong internal labour markets existing at the time of external promotion of unionisation in Japan, again by a post-war military government, unions had to be at the enterprise level to be effective.[29]

Policy refinement: union rationalisation

The 1989 ACTU Congress reaffirmed the 1987 policy premise that union restructuring was central to improving the capacity of the union movement to deliver a greater range and level of services to members and to recruit in areas of employment growth. The 1989 policy established a link between union restructuring and award restructuring: the current structure, reflecting the narrow, occupationally based, constitutional coverage of many unions, had contributed to the problems inherent in the classification structures in existing awards. The policy introduced a new objective, that of union rationalisation. This was justified on the above grounds and also on the basis that inter-union rivalry, a consequence of overlapping membership territories, reduced the capacity of unions to resist anti-union tactics used by employers, for example, 'exemption rates' and other devices whereby employees are appointed to so called 'union free-staff positions'.[30] The Congress therefore supported the active promotion of 'the rationalisation by agreement of union coverage with the aim of significantly reducing the number of unions within each enterprise or industry. Such unions may be occupationally based or industry based.'[31]

The centre-piece of this policy is the creation of three categories of union: 'principal', 'significant' and 'other'. The criteria relating to each category are

Table 7.12 Union rationalisation: ACTU categories 1991

A Principal union—A Principal union shall have the capacity to recruit all employees in a given industry or, in certain cases, defined occupational category and shall recognise significant and other unions in the industry or occupational category and seek to reach agreement with them as to membership coverage and recruitment. Where an existing Principal union has failed to service the needs of the workforce principal status is to be reviewed by the ACTU Executive.

A Significant union—A Significant union is one which has:

i) a substantial number of members in an industry or occupation
ii) agreed to be part of a single bargaining unit with the Principal union
iii) the capacity to maintain and recruit membership provided that, by agreement with the Principal union or unions, a Significant union may be able to recruit membership beyond its existing area of coverage with a view to maximising unionisation; or

Other unions–Other unions do not have a substantial number of members. They may be able to maintain membership on the following basis:

i) they represent those employees who desire to have the union represent them
ii) they will not stand in the way of any employee wishing to join the Principal union
iii) they agree to be part of a single bargaining unit
iv) they service the membership
v) the continuation of award coverage shall be subject to periodic reviews

Source: *ACTU Policies and Strategies as adopted at the 1991 ACTU Congress*, Melbourne, September 9-13, 1991, p. 122.

set out in Table 7.12. The ACTU determines the status of individual unions: a union granted 'principal union' status may extend its membership beyond its constitutional coverage and a union granted 'significant union' status may do likewise if there is no 'principal union' and is so authorised by the ACTU.[32]

The policy advocates that the process of rationalisation of union coverage should occur by agreement between unions with active assistance from the ACTU and with arbitration as a last resort. Further, the terms of any rationalisation should not be dictated or determined by employers and/or governments and consideration is to be given to the wishes of workers concerned and to the occupational nature of their organisation. The primary aim of the rationalisation policy is to reduce the number of unions in each industry and to develop structures enabling inter-union co-operation to extend union coverage to non-unionised sections of the workforce.[33]

The complementary legislation

Unlike the situation in 1982, when the ACTU was not consulted about proposed changes in legislation relating to union structure, legislative changes in 1988 and 1990 were the product of the close alliance between the federal government and the union peak council. The amendments were designed to

1 facilitate union amalgamations;
2 enable involuntary deregistration of small unions;
3 heighten existing barriers to registration of new unions; and
4 increase tribunal powers to determine membership coverage of particular unions.

Amalgamations were facilitated by less onerous voting requirements. Prior to 1988 the legislation required that, in each organisation, at least 50 per cent of eligible members voted and that more than 50 per cent of formal votes favoured amalgamation.[34] The new provisions required only that more than 50 per cent of formal votes supported an amalgamation where a 'community of interest' was declared and in the absence of this there was an additional requirement that at least 25 per cent of eligible members voted.[35] These changes were complemented by reduced opportunities for objections to amalgamations.[36] The then Minister for Industrial Relations, Ralph Willis, said it was widely accepted that Australia had too many unions and small craft-based unions could not effectively represent members' interests due to their limited human and financial resources. Further, small unions could often be seen as inhibiting change in the context of the co-operative approach to industrial relations designed to improve industry and enterprise productivity.[37] Prior to 1988, a union seeking registration required at least 100 members who were 'employees engaged in an industrial pursuit or pursuits ...'[38] There was also the long-standing 'conveniently-belong' provision granting the Registrar discretion to refuse registration if there was already registered an organisation to which members of the applicant might conveniently belong.[39] In 1988, a union seeking registration was required to have a minimum of 1000 members and to be industry-based, unless the Commission was satisfied special circumstances existed justifying registration of craft or occupationally-based associations. Further, the discretion of the Registrar to register a new union notwithstanding the existence of an organisation to which members of the applicant union could conveniently belong, was removed. The Commission was empowered to review the registration of organisations with less than 1000 members, to determine whether their continued registration was justified.[40] The rationale for these changes was to encourage smaller unions to actively pursue amalgamation as they had lagged behind the larger unions in seeking suitable amalgamation partners.[41]

The final change significant for union structure enabled the Commission to grant coverage to a union which the union previously did not have.[42] This extension of power was in the context of a new provision relating to demarcation disputes. Prior to 1988, the Commission did have power to deprive a union of its representation rights,[43] thus the 1988 Act extended tribunal powers over union coverage. The Minister for Industrial Relations expressed government support for moves to rationalise union coverage arrangements where necessary on individual projects and worksites. This reflected government recognition that for some enterprises and projects the continued or potential presence of a multiplicity of unions was a major impediment to higher efficiency and a discouragement to future investment.[44]

In 1990, two new objects were included in the *Industrial Relations Act*: 'to encourage and facilitate the amalgamation of organisations; and to 'encourage and facilitate the development of organisations, particularly by reducing the number of organisations that are in an industry or enterprise'.[45] These objects are to be taken and applied together. Introducing the Bill, the then Minister for Industrial Relations, Senator Peter Cook, emphasised the accommodative function of trade unions in the process of micro-economic reform. The government saw industrial relations as having a key role in this reform, specifically, trade unions choosing to participate in the national industrial relations system had to have the capacity for constructive participation in reform and this depended to a crucial degree on the relevance of their structure. The Minister cited five economic reports to various governments each of which concluded that industrial and administrative efficiency was impeded by the multiplicity of unions. He claimed the union movement recognised the need to rationalise along broad industry lines and to avoid complicating the reform process by involvement of numerous unions in the requisite negotiations. It was held that sharing in the benefits of economic restructuring was clearly in workers' interests and these benefits would be maximised if their unions had the capacity and organisation to identify more closely with the interests of individual industries and enterprises.[46] The amalgamation provisions were telescoped to expedite the amalgamation process. Further, there was a change to the Commission approved exemption from the conduct of a ballot: previously there was no requirement for a ballot in an organisation if the membership of the other, smaller organisation did not exceed five per cent of the total membership. In 1990 this figure was increased to twenty-five per cent.[47] Another significant change enabled the committee of management of an organisation to use the union's funds and other resources to support a proposed amalgamation up to the close of the ballot.[48]

The minimum number of members required for registration was increased to 10 000 unless special circumstances could be established[49] and a second stage was added to the review of registration of small unions: a review of unions with fewer than 10 000 members was to commence in 1993.[50] Factors identified by the Minister as potentially relevant to the Commission's deliberations regarding survival of small unions were :

(i) the absence of another union which could properly represent employee interests in a particular industry;
(ii) the industrial or economic consequences of deregistration particularly if the small union is the major union in the industry or sector; and
(iii) where appropriate, the views of the workers affected as to how their industrial interests should be represented.[51]

This review process was suspended in June 1993[52] as a consequence of an ILO decision in November 1992 which held that the minimum membership provision contravened the ILO convention on freedom of association. (This aspect is further discussed in chapter 8.) Subsequently, the entire process was cancelled[53] with the passage of the *Industrial Relations Reform Act* 1993 which also changed the minimum membership requirement for an association of employees seeking registration to 100 members.[54] Such associations will of course still be required to satisfy the designated Presidential Member that there is no existing registration union to which members of the applicant could conveniently belong.[55]

Finally in 1990, the Commission's power to adjust a union's representative rights by making those rights exclusive, removing them or conferring them was extended from the prevention and settlement of demarcation disputes to disputes generally.[56] Agreed changes to union coverage would continue to be accommodated here. In the exercise of this power the government considered the new object relating to the development of organisations to be especially relevant although the objects of the Act as a whole were to be considered.[57] The government's rationale for the 1990 changes appeared consistent with the 'social engineering' ethos and commitment to 'harmony in industry' discussed by Fisher in the early 1980s (see above).

The union amalgamation and rationalisation activity, when it is union activated and controlled, provides an example of the pursuit of institutional objectives in the interests of future membership objectives. In the short run it may mean a diversion of union resources away from current membership interests: negotiations concerning amalgamation can be lengthy and complex. They can also generate intra-union conflict, as occurred for example in the Transport Workers' Union during 1991 when the Victorian Branch successfully opposed a planned amalgamation with the National Union of Workers which was supported by the federal leadership and other Branches.[58]

The decline in the number of unions and the accelerating rate of decline since 1990, is illustrated in Table 7.13. The total number of unions declined by thirty per cent between 1986 and 1992. The thirty-three per cent rate of decline in the number of unions operating in two or more States (federal unions) was slightly higher than the rate of decline in the number of unions operating in one State only (twenty-eight per cent). The latter group is unaffected by the changes in the federal legislation, although they are unlikely to be immune from political pressures within inter-union forums. Some indication of the transformation of the map of Australian unions is provided in Table 7.14 (see appendix) which provides details of amalgamations finalised in the federal jurisdiction between January 1992 and June 1993. It remains to be seen whether the emergence of a greater number of large unions and the corollary of fewer unions will increase union power in accord with the popular view that power correlates positively with size. It will of course be difficult to isolate this variable because of the many factors which influence union power[59] and the need to distinguish industrial power and political power.

Table 7.13 Number of unions, Australia 1986–1992

	Federal (more than one State)	Single State	Total
1986	139	187	326
1987	136	180	316
1988	131	177	308
1989	131	168	299
1990	127	168	295
1991	119	156	275
1992	93	134	227

Source: ABS *Trade Union Statistics, Australia*, Catalogue. No. 6323.0.

Conclusion

For most of the twentieth century, trade unionism has been a majority movement in this country, with Australia at times among the world leaders in union density levels. ABS surveys indicate however that unionism has been below fifty per cent since the early 1980s. Many of the factors commonly presented to explain the recent decline in unionisation were included in the early model of union growth developed by Shister in the United States.

Despite the decline in union density, Australian unions had the potential to exercise considerable political power during the 1980s due to the prevalence of Labor governments at times when the market context for most unions was unfavourable. Some of the results of the favourable 'power context' were discussed in the previous chapter.

The dominant organising base for Australian unions has been occupation, or more commonly, groups of occupations. Since the early 1980s there has been an accelerating interest in 'industry' unions although the boundaries of industries are far from precise and there are varying concepts of industry. Some are based on outputs and some are based on inputs or processes. It seems too, that many of the newly amalgamated so-called industry unions may have as much in common with general, or conglomerate, unions as they do with the industry form. In the early decades of this century the links, and perceived links, between union organising base and union behaviour were very different from those prevailing since the 1980s. Early moves to create industry unions were associated with radicalism, including notions of over-throwing the capitalist order. Further, the matter of union structure was predominantly privatised, residing largely with unions. Since the late 1980s, the issue has emerged in an engulfing public policy which proclaims union structure as a vital factor in the nation's economic performance and with the law functioning as a major catalyst for change.

Declining density levels and the existence of a large number of small, allegedly inefficient, unions provided the impetus to what has become the virtual nationalisation of union structure. From the late 1980s to the early 1990s the changes sought in union structure became associated with objectives extending beyond the initial desire for more effective representation of members' interests to the need for unions to accommodate micro-economic reform. Supporters of this objective argue that union organising base and union size are a barrier to:

1 union-employer co-operation geared to improving productivity and investment; and
2 the development of unions' capacity to identify more closely with the interests of individual industries and enterprises.

The result of the policy offensive has been dramatic change in the external structure of unions. The changes in the law in January 1994, enabling small unions to seek registration and abolishing the review of existing small registered unions by the Commission, are unlikely to have any impact in the short run. The interpretation of the 'conveniently-belong' provision will be important in the longer term.

The recent changes in external structure may be accompanied by changes in the internal structure and relations of the 'new' unions. Such changes are matters for future research but the important issue of the internal relations of trade unions, the relationship between the leadership and the rank and file members, is the subject of the next chapter.

Notes

1. J. Shister, 'The logic of union growth', *Journal of Political Economy 61*, 1953, pp. 413-433.
2. G.S. Bain and R. Price, *Profiles of Union Growth: A Comparative Statistical Portrait of Eight Countries*, Basil Blackwell, Oxford, 1980, chapter 5.
3. For one discussion of the determinants of growth patterns in Australia see D.W. Rawson, *Unions and Unionists in Australia*, Allen & Unwin, Sydney, (1st ed.) 1978, chapter 2; (2nd ed.) 1986, chapter 3.
4. ABS, *Labour Statistics Australia*, Catalogue No. 6101.0.
5. For a discussion of union membership and gender see J. Benson and G. Griffin, 'Gender differences in union attitudes, participation and priorities', *Journal of Industrial Relations 30*, June 1988, pp. 203-214.
6. ABS, *Labour Statistics Australia*, Catalogue No. 6101.0.
7. ibid. See also P. Dawkins and K. Norris, 'Casual Employment in Australia', *Australian Bulletin of Labour 16*, September 1990, pp. 156-171.
8. ABS, *Trade Union Members Australia*, Catalogue No. 6325.0.
9. ABS, *Manufacturing Establishments selected items of data classified by industry and employment size 1975-86; Manufacturing Industry Selected Items of Data by Employment Size 1986-89*, Catalogue No. 8204.0.
10. See for example density levels for nine countries compiled by the OECD in G.J. Bamber and R. D.Lansbury (eds), *International and Comparative Industrial Relations* (2nd ed.), Allen & Unwin, Sydney, 1993, p. 310.
11. See chapter 6, note 40.
12. For some information on the development of the AWU from the occupational Amalgamated Shearers' Union of Australasia see C. Cameron, *Unions in Crisis*, Hill of Content, Melbourne, 1982, chapter 4.
13. For a detailed discussion of demarcation and jurisdictional disputes see K. Wright, 'Union Demarcation Disputes', in B. Ford and D. Plowman (eds), *Australian Unions-An Industrial Relations Perspective* (1st ed.), Macmillan, Melbourne, 1983, pp. 325-343.
14. C. Fisher, *Industrial Unionism: Some Documents*, Research School of Social Sciences, ANU, Canberra, 1983, pp. 6-10.
15. *ibid.*, pp. 9-10.
16. J. Hagan, *The History of the ACTU*, Longman Cheshire, Melbourne, 1981, chapter 1.
17. This view was put forward during the parliamentary debate on the Conciliation and Arbitration Bill 1972.
18. Conciliation and Arbitration Amendment Bill 1982 and Commonwealth Employees (Voluntary Membership of Unions) Bill 1982.
19. Some of the submissions are included as appendices in Fisher *op. cit.*
20. *ibid.*, p. 12.
21. ACTU, *Future Strategies for the Trade Union Movement*, September 1987, p. 50.
22. *ibid.*, pp. 12-18.

23 *ibid.*, p. 1.
24 *ibid.*, p. 19.
25 *ibid.*, pp. 19-20.
26 These are 1991 figures from *Industrial Relations Index: A Guide to Unions, Employer Groups and the Industrial Relations Industry*, Edition 7, November 1991-March 1992, Information Australia, Melbourne.
27 Department of Trade, *Australia Reconstructed*, Canberra, AGPS, 1987, p. 169.
28 *ibid.*, p. 190.
29 S. Levine, 'Japanese Industrial Relations: An External Perspective', in Y. Sugimoto, H. Shimada and S. Levine, *Industrial Relations in Japan*, Papers of the Japanese Studies Centre, Monash University, November 1982, pp. 48-50.
30 *ACTU Policies and Strategy Statements Adopted by ACTU Congress September 1989*, October 1989, p. 81.
31 *ibid.*, p. 82.
32 ACTU, *Policies and Strategies as adopted at the 1991 ACTU Congress*, Melbourne, September 9–13, 1991, p. 123.
33 *ibid.*, pp. 122-123.
34 *Conciliation and Arbitration Act* s.158N.
35 *Industrial Relations Act 1988* s.246. (No. 86 of 1988).
36 *Conciliation and Arbitration Act*, s.158H; *Industrial Relations Act*, 1988 s.241. (No. 86 of 1988).
37 Australia, *Parliamentary Debates*, House of Representatives, vol. 161, 28 April 1988, p. 2335.
38 *Conciliation and Arbitration Act*, s.132 (1) (c).
39 *ibid.*, s.142.
40 *Industrial Relations Act*, 1988, ss 189 (1) (c) (d) and (j) and 193.
41 Australia, *Parliamentary Debates*, House of Representatives, vol. 161, 28 April 1988, pp. 2335-2336.
42 *Industrial Relations Act 1988*, s.118 (3) (b).
43 *Conciliation and Arbitration Act*, s.142A.
44 Australia, *Parliamentary Debates*, House of Representatives, vol. 161, 28 April 1988, p. 2338.
45 *Industrial Relations Act 1988*, s.3 (j) & (k) inserted by *Industrial Relations Legislation Amendment Act 1990*.
46 Australia, *Parliamentary Debates*, Senate, 23 August 1990, p. 2079.
47 *Industrial Relations Act*,1988 s.253G amended by *Industrial Relations Legislation Amendment Act 1990*.
48 *ibid.* s.237 amended by *Industrial Relations Legislation Amendment Act 1990*.
49 *ibid.*, s.189 (1) (c) amended by *Industrial Relations Legislation Amendment Act 1990*.
50 *ibid.*, s.193A inserted by *Industrial Relations Legislation Amendment Act 1990*.
51 Australia, *Parliamentary Debates*, Senate, 23 August 1990, p. 2080.
52 *The Age*, 18 June 1993, p. 3.
53 Sections 193 and 193A of the *Industrial Relations Act 1988* were repealed by s.76 of the *Industrial Relations Reform Act 1993*.
54 *Industrial Relations Act 1988*, s.189(1)(c) as amended by *Industrial Relations Reform Act 1993*, s.75.
55 *ibid.*, s.189 (l)(j).
56 *Industrial Relations Act 1988*, s.118A inserted by *Industrial Relations Legislation Amendment Act 1990*.
57 Australia, *Parliamentary Debates*, Senate, 23 August 1990, p. 2082.
58 *The Age*, 1 January 1992, p. 1.
59 For a discussion of these see N.F. Dufty and C. Mulvey, *The Sources of Union Power*, Australian Institute for Public Policy, Perth, 1987 and G.S. Bain and R. Price, *Profiles of Union Growth: A Comparative Statistical Portrait of Eight Countries*, Basil Blackwell, Oxford, 1980, pp. 160-162.

Further Reading

Union growth and union density

Australian Bureau of Statistics, *Trade Union Members Australia*, Catalogue No. 6325.0.

Australian Bureau of Statistics, *Trade Union Statistics Australia*, Catalogue No. 6323.0.

G.S. Bain and R. Price, *Profiles of Union Growth: A Comparative Statistical Portrait of Eight Countries*, Basil Blackwell, Oxford 1980, chapters 5 and 10.

J.Benson and G. Griffin, 'Gender differences in union attitudes, participation and priorities', *Journal of Industrial Relations 30*, June 1988, pp. 203-214.

C. Cregan, C. Rudd and S. Johnson, 'Young People and Trade Union Membership', *The Economic and Labour Relations Review 3*, December 1992, pp. 165-179.

G. Griffin, 'White-collar unionism, 1969 to 1981: some determinants of growth', *Journal of Industrial Relations 25*, March 1983, pp. 26-37.

J.D. Hill, 'Australian Union Density Rates 1976-1982', *Journal of Industrial Relations 26*, December 1984, pp. 435-450.

R.D. Lansbury, 'The growth and unionisation of white-collar workers in Australia: some recent trends', *Journal of Industrial Relations 19*, March 1977, pp. 34-49.

R. M. Martin, 'Legal Enforcement of Union Security in Australia', in J.E. Isaac and G.W. Ford, (eds), *Labour Relations: Readings* (2nd ed.), Sun Books, Melbourne, 1971, pp. 166-191.

R.M. Martin, 'Class Identification and Trade Union Behaviour: The Case of the Australian White-Collar Unions', in J.E. Isaac and G.W. Ford (eds), *Labour Relations Readings* (2nd ed.), Sun Books, Melbourne, 1971, pp. 245-263.

D.W. Rawson, *Unions and Unionists in Australia*(1st ed.), Allen and Unwin, Sydney, 1978, chapter 2, (2nd ed.) 1986, chapter 3.

J. Shister, 'The logic of union growth', *Journal of Political Economy 61*, 1953, pp. 413-433.

Patterns of organisation and union mergers

ACTU, *Future Strategies for the Trade Union Movement*, September 1987.

ACTU, *Policies and Strategy Statements Adopted by ACTU Congress September 1989*, October 1989.

ACTU, *Policies and Strategies as adopted at the 1991 ACTU Congress*, Melbourne, September 9-13, 1991.

Business Council of Australia, *Enterprise-Based Bargaining Units—A Better Way of Working*, Report to the Business Council of Australia by the Industrial Relations Study Commission, Volume 1, Melbourne, July 1989, chapters 3, 4 and 5.

Business Council of Australia, 'The Pattern of Union Representation in Business Council Workplaces: 1988-1992', *Business Council Bulletin*, No. 96, April 1993, pp. 34-37.

M. Costa and M. Duffy, 'Trade Union Strategies in the 1990s', *The Economic and Labour Relations Review 1*, June 1990, pp. 145-164.

B. Ellem, 'Solidarity in the Nineties? An analysis of the ACTU Blueprint and the Costa/Duffy Critique', *The Economic and Labour Relations Review 2*, December 1991, pp. 90-113.

C. Fisher, *Industrial Unionism: Some Documents*, Research School of Social Sciences, A.N.U., Canberra, 1983.

G. Griffin, 'Changing trade union structure', in B. Dabscheck, G. Griffin and J. Teicher (eds), *Contemporary Australian Industrial Relations: Readings*, Longman Cheshire, Melbourne, 1992, pp. 211-224.

G. Griffin and V. Scarcebrook, 'Trends in Mergers of Federally Registered Unions, 1904-1986', *Journal of Industrial Relations 31*, June 1989, pp. 257-262.

H. Guille and V. Griffin, 'The Fetish of Order: Reform in Australian Union Structure', *Journal of Industrial Relations 23*, September 1981, pp. 362-382.

J. Hagan, *The History of the ACTU*, Longman Cheshire, Melbourne, 1981.

W.A. Howard, 'Centralism and Perceptions of Australian Industrial Relations', *Journal of Industrial Relations 25*, March 1983, pp. 10-18.

M. Rimmer, 'Long-Run Structural Change in Australian Trade Unionism', *Journal of Industrial Relations 23*, September 1981, pp. 323-343.

K. Wright, 'Union Demarcation Disputes' in B. Ford and D. Plowman (eds), *Australian Unions-An Industrial Relations Perspective* (1st ed.), Macmillan, Melbourne, 1983, pp. 325-343.

Questions

Union growth and union density

1. Explain the variables relevant to union growth in the Shister model.
2. The first evidence of unionism in Australia dates from the 1830s, but it was more than half a century before unions became significant forces. Do you regard this as a slow or rapid growth in the circumstances? Why was it not faster or slower?
3. Discuss the factors influencing union growth patterns in Australia in the 1970s and 1980s.
4. Declining union membership is an international phenomenon. In Australia, it has been particularly evident since the election of a federal Labor government in 1983. What are the major causes of this phenomenon? Do you believe this is a long-term trend?
5. Identify any individual union whose growth pattern has differed from the national pattern and discuss the possible reasons for this difference.

Patterns of organisation and union mergers

6. Until the comprehensive changes in union structure began in the late 1980s Australia had over 300 unions which collectively represented a very complex pattern in terms of organising base. Explain the union behaviour and the legal framework which produced these characteristics.
7. Describe the ways in which the ACTU and the federal government attempted to reduce the number of unions during the late 1980s and explain the considerations which motivated them. Was their analysis flawed?
8. (a) Read the relevant sections of the parliamentary debate (House of Representatives and the Senate) on the 1982 Conciliation and Arbitration Amendment Bill and summarise the arguments in support of the legislative changes relating to union structure.

    (b) Indicate whether you agree or disagree with the arguments presented and the reasons for your views.

9 Discuss the arguments presented by Howard (1983) and by BHP (see document in the Fisher (1983) publication) which challenge the popular view concerning the number of unions in Australia.
10 What were the major findings of the Business Council's Employee Relations Study Commission (publication entitled *Working Relations* (1993)) concerning the impact of legislation relating to union structure on union representation in the large corporate sector?
11 Critically evaluate the following statement:

'The emergence of a small number of large unions resulting from mergers in the federal jurisdiction since the late 1980s will ensure that Australian trade unions generally will be more efficient and more powerful than would be the case if the number and size of unions had remained unchanged since the mid-1980s.'

Exercise

Research the trends in union density based on age and critically evaluate the recruitment strategy discussed in Table 7.7.

APPENDIX

Table 7.14 Union amalgamations Australia: federal jurisdiction, January 1992–June 1993.

Date of amalgamation	Name of amalgamated organisation	Names of unions prior to amalgamation
3 February 1992	Printing and Kindred Industries Union	Printing and Kindred Industries Union Victorian Printers Operatives' Union*
10 February 1992	Construction Forestry and Mining Employees Union	The ATAIU and BWIU Amalgamated Union United Mineworkers Federation of Australia*
2 March 1992	Australian Public Sector, Professional and Broadcasting Union, Australian Government Employment	Australian Public Sector and Broadcasting Union, Australian Government Employment Professional Officers Association, Australian Public Service*
16 March 1992	Australian Postal and Telecommunications Union	Australian Postal and Telecommunications Union Postal Supervisory Officers Association*
18 May 1992	Media, Entertainment and Arts Alliance	Actors Equity of Australia The Australian Journalists Association* Australian Theatrical and Amusement Employees Association*
1 June 1992	CSIRO Staff Association	CSIRO Technical Association CSIRO Officers Association
1 June 1992	Flight Attendants' Association of Australia	Australian Flight Attendants' Association Australian International Cabin Crew Association*

Date	Union	Constituent unions
1 June 1992	National Union of Workers	National Union of Workers The Federated Millers' and Manufacturing Grocers' Employees' Association of Australasia* The Federated Cold Storage and Meat Preserving Employees' Union of Australasia*
1 July 1992	Textile, Clothing and Footwear Union of Australia	The Amalgamated Footwear and Textile Workers' Union of Australia The Clothing and Allied Trades Union of Australia*
1 July 1992	Australian Municipal, Transport, Energy, Water, Ports, Community and Information Services Union	Australian Municipal, Transport, Energy, Water, Ports, Community and Information Services Union Australian Social Welfare Union*
3 August 1992	Australian Liquor, Hospitality and Miscellaneous Workers Union	The Federated Miscellaneous Workers Union of Australia Federated Liquor and Allied Industries Employees Union of Australia*
3 August 1992	Communication Workers Union of Australia	Australian Postal and Telecommunications Union Australian Telecommunications Employees' Association/Australian Telephone and Phonogram Officers' Association*
1 September 1992	Confectionery Workers and Food Preservers Union of Australia	Food Preservers Union of Australia The Confectionery Workers Union of Australia*
1 September 1992	The State Public Services Federation	The State Public Services Federation The University Library Officers' Association*
11 September 1992	Federation of Industrial Manufacturing and Engineering Employees	Federation of Industrial, Manufacturing and Engineering Employees Australian Glass Workers Union*
23 September 1992	Construction, Forestry, Mining and Energy Union	Construction, Forestry and Mining Employees Union The Federated Engine Drivers' and Firemen's Association of Australasia* The Operative Plasterers' and Plaster Workers' Federation of Australia*
1 October 1992	Public Sector, Professional, Technical, Communications, Aviation and Broadcasting Union	Australian Public Sector, Professional and Broadcasting Union, Australian Government Employment Professional Radio and Electronics Institute of Australasia*
27 November 1992	Federation of Industrial, Manufacturing and Engineering Employees	Federation of Industrial, Manufacturing and Engineering Employees The Amalgamated Society of Carpenters and Joiners of Australia* Australian Brushmakers' Union* The Australian Rope and Cordage Workers' Union*

2 February 1993	Australian Muncipal, Transport, Energy, Water, Ports, Community and Information Services Union	Australian Municipal, Transport, Energy, Water, Ports, Community and Information Services Union Australian Shipping and Travel Officers' Association*
2 February 1993	The Australian Maritime Officers' Union	Merchant Service Guild of Australia The Australian Stevedoring Supervisors Association*
2 February 1993	Public Sector, Professional, Scientific Research, Technical, Communications, Aviation and Broadcasting Union*	Public Sector, Professional, Technical, Communications, Aviation and Broadcasting Union CSIRO Staff Association
8 February 1993	Automotive, Metals and Engineering Union	Metals and Engineering Workers' Union The Vehicle Builders Employees Federation of Australia*
1 March 1993	Australian Rail, Tram and Bus Industry Union	Australian Railways Union Australian Federated Union of Locomotive Enginemen* The Australian Tramway and Motor Omnibus Employees' Association* National Union of Rail Workers of Australia*
17 March 1993	Electrical, Electronic, Plumbing and Allied Workers Union of Australia	Electrical Trades Union of Australia The Plumbers and Gasfitters Employees' Union of Australia*
26 March 1993	Construction, Forestry, Mining and Energy Union	Construction, Forestry, Mining and Engineering Union The Federated Furnishing Trade Society of Australasia* The Operative Painters and Decorators Union of Australia*

*Union(s) de-registered in accordance with the requirements of the *Industrial Relations Act*, 1988.
Source: Australian Industrial Registry, Australian Industrial Relations Commission.

Trade Union Democracy

Contents

The case for democracy
The requirements for democracy
The feasibility of democracy
Legal regulation in Australia
- history
- current provisions
- amalgamation and rationalisation

Introduction

The focus of this chapter is the internal government of trade unions. It is concerned in particular with the democratic rights of workers and with the nature and extent of democratic political processes within unions. There is an extensive literature on this aspect of industrial relations and this includes empirical research concerning trade union government in practice.[1] A conversation with any union leader is likely to elicit the information that he or she runs a democratic union and has never lost touch with the rank and file. A similarly universal view concerning the desirability of democracy in unions appears to exist at the political level in democratic states judging by the high incidence of legislation designed to ensure that unions are governed according to democratic form. An important threshold issue in considering trade union government is whether unions ought to be democratic.

The case for democracy

While the issue of union democracy does not attract as much public discussion as its importance may warrant, it certainly does attract a good deal more than does the issue of democratic practice in other institutions. The Australian population may see democracy as a more or less naturally occurring phenomenon, rather than a political system which must be carefully guarded, once it is attained, and such an attitude is understandable among a people whose democratic institutions were awarded, almost from inception, rather than being won painfully from an oppressing ruling elite. Because many unions are formally allied to the ALP,[2] they are political participants, and they take part in a highly polarised political environment. Their political involvement ensures that they are, if not inevitably, at least usually targets for political accusation and abuse. It is probably fair to assume that the relatively frequent adverse comments on the lack of membership involvement in union affairs do not reveal a public concern about democracy so much as an attempt to gain some political advantage, since any defect in unionism can be presented as indicative of virtue on the opposing political side. Australians have often shown themselves tolerant of apparent lapses from democratic norms: *The Age* newspaper in Melbourne reported that in four elections between 1988 and 1990, governments which a majority of electors had voted against were returned to office.[3] That this can occur in Australia is a by-product of a preferential voting system and the distribution of electoral boundaries, neither of which rates much attention in national debate on democratic institutions.

None of this, of course, is intended to suggest that consideration of the question of democratic practice in trade unions is not worthwhile. It is a vitally important issue in our society. If democratic practice elsewhere is not scrutinised as closely, or if the motives of those raising the subject are political rather than altruistic, this does nothing to diminish the importance of union democracy. If there are other institutions in our society, and churches, political parties and sporting and other clubs are sometimes used as examples, which do not accord with the ideals of democratic practice, this does not lessen the need to attempt to secure those ideals and standards in unions.

There are many reasons why it is important that democratic government in unions should be sought, but the overwhelming argument lies in the nature of union membership. In Australia, as in many other countries, joining a union is not a matter of choice for the individual worker. The new recruit may elect to join as a consequence of a personal commitment to unionism, but the worker's beliefs are usually of decidedly secondary importance. The critical decision that places the worker in a union is most likely to have been made by an agreement between management and union officials that all recruits will join the union without regard to their personal preferences.[4] While it is true that where union-employer agreements of this kind operate, a new recruit usually does have the right to be excused membership on conscientious grounds, few people do take that option. A person who is simply not well disposed towards unions is unlikely to take the option to claim conscientious objection. That course is more likely to be followed by one whose zeal was so keen as to amount to an exceptional, or eccentric attitude. It is difficult to know the effect that a pre-employment statement of refusal to join would have on an application for employment, but it is not likely to be favourable. Employers may not be universally enamoured of unionism, but they probably feel that, where, other things are more or less equal between two applicants, they would prefer the person least likely to create tension within the union.

The existence of these union preference agreements, as they are called, has the effect of making a person's ability to obtain and keep a job contingent on their joining the union. People are, in fact, coerced into joining a union, and they may feel no enthusiasm whatsoever for that union. Australian society has elected to tolerate these union-employer agreements on union membership—and it may be noted that not all of these are in forms which would survive legal challenge—for a variety of reasons, but given that they are tolerated, members must be protected against abuse by officials of the unions conscripting them. A very important safeguard is the attempt to try to provide some form of democratic government of unions, to seek to ensure that unions do not operate in ways of which the membership does not approve.

Why is forced membership sought and tolerated? There are cases in which unions have good reason to believe that unless they can achieve 100 per cent membership, union members will face various forms of discrimination on the job. A related problem for unions is that unless recruitment is made at the point of entry, and unless arrangements are made for automatic payroll deduction of union dues, employers may make it extremely difficult for union delegates or shop stewards to either recruit members or collect dues. Even among those favourably disposed towards unionism, the experience of union delegates seems to be that few employees will bother to sign up, or to pay dues regularly if it is an entirely voluntary matter.

There are other reasons for unions to seek these preferential or compulsory arrangements. It is certainly the most efficient and effective means of recruitment to require that employers enroll all new recruits, deduct dues from their payroll and make appropriate payments to the union. It saves a good deal of official time that would otherwise have to be devoted to interviewing and convincing each recruit to join the union, it removes the need for periodic visits to collect dues, simultaneously eliminating the inevitable arguments over the need to pay, and it greatly simplifies union bookkeeping. For some unions, arrangements of this kind are desirable too because they diminish the role of the local delegate or steward. If the delegate succeeds in recruiting and maintaining membership, that delegate inevitably is a figure of authority within the plant or office, at least on local union matters, with a support base independent of union branch headquarters, and some union leaderships may prefer that working members did not attract this kind of following. Like most other holders of elected office, union officials are often not anxious to see potential rivals develop personal followings, and delegates who achieve the status of popular leaders in large plants can become challengers to union office holders. For the most part, of course, the problem for unions is not to restrain or to check the power of delegates, but rather to encourage them to be active and efficient in representing the union. For every workplace in which the union delegate's position is keenly contested and highly valued, there is at least one in which the post is forced on some reluctant person. The reluctant delegate will often undertake the minimum of union functions, and may serve only as a communications point between union, management and membership.

The extent to which apathy is characteristic of union members cannot easily be quantified, but casual observation suggests that it may be considerable. If indeed apathy is generalised, its coexistence with conscripted membership does pose problems for a democratic society. The fact that a person's employment can be made to depend on their union membership does, if this compulsion is to be lawful and tolerated, impose on governments the obligation to ensure that unions do not operate in ways that members find distasteful, nor in ways that do not accord with general social preferences. Some part of this can be achieved by ensuring that unions are subject, generally, to the same legal restrictions as are other organisations and individuals. While that may ensure that unions are forced more or less to conform to social preferences, it does nothing to ensure that the union behaves as its members would prefer. A union may not breach the law, but if its internal rules oppress members' freedoms, or if officials hold their positions through external appointment, or through inheritance, this will be unlikely to satisfy members' preferences.

It is suggested that protection of democratic rights in unions is essential in a democratic society which permits unions to force membership on workers. In the Australian case, where the pressures to join unions are often provided by the awards of government appointed industrial tribunals requiring varying degrees of preference in employment for unionists, the need for these protections is heightened. The outcomes which democratic institutions pursue are not likely to be intrinsically superior, in any sense, to those sought by non-democratic bodies. The value of the democratic system is the means by which desired ends are defined. Democratic bodies select their goals by processes which should approximate the aggregation of the wishes of their members, or at least those of the membership who elect to participate in the choice. As those participants are as likely to include the foolish and the self-interested as the wise and the just, the institution will often seek goals that are undesirable when judged by some standard of efficiency or ethics. The benefit of democracy is that all the choices are made by the members of the institution, and these will all have to live with the consequences of those choices.

In the case of collective bargaining systems it is the compulsory component of collective bargaining and the union's role as representative of employees which similarly provides the primary rationale for requiring that unions be democratic. There are significant differences between countries in terms of the extent of compulsion but all have some measure of compulsion. At one extreme is the United States' legally explicit system of exclusive representation of employees' interest. The majority union, determined by the (majority) vote of all employees in the bargaining unit, is the exclusive representative of all employees in that unit and the collective agreement it negotiates with management is legally binding on all employees whether or not they are union members. Further, management cannot bargain with any other union for any employee(s) and no employee can bargain for terms which differ from those in the collective agreement.[5] In Great Britain on the other hand, the compulsory component is less marked. The collective agreement is not binding on any party and an individual employee can bargain for better or lesser terms. Nonetheless at the plant level there is more intensive regulation, with substantial standardisation of terms and conditions, usually above the national or industry minimum and usually negotiated by shop stewards. These workplace union officials also negotiate on issues not covered by the broader agreements, thereby determining the rules which closely govern the employees' working life.[6]

Another reason for requiring that unions in collective bargaining systems be democratic is that unions are relied upon to fulfil a public responsibility, to become in effect instruments of government. For governments, private regulation of the labour market by unions is the alternative to direct regulation by them. It is argued that governments have delegated their responsibility to regulate to unions and provided a legal framework protecting and promoting unionisation. Unions thereby become an instrument of democratic (public) government performing a public function and, it is argued, should adhere to basic democratic standards expected of public government.[7] This argument is applicable to Australia where government regulation in most jurisdictions is based on compulsory arbitration and the promotion of unionism is an explicit object of a number of industrial relations statutes. As discussed in chapter 6, the compulsory arbitration systems depend upon unions for their effective functioning. The legal support and protection to unions extends to provision of protection for weak unions against competition from other unions through 'conveniently belong' provisions and granting power to unions to sue members for recovery of unpaid dues, fines and levies.[8] This argument for democracy in unions, when expressed in more general terms, is that where government is responsible for some of the power which unions enjoy, it also has a responsibility to see such power is not abused in the context of the relationship between the union leadership and the rank and file.

Finally, the case for democracy in trade union government may also derive from a fundamental purpose of unions in democratic societies, namely to bring a measure of democracy to the workplace. From this perspective, unions cannot serve their basic purpose unless they themselves are democratic. As Summers expresses it:

> 'Employees gain no voice in the decisions which affect their working lives if they have no voice in the decisions of those who represent them.'[9]

The requirements for democracy

Summers identifies the two basic elements of trade union democracy, common to all democratic societies, as responsiveness and respect. These elements, reflected in the expression 'majority rule limited by minority rights' require union decision-making processes to be responsive to the desires of the members and union decisions to respect the individual rights of those affected.[10] As Summers points out, these basic elements often conflict presenting the trade union with the same dilemma as exists in public government namely, accommodating majority rule and minority rights. Responsiveness requires a participatory process, in fact democracy is measured by the process not the outcome. An important distinction in this context is between two forms of representative democracy: 'reflective representation' and 'authoritative representation' which represent two ends of a spectrum of responsiveness. In the case of 'reflective representation' union leaders simply reflect the desires of the members, having been elected because they advocate policies or support values preferred by a majority of the membership. These leaders base their decisions on what they believe that majority wants and a failure by them to do this leads to their removal from office via the electoral process. 'Authoritative representation' involves union leaders exercising authority to decide independently what they believe is good for the members. They hold office, on the basis of rank and file vote, because their judgement and integrity is trusted by the membership. These leaders base their decisions on their judgement of what is good for the members and what the union needs and they are re-elected so long as they exercise honest judgement. According to Summers, the spectrum of responsiveness is broad which means it encompasses significantly different, and often inarticulate, assumptions about the desirable extent and nature of responsiveness: in the United States for example, elected representatives are expected to be largely reflective while in the former West Germany they are expected to be more authoritative.[11]

Accepting the Summers' concept of democracy, a number of specific factors are now identified as necessary conditions for democratic government. They are drawn from the substantial United States literature concerned with the requirements for democracy in unions.[12] This literature emerged when union democracy first became prominent as a public policy issue in that country in the late 1950s and culminated in a substantial body of positive law. Individual and minority rights necessary for democracy include freedom of speech, the right to campaign for office, the right to information and the right to 'natural justice' in the adjudication of disputes between a union and individual members of that union. Freedom of speech, within policy-making forums and during election campaigns, means freedom to criticise elected and appointed officials. For this right to be fully exercised requires there be no monopoly over written channels of communication. Its corollary is freedom to distribute literature and access to the union journal for individuals and candidates wishing to express opinions on the government of the union. All this implies acceptance of the legitimacy of election campaigns. For the right to information to be of value to rank and file members requires information to be user-friendly, timely and readily accessed. The most pertinent information in this context would be the sources and uses of union funds and leadership decisions concerning policy and strategy. It would also include information concerning their rights as union members. This information should be a membership right which stands alone but it is also essential to being able to make an informed choice between alternative leaders or policy and strategy proposals. Assigning this power of knowledge to the membership will enable them to express preferences to which the leaders may respond.

Honesty in financial management is presumed necessary for democracy but is not in itself a component of democratic government. The formal requirements for democracy extend to the adjudication of rights within the union, especially the rights at issue in the union's disciplinary procedures. Other rights could relate to benefits such as eligibility for strike pay or overseas trips. The democratic principles here are adjudication by an impartial body and adherence to natural justice. The former requires that the tribunal not be constituted by current committee of management members or their appointees. In the case of disciplinary matters, the grounds on which charges are made should be precise and substantial. Natural justice requires adequate notice of a hearing, an opportunity to be heard in one's own defence and the member's right of access and challenge to all the evidence brought against that member.

A less frequently cited requirement for democracy concerns the hierarchical distribution of power within the union. This means the assignment of a good measure of self-government to branches of a union. In the Australian context this would mean in the first instance State branches of federal unions but could also mean regional or local (workplace) branches. The rationale for the devolution of power requirement as articulated by Brooks[13] is that dispersion of decision-making power provides an environment in which alternative leaders can develop. Their existence in turn increases the chances that there will be a choice of candidates at State and federal elections. As Brooks argues, growth of leadership does not occur spontaneously, rather it is generated in an environment where decisions have to be made that seem worthwhile and where there is both the authority and opportunity to make such decisions.

Another dimension of the distribution of power within a union is the division of decision-making power between the leaders and rank and file members at any level of the organisation. The membership as a whole cannot continuously determine policy or strategy or manage their implementation. However, a minimum requirement for representative democracy to be realised in formal terms, is that the members should have the formal power to initiate a policy or an issue for decision and to veto policies or decisions of the governing body, under procedures which are practicable yet not readily invoked for spurious reasons. This requirement could also be viewed as one minimum requirement for membership participation. Another minimum requirement is participation in the election process. Important procedural requirements here are

1. minimal restrictions on the right to vote and to nominate for office;
2. honest voting procedures including the right to challenge elections in which irregularities are alleged to have occurred;
3. the principle of one vote one value; and
4. direct election by the rank and file.

The direct voting system increases accessibility of officials to members and increases the power of the rank and file relative to that held under a collegiate electoral system. Apart from these procedural aspects, elections should consistently provide a choice between candidates and between policies, together with some chance of success for those opposing incumbent officials. Although insecurity of office will be a feature of union government, if genuine campaigns for re-election are fought, a corollary is the right of those elected to remain in office for the stated term. If they are removed from office, it must be for serious offences and the power of removal must rest with those who originally elected them.

The above conditions do not constitute a sufficient condition for democracy in practice. They represent the formal requirements for representative democracy. Coleman distinguishes the formal and informal aspects of democratic decision making. The informal aspects are built on the concept of responsive leadership in which the leaders:

> '... (1) make diligent efforts to sound out majority opinion on key issues; (2) clarify their own positions on crystallised issues by a full presentation of their arguments; (3) avoid any action to obstruct the presentation of opposing views; and (4) abide by and fight for the resultant majority opinion.'[14]

The feasibility of democracy

There are a number of factors which operate against the presence of democracy in unions as well as factors or pressures which encourage democracy, or at least the symbols of democracy. The inhibiting factors discussed below include both those applicable to any industrial relations system and some factors which have had particular relevance to Australia. The negative factors include: the 'iron law of oligarchy', a concept developed by Michels; the protection offered to leaders by industrial tribunals; the party political affiliation of unions; the apathy of rank and file members and the electoral advantages which accrue automatically to incumbent leaders.

The leadership of all institutions faces persistently the problem of balancing the needs of the institution itself against the needs of the members. It has been argued by Michels[15] that unions are especially vulnerable to a particular distortion of this dichotomy of needs. Once a union leadership is established in office, the argument goes, it will quickly come to believe that if the union is to serve its membership, the institution's own future and well-being must be secured so that it will be able to serve members into the future. The leadership, according to Michels, will quickly convince itself that the longer term interests of the union are best satisfied if the present leadership retains power, and eventually it will convert the entire reason for existence of the union into the perpetuation in power of the current leadership. In certain circumstances, where there is full democratic participation of the rank and file membership in all major decisions of the union, the perpetuation of the incumbent leadership might very well entail securing for the membership the outcomes which members want. In other circumstances, leaders may be sheltered from accepting the responsibility of failing to achieve members' goals, and the Australian tribunal system does provide some shelter. In a collective bargaining system, a union which did not deliver the gains members expected would be forced to take responsibility for that failure. There could be no escape from this: the union had mounted a campaign to secure certain concessions from the employer, and it had not been good enough to obtain that goal. In the Australian tribunal system, however, union leaders can argue that they have done all that can possibly be expected of them, but that they have been wronged by the bias and intransigence of the tribunal members. Such an argument can protect union leaders from the retribution that failure might be expected to bring, and which it probably would bring where the system does not allow the blame to be shifted to a third party.

Another factor in Australia which allows, apparently, union leaders some further latitude when they fail to make expected gains is the political alliance of many unions with the ALP. The very large public sector union membership, for example, can be convinced that it is an inevitability that its wages and working conditions will be determined entirely by political needs which are so overriding that the unions cannot be expected to prevail against them. In periods of non-ALP government, union failure can be presented to the members as government refusal, on political grounds, to concede anything to its foes. During the period of an ALP government, public sector unions failing to achieve gains for members can argue that the political needs of its allies in government are such that sectional interests of members will need to be held in abeyance to serve the greater needs of all workers, and these will be secured by government policy. That principle was extended considerably in the 1980s and 1990s by the Labor government. Its economic program required a period of wage restraint, and its accord negotiated with the ACTU originally required that government and ACTU should jointly seek from the Industrial Relations Commission wage increases which were limited to a proportion equal to the cost of living increase. As discussed in chapter 16, subsequent renegotiations of that accord reduced the allowable wage increase still further. In 1991, the Industrial Relations Commission awarded a general wage increase of 2.5 per cent, and Australia observed the remarkable spectacle of the ACTU leadership stridently demanding, and most union leaders cautiously following that lead, that members should ignore the Commission, and accept an outcome which would leave many members with a wage increase of less than 2.5 per cent. The relative lack of enthusiasm of union officials, when compared with ACTU officers, for this proposal can probably be explained in terms of the election processes which each group faces (these are discussed below). Before the 1991 episode, the union leaders who succeeded in persuading members not to seek wage increases usually managed this by arguing that it would be fruitless to pursue gains in the Commission against the opposition of the Government (and implicitly the ACTU). In earlier years, of course, many unions had not seen the opposition of the government as being of much consequence. For most of its existence, the opposition of the ACTU to the wage policies, or any other policies, of affiliated unions, would have been unthinkable, for the ACTU has been far from dominant in organised labour.[16] Historically the unions have not always believed that the federal Commission and its predecessors were the only forum in which wage negotiations could take place, but if any unionists still held these views during the 1980s, they were not able to attract much support. Unions have also argued, generally, in support of the wage restraint policies, that to act contrary to the government's wishes would be to damage electorally the ALP government whose plausibility depended heavily on its ability to gain economic improvement by keeping wages from rising. Presumably, although never directly argued, the consequence of damaging the ALP government would be the election of a conservative government which would oppose wage increases for trade unionists! In taking these attitudes, union officials may seem to be placing their terms of office at risk.

Why should a trade union leader carry out a policy of seeking to restrain wages, as required by a political party, rather than seeking the increases which the union's members presumably want? The following may be some of the reasons. Some union leaders may feel that there are more gains, non-wage perhaps, for their members to achieve by doing the bidding of government, rather than seeking to extract concessions from employers. While such a case can be made, it does, implicitly call into question the value of union membership. Since governments are at present unlikely, and possibly unable, to legislate to provide benefits exclusively for unionists, any such non-wage gains would be available to all workers, it may be hard to identify the benefit a union member gains in return for the cost of membership. At least it would seem a more sensible policy to join the political party which provides the benefit, and save the cost of union dues. Obviously, the individual unionist may feel that the protection from victimisation which a union can provide is worth retaining, but surely this too is one of the non-wage benefits that could be provided by legislation.

Secondly, union leaders may support wage policy because of a view that, in pursuing the sectional advantage of the union's members, the interests of other unions may be damaged. It is far from unusual to hear Australian union officials making reference to the 'Australian trade union movement', an expression which conveys the notion of something of broader interests than those of the individual union. Presumably it is concern with sectional interest that induces workers voluntarily to join unions, so concern about the welfare of a 'trade union movement' may not be in accord with their wishes. A third reason may be that there are no trade union leadership positions which represent career peaks for reasonably ambitious people. A significant number of ALP members of Parliament have reached their positions after careers as union officers. For some, it may be that service with a union is seen as a necessary preliminary step to a desired goal in politics. It is not necessary that officials should deliberately seek to use the union and to subordinate the members' welfare to their own ambitions. It is necessary only that an official be convinced that the union as an organisation, as well as its members, might be best served by having a friend in parliament. If the official is to be that friend, it may seem no more than prudent that the union should not buck the system until the election to parliament has been secured.

In non-profit organisations, especially those such as unions in which success or failure cannot easily be reduced to dollar and cents accounting identities, executives can often interpret the goals of the organisation as being outcomes which will benefit themselves. Rarely do such executives deliberately attempt to subvert the institution's goals, but action of this kind is facilitated by the imprecision of goals and performance that characterises all institutions not primarily concerned with profit making. Such considerations, incidentally, are a warning that it is unwise to use business techniques as the model for institutions which are not in fact businesses concerned with profit making.

If the goals of unions as institutions, the personal goals of union officials, or even the goals of the ALP, prevail over the interests of members, this is not, in itself, proof that the union is governed undemocratically. It may just as easily be evidence that the membership is apathetic, uninvolved, and unwilling or unable to indicate to the leadership exactly what it is that members want from their union. The lack of involvement by members can be an indication of support for the leadership, for if the union did take action the members felt was antithetical to their interests, they would be roused to take action. This leads to what is probably the fundamental issue in union democracy. If the rank and file membership can participate, as it chooses, in the affairs of the union, and if the union leadership is responsive to the wishes of participating members, then the major test of democratic government is passed. Normally the business transacted at union meetings has a high proportion of dull and routine matters, likely to deflect the interest of all but the keenest of members, and certainly unlikely to attract many. It would probably not be going too far to suggest that the ruling cliques in some unions have, from time to time, structured meeting agenda so that they interest and attract the attendance of as few members as possible. While that kind of activity may suggest that those responsible have little enthusiasm for rank and file involvement, and that they do use tactics to dilute the force of membership control, the fact is, provided they merely make participation unattractive, as distinct from preventing it, they have not destroyed the principle of democratic government. Where unions adopt strategies which effectively remove the leadership from the control of those who want to participate, then they have destroyed democracy in the organisation.

Pragmatists may wish to argue that concern with democracy can be taken too far, that attention to the niceties of participation can damage the effectiveness of the union. It can be argued that the union is a fighting organisation, that it is contesting with adversaries in business who are concerned with efficiency, not democratic practice. A corporate chief executive who identifies the most efficient method of carrying out his or her work will not seek approval of those methods from subordinates. The chief executive will simply apply those methods and will tolerate no opposition from those who disagree. The union leader who identifies the most effective way of managing union business may not often have this freedom of action, for, ideally, the members must be persuaded, rather than disciplined, if they question the leader's methods. In terms of pure efficiency, the odds may be loaded against the democratic union in contest with the efficient business.

This relative disadvantage can be overstated. A democratic union does not require that a majority of members should sanction every decision made by officials. It does, however, require that an official may be required to account for actions taken which are contrary to decisions taken by the membership, and such an official may well be removed from office. It can probably be argued that the most democratic of unions are, from time to time, authoritarian in their operations; if a union gives an official the authority to execute some action, in undertaking that authorised act, the official may very well require that all members act in a particular way, rather than seeking a majority vote. In the circumstances, it would be argued that, as the course of action had been determined and authorised, members were obliged to act as directed. The critical matters are that an opportunity existed for membership involvement in the decision to act, and that the membership should be able to express its approval or otherwise after the act. Abuses may occur in this process when officials seek approval for very broad objectives, or for courses of action whose meaning is not fully explained to members at the time of seeking approval.

The final factor operating to inhibit democracy in unions is the advantage of union office. A working unionist opposing an incumbent official normally has very restricted opportunity to meet with and to address fellow unionists, and usually to the extent that this is attempted, the candidate must take time off work, and must self-finance travel. Incumbent officials, on the other hand, can make electioneering a part of their regular duties. They can visit large and electorally strategic plants, either ostensibly on union business, or overtly as candidates, call meetings of members at those plants and campaign for votes. The opposing candidate does not have this kind of access to members, may even be unaware of where large numbers are to be found, and must make financial sacrifices to visit workplaces and address those workers who can be notified and who will attend. The incumbent official, however, is paid by the union while doing all these things. In an environment on which level 'playing fields' are much to the fore in public discussion, it may be concluded that in the matter of access to the electorate, a critical issue for democracy, the 'playing field' is all downhill for the incumbent and all uphill for most challengers.

In a democratic state there may be pressure on union leaders to make them conform to the trappings of democracy. Coleman indentifies three sources of pressure:

1 management;
2 certain sectors of the public;
3 the membership.

The weakest pressure for democracy is that from management. Although management pleas for democracy in unions are frequent and although union leaders are often sensitive of criticisms of low participation for example, management interest is not in democracy *per se* but in the extent to which greater membership involvement will produce outcomes more favourable to management interests. Further, it tends to be applied at times when membership pressure is greatest and when the credibility of management views is low, for example during strikes. The second source of pressure for democracy, certain sectors of the public such as civil liberties groups, tends to be greater than that from management because it is usually more consistent and persistent and is from sources regarded as more friendly to unions. Nonetheless, the pressure on union leaders is diminished because the interest of such groups is perceived to be confined to individual rights, specifically formal procedures to protect the dissenter.[17]

The strongest source of pressure is from the members but even their interest in democracy is not an overriding interest. In Coleman's view it is rather sufficient and constant enough to persuade union leaders of 'the advisability of legitimising bureaucratic decision making by dressing it in democratic garb'.[18] Members' attitudes favouring democracy derive from a number of circumstances or sources: union opposition to autocracy (in the workplace); social values supporting democracy; the identifiable stakes or 'bread and butter' issues with which unions are concerned; the desire to counter external critics, that is, a matter of pride; ambivalent attitudes towards their leaders including the need to remind them they are the servants of the members despite the status and power conferred upon them. Coleman stresses there are countervailing attitudes of apathy towards means and an interest in efficiency which are likely to be pervasive when members are reasonably satisfied with leadership results in terms of 'bringing home the bacon'.[19] The symbols of democracy, which do not disturb the real power centres within the union, include the union convention and union elections. It is argued that an examination of the proceedings of the former will show these are in no important sense decision-making bodies and in the case of elections, a rival's chances of defeating an incumbent are reduced to a minimum by advantages accruing to incumbents such as those discussed above. The most compelling source of internal pressure for union democracy is the strength of the value that active membership participation is desirable in the local union. (In the Australian case, this would be the workplace.) The typical leadership response to this pressure, in terms of the symbols of democracy, is to seek to increase meeting attendance levels. Attendance is equated with participation, the ideal outcome being not the creation of a critical decision-making forum but an attentive audience, responding positively but passively to leadership information and advice with any action directed at parties other than the leadership.[20] Another leadership technique is to channel membership energy into what Coleman terms 'educational and community activities' which cost money but do little to disturb the union's real power centres. The use of democratic symbols may be manipulative or may be undertaken in good faith. In the latter and more common case, the leaders believe the organisation requires both 'a bureaucratic mechanism for making and implementing choices of policy and ... faithful adherence to certain ritualistic face-to-face contacts between leaders and supporters'.[21] Another pressure for democracy, or at least the symbols of democracy, is legislation and the history of such legislation in Australia at the federal level is now considered.

Legal regulation in Australia

History

Australia has comprehensive controls on the internal government of trade unions and among democratic nations the volume of regulation is exceeded only by the United States. These controls over the registered rules of the union are contained in federal statute law and in state statute law in New South Wales, Queensland, South Australia and Western Australia (see chapters 12 and 13 for the impact of union registration). The legislation has resulted in a substantial body of case law, especially in the federal jurisdiction, which has established important standards and principles for union government. The focus of this section is the federal law. This extends beyond unions operating under federal awards to the branches of federally registered unions operating under State awards.

Limited controls on union government were introduced in the *Conciliation and Arbitration Act* in 1904 and controls were progressively extended over ensuing decades but especially in 1928 (with some repeals in 1930), 1949, 1951, 1973 and 1976 (changes introduced in the 1980s have been primarily concerned with union amalgamation and rationalisation and are discussed below). The controls apply equally to employer associations registered under the federal Statute but successive legislatures introducing the various controls have been concerned almost exclusively with their impact on trade unions.

The identification of unions with one political party, together with intense political schisms within unions, is conducive to the intrusion of political motives in the area of trade union law generally and union government in particular. In all cases except the significant 1973 changes, the issue of union democracy featured prominently in the election campaigns preceding the amendments to the statute. The parliamentary debates relating to the various bills reveal a belief in a relationship between certain procedures for decision making in unions and certain behavioural outcomes. Those introducing new controls may have genuinely believed intervention was necessary to eliminate malpractice and to increase rank and file involvement. The debates also suggest a significant motive was the belief that the legislation would tell against the more militant and the more radical leaderships.[22] The premise was that such leaders were supported by active minorities and their behaviour tolerated by apathetic majorities. If participation rates for voting in elections and in relation to any proposed industrial action could be increased, unions may become less militant and this could be defended in terms of the object of the Act which sought the prevention of industrial disputes.

The 1904 *Conciliation and Arbitration Act* contained a provision relevant to the individual rights of union members although not explicitly so. One of the grounds for deregistration of a registered organisation was:

> 'that the rules of a registered organisation or their administration do not provide reasonable facilities for the admission of new members or impose unreasonable conditions upon the continuance of their membership or are in any way tyrannical or oppressive.'[23]

In 1928, the Bruce-Page government created a mechanism for individual union members to take their grievances against the union to a third party: members could apply to the Court to seek disallowance of a union rule on the ground *inter alia* that it was tyrannical or oppressive or to seek an order that a particular rule(s) be observed.[24] These provisions gave discretion to the judiciary to determine acceptable standards in relation to the content of union rules. The alternative approach would be to have explicit statutory rights, concerning for example freedom of speech, which arguably would increase the moral force of the law, helping to create acceptance of the legitimacy of opposition. Such rights are contained in the federal statute in the United States, the *Labor Management Reporting and Disclosure Act* 1959. Judicial standards for union practice were slow in emerging in Australia but court decisions have outlawed rules which specify vague offences such as 'acting in opposition to the principles of unionism'[25] and 'any act calculated to weaken ... the federation or its reputation or the confidence of its members in the federation'[26] on the ground that such rules could be a device for suppressing freedom of speech.

In upholding the right of freedom of speech within the union, the Court has distinguished conduct detrimental to the organisation and conduct detrimental to the interests of a particular group. Case law has also established that the rules of natural justice must be observed in union disciplinary proceedings, regarding these as an implied term of the contract between the union and its members. It was not until 1971 however that the Court disallowed a rule of the then Federated Storemen and Packers' Union which gave unqualified power to a federal committee of management to remove a branch committee of management.[27] The provisions for membership influence over rules through an independent intermediary have been used over the decades by opposition factions within unions seeking to gain control of the union. The use of this law peaked during the period from the mid-1940s to the mid-1950s reflecting the intense conflict between two ideologies, those of the Communists and of the Industrial Groups competing for control of particular unions.[28] Neither of these bodies was in any sense endogenous to unionism, but each saw unions as convenient tools for their purposes.

Table 8.1 provides a recent illustration of rank and file members' use of access to a third party (the Federal Court), in this case to challenge disciplinary action taken against them by the United Mineworkers' Union for alleged breach of union rules.

Comprehensive controls on union election procedures began in 1949 with provision for:

1 union members to apply to the Court to conduct an inquiry into an alleged election irregularity;

Table 8.1 Rank and file legal challenge to disciplinary action: an illustration

Miners take legal action against union over hours

By SHANE GREEN,
Industrial Editor

A group of mineworkers is taking Federal Court action against their union after it tried to penalise them for working seven 12-hour shifts a week.

In what is developing into a threshold dispute over changes to the pattern of work, 30 workers at an open-cut coal mine in central Queensland have begun the proceedings after the United Mineworkers Union moved to suspend them from the union.

The Ensham mine has been operating 12-hour shifts for the past year under a deal with two other unions, the electricians' union and the metalworkers' union. Under the arrangement, employees work seven days on, followed by seven days off. The top rate of pay is about $74,000 a year.

The 30 mineworkers were working under the same conditions. But the mineworkers' union objected, describing the conditions as "woeful", and against ACTU policy that 12-hour shifts could be worked for only four consecutive days.

The issues came to a head in February, when the mineworkers' union called on its members at the mine to explain why they were working in breach of the union rules.

Faced with suspension or expulsion from the union, the workers successfully obtained a Federal Court injunction stopping the disciplinary action. A hearing is set down for May.

The secretary of the mineworkers' union, Mr John Maitland, did not respond to calls yesterday. But in the latest issue of the union's journal, Mr Maitland said the deal on 12-hour shifts at the Ensham mine "stinks".

Mr Maitland said the breach of ACTU policy was "even more despicable given that the mining industry is internationally recognised as the most hazardous in the world".

The union has developed a minimum code for the implementation of 12-hour shifts, and members are paying a $10-a-week levy to back the campaign.

The president of the Electrical, Electronic and Plumbing and Allied Workers Union, Mr Graham Gosling, said he understood that the mineworkers' union was planning to throw the 30 workers out of the industry.

Mr Gosling said the company had approached the mineworkers' union about negotiating an enterprise deal when it opened the mine. But the union had rejected the key company demands of 12-hour shifts and seven-day operations.

The company had then approached his union and the metalworkers. 'We have no philosophical policy objections to 12-hour shifts. We have lots of people around the country working those sort of shift arrangements,' Mr Gosling said.

The company declined to comment on the dispute yesterday, and it is unclear who is funding the workers' legal action. The workers could not be contacted for comment yesterday.

A case of union disciplinary action against its members became public in November, when the Maritime Union of Australia fined members $40 for allegedly working too hard. The workers were asked by their employer to work "harder and faster" to save a contract. But the union said the workers were fined for working dangerously.

Source: *The Age*, 16 March 1994, p. 5.

2 the Court to conduct a fresh election if an irregularity was shown to have affected a result; and
3 unions to request that the Court conduct its election.[29]

These provisions, introduced reluctantly by the Chifley Labor government, were in response to intra-party pressure from members supporting the Industrial Groups established within unions to fight Communist Party influence. They coincided with a national miners strike by a union with Communist leadership and represented a shedding by the ALP of a long-standing policy of opposition to state intervention in the internal affairs of trade unions. The precedent established by the Labor government was built upon by the Menzies Liberal-Country Party government in 1951 which legislated for mandatory secret ballots and the right of a group of unionists to request a court supervised ballot.[30] Such ballots resulted in the removal from office of some Communist leaders in the early 1950s, for example in the Federated Ironworkers' Association and the Federated Clerks' Union. In 1973, state controlled elections were made free of cost to the union and since 1976 an election must be conducted by the state (the Australian Electoral Commission) by postal ballot unless the union is granted an exemption by the Court, for example on the ground that voting levels are likely to be higher for a ballot conducted at the workplace. The mandatory postal ballots conducted by the Electoral Office were introduced by the Fraser government. Foreshadowing this provision during the election campaign the then Opposition leader said:

> 'We will take action to prevent militant union leaders dictating to their rank and file members. We will stop dictation to the Australian government by these same few leaders. We are going to give the Australian worker the opportunity to control his own union. Office-bearers of all trade unions and employer organisations registered under the *Conciliation and Arbitration Act* will be elected under Electoral Office supervision by secret ballot.'[31]

Secret ballots of course had been mandatory since 1951.

A study by Rawson[32] of state controlled union ballots for the period 1967 to 1979 shows the mean level of voting in some 86 unions varying from 91 per cent to 26 per cent. Rawson's study suggests a tendency for smaller unions to have higher participation rates but notes that some large unions had mean votes above the overall proportion who voted, namely 40 per cent: the Administrative and Clerical Officers Association (65 per cent), the Federated Storemen and Packers' Union (57 per cent), the Transport Workers' Union (56 per cent) and the Federated Ironworkers' Association (49 per cent). The study finds the size of the section of the union where the election is held to be a more important variable than the size of the union as a whole. Statistical analysis demonstrates that 33 per cent of the variation in voting was explained by the size of the group being polled; the smaller the group, the more likely each individual was to vote. The level of voting in state controlled postal ballots often produces a relatively high vote compared with ballots conducted by other means but as Rawson notes, it is difficult to disentangle the effects of postal voting from the effects of state control.

The absence of any specific reference to election campaigns in the statute law has made this aspect of union government the preserve of judicial interpretation. Until the 1960s the Court appeared to support the principle that the onus was on the individual member to become acquainted with the policies of candidates for office.[33] The Cameron reform of 1973 (see below), introducing to the Act a new object of encouraging democratic control, opened all aspects of union government for Court scrutiny.

In 1976 new requirements concerning disclosure of financial information to members and financial management generally, arose from the Royal Commission into Alleged Payments to Maritime Unions. The Commission investigated payments to maritime unions by shipping companies operating foreign merchant ships in the Australian coastal trade under permits which exempted them from paying the crews Australian award rates and conditions. The Commission concluded that the current law concerning financial administration did not protect the interests of union members.[34]

The 1973 legislative reforms occurred without the partisan rhetoric characteristic of other changes in this area. The reforms initiated by Clyde Cameron, Minister for Labour in the Whitlam government, were a response to his experience as an official of the AWU and his interest in union democracy as a form of government to be pursued for its own sake. Cameron was mindful that the federal law had failed to provide comprehensive minimum safeguards for democracy. Applications before the Court had produced evidence of undemocratic practices which were not outlawed. They included premature removal from (elected) office of political opponents, severe restrictions on the right to nominate for office, vetting and censorship of election material of rival candidates.[35] The 1973 amendments included: a new object of the Act, 'to encourage the democratic control of organisations, and the full participation by their members in the affairs of organisations'; protection of the right of officials to remain in office for the duration of their elected term; and a mandatory direct voting system, as opposed to a collegiate electoral system,[36] (the latter is further discussed below).

Current provisions

The relevant federal legislation covering trade union government is the *Industrial Relations Act*, 1988. Two of the objects of Division 1A Part IX of the Act, carried over from the *Conciliation and Arbitration Act*, are 'to encourage the democratic control of organisations', and 'to encourage members of organisations to participate in the organisation's affairs'.[37] The Act does not recognise unions specifically, it deals merely with 'organisations'. The controls on unions are applied by the Act requiring certain standards of behaviour of organisations if they are to achieve and retain registration. These requirements are for the most part included in Part IX of the Act, although Parts X, XI and XII are also relevant. An organisation may choose not to be bound by any of the requirements of the Act, but if it did so, it would be unlikely to retain registration, and usually only registered organisations have access to the Industrial Relations Commission. In theory, of course, there is no reason why an organisation cannot continue to act as an industrial relations party without registration, and certain employer organisations do so. In the past, unions have also done so, but the post-1983 political climate makes it difficult for them to operate effectively without registration. While it seems probable that the original *Conciliation and Arbitration Act* was not intended to force all parties to use the arbitral system,[38] this does not seem to characterise the 1988 *Industrial Relations Act*.

Lack of registration means only that, as the party concerned may not be recognised by the Commission, it may need to conduct its operations outside the Commission's channels. Currently, the ability of a union to act while unregistered must be questioned following the Builders Labourers affair whereby the collaboration of the Commission, federal and state governments, relevant unions and employers effectively denied the union the capacity to operate after its deregistration. The legitimacy of existence of unregistered organisations is not altered, but the fact seems to be that unregistered or deregistered unions can no longer count on the solidarity of other unions as long as the government-ACTU nexus is preserved.

The essence of democratic government in unions is participation, and the Act does not require that, although its objects seek to *encourage* membership participation. The Act does require that organisations should not impose on members rules that are '... oppressive, unreasonable or unjust',[39] but by far the greatest weight of regulation is given to attempts to control elections, and to eliminate electoral cheating. As discussed above, while rules designed to secure fair elections are a necessary condition for union democracy, they are far from sufficient to secure it.

The regulation of Australian unions seeks also to impose financial controls. Just as it is impossible to pass laws that lead inevitably to democratic practice, although, as argued below, it is certainly possible to go further in this direction than Australia has attempted, it is not possible to legislate to secure honesty in handling union finances. Indeed, it is impossible to achieve honesty through legislation in any circumstances. The main effect of the rules governing financial behaviour is to impose certain reporting requirements on union executives. These are not dissimilar in intent to the rules imposed on companies, and presumably intended to offer the same degree of difficulty of evasion as do corporate regulations. The penalties for breach of the rules, $500 or $1000, do not seem especially severe, and are, in general, less severe than penalties imposed in relation to industrial action, thereby giving some notion, albeit surprising, of the priorities of those framing the Act. It must be borne in mind however, that the fundamental control lies less in the penalty that may be imposed than it does in the capacity of the Commission to review the registration of unions. While prudence necessitates that regulation of the financial affairs of unions should be imposed, the fact is that financial irregularities are not generally believed to be a problem. Whether the requirements to report to the Registrar and to members constitute a major barrier to the dishonest is doubtful. Certainly, regulation has not prevented dubious practice in the corporate sector. Very little is known about the wealth of Australian trade unions in fact. The only detailed study in Australia is that by Wielgosz in 1974,[40] and there it is noted that certain accounting practices, for example carrying real estate on the books at purchase price, made the current wealth of unions difficult to estimate. Unions' financial resources are probably not minimal. Some idea of the incomes of unions can be gauged from the fact that the Commissioner of Taxation reported[41] that for the year 1986-87, taxpayers claimed deductions of $377 021 000 in respect of union dues paid. While this is a considerable sum, it does, of course represent only part of unions' total incomes. Some discussion of the affairs of the Builders Labourers' Federation in the Reports of the Custodian appointed under the terms of the Victorian *BLF De-regulation Act* of 1985 (No.10188) suggested that at one time in Victoria it had assets of $2 877 011. The Custodian's report suggested that it was likely that other funds existed and had been concealed from him. Not all the visible assets were attributable to the Victorian Branch, as some federal funds were held in Victoria.[42]

In large part the *Industrial Relations Act* seeks to ensure that unions are free of financial and electoral misdoing. These are commendable efforts, but they are some way from achieving democracy; electoral and fiscal probity are assured at BHP Pty Ltd, for example, but it is not suggested that these do, or are intended to, secure democracy in the company. It is sometimes suggested that there is little more that legislation can do to ensure democracy. While no amount of regulation can secure democracy if members do not actively seek it, there are certain steps that might be taken to bring union government a little closer to assured democratic government than it may now be.

A first and essential step is to ensure that all candidates for union office have equal access to their electorates. The need for candidates, or their parties, to secure equality of access to the electorate in federal politics underlies much of the relevant law and practice, but the need for similar equality for candidates in union elections has not been addressed. The outcomes of union elections seem frequently to result in long tenure for office holders, and the perpetuation of oligarchies is far from uncommon, suggesting that there is a strong case to be made for equalising the resources available to all candidates for office. Many questions arise as to the extent to which all candidates can obtain equal shares of resources and publicity.

Regulation in this area is difficult indeed. The Federal Court[43] has held that union resources may not be used by officers exercising power within the organisation to support, promote or seek to defeat a candidate during the conduct of an election for officers within the organisation, but the fact is that in the course of official business, union officers do address mass meetings of members, and they do not suspend this activity while seeking election. In the course of those meetings, which are not called to discuss elections, electoral matters may nevertheless arise, and at least an incumbent candidate is drawn to the attention of the electorate in a way that rivals are not.

Rarely of course, do these matters go as far as was reportedly the case during an election in the late 1960s in the United States for the Presidency of the United Mine Workers' Union. The union, it is claimed, circulated a copy of its journal which did not mention the election, but which did, on its twelve pages, contain twenty-four pictures of its incumbent President, a candidate, including one of him unveiling a portrait of himself, presented by a grateful membership. That union experienced more serious events when a candidate for its Presidency, together with his family was murdered by a union faction. In the more law-abiding climes of Australia, the facts seem to be that, without manipulation, intentional or otherwise, the odds in elections are tilted in favour of the candidate who is already a union official, as against a rank and file member.

The Australian Electoral Commission, which now conducts elections for most federally registered unions, has no requirements relating to publication or distribution of election material other than to seek compliance with the law of the land and with union rules where these are applicable. Anecdotal evidence suggests that about twenty-five per cent of Australia's seventy-four federally registered unions (as at June 1993) have a provision in their rules concerning a resume or statement by candidates. Two examples of such rules from the Australian Nursing Federation and the Construction, Forestry, Mining and Energy Union are set out in Table 8.2.

Table 8.2 Examples of union rules relating to election campaigns

Australian Nursing Federation

In elections to fill offices in accordance with these Rules, each candidate may, not later than the time fixed in accordance with these Rules for the close of nominations, submit to the Returning Officer a statement (together with a photograph of the candidate if desired) in support of the candidature. Such statement (together with any photograph so supplied) shall be capable of being reproduced on one side of an A4 sheet and shall not exceed two hundred words. The Returning Officer shall reject any statement or photograph which does not comply with this Rule and may reject any statement or photograph the publication of which may be defamatory or in breach of the law. A candidate whose statement or photograph is rejected shall be given not more than seven days from the close of nominations to supply a replacement statement or photograph on a separate A4 sheet for each candidate. The Returning Officer shall include with the ballot paper delivered to each voter a copy of the statement and photograph printed in relation to each candidate. Where no statement or photograph has been submitted to the Returning Officer by a candidate the Returning Officer shall indicate this on a separate sheet which shall be delivered with each ballot paper.

Source: *Rule 44(d) Elections* (Federal President, Federal Vice-President, Federal Secretary, Assistant Federal Secretary).

Construction, Forestry, Mining and Energy Union

Except in the case of the UMW Division, elections for Divisional Branch Delegates to Divisional Conference shall be in accordance with the following provisions:

> Candidates may include with their nomination form a statement or joint statement not exceeding 200 words containing only the candidate's personal history and only the candidate's policy statement or joint statement.

Source: *Rule 17(iii) (h) Election of Delegates to Divisional Conferences.*

Direct election by the rank and file was identified as one of the formal requirements for democracy. The *Industrial Relations Act* provides specifically for indirect, or collegiate, voting for both full-time and part-time union officials.[44] Collegiate voting is the process whereby those directly elected by the membership, the members of a union committee of management, for example, in turn elect, often from among their own number, the union officials. The system has been used in some unions to ensure that some officials, for example union branch secretaries who are usually the senior full-time officials, may hold their offices without facing the electorate for very long periods. The precise methods by which this is achieved are described by McCallum.[45]

One of the 1973 amendments initiated by Clyde Cameron required, as noted above, the direct election of all union office bearers as a critical part in his long standing campaign to make unions more democratic. The provision[46] allowed unions three years in which to complete the necessary amendments to their constitutions and practices, after which direct elections would be required. By the time the three years had expired, the Whitlam government had left office, and its successor, the Fraser government, included no enthusiasts for the cause of union democracy. It has been suggested that certain unions lobbied the Fraser government to ensure that the Cameron requirements for direct elections should not become law. Whether or not that lobbying did take place, the Fraser government certainly did act to ensure that the requirement for direct election was not enacted. It would be wrong to attempt to blame any particular sector of unionism for so persuading the Fraser government, for none raised any objection whatsoever to retention of what had been shown to be one of the less salubrious aspects of union government.[47]

Cameron's concern had been that the collegiate system allowed union officials to serve for very long periods without their having to face the ballot of rank and file voters. The officials concerned were those who determined union policy, who represented the union at tribunals and in collective bargaining, who managed union assets, dealt with governments, and who were, in popular parlance, union bosses. Cameron is, hopefully, not alone in his view that it is an odd form of democracy which facilitates such shelter from the electorate. There are some Australian union officials whose long tenure may have been secured by the collegiate voting method, but who would certainly have been supported by the rank and file at all times during their tenure. There are others whose official longevity has almost certainly derived from the collegiate process alone. While it is not unusual for sons and daughters to try to emulate the careers of successful parents, there is a surprisingly large number of union officials and ALP politicians who are the second generation in the field. It is difficult to believe that the persistence of such dynasties does not owe something to the collegiate voting system. On the other hand, Broken Hill's Barrier Industrial Council provides, as it often does, a contrary example. One of the Council's more colourful Presidents, W.S. (Shorty) O'Neil, induced the Council to alter the electoral rules so that the President would be elected by direct, rather than collegiate, vote, and he succeeded in retaining the office at annual elections for several years until he reached retiring age. Shorty's successor held the post for sixteen years, then, on retirement was succeeded, at a rank and file election, by Shorty's son, Mr Bill O'Neil. Some labour dynasties, apparently, do not require the aid of the smoke-filled room.

The indirect electoral process can lead to a degree of selectivity in the office-bearers of unions. There is no universal method by which people become paid employees of unions. A relatively junior post may be filled after advertisement, or a known effective delegate may be offered the job, or a person known to senior union officials in other ways may be appointed. Many officials rise through internal promotion, and that process may see them elected, indirectly, as branch secretaries. Thus, a university graduate in an appropriate field may find his or her first paid employment as a union research officer, and progress through the hierarchy to become the chief executive officer of the union, and to do this without ever having been a rank and file member of the union. Clearly, there is nothing wrong with the process, but it is one which can lead union policies into directions which may not sit well with the rank and file. It is, in short, one of the ways in which union leaderships become 'out of touch' with membership needs, or at least can lead the unions to pursue goals that may not be a reflection of the collective aspirations of the rank and file.

The aspirations of such union leaders may be more laudable, have greater long term benefit and be more attuned to current national economic priorities than those the members would prefer, but a society which wants democratic unions would have to opt for a system which ensures that members' preferences are dominant. When the Hawke government took office, the ACTU became, through the accord mechanism, the dominant voice in organised labour, able to persuade and influence its member unions with a completeness that amounted almost to a power to direct affiliates. None of the office holders or executives of the ACTU hold their positions by virtue of rank and file election. Indeed, it is to be noted that three of the best known figures in ACTU history, Albert Monk, Bob Hawke and Bill Kelty have in common at least the fact that they have never attained union office by rank and file vote.

Amalgamation and rationalisation

The matter of union amalgamation (see chapter 7 for detailed discussion) is one which may give rise to some doubt about the priority which the Act gives to promoting union democracy. The amalgamation of unions, involving a vast change to the organising bases and sizes of unions, has been a policy vigorously promoted by the ACTU during the Hawke and Keating governments, and the government has made amendments to the Act providing rules which make it more difficult for members to prevent leaders amalgamating their union with others, and which seek to make it more difficult for small unions to retain registration with the Commission. The ACTU policy on amalgamation has not stemmed from any rank and file demand for it, but it is argued that a small number of large unions would allow the unions to reap considerable economies of scale. Amalgamations have been further justified by the ACTU on grounds which one may suspect to be of slight concern to rank and file unionists. These include concern for the flexibility of Australian business enterprises, scarcely likely to have a high priority with most unionists, a perceived difficulty in establishing enterprise bargaining (which has operated apparently well enough in the past when it has not been inhibited by governments, the Commission or other organisations), and the need to reduce demarcation disputes. The last is unlikely to be a matter which all unionists would support, since demarcation zones have been a source of benefit to many of them, and a policy to end these disputes would promise to restrict their ambitions or to restrict the controls which some could apply. The notion that demarcation issues spring from inter-union differences alone is not supported by the practice of workers. The most persistent inter-worker rivalries may be those between skilled workers whose skills overlap at the margin, and a typical example is the case of boilermakers and fitters. It is part of the folklore of industry that fitters see themselves at the pinnacle of industrial workers.[48] Workplace jokes, for example often suggest that the metrology applied by fitters requires use of a micrometer, while boilermakers need only foot-rulers. The more serious side of their rivalry is that boilermakers are often keen to prove their skills, and fitters just as keen to refuse them access to work they see as compatible with their own skills. These two groups are usually organised by the same union, and the union usually does not encourage them in these craft rivalries, but it is probably politically difficult for the union to try to eliminate them. Similarly, work groups organised by one union, but differentiated only by some managerial decision, for example the assignment of particular work, or employment on different shifts, or in different locations, can often result in demarcation disputes and unions can often do little to ease this.

The *Industrial Relations Act* included provisions designed to ease the difficulties of union amalgamation which had been imposed by the earlier *Conciliation and Arbitration Act*, difficulties consisting in the main of requirements to ensure that the majority of members of each of the amalgamating unions agreed. The amendments to the *Industrial Relations Act* which took effect in February 1991 eased its restrictions still further. It could be argued that the amalgamation proposals accentuate the already considerable thrust of the law to relegate the choices of workers to irrelevancies. Australian legislation has never accepted the right of workers to choose their own union, as is prescribed by the International Labour Organisation's Convention No 87. Article 2 of that Convention is:

> 'Workers and employers, without distinction whatsoever, shall have the right to establish and, subject only to the rules of the organisation concerned, to join organisations of their own choosing without previous authorisation.'

The effect of this convention is further discussed below.

The flavour of the 'official' view on democratic practice is well depicted in Martin's account[49] of the ACTU congress of 1991. The ACTU concept of industry unionism had been challenged, not unexpectedly, by some officials of craft unions, seeking that '........ members of minority unions in a plant or industry should have the right to choose by direct vote whether or not to transfer to a union nominated as their appropriate organisation under the (ACTU) rationalisation plan.'[50] Commendable as this might seem, Martin reports that 'The speeches of (the proposer and seconder)... came under considerable fire. One target was `the right to choose' as an operating principle. A `lovely, emotive phrase', Mr Kelty (ACTU Secretary) called it. But its advocates, he charged, were `not prattling about democracy; they are prattling about anarchy.' Trade unionism was the antithesis of that: `unions bring people together so that individuals don't choose on an individual basis; that is what unions are about.'[51]

The Bismarkian 'the great questions of the day will not be decided by the petty resolutions of minorities and majorities, but by blood and iron' tone of the ACTU view is as difficult to reconcile with the sentiment of ILO Convention No 87 as it is with conventional concepts of democracy and anarchy. No doubt it is considerably easier to proclaim such sentiments before a congress of delegates than before a mass meeting of union members.

Australian legislation has never included any suggestion that persons at a particular workplace should have any voice in deciding which union will represent them. The legislation gives the strong impression that it has been framed to suit the administrative interests of the Commission, the peak organisations and the government, and that it is devoted to maintenance of bureaucratic order rather than furthering members' wishes. The most bizarre section of the legislation may be s.118A which confers on the Commission the ability to alter the rights of unions to represent particular groups. Typically, a union's constitution may have limited its coverage to certain occupations. Section 118A permits the Commission to vary that coverage, either to expand that of an organisation, or to restrict it in other cases, a rule which can *inter alia* award exclusive coverage of an enterprise to one union. While such objectives may be defensible, it is truly remarkable that the Commission may act to make these changes in response to an application not only by a union, but by the Minister for Industrial Relations, or by an employer! Needless to say, there is no provision for input by employees.

Where two or more unions elect to merge, or where their leaders decide to pursue this course, the required indications of rank and file support are slight indeed, but, in contrast to s.118A, there is at least some place for expression of members' interest. In the extreme case, s.253(g) provides that where the smaller of the amalgamating parties does not comprise more than twenty-five per cent of the larger, the larger organisation may apply for an exemption from a ballot. Clearly, protection of the rights of minorities was not included in the Labor government's conception of democracy. At the other extreme, a simple majority of at least one quarter of all the members on the rolls is required, but one might expect that a larger number of amalgamations would fall under s.246 (1) (a), which requires a simple majority of the number of valid votes cast. The Act in its original form provided for 'reviews' of small unions, which were defined as those of fewer than 1000 members, but the 1990 amendment provided that in the period beginning 1 March 1993 and ending on 28 February 1994, unions with less than 10 000 members would be required to demonstrate to the Commission that special circumstances existed which justify their continued registration.[52] If unable to do so their registration would be cancelled. The import of this provision was that, regardless of the wishes of the membership, the Commission could remove the registration of unions which had fewer than this number of members. Again, it is difficult to evade the impression that the legislation existed to serve the interests of others than those who pay the dues, and consequently it sought to structure unions to serve those interests. This is not to suggest that the issue of democracy was ignored. In introducing the 1990 *Industrial Relations Amendment Bill*, Senator Cook, then the Minister, explaining that the amendment would ease the process of amalgamation, noted 'Reference will also be made to the existing object (of the Act) concerning the need for democratic control of organisations'.[53] While this may not quite amount to an overriding commitment to democracy, the Minister was obviously prepared to express measured support for the principle.

As the major force for union amalgamation, ACTU policies on the issue are highly relevant, and the statements of policy and strategy of the ACTU's 1991 Congress[54] express support for democratic union organisations. The ACTU stops well short of suggesting means by which democracy should be promoted or assured, and given the magnitude of the changes involved in the amalgamation and rationalisation program, it may have been prudent to have incorporated some specific protection of democratic practice. The unions are eventually planned to comprise about twenty, suggesting a mean size of about 150 000, thus the membership at any single workplace will be a tiny minority of the whole membership. The amalgamated unions are expected to cover sectors which satisfy very broad definitions of industries, thus there are unlikely to be strong bonds of the kinship of skills which characterise many craft unions, or of common environment which may characterise existing industrial unions.

In these circumstances, the achievement of democratic practice in large and heterogeneous unions is not made easier by size or composition. It is probably made more difficult by the ACTU's intention to ensure that its official and representative positions include, through affirmative action, numbers of females and 'minority groups.'[55] The problem of all quota systems of this type is that they require either that representative bodies are enlarged so that the influence of every member is diluted, or they reduce the degree of representation, and thus the degree of democracy, that is available to members. It may be possible to argue that unions would be more effective in resolving the problems of low female membership and low numbers of female representatives if they sought out and dealt with the issues which apparently make union membership and participation less attractive to women than to men. If that were resolved, the ACTU may not need differential policies for male and female representation.

The affirmative action policies derive from the ACTU's concern that affiliates should demonstrably be democratic institutions in the broadest sense. There are problems for democratic practice in other of the ACTU's broader concerns with democracy: it has argued that unions ought, in multi-union workplaces, to be accorded a hierarchical status.[56] While it is not an inevitable consequence of ranking unions as 'principal', 'significant' or 'other', as is proposed by the ACTU, that the interests of unions of lesser status will be less assiduously protected than members of 'principal' unions, the danger does exist. Even within single unions, members of particular skill or other groups have sometimes felt their minority interests to be neglected by contrast to majorities.[57]

None of these changes to unions, should they eventuate, are intended to or will necessarily cause a lessening of democracy, they merely create an environment in which rank and file participation may diminish. The ACTU has, however, proposed detailed guidelines for the process of amalgamation and for the determination of the relative status of unions in multi-union workplaces. One might expect that procedural matters of this kind would occupy the attention of the largely bureaucratic ACTU staff. The issues of representation of 'minority groups' and of democratic government in unions, while probably only partially responsive to formal resolutions and rules, have not received detailed guidelines. While some attempt has been made to provide detail in the matter of women's representation,[58] nothing appears to have been done to guard against simultaneously diluting the overall representative quality of union government, nor to have identified and remedied the characteristics of unions which have made them relatively unattractive to women, either as representatives or as members.

Employers organisations have entered the debate on union amalgamation, although, naturally enough, the issue of democratic government is not their central concern. On the other hand, the then Confederation of Australian

Industry, now the Australian Chamber of Commerce and Industry (ACCI) took to the International Labour Organisation in 1990, a formal complaint regarding the requirement under sections 193 and 193A of the *Industrial Relations Act* 1988, that the registration of unions with fewer than 1000, and subsequently to rise to 10 000, members should be cancelled, unless 'special circumstances' were shown to exist. The CAI protested that this was inconsistent with ILO Conventions No 87 and 98, covering the right to freedom of association, conventions which the Australian government had ratified. The ILO had elsewhere upheld protests against attempts to impose minimum sizes on unions, minima which in some cases had been less than 100, thus it is not surprising that, in November 1992, the case was upheld.[59] The Minister for Industrial Relations undertook to introduce amending legislation during 1993 to comply with the ILO ruling, and it was eventually suggested that this could be achieved by providing for a lower limit smaller than 10 000 members.[60] It seems clear that the ILO regards any minimum size as contravening rights to freedom of association, thus the government's task became a matter of finding a number which would not draw a further protest. Those concerned about democracy would doubtless prefer that the minimum permissible size for unions was not greater than one. As noted in chapter 7, the *Industrial Relations Reform Act* 1993 amended the minimum membership requirement to 100 and repealed the provisions relating to review of small unions.[61]

The significance of the requirement for a minimum size of unions is that it can reduce the degree of choice available to working people, and it may prevent the registration of unions seeking to cover only persons of a particular trade or occupation. It would also effectively remove the possibility of registering enterprise-based unions, and it is possible to speculate that this, at least as much as the restriction of freedom of association for working people, may have been the matter which attracted the interest of the CAI.[62] Like the ACCI, the Business Council of Australia (BCA) bases its views on union amalgamation primarily on its effect on the practice of industrial relations, and in this context it has noted 'Potential influences on union representation arrangements, including the wishes of employees .... are largely excluded from play'.[63]

If the amalgamation proposals seem to be geared to the interests of trade unionism rather than to the members, this is explicable in that the ACTU, whose officials developed the amalgamation plans, is a council of unions, not of union members. Its concern is necessarily directed, in the first instance, to the welfare of the institutions of unionism. This does not suggest that the ACTU has ignored the issue of union democracy. Its policy and strategy documents refer repeatedly to the desirability of democratic union structures. In proposing that unions should become fewer in number, and consequently bigger, the ACTU has proposed a structural reform which will make the effective participation of individuals even more difficult than it is already, and has done so because it believes this to be more efficient than the existing form. If one accepted the efficiency argument, one might still argue that the concerns of the ACTU about democracy might have been more effective if expressed in terms of guidelines to be followed, using, perhaps, similar logic and format to the proposals addressing women's representation.

The unhappy fact seems to be that the democracy available to an Australian unionist is limited indeed. The most determined participants will find that the aspects of unionism that are susceptible to their wishes are few. The whole shape of the union may be altered by forces which the membership is powerless to influence, and the process that has led to this has been set in train by a group not directly accountable to the rank and file.

Other influences on the conduct and operations of the union may be even further beyond the reach of the rank and file than the aforementioned. In the Australian union of the 1990s, it is apparently no longer unthinkable that employers should be permitted to have a voice on union staff appointments, even if employees are not always consulted (see Table 8.3). In the 1920s, before collective bargaining was legitimised in the United States, 'employee representation plans' were developed as a tactic to deflect working people's attraction to unionism. The plans were intended to establish a form of enterprise unionism, and the resultant organisations were to be staffed and headed by people understanding of and sympathetic to management.[64] The sponsors of the scheme, however, thought it best not be make public their intention to influence and manipulate these 'unions' through selection of their staff.

Table 8.3 Union staff appointments: external influences

New talks may settle battle over ex-BLF officials

BY NICHOLAS JOHNSTON,
Industrial Reporter

Fresh talks between employers and Victoria's main building union may strike a deal that would formally recognise three former officials of the deregistered Builders Labourers Federation as organisers with the union.

The Master Builders Association of Victoria has agreed to talks with the Construction, Forestry Mining and Energy Union in an effort to end the intense battle over the employment of the three ex BLF officials.

Under a proposal to be considered, the men — Mr David Pillar, Mr John Loh and Mr John Setka — would be governed by a code of behaviour in their positions as temporary organisers with the union's Victorian branch.

If they breached the code or disobeyed instructions from the union's secretary, Mr Martin Kingham, they would face dismissal. The association and the union held preliminary discussions last week and are due to hold further talks tomorrow.

But the association still opposes the appointment of the Victorian secretary of the BLF, Mr John Cummins, as an official and this could be a stumbling block.

The BLF was deregistered federally and in Victoria in 1986 after the jailing of the union's federal secretary, Mr Norm Gallagher, for receiving secret commissions.

The move by employers to negotiate with the union represents a softening in their stand. They have said that the move to co-opt the former BLF officials could jeopardise millions of dollars of investment in Victoria's building industry and that the union could even take over the BLF.

A member of the CFMEU's state branch successfully brought a Federal Court injunction against the men's appointments. But the court lifted the injunction last week.

Sources said there was still strong opposition in the union movement to the hiring of the former BLF officials, particularly in the CFMEU's Victorian branch.

Source: *The Age*, 12 November 1993, p. 7.

If the Australian unions are reduced to a small number of large unions, the prospects for membership influence over officials is diminished. A union of, say, 300 000 members will of necessity cover a very large number of establishments, probably only two or three of these will exceed 1000 members. In these circumstances, it will be all but impossible for any opposition group of workers to obtain access to a large number of supporters' votes. The depressing fact is that such unions would almost certainly remain in the grip of incumbent executives, and that effective opposition could only be mounted by groups or organisations which owed their origins to forces outside the unions.

A potential danger resides in the large union, created from the forced merger of distinct organisations, a merger forced without membership enthusiasm. The new unions will be large and nondescript. They will be able to make no claims on the emotional loyalty of members, and when a future government legislates to disallow compulsion to join, and to disallow payroll deduction of union dues, legislation which will surely come, those unions could die a dinosaur's death. The unions that are based in kindred skills and occupations, or in meaningful identified industries will have gone. In their place will be organisations that have no basis for appeal to the loyalty of members, and whose structures have a logic concealed from members.

It is difficult to be optimistic about the future of democracy in Australian unions. In all aspects of life, democracy is one of those qualities which, like youth, is not valued until it is gone, and in trade unionism, it may be especially undervalued while it is present. Current legislation has loaded the dice heavily in favour of incumbent leaderships, and has entrenched the shelter which indirect voting provides for union policy makers. The unions of the 21st century, if unions survive to that era, may be effective or otherwise, but they are unlikely to be responsive to the rank and file. They may well be led by people whose inspiration is not Ernest Bevan, John L. Lewis, Hans Böckler or even Bill Spence, but by people modelled on Arthur Koestler's[65] Gletkin, the soulless bureaucrat who chilled the spines of an earlier generation.

Notes

1 Case studies of union government include E. Davis, 'Participation in six Australian trade unions', *Journal of Industrial Relations 23*, June 1981, pp. 190-215; M. Dickenson, *Democracy in Trade Unions*, University of Queensland Press, St. Lucia, 1982; S.M. Lipset, M.A. Trow and J.S. Coleman, *Union Democracy*, Free Press, Glencoe Illinois, 1956.
2 In chapter 6 the decline in the percentage of unionists in unions formally affiliated with the ALP was noted.
3 *The Age*, 28 May 1991, p. 4.
4 For a discussion of the extent of the closed shop in Australia see chapter 6, pp. 148-150.
5 C. Summers, 'Trade Union Democracy and Industrial Relations-United States', *Bulletin of Comparative Labour Relations*, Special Issue, Bulletin 17, 1988, p. 148.
6 *ibid.*, pp. 149-150.
7 *ibid.*, pp. 151-152.
8 D. Yerbury, 'Legal regulation of unions in Australia: the impact of compulsory arbitration and adversary politics', in W.A. Howard (ed.), *Perspectives on Australian Industrial Relations: Essays in honour of Kingsley Laffer*, Longman Cheshire, Melbourne, 1984, pp. 87-89.
9 Summers, *op. cit.*, p. 152.
10 *ibid.*, p. 146.
11 *ibid.*, pp. 146-147.
12 This includes G. W. Brooks, *The Sources of Vitality in the American Labor Movement*, Bulletin 41, New York State School of Industrial and Labour Relations, Ithaca, New

York, 1960; A. Cook, *Union Democracy: Practice and Ideal*, Cornell University, New York, 1963. J. Seidman, 'Democracy and Trade Unionism: Some Requirements for Union Democracy', *American Economic Review 48*, May 1958, pp. 35-43; C. Summers, 'Internal Relations between Trade Unions and Their Members', *International Labour Review 91*, March 1965, pp. 175-190.
13 G. W. Brooks, *op. cit.*
14 J.R Coleman, 'The Compulsive Pressures of Democracy in Unionism', in W. Galenson and S.M Lipset (eds.), *Labor and Trade Unionism*, Wiley, New York, 1960, p. 207.
15 R. Michels, *Political Parties: A Sociological Study of the Oligarchic Tendencies of Modern Democracy*, Dover Publications, New York, 1959 (1st ed. 1911).
16 R.M. Martin, 'The Authority of Trade Union Centres: The Australian Council of Trade Unions and the British Trades Union Congress', *Journal of Industrial Relations 4*, April 1962, pp. 1-19.
17 Coleman *op. cit.*, pp. 208-209.
18 *ibid.*, p. 211.
19 *ibid.*, p. 210.
20 *ibid.*, p. 212.
21 *ibid.*, p. 213.
22 See for example Australia, *Parliamentary Debates*, House of Representatives, 1951, Vol. 212 : pp. 62-72, 180-227, 228-249 and 268-280.
23 *Commonwealth Conciliation and Arbitration Act* 1904, s.60 (1) (d).
24 *Commonwealth Conciliation and Arbitration Act* 1928 ss 58D and 58E.
25 *Ford v Federated Miscellaneous Workers Union of Australia* (1954) 79 CAR 147.
26 *Wishart v Australian Builders Labourers Federation* (1960) 2 FLR 298.
27 *Higgins v Nicol* (1971) 18 FLR 343.
28 D. Rawson, *Unions and Unionists in Australia* (2nd ed.), Allen & Unwin, Sydney, 1986, chapter 5.
29 *Commonwealth Conciliation and Arbitration Act* 1949 (Act No. 28 of 1949).
30 *Conciliation and Arbitration Act (No.2)* 1951 (Act No. 18 of 1951).
31 *The Age*, 28 November 1975, p. 12.
32 D. Rawson, 'State-controlled union ballots' in B. Ford and D. Plowman (eds), *Australian Unions: An Industrial Relations Perspective* (1st ed.), Macmillan, Melbourne, 1983, pp. 218-240.
33 See for example *Shearer v A.E.U.* (1960) 1 FLR 436.
34 *Report of the Royal Commission into Alleged Payments to Maritime Unions*, AGPS, Canberra, 1976.
35 For details of these cases see C.B. Fox, *Some Aspects of Union Regulation: The Implications for Union Democracy*, Unpublished M.Admin. Thesis, Monash University, 1975, chapter 4.
36 *Conciliation and Arbitration Act* 1973 (Act No. 138 of 1973).
37 *Industrial Relations Act*, 1988, s.187A(a) and (b) as amended by *Industrial Relations Reform Act* 1993, s.74.
38 R.C. McCallum and G.F. Smith, 'Opting Out from Within: Industrial Agreements Under the Conciliation and Arbitration Act 1904', *Journal of Industrial Relations, 28*, March 1986, pp. 57-85.
39 *Industrial Relations Act*, 1988 s.196(c).
40 J.B. Wielgosz, 'Financial Resources of Australian Trade Unions', *Journal of Industrial Relations 16*, December 1974, pp. 314-332.
41 Commissioner of Taxation, *Taxation Statistics 1986-87*, AGPS, Canberra, 1989, p. 105.
42 First Report of the Custodian, 30 November 1987, p. 13, Victoria, Legislative Assembly, Papers Presented to Parliament, Vol. 12, 1987-88.
43 *Scott v Jess* (1984) 3 FCR 263.
44 *Industrial Relations Act 1988* s.197(1)(a).
45 R. McCallum, 'Secret Ballots and the Industrial Relations Bureau: Old Wine in New Bottles', in G. W. Ford, J.M. Hearn & R.D. Lansbury (eds), *Australian Labour Relations: Readings* (3rd ed.), Macmillan, Melbourne, 1980, pp. 375 & 379-382.

46 *Conciliation and Arbitration Act* 1973, s.52.
47 For one perspective on the lobbying see C. Cameron, *Unions in Crisis*, Hill of Content, Melbourne, 1982, pp. 35-37.
48 For a discussion of early attitudes in the context of inter-union relations see T. Sheridan, *Mindful Militants: The Amalgamated Engineering Union in Australia 1920-72*, Cambridge University Press, Melbourne, 1975, chapter 1.
49 R. Martin, 'The ACTU Congress of 1991', *Labour History 62*, May 1992, pp. 138-150.
50 *ibid.*, p. 139 Parenthesis added.
51 *ibid.*, pp. 138-139.
52 *Industrial Relations Act* 1988, s.193A(8).
53 Australia, *Parliamentary Debates*, Senate, 23 August 1990, p. 2081. Parenthesis added.
54 *ACTU Policies and Strategies as adopted at the 1991 ACTU Congress*, Melbourne, September 9-13, 1991, pp. 118-134.
55 *ibid.*, pp. 118-121.
56 *ibid.*, p. 122.
57 P.A. Riach and W.A. Howard, *Productivity Agreements and Australian Wage Determination*, Wiley, Sydney, 1973, pp. 157-159.
58 ACTU, *Policies and Strategies as adopted at the 1991 ACTU Congress*, Melbourne, Spetember 9-13, 1991, pp. 133-134.
59 ILO Committee on Freedom of Association Case No. 1559.
60 *The Age*, Melbourne, 9 June 1993, p. 3.
61 See chapter 7, notes 53 & 54.
62 See Confederation of Australian Industry, *Industrial Review*, No. 71, January 1991, p. 12.
63 Business Council of Australia, *Business Council Bulletin*, April 1993, p. 37.
64 See Neil W. Chamberlain, *The Labor Sector*, McGraw-Hill, New York, 1965, pp. 122-124.
65 A. Koestler, *Darkness at Noon,* Jonathan Cape, London, 1940.

Further Reading

Union democracy: the case for democracy; requirements of democracy; feasibility of democracy.

G.W. Brooks, *The Sources of Vitality in the American Labor Movement*, Bulletin 41, New York State School of Industrial and Labor Relations, Ithaca, New York, 1960.

J.R. Coleman, 'The Compulsive Pressures of Democracy in Unionism', in W. Galenson and S.M. Lipset (eds), *Labor and Trade Unionism*, Wiley, New York, 1960, pp. 207-215.

J.D. Edelstein and M. Warner, *Comparative Union Democracy*, Allen and Unwin, London, 1975.

S.M. Lipset, M.A. Trow and J.S. Coleman, *Union Democracy: The Internal Politics of the International Typographical Union*, Free Press, Glencoe Illinois, 1956.

P. McGrath, 'Democracy in Overalls: The Futile Quest for Union Democracy', *Industrial and Labor Relations Review 12*, July 1959, pp. 503-526.

J. Seidman, 'Democracy and Trade Unionism: Some Requirements for Union Democracy', *American Economic Review 48*, May 1958, pp. 35-43.

C. Summers, 'Internal Relations between Trade Unions and Their Members', *International Labour Review 91*, March 1965, pp. 175-190.

—, 'Trade Union Democracy and Industrial Relations', *Bulletin of Comparative Labour Relations*, Special Issue, Bulletin 17, 1988.

Union democracy and legal regulation in Australia

A. Boulton, 'Government regulation of the internal affairs of unions' in K. Cole (ed.), *Power, Conflict and Control in Australian Unions*, Penguin, Ringwood, 1982, pp. 216-236.

E. Davis, 'Decision making in the AMWSU', *Journal of Industrial Relations 19*, December 1977, pp. 348-365.

E. Davis, 'Participation in six Australian trade unions', *Journal of Industrial Relations 23*, June 1981, pp. 190-215.

E. Davis, 'Trade Union Democracy', in K. Cole (ed.), *op. cit.*, pp. 237-260.

M. Dickenson, *Democracy in Trade Unions*, University of Queensland Press, St. Lucia, 1982.

P. Fairbrother, 'Union democracy in Australia: accommodation and resistance', *Journal of Industrial Relations 28*, June 1986, pp. 171-190.

C.B. Fox, *Some Aspects of Union Regulation: The Implications for Union Democracy*, Unpublished M.Admin Thesis, Monash University, 1975.

W.A Howard, 'Democracy in Trade Unions', in G.W. Ford, J.M. Hearn and R.D. Lansbury (eds), *Australian Labour Relations: Readings* (3rd ed.), Macmillan, Melbourne, 1980, pp. 162-178.

L.S. Merrifield, 'Regulation of Union Elections in Australia', *Industrial and Labor Relations Review 10*, 1957, pp. 252-269.

R. McCallum, 'Secret Ballots and the Industrial Relations Bureau: Old Wine in New Bottles', in G. W. Ford, J.M. Hearn and R.D. Lansbury (eds), *Australian Labour Relations: Readings* (3rd ed.), Macmillan, Melbourne, 1980, pp. 368-394.

D. Rawson, 'State-controlled union ballots', in B. Ford and D. Plowman (eds), *Australian Unions: An Industrial Relations Perspective* (1st ed.), Macmillan, Melbourne, 1983, pp. 218-240.

D.W. Rawson, *Unions and Unionists in Australia* (2nd ed.), Allen and Unwin, Sydney, 1986, chapters 5 and 6.

T. Sheridan, 'Opposition, Factions and Candidates in AEU Elections in Australia 1907-1972', *Journal of Industrial Relations*, 22, September 1980, pp. 293-311.

D. Yerbury, 'Legal regulation of unions in Australia: the impact of compulsory arbitration and adversary politics' in W.A. Howard (ed.), *Perspectives on Australian Industrial Relations: Essays in honouring Kingsley Laffer*, Longman Cheshire, Melbourne, 1984, pp. 82-103.

Questions

The case for democracy: requirements of democracy; feasibility of democracy

1 Identify the most important arguments in favour of the claim that trade unions should be democratic organisations.
2 What are the necessary conditions for democracy in trade unions?
3 Discuss the factors likely to encourage democracy in trade unions and the factors likely to inhibit democracy.

4 (a) Explain why you do, or do not, believe that strong pressures, almost amounting to compulsion to join unions (for example 'no ticket, no start') are consistent with democratic practice.
   (b) Explain why such pressures can, or cannot, be justified in contemporary Australia.

Union democracy and legal regulation in Australia

5 'Legislation designed to bring democracy to Australian trade unions is neither feasible nor desirable'. Explain why you agree or disagree with this statement.
6 'Australia's unions are more highly regulated than in most other capitalist nations, yet there remains more than a lingering suspicion that they are undemocratic'. Discuss.
7 Explain the following statement: 'The legal regulation of trade union government in Australia is desirable even though it provides few explicit democratic rights, places great reliance on the judicial process for protection of such rights, and fails to guarantee democracy in unions'.
8 (a) Do you consider that changes to federal legislation in 1991 and 1992 relating to the registration, amalgamation and coverage of unions would be likely to have an impact on union democracy? Explain your answer.
   (b) In what ways, if any, will amendments introduced by the *Industrial Relations Reform Act* 1993 impact on union democracy?

Exercise

1 Research the outcome to the case referred to in Table 8.1 and discuss the result in terms of the requirements for democracy.

Appendix

Table 8.4 Provisions of the *Industrial Relations Act* 1988 (Commonwealth) relevant to union democracy

Formal Aspect of Union Government	Legal Provision(s)
1. Freedom to join a union	Entitlement to membership if eligible under eligibility rules, unless of general bad character (s261(1)).
2. Freedom not to join a union	A person may apply for a certificate of conscientious objection to union membership. Conscientious objector pays prescribed fee to Registrar (s267(1)).
	A union shall not discriminate against a conscientious objector or seek to influence an employer to so discriminate (s320(2)).
3. Freedom to leave a union	A member may resign by giving 3 months' written notice (s264(1) & (2)(b)).
4. Freedom of speech	Case law only (*note* object s187A(a) & (b)).
5. Right to campaign for office	Case law only (*note* object s187A(a) & (b)).

6.	**Right to information**	Union must inform applicants for membership of the financial obligations of membership and the requirements for and method of resignation (s195(1)(d)).
		Union must make 'specified prescribed information' available to members (s274(1)).
		Union must provide copy of auditors' report and audited accounts to members (s279).
		Union must provide a copy of the rules of the organisation (or branch) upon request and payment of prescribed fee by union member (s289).
		Union must provide to a member upon request a statement concerning membership status (s263).
7.	**Adjudication of rights**	Disputes between a union and any of its members to be decided under the rules (s290(1)). Union may sue for any fine, fee, levy or dues payable (s290(2)). Case law: requirements of natural justice to be met by union.
8.	**Distribution of decision–making power within the union**	
	(a) between different levels of organisation	Case law only. Note that s195(1)(c) (*see below* 9(f)) arose from concern with union rules which enabled a federal committee of management *inter alia* to remove elected State officials from office.
	(b) between leadership and rank & file members (extent of rank and file control between elections)	A union member may seek disallowance of a union rule on grounds that it imposes conditions, obligations or restrictions that, having regard to the objects of the Act and the purpose of registration, are oppressive, unreasonable or unjust (ss196(c) & 208).
		A union member may seek an order that a union rule be adhered to (s209).
		Union rules must provide for the control of committees (i.e. governing bodies) of the union at federal and state level, that is, the 'organisation and its branches' (s195(1)(b)(iv)).
		A union member or group of members who are requested or directed by the leadership to engage in industrial action may apply to the Commission for an order directing that a secret ballot of the 'relevance affected members' be conducted to find out whether they support the industrial action (s130).
		Subject to reasonable provisions in the union's rules in relation to enrolment, every financial member has a right to vote at any ballot taken for purpose of submitting a matter to a vote of members of the organisation, or branch, section or other division thereof in which the member is included (s287).
9.	**Election procedures**	
	(a) Right to stand for office	Candidate for office must be given opportunity to remedy a technical defect in nomination (s197(1)(c)).

(b) Term of office	Maximum of 4 years (s199(1)(a)).
(c) Conduct of election	Elections to be conducted by Australian Electoral Commission unless exemption granted upon union application (ss 210 & 213). Election conducted by Electoral Commission is free of cost to the union (s215(4)).
(d) Method of voting	May be direct voting system or collegiate electoral system (one tier only for full-time positions) (ss 4 &197(1)(a)).
	Secret postal ballot mandatory where election is by a direct voting system (s198(1)) unless Registrar grants an exemption following application by union (s198(2)–(7)).
(e) Minimum voting requirement	No provision (Note that in the case of amalgamation where no community of interest declaration has been made, at least 25 per cent of members on the voters' roll must cast a vote as *pre-condition* for an amalgamation to be approved (s253K)).
(f) Right to remain in office for duration of elected term	Limited specified, grounds upon which an elected official may be removed from office e.g. misappropriation of funds; substantial breach of the rules (s195(1)(c)).
(g) Inquiries into elections	A member who believes there has been an irregularity in an election may apply for an inquiry by the Court into the matter (s218).
(h) Disqualification from office	A person is not eligible to be a candidate for an election if convicted of (i) a prescribed offence which includes an offence under Commonwealth or state law involving fraud or dishonesty and punishable by a minimum of 3 months' imprisonment; (ii) various offences under the *Industrial Relations* Act e.g. offences relating to union elections (ss 227 &228).
	Notwithstanding the above a person may apply for leave to hold union office (ss 229–232).

Source: *Industrial Relations Act* 1988 (Consolidated to 30 March 1994).

9

Management: Theories and Concepts

Contents

The functions of management
- management as 'co-ordination of bargains'
- management as 'control of the labour process'

Frames of reference (ideologies)
- unitary frame of reference
- pluralist frame of reference

Management style

Management strategic choice
- strategic choice: a critique
- strategy: a conceptual refinement

Management strategy: alternative approaches
- strategy: an overview

Management structure

Employee participation in management
- theories of participation
- employee participation and industrial democracy
- employee participation: management motives

Introduction

This chapter considers some contrasting theories concerning the purpose of management in capitalist economic systems together with theories and concepts concerning management objectives and strategies which direct attention to the industrial relations management function in particular. The study of management represents the biggest single growth area in industrial relations research in the 1980s. It is important to appreciate that the sample of frameworks and concepts selected for consideration here, while in the main constituting influential works, are nonetheless only illustrative of the now substantial literature dealing with this group of actors. Further, this chapter does not cover the antecedents of recent works in any detail as this is the province of texts specialising in management.

The functions of management

In studying management in the context of industrial relations it should be recognised that management is concerned with a broader scope of decisions than those relating to the management of labour. Management decisions in the areas of business policy and strategy will influence management behaviour in the industrial relations field. As Dubin expressed it some decades ago:

> Labour decisions are generally instrumental decisions for industrial management. ... The people hired to perform work are viewed by management as instrumental to getting the work done. Management decisions affecting them are designed to make employees effective instruments for accomplishing the firm's primary purposes. In this sense management's labour decisions are secondary to other management decisions.[1]

Thus a foremost consideration for the employer with this management function is to make employees effective in achieving the company's primary purposes of production and profitability. In this sense, industrial relations management decisions are second order choices strongly influenced by first order business policy considerations. This view suggests that the management of industrial relations is pragmatic, always constrained by choices made concerning business policy and strategy, in other words that this management function is always a dependent variable. Some qualifications and challenges to this view emerge in the literature of the 1980s.

Management as 'co-ordination of bargains'

While industrial relations management can be distinguished, a conceptual approach developed by Chamberlain, Cullen and Lewin[2] highlights some commonality between industrial relations management and the function of management in general. Their discussion is built around one of the most controversial issues in labour management, the issue of management prerogatives. The term 'management prerogative', when used in a prescriptive sense, denotes areas of decision making which *ought* to reside exclusively with management and in a descriptive sense indicates those areas which *do* remain exclusively in the control of management. Conflict over managerial prerogatives arises more often in the area of 'management relations' (the deploying, organising and disciplining of the labour force) than in the area of 'market relations' (the economic terms on which labour is hired). Chamberlain *et al.* discuss management prerogatives in the context of the function of management. They note that management prerogatives, or rights, are frequently defended on the basis that management's decision-making authority is grounded in law. Here, management argues that the right to make its own business decisions free from union intervention stems from property rights as the owner or as the agent for shareholders. In other words, management is free to decide how privately held property shall be used. To accede to union demands for greater participation in company operations for example, would require management to abdicate an authority, which it derives from a position of trust, to another group exercising it on behalf of competing interests. Chamberlain *et al.* point out that this argument fails to recognise that property rights confer a control over things not over people.[3] The owners and managers of a factory or a retail store or an office can decide how to employ physical capital but they cannot compel people to implement those decisions. On the strength of ownership or control of physical assets, owners and managers cannot force workers to conform to their decisions concerning either the nature of products or service or the methods of producing or providing them. They must induce employees to conform to those decisions. The inducement will usually take the form of money, though for employees the 'price' for co-operation may also include a voice in certain decisions, for example those concerning production techniques or selection of supervisors. Whether employees can achieve these demands will depend on their bargaining power.[4] From the management perspective, management's ability to avoid employee demands, depends not on its legal status as the owner, or agent for the owners of private property, but on its bargaining power. Thus, 'the function of management when viewed as decision-making, is based not on property law but on broader economic and political considerations'.[5]

Chamberlain *et al.* define the unique function of management as 'the co-ordination of the bargains among all those who compose the business'.[6] It is seen as both an 'inescapable' and 'isolatable' function. It is a function which can be performed only by managers of a company and not by those who make demands on a company. Each individual or group within a company may prefer a different set of company policies and practices or may assign different priorities to existing policies and practices. In addition, there are the demands and preferences of external parties with whom the company deals, including suppliers, customers and regulatory agencies. Chamberlain *et al.* point out that the bargaining which usually precedes decision making typically cannot proceed directly between the parties concerned, particularly when the issue is but one of many which are continuously the subject of bargaining. These include bargains between: functional groups within the management hierarchy, employees; suppliers of material and finance; shareholders and customers and typically also between sub-groups operating within each of these groups.[7] Each interest group tries to influence the conduct of the company in the direction of its preferred policies and practices and does so to the extent of its bargaining power. In carrying out the function of 'co-ordinator of bargains' management has responsibility for securing a complex of bargains (decisions) which will maintain adherence to the company of all those on whom it depends. It exercises this responsibility in the context of an overriding responsibility to secure a profit.

Chamberlain *et al.* identify two implications of this conceptual approach for the alleged invasion by unions of management's prerogatives. First, it suggests that there is no barrier except relative bargaining power to the scope of the subject matter in which the union may become interested.[8] Secondly, it suggests that the extension by unions of their range of decision making within the company does not, indeed cannot, impair the essential function of management. This essential function is the never-ending process of co-ordinating all bargains struck so they are consistent and compatible with all the other decisions being made in the company and so that inflows to the firm cover all outflows.[9]

The labour management function may be constrained by factors other than union pressure, namely legislation (which is true for all areas of management) and in Australia by the decisions of industrial tribunals. The relevance of tribunal decisions for management prerogatives is considered in chapters 10 and 12. The foregoing analysis presumes a pluralist managerial frame of reference. The concept of managerial frames of reference is considered below.

Management as 'control of the labour process'

A different perspective on the function of management is provided by Braverman. As discussed in chapter 2, Braverman applies Marxian concepts to his study of the development of labour processes in capitalist society. For Braverman, the essential function of management in industrial capitalism is control over the labour process.[10] Control is necessary because the labour process becomes the responsibility of the employer, who in purchasing labour power is purchasing something of undefined quality and quantity. Braverman discusses the evolution of management in industrial capitalism which began when a single capitalist employed a significant number of workers. This aggregation of workers required conceptual and co-ordination functions which took the form of management. A rudimentary form of management arose with the aggregation of independent practitioner artisans: co-ordination functions such as the provision of a workplace, the supply of materials, scheduling production and maintaining records. A more sophisticated function, the meshing of different kinds of labour, was necessary for example in civil engineering works and assembly trades such as shipbuilding and coachbuilding. The management function became more important as new industries arose such as sugar refining, soap boiling and distilling. A range of primary processes such as iron smelting, copper and brass working, were completely transformed.[11]

Braverman characterises subcontracting as a transitional form, a phase when the capitalist has not assumed the essential function of management, control over the labour process. In using these systems which existed in the early factories and in mines, as well as for production undertaken in workers' homes, Braverman explains that the capitalist was purchasing finished labour, treating labour purchase in the same manner as the purchase of raw materials, as a definite quantity of work embodied in the product. The reason these systems did not survive in the general case was that they prevented changes in the processes of production, in particular the further development of the division of labour. Subcontracting was jettisoned in favour of direct control over labour power. This system with its fixed hours, systematic control and scope for reorganisation of the labour process, was preferred because it brought much of the potential of human labour within the reach of the capitalist. Capitalist management was to be distinguished from earlier production systems involving large bodies of workers by three factors:

1 the use of hired or 'free' labour;
2 a context of rapidly revolutionising technology, itself influenced in part by employer decisions; and
3 the profit motive—the need to accumulate capital and show a surplus.

Capitalist management, according to Braverman, represents 'a wholly new art of management ⋯ far more complete, self conscious, painstaking and calculating' than its predecessors.[12]

From this perspective management is always conducted in a setting of social antagonism. The sole management motivation for various schemes designed to humanise work or increase worker participation, is to improve labour costs or the firm's competitive market position. In other words, managers seek to ameliorate the antagonistic workplace relations only when this interferes with the orderly functioning of the workplace, be it plant, office, warehouse or store, when productivity levels or absenteeism or turnover levels differ from their expected or desired levels. For Braverman, reforms operating under labels such as job enlargement, quality of working life and the humanisation of work have one overriding purpose: cutting costs, improving efficiency and productivity[13] and 'They represent a style of management rather than a genuine change in the position of the worker'.[14] Any increase in the decision-making power of workers or their discretion under such reforms would be confined to insignificant matters, making choices within fixed and limited alternatives.

Braverman's study includes a detailed analysis of the emergence of modern management based on the principles of scientific management developed by Taylor[15] who had synthesised ideas developing in Great Britain and the United States throughout the nineteenth century. From the labour process perspective, Taylor sought an answer to the specific problem of how best to control alienated labour, that is labour power that was bought and sold. For Braverman, the revolutionary feature of Taylor's approach was that it provided the means for management to achieve control of the actual method of performance of every labour activity, from the simplest to the most complicated. Prior to Taylor's work, Braverman suggests, the general assumption had been that managerial rights in relation to control extended only to the general setting of tasks, not to direct interference in the worker's method of performing them.[16] According to Braverman, Taylor believed that the forms of control he advocated could be applied to labour of all levels of complexity and one of his largest projects concerned an analysis of the complex labour processes of machinists in the machine shop of a steelworks where Taylor had worked as a supervisor.

Braverman's interpretation of Taylor's principles for the reorganisation and subdivision of labour at any given level of technology, illuminate the labour process perspective or radical frame of reference. The first principle of scientific management was the gathering and development of knowledge of labour processes. Braverman calls this 'the dissociation of the labour process from skills of the workers'. The labour process was to become entirely dependent upon the practice of management and thus independent of craft, tradition and the workers' knowledge.[17] The second principle was the concentration of this knowledge as the exclusive province of management. Braverman calls this 'the separation of conception from execution'[18] in preference to its more common description as the separation of mental and manual labour. According to Braverman, the purpose here was to cheapen the worker, by decreasing his training and enlarging his output, and ensure management control. It meant the study of work processes must be reserved to management, the duty of workers being to follow unthinkingly instructions relating to simplified job tasks.[19] The third principle, as characterised by Braverman was 'the use of this monopoly over knowledge to control each step of the labour process and its method of execution.'[20] The essential element here was the systematic pre-planning and pre-calculation of all elements of the labour process which would then exist only as a process in the imagination of managers. Previously it existed as a process in the imagination of the worker.

Braverman argues that modern management came into being on the basis of these principles. It became systematic practice during the period of transformation of labour from processes based on skill to processes based upon science and which became concentrated in the hands of management.[21] Braverman, writing in the early 1970s, argues that Taylorism had become the bedrock of all work design.[22] Its growth coincided with the concentration of production in ever larger corporate units in the latter part of the nineteenth and in the twentieth centuries. It could only become generalised when the scale of production was adequate to support the efforts and costs involved in 'rationalising' it.[23]

Frames of reference (ideologies)

One of the criticisms of Dunlop's model was the neglect of behavioural variables, for example, the motivations of the actors. His only reference to underlying values is in a brief discussion of the ideology of an industrial relations system. As noted in chapter 2, Dunlop defines ideology as a set of ideas and beliefs commonly held by the actors that helps to integrate the system as an entity. The common 'ideas' relate to the role and place of each actor in the system and that defines the ideas which each actor holds towards the place and function of the others. Dunlop recognises that a system would be unstable if there was in fact limited congruence or compatibility between the ideas of the different actors on these matters:

> Thus in a community in which the managers hold a highly paternalistic view toward workers and the workers hold there is no function for managers, there would be no common ideology in which each actor provided a legitimate role for the other; the relationships within such a work community would be regarded as volatile, and no stability would likely be achieved in the industrial-relations system.[24]

A number of models concerning management ideologies and values in industrial relations have been developed and two of these are considered in detail here. One influential framework is that developed by Fox[25] distinguishing two management perspectives on the nature of industrial relations—the unitary and the pluralist perspective or frame of reference. They may be constructed as ideals of how industrial relations ought to be conducted (the core values on which industrial relations practice is based) or as factual characterisations of how they are conducted. Fox explains that management's frame of reference is important because it determines judgement which in turn determines behaviour.

Unitary frame of reference

This perspective sees the natural order in the world of paid employment as characterised by harmony and trust between employer and employees. It finds expression in an emphasis on common objectives and values which are said to unite employer and employees. It is an ideology with 'origins far back in the historical texture of class, status and power; in the constantly asserted and enforced 'right' of the master to demand unquestioning obedience from his servants'.[26] The unitary frame of reference likens a company to a team. There is one source of authority and one focus of loyalty. There are no rival leaders within the team or outside it. Morale and success are closely connected and rest heavily upon personal relationships.[27] From this perspective, conflict is an aberration caused by factors such as outside agitators or perhaps poor communication or abrasive styles of supervision. Trade unions are regarded as unnecessary or damaging. The former view, seeing them as unnecessary, says they achieve nothing that would not otherwise be achieved. They are also of course in competition with management as a focus of employee loyalty. This probably gives rise to the alternative view identified by Fox that unions are damaging, that is unions achieve far too much, for example by pushing up costs, blocking change and frustrating enterprise. This ideology is shown to have a rich yield for managers hence there is a strong incentive to invest in it. Fox identifies three functions of this ideology: a method of self-reassurance; an instrument of persuasion; and a technique of seeking legitimation of authority.[28] His elaboration of these benefits is set out in Table 9.1.

Pluralist frame of reference

From this perspective, management is seen as making its decisions within a set of constraints occasioned *inter alia* by the opposing interests of employees and the possession of some power by those employees. The goals and

Table 9.1 Unitary ideology: the benefits for managers

A method of self-reassurance
'For many managers, the full and complete acceptance of the idea that substantial sections of those whom they govern are in certain fundamental respects alienated is corrosive of self-confidence. This can be a powerful motivation towards believing that a basic harmony of purpose exists, and that any apparent demonstration to the contrary is due to faults among the governed—to stupidity, or short-sightedness, or out-dated class rancour, or an inability to grasp the basic principles of economics, or the activities of agitators who create mischief out of nothing'.

An instrument of persuasion
'Managers seek to persuade their employees and the public at large that industry is a harmony of co-operation which only fools or knaves choose to disrupt. To the extent that they convince their employees their job is made easier; to the extent that they convince the public they gain sympathy whenever their policies are challenged by their workers'.

A technique of seeking legitimation of authority
'The propagation of the idea that the interests of the rulers and of the ruled are identical helps to confer legitimacy upon the regime. Their government is legitimate government; their sanctions are legitimate sanctions; they can be cruel to be kind yet remain free of guilt'.

Source: A. Fox, *Industrial Sociology and Industrial Relations*, Royal Commission on Trade Unions and Employers' Associations, Research Papers 3, H.M.S.O, London, 1966. Reprinted in A. Flanders (ed.), *Collective Bargaining*, Harmondsworth, Penguin, 1969, p. 395.

interests of managers and non-managerial employees are not identical except for a common interest in survival. A certain amount of industrial conflict is both inevitable and legitimate. As Fox expresses it, from this perspective, management prerogatives will be limited in certain respects by the organised expression of such interests of the employees as they feel diverge from those of management.[29]

The pluralist perspective sees the company as a coalition of interests, a miniature democratic state over which managers try to maintain some kind of dynamic equilibrium. Managers with this frame of reference would accept, for example, that there will be a percentage of employees whose loyalty and attachment to the union will be greater than any loyalty they may have towards the company or organisation. Managers would also accept trade unions as legitimate, perhaps on the basis identified by Fox, namely, a social value which recognises the right of freedom of association and of interest groups to combine.

There are many variants to the pluralist perspective but a common feature is the assumption of an approximate balance of power between employers and employees. Power is diffused among conflicting interest groups so that no one party dominates. All parties will get some of what they want; none will get everything they want. The implication of this frame of reference for managers is that the legitimacy of their rule in the eyes of subordinates is not automatic but must be actively pursued and maintained.[30]

Fox provides an illuminating discussion of the implications for industrial relations management of these divergent perspectives.[31] Using the issue of work-group control, restrictive work practices and resistance to change, Fox argues that paradoxically the unitary frame of reference sets out to be a position of management strength but ends by being a position of managerial weakness. The manager with a unitary frame of reference has to interpret restrictive work practices and resistance to change as being due to stupidity or perhaps outdated class antagonism. The manager with a pluralist frame of reference will assess these practices correctly as rational responses by work-groups to protect their interests. These interests could be any or all of the following: employment; earnings; job status; bargaining power, craft or occupational boundaries. Managers who accept the reality of work-group interests which conflict quite legitimately with management's interests will be on the way to what Fox describes as 'imaginative understanding' which he regards as the pre-condition of success in modifying behaviour and therefore for success in productivity bargaining.[32] The pluralist view can understand the work-group or unionists' responses and by understanding them is in a position to change them.

In contrast, the manager whose behaviour is governed or influenced by a unitary frame of reference may resort to management by exhortation, to special pleading to abandon restrictive work practices and pull together for the common good. If this does not work there is nowhere else to go. In other words, a reluctance to accept the full implications of power relations in the workplace increases the difficulty of adjusting to changes in these relations. If there is difficulty in accepting the validity of work-group or union independence and control systems and even greater difficulty in negotiating their codification and change, then this may mean that managerial control systems and work-groups control systems co-exist but are never reconciled:

> 'Management thus preserves the pretence of maintaining its prerogatives but nevertheless connives at the extension of unilateral regulation by work-groups. Precisely because this extension of informal work-group regulation is not met by management, it represents a genuine loss of managerial control. This is the social process by which systematic overtime, overmanning and other diverse manifestations of work-group control have thrived unchecked'.[33]

It is important to distinguish between management attitudes, management behaviour and company policy. This is one distinction emphasised by Purcell in his refinement of the managerial frames of reference concept.

Management style

Purcell has provided a model which seeks to extend the conceptual analysis beyond the rather crude categories of the unitary and pluralist frames of reference.[34] It should be noted that in a later work[35] Fox amplifies and supplements the above frames of reference, for example in developing six patterns of management-employee relations. The Purcell refinement is considered here by virtue of its singular concern with management. Purcell's study of management style is primarily an analysis of originating philosophies and policies which influence action. The analysis is premised on the recognition that companies can make strategic corporate (business) choices and this will include preferences in the way employees are managed. This does not abstract from, or ignore the influence of, environmental factors on management behaviour. Rather it recognises that some part of the explanation of such behaviour may be found in the concept of management style. The concept is specific:

> 'Style implies the existence of a distinctive set of guiding principles which set parameters or signposts for management action in the way employees are treated and particular events handled. Management style is therefore akin to business policy and its strategic derivations'.[36]

Purcell, quoting Argenti, argues that because it is one of those aspects of wider business policy which state in broad terms what may and may not be done, management style is likely to be determined at senior level within a company, by owners or directors. Further, it is likely to be made as a result of moral, political, aesthetic or personal considerations rather than as a result of logical or scientific analysis. Management style is to be distinguished from:

1 outcomes of management-employee interaction;
2 management attitudes, as these do not necessarily translate into action or behaviour;
3 structures; and
4 management practices.

Empirical study of management style would therefore be restricted to those companies with a guiding set of principles which delineate the boundaries and direction of acceptable management action in dealing with employees. To meet Purcell's definition, the guiding principles must be broadly continuous in time and something more than the present whim of a few senior managers in one location. They must be 'reasonably long-standing, firm specific expectations' which mould management actions in the treatment of employees.[37]

Purcell acknowledges the major influence of the frames of reference concepts in initiating the debate on management approaches to industrial relations. He also identifies the limitations of the concepts. First, there are wide variations of values within each perspective. The unitary perspective incorporates the values of loyalty and commitment to employees as well as values which are exploitive of employees. The pluralist perspective incorporates values which are antagonistic to trade unions as well as those which accord legitimacy and support to trade unions. Secondly, the two frames of reference are mutually exclusive and are thereby not useful as a means of articulating the complexity of management style. Thirdly, it is not clear whether they apply to management's dealings with individual employees or with organised labour.[38]

In refining the frames of reference, Purcell develops two dimensions to management style: the individualism dimension and the collectivism dimension. The individualism dimension concerns policies or guiding principles defining the attention to be given to employees and their individual and group needs. The collectivism dimension concerns policies or guiding principles defining behaviour towards trade unions and other types of collective labour organisation. The measure of individualism is the extent to which policies are focused on the rights and capabilities of individual employees, give credence to their feelings and sentiments and seek to develop their capacities and roles. Purcell distinguishes two aspects of collectivism:

1 the degree of collectivism—the existence of democratic structures representing employees which may not be a function of management decisions; and
2 with the degree of collectivism as given, the degree of legitimacy afforded to the collective by management and thereby the extent to which it is accepted or opposed.

The measure of the collectivism dimension of management style is thus the extent to which policy is directed towards inhibiting or encouraging the development of collective representation of employees and allowing employees a collective voice in management decision making.[39] These ideas are represented in Figure 9.1.

Figure 9.1 Management styles: the interconnections between individualism and collectivism

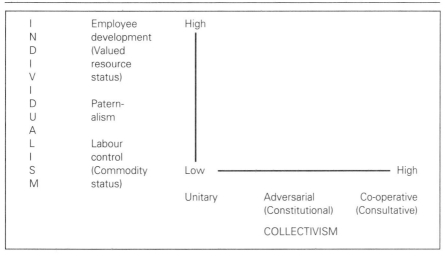

Source: Adapted from J. Purcell 'Mapping management styles in employee relations', *Journal of Management Studies 24*, September 1987, p. 541.

Purcell identifies characteristics of a high, low and paternalistic management style on the individualism dimension. High individualism, or valued resource status for employees, is characterised by careful selection at restricted points of entry; internal training schemes; career progression; extensive welfare provisions reflecting a social responsibility towards employees; payment systems with relatively high rewards including a merit element and the use of performance appraisal. Low individualism, or commodity status for employees, is characterised by an emphasis on cost minimisation, low job security because of a ready willingness to shed labour and generally an absence of the 'investment in employees' characteristics of the high individualism style. The paternalism style uses the concepts characteristic of high individualism to maintain control. Thus, this style emphasises notions of caring, humanity and welfare to legitimise managerial authority and the subordinate position of low level employees who are given limited expectations of changing either their work roles or 'natural' place in the hierarchy.[40]

In the case of the collectivism dimension, a unitary style is characterised by union avoidance. A constitutional (adversarial) style is distinguished by an emphasis on stability, control and the institutionalisation of conflict; defence of management prerogatives and minimising or neutralising union constraints on both operational and strategic management. A consultative (co-operative) style is characterised by an emphasis on building constructive relationships with employee collective organisations and incorporating them into the operation of the company; free flow of information on a whole range of plans and decisions including aspects of strategic management.[41]

Purcell draws on empirical evidence to argue that companies can and do operate along both dimensions independently, that action in one dimension is not necessarily associated with changes in the other dimension of management style. Thus for example, the adoption of, or a move towards, a high individualism style does not inevitably imply a move away from a high (co-operative) or an intermediate (constitutional) collectivism style. A company may choose for example to adopt aspects of both employee development (high individualism) and co-operative collectivism or high individualism in conjunction with unitary collectivism. Purcell cites research into the labour practices of Japanese companies in Britain which has emphasised their distinctive approach of combining union recognition with an emphasis on employee development and commitment. The companies have adopted a carefully considered style linked to business policy for competitive advantage.[42]

Purcell concludes that if the term 'management style' is to be used as meaning something different from management practices, there will need to be clarity concerning the unit of analysis and the type of employees covered by the 'style' policy. In relation to the unit of analysis, Purcell notes the popular assumption that style concerns the whole of the enterprise but cites research to support recognition of distinctive styles (in the proper meaning of the term) for individual divisions or even workplaces, of a large company, often derived from their history and perhaps previous ownership. Purcell thus recognises that while management style is most likely to be set at corporate level, it could in some firms be determined at intermediate or local levels. In relation to the type of employees covered, Purcell notes that a firm may deliberately have a variety of management styles, differentiated between broad occupational groups and their perceived value to the firm. Alternatively, a firm may choose a considered management style toward one group of employees while reacting pragmatically in its management of other groups.[43]

Finally, Purcell points out that many companies may not have any style as defined, no preferred way of managing, but simply respond in an *ad hoc* manner either as a result of change in environmental pressures, the demands and behaviours of the other actors or the personal preferences of individual managers.[44]

Management strategic choice

As noted in chapter 2, the central purpose of Kochan, Katz and McKersie in *The Transformation of American Industrial Relations*[45] is to explain how management operates in industrial relations, how goals are identified and pursued. The concept with which their work is closely identified, the concept of strategic choice or decision, is in fact used in an ambiguous and imprecise manner in this work. This aspect is discussed further below in the summary of Lewin's critique of the concept of strategic choice. It will be evident from other literature summarised in this chapter that this concept has been explored and analysed by other writers in the industrial relations field prior to the publication of the major work by Kochan, Katz and McKersie. They attach significance to management strategic choice or decisions in their analysis of changes in the United States industrial relations system over a twenty-five year period from 1960 to the mid-1980s. Three major areas of change are identified:

1 the decline of unionism and the ascent and eventual dominance of a non-union industrial relations sector;
2 changes in collective bargaining structures and outcomes (the union sector) especially in the early 1980s; and
3 the emergence of new forms of labour-management co-operation at the workplace, such as information sharing programs, autonomous work teams and incentive schemes.

Kochan, Katz and McKersie seek to integrate industrial relations systems theory and theories relating to company business strategies and structure. They are concerned with the relationship between business (corporate) strategies and the company's industrial relations system, that is, industrial relations practices within firms. The primary concern with an industrial relations model rather than with business strategy *per se* means that concepts from literature concerning management values and strategies are complemented by inclusion of variables which will capture the interaction of strategic choices of other actors in the system and the impact of strategic decisions on the goals of the various actors.[46] A central argument, depicted in their diagrammatic representation of a general framework for analysis (see figure 2.1), is 'that industrial relations practices and outcomes are shaped by the interaction of environmental forces *along with* the strategic choices and values of American managers, union leaders, workers, and public policy decision makers'.[47] Kochan *et al.* identify their ultimate purpose as being to develop a more strategic perspective on United States industrial relations and thereby demonstrate that future patterns are not unalterably pre-determined by economic, technological or other environmental forces.[48] Hence they provide a revised theoretical framework which builds on Dunlop's systems concept, wherein external environmental variables were prominent, and also on the contributions of later writers such as Craig and Walker.

The theoretical framework depicted in figure 2.1 implicitly recognises the influence of the values and strategies of unions and third parties on industrial relations outcomes. Nonetheless Kochan *et al.* place management values and strategies at the centre of their analysis. They argue that no one foresaw the decline of unionism and the growing legitimacy of the unitary frame of reference and hence a more powerful theory of managerial values, strategies and behaviour is required. They contend that while traditional industrial relations theory casts management in the role of reactor, that is, as reacting to union demands, pressures and initiatives, there are indications that 'the causal flow has been reversed', that the major initiator of change is now management. Indicators include (1) the innovations in human resource management practices that started in non-union firms and are being increasingly diffused into unionised workplaces and (2) the shift in distribution of decision-making power and authority within management over employment issues from staff to line management and from industrial relations to human resource management.[49]

The writers argue that, since 1960, the other actors have been much slower than the management group to adapt to changes in external environmental variables and to changes in managerial strategies and policies. One illustration of this inertia is that, until the 1980s, most unions in the United States failed to change their behaviour to cope with shifts in technologies and markets which called for new strategies for recruiting and representing workers.[50] Another illustration is the failure of governments to change the

Table 9.2 Three levels of industrial relations activity

Level	Employers	Unions	Government
Long term Strategy and Policy Making	Business Strategies Investment Strategies Human Resource Strategies	Political Strategies Representation Strategies Organising Strategies	Macroeconomic and Social Policies
Collective Bargaining and Personnel Policy	Personnel Policies Negotiation Strategies	Collective Bargaining Strategies	Labour Law and Administration
Workplace and Individual/Organisation Relationships	Supervisory Style Worker Participation Job Design and Work Organisation	Contract Administration Worker Participation Job Design and Work Organisation	Labour Standards Worker Participation Individual Rights

Source: T.A. Kochan, H.C. Katz and R.B. McKersie, *The Transformation of American Industrial Relations*, Basic Books, New York, 1986, p. 17.

industrial relations legal framework to deal with matters such as the serious problems in union representation procedures and the blurring of the distinction between workers and supervisors. A major conclusion of Kochan *et al.* is that unions and government remained locked into what they describe as 'the collective bargaining model of the New Deal' while management reduced its vulnerability to unionism as a consequence of its adaptation to changes in the market context, both labour and product markets.[51]

The more significant theoretical contribution of the Kochan *et al.* work is the three-tier institutional framework distinguishing different levels of activity and decision making within each of the three parties involved in industrial relations: employers, unions and government. Their primary concern with employers, that is management, is evident in the diagram depicting the general framework for analysis (see figure 2.1) which incorporates this three-tier concept in relation to the firm. The three-level framework also reflects the researchers' interest in the relationship between business strategy and industrial relations practice in the firm.

The purpose of their framework, set out in Table 9.2, is to broaden the scope of industrial relations research. Although their predominant concern is to explain the industrial relations activity of management, Kochan *et al.* divide the activities of the three groups of actors into three tiers or levels:

1 the strategic decision-making level;
2 the collective bargaining or personnel policy-making level; and
3 the workplace level where policies are 'played out' affecting employees, supervisors and union representatives.

They argue that hitherto the concept of institutional structure has been too narrow; the focus in research has been on the second level of activity: collective bargaining, its structure, rules and customs.[52] In the Australian context the parallel level would be conciliation and arbitration or the operation of the industrial tribunal machinery.

This second level is the functional level, the management speciality variously titled, 'industrial relations', 'personnel management' or 'human resources management'. In the United States case this 'traditional terrain' of industrial relations activities includes the union negotiating strategies and in the case of government, the development of law and policies specific to industrial relations. Kochan *et al.* use the framework to illustrate the impact of decisions at one level on behaviour and outcomes at the other levels. Thus for example, decisions at level one such as what businesses to invest in, the location of businesses and whether to make or buy components, affect industrial relations at the other levels and should therefore be part of industrial relations analysis.[53] Activities that occur at the third level, the workplace level of the day by day employee-employer relationship, are not under the direct control of the key players at the second level, that is negotiators in the collective bargaining process, company personnel officers nor the control of those at the first level, that is, the level of broad business strategies. However, activities at this level do occur in the context of strategies and agreements (or awards, in the Australian case) determined at level one (business strategy) or level two (collective bargaining).[54]

For the study of management in particular, the framework identifies an important development that the industrial relations system concept does not address: 'the apparent inconsistencies and internal contradictions in strategies and practices occurring at different levels of industrial relations within firms'.[55] An example provided by Kochan et al. is that of a company actively promoting labour-management co-operation at the workplace level (the third level) of their unionised worksites while simultaneously engaging in sophisticated strategies at the first level to ensure any new locations remain union free.[56] The writers identify three advantages of the three-tier framework, which is to be used as a tool of analysis in conjunction with the phenomena of strategic choice and environmental variables, and these are set out in Table 9.3.

Table 9.3 Advantages of the three-tier institutional framework

(1) '—recognises the inter-relationships among activities at the different levels of the system and helps explain the origins of any prevailing internal contradictions or inconsistencies among the three levels'.

(2) '—considers the effects that various strategic decisions exert on the different actors in the system. —[for example, aids understanding of] how unions have responded to the increased importance of decisions made by employers at the top tier. —facilitates analysis of the effects that increased participation in workplace decisions by individuals and informal work groups have for the labor movement and the industrial relations system'

(3) '—encourages analysis of the roles that labor, management, and government play in each other's domain and activities [thereby maintaining] the broad normative perspective that traditionally characterised industrial relations research, theory and policy or prescriptive analyses'.

Source: T.A. Kochan, H.C. Katz and R.B. McKersie, *The Transformation of American Industrial Relations*, Basic Books, New York, 1986, p. 19.

An apposite observation by Strauss however, is that the framework lacks a clear distinction between the first level (strategy) and the second level (bargaining): it is not clear whether the distinction depends on the subject matter, its importance or the rank of the people involved. Strauss says that there is conflicting evidence in relation to the Kochan et al. claim that adoption of new industrial relations policies has been associated with senior management playing a more active role in industrial relations and a decline in the power of the traditional industrial relations department. For example, there is evidence that the status and perhaps the power of human resources departments is growing. Case studies are therefore needed on managerial industrial relations decision making and institutions and 'management governance deserves the same intensive study that union governance received forty years ago'.[57] Kochan et al. have concurred, stressing that more research is necessary to clarify how activities at the various levels interact but warn that sharp distinctions may prove fruitless: to the extent that management and labour transform their relationships in ways that effectively link practices across the three levels, the levels will no longer be separable and a new integrated industrial relations system will become the arena of industrial relations activity.[58]

Strategic choice: a critique

A comprehensive critique of the strategic-choice model of industrial relations is provided by Lewin.[59] The critique is important because of the pervasive use of notions of 'management strategy' and 'strategic choice' in the literature concerned with industrial relations management, including some of the empirical studies reviewed in chapter 10. Lewin provides a critical assessment of contemporary research on industrial relations as a strategic variable in three areas which have received major attention:

1. union avoidance;
2. collective bargaining; and
3. labour-management co-operation.[60]

One aspect of Lewin's critique is summarised here: the research area of union avoidance and specifically the work of Kochan, Katz & McKersie. The key concepts and arguments in their influential work, published in *The Transformation of American Industrial Relations*, have been summarised in chapter 2 and in the above section. The question Lewin considers is whether the 'additive' evidence produced by these researchers supports the theoretical construct of industrial relations as a strategic variable or the accompanying notion of management as the prime mover of modern industrial relations activity.[61]

Lewin observes that the term 'strategy' is used idiosyncratically in the industrial relations strategy literature. In the case of the Kochan *et al.* work, he notes that they appear to argue that the concept of strategy can be applied to and studied at, each of the three main levels of industrial relations activity, namely the strategic, policy and workplace levels (see table 9.2). However they do not appear to offer a consistent, clear, or distinctive definition of strategy or strategic choice in an industrial relations context.[62]

The research concerning union avoidance covers union substitution and union suppression. The former includes management policies and practices to stimulate job satisfaction and positive employee attitudes thereby reducing support for unionism. The latter includes illegal activities and tactics by management such as discharging union activists. Kochan *et al.*[63] argue that chief among the forces affecting declines in union membership are changes in 'basic management values'. As evidence they cite written union-avoidance policy statements and the opening of non-union plants by several large companies including Pepsi-Cola, Procter and Gamble, Mobil Oil, Corning Glass and Pratt and Whitney. Lewin comments that these union-avoidance strategies, as they are termed by the researchers, ostensibly are primarily implemented by disinvesting in unionised plants. Lewin argues however that the Kochan *et al.* multivariate analytical framework (see chapter 2, figure 2.1) was not applied to these cases, thereby weakening empirical support for the conclusion that these events stemmed primarily from managements' strategic choices. No evidence was provided:

1. by which to gauge the effects that competitive forces or relative performance of union and non-union plants may have had on business location decisions and the growth of the non-union component of the companies;

2 to indicate how other factors, such as changing workforce composition or union leadership and behaviour, may have influenced union density in these companies; and
3 to indicate what weight should be assigned to other factors that typically influence business location decisions such as cost of capital, land costs, depreciation, taxes, product distribution channels and transportation costs.[64]

Lewin contends that the Kochan *et al.* research and other research which the authors draw on, seems to suggest that any management objective, action, or choice can be described as strategic, in which case, Lewin concludes, the concept of strategy is vacuous.

Lewin questions the conceptual and empirical validity of treating the strategic choice of union avoidance in isolation from other strategic objectives and policies of the company. He argues that in the 1970s United States companies began to invest, directly and indirectly, in union avoidance because of three factors. First, in the 1960s and 1970s there was a diffusion of knowledge among employers of the costs of unionism: research showing that unions capture a portion of companies' profits and unions and strike activity have negative effects on shareholder equity. Secondly, there was a simultaneous rapid expansion of behavioural science research and consultation acting as a stimulus to employee participation. Thirdly, growing international competition dramatised the labour cost differences between the United States and other nations and also underscored the seeming comparative advantage of non-American companies to enhance employee commitment and loyalty to the enterprise.[65]

Lewin says that management union avoidance behaviour (both union substitution and union suppression) is consistent with the concept of utility maximisation that underlies neoclassical price theory. Thus, increases in economic competition can be expected to influence managerial values which, in turn, affect managers' preferences or choices of business decisions, including those pertaining to industrial relations processes and outcomes. This, Lewin says, helps explain why the long-standing management value orientation of major opposition toward unionism, has increasingly been translated into actual union containment and avoidance behaviour, especially in manufacturing, the stronghold of unionism.

Lewin concludes that Kochan *et al.* and others have not yet conducted the type of research which enables rejection of an alternative explanation (or null hypothesis) of management behaviour. His alternative proposal is that managements' union avoidance activities are as (more) consistent with a reactive behaviour model as with (than) a strategic choice model of industrial relations.[66] He notes it may also be argued that the market-driven 'efficiency' basis of union avoidance behaviour is a smokescreen for the more fundamental reason, namely managements' strong resistance to giving up its unilateral decision-making authority. This interpretation may be relatively more consistent with a 'strategic-choice' than a 'reactive-behaviour' model of industrial relations.[67] Lewin draws similar conclusions in relation to the research concerning collective bargaining and employee participation.

Strategy: a conceptual refinement

Purcell and Ahlstrand[68] provide a further refinement of the concept of management strategy by distinguishing between first, second and third order strategies. Strategic decisions are defined as those actions or plans which have long-run consequences for the behaviour of the firm. Strategy is regarded as a flow of important decisions and the concepts are developed in the context of diversified multi-divisional firms. 'First-order' corporate strategy is concerned with the long-run direction of the firm (mission and goals) and the scope and mix of its activities.[69] Decisions here concern acquisitions or takeovers, major production changes or fixed capital investment. 'Second-order' business strategies are decisions concerned with the structuring of the enterprise and the control systems adopted.[70] Management choices here include:

1. integration or separation of the business, and
2. centralisation or decentralisation of profit responsibility.

'Third-order' strategic decisions are functional decisions in production, marketing and employee relations/industrial relations. The discrete critical choices which comprise employee relations strategy are set out in Table 9.4.

Table 9.4 Management employee relations/industrial relations strategy: 'third order' critical choices

(1)	'the question of management style (whether or not a dominant style is cultivated across the entire corporation)'.
(2)	'the deployment of personnel management resources and the level of decision-making within personnel and industrial relations'.
(3)	'the configuration of internal labour markets, seen especially in job-grading and evaluation systems and labour mobility'.
(4)	'the choice of bargaining and consultative units'.

Source: J. Purcell and B. Ahlstrand, 'Corporate Strategy and the Management of Employee Relations in the Multi-Divisional Company', *British Journal of Industrial Relations 27*, November 1989, p. 404.

In essence, functional strategy is concerned with how the enterprise manages the boundaries of its industrial relations system: 'through corporate-wide systems, divisional-wide arrangements, or localised within the operating subsidiary'.[71]

Purcell and Ahlstrand examine the nature and direction of the linkages between strategic decisions at the corporate level and the functional level through case studies of nine companies, supplemented by a literature review and other data sources. Two examples of the linkages are provided here. The first concerns the possible influence of employee relations management on corporate strategy. Generally, the evidence suggests that the influence is slight with the case studies and the 1985 Workplace Industrial Relations Company Level Survey indicating a decline in representation of this management function on boards of directors, that is, personnel directorships.[72] The researchers conclude that employee relations management and issues are rarely taken into account in the formulation of corporate strategies. The exception is when a strategic decision has distinct industrial relations implications for example plant closure, redundancy or plant run-down. Corporate level strategic decisions may also influence employee relations management. One employee relations strategic decision concerns the level at which bargaining takes place. The choices here are: multi-employer; intra-company (centralised) and intra-company (decentralised). In their case studies, Purcell and Ahlstrand find that where companies had changed their bargaining level in the mid-1980s it was invariably a change deriving from 'second-order' strategy that is, from business style or business structure reasons rather than from strategic thinking within industrial relations. Typically, the stated aim of the change was to link industrial relations outcomes to business performance of divisions or operating units. The style changes which precipitated bargaining level change included greater emphasis on 'entrepreneurship' and 'commercialism'; structural changes included 'the establishment of operating units as separate limited companies'.[73] Another finding was universal resistance from national trade union officers to the moves to decentralise and also frequent resistance from the corporate personnel department whose current role was often at stake.[74]

Management strategy: alternative approaches

Ahlstrand,[75] writing in the late 1980s, argues that it is possible to define three rather distinct approaches to management industrial relations strategy. The distinguishing features of the rational approach, the political approach and the symbolic approach are detailed in Table 9.5. If these distinctions and their underlying assumptions of people and organisations are accepted, it follows that there are a number of definitions of strategy for industrial relations rather than one definition. In the industrial relations literature the rational approach is evident within the British industrial relations 'reformist' movement of the 1960s especially the work of the Royal Commission on Trade Unions and Employer's Associations (the Donovan Commission). This group included Flanders whose study of management initiatives involving productivity bargaining is considered in chapter 18. Ahlstrand observes that the rational approach was also evident in the 1980s 'strategy' debate, in the work for example of Purcell, Timperley and Thurley and Wood.[76] Ahlstrand identifies a consistent theme in the writings of the 1960s and the 1980s: the importance of management education as the means to effective reform. In the 1960s the problems were held to be excessive informality in industrial relations practice, fragmentation and local bargaining. The solution lay in educating managers about new sophisticated managerial techniques such as manpower planning, job evaluation and productivity bargaining and their application by management.[77] In the 1980s strategy debate, similar pleas for strategic thinking by managers were evident. Ahlstrand offers two possible reasons for this: the crisis faced by capital in the recession, the 'challenge from without' and the failure of British management to take heed of the reformists' plea in the 1960s.[78] He observes that the labour process school also imputed rationality to management. While this school's analysis had focused on exposing the exploitative strategies of management rather than the management prescription offered by the reformist school, it did nonetheless assume a deliberateness and a consciousness on the part of management.[79] Ahlstrand contends that two features common to work within this school are:

1. a tendency to see industrial relations strategies following unproblematically from a firm's stated objectives; and
2. an assumption that labour will always be subordinated to capital; if one management strategy begins to fail it will be readily replaced by a more sophisticated, successful strategy.

Table 9.5 Alternative approaches to management industrial relations strategy

Rational approach
- 'stresses long-term planning and the adoption of various prescriptive formulae'; industrial relations problems can be remedied or overcome by careful planning and forethought
- 'assumes management or the dominant coalition is a homogeneous group or is organised around a relatively coherent set of aims'
- is concerned both with goals, for example, productivity improvement, and the means for achieving them, for example, through productivity bargaining
- assumes 'consciousness and deliberateness on the part of management' and that 'management is capable of identifying long-term desirable goals and of implementing and sustaining them'

Political approach
- 'stresses the emergent nature of strategy' and incorporates the notion of accommodation and conflict
- interprets organisations as 'political entities, with political goals, political decisions and political people. As a result, industrial relations strategies are seen as products of complex political processes'
- 'strategies are not the product of a conscious, deliberate and well thought-out process' but rather they evolve over time from 'a complex process of negotiation, compromise and accommodation amongst various competing groups within the organisation'
- 'highlights the fragmented and disparate nature of the management group' and the potential of various competing interest groups and coalitions 'to reshape the content of management strategies'

Symbolic approach
- views strategy in terms of the underlying meaning of what is happening, not in terms of what is happening
- activities of organisations are 'understood not so much by what they do as by what they represent'
- 'organisational structures, activities and initiatives are interpreted in terms of secular myths, rituals and ceremonies'
- explores 'the function that myths, rituals and ceremonies play in day-to-day organisational life'
- suggests 'organisational activities and intiatives may have meaning and significance above and beyond the purely rational functions normally attributed to such phenomena'

Source: Adapted from B. Ahlstrand, *The quest for productivity: A case study of Fawley after Flanders*, Cambridge University Press, Cambridge, 1990, pp. 11-12, 19, 22-23, 26-29.

Just as Purcell's discussion of management style developed from a critique of Fox's managerial frames of reference, so the political approach to management strategy emerged from a critique of the rational approach. Ahlstrand notes that the political approach has been best articulated in the organisational theory literature but is evident in the industrial relations literature. The latter includes: Brown's work on custom and practice; research on managerial and supervisory custom and practice by Armstrong and Goodman and by Brewster and Richbell; the Batstone *et al.* study of management strategies in the British post office; Littler's general study.[80] As indicated in Table 9.5 the political approach 'highlights micro-politics within the management group' and 'stresses the role of subordinate groups in both the determination and the distortion of management strategy'.[81]

The symbolic approach to management strategy had not been applied to the notion of strategy within industrial relations prior to Ahlstrand's study of productivity bargaining at Fawley (see chapter 18). Ahlstrand argues this approach goes one step beyond the political approach in deleting rationality from management strategy. From this perspective what appears to be the case is often not the case. Thus while the rational management goal of productivity bargaining may be productivity improvement, at the symbolic level such management initiative may have more to do with establishing the legitimacy of the management groups which undertook the reform program. As Ahlstrand expresses it '... grand management strategies may be nothing more than coping devices for dealing with seemingly unmanageable problems.'[82] It follows from this approach that while management initiatives may be failing in terms of the rational approach, that is in terms of stated objectives, they may be functional at the symbolic level.

Strategy: an overview

A number of characteristics of management strategy are identified in a secondary analysis of the concept by Dufty and Fells.[83] First, in the broadest sense, a strategy is a means of achieving objectives. It may be characterised as a plan of action for which the prerequisites are the existence of objectives and some freedom of choice when interacting with other actors or with the environment. It is a means of handling the environment which is constantly changing and is often far from benign. Secondly, the formulation of a strategy involves:

1 identifying the issues involved,
2 generating and evaluating alternatives; and
3 choosing the course of action which it is considered will best achieve the objective(s).[84]

Thirdly, strategy formulation and strategy implementation can be distinguished. In the implementation phase, outcomes will be evaluated against the objectives and corrective action taken if necessary. This means strategy development is a continuous process.[85] Fourthly, the purpose of developing a strategy, which is essentially to gain some control over the environment, is as applicable to the industrial relations level (or function) as it is to the company or organisation as a whole. This means that analysis of industrial relations management strategy cannot be undertaken apart from the dynamics of the company or organisation as a whole and its interaction with its environment.[86] This is a central feature of the Kochan, Katz and McKersie analysis considered above.

Dufty and Fells note that the development of the concept and principles of strategy management has been primarily in the area of corporate management and these have their origin in the functional areas of marketing and finance. They observe that many organisations devote resources to developing strategies in order to respond to and exploit their environment and some use strategic planning models. These attempt to chart the company's future course and identify areas of strength and weakness including areas with potential for contraction, rationalisation or even closure. This suggests that strategy is synonymous with a conscious, rational plan. Dufty and Fells, however, identify literature which questions this. They point out that the neo-Weberian idea of 'problematical rationality' applies when considering the notion of strategy. They cite the warning by Thurley and Wood that much of the corporate strategy literature 'assumes an organisational rationality which most industrial relations practitioners and theorists would instinctively reject ... Strategy implementation is always problematical'.[87] In similar vein is the argument by Hyman, from the labour process school, that in the capitalist mode of production, actions by management are beset by contradictions both within management and between management and labour. Thus Hyman concludes that strategy is best conceptualised as 'the pragmatic choice amongst alternatives, none of which prove satisfactory'.[88] In both these cases the writers appear to be referring to what Ahlstrand captures in the concept of the political approach to management strategy (see above).

Management structure

Some of the works discussed above assume management is a homogeneous group. Others recognise the different levels of management and yet others recognise the existence of competing priorities and interests among managers. In practice in all but small companies there will be, to use Dunlop's phrase, a hierarchy of managers. Management covers a wide spectrum from first-line managers or supervisors (marginal managers as they have been termed) to boards of directors.

The organisation and status of the industrial relations function may be influenced by both internal and external factors. The former include the nature of the company structure and ownership and the philosophies of senior management. External factors include the nature of public regulation of industrial relations, and the nature of the trade unions with which the company has to deal. An understanding of the relative importance of these factors for companies requires empirical investigation, with longitudinal case studies providing the most illuminating data.

Gospel defines structure as the organisational forms which management has used for the best pursuit of its strategies.[89] He acknowledges Chandler's[90] original formulation that structure follows strategy but presents the strategy-structure relationship as dynamic and interactive so that structure also facilitates further strategic decisions. Gospel identifies different structural forms used by employers for labour management. There are two indirect (or delegated) forms, the first being 'putting out' and internal subcontracting systems wherein the employer hands production over to a dispersed labour force (known as outworkers in Australia) or to a subcontractor. These systems operate in the clothing and construction industries. The attraction of these systems to management is that they economise on the costs of recruiting, supervising and directly maintaining a labour force. (Marxists, such as Braverman, would explain the decline in these systems in terms of the capitalists' need to control the labour process.) External contracting to smaller firms could be included in this category of labour management. Gospel argues that this structure allows large companies to control employment relations so as to maintain their own permanent labour force while passing on risks to smaller firms and their employees. The second indirect form of labour management is the use of employer associations. The role of these associations in the management of industrial relations in Australia is discussed in chapter 11. As is the case in most Western economies they may be used as an employer collective seeking to provide a united countervailing force to trade unionism and in the case of smaller companies, as a source of expertise and knowledge in a particular management speciality. In Australia however they have also been used by companies which do have the capacity to operate solely with internal systems, for the purpose of handling those areas of labour management which are under the legal control of the industrial tribunals.

The direct form of labour management finds expression in the development of internal management hierarchies. The simplest and earliest forms saw the emergence of the role of the foreman, or first-line manager as this level is now termed. In the early part of this century it was the foreman who controlled both production management and labour management. The foreman was responsible for the planning, allocation, speed and methods of work as well as the personnel functions of hiring, firing, promotion, discipline, payment and grievance handling. Gospel notes that the decline in the authority of the foreman since the First World War[91] has coincided with an elaboration of internal management hierarchies in relation to both line and staff management.

Kochan and Katz[92] identify three basic characteristics of management structure relevant to industrial relations:

1. the number of industrial relations staff vis-à-vis the number of employees in the company. This is said to reflect the priority given to the industrial relations function;
2. the degree of centralisation in decision making on industrial relations issues, that is how decision making or particular activities, are distributed among the different levels of the company. The writers distinguish plant (or establishment) level, divisional level and corporate level. A related feature here is the relative staff allocation at each level;
3. the degree of specialisation in decision making over industrial relations issues, that is, the extent to which decision-making authority rests with specialist industrial relations staff as opposed to operating or line managers.[93]

This third aspect of structure suggests the possibility of lateral shifts in decision-making power while (2) above suggests the possibility of vertical shifts. A distinction is drawn between labour (industrial) relations staff and personnel staff. Responsibilities of the former include: dealing with union organising drives, negotiations and contract administration. The latter are concerned with matters such as recruitment, equal employment opportunity, health and safety and wage and salary administration. However, an increasing number of firms have integrated labour relations and personnel activities within 'a broad human resource management unit'.[94]

Kochan and Katz discuss management structure in the context of the United States collective bargaining system. Noting that the function of an organisational structure is to provide a means for implementing the company's goals and strategies, they point out that in the case of industrial relations functions, the structure is designed to enable management to bargain effectively with the union.[95]

In relation to the second aspect of structure, Kochan and Katz report findings of a survey of 668 companies which they claim contradict one of the most common observations concerning the collective bargaining system in the United States, that it is highly decentralised. The data indicate that control over key strategic decisions such as establishing the discretion limits for management negotiators, determining the issues over which the firm should take a strike and approving the final package, was located at the corporate level in at least two-thirds of the companies surveyed.[96] This was the case even when bargaining was undertaken on a plant-by-plant basis.

The dependence of structure on strategy is illustrated in the shift in power in the United States in recent years from labour relations staff to line managers and, albeit to a lesser degree, to human resource specialists. This lateral shift in management structures is a consequence of shifts in firms' business strategies from those that value labour peace and predictability to strategies of tighter cost controls and greater flexibility in work rules and organisation.[97] Although there was a continuing dependence on labour relations experts for technical expertise, this area has ceased to be a 'powerful fiefdom' of the management hierarchy.[98] The changes include the use of strategic planning groups for labour relations and cross-functional teams to develop new bargaining proposals. Survey data from 1983 showed that the majority of firms assigned primary authority for human resource planning and employee participation programs to human resource executives or line managers. Kochan and Katz suggest if these changes are sustained and widespread, future requirements of industrial relations professionals will be:

1. greater business, analytical, and planning skills;
2. expertise in both traditional labour relations activities and personnel or human resource management activities;
3. a more thorough understanding of operating management issues; and
4. an ability to work as a member of a multi-disciplinary team in implementing labour relations strategies and policies'.[99]

The third aspect of structure identified by Kochan and Katz, the degree of specialisation or the division of responsibility between line managers and specialist (staff) managers, is considered by Flanders in developing lessons of wider application from a study of the first generation productivity agreements in an oil refinery in Great Britain in the late 1950s and early 1960s (see chapter 18). Flanders questions the desirability of the personnel-industrial relations management function being carried out solely by a corps of specialists:

> 'The separation of personnel management from management in general is too artificial not to lead to serious difficulty in practice on both sides. Personnel managers cannot advise line managers intelligently when they have not an adequate grasp of the physical, technical and economic factors in the situation which the line managers are trying to control. Conversely the latter are compelled to treat 'advice' as an 'instruction' if they lack any confident judgement on labour relations though they will still resent it as an interference with their authority. It is typical of a condition of irresponsibility that blame for anything that goes wrong can be placed at somebody else's door, and line management may not be averse to making personnel management the scapegoat for its own deficiencies'.[100]

Flanders argues that all management involves some personnel management and that this function should be strongly integrated with line management. He recognises that acceptance of this view implies that the success of personnel management as a specialised function would be judged by the extent to which the need for it declines.[101] In contrast to the position advocated by Flanders, Ahlstrand's research establishes that the personnel function became very powerful at the Fawley oil refinery, assuming a status higher than that accorded it in British industry generally.[102]

Flanders also considers the issue of lack of management innovation (in the context of Great Britain) and argues that unresolved confusion concerning the division of responsibility between line management and staff contributed to lack of innovation and what he terms 'managerial irresponsibility'. Flanders contends that the majority of (line) managers (both first-line and senior) in British industry readily delegated the industrial relations function to staff specialists. Typical line managers regarded both interest and rights disputes as irritations, as unwelcome diversions from the more important aspects of their work. As Flanders expresses it: 'Trouble-free and frictionless relations are the production man's ideal. To play for safety and to let well alone is the next best thing'.[103] This approach was a product of a lack of knowledge and confidence. For the most part, the day to day running of policy is left to the specialists but in moments of real crisis line managers often must assume real authority—the authority which has been delegated (with varying degrees of clarity/precision) to the staff experts. Thus, argues Flanders, the most complex management decisions, those requiring the most informed judgement were 'as like as not handled by amateurs who trust their hunch as practical men of affairs'.[104] In terms of the quality of management, an important negative consequence is that the position adopted by the line managers may well be in conflict with the policy the company has been following within the confines of the personnel or industrial relations department. Such inconsistency is potentially disastrous in industrial relations management because it has the potential to destroy patiently forged relationships of confidence and perhaps even trust.[105]

Flanders' discussion has relevance for the degree of centralisation of this management function as well as for the degree of specialisation aspect already noted. In terms of the approaches developed by Ahlstrand, Flanders is describing behaviour which may be explained in terms of the political approach. The discussion also reveals some lack of clarity in the formal procedural rules (see chapter 2) within the industrial relations system of a firm, together with some divergence from the formal rules in practice, that is the use of informal procedural rules.

Employee participation in management

This section begins with consideration of some conceptual issues and analytical frameworks relating to employee participation and industrial democracy and this is followed by a critique of popular assumptions concerning management motivations in supporting increased participation.

Theories of participation

Vaughan, writing in the early 1980s, observes that a feature of the debate surrounding the widespread advocacy of increased employee participation in the 1970s was the general absence of detailed supporting arguments or a systematic analysis thereof. He seeks to correct this perceived deficiency by identifying and evaluating the different theories on which the case for increased participation is based.[106] Vaughan identifies three categories of theories of participation and four analytically distinct theories: psychological theory; sociological theory; organisational theory and political theory distinguished in terms of 'basic propositions' or 'core assertions'. The categories of theory are set out in Table 9.6.

Table 9.6 Theories of employee participation: categories

Category 1 includes theories which assert a need or desire by workers to play an active part in the design and control of their own work processes	Psychological Theory
	Sociological Theory
Category 2 includes theories which assert that improved organisational performance will result from worker participation in management decisions.	Organisational Theory
Category 3 includes theories which assert that workers ought to have the right to participate in decisions that will immediately or ultimately affect them.	Political Theory

Source: Adapted from E.J. Vaughan, 'Theories of participation: an analysis of core assertions' in W.A. Howard (ed.), *Perspectives on Australian Industrial Relations: Essays in honour of Kingsley Laffer*, Longman Cheshire, Melbourne, 1984, pp. 166-168.

Vaughan concludes that on an analysis of evidence and argument, each of the theories, with the exception of the psychological theory, provides good reasons for supporting increased employee participation in management. The core assertions for two of the theories, the psychological theory and the organisational theory, are set out in Table 9.7.

Table 9.7 Theories of participation: core assertions

Psychological Theory

1. People apply most effort and intelligence to tasks which they find psychologically satisfying.
2. Psychologically satisfying tasks are those which require skill, self-control and discretion; possess some intrinsic value or meaning to the person performing them; and produce feelings of pride and accomplishment.
3. Non-managerial work and non-professional work, especially mechanised and routine production work, is frequently simple, monotonous, externally supervised and therefore unsatisfying.
4. Work satisfaction and productivity would improve significantly if unsatisfying tasks were redesigned to allow the persons performing them, individually and collectively, to control their own work processes and working arrangements.

Organisational Theory

1. Organisational structure is a major factor determining communication and decision-making processes within industrial organisations.
2. Organisations' environments are increasingly characterised by rapid change and uncertainty.
3. In order to adapt effectively to environmental changes, organisations will need to be managed in a more innovative, flexible and cooperative manner than is observed at present.
4. Existing organisational structures typically impose a rigid division of labour according to technical specialisation, responsibility and authority which permits a very limited use of available intellectual resources and produces interpersonal tensions and management-labour conflict.
5. Organisations would perform more effectively if they were structured in such a way that communication and decision-making processes allowed a free exchange of ideas and a representation of different interests.

Source: E J Vaughan, 'Theories of participation: an analysis of core assertions', in W A Howard (ed.), *Perspectives on Australian Industrial Relations: Essays in honour of Kingsley Laffer*, Longman Cheshire, Melbourne, 1984, p. 169 and pp. 174-175.

Vaughan identifies the weaknesses in the psychological theory as (1) the assumption of a set of universal 'psychological needs' and (2) research results which contradict core assertions for example, evidence that most workers express job satisfaction regardless of the nature of the work.[107] He critically analyses the methods used to justify changes which do not seem to be in high demand by employees and concludes that the theory fails to provide good reasons for supporting increased worker participation in management.[108]

In the case of organisational theories, Vaughan notes the central assumption that structure determines process and that research on organisational processes necessarily commences with an analysis of structure.[109] Regarding the division of labour within the enterprise as the essence of organisational structure, Vaughan summarises the criticisms in the organisational behaviour literature concerning the dominant institutional structural form namely, the bureaucratic division of labour. In this structure, the primary responsibility of managers is to plan, organise and control the work of non-managerial employees and this is based on their assumed technical expertise. The literature criticises this structure on three grounds:

1 that it is irrational;
2 that it generates internal disharmony; and
3 that it exaggerates the true extent of managerial authority.[110]

Arguments relating to the first ground include the diminution in the total amount of intelligence that can be applied to organisational problems when there is a separation between 'thinking' and 'doing' and the findings of research concerning the nature of managerial work. Vaughan cites Mintzberg's[111] conclusions that managerial work is rarely typified by a rational process involving analysis of objectives and alternatives and adoption of the most efficient and effective means. Further, the traditional division of labour is held to be dysfunctional due to the tensions and mistrust which result from the wide gulf between managers and workers. Thirdly, the non-participative structure masks the reality that employee consent to exercise of management authority is frequently a prerequisite for employee co-operation.[112] In concluding that organisational theory provides a strong case for increased participation, Vaughan cautions, as other writers have done, against regarding participatory decision making as a panacea, given the unpredictability of outcomes.[113]

Employee participation and industrial democracy

In the foregoing analysis employee participation and industrial democracy are regarded as synonymous. Teicher,[114] in an analysis of the usage of these terms, distinguishes two broad concepts of industrial democracy: the socialist variant and the collective bargaining variant. He notes that historically, industrial democracy was associated with programs for transition to a socialist society but over time has become identified with its central component, employee participation in management.[115] The socialist variant emphasises direct participation by workers in the government of the organisation. On a strict interpretation of this concept there is no separate management hierarchy but contemporary expositions assume the existence of one. With this variant, employee participation is connected to industrial democracy. The collective bargaining variant accepts the capitalist economic system and that ownership interests are represented by a permanent management hierarchy. Here, industrial democracy is embodied in the institutions and processes of collective bargaining.[116] Teicher notes that limited forms of employee participation could be incorporated in collective agreements and that employees can and should seek greater control over the organisation and conduct of their work. Thus a relationship between employee participation and industrial democracy is presumed as he addresses the usage of the term employee participation. Here Teicher draws upon Vaughan's framework of theories of participation (see above).

Teicher notes that a source of confusion in the literature is the terms employee participation and industrial democracy being used by different individuals to describe the same phenomenon. The various theories reveal diverse views as to:

- whether participation requires involvement in actual decision making;
- the organisational levels at which participation should occur;
- the preferred form of participation; and
- the extent of involvement in decision making.[117]

Teicher identifies two related problems associated with the frequent focus of definitions of employee participation on 'influence on management decision making'.[118] The decision-making focus is seen as restrictive and influence as insufficiently precise in describing the forces mediating the employee-management relationship. Teicher advocates the substitution of power for influence in defining employee participation because this enables the outcome to be predicted.[119] Thus, if managers consult employees on specific matters, the form of influence is specified but knowledge of the parties' relative power is needed to predict the outcome. The focus on decision making highlights the forms and effects of participation but neglects the process element. It 'disguises the routine and implicit way in which power is commonly exercised, and imputes a greater degree of conscious rationality to the process than is often the case'.[120]

The inclusion of power in the definition of employee participation is said to reveal a close connection between employee participation and industrial democracy. Teicher draws on the concept of participatory democracy developed by Pateman[121] to argue that the pre-conditions for industrial democracy are employee participation:

1. at all levels of the organisation; and
2. based on equality of power (full participation).[122]

These aspects form part of a typology of participation illustrated in diagrammatic form in Figure 9.2. The typology uses a framework developed by Pateman as a starting point and draws upon a worker participation matrix developed by Wang.[123]

Pateman regards the degree of participation as being determined by who makes the final decision. She distinguishes:

1. full participation: each member of a decision-making body has equal power to determine the outcome of decisions for example, semi-autonomous work groups under carefully specified decisions.
2. partial participation: workers can only influence a decision; they do not have equal power to decide an outcome, for example, joint consultation.
3. pseudo-participation: employee influence on decision making is more apparent than real.[124]

Lansbury and Gilmour,[125] in a work published in the 1970s, identify types of participation often associated with each of the four levels developed by Wang. These are detailed in Table 9.8.

Figure 9.2 Employee participation and industrial democracy: a typology

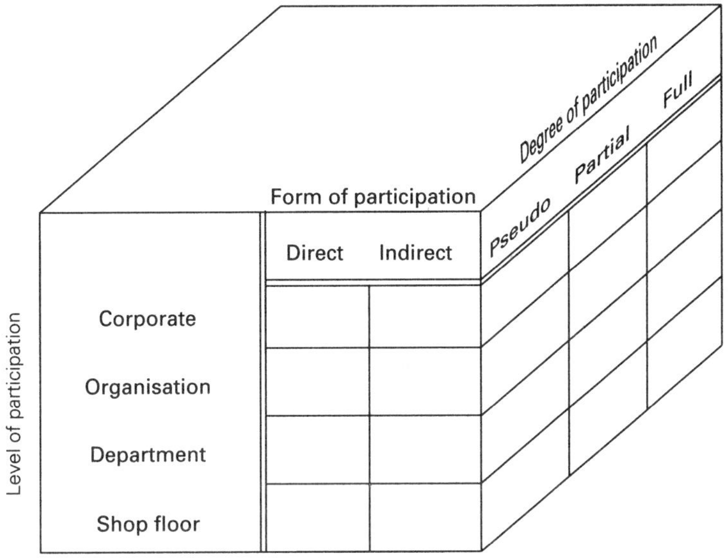

[Figure: A three-dimensional cube diagram with three axes. The vertical axis is "Level of participation" with categories Corporate, Organisation, Department, Shop floor. The horizontal axis is "Form of participation" with categories Direct and Indirect. The depth axis is "Degree of participation" with categories Pseudo, Partial, Full.]

Source: J. Teicher, 'Theories of employee participation and industrial democracy: towards an analytical framework' in B. Dabscheck, G. Griffin and J. Teicher (eds), *Contemporary Australian Industrial Relations: Readings*, Longman Cheshire, Melbourne, 1992, p. 490.

Table 9.8 Forms of worker participation by level

- **Shop floor**
  job enrichment schemes including job rotation and autonomous work groups. The latter may place workers in complete command of their work situation and lead to self-management but typically is confined to more routine aspects of work organisation.

- **Departmental**
  suggestion schemes, mini-work councils, joint consultative committees. Typically involve information being passed down from management to the shop floor. Degree of consultation depends on amount of autonomy given to councils/committees and the scope of their decision-making powers.

- **Organisational**
  Typically joint consultative councils and works councils. Usually consultative only but may have some joint decision-making powers. Decisions usually concerned with expenditure within budgets; office/factory layout; personnel matters such as hiring and firing.

- **Corporate**
  Most common form is the election or appointment of workers' representatives to the company board. May include worker share ownership ranging from no worker board representation to total worker control. In latter case workers may appoint managers who adopt a traditional role.

Source: Adapted from R D Lansbury and P Gilmour, *Organisations: an Australian Perspective*, Longman Cheshire, Melbourne, 1977, pp. 118-120.

Employee participation: management motives

Vaughan[126] writing in the mid-1970s considers management behaviour and its relationship to management attitudes to increases in employee participation. Vaughan notes that the (then) recent support in management theory for participative management relied overwhelmingly on an 'effectiveness-efficiency' argument, regardless of the form of participation being proposed. The common argument was that if employees participated in organisational decision making, they would experience greater job satisfaction, there would be less industrial conflict, communications and information dissemination would be enhanced. The net result wold be an improvement in the quality of decision making and in productivity.[127]

The aspect of concern to Vaughan is the 'concealed premise' in this argument, namely that management behaviour is typically governed by a search for organisational efficiency and effectiveness, by an economic imperative. He suggests that past research concentration on (employee) opposition to management changes, to the exclusion of changes opposed by management has, incorrectly, given credence to this concealed assumption. It is argued that insufficient attention has been given to the political consequences of worker participation, that is, the power and status equalisation implications.[128] Vaughan cites literature which challenges the assumption of management rationality and suggests that any shift in the direction of increased participation is likely to be resisted by management.[129] In other words, that any group or individual which possesses superior power and status is not likely to voluntarily relinquish that position, and in the case of managers their superiority derives primarily from their authority to make and implement decisions.

If this reasoning is accepted, then the fact of management's professed interest in employee participation requires explanation. Vaughan offers three possible reasons. First, in the interests of credibility there is a strong incentive for managers to offer (at least) lip-service support for any proposal regarded as likely to assist the generally accepted function of management, that is, to integrate and co-ordinate company resources to achieve company objectives as effectively and efficiently as possible. There is a parallel here in the oft-cited public support of employers for trade union rights as an expression of democratic values juxtaposed on occasions with a private attitude of 'but not in my factory'. Second, managers may regard employee participation as a means of increasing control over employees over whom they have line authority. In this circumstance managers are making a utilitarian commitment to participation. This is, in effect, pseudo-participation which is used as a means to persuade employees to accept prior management decisions but does not involve the fundamental structural changes essential to genuine participative management. Workers believe they have had some say in decisions and possibly have greater responsibility for their work, but the power relations within the firm are not changed.[130]

The third possible explanation for management support, and the one Vaughan believes is most likely to be invoked by managers, is managers' genuine interest in testing proposals claimed to result in increased efficiency. This is also the socially acceptable reason, the one most amenable to attracting public support.

Conclusion

The theories of industrial relations management summarised here were written within the period from the mid-1960s to the late 1980s. They illustrate the alternative approaches to the study of industrial relations identified in chapter 2 and they are indicative of the burgeoning literature concerned with the hitherto neglected group of actors, the representatives of employers, during the 1980s. Most of the research has been concerned with strategy. This contrasts with trade unions where, in terms of theory, strategy has been a comparatively neglected area.

The material included here shows the continuing refinement of concepts and models and reveals areas of overlap as well as distinguishing features. The cumulative value of research is evident, as is the potential for integration. Strauss for example, in a critique of the Kochan, Katz and McKersie work, implies a weakness of their analysis is that the discussion of the personnel policies of non-union firms present them chiefly as alternatives to those of union firms. He suggests the need for integration of conceptual developments in industrial relations, human resources management and organisational behaviour. The potential diversity of management decisions to which Strauss alludes, has been captured in Purcell's model of management style. The behaviours categorised by Purcell as different styles are regarded as strategies by Kochan, Katz and McKersie. Purcell is concerned with certain management choices which are sometimes made regardless of the position of other actors and the particular features of the environment and his model abstracts from the issue of implementation, in this case, implementation of management style.

The Kochan, Katz and McKersie framework integrates the different levels of decision making by management and here the emphasis is on institutional complexity. Ahlstrand's framework on the other hand, emphasises motivational complexity but overlaps with the Kochan *et al.* framework at the level of the political approach. The distinguishing features of this approach however mesh with the capacity of the three-tier institutional framework to help 'explain the origins of any prevailing internal contradictions or inconsistencies among the three levels'. Ahlstrand is primarily concerned with the motivations and personal goals of managers as one group of actors, as well as implicitly recognising the heterogeneity of management. His theoretical framework emerges from a longitudinal study of management strategy at a particular workplace and is used to explain the endurance and persistent failure of that strategy at a rational level. The study, summarised in chapter 18, also provides vivid illustrations of intra-management relationships and the constraints imposed by unions. This framework of alternative approaches to strategy adds another layer of complexity to the Kochan *et al.* framework. Purcell and Ahlstrand, in the most recent published work on strategy considered here, draw on the political approach and adapt, modify and test the three-tier institutional framework in their examination of the nature and direction of linkages between corporate strategy and (functional) industrial relations strategy. In their analysis, the level at which industrial relations management decisions are made is itself a strategic choice or decision. The summary of theories and concepts relating to industrial democracy and employee participation in management illustrates the diversity of disciplines developing theories and conducting research on this issue. In the industrial relations literature concerned with management, employee participation is seen as one element of management strategy. This literature is complemented by management literature such as Vaughan's examination of management motives in relation to employee participation. Many of the theories and concepts discussed in this chapter have been applied by researchers analysing management in Australia and this is the subject of the next chapter.

Notes

1. R. Dubin, *Working Union-Management Relations,* Prentice Hall, Englewood Cliffs, NJ, 1958, p. 31, cited in H. Gospel, 'New Managerial Approaches to Industrial Relations: Major Paradigms and Historical Perspective', *Journal of Industrial Relations* 25, June 1983, p. 164.
2. N.W. Chamberlain, D.E. Cullen and D. Lewin, *The Labor Sector* (3rd ed.), New York, McGraw-Hill, 1980.
3. *ibid.,* p. 227.
4. This concept is discussed in chapter 17 in the context of collective bargaining.
5. Chamberlain *et al., op. cit.* p. 229.
6. *ibid.*
7. *ibid.,* pp. 228-229.
8. The authors distinguish legally prohibited bargaining subjects for example, discriminatory recruitment practices. These are based on the belief that the interplay of private power may thwart the public interest in some specific respect such as encouraging racial or sex discrimination, not on the principle of an inherent prerogative of management.
9. Chamberlain *et. al., op. cit.,* pp. 229-230.
10. H. Braverman, *Labor and Monopoly Capital,* Monthly Review Press, New York, 1974, p. 63.
11. *ibid.,* pp. 58-60.
12. *ibid.,* pp. 63-65.
13. *ibid.,* pp. 36-39.
14. *ibid.,* p. 39.
15. F.W. Taylor, *Scientific Management,* New York and London, 1947. For details of the separate works in this volume see Braverman *op. cit.,* p. 121, note 10.
16. Braverman, *op. cit.,* pp. 89-90.
17. *ibid.,* p. 113.
18. *ibid.,* p. 114.
19. *ibid.,* p. 118.
20. *ibid.,* p. 119.
21. *ibid.,* pp. 120-121.
22. *ibid.,* p. 87.
23. *ibid.,* p. 101.
24. J.T. Dunlop, *Industrial Relations Systems,* Holt, New York, 1958, Reprint Arcturus Books, 1977, p. 17.

25 A. Fox, *Industrial Sociology and Industrial Relations*, Research Papers 3, Royal Commission on Trade Unions and Employers' Associations, H.M.S.O., London 1966. Reprinted in A. Flanders (ed.), *Collective Bargaining*, Harmondsworth, Penguin, 1969, pp. 391-408. In *Beyond Contract: Work, Power and Trust Relations*, Faber, London, 1974, Fox introduces a third frame of reference—the radical perspective. This prescriptive (as opposed to descriptive) frame of reference shares much with Marxism.
26 Fox, 1974, *op cit.*, p. 250.
27 Fox, 1966, *op. cit.*, pp. 391-393.
28 *ibid.*, p. 395.
29 Fox, 1974, *op cit.*, p. 272.
30 *ibid.*, p. 263.
31 Fox, 1966, *op. cit.*, pp. 407-408.
32 The characteristics of this process, a special case of collective bargaining, are discussed in chapter 18.
33 Fox, 1966, *op cit.*, p. 408.
34 J. Purcell, 'Mapping Management Styles in Employee Relations', *Journal of Management Studies 24*, September 1987, pp. 533-548. There are a number of taxonomies and models similar to that developed by Purcell. See *Further Reading* section at the end of this chapter.
35 Fox, 1974, *op. cit.*, chapter 7.
36 Purcell, *op. cit.*, p. 535.
37 *ibid.*, pp. 534-535 & 546.
38 *ibid.*, pp. 535-536.
39 *ibid.*, p. 533.
40 *ibid.*, pp. 536-538.
41 *ibid.*, pp. 538-539.
42 *ibid.*, pp. 540-541.
43 *ibid.*, pp. 544-545.
44 *ibid.*, p. 546.
45 T.A. Kochan, H. C. Katz and R.B McKersie, *The Transformation of American Industrial Relations*, Basic Books, New York, 1986.
46 *ibid.*, pp. 10-11.
47 *ibid.*, p. 5.
48 *ibid.*, pp. 4-5.
49 *ibid.*, p. 9.
50 *ibid.*, p. 12.
51 *ibid.*, pp. 12-13.
52 *ibid.*, pp. 16-17.
53 *ibid.*, p. 18.
54 *ibid.*
55 *ibid.*, p. 19.
56 *ibid.*
57 G. Strauss, Review Symposium, 'The Transformation of American Industrial Relations' *Industrial and Labour Relations Review 41*, April 1988, pp. 450-451.
58 Review Symposium, p. 452.
59 D. Lewin, 'Industrial Relations as a Strategic Variable', in M.M. Kleiner, R.N. Block, M. Roomkin and S.W. Salsburg (eds), *Human Resources Management and the Performance of the Firm*, Industrial Relations Research Association, Madison, Wisconsin, 1988, chapter 1.
60 *ibid.*, p. 2.
61 *ibid.*, p. 9.
62 *ibid.*, pp. 8-9.
63 Kochan, *et. al.*, *op. cit.*, p. 78.
64 Lewin, *op. cit.*, pp. 12-13.
65 *ibid.*, pp. 14-15.
66 *ibid.*, pp. 15-16.

67 *ibid.*, p. 16.
68 J. Purcell and B. Ahlstrand, 'Corporate Strategy and the Management of Employee Relations in the Multi-Divisional Company', *British Journal of Industrial Relations* 27, November 1989, pp. 396-417.
69 *ibid.*, p. 412.
70 *ibid.*, p. 404.
71 *ibid.*
72 *ibid.*, p. 400.
73 *ibid.*, p. 409.
74 *ibid.*, p. 409-410.
75 B.W. Ahlstrand, *The quest for productivity: A case study of Fawley after Flanders*, Cambridge University Press, Cambridge, 1990, p. 11.
76 See *Further Reading* section for details of these works.
77 Ahlstrand, *op. cit.*, pp. 13-16.
78 *ibid.*, pp. 18-19.
79 *ibid.*, pp. 20-21.
80 The relevant works appear in the *Further Reading* section at the end of this chapter.
81 Ahlstrand, *op. cit.*, p. 25.
82 *ibid.*, pp. 27-29.
83 N.F. Dufty and R.E. Fells, *Dynamics of Industrial Relations in Australia*, Prentice Hall, Sydney, 1989, chapter 8.
84 *ibid.*, p. 215.
85 *ibid.*, pp. 215-216.
86 *ibid.*, p. 217.
87 K. Thurley and S. Wood, 'Business strategy and industrial relations strategy', in K. Thurley and S. Wood (eds), *Industrial Relations and Management Strategy*, Cambridge University Press, London, 1983, p. 222, cited in Dufty and Fells *op. cit.*, p. 216.
88 R. Hyman, 'Strategy or structure? Capital, labour and control', *Work, Employment and Society 1*, 1987, p. 30, cited in Dufty and Fells, *op. cit.*, p. 216.
89 Gospel, 1983, *op. cit.*, p. 170.
90 A. Chandler, *Strategy and Structure : Chapters in the History of American Industrial Enterprise*, Cambridge, Massachussetts, 1962.
91 For an Australian perspective see P. Gilmour and R.D. Lansbury, 'The Changing Role of the Supervisor : Implications for Industrial Relations', *Journal of Industrial Relations* 19, September 1977, pp. 225-240.
92 T.A. Kochan and H.C. Katz, *Collective Bargaining and Industrial Relations: From Theory to Policy and Practice* (2nd ed.), Irwin, Homewood, Illinois, 1988.
93 *ibid.*, p. 198.
94 *ibid.*, pp. 198-199.
95 *ibid.*, p. 199.
96 *ibid.*, pp. 204-205.
97 *ibid.*, pp. 205-206.
98 *ibid.*, p. 207.
99 *ibid.*, p. 206.
100 A. Flanders, *The Fawley Productivity Agreements*, Faber, London, 1964, p. 253.
101 *ibid.*, p. 255.
102 Ahlstrand, *op. cit.*, pp. 224-225.
103 Flanders, *op. cit.*, p. 251.
104 *ibid.*, p. 254.
105 *ibid.*
106 E.J. Vaughan, 'Theories of participation: an analysis of core assertions' in W.A. Howard (ed.), *Perspectives on Australian Industrial Relations: Essays in honour of Kingsley Laffer*, Longman Cheshire, Melbourne, 1984, p. 166.
107 *ibid.*, p. 170.
108 *ibid.*, p. 181.

109 *ibid.*, p. 175.
110 *ibid.*, p. 176.
111 H. Mintzberg, *The Nature of Managerial Work*, Harper and Row, New York, 1973, cited in Vaughan, *op. cit.*, p. 176.
112 Vaughan, *op. cit.*, pp. 176-177.
113 *ibid.*, p. 178.
114 J. Teicher, 'Theories of employee participation and industrial democracy: towards an analytical framework', in B. Dabscheck, G. Griffin and J. Teicher (eds), *Contemporary Australian Industrial Relations : Readings*, Longman Cheshire, Melbourne, 1992, pp. 476-494.
115 *ibid.*, p. 477.
116 *ibid.*, p. 492.
117 *ibid.*
118 *ibid.*, p. 488.
119 *ibid.*
120 T. Schuller, *Democracy at Work*, Oxford University Press, Oxford, 1985, p. 35 cited in Teicher, *op. cit.*, p. 489.
121 C. Pateman, *Participation and Democratic Theory*, Cambridge University Press, London, 1970, p. 70.
122 Teicher, *op. cit.*, p. 492.
123 K.K. Wang, 'A Worker Participation Matrix', *Personnel Practice Bulletin 30*, September, 1974, pp. 264-277.
124 Pateman, *op. cit.*, pp. 68 and 71 cited in Teicher, *op. cit.*, p. 491.
125 R.D. Lansbury and P Gilmour, *Organisations: an Australian perspective*, Longman Cheshire, Melbourne, 1977.
126 E.J. Vaughan, 'Some observations upon the logic of participative management', *Journal of Industrial Relations 18*, September 1978, pp. 220-228.
127 *ibid.*, pp. 221-222.
128 *ibid.*, p. 223.
129 *ibid.*, pp. 224-225.
130 *ibid.*, p. 226.

Further Reading

Functions of management

H. Braverman, *Labor and Monopoly Capital—The Degradation of Work in the Twentieth Century*, Monthly Review Press, New York, 1974.

N.W. Chamberlain, D.E. Cullen and D. Lewin, *The Labor Sector* (3rd ed.), McGraw-Hill, New York, 1986.

Theories of industrial relations management

B.W. Ahlstrand, *The quest for productivity: A case study of Fawley after Flanders*, Cambridge University Press, Cambridge, 1990, chapter 2.

P. Armstrong and J. Goodman, 'Managerial and supervisory custom and practice', *Industrial Relations Journal 10*, Autumn 1979, pp. 12-24.

E. Batstone, A. Ferner and M. Terry, *Consent and Efficiency*, Blackwell, Oxford, 1984.

C. Brewster, C. Gill and S. Richbell, 'Industrial Relations Policy: A Framework for Analysis' in K. Thurley and S. Wood (eds), *Industrial Relations and Management Strategy*, Cambridge University Press, Cambridge, 1983, pp. 62-72.

C. Brewster and S. Richbell, 'Industrial relations policy and managerial custom and practice', *Industrial Relations Journal*, vol. 14, no. 1, 1983, pp. 22-31.

W. Brown, 'A consideration of 'custom and practice'', *British Journal of Industrial Relations*, vol. 10, no. 1, 1972, pp. 42-61.

W. Brown, *Piecework Bargaining*, Heinemann, London, 1973.

R. Edwards, *Contested Terrain*, Heinemann, London, 1979.

A. Fox, *Industrial Sociology and Industrial Relations*, Research Paper No. 3, Royal Commission on Employer Associations and Trade Unions, HMSO, London, 1966. Reprinted in A. Flanders (ed.), *Collective Bargaining*, Penguin, Harmondsworth, 1969, pp. 391-408.

A. Friedman, *Industry and Labour*, Macmillan, London, 1977.

H. Gospel, 'The Development of Management Organisation in Industrial Relations: A Historical Perspective', in K. Thurley and S. Wood (eds), 1983, *op. cit.*, pp. 91-110.

T.A. Kochan, H.C. Katz and R.B. McKersie, *The Transformation of American Industrial Relations*, Basic Books, New York, 1986.

D. Lewin, 'Industrial Relations as a Strategic Variable', in M. Kleiner, R.N. Block, M. Roomkin and S.W. Salsburg (eds), *Human Resources Management and the Performance of the Firm*, Industrial Relations Research Association, Madison, Wisconsin, 1988, chapter 1.

C. Littler, *The Development of the Labour Process in Capitalist Societies*, Heinemann, London, 1982.

D. McDonald, 'The Role of Management in Industrial Relations and Some Views on Its Conceptualisation and Analysis', *Journal of Management Studies* 22, September 1985, pp. 523-546.

M. Poole, 'Managerial strategies and 'styles' in industrial relations: a comparative analysis', *Journal of General Management* 12, Autumn 1986, pp. 40-53.

J. Purcell, 'Mapping management styles in employee relations', *Journal of Management Studies 24*, September 1987, pp. 533-548.

J. Purcell and B. Ahlstrand, 'Corporate Management of Industrial Relations in the Multi Divisional Company', *British Journal of Industrial Relations 27*, September 1989, pp. 396-417.

J. Purcell and K. Sisson, 'Strategies and practice in the management of industrial relations' in G. S. Bain, *Industrial Relations in Britain*, Blackwell, Oxford, 1983.

K. Thurley and S. Wood, 'Business Strategy and Industrial Relations Strategy' in K. Thurley and S. Wood (eds), 1983, *op. cit.*, pp. 197-224.

S.T. Timperley, 'Organisation Strategies and Industrial Relations', *Industrial Relations Journal 11*, 1980, pp. 38-44.

Employee participation in management

M. Gardner, G. Palmer and M. Quinlan, 'The Industrial Democracy Debate', in G. Palmer (ed.), *Australian Personnel Management: A Reader*, Macmillan, Melbourne, 1988, pp. 336-361.

R. Lansbury (ed.), *Democracy in the workplace*, Longman Cheshire, Melbourne, 1980.

C. Pateman, *Participation and Democratic Theory*, Cambridge University Press, London, 1970.

J. Teicher, 'Theories of employee participation and industrial democracy: towards an analytical framework', in B. Dabscheck, G. Griffin and J.

Teicher (eds), *Contemporary Australian Industrial Relations: Readings*, Longman Cheshire, Melbourne, 1992, pp. 476-494.

E. J. Vaughan, 'Some observations upon the logic of participative management', *Journal of Industrial Relations 18*, September 1976, pp. 220-228.

E. Vaughan, 'Structure and strategy in the case for worker participation', *Journal of Industrial Relations 25*, September 1983, pp. 317-326.

E. Vaughan, 'Theories of participation : an analysis of core assertions', in W.A. Howard (ed.), *Perspectives on Australian Industrial Relations: Essays in honour of Kingsley Laffer*, Longman Cheshire, Melbourne, 1984, pp. 165-186.

K.K. Wang, 'A worker participation matrix', *Personnel Practice Bulletin 30*, September 1974, pp. 264-277.

Questions

The functions of management

1. Explain Braverman's view concerning the function of management in capitalist economies.
2. How does Braverman's concept of the function of management differ from that put forward by Chamberlain, Cullen and Lewin?

Theories of industrial relations management

3. Distinguish the 'unitary' and 'pluralist' managerial frames of reference.
4. Explain the 'individualism dimension' and the 'collectivism dimension' in Purcell's concept of management style. In what ways, if any, does this concept illuminate analysis of management behaviour?
5. What do you consider to be the most useful features of the Kochan, Katz and McKersie theoretical frameworks.
6. Summarise the criticisms of the concept of management strategic choice presented by Lewin, drawing on his discussion of research concerning
   (a) collective bargaining and
   (b) labour-management co-operation.
7. Identify the distinctions between the alternative approaches to management industrial relations strategy discussed by Ahlstrand.
8. What factors would be likely to shift the 'locus of innovation' in industrial relations away from management?
9. Explain the generic characteristics of management structure identified by Kochan and Katz.

Employee participation in management

10. Distinguish between 'industrial democracy' and 'employee participation in management'.
11. Do any of the participation theories discussed by Vaughan have relevance or similarity to theories of industrial conflict discussed in chapter 3? Explain your answer.
12. a) Using the typology in Figure 9.2, classify each of the examples of participation cited in Table 9.8.
    b) Are there any examples which cannot be classified? If so, why?

Exercises

1 Identify the reasons put forward by Vaughan in his argument that both sociological and political theories of participation provide a persuasive case for an increase in employee participation in management.
2 Using the typology of employee participation and industrial democracy in figure 9.2. classify any relevant changes in the *Metal Industry Award* during the period of award restructuring from 1987 to 1992. (An alternative to the *Metal Industry Award* may be substituted. This exercise should be undertaken after the section in chapter 18 entitled 'Wages policy and the evolution to enterprise bargaining' has been read.)

10

Management in Australia

Contents

Ideology
Aspects of individualism and collectivism
- steel industry

Strategies
- metal and engineering industry
- mining industry
- communications industry
- small business survey

Structure
Recent developments: the North American influence
Employee participation in management
- management prerogatives and arbitration
- case studies

Introduction

The international trend during the 1980s was for an increasing number of academic researchers in industrial relations to turn their attention to the study of the role of management in industrial relations. This trend is also evident in Australia reflecting what Niland and Turner, writing in the mid-1980s, term 'growing awareness of deficiencies in our knowledge of management ideology and industrial relations strategy'.[1] This chapter summarises some academic research, both surveys and case studies, and draws upon commissioned studies, tribunal decisions and company publications, to provide an Australian focus to the theories and concepts discussed in the previous chapter.

Ideology

A 1984 survey of the membership of the Institute of Personnel Management, Australia provides data on the ideological perspectives of personnel and industrial relations managers from both the private and public sectors. In terms of the Kochan, Katz and McKersie three-tier institutional framework (see chapter 9) these managers work within the functional level, that is, level two. Respondents were asked to indicate which of the statements in Table 10.1 best summed up their view of industrial relations. The table shows the distribution between three frames of reference or ideologies.

Table 10.1 Management frames of reference

Frame of Reference	per cent
Unitary view Employers and employees share common objectives because they are each part of the same team	45
Pluralist view Conflict is inevitable in an organisation because employers and employees have divergent interests and objectives	44
Radical view There is fundamental conflict of interest between employers and employees which reflects the nature of class conflict in capitalist society as a whole	11

Source: S. Deery and P.J. Dowling, 'The Australian Personnel Manager and Industrial Relations Practitioner: Responsibilities, Characteristics and Attitudes', in G. Palmer (ed.), *Australian Personnel Management: A Reader*, Macmillan, Melbourne, 1988, p. 25.

The survey also shows that employment sector, educational level and age acted as moderating variables on the frames of reference adopted by the respondents. Managers from the public sector and younger managers were more inclined to hold pluralist or radical perspectives than private sector or older managers. Managers who did not possess tertiary qualifications were somewhat more inclined to the unitary approach although respondents with trade qualifications were markedly more radical in their ideological frame of reference. The managers were asked their view of trade unions by indicating the extent to which they agreed with the six statements listed in Table 10.2.

Table 10.2 Managers' attitudes to trade unions (percentages) n = 1383

	Strongly agree 1	Agree 2	Indifferent 3	Strongly Disagree 4	Disagree 5	Mean	SD
Trade union membership should be purely voluntary	49	34	5	10	2	1.82	1.05
Trade unions are not acting in the country's economic interest	20	41	17	20	2	2.43	1.08
Trade unions today have too much power	23	40	18	17	2	2.37	1.08
All in all trade unions have more power than management	10	26	18	42	5	3.06	1.12
Unions should be solely concerned with pay and conditions	8	22	13	48	9	3.60	1.14
A trade union should be prepared if necessary to use any form of industrial action which may be effective	2	13	9	47	29	3.89	1.03

Source: S. Deery and P.J. Dowling, 'The Australian Personnel Manager and Industrial Relations Practitioner: Responsibilities, Characteristics and Attitudes', in G. Palmer (ed.), *Australian Personnel Management: A Reader*, Macmillan, Melbourne, 1988, p. 26.

Some 63 per cent of managers considered that trade unions have too much power but only 36 per cent considered that trade unions have more power than management. Only 30 per cent considered that trade unions should be solely concerned with pay and conditions while only 15 per cent believed a union should be prepared if necessary to use any form of industrial action which may be effective. The ambiguity in this last statement precludes a clear picture of these managers' attitudes to the right to strike *per se*. The same could be said for the reference to scope of union activity: there is no indication of what activities 58 per cent of respondents had in mind or how they defined 'conditions', for example how they classified control over the processes of utilisation and deployment of labour or employee or union representation on boards of management. 61 per cent of managers believed that unions were not acting in the country's economic interest although they were not asked whether they believed this was a primary purpose or responsibility of unions.

A policy adopted by the Business Council of Australia in March 1987 entitled 'Towards an Enterprise Based Industrial Relations System' contains features of both the unitary frame of reference and a high individualism management style. The major constituency of the Council comprises the chief executives of about eighty of Australia's largest companies (See Table 11.11 for a list of these companies). The Council's overriding objective was to:

> 'create an industrial relations environment where people can work together most effectively and with greatest satisfaction; where the highest possible productivity becomes the common goal for all; and where healthy enterprise performance provides the best outcomes for employers and employees alike'.[2]

The policy is also directed to reform of the public regulation of industrial relations and the Council proposed a ten to fifteen year strategy for achieving enterprise-by-enterprise legally binding industrial contracts. This was based on gradualism and always trying to work with the wage determination process set by the current government.[3] As part of its strategy the Council established the Employee Relations Study Commission to undertake a review of Australia's industrial relations. The terms of reference of the review stated that:

> 'the overriding aims of changes [to the current industrial relations system] must be to increase the competitiveness and performance of Australian enterprises in providing goods and services internationally and domestically and enhancing personal achievement and satisfaction of individuals at work.[4]

This statement accords 'first-order' management decision status to business policy and gives the appearance of equivalent ranking to labour management. The Study Commission's first Report distinguishes 'industrial relations' and 'employee relations'[5] which could be regarded as proxies for the pluralist and unitary frames of reference respectively. The concepts are introduced in the context of support for a change in the nature of public regulation of industrial relations. There is particular emphasis on the role of the state, both what it is and what it ought to be. 'Industrial relations' assumes employers and employees are inherently at loggerheads and, in the public interest, the outcome of their relationship must be regulated in detail, to protect employees and to control wages and otherwise avoid disrupting the economy. It is interesting that the matter of protection of employees is confronted. Protection of employers is not, however, being expressed as a neutral issue 'control of wages' which may be portrayed as clearly desirable in a non-sectional sense. The report claims that this approach has led to the regulation of substantive rules as well as procedural rules in Australia. It argues this mindset was not inevitable and was now more a product of the structure of existing regulation than anything else. Prevailing Australian values are claimed to be changing and to be more consistent with an 'employee relations' approach. This assumes employers and employees have much more in common than they have differences and in this context public regulation should focus on establishing a well-understood process in which relationships at work are determined. Within the legislative framework, 'employee relations' would cover all aspects of the employer-employee relationship. The main processes of 'employee relations' would be informal, involving direct dealing between the parties. From the national perspective there would be less concern with regulating outcomes (substantive rules) and diversity would be tolerated more readily. These contrasting values are listed in Table 10.3.

Table 10.3 Industrial relations vs employee relations: Business Council of Australia perspective

Industrial Relations	Employee Relations
• Conflict inevitable	• Mutual interests
• Low trust	• Increased trust
• Central control	• Individualism
• Uniformity/equality good	• Flexibility

Source: BCA, *Enterprise-Based Bargaining Units—A Better Way of Working*, Report to the Business Council of Australia by the Industrial Relations Study Commission, July 1989, volume 1, page 5.

The report argues that the adoption of the 'employee relations' approach at the enterprise level was one of the secrets of success of successful enterprises; other factors included the economic environment, the political environment, research and development, competitive strategy and finance.[6] 'Employee relations' is advocated as a desirable management approach but the concept is silent on the issue of the role of the collective voice of employees. In terms of Purcell's concept it is concerned with the individualism dimension only, although some of the characteristics identified in the 'employee relations' approach are implicitly consistent with both views of unionism in Fox's unitary frame of reference that is, unions as either unnecessary or dysfunctional.

Fox has recognised however, that aspects of the unitary ideology may be used as a public relations gloss on what is basically a realistic acccEptance of the true nature of industrial relations. A reading of Business Council views in relation to collectivism, including support for unions which are enterprise based,[7] suggests that elements of the public relations function may be present here. In its third major report, the Employee Relations Study Commission, established by the BCA, identifies three principles which it believes should govern employee representation:

- 'employees should be able to nominate any agent, including a union, to represent them in their relations with their employers
- employees should be able to choose the union which they consider can provide the best representation services, regardless of the nature of the union and of the existing pattern of union representation in the workplace

- unions should not be required to be recognised under any law as a condition of them being able to represent employees in their relations with employers'.[8]

This emphasis on employee rights, rather than union rights, can be found in the legal frameworks of some countries, for example Canada, where union rights to engage in collective bargaining are contingent on employee preferences expressed via secret ballot vote or the signing of union membership cards. The above position advocated by the BCA Study Commission indicates recognition of employee collectives and implies acceptance of their legitimacy when certain conditions are met.

Aspects of individualism and collectivism

Purcell observes that the dimensions of individualism and collectivism developed in his analysis of management style may be useful in classifying aspects of management practice and these could be applied to all firms regardless of whether a style, as defined, existed.[9] Adopting this approach, some management practices in Australia are now classified in terms of Purcell's individualism and collectivism concepts.

The opportunities for employers in the private sector in Australia to adopt, at least overtly, the unitary dimension of collectivism has been obviated by systems of public regulation affording legal recognition and protection for unions and union officials for all of this century. Public employers however, as legislators, have the power to vary those systems in respect of their own employees. Thus for example, the introduction of elements of unitary collectivism (perhaps a more appropriate term would be anti-collectivism) occurred in the South East Queensland Electricity Board (SEQEB) dispute in the mid-1980s when the Queensland government introduced a range of legislation[10] in the electricity supply industry. The legislation *inter alia*, legitimised the employment of workers on individual contracts of service replacing award provisions, repealed many statutory benefits for unions and imposed comprehensive restrictions on industrial action.

A company providing an apparent example of high individualism and co-operative collectivism is ICI Australia Limited, which transformed its management of industrial relations during the latter half of the 1980s. This company, which had 9640 employees in 1992, is the leading Australian company in the industrial chemicals, plastics, paints, commercial explosives and fertiliser markets. It is also a major supplier to many other industries including health care and agrochemicals. The company is 62.5 per cent owned by UK-based Imperial Chemical Industries PLC.[11] The company received substantial media coverage of the changes in its industrial relations practices, in particular the changes occurring at the Botany manufacturing site, heralded as the 'exemplar' of good industrial relations practice. The company's human resources manager at that time, Michael Johnson, said that prior to the transformation the company operated a kind of master and servant law, based on the belief that the workforce was dishonest.[12] It is noteworthy that this company, and the Botany site in particular, has introduced forms of employee participation in management (see below) in the past.[13]

The new approach is illustrated in Table 10.4 which contains an extract from the company's 1992 *Annual Report* dealing with human resources and which is titled 'People'. It is an approach to industrial relations management articulated at corporate level. This is the strategic level in the Kochan, Katz and McKersie three-tier institutional framework discussed in chapter 9. Table 10.5 contains extracts from the Managing Director's Review. The extract includes some references to the product market environment and all the references to employees. Both extracts reveal an integration between corporate strategy and industrial relations, at least in terms of strategy formulation.

The test of whether these recent changes constitute a change in management style as defined, or are simply a pragmatic response to environmental pressures and therefore likely to shift again, can only be applied over a time period which includes significant environmental changes. Further, as with the position of all the actors in the industrial relations system, the rhetoric needs to be tested against the reality.

Purcell notes that companies may have different styles for different sectors of the workforce, reflecting the perceived value of those groups to the

---

Table 10.4 Management approach to industrial relations/human resources management: ICI Australia Limited, 1992

PEOPLE
Core Value:

Appointing leaders who are determined to achieve high and continually improving standards in an environment where people both want to and are able to perform to their full potential.

During the last couple of years the company's total quality management program and workplace reform inititatives have become inextricably linked. The result has been a more fulfilled and committed workforce and a more flexible, profitable approach to business management.

Enterprise agreements at nearly all major sites have allowed businesses to eliminate artificial work boundaries, improve employees' skills acquisition and move towards single status employment conditions.

Simultaneously, TQM has greatly increased employee involvement on issues such as safety, environmental performance and rostering.

This commitment to continuous improvement has had a direct benefit on business performance, with measurable results including a reduction in industrial disputes, lower employee turnover and absenteeism, as well as improved productivity and product quality and the ability of businesses to better match human resources with production demands.

In the area of equal employment opportunity (EEO), the company reviewed its major policies and began examining a number of issues such as ethnic diversity and age discrimination. In May the first ICI–sponsored child care centre opened in East Melbourne for the benefit of working parents. The Botany site was recognised by the NSW Government for its outstanding support of Skillmax, a program to provide professionally–qualified migrants with work experience in their areas of expertise.

In the area of training and development the major focus of the year was to develop career streams for employees in functional areas such as Finance and Technology. About 140 managers also attended programs where their leadership styles were assessed and refined to help them to release the full potential of their employees' talents.

Source: ICI Australia Limited, *Annual Report* 1992, p. 18 (edited).

Table 10.5 Corporate strategy and industrial relations management: ICI Australia Limited, 1992

MANAGING DIRECTOR'S REVIEW

During 1992 ICI Australia enjoyed little relief from the difficult operating environment. The protracted domestic recession, low international chemical prices and dumped imports continued to have an adverse effect on the company's performance.

To counter this the company continued to pay close attention to costs. Most businesses now have their cost base in line with the current level of demand in Australia. Improvements in stock control, debtors and creditors, led to a reduction in trade working capital from 18.1% to 17.3% of sales, freeing up $35 million of cash.

As part of ICI Australia's strategic plan to have a portfolio of world–competitive business units, the company discontinued production at a number of plants which could not achieve a satisfactory rate of return. These included the ephedrine plant at Newcastle (NSW) and Advanced Ceramics' zirconia powders plant at Rockingham (WA).

Other plants closed during 1992 included six plants at Rhodes (NSW), the solvents and silicates plants at Botany (NSW) and the packaged explosives plant at Deer Park (VIC). In total, employee numbers were reduced by 661 in 1992. Some of these redundancies and plant close down costs are reflected in the abnormal items, charged against profit.

ICI employees worked hard during the year improving productivity, applying total quality management (TQM) and implementing workplace reform. Most businesses have improved their performance and, with the exception of Plastics, are profitable.

ICI will emerge from this recession a leaner and more responsive company. It is now in good shape to deal with the fundamental changes in the Australian economy as it moves away from an insulated tariff–protected market to a more open economy with low tariffs and deregulated internal markets such as transport, telecommunications and, eventually, labour.

We will also be better able to deal with international competition as all our businesses benchmark their processes against world best practice. Hundreds of employee teams around the company are actively measuring their performance and seeking continuous improvement in productivity, customer service and quality.

Source: 'Managing Director's Review', ICI Australia Limited, *Annual Report* 1992, pp. 10-11 (edited).

company. The traditional division of Australian public sector workforces into a 'career service' component and a 'temporary employees' component with promotional opportunities and a range of financial benefits confined to the former, is an example of different dimensions of individualism being applied to different groups of employees. A number of inquiries commissioned by governments during the 1970s and early 1980s challenged these management practices on both equity and efficiency grounds.[14]

Steel industry (Quinlan)

Quinlan,[15] drawing on both published sources and company and union documents, analyses the industrial relations practices of BHP, a monopoly employer in the Australian steel industry. The focus is on the period 1945–1975, although practices in earlier and later decades are included. BHP is the largest is the largest private sector corporation in Australia in terms of both capital invested and workforce. Most of the discussion is concerned with a single plant, Port Kembla, the largest steelworks in Australia. Quinlan's view is, however, that management practice at this workplace was typical of the company because of the centralised pattern of BHP management decision making. This case study, which is essentially a study of management strategy, is also suitable for illustrating aspects of the Purcell model of management style. Quinlan adopts the Thurley and Wood definition of management strategy:

> ' ... industrial relations strategies refer to long-term policies which are developed by the management of an organisation in order to preserve or change the procedures, practices or results of industrial relations activities over time.'[16]

Quinlan notes that key elements in this definition are the notions of consciousness, long-term commitment, rationality and choice. He concludes that his study demonstrates that BHP possessed an industrial strategy in terms of the Thurley and Wood criteria but acknowledges further research is required to determine whether strategy could be imputed simply where management displayed a consistent pattern of behaviour over long periods.[17]

In adopting a labour process approach, he argues that management strategy cannot be seen simply in terms of job regulation/bargaining tactics at the workplace level. It is necessary to consider

1. the political, economic and labour-market context in which individual or groups of employers operate;
2. management attempts to manipulate or modify these constraints; and
3. the link between corporate decision making and labour management policies.[18]

Quinlan's analysis predates Purcell's concept of management style but the management practices he discusses could be categorised as being in the range of 'commodity status' and 'paternalism' on the individualism scale and as strongly 'constitutional' or 'adversarial' on the collectivism scale. On the individualism dimension, BHP was vigorous in its pursuit of minimising wage costs and its low wage policy derived from its cheap steel policy. This practice was facilitated by industrial tribunal decisions (NSW Industrial Commission) and, for some of the time period under consideration, by limited union demands. Margins in the steel industry were consistently behind wage movements for similar occupations in other industries. Recruitment practices revealed a strong preference for hiring of unskilled workers from southern Europe, seen to be more adaptable to the rigours of unskilled jobs and subject to less stringent requirements regarding their accommodation. BHP's low wage policy meant it became an 'entrepot' employer of migrant labour because migrants moved on when they became aware of better paying jobs. The company chose a 'continuous replenishment of workers unaccustomed to local conditions'.[19] The company also used aggressive personnel and disciplinary practices, taking full advantage of a unique clause within the steel industry award empowering management to discipline employees through suspension. The company made frequent resort to demotion, suspension and dismissal. Quinlan states:

> 'BHP used this provision to sanction employees refusing overtime, returning late from union meetings, holding meetings within the steelworks, taking part in

unauthorised stoppages, writing graffiti and a wide range of other activities deemed to constitute insubordination. At Port Kembla and Newcastle these powers were invoked literally hundreds of times each year'.[20]

Quinlan discusses the company's rigid division between staff and wages labour documented by Murray and White.[21] This was used to weaken unionism in two ways: promoting workers to staff positions to ensure a reliable skeleton workforce to meet emergency situations such as strikes, and requiring those promoted to relinquish union membership. Workers who refused such promotions were dismissed.

In its collective relations, the company conceded only those rights guaranteed by law and offered the absolute minimum in the way of facilities to union officials. Here again it was assisted by the industrial tribunal. For example, the Commission supported the company's ban on workplace meetings of employees even during crib breaks. Thus full-time union officials were only permitted to enter the steelworks and hold discussions with individual workers during crib breaks and management required that they be accompanied by a security guard at all times. Quinlan notes that this had an intimidatory effect on workers, especially recently arrived migrants. Finally, there were limitations placed on telephone communications between job delegates and full-time officials.[22]

The company strenuously defended management prerogatives in relation to substantive issues not already the subject of external regulation via tribunal intervention. For example, it refused to negotiate with the union on the bonus scheme and health and safety issues. Generally, a litigious approach was adopted, with insistence on all but the most trivial items being referred to arbitration and a marked aversion to both conciliation and direct bipartite negotiation. Decisions were centralised, that is, made at head office level and they included severe restrictions on the scope for local negotiations. Quinlan states this reflected the overriding desire to minimise labour costs and the sensitivity to risks of internal 'flow-on' of concessions granted in any area of the company.[23]

Quinlan's analysis extends to the range of contextual constraints on management including union strategic choices. In summarising his discussion of the interaction between management choices and union behaviour the language of Gardner's model (see chapter 6) is adopted here. The militant communist leadership of the major union, the then Federated Ironworkers' Association, was progressively defeated between 1949 and 1952 (see chapter 8 for discussion of the legal context) and replaced by a right-wing group led by Laurie Short. The new leadership strategy was based on the value of 'leadership discretion', a strong preference for arbitration in terms of union method and a relationship to other unions which was both isolated and conflictual. The decline in union militancy, national leadership attempts to control the activities and independence of shop stewards and the inter-union conflict arising from incompatible strategies among the unions with members at BHP, all facilitated management's preferred and inflexible strategy.[24]

Quinlan outlines the management and union choices which interacted to fuel rank and file dissent and led to a change of leadership in the FIA Port

Kembla branch in 1970. The general approach of management was explained above. Specific management practices included (i) opposition to union preference until 1970; (ii) a 'paternalistic' approach to occupational health and safety; and (iii) a bonus scheme which was complex, 'incomprehensible' to workers and relatively unfavourable. Specific union choices included acceptance of (i) the absence of limits on overtime or shift work; (ii) the principle that a union could not simultaneously pursue arbitration and industrial action; and (iii) the growth of a myriad of minor pay differentials[25] by manipulating the then system of margins for skill determined by the industrial tribunals.

Management did not modify its resistance to union claims despite the change in the union's behavioural character favourable to management, and the low pay status of steelworkers prevailed. Quinlan suggests that a more sophisticated collaboration with the FIA by management may have pre-empted the change of leadership.[26] The new branch leadership adopted the union value of 'united action' and some measure of 'autonomous action'. In terms of union method it reduced reliance on arbitration, adopted more militant tactics and also developed more co-operative relationships with other unions. In terms of the distribution of decision-making power within the union (see chapter 8) the national leadership sought to formalise control at this level proscribing the autonomy of branch officials but also shifted to a position of greater co-operation with other unions. Management also modified its strategy, seeking to isolate the Port Kembla branch via a more conciliatory approach to the (national) union. The 'aggressive challenge to BHP', as Quinlan terms it, did not spread beyond Port Kembla after 1975 because of an adverse shift in the steel industry product market which led to mass labour shedding in the 1980s.[27]

Strategies

Two studies of Australian management strategy in industrial relations are now summarised. The first concerns the 'metal and engineering' industry, the second concerns industrial relations in the mining industry. These are followed by an interview with the Human Resources Manager of a relatively new firm in the communications industry, Optus Communications, and a focus on small business with a summary of the preferences and choices of managers in this sector as revealed in a 1992 national survey. Where applicable, the theories and concepts discussed in chapter 9 are identified.

Metal and engineering industry (Bramble)

Bramble's[28] analysis of industrial relations management strategy in the metal and engineering industry in the 1970s and 1980s is based on case studies of management in seven large plants (ranging from 350 to 1200 employees) and seven small plants (less than fifty employees) in NSW and Victoria. The relationship between certain environmental pressures and the process of change on the shop floor is examined and Bramble concludes that management was the major initiator of change.

In considering the appropriate research approach to the question of management strategy, Bramble refers to literature highlighting the discrepancies between claims of 'strategic management' and management in practice. The practice of management has been observed to involve fragmented, varied tasks and a pre-occupation with *ad hoc* responses to immediate problems. Further, even where a discernible strategy exists, there is the problem of failure of implementation reflected in the distinction between 'espoused' and 'operational' policy.[29] Rivalries and tensions within the management hierarchy may cause a divergence between an objective devised by senior management and the form in which it is implemented at lower levels in the management line. This is one of the problems identified by Ahlstrand in his study of productivity agreements at the Esso oil refinery in England from 1960 to 1985 (see chapter 18) and categorised as the 'political approach' to management strategy (see chapter 9). Bramble concludes that research on management strategy 'has to concentrate on managerial behaviour in practice, as 'operational', and to attempt to deduce any ex-post coherence that may or may not be recognised by senior management'.[30] He regards Mintzberg's concept of 'emergent strategy'[31] as useful because it avoids both over-reliance on corporate plans (the espoused policy) and also moves beyond 'empiricism and impressionism'. The four management strategic choices identified by Bramble are set out in Table 10.6.

Bramble regards the threat to profitability from the prolonged recession and the declining levels of protection as the critical feature of the changed environment. This constitutes a 'general framework' within which three environmental pressures or stimuli are identified as being of particular importance in encouraging management to change their traditional practices. These are: the labour threat (collective and individual); the reorganisation of production methods, and, since 1983, the legal and institutional framework. Each of these pressures is found to affect management in the case study plants in varying degrees. The research showed crucial differences between management behaviours in the large and small plants with very little change evident in the latter group. To illuminate the dynamics of the changes in Bramble's analysis, two specific examples of the impact of environmental change on management strategic choice in the large plants (see Table 10.7) are summarised here: (1) the changing collective labour threat and (2) the reorganisation of production methods.

Table 10.6 Management strategic choices: metal and engineering industry case studies

(1) The professionalisation of industrial relations management.

(2) The development of co-operative relationships with unions at workplace level.

(3) The promotion of increased employee participation in management decision making at workplace level.

(4) The adoption of a two-tier approach to the employment relationship.

Source: Adapted from T. Bramble, 'Political Economy and Management Strategy in the Metal and Engineering Industry', in B. Dabscheck, G. Griffin and J. Teicher (eds), *Contemporary Australian Industrial Relations: Readings*, Longman Cheshire, Melbourne, 1992, pp. 243-245.

Table 10.7 Plant (establishment) characteristics: metal and engineering case studies

Plant	Number of employees	Product	Ownership
T	482	Industrial appliances	Division of Australian PLC
U	1200	Electrical durables	Division of Australian PLC
V	945	Electrical durables	Wholly owned subsidiary of United States PLC
W	493	Metal fasteners	Joint wholly owned subsidiary of two Australian PLC
X	440	Metal fasteners	Wholly owned subsidiary of Australian PLC
Y	380	Electric motors	Division of Australian private company
Z	40	Metal fasteners	Wholly owned subsidiary of United States PLC

PLC = proprietary limited company

Major unions
Amalgamated Metal Workers' Union (now part of AMEU)
Federated Ironworkers' Association (now part of FIMEE)
Vehicle Builders Employees' Federation (now part of AMEU)
All plants except plant Z were unionised

Source: Adapted from T. Bramble, 'Political Economy and Management Strategy in the Metal and Engineering Industry', in B. Dabscheck, G. Griffin and J. Teicher (eds), *Contemporary Australian Industrial Relations: Readings*, Longman Cheshire, Melbourne, 1992, p. 255.

Bramble defines the collective labour threat as the mobilisation of union power in a way detrimental to management's interests. It was manifest in:

1 the use of industrial action directed to individual companies and demands for collective bargaining; and
2 the corollary of a strengthening of union workplace organisation among the major unions.

Three periods were relevant, with the first identified as the most important: 1968-1975; the early 1980s and 1986-1987. The period 1968-1975 saw a 'loss of control' over wages by the federal tribunal following the 1967–1968 *Metal Trades Work Value* case (see chapter 4) and the collapse of legal sanctions against strikes. This followed union movement opposition to the jailing of the secretary of the Tramways Union for the non-payment of fines. The breakdown of the authority of centralised arbitration meant employers could no longer 'hide behind' the bans clause (see chapters 3 and 5). The labour market (a component of the economic environment) was favourable to unions and there was a growth of frequent, fragmented and unregulated enterprise bargaining, especially over wages. These changes were reinforced in 1980-1981 by the unions' 35-hour week campaign which was focused at the workplace level, demonstrating again to management at this level the strength of the metal trades unions.

Bramble concludes that the changes caused the traditional informal pattern of management practices, 'premised on centralised arbitration and union passivity', to become a liability. The resultant 'strategic choice' was a professionalisation of industrial relations management.[32] The characteristics of this change in management are set out in Table 10.8.

Table 10.8 Professionalisation of industrial relations management: metal and engineering case studies

The characteristics of this strategic choice were:

- an increase in functional specialisation—increased numbers of employee relations managers (however styled) at middle and senior levels.

- formalisation of policies and procedures on issues such as discipline, over-award wages and occupational health and safety replacing informal and inter-personal methods of dispute resolution.

- subsequent decentralisation of operational responsibilities to plant level for grievance handling and over-award bargaining within strict guidelines set by senior management and by industrial tribunal policy when applicable.

- consequent increased attention to strategic issues such as development of employee participation programs by senior industrial relations managers.

- reduced dependence on employer associations and industrial tribunals in the handling of rights disputes.

Source: Adapted from T. Bramble, 'Political Economy and Management Strategy in the Metal and Engineering Industry', in B. Dabscheck, G. Griffin and J. Teicher (eds), *Contemporary Australian Industrial Relations: Readings*, Longman Cheshire, Melbourne, 1992, pp. 257-258.

Bramble identifies the 1986-1987 period as also relevant to the changing labour threat by virtue of the prominence of workplace bargaining, occasioned by the Restructuring and Efficiency principle, known colloquially as the 'four per cent second tier' (see chapter 18). A distinction not made by Bramble, but worth noting, is that the workplace bargaining of 1968-1975 and the early 1980s was union initiated and opposed by the federal industrial tribunal while that in the late 1980s was tribunal endorsed. However, the phenomenon of workplace bargaining would have reinforced and justified the professionalisation of industrial relations management regardless of the source of pressure for it.

Another environmental pressure identified by Bramble was the adoption of new production methods. In Dunlop's model this would be classified as a change in the technical context. Bramble concludes that this variable influenced the adoption of two management strategies: increased employee participation in management and increasing use of a two-tier employment relationship. The new production methods involved smaller batch production, usually under the Just-In-Time concept (based on optimisation methods of production scheduling) and the Total Quality Control philosophy. These changes resulted from the continuing recession. They represented an attempt to combine the advantages of Japanese production systems with western technological expertise with emphasis 'now on operational flexibility and market responsiveness'.[33] The significance of the new methods from an employee relations perspective was that they created tight production lines and were extremely dependent on workforce co-operation, thereby delivering strategic power to production workers. A significant specific change identified by Bramble was the transfer of quality control responsibilities from full-time quality control inspectors to production workers and this meant that the latter had to be allowed to stop operations in the case of major faults. This gave these workers considerable strategic power, which Bramble argues made managements keen to develop means of encouraging worker loyalty and commitment to the company.[34] More generally, the introduction of Just-In-Time placed certain behavioural qualities at a premium, reflected in one manager's comment: 'With Just-In-time, we want stable and responsible people—the lack of commitment is the real problem—it's an attitude problem that we'll have to break down'.[35] Bramble found that in each of the six plants using the new methods, management increased employee participation in management in terms of decision making at shop floor level. Bramble describes this strategy as 'an ideological offensive to win over the shop floor'.[36] The increased participation included 'top-down' communications and 'bottom-round' forums such as quality circle and autonomous work groups. In some plants these groups included production workers, tradesmen, technicians and foremen. They were expected to identify, diagnose and solve some of the more common problems on the line.[37] Bramble contrasts these high commitment work relationships with the traditional pattern of workplace relations in the manufacturing sector. According to Ford, writing in the mid-1970s, these were 'stratified, authoritarian and undemocratic', premised on the application of low-discretion work rules and based on the assessment that manual workers were 'obstinate factors of production'.[38]

Management strategy in the seventh plant, which was union free, provided a stark contrast. Here the production methods had removed all operator discretion or physical intervention. The production line was almost entirely automated, causing deskilling and reduced strategic power for production workers; subjective aspects of the job were lost. The outcome was a strong emphasis on 'top-down' communication by management direct to the workforce but no development of 'bottom-round' forums of employee involvement such as occurred in the other plants.[39]

Bramble's model for explaining change is based in part on the labour process approach. The prominence this affords the management objective of control is reflected in his conclusion that:

> 'By impressing on the workforce the centrality of competition and the need to accept an intensification of work effort, by means of 'top-down' briefing groups and quality circles, management may attempt to centralise control and reduce the threat of industrial action, by gaining a more complete ideological hegemony. In this way, the goals of higher productivity may be realised'.[40]

An intervening variable, which Bramble notes facilitated the management strategy of increased employee participation, was the changing policies of the AMWU in response to an adverse market context (see chapter 6). In the early 1980s, in order to protect jobs, the union moved away from its traditional opposition to Just-In-Time and industrial democracy.[41] Quinlan's study of BHP management strategy at the Port Kembla steelworks also discusses union behaviour as an intervening variable (see above pp. 288-290). Bramble draws an interesting parallel between the experimentation by western manufacturing with strategies based on a human relations approach during the 1930s depression and similar strategies in response to the economic crisis of the 1980s.[42]

Bramble identifies the increased use of the two-tier employment relationship as the second strategy for which the changed production methods provided the major stimulus for action. The two-tier relationship involves workforce segmentation: a first-tier or core of workers provided with job security, who, in these plants, were the focus of employee participation programs, and a second-tier or band of peripheral workers exposed to the external labour market.[43] Bramble explains that this enabled management to adjust to variations in product demand without jeopardising the loyalty of the core workforce. These tiers are illustrative, respectively of 'valued resource' status and 'commodity' status on Purcell's individualism dimension discussed above. The strategy as identified by Bramble however, would not meet Purcell's stringent definition of management style. In the 'metal and engineering' plants studied, Bramble found evidence of retention of labour during downturns, even at the cost of temporary overmanning. This reflected a management preference for workforce loyalty, within a first-tier, over production flexibility in the short term. This co-existed with the development of a periphery of casual or part-time workers on short contracts of up to six months. In some plants this tier accounted for up to twenty-five per cent of the workforce.[44]

The other major environmental pressure influencing management choices identified but not summarised here is changes to what Bramble terms 'the legal and institutional framework'.[45] This overlaps in part with Dunlop's power context (see chapter 2) but extends beyond it to include some tribunal decisions, for example the 1984 federal *Termination Change and Redundancy* case (see chapter 12); in Dunlop's system the substance of a decision such as this would be characterised as an output of the system—part of the workplace rules.

Mining industry (Swain)

Swain's[46] study of management objectives and strategies in three iron-ore companies in the Pilbara region of Western Australia draws on the Kochan, Katz and McKersie general framework and the three-tier institutional framework (see chapter 9) and applies and develops the concept of strategic choice articulated by Kochan, McKersie and Capelli.[47] The focus is on the management of change in the face of shifts in product market conditions, both adverse and favourable, and on management choices.

The three companies are: Hamersley Iron Pty Ltd (100 per cent owned by CRA since 1970); Mt. Newman Mining Ltd. (85 per cent owned by BHP) and Robe River Iron Associates (53 per cent owned by North Broken Hill which holds the management contract. This contract was held by Peko Wallsend from August 1986 to 1988 and prior to that by Cliffs Western Australian Mining Co. Pty Ltd.). The study covers the period from the late 1960s to early

1970s, when the companies were established, until 1990. It provides insight into the impact of industrial relations on the management of an organisation and also the effect of management choices upon industrial relations processes and outcomes within the firm.[48] The environment (geography, market etc) and the characteristics of the other actors, is homogeneous and these variables can therefore be discounted as significant in explaining similarities or differences in the enterprise industrial relations systems and their outcomes. This enables the influence of management strategic choice to be isolated.[49]

Swain argues that management objectives in industrial relations in Australia have traditionally reflected criteria determined at the functional level. These criteria have been expressed in terms of:

1 how well the functional rules (both procedural and substantive) have been administered; and
2 the effectiveness of the rules in achieving industrial peace between the parties.[50]

Swain's research shows that a management choice to continue to pursue functional level objectives, as occurred with Mt Newman, had adverse consequences for the company's competitive performance. Conversely, where management chose to link industrial relations objectives to company performance objectives developed at the strategic level, as occurred at Robe River under Peko Wallsend management in 1986 and at Hamersley Iron in 1981, the companies were able to respond readily to an increase in market demand in the late 1980s. This ability depended on their ability to control production which in turn reflected their control of the industrial relations situation at the level of the workplace.[51]

The study finds that management strategic choice concerning three generic features of workplace industrial relations systems influenced company performance. The features were:

1 the management of conflict and delivery of due process;
2 the design and modification of work rules and work organisation; and
3 the motivation and supervision of industrial employees and work groups.

Both Hamersley Iron and Robe River under Peko-Wallsend management achieved flexibility and increased capacity utilisation as a result of their industrial relations choices. Mt. Newman on the other hand experienced low employee productivity and an inability to respond to the market upturn because of its failure to manage the generic features of industrial relations at the workplace level.[52] A critical choice in the successful companies was to judge industrial relations outcomes against corporate performance objectives. In terms of the Kochan *et al.* framework, they changed management objectives in industrial relations from a level two, or functional, focus to a level one, or corporate, focus while Mt. Newman, at least until late 1988, retained the functional focus. This choice then required that management be able to exercise control of the work process.[53] A summary of Swain's study of the objectives and strategies of one company, Hamersley Iron, follows.

During the 1970s, Hamersley Iron attempted to ensure continuity of production by making accommodative arrangements with union site representatives. In 1981 the industrial relations procedures were changed after an appreciation of the relationship between the procedures and the balance of power in the workplace. The company assessed that the recognition which management afforded union convenors (senior shop stewards) and shop stewards, in conjunction with the limited power given to supervisors in the management hierarchy, resulted in the union representative becoming the authority figure in the work-group. The situation was exploited by union representatives who used dispute settlement procedures only when they perceived it was in their interests, otherwise they would have recourse to the Commission.[54] Swain describes this as a 'utilitarian commitment'. The company found that the objective of the procedures namely, to control conflict and promote a harmonious work environment, was not being achieved.[55]

Management decided that open-ended structures with outcomes dictated at enterprise level by site union representatives and at the macro level by the state tribunal were no longer acceptable. The central industrial relations objective became the establishment of the primacy of the employer-employee relationship.[56] The industrial relations strategy objective has been to gain control of matters at the level of the workplace, over work procedures and manning levels. This in turn has meant industrial relations structures and processes which have reinforced and supported the authority of line management. The three major objectives pursued consistently by Hamersley Iron since 1981 are set out in Table 10.9.

The company revealed its planned change in industrial relations strategy during compulsory conciliation proceedings concerning an inter-union dispute which had paralysed mine operations in late 1980 and early 1981. Management regarded the dispute as a product of the power enjoyed by union site representatives who pursued objectives relating primarily to their own status via control of the work process.[57] It decided to 'make a clear distinction between the award conditions and pay rates controlled by the relevant tribunal, and the internal rules and procedures within the company over which the management believed they could claim the right to exercise control under management prerogative'.[58] The power of the site union representatives derived from the company's internal procedures so the company sought to persuade the tribunal and the state union officials to accept its right to determine these. This would enable management to begin the process of reducing shop steward power. Management declared that it was not prepared to take back the striking workers unless they agreed to a new set of industrial relations rules decided by the company. Three days later, the nine unions involved advised the Commissioner of their willingness to return to work. Management interpreted this as confirming their assessment that most conflict at workplace level could be sourced to conflict over the relative status and control of site union representatives who were now united in their concern about a threat to cancel procedures which gave them all power.[59] The Commissioner initially rejected and then, in a significant decision, accepted, the company position on the basis that the customs and practices pursuant to these procedures were outside his jurisdiction.[60]

Table 10.9 Industrial relations strategies: Hamersley Iron Pty Ltd 1981–1990

(1) **Confining the industrial tribunal, the Western Australian Industrial Commission, to the role of external umpire that is, seeking to minimise Commission involvement in the company's internal affairs but at the same time affirming support for the tribunal as an 'umpire'.**

- a strong preference for collective bargaining but registration of agreements as consent awards with the Commission, thus supporting the status and authority of the tribunal.

- avoidance of arbitrated awards where possible but 'in principle' support for the Commission's arbitral function.

(2) **Confining unions to third party status in the workplace and to a decision-making role at the bargaining level remote from the workplace.**

- reduce and confine the status and authority of site convenors and shop stewards, who in most cases are not formally recognised in the union's constitutional hierarchy.

- restriction of convenor and shop steward access to (a) company information and (b) senior management.

- support for legitimacy of unions in Australian industrial relations system.

- strict adherence to the award rights of unions.

- continuous promotion of direct links between employer and employee.

- acknowledgement of authority of state union officials who negotiate with the company representatives within a strictly defined framework.

(3) **Encouragement of culture in which all levels of management share the same attitudes and objectives.**

Source: Adapted from P. Swain, *A Study of the Role of Management and the Influence of Strategic Choice in the Management of Industrial Relations at the Level of the Firm in Three Iron Ore Companies*, Unpublished PhD Thesis, Monash University, 1992, pp. 103-108.

Management also succeeded in its objective of withdrawing from all informal agreements on various aspects of job control—overtime, manning levels, rosters—which it had entered into, usually at workplace level between individual supervisors and convenors.[61] In an arbitrated decision the Commissioner supported management, whose claim was argued on the basis of the right of management to conduct its business as it saw fit. The carefully planned company position was presented as an attempt to bring industrial relations under the control of the recognised parties, the state Commission and the state union officials, to eliminate the control system established by the workplace union representatives.[62] Swain concludes: 'Planned strategy at the corporate level of the company used the bargaining level structures, to control the bottom level which had been calling the tune'.[63]

In 1987 the company obtained a new award, achieved via negotiation, which gave management control of the job process at workplace level. This required that supervisors had the power to determine the manning requirements of their work programs and to implement these without having to obtain the agreement of the union representatives. There was union opposition to the new award in preliminary negotiations in October 1986 but subsequent acquiescence. Management was assisted here by:

1 the changed industrial relations climate in the Pilbara after the Robe River dispute in which Peko-Wallsend closed down the operation on 11 August and dismissed the entire wages workforce;[64] and
2 the change in the power context arising from the March 1987 *National Wage* case (see chapter 18).

Some key characteristics of the new award are set out in Table 10.10.

Table 10.10 Award restructuring: Hamersley Iron Pty Ltd 1986–1987

Characteristics of the negotiated award include:

- horizontal integration of tasks based on multi-skilling
- reduction of wage classifications from 124 to 67 based on broad-banding and job restructuring
- employee classification related to level and type of skill acquisition
- pay levels within each classification related to the performance of work requiring higher levels of skills acquisition and demonstrated competence on a regular basis
- abolition of higher duty payments
- abolition of mid-shift smoko/rest periods to allow continuous work periods

Source: Adapted from P. Swain, *A Study of the Role of Management and the Influence of Strategic Choice in the Management of Industrial Relations at the Level of the Firm in Three Iron Ore Companies*, Unpublished PhD Thesis, Monash University, 1992, pp. 231-232.

As a consequence of the award restructuring, the company was able to increase iron ore shipments by 30.3 per cent between January-June 1988 and January-June 1989.[65]

The case study demonstrates the interrelationships between decisions at the executive level, the formal structures and procedures at the functional level and the industrial relations situation in the workplace.[66] The management choices were almost identical to those made by Peko-Wallsend at Robe River in August 1986 except that Hamersley Iron sought the acquiescence of the State union officials and the Industrial Commission in Perth in removing the convenors' power. The Robe River management strategy included testing the limits of the Commission's conciliation (but not its arbitration) powers by issuing legal challenges to its exercise of those powers.[67]

Communications industry

Table 10.11 contains the text of an interview with the director of human resources at Optus Communications. This company received media coverage during 1994 by virtue of its early application for an enterprise flexibility agreement under the 1993 amendments to the *Industrial Relations Act* 1988 (see chapters 12, 17 and 18 for details of these amendments). The Commission

Table 10.11 Interview with George Webster, Director, Human Resources, Optus Communications, 29 June 1994

Q. How would you describe the management philosophy in employee relations at Optus?

A. Optus works hard to establish direct, frequent and open communication with its employees. We take our obligation for the well being of our staff very seriously and our managers are charged with the responsibility for representing the interests of their staff to higher management.

Optus has developed an extensive internal communication capability; for example, every employee has access to a personal computer and electronic mail is used extensively. Additionally, the Chief Executive and other directors, as appropriate, conduct a live satellite television broadcast to all departments in all locations around Australia following the monthly Board Meeting. This enables us within one or two days to brief our staff on new happenings in the organisation.

Q. How many employees does the company have? Would you provide an occupational profile of your employees and identify the awards and/or agreements applicable to the company.

A. Optus has approximately 3,000 employees — 1,000 in the Customer Service/Telemarketing area, 700 in the engineering disciplines and approximately 150 in sales. We have a single union coverage (the Communication Workers Union) and we have a single Enterprise Agreement which expired recently on 1 March 1994.

Q. Recent media reports have drawn attention to the fact that Optus is seeking an enterprise flexibility agreement under the new federal provisions which became operative on 30 March 1994. Could you explain the company's reasons for this decision?

A. As you are aware we are currently discussing an Enterprise Flexibility Agreement with our staff with a view to finalising this during July. Although media coverage tends to talk of Enterprise Flexibility Agreements as non union or indeed anti union, Optus has taken up the option purely because of its cultural consistency with the type of environment we have established. Simply put, given that we have the opportunity for the first time to talk directly to our staff why would we not do that. It is our view that the majority of our staff would not think highly of us if we chose to talk directly to the union about them given we had the opportunity to talk directly to them. Our approach, therefore, is simply one that I would describe as "pro employee". This is an option, had it been available, that Optus would have pursued in 1992 rather than negotiated a Certified Agreement at that time.

Q. The impressions gained from your comments is that life for employees at Optus may be close to idyllic. Would you agree that real conflicts of interests can arise in the workplace? If so, how are such conflicts resolved within your organisation?

A. Optus now manages its business through about 400 to 500 staff who are in managerial or supervisory positions. By virtue of this fact there will be occasions when we don't "get it right". In other words there may be a failure of implementation *vis-à-vis* the organisational culture and policy intent just as might occur in any organisation. In cases of conflict, resolution will be sought through the management line although often human resources staff will assume an 'honest broker' role to assist settlement.

> **Q. The level of unionisation in the private sector in Australia is reportedly around 30 per cent. Do you know whether union density in your company is above or below this national average for the private sector?**
>
> A. Our policy regarding union membership is simply that such a decision is a personal decision on the part of the employee. Optus commits that it will not discriminate one way or the other regarding that decision. As a result it is around 70 employees or less than 2.5%. I am unsure of the Telecom coverage, but I think you could safely assume it is more in the region of 90%.
>
> **Q. Do you have any general observations on the changes to federal regulation of industrial relations in Australia following the implementation of the *Industrial Relations Reform Act* 1993?**
>
> A. My view regarding the new legislation is that Laurie Brereton should be commended for providing the Enterprise Flexibility Agreement option. I believe there are many organisations who would see this as a more appropriate option given their particular employee relations environment.
>
> **Q. Does Optus distinguish between human resource management and industrial relations management and how many specialist HR or IR staff are employed? Do line managers have specific responsibilities in HRM/IR management.**
>
> A. Optus focus is almost exclusively on employee relations as opposed to industrial relations. We have structured the human resources management function so that the majority of our resources exist out in the line and report directly to line managers. I have a close functional relationship with the line Human Resource Manager and also have a small corporate team to provide assistance. We have introduced induction and training programs which clearly indicate to managers what Optus expects of them regarding their management accountabilities.
>
> **Q. What do you see as the key differences between 'employee relations' and 'industrial relations'.**
>
> A. In my view the difference is very simple. 'Employee relations' rests on the direct relationship between employee and employer. 'Industrial relations', on the other hand, depends more on the relationship between the union and the employer.

approved the company's application in August 1994. The interview illuminates elements of the company's strategy and the ideology on which the strategy is based.

Small business survey (ACCIS)

The 1992 Australian Chamber of Commerce and Industry Survey[68] of firms with fifty or fewer employees confirms both anecdotal and case study evidence that the external constraints on management in small firms are relatively insignificant in relation to changes in the labour process. Firms were asked to indicate whether they had been prevented from implementing any of the changes listed in Table 10.12. Only thirty-eight per cent of respondents, or 250 of the 953 firms, indicated that they had been prevented from introducing change. The relative importance of the sources of pressure against change are also set out in Table 10.12.

Table 10.12 Barriers to labour process changes: Small Business Survey (ACCIS) 1992

Attempted workplace changes
- changes in the arrangement of working hours
- broadening of tasks performed by employees (multi-skilling)
- introduction of training where previously none existed
- significant change in equipment and technology
- introduction of consultative/employee participation arrangements
- significant change in organisational structure
- other changes in work practice

Reasons for inability to introduce change

	As percentage of those unable to implement change (250 firms)	As percentage of all firms (953 firms)
Inadequate financial resources	39%	10%
Resistance from employees	28%	7%
Restriction in award	27%	7%
Resistance from unions	12%	3%
Resistance from supervisors/middle management	10%	3%
Other reasons	4%	4%

Source: Adapted from J. Isaac, S. Kates, D. Peetz, C. Fisher, R. Macklin and M. Short, *A Survey of Small Business and Industrial Relations*, Department of Industrial Relations, Canberra, May 1993, p. 43 & Questionnaire.

A breakdown of 'Other reasons' showed the recession and government policy (the market context and power context respectively) as the main obstacle to introducing one or more of the desired changes. The relative insignificance of unions as a barrier to change is not surprising given the low union density in small firms (see chapter 7) and the fact that fifty-eight per cent of respondent firms were non-union.[69]

The survey also sought information on the preferred framework for setting pay and conditions. This issue approximates the 'union method' area of strategic choice in the Gardner model (see chapter 6). The literature concerned with management strategy has not identified this area of choice in the same manner, nonetheless the Survey does provide some insight concerning the preferences of managers of small firms and also owners, as working owners were present in 77 per cent of firms. For the 93 per cent of respondents covered by an award, in respect of some or all of their employees, nearly two-thirds were covered by an industry award (typically multi-employer occupational awards covering employers who would not be in a strictly homogeneous industry) and one-third by common rule awards.[70] The distribution of types of award coverage is set out in Table 10.13. Sixty-three per cent of respondent firms expressed satisfaction with existing arrangements. The survey found the level of satisfaction declined as firm size increased, from 70 per cent for firms with 1-5 employees to 61 per cent for

Table 10.13 Award coverage preferred framework for determining wages and conditions: Small Business Survey (ACCIS) 1992

Types of award coverage in operation		
	Frequency	Per cent*
Industry award	552	64
Common rule award	292	34
Enterprise award	32	4
Unsure	17	2

*more than one response allowed
N = 869 (firms with awards only)

Preference for alternative arrangements		
	Percentage of those wanting alternative arrangements	Percentage of all firms
Individual contracts	42%	15%
Industry award	21%	7%
Enterprise award	20%	7%
Other	6%	2%

Source: Adapted from J. Isaac, S. Kates, D. Peetz, C. Fisher, R. Macklin and M. Short, *A Survey of Small Business and Industrial Relations*, Department of Industrial Relations, Canberra, May 1993, pp. 15 & 45.

Table 10.14 Who decides industrial relations issues (AWIRS)

	Type of workplace manager				
	Line %	Specialist %	Other %	Most Senior %	Manager beyond workplace %
Levels of overtime	35	14	12	34	5
Staffing levels for particular jobs	25	16	12	35	12
Recruiting non–managerial employees	23	22	10	32	13
Promoting non–managerial employees	14	19	11	38	18
Dismissals	14	22	8	37	19
Changes in work practices	14	23	10	37	16
Allocating resources for in–house training	12	23	11	40	14
Deciding changes to pay of non–managerial employees	8	17	7	35	33
Changes in procedures for disciplining employees	7	23	6	35	29
Employment levels for workplace	6	15	7	41	31
Purchase of major capital equipment	4	8	8	36	44
Referring matters to an industrial tribunal	3	17	5	32	43

Population: Australian workplaces with at least twenty employees.

Figures are weighted and are based on responses from up to 2004 workplaces, where the issues arise.

Source: R. Callus, A. Morehead, M. Cully and J. Buchanan, *Industrial Relations At Work: The Australian Workplace Industrial Relations Survey*, Commonwealth Department of Industrial Relations, AGPS, Canberra, 1991, p. 78.

firms with 21-50 employees. Further, a higher proportion of non-union firms (68 per cent) were satisfied with existing arrangements than unionised firms (55 per cent).[71] The preferred arrangements of the firms dissatisfied with existing arrangements are also set out in Table 10.13.

The researchers note that a breakdown of 'Other' raises the figure for individual contracts and that, of the listed arrangements, individual contracts were given the highest rating by firms of all three sizes.[72] Overall, fifteen per cent of all respondents, including those satisfied and dissatisfied with existing arrangements, identified a preference for individual contracts.[73] This preference could be regarded as a proxy for 'unitary collectivism' but no conclusions can be drawn concerning preferences on the 'individualism dimension' of the management of employees (see chapter 9). The fact that awards may be the product of bargaining or arbitration or some combination of these means that preferences of small employers in relation to industrial relations processes are not revealed.

Structure

The structural characteristics relevant to the industrial relations management function identified in chapter 9 were:

1 the number of industrial relations staff *vis-à-vis* the number of employees in the company;
2 the degree of centralisation of management decision making in industrial relations. This includes the 'level' in the firm at which key industrial relations decisions are made or particular functions are carried out and the relative number of industrial relations staff located at particular levels;
3 the degree of specialisation in decision making over industrial relations issues.

The 1989 Workplace Survey (AWIRS) cross-sectional data provides some information relating to structure, although as Deery and Gahan[74] observe, the Survey's workplace focus restricts understanding of the effect of management decisions made beyond the workplace. The survey material included here reveals the importance of industrial relations decisions by managers beyond the workplace. Table 10.14 provides information relating to the second and third aspects of structure identified above.

The Workplace Survey sought information on the location of management decision-making authority on twelve industrial relations issues. A distinction was drawn between managers at the workplace and managers beyond the workplace and between different types of managers. The types of managers distinguished were: first-line supervisor or line manager; specialist 'industrial relations' manager; other senior manager and most senior workplace manager. The distribution, based on responses from 2004 workplaces with at least twenty employees covering both public and private sectors, is shown in Table 10.14.

In relation to the degree of centralisation in the locus of decision making, the results show that a significant amount, generally over two-thirds, of decision making on these industrial relations issues occurred at the workplace. However, the issues which were more likely to be decided at workplace level were those concerning: the working of overtime; staffing levels; recruitment; promotion and dismissal; work practices and resource allocation for in-house training. Notably, the Survey Report observes that the apparent control by workplace management of day-to-day decisions on these issues may occur only within parameters determined by higher level management, that is the setting of stringent guidelines and reporting procedures for workplace decision making.[75] The researchers did not interview managers 'beyond the workplace' who may of course assess the locus of decision making on these issues differently from the workplace managers.

In relation to the degree of specialisation in industrial relations decision making, the Survey categories are incomplete as they do not distinguish specialist managers from other managers in respect of issues decided beyond the workplace. Where the specialist/non-specialist distinction is made, line managers' control is greatest in relation to overtime decisions followed by staffing levels and recruitment, while decision making by specialist managers peaks in the allocation of resources for in-house training, changes in work practices and changes in disciplinary procedures, followed by recruitment and dismissal decisions. The data also reveal that in relation to all the issues except overtime, senior workplace managers or managers beyond the workplace make the decisions in more than forty-five per cent of workplaces. The Report notes that differences between workplaces not only demonstrate different approaches to managing industrial relations but caution researchers not to generalise about industrial relations management and to recognise the diversity of management styles across different workplaces. However, as the Report acknowledges, the issues are not of equal significance for management and some dispersal of authority is to be expected, for example on the issues of major capital equipment purchases and staffing levels for particular jobs.[76]

Aspects of management structure are considered by Deery and Purcell[77] in analysing the responses of 142 firms respondent to their 1988 postal survey of the industrial relations strategies and policies of the 200 largest organisations in Australia. One area of strategic choice analysed was the staffing of the personnel function at the corporate level. The results showed a positive correlation between the number of specialist managerial staff at this level and two structural variables: size of firm and number of establishments. Two other organisation structural variables, market diversification and devolution of profit centres, showed a negative, although statistically weak, correlation to the size of the corporate personnel function. In other words, the latter was likely to be larger in the case of company focus on a single or related market than in the case of conglomerates and the more decentralised the level of financial accountability, the less likely the company would maintain a large corporate office personnel function.[78]

The relationship between the size of the corporate personnel function and a number of variables relating to industrial relations institutions and practices was also considered. The data showed a positive relationship in respect of the spread of unionism throughout all areas of the firm and union density among white-collar employees, although no such relationship in the case of blue-collar employees. The researchers suggest a possible reason is that the latter may be less likely to be seen as a corporate resource than white-collar employees whose unionisation may spur management to develop company-wide personnel policies and standards as a means of neutralising white-collar union activity. This is the union substitution dimension of a union avoidance strategy. It is argued that the requirements for corporate level staff increase as these policies become more extensive.[79]

A positive relationship was found also in respect of enterprise wide job evaluation with the resource demands of these schemes seen as the probable explanation for this association. The industrial relations institutional variable of joint consultation machinery produced different results for blue-collar and white-collar employees, a positive relationship for the latter but not the former. The writers suggest that while machinery for blue-collar employees seems to form independently of the corporate personnel function a large well-resourced department may encourage joint consultation machinery for white-collar employees.[80] Finally, a positive relationship was found in relation to the degree of centralisation in bargaining level, that is, firms with a large number of corporate personnel specialists were more likely to conduct bargaining at enterprise level than at division, business unit or establishment level than firms with smaller numbers.[81] The researchers conclude that the size of the corporate personnel departments 'is strongly linked to structural factors and to the need to administer the institutions and procedures of industrial relations where these are centralised'.[82]

Recent developments: the North American influence

The burgeoning interest in the 1980s style American industrial relations is suggestive of an opportunistic approach in Australia. The level of American unionisation has declined considerably over recent decades, falling from 23.6% of the labour force in 1973 to 16.3% in 1989.[83] This is probably due more to the failure of American unions to organise new industries, or new sections of industry, rather than to the failure of labour to hold its traditional ground, although both effects are present. There has, however, been some loss of territory by unions, and it has probably been achieved largely by the exercise of choice by unionists. The American labour code permits employees in every bargaining unit to determine, for themselves, which union will represent them. In making that decision, employees can choose, and increasingly have done so, that they want no union at all. Similarly, employees can subsequently hold elections to 'de-certify' the representative union, and to replace it with another, or with no union at all.

From the 1940s through the 1960s, the managers of unionised plants worked in a form of industrial relations partnership with representative unions, but that began to change, and was observable by the 1970s. The political leverage available to unions appears to have weakened since the early 1960s, and their interests may have been less assiduously guarded than they would prefer. The failure of unions to take new ground through the 1970s and 1980s, and the losses unions have suffered in representation elections have been a considerable reversal of trend, and only the credulous would suggest that the shift had taken place in the absence of management involvement. The generation of managers which accepted unions as industrial relations partners presumably did so because the political and economic environments suggested that this was likely to be a profitable course of action. They did not do it out of ideological or other conviction. As discussed in chapter 9, Kochan, Katz and McKersie argue that as a consequence of the change in management attitudes and relative union strength, industrial relations has basically been reshaped.[84] There is considerable argument in the United States as to the extent of this transformation, and whether it is as complete as might be inferred from the discussion.[85] Whatever may be the extent of the transformation, where it has occurred, the old industrial relations practice, of union and management sharing the derivation and administration of rules governing wages, hours and working conditions, has been replaced by processes which see managers seeking to deal with employees as individuals, rather than with their collective representatives. The intent, of course, is to permit managers to take critical decisions without having to consider union policies in their plans.

The relevance of this change in industrial relations, generally described as human resource management, to Australia is, in short run, practical terms, fairly slight. The change in the United States has come about as a consequence of long experience with an industrial relations system which minimises the direct and indirect involvement of government, provides for exercise of choice by union members, and has involved informed and sophisticated managerial appraisals of union leadership, goals and tactics. It has also taken place in a considerably more competitive economic environment than exists in Australia, with consequently greater application of market discipline to managers. While the direct relevance of this experience may be slight, its symbolic influence has been far from negligible. Many Australian managers have expressed interest in the process of human resource management, and many Australian corporations have at least changed titles of relevant staff from Industrial Relations Manager, or Employee Relations Manager, to Human Resource Manager. It is not easy to detect whether there have been changes in substance to accompany the changed style, but there is certainly increased interest in speculating about union-free work-sites. Some legislative changes included in the *Industrial Relations Act*, and ss 118 and 118A are cases in point, do provide for employers to have some voice in the selection of unions to represent their employees—no-one, of course would suggest that Australian workers should be heard on this question—and this may be one step in the direction of human resource management goals.

The interest that Australians have taken in this development is indicative of the fact that managers tend to take a somewhat expedient view of industrial relations. Many of them do not, it would appear, think it worth the effort of seeking to derive stable and effective outcomes from either bargaining or arbitration. A similar attitude exists among union officials. Few of them, obviously, have overtly embraced human resource management policies, but their abrupt switch from the mixed bargaining/arbitration regime of the 1970s to the pure arbitration of the early Accord years was entirely opportunistic, as was the sudden desire to switch back to the mixed regime of the early 1990s. There is of course, every reason to expect business decisions to be made reflecting the advantages of the time, although it would be difficult to argue that union members enjoyed those advantages during the boom years of the 1980s. The point is that while management and labour act in this way, it is unlikely that any form of industrial relations practice will be fully effective in delivering stability and prosperity.

Employee participation in management

In chapter 9 some conceptual issues relating to employee participation in management were introduced. In this section the industrial relations view at tribunal level is considered together with some Australian empirical research.

Management prerogatives and arbitration

In the Australian industrial relations literature, as distinct from management theory or organisational behaviour theory, employee participation has frequently been discussed in terms of management prerogatives. This in turn has been related to decisions of the federal industrial tribunal. In terms of the degree of participation identified in chapter 9, the tribunal decisions referred to below are typically concerned with attempts by unions at 'joint decision making' but also include attempts to introduce 'joint consultation'.

As indicated in chapter 9, the term 'management prerogative' used in a descriptive sense defines those areas or issues which remain exclusively in the control of management; in a prescriptive sense the term denotes areas of decision making which ought to reside exclusively with management. The concept is applicable to any aspect of the employer-employee relationship but the discussion here is concerned with those aspects which writers in the labour process school have defined as 'job control' (see chapter 3) that is, issues relating to the work to be undertaken, the nature, methods and pace of work, together with the location and conditions of work, on any day or shift. These are the areas where conflict over management prerogatives arises most frequently. It is the centre of analysis for the radical frame of reference in which, as McDonald[86] points out, the fundamental premise is that the primary objective of employers and managers is to achieve the control of labour for the purpose of extracting surplus value.

Managerial prerogatives may be restricted or expanded by one or more of the following, either individually or severally: the ideology and power of trade unions or groups of workers; the labour market context; the power context and the technical context. Management practice will also be influenced by management ideology. This section illustrates the perennial conflict over issues relating to job control with the emphasis on the management perspective.

It is important to distinguish between *de jure* and *de facto* restrictions on managerial prerogatives. For example, while the federal industrial tribunal upheld management rights in the area of job control at least until the 1970s (see below) the position in practice may have been less favourable for employers than suggested by tribunal pronouncements. Until the 1980s, many awards, especially federal awards, did not contain any provisions constraining the employer in relation to the dismissal of employees: neither was there any reference to grounds for dismissal or procedures relating to any form of discipline of employees. Further, there was no federal legislation of the kind which existed in some states. This meant that in legal terms the employer had almost unrestricted discretion. In practice, however, in areas of employment where unionism was strong, the metals fabrication sector of manufacturing for example, management freedom was constrained by the power of the union and workers to impose costs on management if a worker was dismissed on grounds or by means that the workers considered unfair.

There has been no overt recognition in Australia of the job property concept which holds that if the means of production are the property of employees, the processes of production belong to the workers. Managers have been inhibited however by the powerful forces of custom and practice, well illustrated in the strong craft tradition of Australian unionism which resulted in the marking out of clear demarcation zones.

It should be noted that many of the restrictions on management's rights to control labour have arisen from sources other than industrial relations forces. In the past managers' willingness to accept a situation in which workers were rarely laid off or fired was partly the product of a largely uncompetitive economy, being in part the *quid pro quo* for a very high level of tariff protection. It was also a reflection of a perceived social ethos, but one ethos whose time was now passed. The rights to particular jobs held by certain craftsmen are often the outcome of licensing restrictions originally aimed at protecting public health and safety. Additionally, the very restrictive tenure provisions observed by many public employers were introduced for the traditional reasons of safeguarding the independence of public servants, rather than as a response to industrial pressure.

During the 1980s, the objective of international competitiveness became pre-eminent and tariff protection was progressively reduced. Management in twentieth century Australia has always operated within the constraints of the conciliation and arbitration systems. These cover about eighty per cent of the total workforce, although coverage may vary between industries and workplaces. In the late 1980s the ethos of international competitiveness and the corollary of increasing efficiency and productivity came to dominate the 'wage' policy of the federal and state industrial tribunals, under the leadership of the former. The policy shift, in conjunction with a favourable labour market context, that is excess labour supply in most areas, presented management with the opportunity to increase the degree of management control, if not to re-establish unfettered management prerogative, in relation to many aspects of work processes and work organisation. The opportunity to regain, or extend, control is to be distinguished from its realisation and the extent of the latter will be established by empirical investigation. Such investigation should also enable the rhetoric of 'employee relations' to be tested for its practical application, including the nature and extent of employee participation in (hitherto) management decisions.

An opportunity for management was provided by tribunal support for a broad negotiating agenda covering most job control issues, in the context of largely tribunal determined wage increases. There was also provision for arbitration in the absence of agreement. The question of the feasibility of these public policy objectives is discussed in chapters 16 and 18.

The legal position of the dominant industrial tribunal in Australia, titled the Australian Industrial Relations Commission since 1989, in relation to management prerogatives may be found in chapter 12. However, an appreciation of the changing views of this important rule-making body may be obtained from the extracts from decisions in Table 10.15. In the early decades the federal tribunal preserved and even promoted management rights. This is exemplified in the oft-quoted remarks of the first President of the then Commonwealth Court of Conciliation and Arbitration, O'Connor J, in a 1906 case involving the Merchant Service Guild of Australasia and the Commonwealth Steam-Ship Owners' Association concerning employment security and wage rates for ships' officers. A similar view is provided by the Court's second President, Higgins J, some sixteen years later. A view more sensitive to employee rights is evident in a 1968 case dealing with a dispute over the redundancy of oil-company clerks resulting from the installation of computers. The extracts from this decision, see Table 10.15, also provide some insights into management practice.

In 1973 Robinson J, in a decision in a rights dispute concerning the work location of an employee of the Dendy Theatre, said that the phrases 'management rights' or 'management prerogatives' had been used to delineate areas of business activity which were properly removed from union interference or influence because they were not 'industrial matters' but added, 'It must be said that the right of management to 'run its own business' is not as untrammelled or clear-cut as it was twenty, or even ten years ago'.[87] Eleven years later, in a test case brought by the ACTU, the Commission agreed that employers should be required by award provisions to consult employees about changes in business operations likely to have employment effects. The Confederation of Australian Industry had argued that such consultation should be voluntary. This would permit management to take the necessary responsibility for the 'change' decision it made and allow appropriate flexibility concerning timing and content. The Confederation also raised the traditional and seemingly circular, management prerogative argument drawing on case law. It argued that the claim did not relate to an industrial matter because it concerned the role and function of the management of an enterprise rather than terms and conditions of employment. Another employer objection put by the Confederation was that unions with a fundamental and long-standing objection to technological change could use such a provision to frustrate change.[88] The final example in Table 10.15 is from the April 1991 *National Wage* case. The statement reflects a tribunal policy which has made most job control issues negotiable as the *quid pro quo* for arbitrated wage increases. In the instance cited here however, the tribunal has arbitrated a universal concession to management control, that is a provision which is to appear in all federal awards, estimated in 1990 to cover about forty per cent of the Australian workforce.

Table 10.15 Management rights and job control: federal tribunal views.

Ships' officers: employment security and wages
'In determining what is fair and reasonable certain rights of the parties must be kept in view. The right of the combination of employees given by the Act is, when the dispute is brought before the Court, to have an award of fair wages, not, as is sometimes urged by those who confuse the constitution of the wages fund with the right to wages, a right to be awarded a fair proportion of the profits. Except in co-operative concerns employees are in no sense partners with their employers. They run no financial risks, and incur no liabilities. On the other hand the right of the employer is to manage his business in his own way without interference of any kind except in so far as the Court may deem it is necessary to interfere for the purpose of making effective the right given by the Act to the combination of employees to fair wages.'
  Merchant Service Guild v Cth Steamship Owners' Assoc. (1906) 1 CAR 4 at 25

A judicial overview
'The court leaves every employer free to carry on his business or his own system, so long as he does not perpetuate industrial trouble or endanger industrial peace; free to choose his employees on their merits and according to his exigencies; free to make use of new machines, of improved methods, of financial advantages, of advantages of locality, of superior knowledge; free to put the utmost pressure on anything and everything except human life.'
  H.B. Higgins, *A New Province for Law and Order* Constable, London, 1922, p. 13.

Oil company clerks: technological change
'We are not prepared to dismiss this application under section 41(l)(d)(iii). On the contrary this is a matter with which we should in the public interest deal. In our view the progressive introduction of automation and mechanisation into industry and particularly into the white collar industry makes it important that this full bench should deal with the particular issues involved.
The history of the introduction of computers by this group of companies was, broadly speaking, not disputed. Over a period of years various kinds of mechanical devices were introduced in the clerical section and early in 1967 the companies decided to lease a new computer and to centralise their accounting systems in Melbourne. After the companies' decision had been made the employees concerned first heard rumours which circulated though the offices that some drastic changes were imminent and at a later date each one concerned was informed officially of what was proposed in his particular case.
The Clerks Union received no official communication from the companies until some months later, indeed, not until after it had made the application to vary the award which is one of the matters now before us. The letter then received was in the following terms: *'To achieve greater efficiency we are making some changes in organisation and procedure and as these may affect some of your members of your union, we feel you might be interested to visit us to learn of our plans.*
If you would care to let the writer know when you will next be in Melbourne, we shall be pleased to arrange a meeting'.
We agree with the statement in H. C. Sleigh Ltd's annual report of 1967 'that a company is not something impersonal, but *people*'. In the particular situation created by the plan to centralise accounts in Melbourne the Company needed to keep this in mind at all stages. When employers are contemplating the introduction of computers and other automatic devices which may have serious effects on employees such as termination of employment or transfer interstate it is essential that both the employees and the union concerned should be informed of and involved in the planning as soon as possible. Many real human problems may be involved which may not be known to company executives and they, with the best will in the world, may take steps which do not help to solve them. It is our view that employees and their welfare are as important in the planning of a change of the kind we have

had to consider as any other aspect of the change and that they, both individually and through their union, should be brought in at the planning stage. When brought into the planning both employees and the union should in their turn attempt to understand the problems which the employer faces and co–operate with him to try to find a reasonable solution.

We realise that the Sleigh group was dealing with a complex situation which, as far as we know, has not occurred before in this industry. But we consider it necessary to set out the facts and make the observations we have made because as the first full bench of this Commission which has had to consider the effects of computers on employment our views should be known for the guidance of both employers and unions. If in the future the Commission's attention is drawn to instances in which the future welfare of employees has not in its view been properly dealt with in company planning the Commission may find it necessary to intervene in the interests of industrial justice.'

Variation-Clerks (Oil Companies) Award (1968) 122 CAR 339 at 344–345.

Consultation re employment effects of organisational change

'We are aware that procedures for notification, consultation and provision of information have generally been settled by negotiation and agreement, and we are of the view that, generally speaking, they are not matters which lend themselves to effective legislation or award prescription.

However, at this stage, we are prepared to include in an award a requirement that consultation take place with employees and their representatives as soon as a firm decision has been taken about major changes in production, program, organization, structure or technology which are likely to have significant effects on employees.

We have decided also that the employer shall provide in writing to the employees concerned and their representatives all relevant information about the nature of the changes proposed, the expected effect of the changes on employees and any other matters likely to affect employees. However, we will not require an employer to disclose confidential information.'

Termination, Change and Redundancy case (1984) 294 CAR 175 at 196

Functional flexibility

'Consistent with the ongoing implementation of the structural efficiency principle determined in the National Wage Case decision of 7 August 1989, any party to a minimum rates award or a paid rates award seeking the increases in wages or salaries allowable under the National Wage Case decision of 16 April 1991 is required to satisfy the Commission:

(e) That there is a provision in the award to the effect that an employer may direct an employee to carry out such duties as are within the limits of the employee's skill, competence and training;'

National Wage case
April 1991, 36 IR 120 at 180–181

Case studies

The experimentation with various forms of worker participation in Australia in the early 1970s, usually introduced by management, was a stimulus to academic research. These schemes were developed during a period of full employment and were widely regarded as a response to the problems of labour turnover and absenteeism. These management initiatives may have led to the emphasis on worker responses to which Vaughan refers (see chapter 9), although some research gives equal consideration to the behaviours of each group of actors. Support for Vaughan's critique of the (then) widespread assumptions concerning management motivations is provided by Gilmour and Lansbury, writing in the latter half of the 1970s. They point to the significance of management resistance to participation. They note that several large Australian companies such as Alcan, CRA, CSR, ICI, Leyland Motors, Phillips Industries and Shell, have experimented with different but limited forms of worker participation in management. These included semi-autonomous work groups at various levels, joint consultation at plant level and some emphasis on communications and training. Significantly, where progress was slow it was often due to resistance from middle managers and first line managers opposed to the changes in their roles.[89]

The 1980s have been characterised by encroachments on management prerogatives through the use of the political method by trade unions that is, via legislation and to a lesser degree, via industrial tribunal decisions. As is evident from the frameworks in chapter 9 and the case studies in this chapter, there has still been room for management strategic choice in the 1980s. Three Australian case studies, highlighting different forms of participation, are now distinguished to provide some appreciation of the diversity of practice and the diversity of research.

Cupper's[90] studies of Dynavac, a small private sector company manufacturing and importing specialised vacuum equipment, provide one of the few documented examples of self-management or comprehensive worker participation. Cupper identifies the following as the factors contributing to the origin and development of self-management:

1 support from Dynavac's owners—the owners' shares were transferred to the Dynavac Charitable Trust in return for a life-time employment contract and the continuation of self-management;
2 a philosophical commitment to the management approach by most employees;
3 a staff size (at the outset twenty-four employees) allowing manageable interaction;
4 low level of union density and no union involvement during the early stages of transition to self-management;
5 the positive influence of the company's field of production and technology, namely specialised engineering. This involves high skill levels and enables clear specification of both job content and responsibility and is thus amenable to job autonomy.[91]

Cupper's second study notes the introduction of a voluntary format for worker participation to replace the compulsory format and he raises the question of whether this may lead to the emergence of a managerial elite. Significantly, the later study concludes that both employee commitment to self-management and the company's commercial viability had been maintained.[92]

Lumley's[93] case study research in 1981-1982 analyses the interaction between employer strategies and union workplace organisation and activity in five South Australian workplaces where union density for non-managerial employees was 100 per cent. The research focus is control over the organisation and conduct of work at workplace level.[94]

The conclusions derive primarily from of a study of a motor vehicle assembly plant and the clerical section of a retail organisation. They are supplemented by data from a light engineering plant, a heavy engineering company and a production facility of a public utility. Lumley finds significant variation in the extent of union involvement within the common institutional framework of compulsory arbitration. There are also differences in management strategies of 'employer control'. In the retail organisation, unilateral management discretion prevailed, with management determining all matters not covered by the award, a position facilitated by the union's discouragement of bargaining by office (workplace) representatives.[95] In the case of the motor vehicle manufacturer, Lumley finds management's long-term objective to be the development of trust and teamwork with employees as a means of generating consensus. The strategies include both worker and union participation in management and, in relation to the nature of the employment relationship, the promotion of job security.[96] Elements of Purcell's 'constitutional collectivism' are also present in management's assertion of its prerogatives juxtaposed with a willingness to negotiate with unions on job control issues in the interests of minimising conflict. The worker participation schemes include suggestion schemes and quality circles culminating in worker-management dinners and family visits to the workplace. In the case of union participation, the focus is on the provision of information to shop stewards: communication meetings detailing plant performance and short-term and long-term plans and attendance at daily vehicle audits. The employment relationship strategy has elements in common with that of the plants in Bramble's case studies: in this instance an assurance of no compulsory redundancy and more rigorous selection standards in conjunction with employment of temporary workers for up to one month.[97]

The most common form of worker participation in management in Australia has been joint consultation. Davis and Lansbury,[98] in their study of the operation of consultative councils at 'top-level' in Telecom, from 1975 to 1987, and in Qantas, from 1981 to 1987, conclude that, in the case of Telecom, the consultation machinery has been a factor promoting improved industrial relations within this enterprise. They cite the work of the council's technological change sub-committee in facilitating agreement on guiding principles and procedures for dealing with this significant matter. The functions of the Telecom Consultative Council parallel that of the Public Service Joint Council which Telecom management and unions had attended prior to Telecom's establishment as a statutory authority. This function was to provide a consultative, non-adversarial setting for union-management meetings on general issues concerning employment with specific matters being reserved for union management negotiations.[99] The Council is empowered to consider and report on any matter referred to it by Telecom (the Commission) and any matter the Council considers to be of general effect or interest in relation to the service of Telecom.[100]

The Qantas Consultative Council was established in 1981 on the recommendation of the then President of the Conciliation and Arbitration Commission, Sir John Moore. The proposal, in the interests of improving dispute settlement procedures, formed part of the settlement terms ending a lengthy dispute with the airline unions.[101] However, the Council was not established as a dispute-settling forum or decision-making authority within the company. Rather, the two principal functions were to 'Consult and act on any matter which it considers is of importance in relation to the Company's operations as they affect its relationship with trade unions, and matters generally affecting company employees'.[102] Davis and Lansbury summarise both union and management views concerning the operation of this consultative machinery. Management views are set out in Table 10.16.

Davis and Lansbury identify three factors which distinguish the two organisations and which account for the greater success of joint consultation in Telecom than in Qantas:

1. the circumstances in which the machinery was established;
2. the resources and time invested in the operation of the council;
3. workforce size, union structure and (consequent) union commitment to the process.

The participants in Telecom were continuing a familiar process while the Qantas Council was an 'imposed' solution established in haste as part of the terms of a dispute settlement. Telecom meetings ran for one and a half to two days while Qantas meetings were typically for half a day. Telecom Council alone had full-time secretarial support. Telecom, with about 94 000 staff, had fewer unions, three were 'enterprise specific' and ninety-one per cent of unionists were in five unions. Qantas with about 14 000 staff had a large number of unions, many of which had only a small percentage of their membership at Qantas and this explained the absence of 'investment' in the process by senior union officials.[103]

Conclusion

The surveys, case studies, commissioned studies, tribunal decisons and company policies summarised in this chapter illuminate many of the concepts and analytical frameworks introduced in the previous chapter. Prior to the mid-1980s, research concerning the industrial relations management function in Australia was confined mainly to surveys of managers' attitudes to industrial relations and studies of employee participation in management. The latter area of research typically did not have a specific focus on management motivations and strategies. There is thus some conceptual discontinuity between this research and more recent analyses, most of which draw upon the theoretical developments concerning industrial relations management emanating from Great Britain and the United States in the mid- to late 1980s.

The recent case studies by Quinlan, Bramble and Swain and other similar studies, represent valuable micro-studies of management at the level of the firm. Quinlan's study of BHP management at the Port Kembla steelworks uses a framework which incorporates concepts and has a scope very similar to the Kochan, Katz and McKersie frameworks though is less detailed and formalised. His analysis is suggestive of effective management control at workplace level for much of the period 1945 to 1975 and provides a stark contrast to the union control at workplace level discussed by Swain and which precipitated changes in management strategy in the Pilbara iron ore industry.

Both the Bramble and Swain studies identify management as the initiator of change but they also illuminate the distinctions in analysis of management

Table 10.16 Management views concerning joint consultation processes: Qantas and Telecom

Positive features (benefits)
Qantas
- a means of detecting and defusing potential industrial relations problems
- enables management to more effectively communicate aspects of the airline business to union representatives in the hope of influencing their behaviour

Telecom
- facilitates early identification of problem issues, acting as 'safety valve'
- enables management to present information to unions on the complex matters facing Telecom that is, acquainting and educating unions about economic and other pressures facing the organisation
- leads to greater mutual understanding
- affords senior managers who attend a greater appreciation of industrial relations
- a useful forum for working on difficult long-term issues, for example technological change and equal employment opportunity
- consolidates improved industrial relations reflected in the low level of disputation and the speed of settlement
- presents a useful model for co-operation at other levels in Telecom

Negative features (criticisms)
Qantas
- places Qantas at a competitive disadvantage, a liability that their private sector competitiors do not have to endure
- unions the major beneficiaries: managers divulge sensitive information re airline operation but unions unwilling to discuss aspects of their activities (demarcation for example) which inhibit airline's performance
- the 'junior' level and discontinuity of union representation
- union use of council as an alternative forum to raise disputes and negotiate industrial issues
- object to overlap of functions between the Council and the Combined Unions Committee conflicting with the unions' preference to integrate these
- unions' attempted use of Council as the single channel of communication between the company and its workforce

Telecom
- slows the decision–making process — anachronistic in a competitive environment with rapid response to economic and commercial developments at a premium
- typically union input is limited and unions are unable to absorb and understand information provided
- non–participation of one major union (the then APTU)
- scant evidence of assisting to eliminate costly demarcation and other restrictive work practices
- perception that (senior) management Council representatives and to lesser extent, union officials, are out of step respectively with middle and lower management and rank and file members.

Source: Adapted from E.M. Davis and R.D. Lansbury, 'Consultative Councils in Qantas and Telecom: A Comparative Study', *Journal of Industrial Relations 30*, December 1988, pp. 559-560 & 563-564.

objectives and practice when viewed through different frameworks. Bramble's study of management from a labour process perspective is premised on the management objective of control, whereas in Swain's study, control is a possible management strategic choice. In the latter study, management objectives are central to the analysis. Swain's research demonstrates explicit and rational strategy as well as both successful and unsuccessful strategy. The Bramble study does not cover the significant shift in tribunal wages policy of the late 1980s but it does illustrate a perennial struggle for management control and the influence of the behaviour of the other actors and environmental variables.

Evidence from a variety of sources points to the ascendancy, especially since the late 1980s, of the unitary ideology with an emphasis on high individualism and some indications, from Swain's major study of the iron ore industry, of an emerging unitary collectivism also.[104] The pervasive rhetoric reflects the socially acceptable face of the unitary ideology, namely 'high individualism' or 'valued resource status'. The support for 'co-operative collectivism' on the other hand is less evident.

The overriding impression from case studies and surveys however, is one of diversity in management practice and more broadly, industrial relations practice. Both forms of research are illuminating; they contribute to an increase in both the standing and the understanding of industrial relations as a practice in its own right rather than as merely an extension of the economic policies of governments. However, the use of theoretical concepts in surveys of management remains relatively limited and there is clearly scope for higher returns from future surveys if the theoretical refinements, including those summarised in chapter 9, are drawn upon.

The diversity in industrial relations practice that co-exists with common conciliation and arbitration frameworks suggests this factor has limited influence. This is not inconsistent with the accepted view of the traditional minimal interference by tribunals with management prerogatives. In chapters 16 and 18, the industrial relations public policy environment in which managers have been operating during the 1980s is discussed in detail. The managements which are now viewing industrial relations outcomes in terms of enterprise performance are making a strategic choice which resonates with *one* of the objectives of public policy operative since the late 1980s.

The employer representations before industrial tribunals mentioned in this chapter are suggestive of a constant employer position in relation to job control issues. However arbitrated decisions on challenges to the boundary between unilateral management decision making and union or employee participation in management decision making are not necessarily indicative of management views. Further, it will be appreciated from a reading of the following chapter that the arguments presented by employer associations before industrial tribunals are not necessarily reflective of current management practice.

Notes

1 J. Niland and D. Turner, *Control, Consensus or Chaos?: Managers and Industrial Relations Reform*, Allen & Unwin, Sydney, 1985, p. 9.
2 Business Council of Australia, *Enterprise-Based Bargaining Units: A Better Way of Working*, Report to the BCA by the Employee Relations Study Commission, July 1989, volume 1, p. ix.
3 BCA, *Business Council Bulletin*, no. 26, August 1986.
4 BCA, 1989, *op. cit.*, p. x.

5 *ibid.*, pp. 5-7.
6 *ibid.*, pp. 4-5.
7 See for example, 'Industrial Relations Reform Bill 1993 Misses the Chance for Real Reform', *Business Council Bulletin*, December 1993, pp. 27-29. In the 1989 Report to the BCA 'enterprise' is defined as a unit with a set of definable human, technological and financial resources. It uses these resources to add value to a product or service that is sold to customers. Enterprises may be independent units (single business) or within a larger corporate group (ANZ Banking Group, BHP). Enterprises are defined by customers and markets (pp. 2-3).
8 Business Council of Australia, *Working Relations: A Fresh Start for Australian Enterprises*, Information Australia and Business Council of Australia, Melbourne, 1993, p. 109.
9 J. Purcell, 'Mapping Management Styles in Employee Relations', *Journal of Management Studies 24*, September 1987, p. 544.
10 *Industrial (Commercial Practices) Act* 1984; *Industrial (Commercial Practices) Act* 1985; *Electricity (Continuity of Supply) Act* 1985; *Electricity (Continuity of Supply) Act Amendment Act* 1985; *Industrial Conciliation and Arbitration Act Amendment Act* 1985; *Electricity Authorities Industrial Causes Act* 1985.
11 ICI Australia Limited, *Annual Report*, 1992, p. 1.
12 *The Age*, 3 April 1991, p. 5.
13 See J. McIntosh and D. Hull, 'Job redesign at ICI Australia' in R.D. Lansbury (ed.), *Democracy in the workplace*, Longman Cheshire, Melbourne, 1980, pp. 68-82.
14 See for example Royal Commission on Australian Government Administration, *Report*, AGPS, Canberra, 1976, chapter 8.
15 M. Quinlan, 'Managerial strategy and industrial relations in the Australian steel industry, 1945-75', in M. Bray and V. Taylor (eds), *Managing Labour?, Essays in the Political Economy of Australian Industrial Relations*, McGraw-Hill, Sydney, 1986, pp. 20–47.
16 K. Thurley and S. Wood, 'Business Strategy and Industrial Relations Strategy' in K. Thurley and S. Wood (eds), *Industrial Relations and Management Strategy*, Cambridge University Press, Cambridge, 1983, p. 198.
17 Quinlan, *op. cit.*, pp. 21 & 46.
18 *ibid.*, p. 24.
19 *ibid.*, pp. 33-34 & 43-44.
20 *ibid.*, p. 38.
21 R. Murray and K. White, *The Ironworkers: A History of the Federated Ironworkers Association of Australia*, Hale & Iremonger, Sydney, 1982, p. 58.
22 Quinlan, *op. cit.*, pp. 38 & 43.
23 *ibid.*, p. 35.
24 *ibid.*, pp. 29-30.
25 *ibid.*, p. 36.
26 *ibid.*, p. 46.
27 *ibid.*, pp. 41-42.
28 T. Bramble, 'Political Economy and Management Strategy in the Metal and Engineering Industry' in B. Dabscheck, G. Griffin and J. Teicher (eds), *Contemporary Australian Industrial Relations: Readings*, Longman Cheshire, Melbourne, 1992, pp. 243-266.
29 C. Brewster, G. Gill and S. Richbell, 'Industrial Relations Policy. A Framework for Analysis', in K. Thurley and S. Wood (eds), *Industrial Relations and Management Strategy*, Cambridge University Press, Cambridge, 1983, cited in Bramble, *op. cit.*, at p. 245.
30 Bramble, *op. cit.*, p. 246.
31 H. Mintzberg, 'Patterns in Strategy Formulation', *Management Science 24*, May 1978, pp. 934-948.
32 Bramble, *op. cit.*, pp. 247-248.
33 *ibid.*, p. 249.
34 *ibid.*, p. 256.
35 *ibid.*, p. 257.
36 *ibid.*, p. 249.

37 *ibid.*, p. 260.
38 G.W. Ford, 'A study of human resources and industrial relations at the plant level in seven selected industries' in *Policies for Development of Manufacturing Industry*, (The Jackson Report), vol. iv, AGPS, Canberra, 1976, pp. 39 & 49 cited in Bramble *op. cit.*, p. 245.
39 Bramble, *op. cit.*, p. 262.
40 *ibid.*, p. 250.
41 *ibid.*, pp. 249-250.
42 *ibid.*, p. 249.
43 *ibid.*, p. 260.
44 *ibid.*
45 *ibid.*, pp. 250-251.
46 P. Swain, *A Study of the Role of Management and the Influence of Strategic Choice in the Management of Industrial Relations at the Level of the Firm in Three Iron Ore Companies*, unpublished PhD thesis, Monash University, 1992.
47 T.A. Kochan, R.B. McKersie and P. Capelli, 'Strategic Choice and Industrial Relations Theory', *Industrial Relations 23*, Winter 1984, pp. 16-39.
48 Swain, *op. cit.*, p. 50.
49 *ibid.*, p. 7.
50 *ibid.*, p. 371.
51 *ibid.*, p. 12.
52 *ibid.*, p. 383.
53 *ibid.*, p. 371.
54 *ibid.*, p. 188.
55 *ibid.*, p. 214
56 *ibid.*, p. 103.
57 *ibid.*, p. 222.
58 *ibid.*
59 *ibid.*, p. 223.
60 *ibid.*, p. 224.
61 *ibid.*, p. 225.
62 *ibid.*, p. 229.
63 *ibid.*, p. 230.
64 For a detailed account of the 1986 Robe River dispute see *ibid.*, chapter 11. See also H. Smith and H. Thompson, 'Industrial Relations and the Law Case Study of Robe River', *Australian Quarterly*, Spring-Summer 1987, pp. 297-304.
65 *op. cit.*, p. 364.
66 *ibid.*, p. 217.
67 *ibid.*
68 J. Isaac, S. Kates, D. Peetz, C. Fisher, R. Macklin and M. Short, *A Survey of Small Business and Industrial Relations*, Department of Industrial Relations, Canberra, May 1993.
69 *ibid.*, p. 9.
70 *ibid.*, p. 15.
71 *ibid.*, p. 44.
72 *ibid.*, p. 45.
73 *ibid.*, p. 59.
74 S. Deery and P. Gahan, 'The Workplace Survey and Management Structures', *Journal of Industrial Relations 33*, December 1991, p. 515.
75 R. Callus, A. Morehead, M. Cully and J. Buchanan, *Industrial Relations At Work: The Australian Workplace Industrial Relations Survey*, Commonwealth Department of Industrial Relations, AGPS, Canberra, 1991, p. 79.
76 *ibid.*, pp. 79-80.
77 S. Deery and J. Purcell, 'Strategic Choices in Industrial Relations Management in Large Organisations', *Journal of Industrial Relations 31*, December 1989, pp. 459-477.

78 *ibid.*, p. 463.
79 *ibid.*, p. 464.
80 *ibid.*, pp. 465-466.
81 *ibid.*, p. 465.
82 *ibid.*, p. 466.
83 M.A. Curme, B.T. Hirsch and D.A. Macpherson, 'Union Membership and Contract Coverage', *Industrial and Labor Relations Review, 44*, October 1990, p. 9.
84 T.A. Kochan, H.C. Katz and R.B. McKersie, *The Transformation of American Industrial Relations*, Basic Books, New York, 1986.
85 See D. Lewin, 'Industrial Relations as a Strategic Variable', in M.A. Kleiner, R.N. Block, M. Roomkin and S.W. Salsburg (eds), *Human Resources and the Performance of the Firm*, IRRA Series, 1987 and Review Symposium: 'The Transformation of American Industrial Relations', *Industrial and Labor Relations Review 41*, April 1988, pp. 439-455.
86 D. McDonald, 'The Role of Management in Industrial Relations and Some Views on Its Conceptualisation and Analysis', *Journal of Management Studies 22*, September 1985, p. 529.
87 *The Cinematograph Exhibitors Association and Australian Theatrical and Amusement Employees Association*, (1973) 152 CAR 66 at 67.
88 Australian Conciliation and Arbitration Commission, *Termination, Change and Redundancy Case*, (1984) 294 CAR 175 at 195.
89 P. Gilmour and R.D. Lansbury, 'The Changing Role of the Supervisor: Implications for Industrial Relations', *Journal of Industrial Relations 19*, September 1977, pp. 225-240.
90 L. Cupper, 'Worker participation in the Dynavac organisation', *Journal of Industrial Relations 18*, June 1976, pp. 124-141; L. Cupper, 'Dynavac revisited; self-management in transition', *Journal of Industrial Relations 21*, March 1979, pp. 51-62.
91 Cupper, 1976, *op. cit.*, pp. 139-141.
92 Cupper, 1979, *op. cit.*, p. 61.
93 R. Lumley, 'Control over the organisation and conduct of work: evidence from some Australian workplaces,' *Journal of Industrial Relations 25*, September 1983, pp. 301-316.
94 *ibid.*, p. 305.
95 *ibid.*, p. 309.
96 *ibid.*, p. 310.
97 *ibid.*
98 E.M. Davis and R.D. Lansbury, 'Consultative Councils in Qantas and Telecom: A Comparative Study', *Journal of Industrial Relations 30*, December 1988, pp. 546-565.
99 *ibid.*, p. 554.
100 *ibid.*, p. 555.
101 *ibid.*, p. 560.
102 *ibid.*, pp. 560-561.
103 *ibid.*, pp. 550-551, 553, 565.
104 Swain, *op. cit.*, p. 233.

Further Reading

Ideology

Business Council of Australia, *Enterprise-Based Bargaining Units: A Better Way of Working*, Report to the BCA by the Employee Relations Study Commission, volume 1, July 1989, chapter 1.

Business Council of Australia, *Working Relations: A Fresh Start for Australian Enterprises*, Information Australia and Business Council of Australia, Melbourne, 1993.

S. Deery and P.J. Dowling, 'The Australian Personnel Manager and Industrial Relations Practitioner: Responsibilities, Characteristics and Attitudes' in G. Palmer (ed.), *Australian Personnel Management: A Reader*, Macmillan, Melbourne, 1988, pp. 15-32.

K. F. Walker, 'Conflict and mutual misunderstanding: a survey of union leaders' and business executives' attitudes to industrial relations', *Journal of Industrial Relations 1*, April 1959, pp. 20-30.

K.F. Walker, 'Personnel officers' perceptions of the industrial relations attitudes of union leaders and business executives', *Journal of Industrial Relations 7*, March 1965, pp. 18-26.

Strategies

T. Bramble, 'Political Economy and Management Strategy in the Metal and Engineering Industry', in B. Dabscheck, G. Griffin and J. Teicher (eds), *Contemporary Australian Industrial Relations: Readings*, Longman Cheshire, Melbourne, 1992, pp. 243-266.

R. Callus, A. Morehead, M. Cully and J. Buchanan, *Industrial Relations At Work-The Australian Workplace Industrial Relations Survey*, Commonwealth Department of Industrial Relations, AGPS, Canberra, 1991, chapter 4.

B. Horstman, 'Labour flexibility strategies and management style', in Dabscheck, Griffin and Teicher (eds), *op. cit.*, pp. 286-305.

W.A. Howard, *Making Industrial Relations Work: A Study of Six Isolated Mines*, Industrial Relations Research Centre, University of New South Wales, Kensington, 1985.

R.D. Lansbury and G.W. Ford, 'The Role of Management in Industrial Relations', in G.W. Ford, J.M. Hearn and R.D. Lansbury (eds), *Australian Labour Relations: Readings* (3rd ed.), Macmillan, Melbourne, 1980, pp. 279-297.

D. Macdonald, 'Management and the Labour Process in two New South Wales Government Organisations', in M. Bray and V. Taylor (eds), *Managing Labour? Essays in the Political Economy of Australian Industrial Relations*, McGraw-Hill, Sydney, 1986, pp. 48-74.

D. Plowman, 'Economic Forces and the New Right: Employer Matters in 1986', *Journal of Industrial Relations 29*, March 1987, pp. 84-91.

M. Quinlan, 'Managerial strategy and industrial relations in the Australian steel industry, 1945-75', in M. Bray and V. Taylor (eds), *op. cit.*, pp. 20-47.

P. Swain, *A Study of the Role of Management and the Influence of Strategic Choice in the Management of Industrial Relations at the Level of the Firm in Three Iron Ore Companies*, unpublished PhD thesis, Monash University, 1992.

Structure

R. Callus, A. Morehead, M. Cully and J. Buchanan, *Industrial Relations At Work: The Australian Workplace Industrial Relations Survey*, Commonwealth Department of Industrial Relations, AGPS, Canberra, 1991, chapter 4.

S. Deery and P. Gahan, 'The Workplace Survey and Management Structures', *Journal of Industrial Relations 33*, December 1991, pp. 502-518.

S. Deery and J. Purcell, 'Strategic Choices in Industrial Relations Management in Large Organisations', *Journal of Industrial Relations 31*, December 1989, pp. 459-477.

P. Gilmour and R.D. Lansbury, 'The Changing Role of the Supervisor: Implications for Industrial Relations, *Journal of Industrial Relations 19*, September 1977, pp. 225-240.

Employee participation in management

M.J. Aitken and R.E. Wood, 'Employee stock ownership plans: issues and evidence', *Journal of Industrial Relations 31*, June 1989, pp. 147-168.

J. Benson, 'Worker involvement: an analysis of the SECV working parties', *Journal of Industrial Relations 24*, March 1982, pp. 41-52.

L. Cupper, 'Worker participation in the Dynavac organisation', *Journal of Industrial Relations 18*, June 1976, pp. 124-141.

L. Cupper, 'Dynavac revisited: self-management in transition', *Journal of Industrial Relations 21*, March 1979, pp. 51-62.

E.M. Davis and R.D. Lansbury (eds), *Democracy and Control in the Workplace*, Longman Cheshire, Melbourne, 1986.

E.M. Davis and R.D. Lansbury, 'Consultative councils in Qantas and Telecom: a comparative study', *Journal of Industrial Relations 30*, December 1988, pp. 564-565.

S.J. Frenkel, 'Explaining the Incidence of Worker Participation in Management: Evidence from the Australian Metal Industry', *Australian Journal of Management 14*, December 1989, pp. 127-150.

S.J. Frenkel and D.L. Weakliem, 'Worker participation in management in the printing industry', *Journal of Industrial Relations 31*, December 1989, pp. 478-499.

R. Lansbury (ed.), *Democracy in the workplace*, Longman Cheshire, Melbourne, 1980.

M. Gardner, C. Littler, M. Quinlan & G. Palmer, 'Management and Industrial Democracy: structure and strategies' in B. Ford & L. Tilley (eds), *Diversity, Change and Tradition*, AGPS, Canberra, 1986.

J.T. Ludeke, 'What Ever Happened to the Prerogatives of Management?', *Journal of Industrial Relations 33*, September 1991, pp. 395-411.

R. Lumley, 'Control over the organisation and conduct of work: evidence from some Australian workplaces', *Journal of Industrial Relations 25*, September 1983, pp. 301-316.

T. Mealor, *ICI Australia: The Botany Experience*, Studies in Organisational Analysis and Innovation, No. 8, Industrial Relations Research Centre, University of New South Wales, October 1992.

Questions
Ideology
1 What are the factors contributing to the apparent ascendancy of a 'unitary ideology' in Australian industrial relations during the period 1987-1993?

2 Assume you are to undertake research relating to the industrial relations management of ICI Australia Ltd or another company with a similar approach to that articulated in the documents included in this chapter. What theoretical concepts and frameworks would you draw upon for your empirical study?

3 Consider the quotation by George F. Baer in chapter 2, question 8. Aside from the terminology, to what extent do you think that the statement reflects the current values of Australian managers?

Strategies

4. Do you consider that any of Lewin's observations concerning the concept of management strategic choice in industrial relations have relevance for the Australian studies of management strategy summarised in this chapter?
5. What differences exist between the concept of union strategy developed by Gardner (see chapter 6) and the concepts of management strategy adopted in the Quinlan, Bramble and Swain case studies.
6. Discuss the factors identified by Bramble which caused
   i the professionalisation of industrial relations management; and
   ii management support for an increase in worker participation in the metal and engineering industry.
7. a Discuss the following statement indicating whether you agree or disagree:

   'Swain's study of management strategy at Hamersley Iron demonstrates the value of the two analytical frameworks developed by Kochan, Katz and McKersie.'

   b Are there any other concepts or theories in the industrial relations literature which may be useful in explaining management behaviour in the Hamersley Iron case study?

Exercises

1. Examine the Annual Reports of BHP in the 1950s or the 1960s as well as in recent years. How would you describe the approach to industrial relations management as reflected in these documents? What other sources could be used to obtain insight into the management approach? Do the reports for the earlier decades provide any indication of the management approach to industrial relations documented in the Quinlan study?
2. a Summarise the union views concerning the operation of joint consultation machinery in Telecom and Qantas.
   b Assume you are an adviser to either Telecom or Qantas senior management. What actions would you recommend that management take to overcome the problems as perceived by managers in relation to the joint consultation process?
3. a Identify the differences and similarities between the participative management schemes at ICI Australia in the 1970s and the approach of the company to industrial relations management in the late 1980s. What are the alternative theoretical frameworks for comparing the two phases of management strategy?
   b Examine ICI Annual Reports in the early 1980s. What are the similarities and differences in relation to the management approach to industrial relations during that period compared with the late 1980s?
4. Establish the reasons for the relative lack of change in management practices in the small plants in Bramble's case studies in the metal and engineering industry. Do the findings correlate with any of the data in the small business survey (ACCIS)?
5. Read all the relevant arguments and recommendations in the BCA publication *Working Relations: A Fresh Start for Australian Enterprises* (1993) relating to trade unions and critically evaluate this employer position concerning the rights of employee collectives.

11

Employer Associations

Contents

Origins and development
Ideology
Functions
- collective bargaining
- specialised services
- relations with the state
- media and public relations

Membership and structure
Internal government

Introduction

As one group of actors within the industrial relations system, employer associations are not functionally equivalent to trade unions. Unlike the trade union constituency, individual employers are often in a position to represent their own interests in relations with other organisations—both trade unions and governments. The need for individual employers to organise is much less strong than it is for individual employees. If employees are to exert any countervailing pressure on employers they need to be organised. Most employees pose no threat individually and the trade union overcomes their individual weakness. Each employer, whether private or public, represents a combination of capital and is more powerful than individual employees. Indeed individual members of an employer association may be as powerful or even more powerful than their representative organisation. Some form of employer associations operate in all countries.

It could be argued that employer associations are not necessary for the practice of industrial relations just as trade unions are not necessary. Small companies however, are especially likely to regard associations as a valuable and desirable resource providing specialist services economically. The use of employer associations is one example of externalising the industrial relations management function rather than relying on internal or direct labour management. Other examples are the use of employment agencies and the use of independent contractors. A company decision to use employer associations may be a strategic decision, a conscious choice by senior management. Alternatively, environmental factors may create compelling pressures to delegate some management functions to employer associations. The use of an employer association may typically begin as the response to the intrusion of an external party: a trade union, an industrial tribunal or a legislature. Varying levels of dependence will then develop from that initial response.

Employer associations are considered here in relation to: origins and development; ideology; functions; structure; membership and internal government. For each of these aspects the chapter draws on an overview of case studies of employer associations in ten industrialised countries by Windmuller and Gladstone.[1] The countries are Australia, France, Federal Republic of Germany, Great Britain, Israel, Italy, Japan, Netherlands, United States and Sweden. This international perspective is followed by a discussion of the Australian case. The material on Australia draws in part on publications by Plowman, an academic who has published extensively on employer associations in Australia. The relatively limited treatment of employer associations by academics generally is usually held to reflect both the attitude of employer associations, who are reputedly often unreceptive to independent investigators and the interests and inclinations of researchers. The latter may have an ideological affinity with worker or union interests or find employer associations less interesting as, unlike trade unions, they are rarely, if ever, the focus of public contests for power. Another feature of this chapter is the identification of differences and similarities between employer associations and trade unions in relation to each of the aspects discussed.

Origins and development

Overview

Windmuller identifies five objectives which acted as an impetus for employers to establish organisations for the pursuit of their collective interests. An individual organisation may have been founded to achieve one or several of the aims listed in Table 11.1. Windmuller distinguishes between trade associations and employer associations on the basis of the chief organisational impetus, the former reflecting the dominance of commercial interests as an impetus to combine, the latter reflecting a concern with issues relating to the employment relationship.[2]

Thus trade associations represent the collective interests of employers in economic or trade matters such as taxation, tariffs, patents and subsidies while employer associations represent the interests of their members mainly or exclusively in relation to issues concerned directly or indirectly with the employment relationship. Writing in the early 1980s, Windmuller observes a trend of the merging of the two functions in the one organisation. Nonetheless 'organisational dualism' had often survived because it brought advantages. First, separate organisations enabled employers whose interest in collective action was confined to one area to accept restraints on autonomy in that area and to pursue separate courses in the other area. The separation would be especially useful for example, for a company whose industrial relations policies were designed to achieve specific corporate objectives without necessarily conforming to the policies of an employers' association but whose trade interests harmonised with those of the industry as a whole or at least with the collective organisational view. Secondly, separate organisations helped employers to confine power sharing with unions to the area covered by industrial relations and to prevent matters of economic policy becoming subjects of bargaining or joint consultation.[3]

This chapter is concerned with employer associations as defined by Windmuller, that is pure trade associations are not considered as their activities are not concerned in any way with industrial relations. Employer organisations with dual functions are necessarily included although the emphasis here is on those activities related to the contract of employment.

Table 11.1 Employer objectives in establishing organisations to represent their collective interests

- to regulate matters of trade and competition by mutual agreement.
- to seek statutory protection in matters of trade, particularly with regard to imported goods.
- to erect a united front in dealing with trade unions.
- to provide services in labour relations and personnel administration.
- to contest the passage of social and labour legislation.

Source: J.P. Windmuller, 'Employers associations in comparative perspective: organisation, structure, administration', in J.P. Windmuller and A. Gladstone (eds), *Employers Associations and Industrial Relations: A Comparative Study*, Clarendon Press, Oxford, 1984, p. 1.

Windmuller notes that there were many cases in the formative period where a single organisation pursued both trade (economic) and labour (social) objectives and sometimes the two objectives were linked. An example was the advancing of arguments by some of the first employer associations against proposals for social reforms through protective labour and social legislation because of their objective of avoiding a competitive disadvantage in international markets.

By about the time of the First World War, most of the countries studied had stable and continuous employer associations, operating both at industry level and at national central levels. The war enhanced the legitimacy and stature of employer associations just as it had done for trade unions. The period of national emergency meant that frequently governments incorporated the associations into economic management decisions, assisting in the setting of priorities for production and distribution and in administering controls over allocation of scarce resources.[4] The position of employer associations was further strengthened in the following two decades, particularly during the 1930s when the economic context was especially adverse for unions although, and partly because of this, this decade also saw a considerable body of statute law enacted concerning industrial relations and with collective bargaining becoming institutionalised in many countries. In a number of countries, Great Britain, the Netherlands, Sweden and Australia to some extent, the role of employer associations as the voice for their constituents expanded in the post-Second World War period, due in part to the greatly strengthened position of trade unions. Even in Germany, Italy and Japan, countries where employer associations had participated in corporatist arrangements with fascist or military dictatorship regimes on the losing side, associations re-emerged quite rapidly despite initial resistance from the Allied military governments. As noted in chapter 7, these governments had influenced the structure of unions as they sought to provide institutional safeguards against a re-emergence of undemocratic forms of government.[5]

The other factor expanding the role and status of employer associations following the Second World War was the changing role of government. Increased government intervention in terms of responsibility for macro-economic management, social welfare programs and regulation of industrial relations meant increased demand for services from member companies in relation to these environmental changes. Further, governments sought to deal with what Windmuller terms 'authoritative representatives of employer views'[6] and this enhanced the importance of central employer federations.

Australia

The origin of employers' associations in Australia can be traced to the early part of the nineteenth century when employers formed temporary alliances to meet special labour problems in particular industries. An example was a meeting of shipowners in 1837 which successfully rejected the demands of seamen and labourers in the Port of Sydney for an increase in their wages from one shilling to three shillings a day.[7] The significant factors in the emergence of permanent associations include both the product market and the labour market interests of employers. One factor was the free trade controversy. Chambers of manufacturers were formed in various colonies to unite employers in their efforts to achieve and maintain tariff protection. A second reason for the formation of employers' associations was to achieve orderly marketing of their products, and to present a common front in the labour market. An example of this type of development was the formation of the Northern Coal Sales Association in 1872, by five leading coal mining companies in NSW. This fixed the price of coal and divided up the market between members.[8] A third factor was the increasing complexity of laws governing industry during the latter part of the nineteenth century. This provided a powerful inducement for the establishment of employers' federations in each colony. A fourth factor was the rapid growth of trade unions in the second half of the nineteenth century, especially after the gold rushes. Two important employers' groups were formed during this period, in the printing and metal trades industries, as a defensive measure against the rising tide of trade unionism, particularly over the issue of shorter working hours.[9] Plowman argues that prior to the Great Strikes of the 1890s, the associations' survival was contingent on the strength of the union challenge. Changes in the power context following the Great Strikes however, provided the impetus for more permanent associations to respond to and combat the new legal framework.[10] This took the form of industrial tribunal legislation in most colonies and at the federal level during the period from the mid-1890s to 1910 (see chapters 6 and 12). Thus the challenge of compulsory arbitration led to the creation of employers' federations in Victoria (1901), NSW (1903) WA (1913) and the reconstitution of moribund federations in Queensland (1904) and SA (1907).[11] By the end of 1904, four parliaments—Victoria, Western Australia, New South Wales and the Commonwealth—had legislated to establish industrial tribunals. Employer associations pursued strategies to restrict the activities of these tribunals and to make them unworkable.[12] In the political arena they used their parliamentary majority to frustrate or restrict legislation in some jurisdictions and to prevent it in others. Associations refused to register with industrial tribunals; established and registered bogus unions; lengthened tribunal proceedings, caused 'log jams' and made frequent use of appellate processes. In the industrial arena, strategies included threatened relocation, capital (investment) strikes, subcontracting, closure of establishments and retrenchment and installing of labour saving machinery.[13]

Initially, many employers regarded the federal arbitration system as a fundamental attack on managerial rights and delayed their registration under the then *Conciliation and Arbitration Act*. However, while individual employers could appear before tribunals, employers' associations could only gain entry if they were registered under the Act. As industrial arbitration became more widely accepted and continued to expand, employers gradually changed from militant opponents to strong supporters of the system. This change in attitude stemmed largely from the belief that once trade unions became well entrenched in the framework of arbitration, the system could be used as an important defence against the excesses of union power. Furthermore, once established, employer associations, like most other organisations, developed a vested interest in their continued survival and saw that the arbitration system provided the assurance of security and development. Employer associations, by and large, became more committed to the arbitration system than some employers, who preferred to engage in direct negotiations with the unions outside the tribunals. The associations sought to expand their role by keeping their members informed of wage movements, preparing cases for various industrial tribunals, and interpreting the complexities of changes in awards and legislation which affected their members' operations. The current functions of associations in Australia are discussed below.

Ideology

Overview

Windmuller concludes that the views generally held by employer associations could not be regarded as an ideology in the sense applicable to a number of trade unions, that is an integrated explanation of history and society or a vision of an ideal future society. Nonetheless generally they did have 'positions and commitments on fundamental political, economic and social issues.'[14] Most of these positions had been articulated by peak federations and four 'domains' are distinguished by Windmuller:

1 the political;
2 the economic order;
3 social policy; and
4 industrial relations policy.

In the political domain, a fundamental position of all employer associations in the countries reviewed was at least an implicit commitment to democratic government. There were probably no differences of principle here although there may have been differences in the basis and interpretation of the commitment. To the extent the associations dealt directly with the concepts of political and economic freedoms there was a fairly uniform view that there was an inextricable link between these freedoms.[15]

In relation to the economic system, the dominant commitment was to 'classic liberalist' ideas involving support for 'free enterprise, private ownership, competitive markets and individual initiative'.[16] This meant strong criticism at times of phenomena seen as barriers to these ideals namely, nationalisation, the regulation of markets and collectivism. Windmuller regards the obvious divergence between commitments and practice as a failing not unique to employer associations; they are held to be as susceptible as other organisations 'to the conflict between seeking to uphold a set of basic principles and simultaneously defending basic material interests.'[17] Windmuller regards social policy as encompassing protective labour law and social welfare law. It was noted above that one of the objectives associated with the formation of employer associations was to resist the passage of such laws. The national studies found the position here to be generally one of opposing advances but not one of retreating from the welfare state *status quo*.

In other words, the policy has been generally conservative if not oppositionist with variation in the strength of the opposition and with no opposition to some specific measures. The philosophical rationale for the opposition has been 'that an overly protective society fosters among its citizenry dependence, idleness, and improvidence, all qualities that hinder progress and may lead to national bankruptcy and decay.'[18] There was also an economic basis for the opposition, namely concern about the adverse impact on production costs, profits and international competitiveness.

In the industrial relations domain associations have generally supported a restricted role for the state, confined to the making of procedural rules and legislating a set of minimum conditions of employment. They have also endorsed collective bargaining which means sharing power with unions. At the same time they are committed to setting limits to this through promotion of the notions of the protection of management's right to manage and the curbing of excessive union power.[19] All this implies a pluralist frame of reference (see chapter 9) although in terms of the historical development of associations, attitudes to unions have included direct opposition to their existence and significant changes in attitudes within associations. For example the National Metal Trades Association in the United States initially sought accommodative relationships with unions and subsequently became militantly anti-union.[20] The managerial frames of reference developed by Fox and the individualism/collectivism dimensions of management style introduced by Purcell (see chapter 9) could also be applied to employer associations.

Australia

Of the four 'domains' of ideology identified by Windmuller, associations in Australia usually confine explicit statements of position to the industrial relations policy domain. However, the then Confederation of Australian Industry provides an example of implicit support for democratic government in the following extract from the President's message in 1990-1991. The President was Ross Berglund, Chairman of Nationwide Realty, East Coast Pty Ltd:

> 'While we can no longer continue to live on the luck that was clearly ours in decades past, we still enjoy a remarkable standard of living, with secure borders and proud tradition of democracy and fair play. I have, during the year spent some time in other countries where these factors do not exist, and where a population fears for the safety of their lives, or struggles to simply survive. Such travels are jolting reminders of the privileges we have in Australia. While we are critical of our performance in Australia, and as we encourage each other to reach out to achieve our potential, we need to recognise what we do enjoy in this country and accept that we have a responsibility not only to preserve it, but to work to see that the rest of the world can also taste the benefits which so often we take for granted. So, as this is the last time I will speak to you as your President, can I leave that as a challenge to all industry—a challenge to recognise what we have and to strive to give opportunity to others. If we do not bridge that gap between the rich and poorer nations then the precious peace which we now enjoy following the collapse of the cold war could well evaporate into a higher level of disorder and insecurity. CAI will have an important role in meeting this challenge.'[21]

The Mission Statement of the Victorian Employers' Chamber of Commerce and Industry includes a reference to both the political and economic domains:

> The Victorian Employers' Chamber of Commerce and Industry is dedicated to helping employers understand and maximise their potential, and through the development and promotion of responsible private enterprise, secure prosperity and freedom for all.[22]

In August 1991 the then Confederation of Australian Industry released a detailed position paper advocating a number of changes in the Australian industrial relations system. Analysis of the Confederation's position is one of the exercises appearing at the end of this chapter. The Confederation's General Council developed six broad policy objectives for industrial relations:

1. labour market flexibility;
2. productivity oriented wages policy;
3. decentralisation;
4. freedom of choice;
5. enterprise emphasis; and
6. individualised approaches.[23]

The Confederation's position in relation to (4) and (5) is set out in Table 11.2.

Table 11.2 Illustrations of industrial relations policy objectives: Confederation of Australian Industry 1991

Freedom of Choice

A related objective is that of freedom of choice. Present arrangements restrict the ability of the direct parties, employers and employees, to determine the way in which their relations should be conducted. They should be able to choose the form of regulation of their arrangements best suited to themselves, without being drawn unwillingly into arrangements made by others. They should also be able to enter into agreements which receive a minimum of scrutiny by others who have no direct interest in their affairs. Of particular importance is the need for employees to have much greater freedom in the choice of their representatives; they should not be constrained in this respect by monopoly powers granted to particular trade unions.

Enterprise Emphasis

The individual enterprise is the generator of output, the source of employment and the only place where productivity growth can be achieved. National growth in productivity is the sum of the efforts made in hundreds of thousands of individual enterprises, and it is not possible to increase national productivity without growth at the enterprise level. These simple propositions must be recognised through a greater enterprise emphasis in industrial relations. This means a greater focus on the practice of industrial relations at the workplace level, and the pursuit of an integrated approach involving human resource development, systems of employee involvement, communication procedures, formal and informal consultation, grievance procedures, negotiation procedures, training arrangements, health and safety and so on.

Human Resources Development

The objective must be the development of mutual understanding, commitment and co-operation in every workplace. CAI is undertaking extensive programs directed towards human resources development. These programs are designed to encourage:
- the introduction of participative management;
- the focusing of industrial relations at the enterprise level;
- the implementation of effective management of occupational health and safety in the enterprise.

Source: CAI, *A New Industrial Relations System for Australia*, August 1991, pp. 1-3 (edited).

An industry association which issues policies on industrial relations is the Metal Trades Industry Association. In 1993 the Association's policy on 'enterprise bargaining, wage fixation and other industrial relations matters' appeared in a published address by the Association's Director of Industrial Relations.[24] The policy emerges in the discussion centred on current public wages policy and union behaviour. It can therefore be distinguished from a stand-alone statement of certain principles. Nonetheless certain 'positions' are evident. These include:

1. support for a reduction in the complexity of industrial relations regulation via a Commonwealth/State Agreement, entrenched in complementary legislation, establishing a common code of minimum wages and employment conditions;
2. a belief that the fundamental objective of the wage fixing system is to improve the competitiveness and productive performance of Australian enterprises, while recognising fairness and equity as important considerations;
3. a 'co-operative collectivism' perspective on relationships in the metal and engineering industry in the late 1980s, juxtaposed with criticism of union behaviour in the early 1990s, behaviour which is at odds with the previous apparent harmony of purpose;
4. a proposal that the terms of enterprise agreements may override the union position where this is in conflict with the express wishes of a two-thirds majority of employees;
5. the right of union members to seek advice from their union in relation to the proposed terms of an agreement;
6. support for an auditing function for the federal industrial tribunal in certifying enterprise agreements;
7. support for adoption in the federal jurisdiction of the New South Wales model of industrial relations regulation,[25] which the Association contends combines the best features of conciliation and arbitration with more freedom to negotiate at the enterprise level.

Functions

The broad categories of functions and activities of employer associations in the ten countries studied are set out in Table 11.3. Gladstone explains that these may be found in an association's constitution or by-laws, either prescribed by specific provisions or suggested by more general provisions. Alternatively, they may result from custom and practice.

Collective bargaining
Overview
Bargaining by employer associations, that is, multi-employer bargaining, is a basic feature of most of the countries studied, including Japan and the United States where enterprise-level bargaining is present. The major bargaining

Table 11.3 Functions of employer associations

- Representation of employers in collective bargaining and associated activities (including interest dispute strategies)
- Provision of specialised services to members
    * information, research and advice
    * representation of members
    * education, training and other specialised services
- Representation of employers vis-à-vis the state and its agencies
- Representation of employers vis-à-vis the media and the public at large
- Provision of forum for exchange of views and the formulation and expression of policies and positions

Source: Adapted from A. Gladstone, 'Employers associations in comparative perspective: functions and activities', in J.P. Windmuller and A. Gladstone (eds), *Employers Associations and Industrial Relations: A Comparative Study*, Clarendon Press, Oxford, 1984, pp. 24-43.

activity is carried out by industry associations and typically the association will have very considerable autonomy in negotiations, if not complete autonomy. Member firms delegate the power to bargain to their associations, either directly or through intermediate organisations. In a number of countries the law allows a collective agreement to be 'extended' to cover an entire industry even if the parties to the agreement do not include all relevant employers (or trade unions). This 'common rule' phenomenon can induce employers to join the employer association in order to have some influence on the content of the agreement.[26] Another incentive for membership and support for multi-employer bargaining is to avoid whip-sawing by unions. Multi-employer bargaining may result in agreements which set either minimum standards or actual standards. Gladstone points to the risk of industry agreements becoming meaningless, especially in the latter case, if additional benefits obtain at the enterprise level, either through supplementary bargaining or unilateral action by individual employers. Two advantages of association bargaining, that is, common conditions, are then lost. These are:

1 the lessening of competition and bidding for labour in a tight market;
2 the protection of the viability of marginal firms in the industry.

Maintaining internal discipline, as Gladstone points out, is always a difficult matter for associations.[27] Where these expressions of autonomy occur the delegation to the association of the power to bargain becomes a very qualified delegation.

While employer associations may be primarily concerned to ensure that the provisions of agreements are not exceeded, they also police, and seek to enforce adherence to the minimum standards in order to prevent the undercutting of minima that enables some firms to gain competitive advantages. As Gladstone notes, they are assisted here by trade union vigilance, grievance procedures and labour courts.[28] The association negotiating teams usually comprise the chief executive officer (however styled) and other senior officers, with back-up support from other staff members who have assisted in planning the association's bargaining position and supporting arguments.

Gladstone also notes instances where the association president, other prominent elected officials or representatives from major firms are part of the negotiating team.[29]

Little information emerged from the country studies on association methods for determining bargaining positions. This is, understandably, an elusive aspect of association activities. The limited evidence suggests

1. some use of policy or study committees which 'factor in' positions emerging from association forums such as councils or general assemblies;
2. a very significant role for representatives of larger, more influential firms and association staffs;
3. attention to the interests of small and medium-size firms by larger firms and especially by staff, to preserve harmony and the integrity of the organisation;
4. formation of caucuses by small and medium-size firms to defend their special interests, given their perception of being neglected and their frequent major stake in bargaining outcomes; and
5. the likelihood of difficult decisions such as the choice between a strike or a settlement affordable to the large firms but likely to cause hardship to the small firms in the membership.[30]

At the peak council, or central confederation, level some organisations are excluded from engaging in collective bargaining either by custom and practice or by their constitution, as in Japan for example. In countries where peak councils are involved in bargaining it is most often framework bargaining. This seeks to establish a broad framework for relations between the parties and their affiliates as a semi-permanent or long-term arrangement. Flanders termed these matters 'procedural rules' and in these cases the negotiated rules may be a substitute for legislated procedural rules. Peak councils may also negotiate semi-permanent nation-wide agreements on substantive issues: this occurred in France in the late 1960s and early 1970s, the subject matter of agreements being: salaried-status for blue-collar workers; job security; and vocational training.[31] Where peak councils act as employer agents in traditional collective bargaining it is usually designed either to be supplemented by industry or enterprise level bargaining or to reflect a social partnership or corporatist[32] arrangement seeking to control wage increases. Examples cited are Sweden and the Netherlands. Australia is cited as an exception to the rule concerning the bargaining activities of central federations: specifically the national wage case submissions of the Confederation of Australian Industry (now the Australian Chamber of Commerce and Industry) which 'have a significant influence on collective bargaining settlements and awards under the Australian compulsory arbitration procedures'.[33]

Australia

Employer association functions include the representation of member companies in both interest and rights disputes. In the case of interest disputes, that is industrial relations rule-making, employer association activity has been concentrated, at least until the early 1990s, around the rules which appear in tribunal awards and, to a lesser degree, certified agreements. This is due to the dominance of conciliation and arbitration in Australia for most of this century. It has meant that typically the Australian equivalent of the collective bargaining function, especially in recent decades when tribunal control has been considerable, is representation before industrial tribunals and any associated negotiations. Nonetheless, there are long-standing examples of multi-employer 'good faith' bargaining where a comprehensive agreement is negotiated outside the tribunal, with certification of the agreement, or the creation of a consent award, by the Commission largely a formality. An employer association which has participated in this form of negotiation, especially since the 1970s, is the Oil Industry Industrial Committee which was established in the late 1940s to represent the oil companies. In 1994 it represents the Ampol, BP, Caltex, Esso, Kemcor, Mobil and Shell companies. In the 1970s the Committee negotiated oil industry consent awards with a coalition of unions led by the ACTU. These were supplemented by agreements specific to particular occupational groups and others specific to company sites. In the late 1980s the Committee provided a forum for a review of employer (enterprise) industrial relations strategy. This resulted in the negotiation of company consent awards for most employees, one exception being transport workers, for whom an industry award prevails. In the 1990s, the Committee conducts any industry negotiations and seeks to develop an industry position on the parameters for company level negotiations.

Presentation of the employer case in the high profile tribunal cases, such as national and state wage cases and other test cases, is a major activity of the employer peak councils, although this function is also undertaken by a small number of industry associations and individual companies as is evident from the parties listed in Table 11.4.

The major awards cover hundreds or thousands of companies[34] (see Table 15.6 for coverage in terms of employees). This has contributed to the technical legalistic nature of tribunal operations which makes it difficult for smaller companies and organisations to handle representation themselves. Typically, the association processes logs of claims served by unions on association members and represents members in negotiations, often strategic negotiations (see chapter 17). In the ensuing tribunal proceedings, the association prepares cases and acts as advocate for member companies in relation to the issues not resolved by negotiation. Employer association officials, like full-time union officials, develop skills and knowledge specific to the operation of the tribunals and become familiar with the culture. This is especially the case for research and advocacy activity. From time to time, company managers participate in the tribunal rule-making processes as expert witnesses but for them it is probably an alien environment, notwithstanding that their evidence may be vital for the case. Typically, the management of the employer case is controlled by association officials.

The emergence of enterprise bargaining in the federal jurisdiction and some state jurisdictions in the early 1990s has placed a premium on the provision of specialised services by associations (see below). However, for as

> **Table 11.4** Employer representation: *National Wage case*, April 1991
>
> Confederation of Australian Industry and respondent members of the Chamber of Commerce and Industry, South Australia Inc., Northern Territory Confederation of Industry and Commerce Inc., Municipal Association of Victoria, Confederation of A.C.T. Industry and Brisbane City Council.
>
> The Victorian Employers Federation.
>
> Printing and Allied Trades Employers' Federation of Australia.
>
> Metal Trades Industry Association of Australia and the Engineering Employers Association, South Australia.
>
> Australian Road Transport Industrial Organisation.
>
> National Transport Federation Limited.
>
> Meat and Allied Trades Federation of Australia (intervening).
>
> National Farmers' Federation (intervening).
>
> Australian Federation of Construction Contractors (intervening).
>
> Australian Wool Selling Brokers Employers Federation (intervening).
>
> Australian Bankers' Association and the Australian and New Zealand Banking Group Limited, National Australia Bank Limited, Westpac Banking Corporation, Bank of New Zealand, Banque Nationale de Paris, Australian Bank Limited, Rural Industries Bank of Western Australia, State Bank of South Australia, Tasmania Bank, SBT Bank, Cardlink Services Limited and Primary Industry Bank of Australia (intervening).
>
> Australian Chamber of Commerce (intervening).
>
> Source: Australian Industrial Relations Commission, *National Wage case*, April 1991, Print J7400, pp. 82-83.

long as tribunal awards operate as minima and awards continue as a precondition for enterprise bargaining, the function of multi-employer representation before industrial tribunals will remain a significant function for industry and regional associations.

Specialised services

Overview

Specialised services provided by employer associations are a prime reason for membership. Gladstone identifies three categories of such services:

1. information research and advice;
2. representation and assistance to individual members in disputes, usually rights disputes; and
3. education and training services.

The demand for the specialised service function increases with the complexity of the legal and institutional framework for industrial relations and decreases with the increase in the number of firms developing in-house services. However, the provision of comprehensive services by associations may delay the professionalisation of the industrial relations management function.

All employer peak councils and most larger industry associations provide a flow of general information on industrial relations matters. This includes:

1. legislative changes and case law relating to the various statutes which constrain and guide employer behaviour; and
2. collective bargaining, where the information includes wage and salary trends, details of recent settlements and economic analyses, both industry and national.

Special information may also be provided on request, frequently with a fee set to cover costs.[35] Advisory services, in the form of authoritative information concerning the legal and contractual rights and obligations of member companies, is an important function due to the increasing complexity of the legal environment. Areas cited by Gladstone in which advice is increasingly sought include: options provided by government incomes policies; obligations under health and safety and anti-discrimination legislation; obligations concerning trade union recognition and, in some cases, advice concerning union avoidance tactics. Another form of advice is the interpretation of the often complex provisions of collective agreements, or in the case of Australia, tribunal awards, together with court decisions relating to these provisions.[36]

Associations also represent members in interest dispute negotiation at enterprise level and in rights disputes at both enterprise level and at arbitration. In the case of interest disputes where the association does not appear at the negotiating table as an agent for the employer, it may nonetheless be on hand to provide advice during negotiations. Gladstone notes that while such representation is first and foremost a membership service, it does facilitate adherence to association policies and directives.[37] In a number of countries it is common practice for associations, usually industry associations, to become involved in negotiation of rights disputes by virtue of their specific inclusion at a particular level of the grievance procedure. Gladstone cites the British engineering industry where the final stage in the general disputes procedure involves 'going to York', the location of the headquarters of the Engineering Employers Federation. At this stage the Federation becomes involved as does the central office of the Amalgamated Engineering Union.[38] It is also common practice for associations, usually industry level associations, to act as advocate for individual companies in rights disputes hearings and the precedents created by the arbitration decisions may have repercussions for the entire association membership.[39]

As with other association services, the range of services in the area of education and training will be influenced by membership demands, in turn influenced by alternative sources and their relative costs. Larger firms may be independent of associations in this area, as they are in relation to enterprise-level bargaining for example. Their internal training programs may compensate for the absence of association programs or eliminate the need for them, especially if such programs are accessible to smaller firms in the industry. Where associations do provide these services they include:

1. management development programs, including those specific to industrial relations and human resource management as is provided by Nikkeiren in Japan for example; and
2. vocational training, sometimes organised or sponsored jointly with trade unions as occurs in Sweden and the Netherlands.

Associations may not have the expertise and personnel to provide programs directly so they may instead sponsor programs offered by others such as universities or government agencies, or sponsor conferences and symposia, for example the special assemblies devoted to particular labour themes held by the CNPF, the National Council of French Employers. Other less common services include responsibility for:

1. administering industry pension and welfare schemes. This may be assumed either independently or jointly with trade unions; and
2. recruitment, usually confined to a few industries such as shipping, long-shoring and printing.[40]

Australia

Employer associations in Australia provide all of the above specialised services. One important service provided to members is award interpretation. In many cases management will have had no involvement in the making of the rules which appear in awards. Where rules are ambiguous or complex, as occurs from time to time, employers will not have the benefit of knowing what was in the mind of the parties who negotiated the new rules(s) or of the arbitrator(s), as the case may be. Employer dependency on award interpretation services will be heightened in circumstances where there is multiple award coverage within the company. This characteristic, in conjunction with small company size, means the employer association provides a vital function here and does so with the benefit of economies of both scale and specialisation. In the manufacturing sector, for example, only nine per cent of establishments employ more than 100 people and over forty per cent employ fewer than ten people.[41] A similar rationale applies to the award information services provided by employer associations. Even employers who rely on associations for little else in industrial relations may benefit from the efficient and timely production and distribution of information concerning award amendments and major tribunal decisions.

In the case of rights disputes, for example a union challenge to an employer decision to dismiss an employee, or conflict over the meaning of a clause concerning rosters or overtime, the employer association will again act as negotiator and advocate if required. Employer association officials sometimes refer to this area of activity as 'putting out the spot fires'. Some members will use the association solely in an advisory capacity, checking their planned action with the association but handling the face-to-face negotiation independently. Company resources are likely to be more significant in determining the extent of association involvement in rights disputes than in the case of interest disputes. Another important factor will be the culture within the industry or the company concerning the operation of grievance procedures.[42] A company policy seeking internal resolution as a preferred outcome will diminish the association role. In cases where a union briefs counsel to appear in a rights dispute, this form of representation is likely to be matched by the employer association.

It was noted above that association participation in negotiations may be due to their specific inclusion in a grievance procedure. This is the case in the 'Avoidance of Industrial Disputes' clause in the *Metal Industry Award*. It applies to those companies or sectors of the industry which did not have existing procedures when the clause was introduced. It provides for up to four stages of discussion depending on a range of factors: issues involved; size and function of the plant or enterprise; and union membership of the employees concerned. The third and fourth stages of discussion provide for the involvement of employer organisation Branch representatives and National Officer respectively. The clause emphasises a negotiated settlement but there is provision for joint or unilateral reference to the federal tribunal for assistance in dispute resolution in the absence of bipartite agreement.[43] The *Metal Industry Award* has a separate dispute settlement procedure for unfair dismissals which allows for the union representative to 'take the matter up with the employer or his or her representative'.[44]

Employer associations also undertake an educational function. The larger associations conduct seminars and workshops designed to provide managers with information and skills, especially in relation to the handling of conflicts arising under grievance and disciplinary procedures. In the event that comprehensive enterprise agreements become the norm in Australia, the educational function of employer associations is likely to increase, especially in relation to negotiation skills.

The increased prominence of negotiations since 1987 (see chapter 18) has generated educational material for managers. For example recent MTIA publications include: *Award Restructuring: Consultation, Training and Award Flexibility* (1990); *Implementation Manual: Supplement for Supervisors* (1990); *Building Enterprise Productivity* (1991); *Bargaining for Best Practice* (1993). In 1990 MTIA was also a joint publisher, in conjunction with the Metal Trades Federation of Unions and the Australian Council of Manufacturing, of *Award Restructuring: Implementation Manual for the Metal and Engineering Industry*. This publication was confined to material jointly agreed between the parties and comprised technical advice and information concerning agreed procedures for implementation with a view to avoiding procedural disputes.

An initial dependence on an employer association may be a difficult habit to break. The employer association representative by virtue of his or her specialisation commands expert power and is usually a fairly formidable figure to the plant industrial relations or personnel manager. The representative has access to a wider range of information, because of the research function of the association, experience of a wide range of disputes and a good understanding of the goals of trade unions. Thus, in a number of respects, an external adviser may be better equipped than company management. These advantages need to be balanced against the fact that such advisers inevitably will be less attuned to local needs and less concerned with medium and long-term issues. Most significantly they may not be in tune with other management policies and strategies.

This disadvantage may disappear however if the emerging trend of employer associations offering customised services continues to develop. Since the shift in wages policy in 1987 to include a concern for enterprise competitiveness, there has been pressure on associations to tailor advice to company specific needs. Increasingly negotiations have included the objective of identifying factors critical to organisational success. The change in the emphasis in association services is well articulated by Boland: 'Our staff have had to become adept at offering advice to members in the context of an integration between the enterprise's business strategy and industrial relations management. This has been a distinct shift in the function of the MTIA' (see Table 11.5).

A development associated with both the shift in focus of wages policy and the emergence of a 'training industry' in Australia during the 1980s, is the emergence of competitors to employer associations. The service providers with whom associations now have to compete for the industrial relations business of employers are law firms, management consultants and lobbyists. One consequence of the increased competition may be some 'unbundling' of association services available to members. In other words, member companies may be able to exercise choice in the services they purchase rather than paying a single membership fee and perhaps using some services and not others, all of which historically have been available for a particular fee.

An industry employer association with a distinctive position in Australian industrial relations is the Metal Trades Industry Association. As the name indicates, the Association represents employers in the 'metal trades' or the

Table 11.5 Interview with Roger Boland, Director, Industrial Relations, Metal Trades Industry Association, 3rd August 1993

Q. What are the most significiant industrial relations functions of the MTIA?

A. I suppose the most significant function is the telephone advisory service for our members where they can ring up with a very simple question, for example, the award entitlement for a fitter, or a workers' compensation inquiry or the meaning of a section of the Occupational Health & Safety Act, and get a ready answer. The service is highly regarded, especially among the small and medium sized businesses within our membership. In fact, I think you could say that is the principal industrial relations service of our Association. The New South Wales Branch, for example, would receive an average of 400 inquires each week.

Another significant industrial relations function is the representation of members in enterprise bargaining, both within the enterprise and within the arbitration system. We assist members in negotiation and then follow through with assistance to obtain certification or ratification of any agreement. The Association may also become involved when members request assistance when they are faced with an industrial dispute, that is, industrial action. We may then assist with negotiation and once again offer advice through all phases of the process until an agreement is certified by the federal Commission or a state tribunal.

The industrial action in a particular enterprise is usually short–lived. A stoppage of more than two weeks would be extraordinary, although in May–June, 1991 there was a strike of about four weeks duration when the unions applied sustained pressure against Email Ltd to obtain a 4.5 per cent wage increase. In recent weeks in Victoria there have been a couple of disputes over wages where the industrial action has lasted for two weeks. The enterprises where industrial action arises usually have high levels of union density.

The MTIA also represents employers at an industry level: the *Metal Industry Award* is still very important in the overall system in Australia. We also represent the 'metal and engineering industry' in national wage case hearings. The association has assumed a high profile in this forum in recent years, having split from the then Confederation of Australian Industry (CAI) in late 1986. Thus, in the last six or so national wage cases, MTIA has presented an independent submission tailored to the needs of our members in the metal and engineering industry.

As a member of the Confederation, the Association was not able to adequately represent our own industry views within the national wage case hearings and the employer peak council was adopting an increasingly different view from our own position. MTIA came to the view in late 1986 that we were getting nowhere in industrial relations. The relationship with the unions was adversarial and we were constantly brawling. So in the interests of a better relationship we proposed a compact with the unions. This was a significant turning point in the employer/union relationships in the metal and engineering industry and in the period 1987–92, in cooperation with the metal unions, we achieved more in the way of labour market reform than in the previous 50 years.

Q. Have there been any major changes in the work of Association officials since 1987, that is, since the federal Commission's shift to greater emphasis on negotiation and productivity, especially negotiation at enterprise level?

A. Since the adoption of the enterprise bargaining framework in the industry in June-July, 1991 (which the Commission approved in October, 1991) our focus has been enterprise bargaining. Thus our work has moved away from the traditional industrial relations functions, for example handling over-award claims and summary dismissals, to a broader range of issues. We have had to train staff in a wide range of new skills relating to quality, benchmarking, performance measurement, new production techniques and so on. Our staff have had to become adept at offering advice to members in the context of an integration between the enterprise's business strategy and industrial relations management. This has been a distinct shift in the function of the MTIA.

Q. What union amalgamations have occurred in the metal and engineering industry in recent years? From the MTIA perspective, have these amalgamations made any difference to the negotiations with the metal unions?

A. The AMWU amalgamated with ADSTE in 1991 to form the MEWU. Early this year, the Metals and Engineering Workers' Union merged with the Vehicle Builders Employees' Union to form the Automotive, Metals and Engineering Union (AMEU). Recently, there was an unsuccessful attempt to merge also with the PKIU. I understand that there are discussions concerning a possible merger with the Food Preservers Union. The FIA merged with the ASE and Glass Workers' Unions to form the Federation of Industrial, Manufacturing and Engineering Employees (FIMEE) in July, 1991. There is currently discussion concerning the possibility of an amalgamation between FIMEE and the Australian Workers' Union.

At the industry level, the unions have negotiated as a coalition, the Metal Trades Federation of Unions for some twenty–two years and the position hasn't changed much at this level as a result of the amalgamations. The amalgamations have not altered the number of union representatives at the negotiating table. There are still typically about twenty representatives on the union side with about six to eight representatives on the employer side.

Q. Do you consider that union amalgamations have altered the day–to–day dealings between management and unions at the shopfloor level in companies which your Association represent?

A. Our members observe that there is a lot of tension between the Automotive, Metals and Engineering Union and the Federation of Industrial, Manufacturing and Engineering Employees. These two major unions are in conflict, vying for territory, with FIMEE seeking to establish a strong 'right–wing' union bloc. In negotiations at enterprise level, we find often that the differences between the unions are greater than the differences between the employer and employees and this intrudes on negotiations making it difficult to achieve unanimity.

Under the terms of the Commission's decision of October, 1991 unions are required to operate as a single bargaining unit (SBU). It is our experience that the spirit of this is often not observed. In protecting their own interests, trade unions have sought in some cases to dominate both the selection and operation of single bargaining units and pay only lip–service to the requirement that these negotiating mechanisms should operate as a single unit with the principal responsibility for negotiating workplace change. Under Division 3A of the Industrial Relations Act, there is no requirement for unions to operate as a single bargaining unit. Consequently, the AIRC's wage fixing principles regarding SBUs are often bypassed by the making of a certified agreement.

It seems that in some cases the union amalgamations have not produced integrated organisations. Some unions are continuing to operate as a separate entity. This appears to be the case, for example, with the VBEF, although this union's amalgamation with the MEWU is a recent one. The continued independence appears to be a reflection of very different union cultures but it may be that the differences will diminish over time. The Australasian Society of Engineers (ASE) and the Federated Ironworkers' Association (FIA) which amalgamated in 1991 to form the FIMEE appear to have blended very well and are operating as a single integrated entity.

Q. **The popular perception of employer associations is that there is little interest among members in attaining positions on the governing bodies and that positions are rarely, if ever, contested. Is that the case with the MTIA?**

A. There is no shortage of candidates for Branch Council elections. In the industry it is a position of high prestige. The structure of the MTIA includes Branch Councils in the various States, for example, New South Wales Branch Council comprises of 32 chief executives elected by the membership in that State and there is a similar number in Victoria. Queensland Branch Council has some 21 councillors, again elected by the membership in that State.

The National Executive meets quarterly. The National Executive is constituted by the Executive of each Branch, Branch Councils are elected annually. Companies represented on MTIA's Councils include Email, Clyde Industries, Holden Engine Company, Hoover, Pacific BBA, Siemens, Telecom, South Pacific Tyres. Small business is also well represented by such firms as G & J Dowrie, George and Courtier, M. Brodribb Pty Ltd and Carruthers Bros.

Q. **Does the Association have different categories of membership based on company size or other factors and is there any differentiation in the range of industrial relations services available.**

A. MTIA membership is about 6500 employers and these companies pay subscriptions on a total of 300 000 employees, with the subscription level being determined by the number of employees in the company.

There are two classes of membership. The first class relates to companies principally engaged in the 'metal and engineering industry' and these members have voting rights. The number of votes each member may exercise at a properly constituted meeting or election is determined by the number of employees employed. Thus a large company may have four or five votes and a small company one or two votes. The other class of membership is associate membership. This entitles these companies to various industrial relations services that MTIA provides. These are companies not principally engaged in the 'metal and engineering industry' or not employing persons in a metal trades or engineering occupation.

Q. **Does the Association have any information concerning the responses of members operating in the Victorian jurisdiction to the choices available to employers under the Victorian *Employee Relations Act* 1992?**

A. The predominant view is that it is not worth the trouble to seek a collective agreement under the Victorian legislation. To do so would attract a hostile union response and most MTIA members do not want a confrontation with unions.

So employers with members under the old Clerks State Award, for example, might have preferred to negotiate a collective agreement but when they were presented with the Federated Clerks' Union log for a federal award their response was typically, 'well, this is inevitable, we will not oppose this'.

Their preferred position may have been a collective agreement, probably ideally one that didn't involve trade unions. Trade unions are however, a fact of life and given the prospect of confrontation with what is, relatively speaking, one of the strongest and best organised trade union movements in the world, employers have generally not resisted a transfer to the federal jurisdiction.

'metal and engineering' industry. This industry, so-called, has long been a watershed for industrial relations rule-making within the federal tribunal system. This status has been retained in the late 1980s and early 1990s with negotiated outcomes on procedural rules between the Association and the Metal Trades Federation of Unions forming the basis of the national wage case decision on a number of occasions. The text of an interview with the Association's Director of Industrial Relations, Roger Boland in August 1993 is set out in Table 11.5. The comments by this senior officer illustrate the functions of employer associations discussed above, together with some of the aspects to be discussed below.

The 1989 Workplace Survey provided information on the functions undertaken by employer associations in Australia from a user perspective. The Survey defines associations as 'organisations which included an industrial relations function in the range of services and advice they provided'.[45] The extent of use of different types of service is set out in Table 11.6. The aggregate picture shows the primacy of the information service function and also that one quarter of workplaces made no use of association services. A breakdown of the data by size of workplace (not shown in the table) revealed more direct involvement in workplace activity in larger workplaces. For example, fifty-nine per cent of workplaces with 500 or more employees sought advice about dealing with unions compared with eleven per cent overall.[46] The data on union density (see chapter 7) show significantly lower density levels in small workplaces which probably explains, at least in part, the variations in use of this specific service.

Relations with the state

Overview

A major and pervasive function of employer associations is to 'represent, promote and protect' employer interests in relation to decisions made by the various agencies of the state, legislative bodies in particular but also judicial and administrative agencies. As noted above, one important reason for the emergence of employer associations was to seek state protection in product markets. This concern extended to a determination to influence the direction, scope and content of state decisions in matters relating to the contract of employment. Gladstone suggests that strong employer associations will pursue and defend members' interests in this arena tenaciously, citing the unsuccessful action by the Confederation of German Employers Associations, the employer peak council in the Federal Republic of Germany, against the so-called 'parity co-determination' legislation of 1976. The association's lobbying failed to prevent passage of the legislation and subsequent legal action to have the new law declared unconstitutional was also unsuccessful.[47] Two examples of lobbying to change the *status quo* cited by Gladstone are the pressure from the Confederation of British Industry which influenced the adoption of the 1971 *Industrial Relations Act* and the unsuccessful lobbying by Australian employer associations in the 1920s seeking legislation to abolish compulsory arbitration.[48]

More generally, lobbying may be directed to resisting the trend to increased regulation *per se*, perhaps because of an in-principle preference for minimal

Table 11.6 Types of employer association services used (AWIRS)

Services used	% of workplaces using this service
Information on awards	56
Advice on dismissals	12
Dealing with unions	11
Legal advice	7
No services used	24

Population: Australian workplaces with at least 5 employees and who are members of an employer association. Figures are weighted and are based on responses from 1501 workplaces, representing 77 800 employers.

Note: Some workplaces used several services.

Source: R.Callus, A. Morehead, M. Cully and J. Buchanan, *Industrial Relations At Work : The Australian Workplace Industrial Relations Survey*, Commonwealth Department of Industrial Relations, AGPS, Canberra, 1991, p. 48.

regulation as well as because of the financial costs.[49] Lobbying is not confined to formal institutionalised consultative machinery but such machinery, usually tripartite, is a major vehicle for the expression of association views, as well as a means of accessing government views. Gladstone notes that typically associations attach importance to these avenues for lobbying; they exercise care in selection of appointees and closely monitor their contribution.[50]

Central federations or peak councils take the lead in this employer association function, although associations at 'subordinate levels' may undertake this activity if substantial government intervention in industrial relations occurs at state or regional level. Further, industry associations may be strong lobbyists in relation to industry specific matters, safety regulations in the mining industry for example.[51] Gladstone argues that one reason why associations strive for consensus when developing policy positions is that effective lobbying requires a belief by government decision-makers that the association is representative of members' interests. He suggests that the infrequent public disclosure of internal dissent distinguishes employer associations from trade unions, the comparatively closed nature of their decision-making processes making the presentation of a solid front, or at least the appearance thereof, easier.[52]

Unlike trade unions in at least three of the countries studied, Australia, Sweden and Great Britain, employer associations do not seek formal affiliation with political parties, nor do they support particular parties during election campaigns. There may however be a measure of informal affiliation, described by Gladstone as 'an affinity ... for parties whose philosophy generally corresponds to the dominant 'ideology' of employers'.[53] He suggests however that the critical factor in exerting decisive influence on legislators and public policy decision-makers is 'a favourable current of public opinion', being more important than either ideological compatibility or making financial contributions to all major parties. Gladstone argues that employer associations recognise that public opinion can be cultivated and this explains the high ranking of the association function of fostering and maintaining public and media relations.[54]

Australia

Employer associations in Australia are active political lobbyists, making representations and submissions to government concerning industrial relations legislation and government policy at both federal and state levels. Here the employer association will be seeking to maintain or create a legal and political environment beneficial to its membership and perhaps also an environment which furthers the institutional needs of the association.

Employer associations, unlike a significant percentage of unions, are not formally affiliated with political parties. Many associations do however have informal links with non-Labor parties reflecting some degree of ideological affinity. These links become visible from time to time when senior officials of employer associations obtain political office, for example, Ian McPhee, a former executive director of the VCM became a Minister in a federal Liberal-National government; Phil Gude, a former officer of the then Victorian Chamber of Commerce became a Liberal member of parliament in Victoria and Minister for Business and Employment in the Kennett government elected in 1992. Ian McLachlan, the federal opposition shadow minister for national development, was president of the National Farmers' Federation during the 1980s. These career paths are an important factor in the informal networks within which continuous lobbying occurs and they have parallels in the comparable career paths of many union officials in Australia. Like trade unions, employer associations have to seek concessions from either political party. They may have party political preferences but unlike trade unions, the party in office may not always be a significant factor in determining the benefits conceded to them.

As noted above, lobbying activity may be *ad hoc* or occur within formal tripartite structures (both permanent and temporary) established by government for consultation with unions and employers. An example of a permanent structure in the federal jurisdiction is the National Labour Consultative Council. Employers are represented on this body by the employer association peak council, the Australian Chamber of Commerce and Industry (ACCI). This is one of many tripartite advisory bodies where the ACCI is represented, along with the federal government and usually also the ACTU. These include: National Board of Employment, Education and Training; National Occupational Health and Safety Commission; Economic Planning Advisory Council; Social Security Advisory Council; Commonwealth/State Training Advisory Committee; Australian Manufacturing Council; National Health and Medical Research Council; TPC Consultative Committee; National Training Board; Trade Negotiations Advisory Group; Indicative Planning Council for the Housing Industry; Technology Transfer Council. This representation reflects the peak council's major function as lobbyist, its concern with the product market interests of affiliated associations and recognition of the overlap between social policy, economic policy and industry policy, notwithstanding the organisation's predominant concern with industrial relations.

The importance of industrial relations regulation at state level in Australia ensures a lobbying function for regional associations, especially the multi-industry umbrella associations. They have been active lobbyists in relation to the occupational health and safety and workcare statutes introduced by state Labor governments during the 1980s. In Victoria in 1985, employer associations such as the then Victorian Employers' Federation and the Australian Chamber of Manufactures (Victorian Division), opposed, unsuccessfully, the principle of statute based union representation on workplace occupational health and safety committees. In 1992, however, lobbying by VECCI via representation on regulatory committees led to substantial revision of what the association regarded as an 'onerous package' of plant safety legislation to be introduced by the Kirner government.[55] An example of successful lobbying to protect the *status quo* is provided by employer associations in New South Wales in 1986-1987. They succeeded in achieving withdrawal of a Bill which sought to prevent actions in tort in relation to industrial action (see chapter 5) unless leave had been granted by the Industrial Commission of New South Wales.[56] At the federal level in 1987 there was similarly strong and successful lobbying by employer associations against proposed legislation also seeking to soften the impact of common law and statutory sanctions relating to industrial action.[57]

Media and public relations
Overview
The prominence of this function is of relatively recent origin although Gladstone notes that some associations continue to prefer a low public profile citing the Australian Mines and Metals Association as an example.[58] As noted above, public relations is important for influencing public opinion which in turn is a critical factor in successful lobbying of government. Media relations assume importance because the mass media is the most important means for associations to convey their views and policies to the general public. In addition to seeking to influence community attitudes toward specific policies and positions, associations will also seek to promote a favourable general image and this will include counteracting any portrayal of negative images, by trade unions for example.[59]

In addition to media statements and interviews, associations use their own publications as a means of image promotion and to disseminate information and ideas. They often target specialised audiences, such as teachers and students, and it is in relation to this aspect of their activities that they are likely to provide objective material on social policy and industrial relations issues as well as promotional material. The country studies attested to the extensive use of publications—advisory, instructional and promotional—produced by major national associations by their branches and/or affiliates. While associations typically assume these functions independently, in countries with an embedded 'social partnership' they sometimes participate jointly with trade unions in education and promotion activities.[60]

Australia
The major employer associations, in particular the ACCI and the Business Council of Australia, seek to raise the profile of business in the media and in the community generally. In September 1993, employer associations in Australia, under the leadership of ACCI, commenced a public relations

offensive against certain aspects of proposed legislation by the Keating government. Their opposition focused on planned restrictions on employer access to sanctions in relation to secondary boycott industrial action and the limitations on access of non-unionised employees to legally enforceable, that is industrial tribunal endorsed, enterprise agreements. The associations proclaimed that the government failed to 'adequately consult' them and they signalled their intent to lobby the Australian Democrats and the Greens who hold the balance of power in the upper house of the federal parliament.[61]

In October 1987, the Business Council of Australia established an Employee Relations Study Commission chaired by an academic, Professor Fred Hilmer, Dean, Australian Graduate School of Management, University of New South Wales, to advise the Council on changes needed to create an industrial relations environment consistent with Council policy and to stimulate debate and processes of change.[62] The Commission's third and final report on reform of Australia's industrial relations framework, *Working Relations: A Fresh Start for Australian Enterprises*, was released at a media conference in August 1993. The work of this Commission and the publicity associated with it, provides an illustration of the blending of the lobbying, educational and public relations functions of this influential association. A major finding of the final report is that fundamental changes in bargaining structures and employee representation arrangements are necessary if Australian enterprises are to close the gap with their best international competitors.[63]

The public relations function of the Victorian Employers' Chamber of Commerce and Industry is illustrated in its support for the Premier Town Contest and its presentation, on an annual basis, of the Victorian Community Service Award through the Develop Victoria Council.[64]

Membership and structure

Overview

Information on employer association membership densities are 'crude estimates at best' due to the disinclination of associations to disclose details. This is another point of distinction with trade unions. The unit of measurement is typically the proportion of enterprises or plants which belong or employees working in member firms as a proportion of all employees. Most of the countries in the Windmuller and Gladstone-edited volume show high to very high density for the peak councils, especially in terms of the latter measure. Windmuller concludes that overall, employers are at least as well organised as unions and probably better organised in a number of countries.[65] However aggregate, that is nation-wide, membership levels may be higher than the average density for industry associations because of peak council willingness to accept individual companies, usually conglomerates, into membership without industry association membership as a precondition. This may suit the preference of such companies for autonomy in industrial relations management.

Another feature distinguishing employer associations from trade unions is the virtual absence of coercive pressure to join. Windmuller cites the rare example of an employer association closed shop in the Dutch printing industry where an association-union agreement supports a closed shop for both parties.[66] Further, association recruitment activity is low profile, characterised as 'discreet solicitation' by Windmuller, with the emphasis on inducement and peer pressure. The inducements cover the range of functions discussed above, supplemented in some cases by the establishment of special membership categories with fewer obligations attached. Nonetheless, as Windmuller points out, for many companies, in particular the larger and more powerful companies, remaining independent of an association is a practicable option.[67]

The universal dominant characteristic of the structure of employer associations in terms of organising base is complexity. This is due to the number of organising principles which determine structure and the fact that they are 'partly competitive and partly overlapping'. Windmuller identifies the main organising principles as:

1 function;
2 industry or economic activity;
3 territory;
4 ownership; and
5 size.[68]

In relation to function, the structural distinction is between: exclusively trade associations (which are not considered here); associations concerned solely with members' industrial relations interests; and multi-function associations concerned with both 'economic' and 'social' issues, to use the European terminology. Association structure based on function is usually found in the manufacturing sector, being rare in the primary and tertiary sectors. The country studies point to a growth in multi-function associations through mergers, both to reduce employer membership costs and in response to the increasing convergence between 'economic' and 'social' issues. Windmuller cites the unified Confederation of British Industry established in 1965 as an example, one which involved a number of parallel mergers at the industry level, but he notes that peak council affiliates do not necessarily follow the peak council's action and thus mergers may present problems.[69] At peak council level, the two major functionally distinct federations of associations in Germany provide an example of the use of 'close policy co-ordination' as an alternative to merger. Organisation based on industry is a common structural feature, with industry associations accounting for most of the membership of employer peak councils. Testifying to the complexity of structure however, is the fact that some industry associations approximate federations of associations. Examples cited are Great Britain's Engineering

Employers Federation, comprising eighteen fairly autonomous local and regional associations and, in the Dutch construction industry, the federation of 'specialised' associations. Another common feature is the pre-eminence of associations based on the metals sector. They tend to be leaders among employers, negotiating key agreements with unions. Similarly, unions in these industries are frequently leaders among unions. Windmuller speculates that the prominence of both parties is due to:

1 the industry's status as a highly capitalised sector of the economy and frequent leader in export trade; and
2 the large numbers of relatively well-paid employees.[70]

The country studies reveal no common factor in the definition of industry; both wide and narrow definitions are used and this results in very wide inter-country variance in the number of employer associations per comparable geographic level. This contrasts with trade unions where inter-country variance in the number of unions can be explained by the relative importance of 'craft' and 'industry' as an organising base.[71]

The country studies show 'consistently, greater fragmentation' among employer associations, that is, the number of affiliates of employer association peak councils is usually greater, and sometimes much greater, than the number of affiliates of trade union peak councils. Windmuller offers two alternative possible explanations for this:

1 for a 'community of interest' of employers to exist in the minds of employers it has to be defined more 'narrowly' than is the case for employees; and
2 employee solidarity is feasible in organisations with significantly broader and more diffuse bases than is the case for employer associations.[72]

Organisation based on territory or region is typically second only to 'industry' and in some cases is the most important organising principle. The key to the significance and autonomy of regional associations is the structure of collective bargaining. Where this is decentralised on a regional basis the geographic units assume importance. Windmuller cites as one example the high level of autonomy at the local and regional levels of employer associations in the United States. Control over bargaining also explains self-sufficient associations in some urban areas such as San Francisco where heterogeneous firms are 'united' by location rather than by industry.[73] It was noted in chapter 6 that power in trade unions is similarly likely to reside at the level where the industrial relations rule-making function is carried out.[74]

Another organising base for employer associations is ownership, the distinction being between private and public ownership. Where public sector organisations have formed employer associations, generally they do not seek membership in employer association federations representing private sector companies. Australia provides an exception with the associations representing local government employers being members of private sector multi-industry federations. Further, where such integration occurs, the public sector organisations will usually join at a level divorced from the bargaining level and the membership will be conditional, for example, exemption from any endorsement of association views on public policy issues.[75]

'Size of firm' is not a common organising principle for employer associations but where it operates it usually applies to small firms. In the case of associations open to firms of all sizes, differences in objectives and in bargaining positions based on firm size generates intra-association conflict. One result may be large firms demanding special status or conversely, policy autonomy. Another outcome may be the formation of a break-away association, with membership confined to small and medium-sized firms. Such associations are likely to adopt a position of stronger opposition to unions and other 'pluralist' industrial relations legislation, perhaps to approximate Purcell's 'unitary collectivism' (see chapter 9). Windmuller suggests this is probably because 'they contain more members operating at the margin of economic viability'.[76]

Australia

There is comparatively little information concerning the number, size and membership of employer associations in Australia. This is due to the aversion to disclosure noted above and to the fact that the Australian Bureau of Statistics does not publish data on employer associations in contrast to the detailed information provided on trade unions. Some limited data are provided by the Workplace Survey which found that 72 per cent of all private sector workplaces with 5 or more employees had membership of employer associations; the industry breakdown for this sector showed the highest membership density to be in construction (94 per cent) and the lowest density to be in recreation, personal and other services (53 per cent). The Report suggests that the lower density for workplaces that were part of a larger organisation (57 per cent) compared to single workplaces (72 per cent) may reflect the fact that workplace managers in the former group obtained advice internally, unaware of the company's membership of an association.[77] In that event, the Survey figure understates employer association membership.

The organising principles discussed above are all evident in Australian employer associations with 'industry' or 'economic sector' being the most common principle. Plowman includes the craft (or occupational) organising principle but typically these associations have no industrial relations function and therefore do not meet the Windmuller definition. Industry associations may be single industry or multi-industry umbrella associations. In relation to organisations based on territory, associations may be national (more than one state) or single state. A number of associations in both categories operate regional branches. Examples of associations based on each of these organising principles are provided in Table 11.7. The overlapping nature of the organising principles within individual associations is apparent. All of the associations listed, with the exception of the Oil Industry Industrial Committee, are multi-function associations.

Table 11.7 Employer associations: organising principles

Craft (or occupation)
Master Painters, Decorators and Signwriters' Association
Pharmacy Guild of Australia
Australian Dental Association
Roof Restorers' Association

Industry (economic activity)
Australian Mines and Metals Association (about 200 member companies)
Master Builders—Construction and Housing Association of Australia (over 17 000 firms)
Oil Industry Industrial Committee (7 member companies)
Metal Trades Industry Association (6500 member companies)
Private Hospitals' Association of Victoria (63 member hospitals)

Multi-industry (umbrella)
Australian Chamber of Manufactures (about 9000 member companies)
Victorian Employers' Chamber of Commerce and Industry (about 8000 member companies)[78]

Territory (region)
Victorian Employers' Chamber of Commerce and Industry (about 8000 member companies)

Size of firm
Small Business Association of Victoria (a subsidiary of VECCI)
Business Council of Australia (82 member companies)

Peak council
Australian Chamber of Commerce and Industry (14 State/Territory employer associations and 26 (national) industry employer associations)

Plowman points out that few industry associations have exclusive jurisdiction over the industry territory and will frequently seek some accommodation with the craft or occupational associations within the industry.[79] The membership of the Victorian Employers' Chamber of Commerce and Industry (VECCI) and the Australian Chamber of Manufactures (ACM) is diverse. It includes single industry and craft employer associations as well as individual companies. Plowman argues that, in the case of the employer associations which recruit across industries, many of the individual members are small employers who may resent the domination of the industry association by larger companies. The small companies may seek assistance from the umbrella association in ensuring that the industry association and unions do not collude at their expense.[80] The VECCI membership comprises about 8000 member companies and it also has about seventy single industry associations as members. Employee relations services to members are organised around six industry sectors: Building and Construction; Commercial, Retail and Business Services; Hospitality, Tourism and Leisure; Local Government; Manufacturing, Wholesale and Transport; Health, Community Services and Education. In 1992 there were thirty-seven staff providing representation and advisory services in employee relations. In addition to the advisers appointed to specific industry sectors there are specialist staff appointed in the areas of occupational health and safety and training and education.[81]

The Victorian Office of the ACM employs about fifty staff to deal with the labour market interests of members. 'Industrial relations' personnel are distinguished from 'employment, education & training' personnel. The former services are organised around four industry groupings: consumer products industries; general and service industries; metals, engineering and construction industries and textiles, clothing and footwear. In 1993, the Victorian Office had a membership of around 6000 companies and up to fifty affiliated associations (identified as 'Affiliated Groups').[82]

The primary organising principle for the Business Council of Australia is size of firm. The Council has two tiers of membership 'Council Membership' and 'General Membership'. The former is the more important with the higher subscription rate and with eligibility, which is self-limiting, based primarily on the criterion of scale in terms of 'the contribution to the economy of Australia', although this is qualified by the need for regional and business sector balance. The eighty-two major companies, including three government trading enterprises, who were members of the Council in 1992 are listed in the Appendix (Table 11.11). Membership is by companies but participation in the Council is restricted to either the chief executive or chairman, if the latter is a company employee. General membership is available to companies and associations operating in Australia. Membership in this category entitles companies to raise matters for consideration by the Council and to advisory services in respect of government-company relations and economic matters.

Plowman[83] distinguishes between autonomous, dependent and semi-autonomous single industry associations on the basis of the extent to which they contract out their industrial relations functions to other employer associations. Autonomous associations provide members with an extensive range of specialist services because of their size and resources. Such associations usually represent employers in large industries, for example mining, banking and metal fabrication. They include the Australian Bankers Association, the Metal Trades Industry Association and the Australian Mines and Metals Association. Most associations may be characterised as semi-autonomous. They provide some services directly, for example award interpretation and negotiations with unions in rights disputes and certain interest disputes; they also contract out some services, for example negotiations or advocacy in major rights or interest disputes. The Private Hospitals' Association of Victoria is in this category, drawing from time to time on the specialist services available from VECCI, with which it is affiliated. Dependent associations rely exclusively on another employer association for industrial relations services. They are usually small and do not employ specialist staff. Some examples are the Plastic Fabricators' Association and the Wool Textiles Manufacturers of Australia which rely on the State Offices of ACM; and the Small Business Association of Victoria and the Bus Proprietors' Association of Victoria which rely on VECCI for staffing and services.

A pre-condition for trade union viability in Australia this century has been registration or recognition by federal or state industrial tribunals (see chapters 6 and 12). This is not the case for employer associations and they tend to approach the matter of registration more cautiously than trade unions as there may be strategic advantage in remaining unregistered. The essential requirement for registration of an employer association under federal legislation, operative from 2 January 1994, is that the association had in aggregate, over the six months preceding application, employed on average at least 100 employees.[84] The provisions for registration and the regulation of employer associations are the same as for unions under all the compulsory arbitration statutes. Thus registered employer associations are subject to the same controls over their internal governments as registered trade unions (see chapter 8). However the legislation introduced by both political parties invariably has been directed to, or motivated by, its impact on trade unions and its practical relevance to employer associations is limited (see below).

The decision by an employer association on whether or not to apply for registration involves the consideration of several factors. Once registered, an employer association is entitled to initiate proceedings before the relevant industrial tribunal (federal or state). Associations not registered may, however, seek leave to appear in a case. In the latter circumstance in the federal jurisdiction, decisions made by the tribunal will not be automatically binding on all members of the unregistered employer association, although some of its members may be covered as individual respondents to the award. The advantages of registration for an employer association are:

1 the right to initiate claims and to intervene in proceedings before the tribunal;
2 the aid to membership recruitment which derives from the association's status as a registered body; and
3 a factor related to 2: the association's familiarity with the tribunal 'system' enables it to facilitate proceedings for member companies.

On the other hand, the main advantage which employer associations see in not registering is that they have the choice of appearing in a case without automatically involving all their members. Sometimes similar bodies will vary in their attitudes to this issue: the Australian Chamber of Manufactures for example, is registered under the federal statute and the Victorian statute but not the NSW statute. However, the growing dominance of the federal over state tribunals on major industrial issues appears to have led to an increasing proportion of employer associations registering under the federal legislation. In October 1993, there were eighty-two employer associations registered, compared with sixty-four trade unions. Victoria provides for 'recognition' of representative associations rather than registration.[85] There are no statutory controls on the internal governments of recognised associations in Victoria. In March 1993 there were 191 recognised employer associations and 120 recognised trade unions. This 'recognised' status has diminished relevance however under the *Employee Relations Act* 1992 (see chapter 13).

In the case of industrial affiliations, the aggregate picture of employer associations is more complex than it is for trade unions. This is because of the greater number of employer associations, the frequent difficulty of isolating their industrial relations activity and the greater inclination of small employer associations to affiliate with one or more larger associations to obtain specialist services than is the case with small trade unions. The complexity is a reflection of the absence of barriers to affiliation and the continuing conflict between the desire for independent representation of special interests and the desire for strong representation (through larger associations) of common interests. At the national level the employer 'equivalent' to the ACTU has been the Australian Chamber of Commerce and Industry (formerly the Confederation of Australian Industry). In 1992 its membership comprised forty member organisations (twenty-six national industry and fourteen

State/Territory associations), together with four affiliated associations which collectively represented about 100 000 Australian businesses (see Appendix Table 11.12). Disaffiliation from both the union and employer peak councils is a simple matter but during the 1980s only the employer peak council experienced disaffiliations. The MTIA withdrew in 1987, arguing that there should be concentration solely on industrial relations issues if the peak council was to achieve a national leadership role, and the Australian Bankers' Association withdrew in 1988.

Other national employer associations which disaffiliated were the Australian Hotels Association, the Australian Retailers Association, the then Master Builders' Federation, the Federation of Australian Radio Broadcasters and the National Farmers' Federation. By the early 1990s most of these associations had rejoined the national peak council (see Appendix Table 11.12). One exception was the high profile National Farmers Federation which joined the Australian Federation of Employers established in 1986 and remains the only sizeable affiliate of an organisation designed to provide a national voice for small business.[86] Plowman documents the conflicts between this Federation and the mainstream multi-industry employer associations, conflict based *inter alia* on major differences concerning the methods for achieving reform in industrial relations.[87] A key difference is that the mainstream associations favour gradual devolution of industrial relations practice to an enterprise focus through adaptation of existing institutions rather than revolutionary change.

Unlike the ACTU, the ACCI must co-exist with another major employer association, the Business Council of Australia, operating in its major areas of activity that is political lobbying and advocacy on major cases before the federal industrial tribunal. The position is similar in the various states. The union trades and labour councils (however styled) are usually the only industrial bodies with which unions affiliate but in the case of employer associations there will be a number of associations lobbying state governments and there will be greater diversity of representation in state wage cases. As noted above, there is also greater volatility in employer association affiliations than is the case with trade unions. These differences are in part a reflection of the distinguishing features of the relationship between individual employers and their associations. These internal relations are now considered.

Internal government

Overview

A number of the features of the internal government of employer associations identified by Windmuller have parallels in the government of trade unions (see chapter 8). These are:

1 a formal structure which meets many of the procedural requirements of democracy;
2 some divergence between formal decision-making structures and actual practice, with 'power centres and pressure groups existing informally and operating through informal channels to supplement and sometimes to bypass the formal structure';[88] and

> **Table 11.8** Employer associations: internal government structure
>
> **General meetings (assemblies)**
> Usually held annually or less frequently. Functions include: (1) to serve as a sounding board for rank and file views; (2) to ratify, rather than to seriously challenge, decisions that may be required to be made under the association's constitution. A significant decision at this level may be the election of executive committees but otherwise real power is not exercised at this level. Not all associations have such a level in the formal structure.
>
> **Councils (for example general councils, executive councils)**
> Meet more frequently than general assemblies, usually about four to six times per year. They comprise elected or designated members whose constituency may be based on an industry or region. Functions may include: (1) election of officers, executive committee and other standing committee members (if not undertaken by a general assembly); (2) scrutiny of financial accounts. These bodies exercise some influence but this is not the decisive level in association policy development because they lack the necessary 'continuity and compactness'.
>
> **Executive board (however styled)**
> Meets frequently, monthly or more often. Usually the most important decision–making level. Typically decisions cover matters such as senior staff appointments, bargaining positions, strike or lockout strategies and budget allocations. Sometimes these matters are delegated to key standing committees.
> Membership is usually limited to twenty to thirty representatives of the most important companies, regions or branches. The authority of this level of government will be determined more by the calibre and status of the representatives, in both personal terms and corporate terms, than by the formal structure, that is, the association rules or by–laws.
>
> **President (chairperson)**
> Usually an honorary position held by a leading employer. In the past the expectation was that the 'eminent incumbent' would devote a reasonable share of his time to association affairs especially for representational purposes but nonetheless be primarily concerned with the management of his own enterprise. Increasingly this position is becoming full-time or near full–time and where this occurs it will impact upon the traditional demarcation of functions between the president and the chief executive wherein the former had no involvement in the day by day internal management of the association.
>
> Source: Adapted from J.P. Windmuller, 'Employers associations in comparative perspective: organisation, structure, administration', in J.P. Windmuller and A. Gladstone (eds), *Employers Associations and Industrial Relations: A Comparative Study*, Clarendon Press, Oxford, 1984, pp. 15-16.

3 delegation of substantial authority to full-time officials, executive committees (however styled) and other key standing committees.

The various levels, three or four being the norm, of the governing structures of employer associations are explained in Table 11.8.

Features of employer association internal government which in the general case provide a contrast to trade unions are:

1 unopposed elections as the norm;
2 voting systems usually based on criteria other than one member—one vote, for example, voting entitlements weighted by number of employees, size of payroll or association dues;
3 the absence of committed groups of active members willing to devote time to the association; and
4 the impression, if not the reality, of consensual decision making.

Windmuller attributes the vastly different political cultures of employer associations and trade unions first to the fact that 'tangible rewards' for employers and managers derive from their performance and advancement in their own companies rather than in associations to which the company belongs and secondly, to the preference for 'privatising' internal controversy with the corollary of an absence of displays by representatives in association meetings of 'their rhetorical skills or charismatic qualities to their constituents'.[89] A common feature of employer association internal government and one which is often a feature of trade unions, is oligarchy. However, as Coleman has noted in the context of trade union governments, it is still possible to reflect membership wishes through this form of government.[90]

An aspect of internal government where the difference between employer associations and trade unions is marked is that of authority and discipline. The key determinant of behaviour here is the fact that associations are 'alliances of competitors and individual decision-making units'[91] as well as being the collective voice for common interests. This characteristic may explain members' rejection of association policies or decisions in response to pressure from various sources including: union company by company campaigns designed to break employer solidarity; the pursuit of a competitive advantage in either product or labour markets; the objective of maintaining viability of a marginal company. These examples involve a breaking of ranks between individual companies and an association. Another manifestation of a breakdown of solidarity is between an industry association and an employer peak council.

The key difference with unions is employer association disinclination to discipline member companies in any way for disregarding association decisions. In some cases, for example the Dutch Christian Employers Union (NCW) and the Federation of Dutch Industries (VNO), there is explicit rejection of penalties. Another method is to define the problem away by avoiding formal policies and simply providing advice to members, which Windmuller indicates is the case with some Australian associations.[92] The most forceful attempt to impose discipline takes the form of the issuing of reprimands and peer group pressure, that is expressions of disapproval. Windmuller cites the practice of the Confederation of German Employers Associations (BDA) which expects affiliate adherence to governing body decisions but concedes that its wage policies have the status of non-binding recommendations.[93]

Australia

Employer associations in Australia, like trade unions, range from large complex organisations employing scores of staff to small specialist organisations with no full-time staff. Formal employer association structures have much in common with unions. The supreme governing body is an elected council which determines policy and which elects an executive committee to which is delegated varying degrees of decision-making autonomy and responsibility for day by day management. Just as the specialist staff within unions are sometimes not drawn from the occupations or industries the union represents, so employer association officials may not be employers nor have worked as managers within the member companies. This is particularly true for those whose skills are geared to the advocacy function within industrial tribunals.

The governing structure of associations varies with size and with the range of interests represented, for example trade, regional or company-based divisions of interests. Multi-industry associations usually have constitutions in which members have ultimate control over policy decisions through a structure of representative committees. The central policy-making body is usually a general council. Sub-committees of the council may be advisory or may be delegated to act within a general mandate. The Victorian Employees' Chamber of Commerce and Industry has a twenty-five member Executive Council with representation from each of six industry groups:

1 Building and Construction;
2 Commercial, Retail and Business Services;
3 Health, Community Services and Education;
4 Hospitality, Tourism and Leisure;
5 Local Government; and
6 Manufacturing, Transport and Wholesale.

The members of this Council in most cases hold the position of managing director/chief executive of the organisation they represent. In this association the executive board (see Table 11.8) takes the form of a six member board of directors.

Typically, elections to association offices are not contested, indeed there is often a reluctance by members to give time to running associations. Employer associations are not part of the career path for managers; their careers are more likely to benefit from efforts spent running the companies they are representing. As noted in chapter 8, all registered organisations must have elections conducted by the Australian Electoral Commission unless granted an exemption. Anecdotal evidence suggests that in elections conducted by the Commission it is common in the case of employer associations for the number of nominations to equal the number of vacancies and for the nominees to be declared elected without contest. While this also occurs in the case of trade unions, it is a far more frequent occurrence for employer associations.

The fee structure tends to be based on membership (company) size, that is financial resources. Voting strength is often in proportion to fees. A few trade unions base membership fees on members' income but this does not affect voting strength. In other words, an employer association is not a fraternal organisation. It is a service for which the employer pays. The more the company pays, the more it gets. It is not meant to be and is not democratic.

While employer associations enjoy a prominent role in Australian industrial relations they are nonetheless constrained by their constituents in significant ways. The delegation by the individual member companies of part of the management function to an association is a very conditional delegation. The individual member will not hesitate to revoke that delegation if it is assessed that the position being taken by the association is against the interests of the company.

In the matter of internal authority and discipline there are significant differences of degree between employer associations and trade unions. Employer associations in Australia do not discipline or expel members who choose to act alone or to defy association policies. They have little if any control over members. This reflects in part the values or ideology of the membership, certainly that of the owner/managers whose inherent characteristics make them more difficult to control, individualists seeing their welfare depending on their own efforts. Notions of class collaboration and class interests are alien. Associations do not act against recalcitrant members for fear of splitting the association. Rather, they rely on persuasion. Employers, for their part, generally regard their associations as little more than advisory agencies and want to be left alone to manage their business affairs. This means that they do not expect their associations to direct them and, for example, will not surrender their right to concede a union's demand in order to avoid a dispute. The principal allegiance of a member organisation is to its own firm rather than to its association and it is generally cautious of surrendering its autonomy for the sake of the common good.

When confronted with the dilemma of acting in their own interests or the interests of employers as a class, employers are far more likely than employees to choose the former. In addition to the matter of values, the nature of the relationship between association members, that is the fact that they may be direct competitors, may reinforce this behavioural characteristic. Employers may also have more objective pressures than the pressure of class solidarity, for example debts to be paid. Thus an employer association's strategic decision to oppose a union claim, for example to offer no wage increase, may be ignored due to one or more of the above factors. The capacity to resist will depend on liquidity, inventory and the extent and nature of competition. An employer may know for example that if he or she concedes, a rival (another member of the association) will be forced out of business. An employer may also know that if all employers covered by the award or agreement resist and this precipitates a strike, the employer who gives in may benefit from increased business. Some employers can resist, some cannot, some gain by conceding, some do not.

The inability of employer associations to enforce their strategy is illustrated in employer responses to a 1981 wages and conditions claim by the then Federated Storemen and Packers Union in Victoria. The employer associations were the then Victorian Employers' Federation and the Victorian Chamber of Manufactures. During September, negotiations took place on the union's thirty point log of claims with little progress and employer association officials advised the union they were not in a position to negotiate on any items in the log. The union response was to call a general meeting of members which voted for indefinite strike action. The union then by-passed the employer associations and wrote directly to the chief executives of the 350 or so companies, claiming the associations were misrepresenting the union position. Within days, the union had reached a settlement with a number of companies on wages (a $30 increase and no absorption of over-award wages). As soon as a company signed an agreement on wages, production was resumed. The employer associations called a meeting of members attended by 150 member companies. The meeting voted overwhelmingly to direct the associations to agree to the union's wage demands.[94] The preferred process for employer associations in this case would presumably have been arbitration, for two reasons: first, the difficulty of developing a single negotiating position on behalf of a diverse constituency in terms of capacity and inclination to resist the claim; secondly, the shifting of responsibility for outcomes to a third party, thereby avoiding the internal political tensions which may arise for officials when they are responsible for negotiating a compromise position. Trade unions may on occasion have these same preferences for the same reasons.

Another circumstance where individual rather than class interest may govern behaviour is in relation to labour markets with excess demand. Employers may agree at association level not to bid up wages but it has often been demonstrated that some of them will bid up wages in their own interests. In trade unions, officials can more readily convince members that they may gain in the long run from a short-term sacrifice. On occasions employer associations meet with a veneer of success in seeking to superimpose a notion of class welfare on to existing employer objectives involving company welfare or personal welfare. This occurred in the late 1960s in the metal trades when the member companies backed their associations (MTIA and ACM) with words in advocating absorption of over-award wages (see chapter 4 for an account of this dispute). Employers carried resolutions asking their associations to take a position before the federal tribunal which they did not intend to observe. At the same time award rates were falling further and further behind market rates. An illustration of an employer association acting under an obligation to hold the line in the face of contrary behaviour by members, is provided by the standard hours of work claim lodged by the MTIA in April 1981. The claim sought to have the relevant award provision amended to provide that ordinary hours of work would be forty hours for two years.[95] Simultaneously many association members were conceding a thirty-eight hour week in negotiations and some were conceding a thirty-five hour week.

The Workplace Survey provided some data concerning the internal relations between employer associations and their members. Table 11.9 shows the responses from workplace managers in workplaces with twenty or more employees concerning the extent to which they sought and followed association advice in relation to five issues : training and skills formation; payment of over-awards; handling of industrial action at the workplace; dismissals; negotiating with unions. The responses confirm the character of the internal relationship discussed in this section. They show that managers discriminated between issues, being most likely to seek and follow advice in dealing with industrial action and negotiating with unions (interest and rights disputes are not distinguished) and much less likely to do so in relation to training and skills formation and over-award payments.

Employers do not hesitate to transfer their allegiance to another association if they are not satisfied with the service. Trade unionists similarly, may vote with their feet where a choice of union exists but for employers there is no equivalent to the compulsory membership requirement which exists for some sections of the workforce. An individual employer may regard association membership as essential, as a guide through the labyrinth of industrial tribunal activity or as a countervailing power to union aggression, but that is the employer's choice. Thus for employers, any dissatisfaction with the services provided by a particular association may well be met by resignation.

Table 11.9 Extent to which member workplaces follow advice of employer associations on workplace issues (AWIRS)

Issue	Closely follow advice per cent	Follow with some modifications per cent	Do not follow advice per cent	Do not seek advice per cent
Training and skills formation	23	33	3	41
Payment of over-awards	26	25	6	43
Handling of industrial action at the workplace	46	31	2	21
Dismissals	41	22	4	33
Negotiating with unions	48	30	2	20

Population: Australian workplaces with at least twenty employees and which are members of an employer association. Figures are weighted and are based on responses from up to 1317 workplaces where the issue arises.

Source: R. Callus, A. Morehead, M. Cully and J. Buchanan, *Industrial Relations At Work: The Australian Workplace Industrial Relations Survey*, Commonwealth Department of Industrial Relations, AGPS, Canberra, 1991, p. 83.

To the extent that there is internal conflict within employer associations, it is unlikely there will be recourse to third parties (the state) to resolve that conflict. Employer associations have been able to act with little regard for the requirements of the federal industrial relations statute concerning the government of registered organisations because these provisions have to be activated by an aggrieved member of the association. Further, for the most part an association is not able to impose costs on members sufficient to warrant recourse to legal remedies. Much of the structural diversity in employer associations reflects conflicting interests between employers. Sometimes the response to conflicting interests is to create a new association structured to defend and promote those interests, often narrower than that of the established association. Thus there is the Retailers Council of Australia representing large department stores and numerous others representing other interests, for example the Electrical Retailers Association and the Mixed Business Association. The Business Council provides another example. The BCA was the result of a merger between the Australian Industries Development Association and the Business Roundtable and reflected dissatisfaction with the performance of the employer peak council, the then Confederation of Australian Industry.

Industrial relations activity among employers, at the state level, tends to be concentrated within the state Chambers of Manufactures, the state Employers' Federations and the Metal Trades Industry Associations. In some states there is a considerable rivalry between these three organisations for the leadership of employers in industrial matters. Some state bodies do, however, exchange information and there are *ad hoc* meetings on common problems at the staff level. Each of these associations varies considerably in the degree of cohesion between their state branches and between the federal and state bodies. Those industry associations which operate under a mixture of state and federal awards show less cohesion than those operating solely under federal awards. There is a certain amount of membership overlap between registered employer associations, but jurisdictional disputes are usually settled privately. Registered organisations of employers appear to be unwilling to publicly contest the right of other employers to have the representation of their choice. Typically, an employer willing to join an association will have a range of choice and may, in fact, belong to several associations at the same time. No pressure appears to be exerted on individual employers to join particular associations, although associations do actively compete for membership. Employer association representation at national wage cases reflects the comparative lack of organisational unity at federal level.

Conclusion

Many of the functions of employer associations represent a contracting out of the management industrial relations function. Typically there will be an inverse relationship between the volume and quality of resources allocated within a company for this function and the extent of dependence on an employer association. While company size is an important factor here, in the Australian case the prevalence of conciliation and arbitration systems, the associated wide scope of tribunal awards and tribunal-specific skills, have ensured a prominent place for employer associations in the process of workplace rule-making. The international overview which has been used in this chapter has served however to identify many similarities between associations in Australia and associations in the country studies in the Windmuller and Gladstone volume.

The changes in the power context in Australia in recent years have changed the focus of industrial relations practice. This has significant consequences for the work of employer associations, in particular the need to tailor services and advice to the individual needs of member companies. A complicating factor is the emergence of competitors, such as law firms and management consultants, for the industrial relations business of companies. A positive prognosis for employer associations would see them drawing successfully on their competitive tradition and perhaps possessing a competitive edge at the operational level. The fact that the majority of members of most employer associations are small to medium-sized firms however would suggest a continuing need for employer association advice. Unless there is a dramatic change in what is virtually a tradition of volatility, quite apart from the complexity, in the legal framework in which Australian industrial relations is conducted, the 'specialised services' functions of employer associations are likely to remain in high demand.

Notes

1. J.P. Windmuller, 'Employers associations in comparative perspective : organisation, structure, administration' and A. Gladstone, 'Employers associations in comparative perspective : functions and activities' in J.P. Windmuller and A. Gladstone (eds), *Employers Associations and Industrial Relations : A Comparative Study*, Clarendon Press, Oxford, 1984, pp. 1-43.
2. Windmuller, *op. cit.*, p. 1.
3. *ibid.*, pp. 2 & 9.
4. *ibid.*, pp. 3-4.
5. *ibid.*, pp. 4-5.
6. *ibid.*, p. 5.
7. J.T. Sutcliffe, *A History of Trade Unionism in Australia*, Macmillan, Melbourne, 1921, p. 13.
8. R. Gollan, *The Coalminers of New South Wales*, University Press, Melbourne, 1963, p. 14.
9. J. Niland, *The Movement for a Shorter Working Day in New South Wales, 1855-1875*, unpublished M. Com. thesis, University of NSW, 1966.
10. D. Plowman, *Holding the Line: Compulsory Arbitration and National Employer Co-ordination in Australia*, Cambridge University Press, Melbourne 1989, p. 1.
11. *ibid.*, p. 8.
12. *ibid.*, p. 11.
13. *ibid.*, pp. 11-17.
14. Windmuller, *op. cit.*, p. 5.
15. *ibid.*, p. 6.
16. *ibid.*
17. *ibid.*
18. *ibid.*, p. 7.
19. *ibid.*
20. *ibid.*, p. 3.
21. Confederation of Australian Industry, *Annual Report 1990-91*, p. 4.
22. Victorian Employers' Chamber of Commerce and Industry, *Annual Review 1992*.
23. Confederation of Australian Industry, *A New Industrial Relations System for Australia*, Psicomp, Melbourne, August 1991, p. 1.
24. R. Boland, 'The Shift to Enterprise Bargaining: Addressing the Core Issues' IIR Enterprise Bargaining Conference, Hotel Nikko, 21 June 1993.
25. See chapter 13 for details of this legal framework.
26. A. Gladstone, 'Employers associations in comparative perspective: functions and activities' in J.P. Windmuller and A. Gladstone, *op. cit.*, p. 37.
27. *ibid.*, p. 38.
28. *ibid.*
29. *ibid.*, p. 39.
30. *ibid.*
31. *ibid.*, pp. 35-36.
32. For a discussion of this concept see chapter 6.
33. *ibid.*, p. 37.
34. Business Council of Australia, *Working Relations: A Fresh Start for Australian Enterprises*, Information Australia, Melbourne 1993, p. 35.
35. Gladstone, *op. cit.*, pp. 30-31.
36. *ibid.*, pp. 31-32.
37. *ibid.*, p. 32.
38. *ibid.*, p. 33.
39. *ibid.*
40. *ibid.*, p. 34.

41 Australian Bureau of Statistics, *Manufacturing Establishments, Select Items of Data Classified by Industry and Employment Size*, Cat. no. 8204.1.
42 For a discussion of the operation of grievance procedures in Australia see chapter 17.
43 *Metal Industry Award 1984-Part 1*, clause 6(j).
44 ibid., clause 6(d)(vii).
45 R. Callus, A. Morehead, M. Cully and J. Buchanan, *Industrial Relations At Work : The Australian Workplace Industrial Relations Study*, Commonwealth Department of Industrial Relations, AGPS, Canberra, 1991, p. 47.
46 ibid., p. 48.
47 Gladstone, *op. cit.*, p. 25.
48 ibid., pp. 25-26.
49 ibid., pp. 26-27.
50 ibid., p. 28.
51 ibid., p. 26.
52 ibid.
53 ibid., p. 27.
54 ibid.
55 Victorian Employers' Chamber of Commerce and Industry, *Annual Review 1992*, p. 14.
56 P.A. Lawson, 'Employer Matters 1987', *Journal of Industrial Relations 30*, March 1988, pp. 142-143.
57 ibid., p. 142.
58 Gladstone, *op. cit.*, p. 28.
59 ibid., p. 29.
60 ibid.
61 *The Age*, 23 September 1993, pp. 3 & 16.
62 Business Council of Australia, *Enterprise-Based Bargaining Units: A Better Way of Working* Volume 1, Melbourne, 1989, p. vii.
63 *Business Council Bulletin*, August 1993, pp. 6-8.
64 Victorian Employers' Chamber of Commerce and Industry, *Annual Review*, 1992, p. 19.
65 Windmuller, *op. cit.*, p. 22.
66 ibid., p. 20.
67 ibid., p. 21.
68 ibid., p. 7.
69 ibid., pp. 8-9.
70 ibid., p. 11.
71 ibid., p. 10.
72 ibid.
73 ibid., p. 12.
74 see chapter 6, p. 32.
75 Windmuller, *op. cit.*, p. 12.
76 ibid., pp. 13-14.
77 Callus, et al., *op. cit.*, pp. 47 & 247.
78 On 1 July 1991, the Victorian Employers' Federation amalgamated with the State Chamber of Commerce and Industry to form the Victorian Employers' Chamber of Commerce and Industry.
79 D. Plowman, 'The Role of Employer Associations' in G.W. Ford, J.M. Hearn and R.D. Lansbury (eds), *Australian Labour Relations: Readings* (4th ed.), Macmillan, Melbourne, 1987, p. 237.
80 Plowman, 1987, *op. cit.*, p. 236.
81 Victorian Employers' Chamber of Commerce and Industry, *Annual Review*, 1992, pp. 27-28.
82 *Industrial Relations Index*, July 1993-November 1993, Edition 12, Information Australia, pp. 222-225.
83 D. Plowman, 'Employer Associations: Challenges and Responses' in G.W. Ford, J.M. Hearn & R.D. Lansbury (eds), *Australian Labour Relations: Readings* (3rd ed.), Macmillan, Melbourne, 1980, pp. 248-278.

84 *Industrial Relations Act* 1988 s.189(1)(b) as amended by *Industrial Relations Reform Act* 1993, s.75.
85 *Employee Relations Act* 1992 (Victoria), Part 12. The nature of recognition is discussed in chapter 13.
86 D.H. Plowman, 'Economic Forces and the New Right: Employer Matters in 1986', *Journal of Industrial Relations* 29, March 1987, p. 85.
87 *ibid.*, pp. 84-86.
88 Windmuller, *op. cit.*, p. 14.
89 *ibid.*
90 J.R. Coleman, 'The Compulsive Pressures of Democracy in Unionism', in W. Galenson and S.M. Lipset (eds), *Labour and Trade Unionism*, Wiley, New York, 1960, p. 208.
91 Windmuller, *op. cit.*, p. 19.
92 *ibid.*, p. 20.
93 *ibid.*
94 B. Dobson, 'Employer Matters in 1981', *Journal of Industrial Relations* 24, March 1982, pp. 113-114.
95 *ibid.*, p. 114.

Further Reading

F.T. De Vyver, 'Employers' organisations in the Australian industrial relations system', *Journal of Industrial Relations* 13, March 1971, pp. 30-51.

F.T. De Vyver, 'Employers' associations developments', *Journal of Industrial Relations* 14, December 1978, pp. 447-454.

N.F. Dufty, 'Employers Associations in Australia', in J.P. Windmuller and A. Gladstone (eds), *Employers Associations and Industrial Relations: A Comparative Study*, Clarendon Press, Oxford, 1984, pp. 115-148.

A. Gladstone, 'Employers Associations in Comparative Perspective: Functions and Activities', in Windmuller and Gladstone (eds) *op. cit.*, pp. 24-43.

J.M.C. King, 'Incentives, goals and role conflicts in an employers' association', *Journal of Industrial Relations* 12, March 1970, pp. 98-107.

D.H. Plowman, 'Economic Forces and the New Right: Employer Matters in 1986', *Journal of Industrial Relations* 29, March 1987, pp. 84-91.

David Plowman, 'Employer associations and industrial reactivity', in B. Dabscheck, G. Griffin and J. Teicher (eds), *Contemporary Australian Industrial Relations: Readings*, Longman Cheshire, Melbourne, 1992, pp. 225-242.

D. H. Plowman, 'Countervailing Power, Organisational Parallelism and Australian Employer Associations', *Australian Journal of Management* 14, June 1989, pp. 97-113.

D. Plowman, *Holding the Line Compulsory Arbitration and National Employer Co-ordination in Australia*, Cambridge University Press, Melbourne, 1989.

D.H. Plowman, 'Employer associations: challenges and responses', *Journal of Industrial Relations* 20, September 1978, pp. 237-263.

D.H. Plowman, 'Industrial legislation and the rise of employer associations, 1890-1906', *Journal of Industrial Relations* 27, September 1985, pp. 283-309.

D.H. Plowman and M. Rimmer, *Bargaining Structure, Award Respondency and Employer Associations*, Industrial Relations Research Centre, University of New South Wales, Kensington, 1992.

J.P. Windmuller, 'Employers associations in comparative perspective: organisation, structure, administration' in Windmuller and Gladstone (eds), *op. cit.*, pp. 1-23.

Questions

Origins and development

1 What are the major objectives of employers in establishing organisations to represent their collective interests?
2 Identify the significant factors in the establishment of permanent associations of employers in Australia.

Functions

3 Identify and illustrate each of the traditional functions of employer associations in Australia.
4 What changes, if any, are likely in the major functions of employer associations in Australia during the next few years? In particular, explain the likely impact of environmental factors on function.
5 Critically evaluate the following statement indicating whether you agree or disagree:

'There are significant similarities between employer associations and trade unions in terms of their use of the political method to achieve objectives.'

Membership and structure

6 Explain the various principles on which employer associations are organised and provide an example of each.

Internal government

7 Identify and explain the major differences in the operation of the internal governments of employer associations and trade unions in Australia.
8 Read the MTIA view concerning enterprise bargaining in the metal and engineering industry from 1991-1993 (see Appendix Table 11.10). What does this evaluation reveal about
   i employer ideology; and
   ii the relationship between employer associations and individual member companies?

Exercises

1 Identify any changes in employer representation in national wage cases during the period 1987 to 1993 and establish the reasons for the changes.
2 Read the 1991 publication by the Confederation of Australian industry entitled *A New Industrial Relations System for Australia* and provide a summary of the position paper in relation to:
   i   managerial frames of reference (chapter 9)
   ii the role of the state (chapters 12 & 13)
   iii trade union power (chapter 6)
3 Drawing upon the material contained in this chapter, indicate what may be concluded about the functions and the internal government of the Australian Chamber of Manufactures from the extract from an ACM publication contained in Table 11.13.

Appendix

Table 11.10 Enterprise bargaining in the metal and engineering industry 1991-1993: the MTIA view

Background

In June–July 1991 an industry framework for enterprise bargaining was negotiated between MTIA and the Metal Trades Federation of Unions (MTFU). The Agreement became the vehicle for the October 1991 National Wage Case and was effectively endorsed by the full bench in that Case.

MTIA/MFTU Agreement

The Agreement identified seven major aspects of workplace change that might be addressed in enterprise negotiations:–

- Work flexibility;
- Work organisation (that is, job design);
- Skills development (that is, training);
- Absenteeism, turnover, disputation;
- Performance improvement program;
- Single bargaining units;
- Award restructuring issues.

The pursuit of a broad workplace change agenda yielded excellent results for both employers and employees. It helped in shifting the focus away from traditional industrial relations values, to issues going directly to a firm's competitiveness and, at the same time, offered the opportunity for greater employee participation and the achievement of greater job satisfaction.

MTIA saw the industry framework as a transitionary mechanism in facilitating the shift to enterprise bargaining. The framework was designed to maintain stable industrial relations; avoid the prospect of excessive wage outcomes; achieve genuine workplace reform across a broad front—not just an enterprise here and there; and to assist in changing outdated industrial relations values.

MTIA Proposals for a New Framework

The MTIA/MTFU Framework expired on 1 January 1993 and MTIA sought to negotiate a new framework with the unions in order to maintain the momentum of workplace reform in a stable industrial relations environment. Consequently, late last year, MTIA put to the unions a set of guidelines designed to assist and encourage ongoing reform at the enterprise level on a broad front. MTIA's guidelines included a proposal that 'any wage increase shall be determined at the enterprise level on the basis of changes which have been implemented to improve the productive performance of the enterprise'.

In other words, wage increases would not be set at the industry level. Instead, it was time to take the next step in decentralising wage fixing by placing the responsibility on individual enterprises to determine their own wages within the terms of an agreed bargaining framework which placed the emphasis on improved productive performance.

Unions Reject MTIA Proposals

The unions rejected MTIA's proposals, insisting that the only basis upon which an industry framework could be agreed was a six per cent wage increase to the end of 1994 to apply to all employees in the industry. MTIA declined to negotiate an industry framework on that basis and any chance of maintaining a managed approach to enterprise bargaining has now faded.

MTIA's refusal to submit to the metal unions demands is understandable. Current business conditions remain extremely difficult. The Nineties will be a very cautious and tough period, characterised by fierce competition in manufacturing and small margins for error. Securing economic recovery for Australia and at the same time building higher competitiveness for our industries, must be our top priority. Wage outcomes must reinforce this priority, not present more risks. An across-the-board wage increase which had no connection with the national imperative of increasing productivity was, and remains, unacceptable to MTIA.

Unions' Company by Company Campaign

Since MTIA's rejection of the across–the–board claim, the unions have pursued a company by company campaign for wage increases. The campaign is likely to continue throughout the remainder of 1993, and is set to intensify following the resolution of union shop stewards in April to give added impetus to the campaign by vigorously targeting 'key corporations, industry sectors and regional areas'. The current mindset of the unions in relation to enterprise bargaining can best be summed up in the descriptive phrase they are using; 'catch and kill your own'.

Since the start of the unions' company by company campaign late last year, it is claimed that agreements have been made in relation to some ninety–six enterprises. The agreements obviously vary from one enterprise to another, but a very common element is a concession to the unions' claim for [a] six per cent wage increase for the period to the end of 1994, 'with the opportunity to negotiate additional increases in that period, depending on various criteria agreed within the enterprise'. The basis of the wage increases vary, although there are a number where the increases are referred to as 'economic adjustments' and are unconditional. On the other hand, more recent agreeements involve wage increases which are in some way linked to improving the productive performance of the enterprise.

However, the unions have boasted in a recent Shop Stewards Newsletter that of the agreement so far negotiated 'the six per cent rises involve no trade–offs, or measured productivity before payment...'

It is fair to say that the union's perception of the six per cent wage increase is that it is payable simply on the basis of allowing the reform process, commenced under the 1991-92 enterprise bargaining round, to continue to be implemented without any new initiatives being introduced to improve the productive performance of the enterprise. This attitude is having a suffocating effect on attempts to achieve genuine outcomes from enterprise bargaining and in many cases amounts to double counting, given that enterprises paid a 4.5 per cent wage increase in 1991–92.

Source: R. Boland, 'The Shift to Enterprise Bargaining: Addressing the Core Issues', Address to IIR Enterprise Bargaining Conference, Hotel Nikko, 21 June 1993, pp. 14-17.

Table 11.11 Business Council of Australia: Council Membership 1992

Alcan Australia Limited
Alcoa of Australia Limited
Amcor Limited
ANZ Banking Group Limited
Australian and Overseas
    Telecommunications Corporation
Australian Gas Light Company
Australian Mutual Provident Society
AWA Limited
BHP Company Limited
Blue Circle Southern Cement Limited
Boral Limited
BP Australia Limited
Bundaberg Sugar Co. Limited
Burns Philp & Co. Limited
Cadbury Schweppes Australia Limited
Caltex Australia Limited
Coca-Cola Amatil Limited
Coles Myer Limited
Colonial Mutual Life Assurance Society
    Limited
Commonwealth Bank of Australia
CRA Limited
CSR Limited
Dalgety Farmers Limited
Dow Chemical (Australia) Limited
Du Pont (Australia) Limited
Email Limited
Esso Australia Limited
FAI Insurance Limited
Ford Motor Company of Australia Limited
Foster's Brewing Group Limited
General Motors Holden's Automotive
    Limited
George Weston Foods Limited
Goodman Fielder Wattie Limited
IBM Australia Limited
ICI Australia Limited
James Hardie Industries Limited
James N. Kirby Pty Limited
Jardine Matheson (Australia) Limited
Kodak Australasia Pty Ltd
Kraft Foods Limited
Leighton Holdings Limited
Lend Lease Corporation Limited
Mayne Nickless Limited
McDonald's Australia Limited
McPherson's Limited
Metal Manufactures Limited
MIM Holdings Limited
Mitsubishi Motors Limited
Mobil Oil Australia Limited
National Australia Bank Limited
National Mutual Life Association of
    Australasia Limited
Newcrest Mining Limited
North Broken Hill Peko Limited
Optus Communications Pty Ltd
P & O Australia Limited
Pacific Dunlop Limited
Pancontinental Mining Limited
Pasminco Limited
Pioneer International Limited
Pratt Industries
Qantas Airways Limited
Renison Goldfields Consolidated Limited
Rothmans Holdings Limited
Santos Limited
Shell Australia Limited
Smorgon Consolidated Industries
South Australian Brewing Holdings
    Limited
Spicers Paper Limited
The Commonwealth Industrial Gases
    Limited
The Seven Network
TNT Limited
Toyota Motor Corporation Australia
    Limited
Tubemakers of Australia Limited
Unilever Australia Limited
United Australian Automotive Industries
    Limited
W.D. & H.O. Wills Holdings Limited
W.G. Goetz & Sons Limited
Wesfarmers Limited
Western Mining Corporation Holdings
    Limited
Westfield Holdings Limited
Westpac Holding Corporation
Woodside Petroleum Limited

Source: Business Council of Australia 1991-92 Annual Report in *Business Council Bulletin*, no. 92, November 1992.

Table 11.12 Australian Chamber of Commerce and Industry: Member Organisations 1992

State/Territory Associations
  Victorian Employers' Chamber of Commerce and Industry
  South Australian Employers' Federation
  Chamber of Commerce and Industry of South Australia
  Chamber of Commerce and Industry of Western Australia
  Northern Territory Chamber of Commerce and Industry
  Queensland Confederation of Industry
  State Chamber of Commerce and Industry (Queensland)
  Employers' Federation of New South Wales
  State Chamber of Commerce (New South Wales)
  Chamber of Manufactures of New South Wales
  Confederation of Australian Capital Territory Industry
  ACT Chamber of Commerce and Industry Ltd
  Tasmanian Confederation of Industries
  Tasmanian Chamber of Commerce

National Industry Associations
  Agricultural and Veterinary Chemicals Association Australia
  Association of Employers of Waterside labour
  Australian Associated Brewers
  Australian Bus and Coach Association
  Australian Chemicals Specialties Manufacturers Association
  Australian Hotels Association
  Australian Maritime Employers' Association
  Australian Mines and Metals Association
  Australian Paint Manufacturers' Federation Inc.
  Australian Sugar Refiners' Industrial Association
  Australian Chemical Industrial Council
  Commonwealth Steamship Owners' Association
  Electrical Contractors' Association of Australia
  Grocery Manufacturers of Australia Ltd
  Housing Industry Association
  Insurance Employers' Industrial Association
  Iron and Steel Industry Association
  Local Government Industrial Association
  Master Builders—Construction & Housing Association Australia
  Meat and Allied Trades Federation of Australia
  Oil Industry Industrial Committee
  Pharmacy Guild of Australia
  Printing and Allied Trades Employers' Federation of Australia
  Retailers Council of Australia
  Victorian Automobile Chamber of Commerce
  Growers' Conciliation and Labour League

Associate Members
  Australian Bankers' Association
  Australian Federation of Construction Contractors
  Australian International Airlines Operations Group

Source: Australian Chamber of Commerce and Industry, *Annual Report* 1991-1992.

Table 11.13 Extract from ACM *Bulletin*

AUSTRALIAN CHAMBER OF MANUFACTURES

MEMBERS URGED TO TAKE A ROLE IN ACM ELECTIONS

I urge all Members to take an active interest in the upcoming elections for ACM National Council.

From Allan Handberg's Desk

The election is being conducted by the Australian Electoral Commission and nominations for all 22 positions are being called in this edition of ACM Bulletin (see page 3).

ACM is your organisation - and the ACM National Council has the decisive role in determining ACM objectives, priorities and strategies.

Your active participation - either by standing for election or by nominating a fellow Member - consequently can assist in establishing ACM's policy and direction.

Within the appropriate categories, all Members of ACM have a right to make nominations and to be nominated and elected.

The full Council meets bi-monthly, but in addition Councillors also may participate in various policy committees and ACM activities.

This year's election is the first under constitutional changes foreshadowed at the time of the 1992 election.

To facilitate continuity in the Council's deliberations, one aspect of these changes provides for an election for half the Councillors each year instead of holding elections for the full Council every two years.

Since this is the first election under the new arrangements, 11 positions on this occasion are for two year terms and 11 for one year.

The Electoral Commission's notice on page 3 sets out further details of the various positions, how to obtain nomination forms and so on.

Members seeking advice about the Industry or Regional Group of their company or other related information should contact Gary Stoneham (03) 698 4347 or Dianne Bloemhoff (03) 698 4396 in Melbourne, Brian Martin (02) 372 0430 or Mark Fogarty (02) 372 0490 in Sydney, or their ACM Branch Manager. ▲

Allan Handberg

National Chief Executive

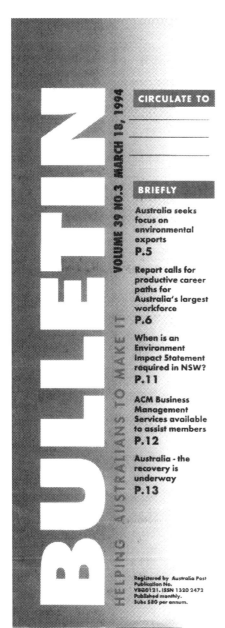

The Deputy Leader of the Opposition, Dr Michael Wooldridge, was a guest at this week's ACM luncheon for Chief Executives of member companies.

Pictured (from left): Norman Tims, Chairman and Managing Director, Charles Tims Pty Ltd; Ken Windle, Managing Director, Glaxo Australia Pty Ltd; Roger Pickford, Managing Director, Bush Boake Allen Australia Ltd; Anita Roper, National Manager, Strategy and Industry Policy, ACM; Dr. Michael Wooldridge and Allan Handberg, National Chief Executive, ACM.

Source: ACM *Bulletin*, volume 39, No. 3, March 18, 1994, p. 1.

12

Federal Labour Law

Contents

Constitutional power
Other consitutional heads of power
- trade and commerce power
- the corporations power
- the external affairs power
- the defence power
- the public service
- the Territories power
- the 'incidentals' power

Commonwealth law regulating industrial relations
Institutions
The power of the Australian Industrial Relations Commission
- industrial disputes
- the question of the matter in dispute
- the requirement that a dispute 'extend beyond the limits of any one State'
- the question of parties
- ambit of the award

Conciliation and arbitration: legal procedures
The award
Agreements
Enforcement of awards and agreements
Interaction of contract and award
Awards and collective bargaining
National wage cases
Registration of associations

Introduction

Australia, being a federation of states, has a Commonwealth Parliament with express power to make laws conferred on it under the Constitution of the Commonwealth of Australia, and each state has its own separate express lawmaking powers under its state constitution. The Commonwealth Constitution contains a specific power with respect to labour relations, s.51(35), which gives the Commonwealth Parliament power to make laws with respect to:

'conciliation and arbitration for the prevention and settlement of industrial disputes extending beyond the limits of any one state'.

Whilst the federal parliament has this power to make laws with respect to labour relations, this power is not one which is conferred exclusively on the federal parliament. The parliament of each state in Australia concurrently holds power to make laws relating to labour relations. In Victoria, for example, the parliament has the power to make laws with respect to and for the good government of Victoria. There is no express power in respect of labour relations. However this broad power does enable the parliament to make laws with respect to labour relations. Each state within Australia has chosen to make such laws. As a result, there are several systems of dispute resolution in Australia, one at Commonwealth level and one in each of the states of Australia. They are separate and distinct systems. However, over the years, the state parliaments have tended to follow the model established under the legislation made by the federal parliament, so that state parliaments have established conciliation and arbitration systems even though the state parliaments are not confined by the terms which are express in s.51(35) of the Commonwealth Constitution.

This chapter examines the origin of the federal power with respect to labour relations, the scope of that power and the reasons for the development and operation of the system. Approximately forty per cent of Australian employees are covered by Federal Awards—the rest being covered by awards of State Industrial Tribunals or in so-called 'award free' areas. However, the federal system has tended to be dominant for two reasons: the first is that if there is a clash between a federal and state award, the federal award will prevail to the extent of inconsistency;[1] and secondly state industrial tribunals have tended to follow the lead of the federal tribunal, in particular in following the principles of *National Wage* cases.[2]

Constitutional power

The main power, however, which the Commonwealth Parliament has to make laws with relation to labour relations as indicated is contained in s.51(35). From an examination of the words of this section, it can be seen that the very processes by which industrial disputes are to be settled is enshrined in the Constitution—s.51(35) refers expressly to 'conciliation' and 'arbitration'. Why was this method for dispute resolution chosen and why was it expressed in the Australian Constitution? Why was the new Commonwealth not given power to make laws with respect to collective bargaining or to enact legislation proclaiming minimum pay and conditions? Why indeed was there an express power inserted in the Commonwealth Constitution in respect of labour relations? Why had the colonies already begun to make laws with respect to industrial regulation?

These questions can be answered by reference to the thinking of the (so-called) forefathers at the time of the deliberations taking place in Australia, which spanned most of the 1890s, to determine the establishment of the new Commonwealth Parliament. Representatives from the then colonies of Australia gathered together to debate the question of federation and what powers the new federal parliament should have. The strikes of the 1890s are thought to have been influential in the decision to include an express power in the Constitution giving the federal parliament power to make laws with respect to labour relations. Strikes had taken place in the maritime and shearing industries; these strikes had gone beyond the boundaries of any single state colony and the concern of some of the constitutional forefathers was to ensure that the Commonwealth Parliament had power to make laws to settle disputes which were beyond the control of any one state. In other words, the concern was that the federal parliament should have power to settle disputes which were interstate in nature. The problem of course was to determine what the method for dispute settlement should be.

The New Zealand Parliament had already established a system of compulsory conciliation and arbitration[3] and it was perceived as providing a good model for the resolution of industrial disputes. It is said that 'During those last years of the nineteenth century New Zealand was viewed by the world as a progressive social laboratory. Visitors and overseas audiences sought information about the substance, implementation, and operation of major reforms, particularly in labour areas. ... The *Industrial Conciliation and Arbitration Act* 1894 was another key part of those social and industrial reforms.'[4] Voluntary mediation which had been tried in some of the Australian colonies was also regarded as having failed. In this context, it was thought that a process of conciliation should be used and if that was not successful there should be legal power in respect of arbitration.

Hence, without a great deal of debate, the constitutional forefathers ultimately adopted conciliation and arbitration as a method of interstate industrial dispute settlement. The particular form of the power was proposed by Henry Bourne Higgins, later to become the second President of the Court of Conciliation and Arbitration. However, this power was only adopted by the resolution of the constitutional forefathers in its third attempt, and then only by a majority of twenty-two to nineteen votes. The reluctance concerned not the form of process for the resolution of industrial disputes but the question to what extent a federal parliament should have such powers—the concern was that state rights would be ignored or downgraded. When the Constitution Act was enacted, s.51(35) in the form outlined above was included.[5]

Although s.51(35) was seen as the main power with respect to making laws for labour relations in Australia, there are other powers in the Constitution which have enabled parliament to make laws with respect to labour relations from time to time. These are broader powers relating to corporations where under s.51(20) of the Constitution the Commonwealth Parliament has power to make laws with respect to 'foreign corporations and trading or financial corporations within the limits of the Commonwealth'; there is also the trade and commerce power under s.51(1) of the Constitution which gives the Commonwealth Parliament power to make laws with respect to 'trade and commerce with other countries, and among the states'. These powers have been used from time to time to regulate industrial relations in the waterfront, maritime and airline industries in Australia and also to enact provisions such as s.45D of *Trade Practices Act* 1974 (Cth). There is further the external affairs power, the Territories power and the defence power.[6]

Other constitutional heads of power

Whilst s.51(35), together with s.51(39) of the Constitution (the 'incidentals power' discussed further below), have been of fundamental importance in moulding the legal framework of Australian industrial relations, other heads of power have from time to time been used to control labour relations at federal level and may be utilised more fully in the future.

Trade and commerce power

Section 51(1) gives the Commonwealth Parliament power to make laws with respect to 'trade and commerce with other countries, and among the States'.

This power has been used to regulate industrial relations in the following industries: maritime, airlines, waterfront. It has enabled direct regulation of such industries without the limitations of the s.51(35) and in particular without the need to establish 'interstate disputes'.

The secondary boycott provisions in the *Trade Practices Act* relied in part on the trade and commerce power.[7] These have now been transferred to Part 6 Div 7 of the *Industrial Relations Act* 1988 (Cth) and continue to make use of the trade and commerce power.

The corporations power

Section 51(20) gives the Commonwealth Parliament power to make laws with respect to 'the foreign corporations and trading or financial corporations formed within the limits of the Commonwealth'.

The use of this power to regulate labour relations has not to date been extensive but it has been used in some important areas.

Section 45D of the *Trade Practices Act* 1974 (Cth) relied heavily on the corporations power and the transfer of the boycott provisions to the *Industrial Relations Act* 1988 (Cth) has made use of the concept of the 'constitutional corporation' to proscribe boycott conduct. The independent contractor provisions in the *Industrial Relations Act* 1988 (Cth) whereby there was power (formerly in the Commission now in the Industrial Relations Court) to review the fairness of contracts between independent contractors, and foreign, trading or financial corporations,[8] relies on the corporations power.

The *Industrial Relations Reform Act* 1993 (Cth) has made use of the corporations power to enable enterprise flexibility agreements to be made and implemented between groups of employees and constitutional corporations, as defined. Thus, the use of the corporations power from the end of March 1994 has been extensive to promote enterprise bargaining and agreements.

The external affairs power

The power to make laws with respect to 'external affairs' is given to the Commonwealth Parliament in s.51(29) of the Constitution.

This power was not used extensively in labour relations until 1994. The *Racial Discrimination Act* 1975 (Cth) was enacted using the external affairs power to give effect to the *International Convention on the Elimination of All Forms of Racial Discrimination*. The *Sex Discrimination Act* 1984 (Cth) also used the external affairs power to bring in international standards in the field of sex discrimination.

The *Industrial Relations Reform Act* 1993 (Cth) utilises the external affairs power to give effect to International Labour Organisation Conventions (to which Australia is a signatory or has ratified) in the areas of minimum wages, equal pay for equal work, termination of employment and unfair dismissal and parental leave. Thus, it has been used in a novel way in Australian labour relations law to introduce a floor of rights or the potential for uniform conditions to be declared. This represents quite a radical departure from previous government legislation in the field—which tended to rely mainly on s.51(35) of the Constitution and to leave the declaration of standards to the Commission through dispute settling powers. The extent to which this power will be able to validly sustain legislative proscription of minimum standards by the Commonwealth Parliament remains to be seen as its constitutional validity is the subject of challenge. It has been thought that since the *Tasmanian Dams* case[9] the Parliament can make laws to give effect to international conventions by using the external affairs power.

The defence power

Section 51(6) of the Consitution gives the Commonwealth Parliament power to enact laws with respect to 'the naval and military defence of the Commonwealth and of the several States, and the control of the forces to execute and maintain the laws of the Commonwealth'. This power has been used to directly legislate for wages in war time and beyond.

The public service

Section 52 of the Constitution gives the Commonwealth Parliament exclusive power to legislate in respect of Commonwealth employees. Section 52 provides:

> 'The Parliament shall, subject to this Constitution, have exclusive power to make laws for the peace, order, and good government of the Commonwealth with respect to—
> ...
> (ii) Matters relating to any department of the Public Services the control of which is by this Constitution transferred to the Executive Government of the Commonwealth.'

This power enacted the *Public Service Act* 1922 (Cth), and the provisions in the *Industrial Relations Act* 1988 (Cth) now apply to public servants, shorn of the need to satisfy jurisdictional requirements as required by s.51(35).

The Territories power

Section 122 of the Constitution provides:

> 'The Parliament may make laws for the government of any territory surrendered by any State to and accepted by the Commonwealth, or of any territory placed by the Queen under the authority of and accepted by the Commonwealth, or otherwise acquired by the Commonwealth, and may allow the representation of such territory in either House of the Parliament to the extent and on the terms which it thinks fit.'

Some parts of the *Industrial Relations Act* use the territories power—e.g. s.141 enables common rules to be made by the Commission in respect of the Territories. Further, disputes in the Territories do not have to meet the other requirements of s. 51(35): there is no need to establish 'interstateness' and industrial disputes.

The 'incidentals' power

The Commonwealth Parliament has power in s.51(39) to make laws with respect to:

> 'Matters incidental to the execution of any power vested by this Constitution in the Parliament or in either House thereof, of the Government of the Commonwealth, or in the Federal Judicature, or in any department or office of the Commonwealth.'

This power has been used, together with s.51(35) of the Constitution to regulate trade unions: to provide for trade union registration, provision of legal status trade union registration, the working of union elections and so on.[10]

Commonwealth law regulating industrial relations

It was in 1904 that the Conciliation and Arbitration Act was first enacted. H.B. Higgins, who was not only influential in the federation debates as to the form of the federal labour power but who became the second President of the Court of Conciliation and Arbitration and a judge of the High Court of Australia, wrote in his collection of essays, 'A New Province for Law and Order',[11] that the aim of this new legislation was to replace 'the rude and barbarous processes of strikes and lock-outs' with a system which established the resolution of industrial disputes by formal mechanisms. The system which was established has often been described as one of 'compulsory arbitration'. The main emphasis of the dispute settlement process was to be on conciliation —the newly established Court of Conciliation and Arbitration would endeavour to resolve any dispute reported to it by conciliation, a form of mediation. If a settlement was not reached, the Court would arbitrate the matter. The original idea was that the emphasis would be on conciliation, with arbitration playing a background role.[12] Once a determination of the Court was made, the award was legally enforceable (hence the compulsory nature of the arbitration), and both employer and employee would be bound by the terms of the particular award.

The *Conciliation and Arbitration Act* 1904 was operative for some eight and a half decades, although it was amended on numerous occasions over this period of time. On 1 March 1989, the *Industrial Relations Act* 1988 (Cth) became operative. This legislation provided for some major changes with respect to Australian labour relations but there was no change in the formal method of resolving disputes by conciliation and arbitration. This Act has in turn been amended to promote and facilitate bargaining and major amendments were made by the *Industrial Relations Reform Act* 1993 (Cth) operative from 30 March 1994.

Institutions

The first tribunal to be established by the *Conciliation and Arbitration Act* 1904 (Cth) was the Court of Conciliation and Arbitration. It was set up to settle interstate industrial disputes by the process of conciliation and arbitration. The functions of the Court were to make awards, either by means of conciliation or arbitration, which would bind employers and employees, or unions which represented employees. In addition to the award-making function, the Court was given the power to enforce awards and interpret awards. Thus, the Court was maker of industrial awards and interpreter and enforcer of those awards.

However, in 1959, the *Conciliation and Arbitration Act* was amended to separate these functions and to give responsibility to different bodies for those functions. This followed a decision of the High Court and the Privy Council in the *Boilermakers'* case[13] which decided that because of the constraints in the Constitution, a Court which was established under Chapter 3 of the Constitution could only perform judicial functions (those functions which were involved in the interpretation and enforcement of awards) and could not also perform arbitral functions (which were involved in the making of awards). The Industrial Court was then established to exercise judicial functions, whilst the arbitral functions were transferred to a newly established Conciliation and Arbitration Commission.[14] Whilst the names of these institutions have changed, the two functions remain performed by separate bodies.

The arbitral functions are now performed by the Australian Industrial Relations Commission, which replaced the Conciliation and Arbitration Commission by the enactment of the *Industrial Relations Act* 1988 (Cth).

The Australian Industrial Relations Commission is presided over by the President who is required by the Act to hold the qualifications necessary for judicial appointment, as well as the appropriate skills and experience in industrial relations. There is provision for appointment of two Vice-Presidents. The President is assisted by a group of Senior Deputy Presidents and Deputy Presidents who like the Vice-Presidents may be legally qualified, but are required to hold appropriate training and experience in industrial relations.[15] The other members of the Commission are Commissioners who are appointed on the basis of their skills and experience in the field.

The President, Vice-Presidents, Senior Deputy Presidents and Deputy Presidents are known as 'presidential members', have the same rank and status as a judge of the Industrial Relations Court of Australia (formerly Federal Court) and may be called 'The Honourable'. It is suggested that this status of presidential members owes its existence to the former Court of Conciliation and Arbitration and that when the functions were divided those who were appointed to the Commission only could not be seen to be 'inferior' to their judicial colleagues in the Industrial Court.[16] Indeed until 1972, legal qualifications were necessary for appointment to the position of Deputy President, and after that date only the President is required to be a lawyer. However, the trappings and status of judicial appointment are retained in the rank and styling of the judges.

The Commission now has a separate Bargaining Division established under Part VIB, Division 5 of the Act. The Division is presided over by a Vice-President and other members of the Commission who have been assigned to it. The Division generally performs functions of conciliation in respect of enterprise agreements, ensures the parties are bargaining in good faith and facilitates the making of agreements.

The Registrar is appointed to deal with and oversee administrative matters relating to the Act.

From 1976 to 1994, the Federal Court of Australia performed the judicial functions after the enactment of the *Federal Court of Australia Act* 1976 (Cth) which established the Federal Court of Australia and transferred the Industrial Court's jurisdiction to the new Federal Court. The Federal Court did not have exclusive jurisdiction in labour law for its jurisdiction also included matters such as administrative law, tax, and trade practices. In industrial law matters it could deal with questions of law arising under federal awards which are referred to it; it could hear and adjudicate on enforcement proceedings instituted by employers or employees or unions; it could make rulings on irregularities of trade union elections or union membership and had a jurisdiction to deal with offences under the *Industrial Relations Act*. These functions in industrial law were transferred on 30 March 1994 to a newly-established specialist labour court, the Industrial Relations Court of Australia, presided over by Justice Wilcox of the Federal Court of Australia. A significant point is that, although the Industrial Relations Court (and Federal Court before it) does not have jurisdiction to deal with the merits of any industrial dispute, the court is and has been influential in the matters already delineated in federal labour relations law.

There can be an appeal from decisions of the Industrial Relations Court to the highest court of judicial authority in Australia, the High Court of Australia, only with the leave of the court. However, the High Court of Australia is, and has been, important in Australian federal labour relations law because of its powers in interpreting s.51(35) of the Constitution and the federal industrial relations legislation enacted pursuant to it. The High Court deals with questions whether the Australian Industrial Relations Commission has validly taken jurisdiction over a dispute and whether it has acted within its jurisdiction. The High Court cannot adjudicate on the merits of an industrial dispute or whether the Commission has settled the matter appropriately. However, the High Court, through its original jurisdiction contained in the Constitution,[17] has shaped and moulded the legal framework in which Australian Industrial Relations operate today. This legal framework is discussed below.

The power of the Australian Industrial Relations Commission

(a)   Industrial disputes

Section 51(35) of the Constitution has limited the Federal Parliament's power to make laws with respect to 'industrial disputes'. This expression in turn has been defined in the relevant industrial legislation enacted pursuant to this power. However, the main substance to the definition has been given by the High Court in its interpretation of this expression in both the Constitution and Act. The Commission can only validly take jurisdiction over a dispute which falls within this definition of 'industrial dispute'. The concept of industrial dispute is relevant also to the making of certified agreements.

The early view

A very significant decision occurred in 1908 in the case of the *Jumbunna Coal Mine No Liability v Victorian Coal Miners' Association*[18] when a question arose as to whether a union with members in one state only, the Victorian Coalminers Association, could register as an organisation under the provisions of the *Conciliation and Arbitration Act* 1904. In the course of the decision in which the court held such an association could be registered and that the registration provisions were a valid exercise of s.51(35) and s.51(39) (the incidentals power) of the Constitution, the members of the High Court considered the definition of industrial dispute. Their Honours interpreted this expression broadly. Griffith CJ held: 'An industrial dispute exists where a considerable number of employees engaged in some branch of industry make common excuse in demanding from or reprising to their employers (whether one or more) some change in the conditions of employment which is denied to them or asked of them.'[19] O'Connor J stated: '"Industrial dispute" was not, when the Constitution was framed, a technical or legal expression. It had not then, nor has it now, an acquired meaning. It meant just what the two English words in their ordinary meaning conveyed to ordinary persons, and the meaning of these words seems to be now much what it was then.'[20]

However, from the late 1920s a narrowing of this expression occurred over the years because the High Court interpolated a notion that an industrial dispute, within the meaning of the Constitution, had to be a dispute in an 'industry', thereby excluding certain professions, such as school teachers,[21] and certain employees of governments, such as fire-fighters,[22] and clerical workers in the New South Wales Department of Motor Registration.[23]

Various tests or definitions of 'industrial dispute' were used by the High Court over the years until 1983. These included:

i The capital and labour test

In the *Municipalities* case,[24] the High Court held the labourers employed by local government could be covered by a federal award because they were engaged in an 'industrial dispute' with their employers. Isaacs and Rich JJ held that 'Industrial disputes occur when, in relation to operations in which capital and labour are contributed in co-operation for the satisfaction of human wants or desires, those engaged in co-operation dispute as to the basis to be observed, by the parties engaged, respecting either a share of the product or any other terms and conditions of their co-operation'.[25]

This test enabled employees such as journalists[26] to come under federal awards, but excluded school teachers employed by state education authorities as the capital and labour test was not relevant to public education.

ii Incidental to industry

Insurance and banking clerks[27] were regarded as providing services which were essential or incidental to industry and so would come under federal awards, as were employees of credit unions.[28]

iii Two-tier test relating to work of employee and work of employer

In the *Professional Engineers'* case[29] Dixon CJ proposed two tests for determining whether there was an industrial dispute. In essence, the work of the employee was to be examined first: if the work was of a manual nature, the employee could be engaged in an industrial dispute, regardless of the nature of the employer's business. If the employee's work was 'neutral' in the sense that it did not lead to the conclusion that it could be involved in an industrial pursuit, the employer's business or undertaking should be examined: if the employer's business was 'an undertaking for some productive purpose or some purpose of transportation and distribution'[30] then the worker could be involved in an 'industrial dispute'.

Applying these tests, some employees were excluded from federal award coverage: firefighters;[31] university academics;[32] employees of the NSW Department of Motor Transport;[33] employees of credit unions.[34]

Return of the broader view

However, in 1983, the High Court reverted to the broad definition given in the *Jumbunna* case. In the *Australian Social Welfare Union* case,[35] a case which is regarded as revolutionary in its application because of its impact and overturning of previous High Court authority. The High Court held that any dispute between an employer and employee about the terms and conditions of employment would be regarded as an industrial dispute—the definition was neither to be technical or legal in its expression and should have the meaning which a person in the street would give it. The Court reviewed all the previous case law in the area and expressly rejected the notion that industrial dispute was confined to dispute in industry. The previous cases involving these definitions were overturned and *State School Teachers* case was expressly overruled.

This broad definition of industrial dispute gives the Australian Commission reasonably wide powers over most Australian employers and employees. There is one area however which remains open for future resolution and possibly restriction of the broad view. In the *Australian Social Welfare Union* case, the High Court left open the question whether those persons involved in what it called the 'administrative services of the state' could be involved in an industrial dispute. It had always been a difficult question to determine the extent to which the Federal labour power should encroach on state government employees. Despite Dixon CJ in the *Professional Engineers'* case stating that 'That which is naturally within s.51(35) cannot cease to be so because it is governmental',[36] various government employees *were* excluded (e.g. state school teachers and clerical workers in the NSW government department).

If the expression 'administrative services of the state' is interpreted broadly to mean most state government employees, then naturally the potential for the coverage of the federal labour power is more limited. However in the case of *Re Lee; Ex parte Harper*,[37] concerning registration of teachers' unions, the High Court decided that school teachers, even though they were employed by state government Education Departments, would be able to be engaged in an industrial dispute. Although a final definition of administrative services of the state was not given, the High Court suggested that the relevant test would be whether the constitutional integrity of the states would be affected by a federal award covering state employees. To date, this question has not been resolved, although in the *State Public Service Federation* case the Court seemed to adopt a view in keeping with that of *Re Lee; Ex parte Harper* about the constitutional integrity of the state.

Today, most employees would be able to be engaged in an 'industrial dispute' within the definition of the Act and the Constitution. The question may concern a very small group of state government employees, for example senior officials within State Treasury Departments, as to whether federal awards could apply to these people. These questions remain for future resolution and are most important in states where employees wish to move to federal award coverage because of dissatisfaction with the state system.[38]

(b) The question of the matter in dispute

'Industrial disputes' as defined in s.4(1) of the *Industrial Relations Act* 1988 (Cth) mean disputes 'about matters pertaining to the relations of employers and employees'. In the original definition in the *Conciliation and Arbitration Act*, there were enumerated in paragraphs various examples of what were industrial matters, as they were then known.[39] Despite the definition having on its face a broad meaning, the High Court has held that not every matter which is or might be the subject of dispute between employers and employees comprise subject matter over which the Commission will be able to validly exercise its jurisdiction or include in industrial awards or agreements.

One of the main problems over the years has been the extent to which issues which might encroach on prerogatives of management or areas which are regarded as being within the sole domain of management could come within an industrial award. For example, trading hours of a business might be regarded as being something which the employer should determine and not be the subject of any agreement or arbitrated award between employers and employees.[40] The notion of managerial prerogatives was seen to underpin many decisions of the High Court and operate to exclude some matters from awards. In recent times, matters such as staffing levels, or whether technological change should be introduced into the workplace without prior consultation, have been regarded as being matters pertaining to the employer/employee relationship and therefore arbitral matters. There has been a whittling down of the concept of managerial prerogative. The view which the High Court now adopts on this matter is that to focus on whether the matter is a prerogative of management may be asking in effect the wrong question—the question is whether the matter pertains in a direct, and not consequential, way to the relationship of employer as employer and employee as employee.[41]

What matters has the High Court decided are matters pertaining to the relationship of employer and employee? These include issues about the level of staffing of employees within an employer's business;[42] obligations imposed on an employer to make contributions to superannuation schemes;[43] matters relating to the preferential employment of unionists over non-unionists.

There are, however, many matters which the High Court has decided are not matters pertaining to the employer/employee relationship. These include a system of deduction of union dues from salary to be paid to the union;[44] provisions which compel employers to make superannuation payments in respect of non-unionists to a nominated superannuation fund;[45] and disputes about compulsory unionism.[46] It would seem also that matters relating to some political issues may not be able to be arbitrated upon and matters which perhaps affect general environmental considerations rather than the health and safety of the workforce may not also be the subject of awards.

One of the areas which has troubled the High Court is whether the Australian Commission can make awards reinstating workers who are regarded as being unfairly dismissed. This has been a source of jurisdictional difficulty because the view was taken by the High Court that disputes about fairness of dismissal and whether employees should be reinstated were disputes about the relationship between persons who were former employers and ex-employees,[47] the employer-employee relationship having ended with the dismissal. However, there were additional problems concerning jurisdiction in respect of these types of matters, including whether an interstate dispute was involved and whether the Commission would be exercising judicial and not arbitral powers. In recent times the High Court has held that where disputes about dismissal and reinstatement have an impact on the security of employment for any remaining employees then the definition of matter will be fulfilled.[48] Some recent decisions of the High Court have confirmed that the Commission may be able to exercise powers to reinstate an unfairly dismissed worker.[49] However reforms in 1993 to the *Industrial Relations Act* have largely overcome this problem in any event as the Industrial Relations Court has been given reinstatement powers in respect of unlawful termination and the Commission may conciliate first to try to resolve the matter.[50]

Another area which caused problems was whether employers and employees could have provisions in an award dealing with rates of pay for independent contractors. Again, the difficulty was that an independent contractor was not an employee and could not therefore be directly regulated by an industrial award. There were difficulties then as to whether the employer and the union could be bound in respect of persons who were not directly parties to an award—could an award prohibit employers from engaging independent contractors except on certain terms and conditions? This question is an important one for unions and employees who see that their security of employment might be threatened by employers engaging contractors more cheaply. The question was answered in the negative by the High Court.[51] The *Industrial Relations Act* was amended in 1992 to enable the Australian Commission (and now the Industrial Relations Court of Australia) to review the fairness of contracts made with independent contractors. But, on the current state of the law, it still does remain a matter outside the province of the Commission to determine directly by industrial award.

Given that not all matters in dispute between employer and employee can validly be the subject of a federal award, some issues must be left to the parties themselves to resolve and be the subject of agreement. If an agreement dealing with such issues which are not regarded as matters relating to the employment relationship is made, the agreement cannot be certified under the Act as the agreement provisions are circumscribed by the requirement that they be about 'matters'. If the agreement cannot be certified there may be problems of enforcement.

The wide scope of matters included in the contents of the federal *Nurses (Victorian Health Services) Award* 1992 in Appendix A indicates the very wide range of arbitral matters which are usually included in some detail in federal awards.

(c) The requirement that a dispute 'extend beyond the limits of any one state'

It will be recalled that one of the concerns of the founders of the federation was that there should be a mechanism whereby disputes which were truly interstate in nature could be resolved at Commonwealth level. The concern of those wanting to forward or promote the interests of states' rights was that such a federal power would be used to encroach on states' rights. As it has turned out, the interstateness requirement is fairly easily fulfilled or satisfied by the device of the creation of a 'paper dispute', the legality of which has been accepted by the High Court. Thus, the fears of those wishing to preserve state rights have been well-founded.

Section 4(1) of the *Industrial Relations Act* defines 'industrial dispute' to include a dispute 'extending beyond the limits of any one state' and also a situation that is likely to give rise to an industrial dispute extending beyond limits of any one state. What disputes will fulfil these requirements? A national dispute which traverses the several Australian states will meet this requirement. Also, if the dispute is seen on its face as a local dispute but in reality is part of an interstate dispute of an ongoing nature—for example a demarcation dispute which might surface at any one site and is part of an ongoing problem—this is regarded as fulfilling the interstateness requirement.[52]

By far the most common way for the parties to initiate an interstate dispute is to serve a log of claims including a set of demands on employers in more than one state. When the employers fail to comply with any or all of the demands, a dispute arises and it is generally regarded as an interstate dispute. There is then no need for direct industrial action on the part of union or employees—it is all created on paper,[53] hence the term 'paper dispute'. However the High Court has developed a notion which has the potential for sifting out disputes which are not genuinely interstate but which are intrastate disputes created *solely* for the purpose of attracting the jurisdiction of the Australian Commission. The notion of 'genuineness' was used in the case of *R v Gough; Ex parte BP Refinery Pty Ltd*[54] where the High Court regarded the dispute as a single dispute in Victoria and not extending beyond the limits of any one state, even though the paper dispute appeared to be interstate. A log of claims had been served on BP Refinery (Westernport) Pty Ltd which was engaged in refining of petroleum products and a few (of many of the hundreds of) agents who were engaged in distribution of petroleum products interstate. It was decided by the court that the interests of the agents and of BP would be quite different—in effect they were not part of the same industry and there was not truly or genuinely an interstate dispute. The issue has arisen more recently in the *Aberdeen* case[55] where the court revived a notion of community interest to determine where there would indeed be an interstate dispute. In this case, employers in NSW, Queensland and South Australia were served with a log of claims which they rejected. The employers were owners and operators of meat processing establishments, of which twenty-three were in NSW, six in Queensland and one in South Australia. The employers engaged in slightly different activities from each other. The range of activities included abattoirs, boning, ham and bacon manufacturing and retail butchers shops. The employers suggested that the real aim of the log was to bring the NSW employees, who were covered by NSW awards, under federal awards and that the real dispute was in NSW only. The High Court held that there was a real and genuine interstate dispute because the dispute was in a single industry, the meat processing industry, and the union genuinely intended to pursue the demands interstate.

(d)   The question of parties

Once an award is made, the parties to the dispute normally become parties to the award.[56] The award binds those parties in much the same way as a contract would bind the parties to the contract. It would be thought that once an award was made in a particular industry binding the parties to the dispute, it would be easy to extend the terms and conditions contained to the whole of the industry, to make the award a common rule throughout industry. However, the High Court has held that s.51(35) of the Constitution does not enable the Commonwealth Parliament to legislate to give the Commission power to make a common rule.

Section 38(f) was once contained in the *Conciliation and Arbitration Act* permitting awards to be made common rules, but was declared by the High Court to be beyond power in *Whybrow's* case.[57] The reasoning of the court was that the notion of arbitration meant that there had to be parties to a dispute: if the award were to extend to persons who were not in dispute this would be beyond the arbitral power. Thus a common rule is not possible within the Federal system, although the states do not have the same constitutional constraints and common rules are generally permitted in the state industrial relations systems. The common rule is only available to parties in the territories by virtue of the Parliament's use of the power to make laws with respect to territories which is contained in the Constitution. *De facto*, a common rule can prevail because unions can ensure that they serve a log of claims on *all* relevant employers who are in the industry and the employer association to which employers belong. This method ensures there will be extensive coverage of the award. *De facto* then there will be a common rule, but it is more costly and less efficient for the parties.[58]

Section 149 of the *Industrial Relations Act* 1988 (Cth) provides that members of organisations which are parties to the award or agreement are parties to the award or agreement. This means that unionists who are members of a trade union, which is a party to the award or agreement, are themselves parties to that award or agreement, and employers which belong to an employer association which is bound, are also parties. This situation prevails so long as the individual employer or employee is a member of the relevant association (unless of course the employer has been separately served with a log of claims and becomes in its own right a party to the dispute and then the award).

The non-unionist

The position of non-unionists within federal labour law is curious. A non-unionist is technically not a party to the award. The union which initiates claims represents present or future members but does not represent non-unionists, so they will not be bound by an award. In an extremely important decision of the High Court in 1935, the *Metal Trades* case,[59] it was held that although non-unionists would not be parties to an award, an award could be made binding employers and employees as to the terms and conditions on which non-unionists could be employed. The High Court decided that the unionists would have an industrial interest in the terms and conditions on which non-unionists would be employed. These principles were reiterated more recently in the *Re Finance Sector Union* case.[60]

The *Metal Trades* case leads to the curious result that whilst non-unionists are not parties to the award they can receive the benefit of the terms and conditions of an award. An employer is under a duty to comply with the award in respect of non-unionists (so long as the terms of the award cover unionists) but the non-unionists have no rights themselves under the award. This ordinarily would mean that the non-unionists cannot enforce the awards themselves but an employer would be in breach of an award if the non-unionist did not receive the appropriate pay under the award. However, by statutory amendment in 1991, the *Industrial Relations Act* now permits, by s.178(5)(ca), the non-unionist who is entitled to the benefits of an award to institute proceedings to enforce an award. Today, therefore, the non-unionist does not suffer the disadvantage of not being able to directly enforce the award but legally the non-unionist still remains not a party to the award.

The same principles in relation to parties to and non-unionists apply to certified agreements.[61] However, it should be noted, given the different nature of enterprise flexibility agreements which do not have the same dependence as a matter of practice on unions or the same jurisdictional requirements as awards or certified agreements, s.149(4) of the federal Act provides that an enterprise flexibility agreement will bind each employee of the corporation covered by the agreement. Thus, a non-unionist employee may be a party to the agreement in his or her own right and not simply by virtue of union membership.

(e) Ambit of the award

The notion of ambit is an important one in jurisdictional terms for the Australian Commission. The award can only be made within the ambit or the four corners of the industrial dispute. The log of claims, then, serves another purpose—that of defining the scope of the original industrial dispute. If there is no ambit or insufficient ambit for the industrial award the Commission cannot validly make an award, or if it does, the legality of the award may be challenged subsequently by either party. This means that a demand for wages of $500 per week cannot be settled by arbitration of an amount in excess of $500 per week; or a clause dealing with staffing levels cannot be inserted where there was no demand or dispute about this matter originally.

In the case of *Re Bain; Ex parte Cadbury Schweppes*,[62] it was suggested that the notion of ambit is more important in the case of arbitration rather than conciliation. If this is so, then where the dispute proceeds to arbitration the ambit will have to be set out fairly precisely. It seems logical that in the case of conciliation the same attention to the scope of the dispute is not given because the nature of the ambit of the dispute may be able to be 'reworked' by the parties during the course of conciliation. Further if the aim of conciliation is amicable resolution of the dispute, then it would not be sensible to allow a rigid, technical view of ambit to stand in the way of a settlement.

Recently, the High Court has developed the notion of 'industrial reality' in relation to ambit. The doctrine of ambit has been seen as resulting in outrageous or at least ambitious demands because of the need for the one log to sustain an award and as many variations of that award as possible. If one log containing all the demands imaginable is served in order to sustain many variations, this has obvious implications for cost and efficiency.

However, in *Re State Public Services Federation; Ex parte Attorney-General (WA)*[63] the High Court decided that claims for wages of $5000 per week for all employees, plus an allowance of $2500 per week to be indexed to changes in the cost of living, was so extravagant as to lack industrial reality. The court took the view that what was really being sought was for the Commission to exercise a general power of industrial regulation which it cannot do because of constitutional and statutory constraints.

Conciliation and arbitration: legal procedures

The *Industrial Relations Act* 1988 (Cth) lays down some of the procedures to be followed.[64]

Once the Commission has determined that there is an 'industrial dispute' within the meaning of the Act, it shall make a dispute finding pursuant to section 101 of the *Industrial Relations Act* 1988 (Cth), determining who are the parties to the industrial dispute and the matters in dispute. The Commission is under an obligation to attempt to settle the dispute by conciliation—unless the relevant Presidential Member is 'satisfied that it would not assist the prevention or settlement of the alleged industrial dispute'.[65] Conciliation can take the form of conferences amongst the parties and their representatives in the absence of the Commission or such conferences may be presided over by the member of the Commission.[66] If the parties have reached an agreement or there is no likelihood of reaching agreement, the conciliation phase will have ended[67] and the matter will be referred to arbitration.[68] The same member of the Commission who was involved in the conciliation phase will arbitrate unless one of the parties to the proceeding objects.[69]

Usually, a single member of the Commission will exercise the powers of the Commission,[70] but some important matters have been made the province of a Full Bench of the Commission: these include matters relating to general conditions such as standard hours of work, or minimum wages on grounds relating to the economy or without report to work performed or the industry in which the workers are employed,[71] hence National Wage decisions are undertaken by a Full Bench.[72] The Full Bench may also have matters referred to it[73] and acts as an appellate body from decisions of single members of the Commission.[74]

The Commission is charged under the Act with the function of preventing and settling industrial disputes by conciliation and arbitration[75] but it is not a responsibility which can be exercised in any way the Commission thinks fit. In performing its functions, the Commission must take into account the public interest,[76] including the objects of the Act and state of the national economy and the likely effect of the decision on the economy, in particular inflation and the level of employment;[77] the principles in the *Racial Discrimination Act* 1975 (Cth), the *Sex Discrimination Act* 1984 (Cth) and the *Disability Discrimination Act* 1992 (Cth);[78] the provisions of State or Territory laws with regard to safety, health and welfare of employees in relation to their employment.[79] The Commission is under an obligation to perform its functions as quickly as possible;[80] it is not bound to act in a formal manner; it is not bound by the rules of evidence—it may inform itself on any matter in such manner as it considers just; it shall 'act according to equity, good conscience and the substantial merits of the case without regard to technicalities and legal forms';[81] and it may require evidence to be presented in writing or orally.[82]

There are also particular powers of the Commission, for example, to take evidence on oath or affirmation, to give directions in the course of or for the purpose of, the hearing or determination of the industrial dispute, to sit at any place, and to conduct its proceedings in private.[83]

Probably due to its origins as a Court presided over by a judge of the High Court, the Commission retains some of the trappings of a court—it sits in hearing rooms set up like a court; barristers or solicitors may represent the parties;[84] leave can be given to interested persons to intervene;[85] parties, witnesses and other persons can be summoned to attend and persons can be compelled to produce documents.[86] However, there has been an emphasis on informality (unlike that of the courts) by s.110(2)(b) which provides that the Commission is not bound to act in a formal manner.

There are appeal mechanisms in Part II, Division 4 of the legislation, too, which are strictly governed by legal procedure.

The award

There are various legal requirements in the Act in respect of the award. The award must be in writing; the commencement date and the duration of the award must be specified; the award shall be expressed in a way which avoids unnecessary technicalities.[87]

The outcome of the process of conciliation and arbitration is a legally-binding document. The terms may have been reached by settlement imposed by the Commission, by a combination of conciliation and arbitration or by conciliation alone. If it is the latter, a consent award will be made or a certified agreement may be the end result.

The award can be varied subsequently upon application of a party[88] but the doctrine of ambit is important and an award may only be varied within the ambit of the original industrial dispute. Hence the original four corners of the dispute play an important part in enabling variations to be made. Sometimes, the variation may apply only to employees in one state or a small geographical area. The interstateness requirement is met by the original interstate dispute and does not have to be separately established for each variation. This then gives a measure of flexibility to the award and variation.

Agreements

Alternatively, the parties may have settled their differences and resolved upon the terms of an agreement which they wish to be certified as an agreement. The Commission is under an obligation to certify the agreement unless to do so would disadvantage the employees and be against the public interest.[89] Such agreements, however, are not free of the Constitutional limitations: there must be an 'industrial dispute' as defined or a situation which may give rise to an industrial dispute, and the contents of the agreements must be those which the Commission could legally include in an award. The passage of the *Industrial Relations Act* 1988 saw greater statutory regulation in relation to *certified agreements*. In particular significant changes were introduced in 1992 in the context of conflict between the federal government and the Commission concerning enterprise bargaining (see chapters 16 and 18 for details of this conflict). The provisions were further refined in the *Industrial Relations Reform Act* 1993. A significant difference between the traditional use of certified agreements and the 1990s provisions lies in the nature of tribunal discretion to refuse to certify agreements. In the past the tribunal enjoyed largely unfettered freedom to withhold certification in the 'public interest', usually in defence of tribunal wage-fixing principles. The position in 1994 is that certain pre-conditions for Commission certification and for refusal to certify are tightly proscribed while other provisions continue to provide the tribunal with a power of veto, usually based on the public interest. The proscribed pre-conditions for certification of an agreement include the following:[90]

1. the existence of one or more awards covering the employees to whom the certified agreement is to apply (an award 'safety-net');
2. the inclusion in the certified agreement of certain subject matter, for example:
   a procedures for preventing and settling rights disputes; and
   b consultative machinery to deal with changes to the organisation or performance of work (unless the parties agree not to include such a provision);
3. evidence that reasonable steps have been taken by the parties to
   a consult employees about the agreement during negotiations; and
   b inform employees about the terms of the agreement and in particular about a number of specified aspects such as the effects of the terms and the consequences of certification.

The proscribed circumstances in which the Commission *must* refuse to certify an agreement include the following:

1. where the Commission thinks that 'a provision of the agreement discriminates against an employee because of, or for reasons including race, colour, sex, sexual preference, age, physical or mental disability, marital status, family responsibilities, pregnancy, religion, political opinion, national extraction or social origin'[91]
2. except where an agreement applies to a single business, a part of a single business or a single place of work—'the Commission thinks that certifying the agreement would be contrary to the public interest'.[92]

The second example above is one of a number of instances where the legislation provides the tribunal with wide discretion, although in the above case it only applies where the agreement covers more than one business. A second instance of some discretion in the Commission derives from another pre-condition for certification, namely, that the agreement does not disadvantage employees in relation to their terms and conditions of employment. This is referred to as the 'no disadvantage' test and the Act provides that employees will be disadvantaged only if:

'(a) certification of the agreement would result in the reduction of any entitlements or protections of those employees under:
  (i) an award (as defined in subsection (6)); or
  (ii) any other law of the Commonwealth or of a State or Territory that the Commission thinks relevant; and

(b) in the context of their terms and conditions of employment considered as a whole, the Commission considers that the reduction is contrary to the public interest.'[93]

The reference point for the 'no disadvantage' test is a federal *or* state award but not a certified or enterprise flexibility agreement or a Commission order for minimum entitlements. The discretion of the Commission here derives from its interpretation of the public interest. A third instance of discretion is the power of a full bench of the Commission to review the operation of a certified agreement after allowing the parties to the agreement to be heard. It also has the power to vary or terminate the agreement if, inter alia, it finds that continuation of the agreement would be unfair to the employees affected.[94] These examples, which are not exhaustive, illustrate the wide and complex range of third party controls. They build upon a longstanding feature of tribunal operation, namely the right of the Commission to refuse to give legal effect to agreements negotiated, whether or not with tribunal assistance in the capacity of conciliator.

The *Industrial Relations Reform Act* 1993 (Cth) has further amended the agreements provisions and enabled another type of agreement, an *enterprise flexibility agreement*, to be made. Enterprise flexibility agreements do not require an 'industrial dispute' to exist. The reason is that these provisions[95] rely for their constitutional validity on the corporations power and are not constrained by the interstate industrial dispute requirement of s.51(35) of the Constitution.

The provisions relating to this type of agreement widen the scope of employers and employees eligible to participate in the legislative framework for negotiating agreements based on improving efficiency and productivity. In essence this means enabling participation where registered unions are either totally absent, inactive or perhaps even unwelcome. Tribunal involvement is necessary for approving the implementation of the agreement but it may also include conciliation, just as in the case of certified agreements. There are a number of distinguishing features of this instrument.

One distinguishing feature is that the employer party to the agreement must be a 'constitutional corporation' as defined in s.4(1) of the Act. Thus, the employer must be a financial or trading corporation or a foreign corporation. Another feature is that the application requesting the Commission to approve implementation of the agreement is the prerogative of the employer.[96] Perhaps the most significant feature is that it is not necessary for a registered union to be a party to an enterprise flexibility agreement in order for the Commission to approve it. Unions have the right to participate in negotiations and to make submissions in relation to employer applications.[97] They may also choose to be bound by the agreement but they cannot veto it.[98] The key factor here is that one pre-condition of approval is for the Commission to be satisfied that the majority of employees covered by the agreement have genuinely agreed to be bound by it. Otherwise, however, the nature and scope of the Commission's discretion and veto powers are similar to those for certified agreements. This means, for example, that there must be an award in existence and that the agreement must not disadvantage employees who are covered by the agreement.[99] However, despite the use of the corporations power in the Constitution to enact these provisions, the agreement must be 'about matters pertaining to the relationship between employers and employees',[100] so that the principles relating to 'matters' discussed earlier in this chapter are relevant to enterprise flexibility agreements.

Enforcement of awards and agreements

Awards are legally enforceable and certified and enterprise flexibility agreements are enforceable as though they are awards. Agreements which are not certified or implemented by the Commission will not be enforceable unless they are incorporated in the employee's contract of employment or regarded as being the subject of a separate, binding contract.

Section 178 of the *Industrial Relations Act* governs enforcement of awards and agreements. Fines can be imposed on employers for breach and payment of amounts owing ordered (for a period of up to six years).

Enforcement was the jurisdiction of the Federal Court or a court of appropriate jurisdiction until end of March 1994. Since that date the Industrial Relations Court of Australia performs the function of enforcement previously undertaken by the Federal Court.

Interaction of contract and award

Whilst the award specifies the minimum terms and conditions to which employees are entitled, each employee will still have a contract of employment, whether that contract is in writing or oral. Usually at the time an employee is engaged, it will be understood that the employee is being engaged according to the terms of a particular award. This means that the terms of employment will be governed by the contract entered into between the employer and the employee with its terms as expressly agreed and all the implied terms which the law regards as relating to that particular relationship,[101] plus the award conditions.

In the case of *Gregory v Philip Morris Ltd*,[102] the Federal Court of Australia decided that in most instances the terms of a federal award are incorporated into, and become terms of, the contract of employment. This meant that the individual employee not only had a right to enforce the award under s.178 of the *Industrial Relations Act* but could also institute proceedings for breach of contract for which remedies at common law will be available in the courts. This was particularly significant in the area of unfair dismissal. In 1984 in the *Termination, Change and Redundancy* case[103] the Australian Commission decided in a test case that (amongst other matters) clauses could be inserted in federal awards prohibiting employers from dismissing employees 'harshly, unjustly or unreasonably'—this unfair dismissal provision was to apply whether the employee had received appropriate notice or not under the award to terminate the relationship. In *Gregory v Phillip Morris*, the Federal Court regarded the term in the award as being incorporated into the plaintiff employee's contract of employment. When the employee was dismissed unfairly by his employer, the employer was not only fined for breach of award but the employer was ordered to pay damages as compensation for the breach of contract which was suffered. This case has also been followed in the case of *Gorgevski v Bostik (Australia) Ltd*[104] where the Federal Court gave an employee, who had been unfairly dismissed for smoking in a non-smoking zone delineated by the employer in the employer's premises, the sum of nearly $200 000 in damages.

The basis for incorporation has not yet been determined by the High Court. In *Gregory's* case, two judges of the Federal Court determined that the nature of incorporation was by implication as a matter of law, regardless of the intention of the parties, and was necessary to give business efficacy to the employment contract.[105] A third judge took the view that as an award was made pursuant to statute, the award imposed on the party a statutory duty and any breach of that award would be a breach of statutory duty for which damages could arise.[106] The decision in *Gregory's* case was overruled by a majority of the Full Court of the Federal Court in *Byrne v Australian Airlines Ltd*.[107] The court held that an award term was *not* automatically incorporated into the contract of employment and that it was not necessary to imply that award term for reasons related to business efficacy. Thus, for a period of some 6 years, due to the interaction of unfair dismissal clauses in awards and the contract of employment, unfairly dismissed employees could obtain often quite large monetary compensation under the law of contract. *Byrne's* case is on appeal in the High Court so that the legal principles on interaction of contract and award are yet to be finally determined by the highest judicial authority in Australia.

Awards and collective bargaining

At the time the *Conciliation and Arbitration Act* 1904 was enacted, it was considered that collective bargaining would be the main form for resolution of disputes between employers and employees and the determination of terms and conditions of employment, so that only in the cases where there was difficulty would the independent arbitrator step in to conciliate and, if that failed, to impose settlement by arbitration. Collective bargaining has, therefore, always co-existed with arbitration and operated side by side and its importance has altered—enlarged or expanded or diminished—over the years.

However collective bargaining has always operated in the form of over-award payments. Given that awards provide for *minimum* terms and conditions of employment, it has always been open to the parties to negotiate to receive better pay and conditions than provided under the award. The main process for this negotiation is usually collective bargaining undertaken by the union and enforcement of the over-award payment would be a matter of contract law. There are doubts as to the enforceability of collective agreements which are not incorporated as part of an individual employee's contract of employment or which are not registered under relevant industrial legislation. Over-award payments can of course be negotiated individually by an employee with his or her employer and the matter would then become one of contract law.

Collective bargaining may result in an agreement—in order to be enforceable, the party should register that agreement under the provisions now contained in Part VIB, Division 2 (certified agreements) and Division 3 (enterprise flexibility agreements) of the *Industrial Relations Act*. However, it is and always has been the case in respect of certified agreements (and this is a point which is not often understood), that the jurisdictional requirements must still be fulfilled. The parties must still satisfy the Commission that there is an industrial dispute relating to a matter within the Commission's jurisdiction (or a situation which may lead to an industrial dispute), and that the dispute is interstate in nature. Then the Commission is under a duty to register the agreement unless it is of the view that the employees would be disadvantaged and that it would not be in the public interest to register the agreement. The powers of the Commission are circumscribed by the legislation. More flexibility is obtained through enterprise flexibility agreements but these too are subject to legal and other requirements as discussed in the section in this chapter on Agreements.

It has always been difficult to know the extent to which parties can opt out of the system of conciliation and arbitration. When a fairly tightly-controlled centralised wage-fixing system was in operation, the airline pilots learnt in a rather dramatic way that they were not able to unilaterally opt out of the federal system. They had sought wage increases far in excess of the guideline operating under the national wage cases; their employers did not agree to the wage increase demanded; the union refused to give a continuing commitment to the centralised system of wage fixation; as a consequence the existing awards were cancelled. In the meantime, the union members undertook industrial action, resigned their employment *en masse*, and were sued in the industrial torts.[108] However, the parties, it would seem, could have bilaterally agreed that they would opt out of the federal system. In Victoria, the legislature took the view that all awards should be cancelled and then parties decide whether they would opt back into the system by consent or remain outside the system—see the *Employee Relations Act* 1992 (Vic). The mechanism adopted by the federal parliament in the major reforms of 1993 was to retain the award system as a safety net and to permit parties to negotiate for agreements, subject to Commission approval and control. The legislation attempts to shift the focus of resolving disputes away from arbitration to negotiation and conciliation, and for the parties to be responsible for their own agreements. Any 'opting out', if it can be referred to as such, is within a quite strictly controlled framework. The new legislative provisions of 1993 should be seen as part of the changing cycle in the life of federal industrial regulation and the role of collective bargaining *vis-à-vis* arbitration and awards.

National wage cases

The national wage cases have performed an important role within the Australian system of industrial relations. The standard procedure is for the ACTU to bring a test case to determine whether adult minimum wages should increase on account of national economic indicators rather than anything relating to the industry itself. This is usually done by seeking a variation of an award such as the *Metal Industry Award*. Peak employer and employee organisations make submissions as do the Governments, of the Commonwealth and the states, under the powers that parties have to intervene in Commission proceedings. These matters have to be considered by a Full Bench of the Commission of which at least two members must be presidential members. The practice has been for a Full Bench of five persons to be convened. Once a decision is made to vary the Metal Industry award, the principles contained in that *National Wage* decision can be used to vary other awards. The wage increases do not flow automatically. Each award must be varied to reflect the amount on account of national wage increase. This can be done on paper by a Commissioner simply dealing with the application to vary the award and in effect rubber-stamping the decision of the Commission. Sometimes, employees complain that they are not receiving the latest wage increase and when the matter is investigated, the appropriate award variation has not occurred.

Even though the Commission legally cannot prescribe minimum wages due to constitutional and legislative constraints, the Commission *de facto* regulates wages through the National Wage decisions. The constitutionality of this function has never been directly challenged in the High Court, but the Commission has frequently asserted that it is not an economic tribunal or an economic legislature but a dispute settler.[109] Certainly, as a matter of technical procedure, the Australian Industrial Relations Commission's functions in altering minimum wages arise out of dispute settling and award varying procedures. The role can be traced back to the decision in *Ex parte H V McKay* (the *Harvester* case)[110] where the President of the (then) Arbitration Court was given responsibility under excise tariff legislation for determining 'fair and reasonable' wages. The decision in this case and the methods of determining wages were later applied in decisions for altering minimum wages.[111] The Commission builds up a body of jurisprudence which will be applied, reconsidered, revised or reformulated in later cases. It should be noted that the reforms of 1993 give the Australian Commission power to declare minimum entitlements in respect of wages and equal pay in certain circumstances.[112] It may be queried whether in the long term national wage decisions will continue to play the same important role, and whether the Commission's general powers to declare minimum entitlements (based on constitutional heads of power other than s.51(35)) may render such decisions otiose.

Registration of associations

In the original Act of 1904, provision was made for the registration of associations of employers and registration of associations of employees. These registration provisions encouraged the existence of unions and meant that in Australia the struggle for survival and recognition of unions which took place in many countries was unnecessary. Registration not only meant in effect legal recognition but legal status too was conferred on unions. Today, s.192 of the *Industrial Relations Act* provides:

192   An organisation;

(a) is a body corporate;
(b) has perpetual succession;

(c) has power to purchase, take on lease, hold, sell, lease, mortgage, exchange and otherwise own, possess and deal with any real or personal property;
(d) shall have a common seal; and
(e) may sue or be sued in its registered name.

These registration provisions rely on s.51(35) and s.51(39) (the incidentals power) of the Constitution.[113] In the *Jumbunna* case, the validity of the registration provisions were upheld by the High Court. Griffith CJ explained the necessity for registration:

> It is plain that communication with all the individual disputants or probable disputants would be impracticable for either purpose. It would, therefore, be expedient, and indeed necessary to make provision for representation. And I can see no reason why the parliament should not provide that existing State organisations, representative of bodies of employers or employees should be recognised as representatives for the purpose of the law which they pass to deal with the matter. Nor can I see any reason why they should not authorise the constitution by new organisations for the specific purposes of the Act. And they might confer upon such organisations of either kind such powers as are incidental to the discharge of these functions ... But beyond such limits it seems to me that they could not go in this respect. The parliament has no independent power to create corporations, except in the cases specified in s.51 pl(xiii) (banks) and, possibly, in s.51 pl(xx). And, since the powers and functions of every corporation limited by its constitution, it follows that the parliament cannot confer upon a corporation created by its powers or functions for the exercise of which alone it could not create a corporation. It could, however, I think, create a corporation as a means to the execution of an express power and confer on it such powers and functions as are incidental to the execution of that power.[114]

O'Connor J, in the *Jumbunna* case, after discussing the nature of disputes covered by the Constitution, stated:

> [It] was open to the legislature to adopt any method which they deemed effective for prevention and settlement by conciliation and arbitration. They might, if they had thought fit, have dealt with the individual workman or employer as the unit of combination, and provided for the registration of all workmen and all employers in a trade as a step in aid of procedure. It was equally open to them to take the State trade union or association as the unit of combination, and provide for their registration as a step in the same direction. For, as the individual workman may in combination with other workmen in his own or another State become concerned in an industrial dispute extending beyond the limits of any one State, so a State trades union or State association of workmen may, by combination with trade unions or associations of workmen in another State, become concerned in such a dispute.
>
> It follows that the power of Parliament would extend to the creation of organisations such as those contemplated by the Act, even though they might be incapable at the time of registration of being in themselves parties to an industrial dispute within the meaning of the Constitution, provided that they are so constituted as to be capable of becoming at any time parties to such a dispute as members of a combination of the organisations of more than one State acting together in carrying on an industrial dispute for the attainment of a common end.[115]

The validity of the registration provisions having been upheld, unions today usually seek the course of registration. It gives them corporate status, they can act independently of the membership from time to time (although of course there will be the need for authority to act) and can be party principals in matters before the Commission as well as parties to awards and agreements. One disadvantage has been the ability to be sued in their name which has opened up the way for liability in tort.[116]

Once registered, unions are subject to the safeguards and sanctions of the Act. They must have rules which comply with certain requirements,[117] which can be altered only in accordance with certain procedures and can be enforced in the courts. Election of office bearers is controlled by compulsory ballot in approved form and the Industrial Relations Court (and formerly the Federal Court) has jurisdiction to deal with applications in respect of alleged election irregularities. There are controls on who can hold office and admission of persons as members, as well as amalgamation of unions. The Court may also rule on eligibility for membership, as in the High Court case where the court had to determine whether enrolled nurses, nursing aides, trainee or student nurses were eligible for membership of the Royal Australian Nursing Federation.[118]

Having said that most unions will seek registration, it is not absolutely essential for the creation of an industrial dispute and subsequent award coverage for members of a union to be involved. In the case of the Australian Football League Players Association, an association which was not registered, Deputy President Polites of the Commission held that the players could collectively incite an industrial dispute over which the Commission could take jurisdiction.[119]

A sanction is that of deregistration of unions. Although regarded as of doubtful punitive value because the union is placed outside the controls of the Act, deregistration deprives the organisation of its legal status. The association may however continue to exist as an unincorporated association, as it is not made defunct as an association.[120]

Notes

1 See s.109 of the Constitution and s.152 of the *Industrial Relations Act* 1988 and see chapter 13.
2 This lead at federal level has not always been the case: see, e.g., the decision to limit standard working hours to 40 per week was first made at state level.
3 See *Industrial Conciliation and Arbitration Act* 1894 (NZ).
4 K. Hince 'From William Pember Reeves and William Francis Birch: from conciliation to contracts', chapter 1 in R. Harbridge (ed.), *Employment Contracts: New Zealand Experiences,* Victoria University Press, Wellington, 1993, p. 9.
5 For extensive discussion of the origin of Australian arbitration, see S. Macintyre and R. Mitchell, *Foundations of Arbitration: the Origins and Effects of State Compulsory Arbitration 1890-1914* , Melbourne, Oxford University Press, 1989.
6 See this chapter pp. 372-373.
7 The validity of these provisions relying on s.51(1) was upheld in *The Seamen's Union of Australia v Utah Development Company* (1978) 144 CLR 120.
8 Section 127A and B.
9 *The Commonwealth v Tasmania* (1983) 158 CLR 1.
10 See also chapter 8.
11 London, Constable, 1922, p. 2.
12 See again H.B. Higgins, 'A New Province for Law and Order', London, Constable, 1922, p. 2.

13 *R v Kirby; Ex parte Boilermakers' Society of Australia* (1956) 94 CLR 254 (High Court); affirmed 95 CLR 529 (Privy Council).
14 On the transfer of jurisdiction and appointment of personnel to these functions, see B. d'Alpuget, *Mediator: A Biography of Sir Richard Kirby*, Melbourne University Press, Melbourne, 1977.
15 In practice, their most commonly held formal qualification is a law degree.
16 See further B. D'Alpuget, *Mediator: A Biography of Sir Richard Kirby*.
17 Section 75(3) and (5) of the Constitution. Since the enactment of the *Industrial Relations Reform Act* 1993, the High Court may refer matters of jurisdiction to the Industrial Relations Court of Australia.
18 (1908) 6 CLR 309.
19 At 332.
20 At 365.
21 *Federated State School Teachers Association of Australia v Victoria (the School Teachers case)* — (1929) 41 CLR 569.
22 *Pitfield v Franki* (1970) 123 CLR 448.
23 *R v Holmes: Ex parte Public Service Association of New South Wales* (1977) 140 CLR 63.
24 *Federated Municipal and Shire Council Employees' Union of Australia v Melbourne Corporation* (1919) 26 CLR 508.
25 At 554.
26 *Proprietors of the Daily News Ltd v Australian Journalists Association* (1920) 27 CLR 532.
27 *Australian Insurance State Federation v Accident Underwriters' Association and Bank Officials Association v Bank of Australasia* (1923) 33 CLR 517.
28 *R v Marshall; Ex parte Federated Clerks Union of Australia* (1975) 132 CLR 595.
29 *R v Commonwealth Conciliation and Arbitration Commission; Ex parte The Association of Professional Engineers* (1959) 107 CLR 208.
30 At 236.
31 *Pitfield v Franki* (1970) 123 CLR 448.
32 *R v McMahon; Ex parte Darvall* (1982) 151 CLR 57.
33 *R v Holmes; Ex parte Public Service Association of New South Wales* (1977) 140 CLR 63.
34 *R v Marshall; Ex parte Federated Clerks' Union of Australia* (1975) 132 CLR 595.
35 *R v Coldham and Others; Ex parte Australian Social Welfare Union* (1983) 153 CLR 297; 57 ALJR 574.
36 At 234.
37 (1986) 60 ALJR 441.
38 This is particularly true of Victoria where the *Employee Relations Act* 1992 (Vic) abolished awards from March 1993 and left employees with *voluntary* arbitration.
39 'Industrial matters' in the *Conciliation and Arbitration Act* 1904 (Cth) means all matters pertaining to the relations of employers and employees and, without limiting the generality of the foregoing, includes —
   (a) all matters or things affecting or relating to work done or to be done;
   (b) the privileges, rights and duties of employers and employees;
   (c) the wages, allowances and remuneration of persons employed or to be employed;
   (d) the piece-work, contract or other reward paid or to be paid in respect of employment;
   (e) the question whether piece-work or contract work or any other system of payment by results shall be allowed, forbidden or exclusively prescribed;
   (f) the question whether monetary allowances shall be made by employers in respect of any time when an employee is not actually working;
   (g) the hours of employment, sex, age, qualification and status of employees;
   (h) the mode, terms and conditions of employment;
   (i) the employment of children or young persons, or of any persons or class of persons;
   (j) the preferential employment or the non-employment of any particular person or class of persons or of persons being or not being members of an organisation;
   (k) the right to dismiss or to refuse to employ, or the duty to reinstate in employment, a particular person or class of persons;

(l) any custom or usage in an industry, whether general or in a particular locality;
(m) any shop, factory or industry dispute, including any matter which may be a contributory cause of such a dispute;
(n) any question arising between two or more organisations or within an organisation as the rights, status or functions of the members of those organisations or of that organisation or otherwise, in relation to the employment of those members;...
(p) any question as to the demarcation of functions of employees or classes of employees, whether as between employers and employees or between members of different organisations; and
(q) the provision of first-aid equipment, medical attendance, ambulance facilities, rest rooms, sanitary and washing facilities, canteens, cafeteria, dining rooms and other amenities for employees.

and includes all questions of what is right and fair in relation to an industrial matter having regard to the interests of the persons immediately concerned and of society as a whole.

40 See *R v Kelly; Ex parte State of Victoria* (1950) 81 CLR 64.
41 See *Manufacturing Grocers' Employees Federation of Australia and Association of Professional Engineers, Australia; Ex parte Australian Chamber of Manufacturers and Victorian Employers' Federation* (1986) 160 CLR 341; 60 ALJR 347.
42 See *Re Cram Ex parte New South Wales Colliery Proprietors' Association* (1987) 163 CLR 117, 72 ALR 161.
43 See *Manufacturing Grocers' Employees Federation of Australia case.*
44 *R v Portus; Ex parte Australia and New Zealand Banking Group Limited* (1972) 127 CLR 353. This scheme was recently considered again by the High Court in *Re Alcan Australia Limited; Ex parte Federation of Industrial Manufacturing and Engineering Employees* (unreported decision, 25 August 1994) where the High Court upheld its decision in *Portus* stating that the relationship in a system for deduction of union dues is that of employees as union members, not as employees.
45 See *Re Finance Union Sector Union case.*
46 *R v Holmes; Ex parte Altona Petrochemical Co* (1972) 126 CLR 529.
47 See *R v Portus; Ex parte City of Perth*, per Stephen J at 329.
48 See *Re Ranger Uranium Mine Pty Ltd; Ex parte Federated Miscellaneous Workers' Union of Australia* (1987) 163 CLR 656; 62 ALJR 47.
49 See, e.g., *Re Boyne Smelters Ltd; Ex parte Federation of Industrial Manufacturing and Engineering Employees of Australia* (1993) 112 ALR 359 and *Re Printing and Kindred Industries Union; Ex parte Vista Paper Products Pty Ltd* (1993) 113 ALR 421.
50 Part VIA, Division 3.
51 See *R v Judges of the Commonwealth Industrial Court; Ex parte Cocks* (1968) 121 CLR 313.
52 See, e.g., *R v Turbet and Metal Industry Association; Ex parte The Australian Building Construction Employees and Builders Labourers Federation* (1980) 144 CLR 335.
53 This method of dispute creation was held by the High Court to be valid in *R v. Commonwealth Court of Conciliation and Arbitration and the BLF; Ex parte Jones; Ex parte Cooper* (1914) 18 CLR 224.
54 (1966) 114 CLR 384.
55 *Re Australasian Meat Industry Employees' Union; Ex Parte Aberdeen Beef Co Pty Ltd* (1993) 112 ALR 35.
56 See s.149 *Industrial Relations Act* 1988.
57 *Australian Boot Trade Employees' Federation v Whybrow* (1910) 11 CLR 311.
58 In the Metal Industry award, there are approximately 12,000 employer respondents.
59 *Metal Trades Employers Association v Amalgamated Engineering Union and Others* (1935) 54 CLR 387.
60 *Re Finance Sector Union of Australia; Ex parte Financial Clinic (Vic) Pty Ltd* (1993) 114 ALR 321. This case confirmed the decision in the *Metal Trades* case, but held that an award could not be made directing employers to make contributions to a nominated superannuation fund in respect of non-unionist employees.

61 Section 149(2) *Industrial Relations Act* 1988.
62 (1984) 159 CLR 163; 51 ALR 469.
63 (1993) 113 ALR 385.
64 The actual processes of conciliation and arbitration are described and analysed in chapter 15.
65 Section 100(1).
66 Section 102(2), the Commission also has power under s.119 to call compulsory conferences
67 Section 103(1).
68 Section 104(1).
69 Section 105(1). See also s.105(2) which sets out when a member of the Commission shall not be taken to have exercised conciliation powers (e.g. merely because the members arranged a conference for the parties to confer amongst themselves at which the member was not present).
70 Section 31.
71 Section 106(1).
72 Full Bench is defined in the Act to mean a Bench of at least three persons, two of whom must be Presidential members: s.30(2).
73 Section 107.
74 Section 45.
75 Section 89.
76 This is discussed further in chapter 15.
77 Section 90.
78 Section 93.
79 Section 97.
80 Section 98.
81 Section 110(2).
82 Section 110(4).
83 Section 111(1).
84 See s.42(3) which outlines when legal representation is permitted.
85 Section 43.
86 Section 111(1) para (s).
87 See generally Part VI, Division 6.
88 Section 113.
89 See s.170MA–MN.
90 See s.170MC. This list is not exhaustive. The 'no-disadvantage' test is discussed further below.
91 Section 170MD(5).
92 Section 170MD(1)(b).
93 Section 170MC(2).
94 Section 170MM.
95 Section 170NA–NP.
96 Section 170NA(2).
97 Section 170NB.
98 Section 170NP.
99 Section 170NC. Curiously, 'award' is limited to Federal Award; c.f. p. 387.
100 Section 170NA(1).
101 See chapter 1. These include duties of fidelity, to take reasonable care, etc.
102 (1988) 80 ALR 455.
103 (1984) 294 CAR 175; 8 IR 35.
104 (1992) 41 IR.
105 Wilcox and Ryan JJ.
106 See judgment of Jenkinson J.

107 (1994) 120 ALR 274.
108 See chapter 5.
109 See, e.g., *National Wage* case, 23 September 1983, (1983) 291 CAR 3; 4 IR 429.
110 (1907) 2 CAR 1.
111 See generally chapter 12, McCallum and Pittard, *Australian Labour Law: Cases and Materials*, Butterworths, Sydney, 1994.
112 Part VIA, Division 1, *Industrial Relations Act* 1988.
113 See discussion under 'Other Constitutional Heads of Power' this chapter.
114 (1908) 6 CLR 309 at 334–5.
115 At 353.
116 See chapter 5.
117 See Part I, Division 2.
118 *Re Royal Australian Nursing Federation; Ex parte New South Wales Nurses' Association* (1986) 67 ALR 172.
119 See also *Re Ansett Transport Industries (Operations) Pty Ltd* 8 ALR 587.
120 See chapter 5.

Further Reading

R.C. McCallum and M.J. Pittard, *Australian Labour Law: Cases and Materials* (3rd ed.), 1994, chapters 5, 6, 7, 8, 10.

W.B. Creighton and A. Stewart, *Labour Law—An Introduction* (2nd ed.), The Federation Press, 1994.

Questions

1 Do you think that the institutional changes which have occurred to the structure of the Commission and the court have influenced Australian industrial relations? If so, explain in what way?

2 To what extent should Australian workers have a right to strike, given the formal mechanisms which exist for dispute resolution?

3 How important do you regard the legal framework in which Australian industrial relations operates? To what extent have decisions on jurisdiction influenced the course of Australian industrial relations?

4 Consider s.51(35) of the Constitution. To what extent might this section become less significant in labour law and relations following the increased use and flexibility of the corporations power (s.51(20)) and the external affairs powers (s.51(29))?

5 Consider the reforms introduced by the *Industrial Relations Reform Act* 1993. Do you think that they are novel or revolutionary in Australian industrial relations? Can they simply be seen as part of a cycle in which bargaining and agreements have a changed role over time?

Appendix A

Nurses (Victorian Health Services) Award 1992
This is an edited federal award (Print K6359)

Part A—Preliminary

1—Title
2—Division into parts

This award is divided into the following parts:

Part
A   Preliminary
B   Registered Nurses
C   Enrolled Nurses
D   Mothercraft Nurses

3—Arrangement

Part A—Preliminary

Subject matter	Clause No.
Title	1
Division into parts	2
Arrangement	3
Incidence and Application	4
Parties Bound	5
Supersession and Savings	6
Date and Period of Operation	7
Definitions	8
Leave Reserved	9

Part B—Registered Nurses

Subject matter	Clause No.
Accident Pay	25
Advertisement of Position	9
Allowances	24
On call	
Re call to duty	
Travelling	
Uniform and laundry	
Shift	
Meal	
Telephone	
Award Modernisation	36
Enterprise Agreements	
Existing flexibility	
Facilitative	
Classification In Grades	5
Classification Structure Private Hospitals	8
Day off each week	14
Deduction for Accomodation—Non Public Health Sector	12
Deduction for Accommodation—Public Health Sector	12A
Definitions	3
Higher Duties	7

Hours of Work	13
Introduction of Change	34
Leave Entitlements	
Annual Leave	26
Compassionate Leave	29
Examination Leave	32
Jury Service	30
Long Service Leave	28
Parental Leave	31
Sick Leave	27
Trade Union Training Leave—Public Sector	33
Modes of Employment	4
No Extra Claims	2
Overtime	19
Payment of Salaries	26
Posting award	1
Proportion of nurses to patients	16
Prevention and Settlement of Disputes	35
Provision of accommodation and other necessary requirements	23
Public Holidays	22
Redundancy—Private Sector Only	37
Reserved	10
Reserved	11
Rest Intervals	15
Right of Entry	39
Rosters	17
Salaries	6
Payment of salaries	6(c)
Saturday and Sunday Work	20
Summer Time	18
Termination of Employment	38
Terms of Employment	13
Time and salaries records	21

[There follows clauses in relation to Enrolled Nurses and to Mothercraft Nurses.]

4—Incidence and Application

(a) This Award shall apply to the employment of Registered Nurses, State Enrolled Nurses and Mothercraft Nurses in the State of Victoria PROVIDED it shall not apply to persons employed under the *Public Service Act 1974* (Vic).
(b) Part A of this Award shall apply to the employment of all employees to whom this Award applies.
(c) Part B of this Award shall apply to the work and employment of Registered Nurses.
(d) Part C of this Award shall apply to the work and employment of Enrolled Nurses.
(e) Part D of this Award shall apply to the work and employment of Mothercraft Nurses.

5—Parties Bound

This award shall be binding upon:
(a) the employers referred to in Schedule A hereto and the employers of persons in the places referred to in Schedule A hereto in respect of all their employees for whom provision is made herein;
(b) the Australian Nursing Federation;
(c) the Health Services Union of Australia in respect of Parts A, C and D.
(d) the Health Services Union of Australia in respect of Part B to the extent that Part B extends to the employment of Registered Psychiatric Nurses and Registered Mental Retardation Nurses who were at the date of commencement of this award financial members of the Health Services Union of Australia.

(e) The Victorian Employers' Chamber of Commerce and Industry, and its members; and
(f) The Australian Chamber of Manufactures, and its members.

6—Supersession and Savings
...

7—Date and Period of Operation
This Award shall come into force on 23 December 1992 and remain in firce for a period of twelve months.

8—Definitions
For the purposes of this award:
(a) 'Registered Nurse' shall mean a person whose name appears in any section of the Register maintained by the Victorian Nursing Council excluding a State Enrolled Nurse or Mothercraft Nurse.
(b) 'Enrolled Nurse' and 'State Enrolled Nurse' shall mean a person registered as such by the Victorian Nursing Council.
(c) 'Mothercraft Nurse' shall mean a person, other than an enrolled nurse, registered by the Victorian Nursing Council as a Mothercraft Nurse.
(d) 'Public Sector' shall refer to employment under this award in respect of a respondent or place of work identified in Schedule B.
(e) 'Private Sector' shall refer to any employment in this award not in the public sector.
(f) 'Union' within the respective parts of this award shall mean those unions set out in clause 5 as being respondents to that part.

9—Leave Reserved
Employers bound by this award shall have leave reserved to make an application to set aside this award during its currency.

Part B Registered Nurses

1—Posting Awards
A copy of this Award shall be posted up by the employer in a conspicuous place accessible to all employees.

2—No Extra Claims
It is a term of this Award (arising from the decision of the Australian Industrial Relations Commission in the National Wage Case of April 1991, the terms of which are set out in Print J7400) that the union undertakes for the duration of those principles determined by that Commission, not to pursue any extra claims, award or overaward, except when consistent with those principles.
[There follows 10 pages of the award containing definitions of terms relevant to the award.]

Full-time employment
(a) A full-time employee is one who is employed and who is ready, willing and available to work a full week of 38 hours or an average of 38 hours as per subclause 13(d) at the times and during the hours as may be mutually agreed upon or in the absence of such agreement as prescribed by the employer.

Subject to the provisions of subclause 13(a) such employee shall be paid the weekly salary appropriate to the employee's classification, irrespective of the number of hours worked not exceeding 38, or an average of 38 per week.

Part-time employee
(b) (i) A part-time employee is one who is employed and who is ready, willing and available to work on a regular basis any number of hours up to but not exceeding 38 hours in any one week (or 76 in a fortnight) provided that the number of hours

worked may vary from week to week by mutual agreement. Such employee shall be paid per hour worked an amount equal to one thirty-eighth (1/38th) of the weekly salary appropriate to the employee's classification, provided that Clauses 14 and 15 will also apply to part-time employees, and payment in respect of any period of Annual Leave or Long Service Leave to which an employee may become entitled shall be on a pro rata basis.

(ii) Payment in respect of any period of paid Sick Leave (where an employee has accumulated an entitlement) and Compassionate Leave shall be made according to the number of hours the employee would have worked on the day or days on which the leave was taken so as not to reduce the employee's salary below that level which such employee would have received had such employee not been absent.

Casual employee

(c) (i) A casual employee is one who is engaged in relieving work or work of a casual nature and whose engagement is terminable by an employer in accordance with the employer's requirements without the requirement of prior notice by either party, but does not include an employee who could properly be classified as a full-time or part-time employee under subclauses 4(a) and 4(b).

(ii) A casual employee shall be paid per hour worked an amount equal to one thirty-eighth (1/38th) of the weekly salary appropriate to the class of work performed plus 25%.

(iii) In addition, a casual employee shall be entitled to receive the appropriate uniform and other allowances prescribed herein.

(iv) The provisions of Clause 26 Annual Leave, Clause 28 Long Service Leave, Clause 32 Sick Leave, Clause 29 Compassionate Leave, and Clause 43 Termination of Employment, shall not apply in the case of a casual employee.

5—Classification in Grades

[There follows extensive classifications into grades of the nurses.]

6—Salaries

[There follows salaries for grades of nurses.]
[There is also provision for payment as follows.]

Payment of Salaries

(c) Salaries shall be paid during working hours on a week day being not more than five days following the end of the pay period provided that—

(i) when a Bank Holiday occurs between the end of the pay period and the usual pay-day payment may be postponed by one day for each Bank Holiday so occurring during that period but payment must still be made on a week day (the expression 'pay-day' in this Clause includes the week day designated as a pay-day pursuant to this proviso);

(ii) an employee who is rostered off duty on the pay-day, but who works any period of rostered duty between 10.00 a.m. on the Monday preceding the pay-day and the pay-day itself shall be paid during working hours before completing duty prior to pay-day;

(iii) when an employee does not work a rostered period of duty between 10.00 a.m. on the Monday preceding the pay-day and the pay-day itself, payment may be postponed until that employee's next rostered period of duty but the employee's salary shall be available for collection on the pay-day;

(iv) an employee shall be supplied at the time of receiving his or her pay with a statement in writing showing or from which may be calculated the amount of ordinary pay, overtime, penalty rates and allowances; and the amount of deductions for any purpose in respect of the amount paid;

(v) where the system of working provides for the taking of Accrued Days Off and an employee's employment is terminated:
(1) one or more ADOs have been granted in advance; or

(2) an ADO has been taken during the work cycle during which the employee is terminated, the salary due to that employee shall be reduced by the total of the ADOs taken in advance, and/or the total un-accrued portion of the ADO granted in that work cycle as the case may be;

(3) an employee who has not worked a complete twenty day four week cycle (or 5 week cycle) as the case may be, shall receive pro rata accrued entitlements for each day worked or regarded as having been worked (i.e. paid leave) in such cycle payable for the accrued day off.

7—Higher Duties

13—Hours of Work

Hours for an Ordinary Weeks Work

(a) The hours for an ordinary week's work shall be 38, or be an average 38 per week in a fortnight or in a four week period (or by mutual agreement, a five week period in the case of an employee working 10 hour shifts) and shall be paid either:
  (i) in a week of five days in shifts of not more than eight hours each; or
  (ii) by mutual agreement in a week of four days in shifts of not more than 10 hours each; or
  (iii) by mutual agreement, provided that the length of any ordinary shift shall not exceed 10 hours; or
  (iv) in 76 hours per fortnight to be worked as not more than 10 days of not more than eight hours each; or
  (v) (1) In 152 hours per four week period to be worked as 19 days each of eight hours.
   (2) Employees in the Private Sector who, pursuant to paragraph 18(a)(v) above receive an accrued day off (ADO) may, with the consent of the employer accumulate such ADO's up to a maximum of six (6) in any one year. Accumulated ADO's must be taken in the year in which they accumulate. In the case of termination of employment for whatever reason, accumulated ADO's will be paid to the employee by the employer.
   (3) Subject to the Roster provision Clause 17 not more than 48 ordinary hours be worked in any week.
   (4) With the exception of time occupied in having meals (which shall be a period of not less than 30 minutes for each meal) with one additional break if same is required by the employer, the work of each shift shall be continuous provided that no such additional break shall be required in respect of rostered hours of ordinary duty finishing on the day after commencing duty or commencing after midnight and before 5.00 a.m. Provided that, an employee of a Private Hospital, who is not relieved from duty during the rostered meal interval as prescribed by this clause shall, in addition to any other payment of allowance provided in this Award, be paid for the meal interval at the ordinary time rate of pay, or by mutual agreement be granted time off in lieu thereof.

(b) Subject to the Roster provision, Clause 17, of this Award not more than 48 ordinary hours be worked in any week.

(c) With the exception of time occupied in having meals (which shall be a period of not less than 30 minutes for each meal) with one additional break if same is required by the employer, the work of each shift shall be continuous provided that no such additional break shall be required in respect of rostered hours of ordinary duty finishing on the day after commencing duty or commencing after midnight and before 5.00 a.m.

14—Day Off in Each Week

(a) All employees shall receive at least one clear day off in each week in the case of day-shift employees and one clear night off in each week in the case of night-shift employees.

(b) Provided that during any working period not exceeding three consecutive weeks, the day or night off may, with the approval of the Director of Nursing, be allowed to stand over, and be taken at a time mutually agreed upon in any one consecutive period equivalent to one day or night, as the case may be, for each week in the period concerned.

15—Rest Intervals

At a time suitable to the employer two rest intervals of ten minutes each shall be given to all employees during each day or rostered shift and shall be counted as time worked.

16—Proportion of Nurses to Patients

(a) (i) The provision of this clause shall not operate so far as employees at benevolent homes or at the Melbourne Convalescent Home for Men, Cheltenham, and the Melbourne Convalescent Home for Women, Clayton are concerned.
 (ii) The proportion of nurses to patients in private intermediate or community hospitals shall be as provided in the regulations relating to private hospitals under the *Health Act 1958* (Vic.); but,
 (iii) in all other places the proportion on duty shall be as follows:
  (a) Day Shift—One nurse to each ten or fraction of ten patients.
  (b) Night Shift—One nurse to each fifteen or fraction of fifteen patients.

17—Rosters

[There follows detailed clauses as to Rosters.]

19—Overtime

(a) All work done in excess of the ordinary hours prescribed shall be paid at the rate of time and a half for the first two hours and double time thereafter. For the purpose of this clause each day or shift shall stand alone.

Rest Periods—Affected by Overtime (Including Saturdays and Sundays)

(b) (i) When overtime work (including recall to duty) is necessary it shall, wherever reasonably practicable, be so arranged that employees have at least ten hours continuously off duty between the work of successive shifts.
 (ii) An employee (other than a casual employee) who works so much overtime between the termination of her/his last previously rostered ordinary hours of duty and the commencement of her/his next succeeding rostered period of duty that she/he would not have had at least ten hours continuously off duty between those times, shall subject to this subclause, be released after completion of such overtime worked until she/he had ten hours continuously off duty without loss of pay for rostered ordinary hours occurring during such an absence.
 (iii) If on the instructions of her/his employer such an employee resumes or continues work without having had such ten hours continuously off duty she/he shall be paid at the rate of double time until she/he is released from duty for such rest period and she/he shall be entitled to be absent until she/he has had ten hours continuously off duty without loss of pay for rostered ordinary hours occurring during such an absence.
 (iv) In the event of any employee finishing any period of overtime or recall at a time when reasonable means of transport are not available for the employee to return to her/his place of residence the employer shall provide adequate transport free of cost to the employee.
(c) (i) In lieu of receiving payment for overtime worked in accordance with this clause, employees may, with the consent of the employer, be allowed to take time off, for a period of time equivalent to the period worked in excess of ordinary rostered hours of duty, plus a period of time equivalent to the overtime penalty incurred. Such time in lieu shall be taken as mutually agreed between the employer and the employee, provided that accrual of such leave shall not extend beyond a 28 day period.
 (ii) Where such accrued time has not been taken within the 28 day period, such time shall be paid in accordance with this clause at the rate of pay which applied on the day the overtime was worked.
 (iii) For the purposes of this clause, in accruing or calculating payment of overtime, each period of overtime shall stand alone.

(d) In the public sector this clause shall apply to part-time employees only with respect to shift lengths referred to in Clause 18 Hours of work. Any part-time employee working in excess of 38 hours in any week shall be regarded as a full-time employee for the period so worked.

20—Saturday and Sunday Work

(a) Payment for all ordinary work performed between midnight Friday and midnight Sunday (inclusive) shall be paid for at the rate of time and one half.
(b) If the Saturday and Sunday work involves duty in excess of the prescribed ordinary rostered hours the excess period shall be paid at the rate of double time.
(c) This clause shall not apply to DIrector of Nursing and Deputy Director of Nursing.

21—Time and Salaries Records

[There follows detailed provisions as to time books and records to be kept and inspections by union Executive Secretary.]

23—Provision of Accommodation and Other Necessary Requirements

(a) Suitable healthy accommodation shall be provided for resident employees. Wherever possible, single bedrooms shall be provided. Separate beds shall be provided for each employee and in no case shall more than two employees be required to occupy the same bedroom. Separate accommodation distinct from that provided for day shift shall be provided for employees on night duty.
(b) An employer shall provide at some reasonably convenient place a dressing room/rest room, bathroom or shower room and a meal room for non-resident employees. The provisions of this subclause shall not be construed so as to require an employer to provide separate facilities for the exclusive use of non-resident employees covered by this Part of this Award.
(c) Adequate supplies of rubber gloves and all necessary safety appliances shall be kept and maintained at each institution and provided free of cost to employees for use as required.
(d) Linen, cutlery, crockery and blankets shall be provided free of cost to the employee.

24—Allowances

On call allowance

...

Recall allowance

...

Travelling allowance

...

Uniform and laundry allowance

...

Shift allowance

(e) (i) In addition to any other rates prescribed elsewhere in this Part of this Award an employee whose rostered hours of ordinary duty finish between 6.00 p.m. and 8.00 a.m. or commence between 6.00 p.m. and 6.30 a.m. shall be paid an amount equal to 2 1/2 per cent of the rate for Registered Nurse Grade 1 in paragraph 6(a)(iv) per rostered period of duty.
 (ii) Provided that in the case of an employee working on any rostered hours of ordinary duty, finishing on the day after comencing duty or commencing after midnight and before 5.00 a.m. he or she shall be paid an amount equal to 4 per cent of the rate for Registered Nurse Grade 1 in paragraph 6(a)(iv) for any such period of duty and provided further that in the case of an employee permanently working on any such rostered hours of ordinary duty shall be paid an amount equal to 5 per cent of the rate for Registered Nurse Grade 1 in paragraph 6(a)(iv) for any such period of duty. 'Permanently working' shall mean working for any period in excess of four consecutive weeks.
 (iii) Provided that the shift allowance shall be calculated to the nearest 10 cents, an exact amount of 5 cents in the result going to the higher figure.
 (iv) Provided further that this clause shall not apply to Director of Nursing and Deputy Director of Nursing.

Meal Allowance
(f) An employee shall be supplied with an adequate meal where an employer has her/his own cooking and dining facilities or be paid meal money in addition to any overtime payment as follows:
   (i) when required to work after the usual finishing hour of work beyond one hour (Monday to Friday inclusive), or in the case of a shift worker when the overtime work on any shift exceeds one hour—$6.20. Provided that where such overtime work exceeds 4 hours a further meal allowance of $4.95 shall be paid;
   (ii) when required to work more than 5 hours overtime on a Saturday or on a Sunday, or more than 5 hours by a shift worker on her/his rostered day off—$6.20 and a further $4.95 when required to work more than 9 hours on such day. These foregoing provisions shall not apply where an employee could reasonably return home for a meal within the period allowed;
   (iii) on request meal money shall be paid on the same day as overtime is worked.

Telephone Allowance
(g) Where an employer requires an employee to install and/or maintain a telephone for the purposes of being on call the employer shall refund the installation costs and subsequent three-monthly rental charges on production of receipted accounts.

25—Accident Pay

...

34—Introduction of Change

Employer's duty to notify
(a) (i) Where an employer has made a definite decision to introduce major changes in production, program, organisation, structure or technology that are likely to have significant effects on employees, the employer shall notify the employees who may be affected by the proposed changes and their union or unions.
   (ii) 'Significant effects' include termination of employment, major changes in the composition, operation or size of the employer's workforce or in the skills required; the elimination or diminution of job opportunities, promotion opportunities or job tenure; the alteration of the hours of work; the need for retraining or transfer of employees to other work or locations and the restructuring of jobs. Provided that where the award makes provisions for alteration of any of the matters referred to herein an alteration shall be deemed not to have significant effect.

Employer's duty to discuss change
(b) (i) The employer shall discuss with the employees affected and their union or unions, inter alia, the introduction of changes referred to in subclause 34(a), the effects the changes are likely to have on employees, measures to avert or mitigate the adverse effects of such changes on employees and shall give prompt consideration to matters raised by the employees and or their unions in relation to the changes.
   (ii) The discussion shall commence as early as practicable after a definite decision has been made by the employer to make the changes referred to in subclause 34(a).
   (iii) For the purposes of such discussion, the employer shall provide in writing to the employees concerned and their union or unions, all relevant information about the changes proposed; the expected effects of the change on employees and any other matters likely to effect employees provided that any employer shall not be required to disclose confidential information the disclosure of which would be inimical to the employer's interests.

35—Prevention and Settlement of Disputes

(a) Should a grievance or claim arise between the employer and any employee the parties shall confer in good faith with a view to resolving the matter by conciliation in accordance with the following procedure:
   (i) Should any matter occur which gives cause for concern to an employee, he/she shall raise such matter with his/her immediate supervisor.

(ii) If not settled to his/her satisfaction within 48 hours, the employee concerned shall draw such matter to the attention of the employee appointed and recognised as the local Union representative of the employee concerned. Such local Union representative shall submit the matter to the most senior employee responsible for supervision.

(iii) If still not satisfactorily settled within a further 48 hours, the local Union representative shall submit the matter to the appropriate senior executive officer or such other officer nominated by the employer.

(iv) If not settled after a further 7 days (or such longer period as may be mutually agreed) or where a matter of policy is concerned, the matter shall be referred by the senior executive officer to the next meeting of the Staffing Committee or Council/other Authority, whichever is appropriate.

(v) If not settled the matter shall be further discussed between the union and the appropriate representative of the employer.

(vi) Nothing contained in subparagraphs 35(a)(ii), 35(a)(iii) and 35(a)(iv) shall prevent either the employer Association or the union from becoming involved at an earlier stage should they consider it necessary.

(vii) If settlement has not been reached the matter then shall be referred to the employer Association and the union for further discussion.

(viii) If the matter is still not settled, either party shall refer it to the Industrial Relations Commission.

Disciplinary Procedure

(b) (i) Where disciplinary action is necessary, the management representative shall notify the employee of the reason, The first warning shall be verbal and will be recorded on the employee's personal file.

(ii) If the problem continues the matter will be discussed with the employee and a second warning in writing will be given to the employee and recorded on the employee's personal file. The local union representative shall be present if desired by either party.

(iii) If the problem continues the employee will be seen again by management. A final warning in writing may be given. The employee has the right to union representation.

(iv) In the event of the matter recurring, then the employee may be terminated. No dismissals are to take place without the authority of senior management.

(v) Summary dismissal of an employee may still occur for acts of 'serious and wilful misconduct'.

(vi) If a dispute should arise over the disciplinary action, the course of action to be followed is that the matter shall be referred to the appropriate reference body for resolution. Such resolution shall be accepted by the parties as final.

(vii) If after the warning, a period of twelve months elapses without any further warning or action being required, all adverse reports relating to the warning must be removed from the employee's personal file.

37—Redundancy—Private Sector only
Discussion before Termination

(a) (i) Where an employer has made a definite decision that the employer no longer wishes the job the employee has been doing done by anyone and this is not due to the ordinary and customary turnover of labour and that decision may lead to termination of employment, the employer shall hold discussions with the employees directly affected and with their union or unions.

(ii) The discussions shall take place as soon as is practicable after the employer has made a definite decision which will invoke the provision of paragraph 37(a)(i) and shall cover, inter alia, any reasons for the proposed terminations, measures to avoid or minimise the terminations and measures to mitigate any adverse effects of any terminations on the employees concerned.

(iii) For the purpose of the discussion the employer shall, as soon as practicable, provide in writing to the employees concerned and their union or unions, all relevant information about the proposed terminations including the reasons for the proposed terminations, the number and categories of employees likely to be affected, and the number of workers normally employed and the period over which the terminations are likely to be carried out. Provided that any employer shall not be required to disclose confidential information the disclosure of which would be inimical to the employer's interests.

Transfer to lower paid duties

(b) Where an employee is transferred to lower paid duties for reasons set out in paragraph 37(a)(i) the employee shall be entitled to the same period of notice of transfer as she/he would be entitled to if her/his employment had been terminated, and the employer may at the employers option, make payment in lieu thereof of an amount equal to the difference between the former ordinary time rate of pay and the new lower ordinary time rates for the number of weeks notice still owing.

Severance pay

(c) (i) In addition to the period of notice prescribed for termination in this part and subject to further award of the Commission, an employee whose employment is terminated for reasons set out in paragraph 37(a)(i) shall be paid the following amount of severance pay in respect of a period of continuous service.

Period of continuous service	Severance pay
less than one year	nil
1 year but less than 2 years	4 week's pay
2 years but less than 3 years	6 week's pay
3 years but less than 4 years	7 week's pay
4 years and over	8 week's pay

(ii) Provided that the severance payments shall not exceed the amount the employee would have earned if employment with the employer had proceeded to the employee's normal retirement date.

Definitions

(iii) 'Week's pay' means the ordinary time rate of pay for the employee concerned.

Continuous service

(iv) For the purposes of this clause, continuity of service shall be calculated in the manner prescribed by subclause 28(b) of this part.

Employee Leaving During Notice Period

(d) An Employee whose employment is terminated for reasons set out in paragraph 37(a)(i) may terminate her/his employment during the period of notice and, if so, shall be entitled to the same benefits and payments under this clause had she/he remained with the employer until the expiry of such notice. Provided in such circumstances the employee shall not be entitled to payment in lieu of notice.

Alternative Employment

(e) An employer, in a particular redundancy case, may make application to the Commission to have the general severance prescription varied if the employer obtains acceptable alternative employment for the employee.

Time off During Period of Notice

(f) (i) During the period of notice of termination given by the employer an employee shall be allowed up to one day's time off without loss of pay during each week of notice for the purpose of seeking other employment.

(ii) If the employee has been allowed paid leave for more than one day during the notice period for the purpose of seeking other employment, the employee shall, at the request of the employer, produce proof of attendance at an interview or she/he shall not receive payment for the time absent.

(iii) For this purpose a statutory declaration will be sufficient.

Notice to Commonwealth Employment Service

(g) Where a decision has been made to terminate employees in the circumstances outlined in paragraph 37(a)(i), the employer shall notify the Commonwealth Employment Service thereof as soon as possible giving relevant information including the number and categories of the employees likely to be affected and the period over which the terminations are intended to be carried out.

Employees with Less Than One Year's Continuous Service

(h) This Clause does not apply to employees with less than one year's continuous service.

Employers Exempted

(i) Subject to an Award of the Commission, in a particular redundancy case, this clause shall not apply to employers who employ less than 15 employees, whether under this part and/or otherwise.

Employees Exempted

(j) This clause shall not apply where employment has been terminated because the conduct of an employee justifies instant dismissal or in the case of casual employees, or employees engaged for a specific period of time or for a specified task or tasks.

Superannuation Benefits

(k) (i) Subject to further award by the Commission, where an employee who is terminated receives a benefit from a superannuation scheme, she/he shall only receive under subclause 37(c) the difference between the severance pay specified in that subclause and the amount of the superannuation benefit she/he receives which is attributable to employer contributions only.

(ii) If this superannuation benefit is greater than the amount due under subclause 37(c) then she/he shall receive no payments under that clause.

Transmission of Business

(l) (i) Where a business is, before or after the date of this part, transmitted from an employer (in this subclause called 'the transmittor') to another employer (in this subclause called 'the transmittee') and an employee who at the time of such transmission was an employee of the transmittor in that business becomes an employee of the transmittee:

(1) the continuity of the employment of the employee shall be deemed not to have been broken by reason of such transmission; and,

(2) the period of employment that the employee has had with the transmittor, or any prior transmittor shall be deemed to be service of the employee with the transmittee.

Definitions

(ii) For the purposes of this subclause the following definitions apply:

'Business' Includes trade, process, business or occupation and includes part of any such business.

'Transmission' Includes transfer, conveyance, assignment or succession whether by agreement or by operation of law.

'Transmitted' has a corresponding meaning.

Incapacity to Pay

(m) An employer, in a particular redundancy case, may make application to the Commission to have the general severance pay prescrption varied on the basis of the employer's incapacity to pay.

38—Termination of Employment

Public Sector Termination

(a) Except where the conduct of an employee justifies instant dismissal twenty-eight days notice of termination of employment may be given by either employer or employee, or in lieu thereof twenty-eight days salary shall be paid or forfeited as the case may be.

Private Sector Termination

Notice of Termination by the Employer

(b) (i) (1) In order to terminate the employment of an employee the employer shall give to the employee the following notice:

Period of Continuous Service	Period of Notice
less than 3 years	2 weeks
3 years but less than 5 years	3 weeks
5 years and over	4 weeks

(2) In addition to the notice in subparagraph 38(a)(i), employees over 45 years of age at the time of the giving of the notice with not less than two years continuous service, shall be entitled to an additional weeks notice.

(3) Payment in lieu of the notice prescribed in subparagraph 38(b)(i)(1) and/or 38(b)(i)(2) shall be made if the appropriate notice period is not given. Provided that employment may be terminated by part of the period of notice specified and part payment in lieu thereof.

(4) In calculating any payment in lieu of notice, the wages to be used shall be those the employee would have received in respect of ordinary time she/he would have worked during the period of notice had her/his employment not terminated.

(5) The period of notice in this clause shall not apply where the conduct of an employee justifies instant dismissal or in the case of casual employees or employees engaged for a specific period of time or for a specified task or tasks.

(6) For the purposes of this clause, continuity of service shall be calculated in the manner prescribed by subclause 28 (b).

Notice of Termination by the Employee

(ii) (1) The notice of termination required to be given by an employee shall be the same as that required of the employer, save and except that there shall be no additional notice based on the age of the employee concerned.

(2) Subject to financial obligations imposed on an employer by any Act, if an employee fails to give notice the employer shall have the right to withhold moneys due to the employee with a maximum amount equal to the ordinary time rate of pay for the period of notice.

Time Off Work During Period of Notice

(iii) Where an employer has given notice of termination to an employee, an employee shall be allowed up to one days time off without loss of pay for the purpose of seeking other employment. The time off shall be taken at times that are convenient to the employee after consultation with the employer.

Statement of Employment

(iv) The employer shall upon receipt of a request from an employee whose employment terminates, provide to the employee a written statement specifying the period of her/his employment and the classification and/or the type of work performed by the employee.

39—Right of Entry

(a) Employees of any establishment subject to this award may, with the consent of the person in charge of such establishment (which consent shall not unreasonably be withheld) be interviewed by the Secretary or another accredited representative of the Australian Nursing Federation (Victoria Branch), or have their union contributions collected.

(b) Where possible, one week's notice shall be provided in writing by the Australian Nursing Federation (Victoria Branch) and subject to subclause (c) such notice shall be accepted by the employer. In the private sector the Australian Nursing Federation (Victoria Branch) would also notify the employer of the reasons for the meeting. The Australian Nursing Federation (Victoria Branch) shall endeavour to accommodate any reasonable request by the employer to alter the date and/or time of the proposed interview.

(c) Union interviews shall not interfere with the efficient running of the employer's business.

[There follows Part C containing terms for Enrolled Nurses and Part D containing terms for Mothercraft Nurses.]

13

Legal Regulation of State Systems

Contents

State industrial regulation
Institutions and jurisdictions
- New South Wales
- South Australia
- Tasmania
- Queensland
- Western Australia

Role of state tribunals in unfair dismissal
Union registration and legal status
- effect of registration at state level
- the problem of dual registration
- possible solutions

Awards and agreements
- workplace agreements in Western Australia
- unions and agreements

Deregulation of labour law: the Victorian example
- employment agreements
- awards: voluntary arbitration
- award enforcement
- unfair dismissal
- institutions in Victorian industrial law
- industrial action
- secret ballots
- Victoria: concluding comments

Dominance of the federal system and co-operation between federal and state systems

State industrial regulation

Each State in Australia retains concurrent power with that of the Commonwealth Parliament in respect of labour relations. Consequently, each State has enacted separate and distinct systems of regulating industrial disputes and settling terms and conditions of employment. These systems operate to affect some 46% of Australian employees. (See Table 13.1 for state coverage.)

The legislation governing the regulation of state industrial relations is as follows:

> *Industrial Relations Act* 1991 (NSW)
> *Employee Relations Act* 1992 (Vic)
> *Industrial and Employee Relations Act* 1994 (SA)
> *Industrial Relations Act* 1979 (WA), together with the *Workplace Agreements Act* 1993 (WA) and the *Minimum Conditions of Employment Act* 1993 (WA)
> *Industrial Relations Act* 1984 (Tas)
> *Industrial Relations Act* 1990 (Qld)

The regulation of industrial relations commenced in colonial days and, although the historical development and evolution of each state system is both fascinating and important, this chapter deals with the current legislative framework.[1]

Significantly, although the state constitutions were not subject to the same constraints of s.51(35) in the Commonwealth constitution, the state legislatures chose to establish independent, government appointed tribunals to both resolve industrial disputes and generally (and in most cases) set the terms and conditions of employment. The methods of dispute resolution, too, have generally parallelled that in the federal sphere—conciliation and arbitration (usually of a compulsory nature). Thus we have not seen, until the recent Victorian example, radical departures from the federal model. Differences, of course, occur in emphasis, culture and practice, but the states have not been the initiators of different legal frameworks, such as the establishment of collective bargaining with the protection of minimum wages and conditions legislation. Such a system has always been open to the states but it is not a path down which state legislatures, speaking generally, chose to travel.

Institutions and jurisdictions

The nature of the institutions and the scope of their jurisdictions differ amongst the states. These features in all states, except Victoria, are examined below. The Victorian system is treated separately as an example of the radical move to deregulation of labour relations.

New South Wales

The *Industrial Relations Act* 1991 (NSW) ('The NSW Act') establishes a number of institutions with specific powers and jurisdictions. They are the Industrial Relations Commission of New South Wales, Conciliation Committees and the Industrial Court of New South Wales. In addition, there is the newly established position of Commissioner for Enterprise Agreements. Part 2 of

Table 13.1 Coverage of workers by State awards, and also by breakdown of male/female workers.

State or Territory	Number of employees ('000)	Covered by awards, determinations and collective agreements			Not covered by awards etc.
		Federal	State	Total(a)	
		–per cent–			
Males					
New South Wales	1,070.3	32.8	40.6	74.1	25.9
Victoria	919.1	45.7	28.1	78.2	21.8
Queensland	472.7	28.9	48.6	79.4	20.6
South Australia	267.7	41.4	36.5	79.6	20.4
Western Australia	267.6	24.7	50.2	75.5	24.5
Tasmania	78.2	49.7	35.3	86.3	13.7
Northern Territory	33.4	84.9	*1.3	86.4	13.6
Australian Capital Territory	65.0	83.2	*0.7	84.6	15.4
Australia	3,174.1	38.0	37.3	77.3	22.7
Private	2,229.2	33.8	32.0	68.4	31.6
Public	944.9	48.0	49.9	98.2	1.8
Females					
New South Wales	839.2	18.5	59.2	78.5	21.5
Victoria	691.9	27.6	54.8	87.3	12.7
Queensland	371.5	16.0	68.5	85.0	15.0
South Australia	219.4	23.4	61.6	86.3	13.7
Western Australia	224.6	16.3	65.7	82.5	17.5
Tasmania	51.7	27.3	61.0	89.4	10.6
Northern Territory	22.3	88.1	*1.3	89.6	10.4
Australian Capital Territory	57.6	84.7	*2.2	87.7	12.3
Australia	2,478.2	23.2	58.4	83.5	16.5
Private	1,728.3	19.0	56.0	77.6	22.4
Public	749.9	33.0	63.9	97.3	2.7
Persons					
New South Wales	1,909.5	26.5	48.8	76.1	23.9
Victoria	1,610.9	37.9	39.6	82.1	17.9
Queensland	844.2	23.2	57.3	81.8	18.2
South Australia	487.1	33.3	47.8	82.6	17.4
Western Australia	492.3	20.8	57.3	78.7	21.3
Tasmania	129.8	40.8	45.6	87.5	12.5
Northern Territory	55.7	86.2	*1.3	87.7	12.3
Australian Capital Territory	122.6	83.9	1.4	86.0	14.0
Australia	**5,652.2**	**31.5**	**46.5**	**80.0**	**20.0**
Private	3,957.4	27.3	42.4	72.4	27.6
Public	1,694.8	41.3	56.1	97.8	2.2

(a) Includes a small number of employees covered by unregistered agreements or unknown awards, determinations or collective agreements.

Source: Australian Bureau of Statistics, Catalogue No 6315.0, May 1990. Inquiries have indicated that these were the most up-to-date figures published, at the time of the book going to press.

the NSW Act establishes the Industrial Relations Commission of New South Wales which consists of a President, Vice President, Deputy President and Conciliation Commissioners. To be appointed as a member of the Commission, the person must have 'the skills and experience in the field of industrial relations that are appropriate for the office to which the person is recommended for appointment'.[2]

Under s.8(1) of the Act, the Commission has power to make an award relating to any conditions of employment which include the rates of wages payable to employees, the number of hours and the times to be worked in order to entitle employees to those wages, overtime and holiday rates, deductions to be made from wages of employees etc., the quantity of work to be done or services to be provided in connection with wages payable to employees, and any other industrial matter, whether or not it relates to the proceeding matters. Chapter 3 of the Act sets out the power of the Commission to deal with a 'question, dispute or difficulty concerning an industrial matter' and empowers the Commission to deal with the dispute by conciliation and if conciliation does not settle the question, dispute or difficulty, then the Commission has power to deal with it by arbitration.[3]

An innovative aspect of the NSW legislation is that it draws a distinction between *grievance* disputes which are dealt with under Part 1 of Chapter 3 and *rights* disputes. There is a procedure for reference of such grievance disputes to the Commission and the Commission is not empowered to deal with the grievance or question, dispute or difficulty unless it is satisfied that procedures in the award or agreement for its settlement have been complied with 'as far as is reasonable practicable in the circumstances'.[4] If agreement is not reached, the Commission may determine the grievance, question, dispute or difficulty by order, but it is limited in its powers of altering the substance of the employment relationship—it may only change the conditions of employment fixed by the award or agreement with the concurrence of the parties to the award or agreement.[5]

'Industrial matters' are defined in s.4(1) to mean

> 'matters or things affecting or relating to work done or to be done, or the privileges, rights or duties of employers or employees in any industry, and not involving questions which are or may be the subject of proceedings for an indictable offence and, without limiting the scope of those matters or things, include all or any of the matters relating to ...'

and matters are then set out in paras (a)(i), particular matters such as wages, hours of employment, mode, terms and conditions of employment etc. The Commission has express power to determine any question as to the demarcation of the industrial interests of industrial organisations of employees.[6]

The Act sets out a number of procedural requirements. The Commission may determine its own procedure (subject to the Act); it must act as quickly as is practicable, it is not bound to act in a formal manner; it is not bound by the rules of evidence and may inform itself on any matter in any way that it considers to be just; it must act according to equity, good conscience and the substantial merits of the case without regard to technicalities or legal form;

and it may conduct its proceedings either publicly or privately.[7] The Commission can exercise its functions either on its own initiative, on application in accordance with the Act and the rules or in other circumstances proscribed under the Act. Consent of the Commission must be obtained before parties may be represented by a legal practitioner.[8]

Conciliation Committees may be established to operate in relation to an identifiable industry or enterprise. These Committees are to consist of a conciliation commissioner who will be chairperson of the Committee and an equal number (the number to be determined by the Commission) of representatives of employers and representatives of employees.[9] The Conciliation Committee may exercise the functions of the Commission under the Act with respect to an industrial matter, but only in respect of the industry or enterprise for which the committee is established.[10] The Conciliation Committee is subject to the same general procedures of the Commission in respect of not acting formally, not being bound by the rules of evidence and so on.

The Industrial Court of New South Wales, consisting of a chief judge and such other judges as are appointed, is a superior court of record. The Industrial Court exercises jurisdiction with respect to offences under the Act, hearing offences in respect of engaging in unlawful industrial action,[11] procedures in respect of boycott conduct, and appeals on questions of law.[12]

Another officer within the system is the Commissioner for Enterprise Agreements who is charged with the responsibility under s.144(1) of the NSW Act to review the operation of the provisions relating to enterprise agreements, to advise any person in relation to an enterprise agreement when asked for assistance, to promote the use of enterprise agreements, and to report annually to the Minister on the Commissioner's activities.

Each enterprise agreement which is lodged for registration with the Industrial Registrar must be sent to the Commissioner for Enterprise Agreements who must then arrange a meeting of the parties to the enterprise agreement to establish that the parties understand their rights and obligations under the agreement and the conditions of employment under any award, former industrial agreement or other enterprise agreement applying to the parties. The Commissioner must then issue a certificate stating that the parties have the necessary understanding.

Enterprise agreements are designed to regulate (wholly or partly) the conditions of employment of persons who are employed in a single enterprise in any one or more trades or occupations.[13] An enterprise agreement will not have any effect unless it is registered and it will be enforceable as if it were an award. The NSW Commission is able to exercise functions of conciliation with respect to the enterprise agreement but only with the concurrence of each party to the agreement.[14]

Section 122 of the Act spells out the minimum conditions of employment for enterprise agreements (including minimum sick leave, ordinary hours of employment and rates of wages). There are positions governing formal matters (to be in writing) and length of life of the agreement.

South Australia

The *Industrial Relations Act* (SA) 1972 regulated the dispute resolution and award functions in South Australia, until the repeal of that Act by the *Industrial and Employee Relations Act* 1994 (SA).[15]

Although the 1994 Act has significantly changed this state system, the Industrial Commission of South Australia continues in existence as the Industrial Relations Commission of South Australia. It has two Divisions, the Industrial Relations Division and the Enterprise Agreement Division. It comprises a President, Deputy Presidents and Commissioners. The jurisdiction of the Commission is conferred by s.26 of the 1994 Act—the Commission has jurisdiction to approve enterprise agreements and awards which regulate remuneration and other industrial matters, to resolve industrial disputes and 'to hear and determine any matter or thing arising from or relating to an industrial matter as well as exercising other jurisdiction conferred by the Act'.

'Industrial matter' is now defined in the SA Act to mean 'a matter affecting the rights, privileges or duties of employers or employees (including prospective employers and employees), or the work to be done in employment' and there follows a list of matters in paragraphs (a) to (n) which are examples of such matters contained within the general element of the definition.[16] 'Industrial dispute' is defined in s.4(1) of the Act to mean 'a dispute about an industrial matter or a threatened, impending or probable dispute about an industrial matter'. The South Australian Act has, like most of the other State Acts, retained definitions of industrial disputes and industrial matters which are similar to the definitions at federal level in the *Industrial Relations Act* 1988 (Cth).

The Industrial Relations Commission may make an award about remuneration as well as other industrial matters.[17] It is under an obligation in exercising its jurisdiction to 'make every practical attempt to conciliate, to prevent impending industrial disputes and to settle existing disputes and claims by amicable agreement'.[18] In addition, in resolving or preventing industrial disputes, the Commission may exercise powers of mediation[19] and call voluntary or compulsory conferences.[20]

Like the powers possessed by the Australian Industrial Relations Commission and the New South Wales Commission, the South Australian Commission has power to sit at any place, and is not bound by the rules of evidence. As with developments at federal level, there is a strong emphasis on conciliation and attempts at amicable agreement.[21] The 1994 Act provides minimum entitlements in Schedules for sick leave, annual leave and parental leave, but the Full Commission has power to review the minimum standards in each of these areas and substitute a 'fresh minimum standard'.[22]

Approval by the Commission of industrial agreements was necessary under the former Act as it is for enterprise agreements which are a significant feature of the 1994 Act. Thus, although there is provision for the parties to make agreements, they are subject to control by the Commission.[23] The controls mainly require the Commission to be satisfied that reasonable steps were taken to ensure the employees understood the effect of the agreement, that they entered into it without coercion or properly authorised their union to enter into it, that it is in the employees' 'best interests' and that it does not provide for terms and conditions which are inferior to existing awards and the Schedules of minimum entitlements.

The Industrial Court of South Australia continues as the Industrial Relations Court of South Australia constituted by a Senior Judge, judges and industrial magistrates. Its jurisdiction is interpreting awards or enterprise agreements, hearing questions of law referred to it by the Commission, determining jurisdictional and other questions about the validity of determinations of the Commission, and hearing and determining claims in respect of sums due to employees or former employees under an award, enterprise agreement or contract of employment.[24] There can be appeals from orders or decisions of the Court to the Full Court, and appeals from orders of the Court consituted by an industrial magistrate to a single judge of the Court.[25]

The 1994 Act created a new office, that of Employee Ombudsman. The Employee Ombudsman has functions which include advising employees on their rights and obligations under awards and enterprise agreements and/or available avenues for enforcing their rights; investigating claims by employees or their unions as to coercion in negotiating enterprise agreements and scrutinising enterprise agreements lodged for approval under the Act.[26] The Employee Ombudsman is also one of the inspectors who ensure compliance with Act, enterprise agreements and awards.[27]

The South Australian legislative scheme follows the same structural division as the federal system, whereby award-making and agreement approval are given to the Commission and enforcement and interpretation powers are given to a separate body, the Industrial Relations Court. Unlike the federal system, there are no constitutional requirements which force such a separation of functions. Interestingly, whilst the system has been one of conciliation and arbitration, 'arbitration' is a term avoided in the Act.

Tasmania

The Tasmanian system and the Victorian system of industrial regulation with their original and long-standing emphasis on committees of employer and employee representatives were very similar until relatively recently. In 1984, the Tasmanian system was amended to bring the system closer to the federal model of conciliation and arbitration.

The Tasmanian Industrial Commission consists of Commissioners, one of whom shall be President, and some others Deputy President, and the Enterprise Commissioner.[28] The jurisdiction of the Commission is set out in s.19(1) of the *Industrial Relations Act* 1984—the Commission 'has jurisdiction to hear and determine any matter arising from, or relating to, an industrial matter'. 'Industrial matter' means 'any matter pertaining to the relations of employers and employees' and without limiting its general definition there are listed matters in sub-paragraphs which include rates of pay, hours of work etc. The definition of 'industrial matter' however contains a number of exclusions—industrial matter does not include a matter relating to, for example, the opening or closing hours of an employer's business premises, the entitlement to long service leave, compensation in respect of injuries or diseases suffered in the course of employment, deduction of union dues, preferential employment, bonus payments made at the discretion of the employer, insurance of employees, or appointments or promotions other than in respect of the qualifications required for advancement. The Tasmanian Industrial Commission cannot then order preference to unionists in employment or permit the establishment of a system of 'check-off' (deduction of union dues from wages). These would have to be agreed to by employer and union and these may well be problems of enforcement of such agreements.

Applications can be made to the President for hearing before a Commissioner in respect of an industrial dispute which has arisen or which is considered likely to arise[29] and the Commission may, for the purpose of preventing, settling or attempting to prevent or settle, an industrial dispute summon persons to attend at conferences.[30] The Commission may make an order requiring something to be done or action to be taken for the purpose of preventing or settling the industrial dispute.

The Commission has power to make awards in respect of state employees in the public sector.

There is provision for the making of industrial agreements and enterprise agreements. The Enterprise Commissioner has the function under s.61ZC(1) of reviewing the operation of the provisions relating to enterprise agreements, promoting the use of the enterprise agreements, and reporting on matters relating to the development and operation of enterprise agreements. The Enterprise Commissioner is specifically charged under s.61J(1) with approving an enterprise agreement unless certain stated conditions are made out— for example that the conditions of employment are less than the minimum conditions specified in the Act. Once an enterprise agreement is registered it is enforceable as if it were an award.[31] Employee committees can be formed in order to represent employees in an enterprise with respect to negotiating or making, varying or terminating an enterprise agreement.[32]

Freedom of association is encouraged in s.87 which provides that 'it is not compulsory for any person to be or not to be a member of, or to join or not to join, any organisation or association'.

A Magistrate determines proceedings for an offence against the Act or the Tasmanian system.

Queensland

The *Industrial Relations Act* 1990 (Qld) was enacted following a major overhaul of the Queensland system.

The Queensland Industrial Relations Commission took over the functions of the already established Industrial Conciliation and Arbitration Commission. The Commission consists of at least six Industrial Commissioners, presided over by a Chief Industrial Commissioner. The Commission has conferred on it a general jurisdiction[33] to hear and determine all questions of law or fact brought before it for the purpose of regulating any calling, all questions arising out of an industrial matter or involving the determination of the rights and duties of any person in respect of an industrial matter, or questions that it considers expedient to hear and determine in respect of the industrial matter, any industrial dispute, appeals under the Act and matters committed to the Commission by the Act. An industrial matter is defined as a matter affecting work, privileges, rights and duties of employers and employees, any matter which in the opinion of the Industrial Court or Industrial Commission is or has been or may be a cause or contributory cause of a strike, lock-out or industrial dispute and, industrial matter is more particularly described in certain sub-paragraphs of the definition section.[34]

Disputes may be notified to the Industrial Commissioner who must attempt to conciliate the matter and if that is not successful to arbitrate the matter.[35]

The Industrial Magistrate's Court is the Court of Record and constituted by an Industrial Magistrate sitting alone.[36] The Commission is empowered to remit to an Industrial Magistrate for investigation and report to the Commission, for taking of evidence, or for the hearing and determination of any industrial matter or aspect of it or of any matter or question that arises in connection with that matter.[37] The Industrial Magistrate has jurisdiction to hear and determine proceedings in relation to offences under the Act, claims in respect of wages due and payable, claims for damages for breach of an agreement made under an award, industrial agreement, certified agreement or enterprise flexibility agreement.[38]

Major amendments to the Queensland Act made by the *Industrial Relations Reform Act* 1994 (Qld) mirrored the federal reform legislation of 1993. Thus, the Queensland system now makes provision for the approval of enterprise flexibility agreements (shorn of the 'constitutional corporation' limits in the federal Act) and certified agreements in the same way as the federal model.[39] Further minimum entitlements covering a range of matters, including different types of leave and termination requirements, are set down in Part 11 of the Act.

Western Australia

The Western Australian Industrial Relations Commission is constituted under s.8 of the *Industrial Relations Act* 1979 and consists of a President, a Chief Commissioner, a Senior Commissioner and a number of other commissioners.[40] The President of the Commission must be legally qualified, that is to be or have been a barrister or solicitor of the High Court or a State or Territory Supreme Court of not less than five years standing.[41] The Chief Commissioner must be either experienced at a high level in industrial relations or have obtained a University degree or similar educational qualification which has substantial relevance to the duties of Chief Commissioner.[42]

The Chief Commissioner performs the function of allocating work amongst the Commission and assigning and appointing commissioners for the purposes of constituting the full bench for the Commission in court session.

The main jurisdiction of the Commission is set out in s.23(1) of the Act which provides 'Subject to this Act, the Commission has cognizance of and authority to enquire into and deal with any industrial matter'. There are limits to the jurisdiction set out in s.23(3) which include a provision which does not enable the Commission to provide for preference or to provide for compulsory unionism.

In addition, under s.24, the Commission has jurisdiction to determine whether proceedings relate to an industrial matter and the finding is to be final. 'Industrial matter' is defined in s.7(1) to mean 'any matter affecting or relating to the work, privileges, rights or duties of employers or employees in any industry or of any employer or employees therein and, without limiting the generality of that meaning, includes any matter relating to ...' and there follows a list of subjects in paragraphs (a) to (m).[43]

The Commission is under an obligation to endeavour to resolve a matter referred to it first of all by conciliation which includes arranging conferences of the parties or their representatives presided over by the Commission, arranging for conferences amongst the parties at which a member of the Commission is not present, giving directions and making orders to enable conciliation or arbitration to resolve the matter and so on. When the Commission cannot resolve the matter by conciliation, the Commission may proceed to determine the matter by arbitration.[44]

The Commission must make a determination in the form of an order, award or declaration[45] and the award is to bind 'all employees employed in any calling mentioned therein in the industry or industries to which the award applies; and all employers employing those employees'.[46] Thus, the constraints of parties and the 'no common rule' doctrine at federal level does not exist in WA and the other states.

There is provision for registration of industrial agreements under s.41, where an agreement has been made 'with respect to any industrial matter or for the prevention or resolution under this Act of dispute, disagreement, or questions relating thereto'. The Commission is the body empowered to register the agreement as an industrial agreement, but before doing so, the Commission may require the parties to effect any variation the Commission considers necessary or desirable 'for the purpose of giving clear expression to the true intention of the parties'.[47] An industrial agreement cannot be registered if the agreement applies to more than a single enterprise which is defined as more than one business, project or undertaking or the activities carried on by more than one public authority, and the term of agreement is contrary to the Act or any general order made under s.51 in relation to national wage decisions.[48]

The Commission has power to call compulsory conferences[49] and can make various directions as appropriate.[50]

The Commission in Court Session has power to make orders relating to minimum conditions, but cannot exercise that power if a minimum condition is prescribed by the *Minimum Conditions of Employment Act* 1993 (see below).

There are also specialist bodies, the Government School Teachers Tribunal, the Public Service Arbitrator and Appeal Boards, the Railways Classification Board and the Promotions Appeals Board which are set up under the legislation with express jurisdiction, powers and composition.

Enforcement of the Act, awards and industrial agreements is within the jurisdiction of the Industrial Magistrates Court. The Industrial Magistrates Court, if there is contravention or failure to comply with an order or award, may issue a caution or impose a penalty which the Court considers just, but which, under the present law, must not exceed $1000 in the case of an employer, organisation or association, and $250 in any other case. The Court can order payment of award wages due.[51] There may be an appeal to the Full Bench from a decision of the Industrial Magistrates Court.

Another entity relevant in the Western Australian system is the Western Australian Industrial Appeals Court, established under s.85 of the *Industrial Relations Act*. The members of the Court are the judges nominated by the Chief Justice of Western Australia and consist of the Presiding Judge, the Deputy Presiding Judge and two ordinary members. The jurisdiction of the Court is an appellate one—it is empowered to determine appeals under s.90 (which deals with appeals from decisions of President, Full Bench, or the Commission in Court Session on errors of law) and s.96K which enables an appeal from a decision of an industrial magistrate in respect of discrimination against persons because of membership of an organisation, refusal to employ, discriminatory and injurious acts against a person who perform work for employers because of membership or non-membership of an employee organisation and discriminatory and injurious acts against persons because of non-membership of an employee organisation.

The industrial inspectors are appointed under s.98 for the purpose of enforcing the observance of the legislation.

The *Industrial Relations Act* 1979 (WA) is the main Act establishing the institutions and governing industrial regulation in Western Australia. However, in a move which has paralleled to some extent developments in Victoria with the enactment of the *Employee Relations Act* 1992 and at federal level with the *Industrial Relations Reform Act* 1993, the legislature in Western Australia has introduced changes to the WA industrial relations system by amending the *Industrial Relations Act* 1979 (WA), and enacting separate legislation which interlocks or overrides the 1979 Act.

The main changes relate to facilitating the employers and employees to make workplace agreements, ending compulsory unionism and providing for a minimum set of wages and conditions for non-award employees. Unlike the Victorian system, however, awards have not been abolished but there is provision for opting out of awards and to have collective or workplace agreements govern the terms and conditions of employment.

The amending or interlocking legislation is as follows:

Industrial Relations Amendment Act 1993 (WA); Minimum Conditions of Employment Act 1993 (WA); and Workplace Agreements Act 1993 (WA).

The new workplace agreements legislation is examined further under section Awards and Agreements.

Role of State tribunals in unfair dismissal

An important industrial issue which has often been resolved by the state industrial tribunals is that of unfair dismissal. As we have seen, the State Parliaments have not the same constraints as the Federal Parliament has under s.51(35) of the Constitution. Thus, they have been able to enact provisions which confer a jurisdiction on the relevant state industrial tribunal to deal with the unfair dismissal of a worker and to make orders which may achieve reinstatement, re-employment or compensation depending on the powers chosen to be conferred on the tribunal. As there have until recently been considerable doubts as to the legality of the Federal Commission making orders of reinstatement, the states have become very important in this industrial issue. These jurisdictions are examined as to the role and powers of the industrial tribunal in the states.

Part 8 of Ch 3 of the *Industrial Relations Act* 1991 (NSW) confers an unfair dismissal jurisdiction on the NSW Industrial Commission—if an employer dismisses or threatens to dismiss a person who is an employee of the employer and the dismissal is harsh, unreasonable or unjust, the employee (or an industrial organisation of employees on the person's behalf) may apply to the Commission for relief.[52] The Commission must try to settle the claim by conciliation. When all reasonable attempts to settle in that manner have been made but have been unsuccessful, the Commission can make an order.[53] The Commission has a number of alternative orders. The Commission may order reinstatement of the applicant in his or her former position on terms not less favourable to the applicant and to order payment of an amount the applicant would have received had he or she not been dismissed. Where reinstatement is not applicable the Commission may order re-employment of the applicant on terms and conditions determined by the Commission in another position that the employer has available and which, in the opinion of the Commission, is suitable and make payment[54] of an amount the applicant would have received but for the dismissal. Where either reinstatement or re-employment is impracticable, the Commission may order compensation to a maximum of six months pay for the applicant. The NSW Commission, unlike the Victorian Commission, may order monetary compensation as an alternative to either re-employment or reinstatement. This is a remedy which is often utilised in instances where the employer/employee relationship has broken down to such an extent that it is not possible to order the parties to resume that relationship.

An important power and role of the Industrial Commission of South Australia was its jurisdiction in respect of unfair dismissals—s.31(1) of the South Australia *Industrial Relations Act* 1972 provided that an employee could, within twenty-one days after dismissal, apply to the Commission for relief under the section. Where the Commission determined that the dismissal was 'harsh, unjust or unreasonable' the Commission had power to order re-employment in the employee's former position or re-employment in another position if re-employment in the former position was impracticable. Where re-employment in either manner was not an appropriate remedy, the Commission may order the employer to pay compensation.[55] Section 31(4a) sets out an upper limit by salary in respect of compensation.

These provisions are essentially now contained in Ch 3 Part 6 of the 1994 SA Act but the ILO Termination of Employment Convention now applies to determine when dismissal is harsh, unjust or unreasonable. Further procedures relevant to this question are laid out expressly (in Schedule 8).

As with some of the other jurisdictions, there is an express reinstatement and re-employment jurisdiction given to the Queensland Industrial Relations Commission under Part 11, Division 4 of the *Industrial Relations Act* 1990 (Qld). Application can be made to the Commission by an employee dismissed from employment (application should be made within twenty-one days after the dismissal or within a longer period if the Commission permits); application can be made by the employee himself or herself or an industrial organisation to which the employee belongs acting on behalf of the employee and with the employee's consent. The parties must explore the possibility of resolving the matters by conciliation and be fully informed of possible consequences of further proceedings, before the Commission hears the application. There is then an emphasis on the parties endeavouring to resolve the problem first by conciliation.

The Commission may order reinstatement or re-employment, or if neither of those are considered appropriate, the employer may be ordered to pay the employee an amount of compensation determined by the Commission. The Queensland provisions now essentially mirror the unlawful termination of employment law at federal level, so that the remedies will be available for dismissals on prohibited grounds and not for a valid reason which includes a harsh, unjust or unreasonable dismissal.

In Western Australia there is an express unfair dismissal jurisdiction set out in s.23A of the *Industrial Relations Act* 1979 whereby if the Commission has referred to it a claim of harsh, oppressive or unfair dismissal then the Commission can order compensation and order reinstatement or re-employment or make an ancillary order. Compensation is not generally available as a remedy unless the employer has not complied with a reinstatement or re-employment order, in which cases compensation is subject to a maximum of six months wages of the dismissed employee.

The Tasmanian unfair dismissal jurisdiction is derived from its general jurisdiction over industrial disputes which are defined to include disputes relating to the engagement, dismissal or reinstatement of an employee.[56] There are no express powers of reinstatement or compensation contained in the Act but the Tasmanian Commission would be limited to its normal powers over a dispute which would include reinstatement.

The states, thus, have different ways of approaching this important jurisdiction. The Victorian approach is outlined in the section Deregulation of Labour Relations. The state powers in this area have been an important source of relief for unfairly dismissed workers. Even after the federal reforms of 1994, they will continue to be so unless the state remedy is not regarded as an 'adequate alternative remedy' in which case the federal law will apply. Not only did the states provide significant job protection to employees which was lacking under federal law but the relief was generally unavailable under principles of contract law.

Union registration and legal status

Effect of registration at State level

At federal level, registration of organisations of employees confers corporate status on unions pursuant to s.192 of the *Industrial Relations Act* 1988 (Cth). At state level, different approaches have been taken to union registration. Some states have permitted registration of unions to grant that union corporate legal status, whilst other states have permitted a system of registration or recognition as in Victoria, where recognition of a union does not confer corporate status on that organisation. The states which have enacted legislation conferring corporate status on registered unions are New South Wales, Queensland, Western Australia and South Australia. In Western Australia, for example, Division 4 of the *Industrial Relations Act* 1979 (WA) deals with industrial organisations and associations and details qualifications for and the basis for registration of organisations of employees and organisations of employers. Ordinarily, an association of at least 200 employees may apply to be registered under the Act and if there are fewer than 200 employees, then the Full Bench of the WA Commission must be satisfied that there is a good reason, consistent with the objects set out in s.6 of the Act, to permit registration. There are certain requirements as to registration and the nature of the rules in relation to secret ballots.[57] Pursuant to s.60, the organisation when registered 'shall, upon and during registration, become and be, for the purposes of this Act, a body corporate by the registered name, having perpetual succession and a common seal, but, subject to this Act, an organisation may at any time, with the consent of the Full Bench, change its name...'. Under s.60(2) an organisation can sue and be sued, can hold property etc. There are also provisions relating to amalgamation set out in s.72.

The problem of dual registration

Given the federal nature of our system of industrial relations, problems arise in terms of the legal status of unions. For example, there may be in existence several separate state unions which come together to form a federal union, and the federal union seeks registration. State unions have already been registered at ftate level and have independent corporate legal status. Those state unions then become branches of federal unions and the question arises whether the branch of the federal union is one and the same body as the state registered union or whether in fact there are two separate bodies. What tends to happen is that the state bodies—whether they be branch or state registered unions—operate as the one organisation. They will have the one set of accounts, they will have one election for the office bearers to both branch and state union, their property will be the same and so on.

The situation can also occur in reverse where the federal body is the first body to be in existence and to obtain union registration. Branches exist in the various states and those branches may see advantages in registering at state level as separate organisations in order to participate in the state system of industrial relations. The same problems arise—they are often administered as one and the same body.

This causes difficulty for members—are they members of the branch or the state union or both; to whom does the property of the union belong; to whom do the funds of the union belong and so on?

The problem came to a head in the celebrated case of *Moore v Doyle*[58] in which a factional dispute had arisen between a federal union and that union's own state branches. It concerned the Transport Workers' Union of Australia, a registered organisation under the then *Conciliation and Arbitration Act* 1904 (Cth) and a branch of the Transport Workers' Union which was registered as both a trade union and an industrial union under two state Acts—the *Trade Union Act* and the *Industrial Arbitration Act* of New South Wales. The litigation arose when a member of the federal union took proceedings under s.141 of the 1904 Act against the Committee of Management of the federal body, the Committee of Management of the New South Wales branch and the organisation itself in order to obtain performance and observance of the union rules in relation to conduct of the state branch. The particular issue in question was whether persons who were not employees but owner drivers of trucks could become members of the branch and the federal organisation. There were different laws at federal and state levels on this question—such individuals could not be admitted to membership of the federal body and the rules at that time could not be altered to allow their membership; whereas in New South Wales s.88E of the then *Industrial Arbitration Act* permitted persons who were not employees but performed certain classes of work (and were therefore deemed employees) to become members of the state union. Therefore there was a problem in terms of eligibility to membership to the different unions.

The three judges of the then Industrial Court who heard the matter (Spicer CJ, Smithers and Kerr JJ) said:

> 'The cases in both State and Federal jurisdictions and the rules of many organisations and trade unions show that the constitutions of the Federal and the corresponding State body often differ to some extent so that membership of the trade union and the State branch of a Federal organisation, if full use is made of the range of eligibility, must be different. The cases also show that the rules of the Federal organisation and the corresponding State trade union each provide for a contribution fee but in all or almost all cases only one fee is collected and this is treated as satisfying the requirements of membership in both the Federal and the corresponding State registered body. Very frequently the rules of the Federal organisation and of the trade union on other matters are different from and inconsistent with one another and often the rules require different officers to be filled in a State branch of the Federal organisation and in the trade union.
>
> In the great majority of cases the trade union and the branch of the Federal organisation are administered as though they were the same body with one set of assets, one system of banking, one set of books, one register of members, one set of officers, one election of officers for both bodies, and one system of meetings of a Committee of Management to handle the affairs of the trade union and the State branch of the organisation. Despite differences in the constitution rule of the Federal and the corresponding State body, members of one who are not eligible to be members of the other are often treated as members of both and often vote in elections of the body to which they are not entitled to belong. Generally, one application form is filled in and this sometimes satisfies the provisions of rules of the organisation and the trade union, but often there are different rules as to applications. Sometimes, as the cases show, the real and effectively-operating body is the State branch of the Federal organisation with the corresponding trade union existing as a mere fiction and it has occurred that a trade union has been held to be non-existent and liable to be deregistered by the State authority. In other cases it is the trade union which is the living body at a State branch of the Federal organisation which may be a shadow or fiction having no real existence. In yet other cases the affairs of the State branch of the Federal organisation and of the

corresponding trade union are administered under some practically-evolved set of rules which are an administrative amalgam of the registered rules of the State branch and the trade unions but are not the actual rules of either. The trade union and industrial arbitration acts of some of the States appear to proceed upon the basis that the State trade union and Federal industrial union is an autonomous body corporate or separate legal entity not under control of bodies outside itself, whereas the State-registered body is usually treated as being part of a Federal organisation and is, in fact, subject to control by a Federal council or Committee of Management.'[59]

This case highlighted and identified the problem of dual registration, a problem which in essence has arisen from our federal and state regulation of industrial relations.

Possible solutions

The Industrial Court in *Moore v Doyle* made a plea to the Parliament to introduce legislation to correct the situation. Following the case, a Committee of Enquiry was established to review the problem, which has become known as the '*Moore v Doyle* problem'. The Committee was chaired by Justice Sweeney. The Committee recommended that state laws be amended to permit the registration of branches of federally registered unions which would not entail the giving of legal status to those branches—in other words, legislation should be changed so that branches would have the right to participate in state industrial relations systems without the necessity for corporate legal status being conferred upon them. This proposal did necessitate some changes at federal level which were indeed made, but, until recently, no state had legislated to resolve the problem. It was the South Australia Parliament which first amended its *Industrial Relations Act* (SA) 1972 to provide for two types of registration: state unions which participate in the state system are to still be able to be registered and obtain corporate status; branches of federal organisations which wish to participate in the federal system as well as the state system can be registered under the State Act but no corporate legal status is conferred upon them. These provisions are now in the *Industrial and Employee Relations Act* 1994 (SA).[60]

Other solutions to the problem of dual personality have been suggested. Justice Gray of the Federal Court of Australia in the 1985 decision of *Bailey v Krantz*[61] considered the question of registration of a branch of a Federal union under South Australian law. It was held by Gray J that such registration did not create a corporation under state law because, as the federal union was already registered and therefore a corporation under federal law, a state law providing or giving corporate status to a branch of such union would be inconsistent with the federal law and pursuant to s.109 of the Australian Constitution, the federal law would prevail and the state law would be rendered inoperative.[62]

In a later case, *Sharpe v Goodhew*[63] Pincus J of the Federal Court held that a branch of a union which was registered at federal level could be incorporated under the then *Industrial Conciliation and Arbitration Act* 1961 (Qld). There has been, then, conflicting authority between judges in the Federal Court.

More recently in the case of *Frizziero v Rice*[64] the question posed for a full bench of the Federal Court was whether a branch of the Confectionery Workers' Union of Australia had been registered under South Australian labour laws, and, if so, whether such registration created an incorporated body under this State law. However, the Federal Court did not answer the second part of the question because it decided as a matter of fact that a branch had *not* been registered under state law. Hence the matter remains for resolution.

In South Australia, the legislation was amended in the way outlined above to provide for some non-corporate registration of unions. In Victoria and Tasmania, the state systems of industrial regulation have never provided for incorporation of state registered unions so the problem does not arise. In Victoria, even when the legislation was amended in the 1980s and early 1990s to establish a system along the lines of the federal system of conciliation and arbitration (this system has now been replaced by a system of voluntary arbitration), provision for the first time was made for registering unions. The system was not one of registration but rather one of recognition. In order to have certain rights and privileges under the legislation, for example, in order to be able to be a party to a registered agreement, to nominate representatives on the then Conciliation and Arbitration Boards and so on, a union of employees had to be recognised under the Act. This recognition gave rise to certain rights but it did not give rise to corporate legal status.[65]

The problem of dual registration of trade unions remains one for consideration by state legislatures.

Awards and agreements

Each state system has provisions as discussed for making awards which can be enforceable and binding. The state systems have always had provision for some form of registration or certification of industrial agreements so that in these systems, too, some form of collective bargaining has operated side-by-side with the more formal processes of dispute resolution. There have been initiatives at federal level to promote enterprise and collective bargaining and these initiatives have also occurred in most of the states. In Victoria, under the *Employee Relations Act* 1992, the Victorian Parliament took the step of forcing all parties out of the award system, establishing a system of voluntary arbitration and leaving parties to negotiate either individual or collective employment agreements. Section 8 of the Act governs both collective and individual employment agreements so that some form of bargaining—either individual or collective is in place in Victoria. These are analysed in the section Deregulation of Labour Law: The Victorian Example.

The New South Wales Act has been amended to facilitate enterprise bargaining as has the Tasmanian legislation and more recently the legislation in Queensland, South Australia and Western Australia.[66] The Western Australian *Workplace Agreements Act* 1993 (WA) is analysed as an example of how the move to bargaining can be superimposed on existing systems. It will no doubt be the subject of further amendment but the example is illustrative of problems of change at state level.

Workplace agreements in Western Australia

The *Workplace Agreements Act* 1993 (WA) commenced operation on 1 December 1993. The Act has the effect of overriding the *Industrial Relations Act* 1979 as s.4 provides 'This Act has effect despite any provision of the *Industrial Relations Act* 1979'.

The Act has the effect of enabling workplace agreements to be made and for awards, then existing or future, *not* to apply so long as the workplace agreement is in force. A workplace agreement is defined as an agreement made between employers and employees, and which provides for some or all of the rights and obligations that employers and employees have in relation to one another, including rights and obligations that are to take effect after termination of employment.[67] A workplace agreement may cover a single workplace, or a number of workplaces, and it may apply to the employment relationship between the parties in any place or circumstances. Contracts of employment can still be entered into.[68] There is provision for making of collective workplace agreements in s.9, and also workplace agreements entered into between an employer and one of the employer's employees (s.10). A workplace agreement will bind parties to the agreement and successors and transmittees of an employer's business.[69]

There is provision for entitlement to be represented by a bargaining agent and a bargaining agent may be 'any person or group of persons'.[70] Written authority must be given for the appointment of a bargaining agent as provided in s.15(3) of the Act. It is to be noted that it is not to be assumed that a trade union is to be the bargaining agent.

Section 17 of the Act ensures that the *Minimum Conditions of Employment Act* 1993 has effect to imply provisions in a workplace agreement (see below). There are also requirements as to content of the agreement. For example, in every workplace agreement, there is to be implied a provision that an employer must not unfairly, harshly or oppressively dismiss from employment any employee who is a party to the agreement. This cannot be excluded by agreement.[71] The workplace agreement must be in writing, must name the employer and the employee or employees between whom it is made and be signed by each of them.[72] In addition, the workplace agreement must set out provisions for dealing with any question or dispute which arises between the parties as to the effect of the agreement[73] and an agreement must not require persons to be members of organisations.

A collective workplace agreement must be registered under ss 31 or 32 of the Act whilst an individual workplace agreement has effect whether or not it is registered.

The Commissioner must be satisfied that the agreement complies with the Act, that each party to the agreement seems to understand his or her rights or obligations under the agreement, that no party was persuaded by threats or intimidation to enter into the agreement and that each party to the agreement genuinely wishes to have the agreement registered. These provisions which have to be satisfied are set out in s.30(1). If the Commissioner is not satisfied of those matters, then the Commissioner must refuse to register the agreement unless the Commissioner can utilise the partial registration of collective workplace agreement set out in s.32.

It should be noted that s.33 sets out the position where an individual workplace agreement has been lodged for registration but registration is refused by the Commissioner. The agreement will cease to have effect and either party may recover from the other an amount which if the agreement had not taken effect he or she would have been entitled to receive.

There can be an appeal to the Supreme Court against the Commissioner's refusal to register an agreement. There are various requirements as to the employer's keeping of records, and enforcement is to be in the Industrial Magistrates Court.

The *Minimum Conditions of Employment Act* 1993 (WA) was also operative on 1 December 1993. The general thrust of the legislation is that minimum conditions of employment are to bind all employees and employers and are taken to be implied in any workplace agreement, any award or in a contract (if the contract of employment is not governed by a workplace agreement or an award).[74] Any provision which is less beneficial than that in the minimum condition, will not have an effect. The minimum rates of pay are to be announced by the Minister and published in the gazette and the Commission in Court Session is to review the minimum weekly rates of pay and make a recommendation to the Minister by 31 May each year. The Minister is under an obligation to determine the minimum weekly rates of pay by either accepting the Commission in Court Session's recommendation or determining a rate or rates different from the recommendation. Provisions are set out in:

Part 4, Division 2, dealing with Leave, Illness or Injury;
Part 4, Division 3, Annual Leave;
Part 4, Division 4, Bereavement Leave;
Part 5, Division 5, Public Holidays;
Part 5, Division 6, Parental Leave; and
Division 4, Part 5, Minimum Conditions of Employment Changes with Significant Effect and Redundancy.

The WA legislative framework is detailed in respect of parties opting out of the concilation and arbitration processes and opting for workplace agreements by negotiation. The system is controlled and very specific as to legislative requirements and Commission power and functions. 'Opting out' is not achieved in the context of award abolition as in Victoria but is voluntary. Even so, the legal framework is detailed because of the demand for checks and protections within the system.

Unions and agreements

One question which has always remained a sensitive one for unions is whether unions have to be parties to collective agreements. In Victoria, the union cannot be a party to the agreement but could be authorised by the relevant employees to negotiate the agreement on their behalf. The role of unions in the Victorian system has been very much downgraded. In WA, the union will not necessarily be the bargaining agent. In New South Wales, in other contexts too, this 'downgrading' of unions has taken place—for example, unions no longer are required to make application to the Commission in respect of unfair dismissals; application can now be made by the individual employee and only if that individual so chooses can the union be involved in making the application on the dismissed employee's behalf.

Deregulation of labour law: the Victorian example

Section 1 of the *Employee Relations Act* 1992 (Vic) (the Act), which repealed the *Industrial Relations Act* 1979 (Vic), states that one of the purposes of the Act is that it makes 'fresh provision with respect to the law relating to employee relations in Victoria'. In fact, this Act, which was enacted in November 1992 and became fully operative on 1 March 1993, has effected substantial and fundamental changes to the Victorian system of industrial relations and law. The main changes are the introduction for the first time of voluntary arbitration and the facilitation of the making of employment agreements between employers and employees.

These changes are broadly in line with changes which have already taken place in New Zealand in the *Employee Contracts Act* 1991 (NZ), and go well beyond the changes effected in New South Wales by the *Industrial Relations Act* 1991 (NSW) in terms of deregulation of employer-employee relations. The new emerging philosophy of the 1990s for industrial relations in Victoria and New Zealand seems to be to encourage individual agreements, to move reliance away from protective awards and to de-emphasize, or exclude in certain cases, the role of trade unions. In Victoria, this philosophy is implemented first by enabling the employment agreements to be entered into from 27 November 1992 and secondly, by the abolition of all existing awards made by the Industrial Relations Commission under the *Industrial Relations Act* 1979 (Vic) from 1 March 1993 (see s.172(6) *Employee Relations Act* 1992 (Vic)). Until a new award is made covering the employee or an agreement is entered into between employer and employee, by virtue of s.24(3), each employee is covered by an individual employment agreement which contains the same terms and conditions as those which applied to the parties under the expired award.

The implication of these provisions is clear: from 1 March 1993 all employees formerly under awards are covered by individual employment agreements; the terms of employment will continue to be covered by agreements—either collective or individual—if only one of the parties wishes to proceed to agreements rather than awards. Certainly, if both employer and union (and/or employees) agree, the matter or industrial dispute could be brought before the new Employee Relations Commission, which replaces the Victorian Industrial Relations Commission as the main dispute-settling body. The Employee Relations Commission must attempt to settle the dispute by conciliation and then if that fails, by arbitration. However, if one party does not want to go to the Commission, then the matter must be negotiated to achieve a collective agreement or an individual agreement.

If the employer does not agree to the Commission's jurisdiction and does not wish the terms of the old award to prevail, the employer can simply make a new agreement, containing the minimum terms and conditions which are laid out in Schedule 1 to the Act. These relate to a limited range of employment conditions: pay, annual leave, sick leave and maternity, paternity and adoption leave. So effectively for many employees a reduction in pay and conditions could have taken place immediately upon the implementation of the relevant provisions in the Act. Further, the *Annual Leave Payments Act* 1992 (Vic), operative on 28 October 1992, effectively abolished payment of the 17.5% annual leave loading by making provisions for its payment unenforceable in existing awards. Parties can however agree to include such leave loading in any agreement made.

In the Act, there are now severe restrictions on strike activity and provisions for secret ballots to take place before strikes can occur. The system for recognition of associations remains as under the *Industrial Relations Act* 1979 (Vic) with the association not receiving legal status by virtue of recognition. The Act has major consequences for enforcement as enforcement proceedings are now the exclusive jurisdiction of the Industrial Division of the Magistrates' Court. The main provisions in the Act will be analysed in more detail below.

Employment agreements

Collective and individual employment agreements

Employment agreements, as stated earlier, may be collective or individual. Collective employment agreements (s.8) may be entered into by an employer with any or all of the employees employed by the employer (s.8(1)), or two or more employers may enter into a collective agreement with any or all of their employees (s.8(2)). Negotiations by the employer may be with the employees themselves or, if the employees wish, any representative or committee of employees authorised by the employees to represent them (s.8(3)). The agreement, which must be in writing, must specify the expiry date, which should be no more than five years after the agreement's operative date. Collective agreements cannot be varied during their life (except to remove ambiguity on uncertainty). Collective employment agreements are to be lodged with the Chief Commission Administration Officer but there is no supervision, control or approval of such agreements by the Employee Relations Commission.

Any employee not covered by a collective agreement may enter into an individual agreement with his or her employer.[75] Even where a collective agreement applies, s.9(2) provides that an individual agreement may be entered into by the employee and employer. Negotiations by the employer can be with the employee directly or an authorised representative of the employee.[76] There is no lodging requirement for individual employee agreements but the number of such individual agreements must be notified to the Chief Commission Administration Officer each year.

Minimum terms of employment agreements

Minimum terms which must be contained in either collective or individual agreements are set out in Schedule 1 to the Act. These matters relate to pay, minimum leave (four weeks' holiday leave with pay), sick leave (one week per year) and maternity, paternity and adoption leave (up to 52 weeks, unpaid, subject to conditions in the Schedule). The minimum wage must be equal to the base hourly or weekly rate for the job classification in the former award for the employee (there are ambiguities in the interpretation of this condition). Prima facie this schedule of minimum conditions provides protection for employees but the protection is limited. Many sick leave provisions in awards were more generous (providing for accumulation of sick leave) and the wage rates only provide for the base rate—over time the original job classification under an expired award will become increasingly meaningless so that historical protection of minimum wages will be eroded. Maternity leave which existed in awards was paid leave for a certain period—under the Schedule it is unpaid leave. Moreover, many matters now regarded as standard in awards—superannuation, notice for termination of the employer-employee relationship, redundancy pay, tea breaks, allowances for uniforms etc.—are not included in the schedule of minimum conditions.

Employment agreements, whether collective or individual, are required to contain provisions relating to grievance procedures and the standing down of employees. Section 14(4) of the Act specifies that employee agreements must lay down procedures 'to be followed to prevent or settle claims, disputes or grievances that arise during the currency of the agreement', and to make provision for standing down employees, who because of a strike, stoppage of work or breakdown of machinery for which the employer is not responsible, cannot usefully be employed.

Enforcement of employment agreements

Proceedings for breach of employment agreements now rest exclusively within the jurisdiction of the Industrial Division of the Magistrates' Court[77] which is given 'jurisdiction to hear and determine any cause of action for damages, or any claim for equitable relief, arising out of or related to a breach of an employment agreement, irrespective of the amount claimed or the value of the relief sought'.[78] However, there is a limit on the amount of damages ($5000) which can be awarded by the Industrial Division of the Magistrates' Court in respect of damages against any individual employee—the amount which can be awarded against an employer in proceedings for breach of the agreement are unlimited.

A party to an individual agreement is the employee himself or herself. A collective agreement, although it may be negotiated collectively with employees, appears to be with the employees individually so that each employee is a party to the collective employment agreement. Parties themselves may institute enforcement proceedings. It is only in cases where the employee is owed money that a recognised association of the employee may institute proceedings within twelve months of the employee's entitlement arising[79] otherwise the individual will be responsible for such enforcement (except in the alternative procedure—see below). The role of unions may be less prominent in enforcement: one could imagine that if the employees have not collectively negotiated the agreement through the union or a union representative the union may be reluctant to assist in any proceedings which an employee wishes to institute for breach of the agreement.

It is an offence under s.163 of the Act to fail to comply with a provision of an employment agreement and a fine can be imposed for failure to comply. Part 15, ss 153-162, govern prosecutions for offences. If an employee does not want to bring an action for breach of agreement, an alternative is for authorised persons to institute proceedings for an offence for breach of agreement and for an order to be made under s.161 for an amount owing to the employee to be paid by the employer. There are disadvantages of this course of action. First by virtue of s.154(1), persons who can bring proceedings are those authorised by the Minister, the Chief Administrator (i.e. the Secretary to the Department of Business and Employment) and an officer of the department of Business and Employment (in the latter two cases only where the Minister has authorised the Chief Administrator or an officer of the Department to give such authorisation). A union, then, has no right under the Act to institute proceedings for an offence although presumably may be an authorised person, so again the role of unions is diminished or may even be excluded. (Under the 1979 Act, unions were not given the right to prosecute.) Secondly, the amount which an employer can be ordered to repay is limited to an amount in respect of a period up to twelve months,[80] as compared to common law claims for breach of contract. These provisions seem to make it a criminal offence for an employer or an employee to breach an award. It should be queried whether this is appropriate for industrial relations matters.

Legal problems in employment agreements

When the Act was first enacted, it was not clear whether two groups of employees were covered by the Act:

i employees who have been engaged after 1 March 1993 and who would have been covered by an award had they been employed whilst awards were in force (before 1 March 1993);
ii employees engaged after 1 March 1993 who are in previously 'award-free' job classifications (e.g. executives, managers etc.).

The Act was not clear as to the effect on workers in groups i and ii above as it was strongly arguable that the Act applied only to those covered by awards before 1 March 1993 and employed before that date by the employer.

Further, an employment agreement was defined as an employment agreement entered into Part 2 of the Act: was it then possible to expressly declare that the agreement was one which is not entered into under Part 2 of the Act and thereby avoid entirely the protection of the minimum conditions contained in Schedule One of the Act? If this device was available it could cover not only groups i and ii above but also workers employed before 1 March 1993 under an award and who renegotiate their contracts of employment with the same employer.

These legal questions were fundamental to the operation of the Act and were resolved by legislative amendment to the 1992 Act. The scope of coverage of the Act also had implications for enforcement, including the appropriate forum for taking action. However, the loophole in the drafting and the uncertainties of application of the Act as originally enacted caused problems for a smooth start to a dramatically new system.

Consequences of employment agreement provisions

The impact of the negotiation of collective or individual agreements remains to be seen. In cases of union strength, the parties may be able to negotiate better than previous award conditions—but presumably these would already have been reflected in more generous over-award conditions in contracts of employment, so no significant changes will emerge. However, union muscle is arguably more controlled by the compulsory requirement for secret ballots to be called and legislative procedures to be complied with, otherwise strike action will be regarded as unlawful (which will attract penalties for the union or employees or both). Other restrictions in s.36(1) curtail the taking of strike action (by making many strikes unlawful and an offence) and therefore the ability to use union muscle without incurring penalties. The philosophy of the Act is clear—if an employer does not want to submit to conciliation or arbitration, either collective or individual agreements may be negotiated. If collective agreements are negotiated, there is not only no guaranteed right to engage in industrial action by employees to bring about a settlement of the terms of the agreement but severe restriction of strike action (see Industrial Action below). Thus even in industries where unions are strong, their effectiveness in negotiations may be diminished. In other instances, given current economic conditions, inadequate protection of minimum pay and conditions means that employees in industries where unions are weak, or where the employees themselves lack negotiating strength for various reasons (lack of market power, negotiating skills, migrant workers etc.), will be severely disadvantaged. Very few individual employees would have adequate bargaining power to negotiate satisfactory individual employment agreements.

Awards: voluntary arbitration

Conciliation and arbitration by consent

Under the Act, it is still possible to make use of an independent third party, the Employee Relations Commission, to first conciliate on an industrial dispute and then to arbitrate on that dispute if conciliation fails to produce a settlement. However, there are several restrictions on invoking the Commission's jurisdiction. The Commission must not convene proceedings in relation to an industrial matter or dispute unless three conditions are met:

- first, all the parties to the matter or dispute must consent to the Commission exercising its powers under the Act;
- secondly, the parties must undertake not to engage in any industrial action over the matters in dispute; and
- thirdly, the parties must agree to accept the outcome of the proceedings.[81]

If one party does not agree to submit to the Commission's jurisdiction, then the Commission cannot exercise any of its powers. The emphasis then has changed completely from the *Industrial Relations Act* 1979 (Vic) where a dispute could be notified by one party and so long as the then Industrial Relations Commission validly had jurisdiction, an award could be made binding the parties. The system is now one of voluntary arbitration, with a publicly funded conciliation and arbitration service.

Section 98(1) sets out the general powers of the Commission in relation to industrial matters or disputes—the Commission may attempt to settle the matter or dispute informally, it can mediate or attempt to conciliate the parties to the dispute or it can arbitrate the matter of the dispute, it can make an award in relation to all or any part of the matter or dispute, or it can vary or revoke an award. The Commission's powers are further limited—it cannot make an award in relation to preferential employment of employees, nor can it make an award 'unless the scope of the award is confined to an industry and the award applies to a majority of the employees of each employer who is to be bound by the award'.[82] Awards no longer operate as common rules in the industry. The Commission cannot make an award in relation to long service leave with pay, basic entitlements to long service leave being set out in Part 5, Division 6. Some matters are within the jurisdiction of the Commission in Full Session—these include matters relating to standard hours of work in the industry, rates of pay on grounds predominantly related to the Victorian economy etc. and annual leave with pay. This provision echoes very much that in the *Industrial Relations Act* 1988.

The award itself must avoid any unnecessary technicalities of expression and be worded so as to best express the wishes of the parties or the decision of the Commission, it must be signed appropriately[83] and it must be in writing. The award has to specify a date of operation[84] and must have a date for expiry no more than five years from the operative date.[85] Awards cease to operate when they expire but if no new award is operative from that date then the employer and employee will be bound by an individual employment agreement with the same terms and conditions as those which governed the expired award.[86] Awards, like employment agreements, must contain disputes or grievance clauses and also stand-down clauses. The minimum terms and conditions to be contained in awards are those contained in Schedule 1 and where there are conditions less favourable than those contained in Schedule 1, the award conditions will not be operative.[87]

It is important to note that any award made under the *Employee Relations Act* after the commencement of s.25(3) must not contain a provision

> 'which limits the working of ordinary hours to specified days of the week or provides for additional payment through ordinary hours worked on specified days of the week. An award made after that commencement may, however, limit the working of ordinary hours to an average of five days per week over the period of a roster cycle or require additional payments for work performed on public holidays'.

Awards will not be able to contain penalty rates unless for work on public holidays so the idea is to enable a much more flexible system of payment of wages. This will affect particular employees, for example, shop assistants and, in some instances, nurses.

Award enforcement

Section 163 also applies to awards — 'A person must comply with every provision of an award or employment agreement that applies to the person and that imposes an obligation on that person'. Penalties for breach of s.163 depend on whether the offence is a first, second, or third or subsequent offence. Proceedings can be taken in the Industrial Division of the Magistrates' Court for an offence and the court can order the amount of underpayment to the employee (s.161) or the money can be recovered pursuant to s.160. In respect of the latter, the employee's recognised association may institute proceedings, but for prosecution of an offence, the association must be a 'person authorised' under s.154(1) to bring proceedings (see also section Employment Agreements, Enforcement for limitations on these proceedings).

Unfair dismissals

Provisions for employees seeking a remedy against an unfair dismissal or a threatened dismissal are still available in the Act and they are very similar to the provisions which existed in the amended *Industrial Relations Act* 1979 (Vic), except that it is now the Employee Relations Commission which hears proceedings for unfair dismissal. Those employees who can seek redress before the Commission are those who are 'engaged in a classification of work which was governed by an award at the commencement of this Division' (1 March 1993). Over time, employees' jobs may not relate easily to job classifications under former awards, so this remedy will become less available.

Applications must be made within ten business days after a dismissal to the Chief Commission Administration Officer who will refer the application to the Commission after first being satisfied that the employee has made out a prima facie case and that the employee or a recognised association on the employee's behalf has attempted to resolve the matter directly with the employer or any recognised association to which the employer belongs.[88] An employee cannot make application for unfair dismissal if the employee has a right of appeal or review under any contract, or has a right of appeal or review under legislation such as the *Public Service Act* 1974 (Vic) or the *Teaching Service Act* 1981 (Vic). Further, the employee must have been continuously employed by the employer for at least six months (on a full-time, part-time or casual basis).

The Employee Relations Commission's powers do not differ from those of the Industrial Relations Commission under the former Act: if the Commission is satisfied that the dismissal or threatened dismissal is 'harsh, unjust or unreasonable', it may order the employer to either re-employ the employee in that employee's former position 'on terms which are not less favourable to the employee than if the employee had not been dismissed; or not to dismiss the employee'.[89] Where a re-employment order is made, the Commission may order the employee to receive the amount he or she would have been entitled to receive as wages during the period when the employee was not employed.[90] The Act specifically provides that the only powers the Commission may exercise with respect to harsh, unjust or unreasonable dismissal or threatened dismissal are those contained in ss 42(1) and (2). This section ensures that the Commission cannot make compensation orders in instances where it is not satisfied that re-employment is an appropriate order. The section therefore avoids the difficulties of interpretation which existed under the *Industrial Relations Act* 1979 (Vic) and which were finally resolved by the High Court in *Downey v Trans Waste Pty Ltd*[91] in effect declaring that the tribunal could not order compensation, as an alternative to reinstatement for an unfairly dismissed worker.

Institutions in Victorian industrial law

The Employee Relations Commission

The powers of the Employee Relations Commission (already discussed) are set out in Part 8 of the Act. Schedule 3 of the Act however contains the appointment and conditions of employment of members of the Commission. The Commission consists of a President, Deputy Presidents and Commissioners. The President must be qualified as a legal practitioner for a period of at least five years and be a person who in the opinion of the Governor in Council is suitable to be appointed President because of his or her skills and experience in the field of employee relations. The Deputy Presidents however may either be legal practitioners of at least five years' experience or persons who have had experience at a high level in industry or commerce or government, and also be persons who in the opinion of the Governor in Council are suitable to be so appointed because of skills etc. in the field of employee relations. To be eligible to be a Commissioner the person must, in the opinion of the Governor in Council, have 'appropriate skills and experience in the field of employee relations'.

Persons may hold appointment until they are either sixty-five years of age or removed from office by the Governor in Council under clause 7 which lays down certain conditions (e.g. if both Houses of Parliament in the same session ask the person to be removed from office, if the person becomes bankrupt, if the person is convicted of an indictable offence or which if committed in Victoria would be an indictable offence, or if the person engages in paid employment contrary to Clause 8 which requires the person to obtain the consent of the Minister for engaging in outside employment). Whilst the Commission ordinarily acts by one member sitting alone, the Commission may operate as the Commission in Full Session (consisting of three or more members, one of whom is to be the President or Deputy President—s.85(1)) and can hear appeals from awards made, or decisions not to make awards, by a single member of the Commission or a decision in respect of recognition of an association.

The Chief Commission Administration Officer

The Chief Commission Administration Officer, whose functions are set out in Part 9, Division 2, has in effect taken over the role of the Registrar under the former Act but with some differences. The Officer must direct the business of the Commission Administration Office—this is the registry to the Commission and keeps a register of recognised associations, up to date copies of awards and a register of collective employment records. The Officer gives priority to the needs of the Commission, reports annually to the President of the Commission and carries out the Commission's orders. The Chief Commission Administration Officer has functions in relation to unfair dismissal as already discussed but also has the power to 'investigate the role, performance and functions of any association of employees or employers if requested to do so by the Minister'.[92] The reasons for and the consequences of such investigation are not set out.

Associations

Applications must be made to the Employee Relations Commission for associations of either employers or employees to be recognised with respect to an employer, an industry or an award. The Commission is under an obligation[93] to hold a hearing on the application, to hear submissions from the applicant and any other person or body and to take evidence on the application. Conditions laid out in s.136(1) must be met before the Commission can grant an application for recognition—these are that the applicant must be a 'genuine association with respect to the employer or business concerned' and that, in respect of an association of employees, 'the association has been authorised by an employee engaged by the employer or in the industry concerned to represent the employee in negotiations or proceedings'. Recognised associations are entitled to appear before the Commission in matters affecting interests of their members, to represent members in relation to employment agreements to be made under the Act or to represent any members seeking to recover a payment under ss 160 or 162 (in relation to unpaid superannuation). As with the previous Act, recognition does not confer corporate status on the association so that the Act continues to provide a solution to the problem of legal personality of state unions identified in *Moore v Doyle*.[94]

Industrial action

Unlawful industrial action: offences and the industrial torts

It was previously left to the common law to define what industrial action may attract civil liability in the industrial torts in Victoria. The Act has introduced the concept of unlawful industrial action which severely restricts the freedom to undertake industrial action. Section 36(1) provides that participation in industrial action is unlawful if one of eight matters set out in sub-para (a) to (h) is applicable. These include: industrial action which occurs whilst a relevant award or collective employment agreement is in force; industrial action not authorised by secret ballot (see below); industrial action relating to a claim, dispute or grievance where there is a procedure set out in the relevant award which has not been followed; industrial action which is in relation to an essential service or is vital to industry as defined in the *Essential Services Act* 1958 (Vic) and the *Vital State Industries (Works and Services) Act* 1992 (Vic); industrial action engaged in for the purpose of causing loss or damage to the business of an employer other than employer which employs those undertaking the industrial action (that is, secondary boycotts). Section 36(4) provides that industrial action is not unlawful if it is not unlawful under subsection (1) and the industrial action 'relates to the negotiation of an award or collective employment agreement for the participants'. Thus an extra hurdle, having avoided the conditions in s.36(1), is the reason for the industrial action. Any political strike, even though authorised by secret ballot, is unlawful as is any secondary boycott, sympathy strike and rights dispute. Employees under a federal award will not be subject to those provisions. There are penalties for individuals (up to $1000) and others (up to $50 000 for a body corporate) who engage in unlawful industrial action.[95]

Further, if strike action is not unlawful, then legal action in the industrial torts (conspiracy, intimidation, inducing breach of contract and causing loss to business, trade or employment) may not be instituted.[96] The effect of the immunity is doubtful. First, in most instances strike action will be regarded as unlawful and the parties open to legal suit. Secondly, picketing remains an exception to this immunity[97]—where picketing activities are involved proceedings in the industrial torts may be brought at any time.

In any event, if strike action is regarded as unlawful, it may aid the success of an industrial tort action because it is easy to establish unlawful means for the purpose of interference with contractual relations (indirect form), civil conspiracy by unlawful means and intimidation. These provisions were operative from 4 January 1993.

Secret ballots

Industrial action will be unlawful if it is undertaken without a secret ballot being held for members or if it is not authorised by a secret ballot.[98] The provisions in the Act dealing with secret ballots are brief[99] but the main code of practice detailing the secret ballot is set out in Schedule 2 which contains forty clauses. These clauses outline when a ballot can be held, who must be informed, how it is to be conducted, how questions are to be expressed etc. A ballot authorising industrial action may only authorise such action for a maximum of five days. The action is limited to taking place within a period of twenty-eight days from the final date for the return of the ballot papers.

Victoria: concluding comments

Parties who wish to avoid the operation of the new Victorian employee relations law may attempt to bring their disputes within the jurisdiction of the Australian Industrial Relations Commission. Amendments enacted by the Federal Parliament in the *Industrial Relations Legislation Amendment Act (No. 2) 1992* restrict the Australian Commission's ability to refuse to hear an industrial dispute on the ground that it should be dealt with by a State industrial tribunal where that State tribunal does not have the power of compulsory arbitration,[100] thereby making it easier to obtain a federal award for employees in Victoria.

The federal parliament has now enacted legislation to attempt to broaden the scope of the federal Act. Many legal issues require resolution at Victorian level and over time the extent of the use of employment agreements as opposed to voluntary arbitrations will be revealed. The trend thus far has been for unions to seek federal award coverage, leaving the main role played by the Victorian Commission confined to unfair dismissal, as this does not rely on arbitration by consent, and updating old awards as to wage rates.

Dominance of the federal system and co-operation between federal and state systems

Given the existence of six separate state industrial relations systems and one federal system, there is always the possibility for there to be inconsistencies between statute law made by the Federal Parliament and those made by the States and also between awards or orders of the respective state and federal commissions. Section 109 of the Constitution[101] which is echoed in s.165 of the

Industrial Relations Act 1988 provides for the resolution of any inconsistency. When an inconsistency occurs between a federal and state law or award, the federal law or award is to operate, and a state law or award to the extent of the inconsistency is invalid. The meaning of invalid is simply inoperative—the sections do not repeal any existing state law or awards. If the federal law which is inconsistent is subsequently repealed or made no longer inconsistent, the then state law or award will revive in operation.

Although there is such a mechanism for ensuring dominance of the system, it is sometimes difficult to ascertain whether there is indeed an inconsistency. Inconsistency can arise where there is a direct clash between the legislative provisions or where the federal law or award is taken to cover the whole subject matter involved and therefore exclude the operation of state law. There have been many High Court decisions on the problem of when the laws are inconsistent.

There are other provisions which are designed to avoid the problem arising. In s.111(1)(g) of the *Industrial Relations Act* 1988 (Cth), there is provision for the Commonwealth to dismiss a dispute or refrain from hearing an industrial dispute if it is considered that the dispute is being dealt with or should be dealt with by a state arbitrator. This means that the Federal Commission can leave it to the state industrial body to resolve the matter where appropriate. There are certain controls now included in the legislation to prevent the Commission exercising its power and refraining from hearing a dispute in the case of the Victorian Employee Relations Commission—this was inserted to permit parties who were wanting to move out of the system of voluntary arbitration into the federal system to do so with greater ease. There is also provision in the Federal Act for the Commonwealth Tribunal to deal with the matter.

In addition, there are provisions designed to provide co-operation between state and federal industrial tribunals. These include provision for joint appointments to the Federal Commission as well as to State industrial authorities.

The question is posed: what is the future of the separate state systems of industrial relations? Table 13.1 indicates the percentage of workers covered by state as opposed to federal awards and some changes over recent years. Very frequently, the choice as to federal or state coverage was determined historically, by early decisions relating to union structure and organisation or by decisions on federal jurisdiction which (until recently) excluded certain groups from federal coverage (for example teachers). Perceptions of the parties as to which system (federal or state) may best secure their interests has no doubt been, and will continue to be, an important factor in the choice of federal or state award coverage. Whilst it is too early to form a final judgment, the tendency in Victoria appears to be for many groups to be seeking federal awards or wishing to use the federal system. In some cases this move federally commenced soon after the more expansive view of the federal jurisdiction taken by the High Court in the 1980s,[102] but the system of deregulation and voluntary arbitration introduced in 1992 in that state precipitated attempts, including by state government employees, to seek federal coverage. Changes in Queensland which largely mirror the federal enterprise bargaining developments are unlikely to have an impact on federal/state coverage. Developments in New South Wales, Tasmania, South Australia and Western Australia, although quite significant in the latter two states, are not likely in themselves to lead to changes.

From time to time, the question of the States handing over to the Commonwealth their powers in respect of labour relations has been raised, but politically this seems a solution which is not without the bounds of reality.[103]

Notes

1. See the significant contribution of S. Macintyre and R. Mitchell (eds.), *Foundations of Arbitration: The Origins and Effects of State Compulsory Arbitration, 1890-1914*, Oxford University Press, 1989.
2. Section 316(2).
3. See ss 205, 206 and 207 of the New South Wales Act.
4. Section 189.
5. Section 191.
6. Section 220.
7. Section 354.
8. Section 359.
9. Section 329(1).
10. Section 347(1).
11. Section 216.
12. Section 383.
13. Section 115.
14. See ss 117 and 118.
15. This Act mainly commenced operation on 8 August 1994.
16. 'Industrial matter' was defined in s.6(1) of the now repealed Industrial Relations Act (SA) 1972 to mean 'any matter, situation or thing or any industrial dispute affecting or relating to work done or to be done or the privileges, rights or duties of employers or employees or persons intending to become employers or employees in any industry' and the definition also provided, without limiting the foregoing that it includes any 'matter, situation or thing affecting or relating to' and there followed enumerated paragraphs (a) to (k) which listed such matters as wages, hours of employment, relationship of employer and apprentice, employment of any person or any class of person in an industry, a demarcation dispute, the dismissal of an employee and so on.
17. Section 90(1).
18. Section 192.
19. Section 197.
20. Sections 200 and 201.
21. See also the objects of the 1994 Act in s.3.
22. See Ch 3, Pt 1, General Conditions of Employment, 1994 Act.
23. See Ch 3, Pt 2, particularly s.79 of the 1994 Act.
24. Sections 11, 12 and 14.
25. Sections 188 and 187.
26. See generally Ch 2, Pt 6, Div 1.
27. Section 65.
28. Section 5.
29. Section 29.
30. Section 30.
31. Section 61M(1).
32. See Pt 4A, Div. 2.
33. Section 31.
34. Section 6.
35. Section 187.
36. Section 51.
37. Section 52.

38 Section 52(d).
39 Part 10A, Queensland Act.
40 Section 8(2).
41 Section 9.
42 Section 9(2).
43 Industrial matter has a special meaning in relation to a person who is defined as a teacher and is employed under the *Education Act* 1928 (WA).
44 See s.32(6).
45 Section 34.
46 Section 37(1).
47 Section 41(2)(3).
48 Section 41A.
49 Section 44.
50 Section 44(6).
51 See s.83.
52 Section 246.
53 Section 248.
54 Section 250(1)(2).
55 Section 31(3) of the former 1972 Act.
56 Section 3(1) *Industrial Relations Act* 1984 (Tas).
57 See for example s.56 relating to election by secret ballot, s.57 election by secret postal ballot.
58 (1969) 15 FLR 59.
59 At 120-3.
60 See chapter 4.
61 (1985) 13 IR 339.
62 Section 109 of the Constitution provides:
    'When a law of a State is inconsistent with a law of Commonwealth, the latter shall prevail, and the former shall, to the extent of its inconsistency, be invalid.'
63 (1990) 96 ALR 251.
64 (1992) 110 ALR 549.
65 See former *Industrial Relations Act* 1979 (Vic).
66 For discussion of these provisions relating to agreements in New South Wales, Tasmania, Queensland and South Australia, see section 'Institutions and Jurisdictions'. For discussion in Victoria, see 'Deregulation of Labour Law: The Victorian Example'; for Western Australia, see 'Workplace Agreements in Western Australia' below.
67 See s.5(1).
68 See s.5(3).
69 See s.12(1).
70 See s.15(2).
71 See s.18.
72 See s.20.
73 See s.21.
74 See s.5.
75 Section 9(1).
76 Section 9(3).
77 Section 19(3).
78 Section 19(1).
79 Section 160(3).
80 Section 161(2).
81 Section 92(2).
82 Section 92(2)(c).
83 Section 20(1)(c).
84 Section 22(1).
85 Section 24(1).

86 Section 24(3).
87 Section 25(5).
88 Section 41(2).
89 Section 42(1).
90 Section 42(2).
91 (1991) 172 CLR 167.
92 Section 106.
93 Section 135(2).
94 (1969) 15 FLR 59 (previously discussed).
95 Section 36(2).
96 Section 37(1).
97 Section 37(2).
98 Section 36(1)(g).
99 Section 51 and see s.52 which sets out offences in relation to the ballot.
100 By amendments to s.111(1)(g) of the federal Act.
101 See footnote 62 this chapter and chapter 12.
102 See chapter 12.
103 See Hancock Committee Report.

Further Reading

Alley's Industrial Law, Victoria , B. Mueller and D.B. Moore (eds), Butterworths, Sydney (updated), now *Employee Relations: Victoria*.

J. Benson, G. Griffin and K. Soares, 'The Impact of Unfair Dismissal Legislation in the Victorian Jurisdiction', *Australian Journal of Labour Law 2*, 1989, p. 141.

S. Jamieson, 'Enterprise Agreements in New South Wales: A New Era?, *Australian Journal of Labour Law 5*, 1992, p. 84.

J.T. Ludeke (The Hon.), 'Enterprise Bargaining and its Consequences', *Australian Law Journal 66*, 1992, p. 509.

G. McCarry, 'A Disputatious Dispute Procedure: The Industrial Relations Act 1991 (NSW)', *Australian Journal of Labour Law 5*, 1992, p. 177.

S. Macintyre and R. Mitchell, (eds), *Foundations of Arbitration: The Origins and Effects of State Compulsory Arbitration, 1890–1914*, Oxford University Press, Melbourne, 1989.

M. Pittard, 'A Personality Crisis: The Trade Union Acts, State Registered Unions and their Legal Status', *Monash University Law Review 6*, 1980, p. 49.

M. Pittard, 'Legal Regulation of Collective Agreements in Victoria', *Australian Journal of Labour Law 3*, 1990, p. 271.

M. Pittard, 'The Fundamental Transformation of Employee Relations in Victoria', *Australian Business Law Review 21*, 1993, p. 220.

J. Shaw, 'The Greiner Government's Industrial Relations Laws—An Experiment in Deregulation', *Australian Journal of Labour Law 5*, 1992, p. 101.

D.W. Smith and D.W. Rawson, *Trade Union Law in Australia: The Legal Personality of Australian Trade Unions*, Butterworths, Sydney, 198?.

A. Stewart, 'A Quiet Revolution: Unfair Dismissal in New South Wales', *Australian Journal of Labour Law 5*, 1992, p. 69.

Questions

1 What advantages are there for unions or employees to have their disputes settled and their terms and conditions of employment covered federally? Are there any advantages of State systems over the Federal system?
2 Outline the *'Moore v Doyle'* problem of dual registration of trade unions.
3 State Parliaments are not constrained in the same way as the Federal Parliament by equivalents of s.51(35) of the Constitution. Given this, why is it that State Parliaments have generally chosen to set up systems of industrial regulation which mirror in large part the Commonwealth system?
4 What rights does a worker who believes he or she has been unfairly dismissed have in respect of the dismissal? In what sort of cases will reinstatement or re-employment be an appropriate order for a tribunal to make where an employee has been unfairly dismissed?
5 What are the advantages or disadvantages which the Victorian system of collective bargaining or individual bargaining has in relation to the Western Australian system of opting out of awards to workplace agreements?
6 What role do you see state systems will play in the future, especially following reforms at federal level which rely on the corporations and external affairs powers in the Constitution? What factors will unions and employers take into account in deciding whether to have disputes resolved under federal or state industrial laws?

14

Workplace Safety and Equity

Contents

Workplace health and safety
- workplace safety: an industrial relations issue
- problems for federal jurisdiction and safety issues
- standard setting and the Australian Commission
- safety standards by legislative prescription

Workplace equity: discrimination and equal opportunity
Industrial awards, agreements and equity
- wages
- parental leave
- discrimination and dismissals

Negotiating agreements
Unlawful discrimination in the workplace under statute
- sexual harassment
- affirmative action

Introduction

The legal framework in which industrial relations operate at federal level and in the states is governed by the relevant industrial relations legislation. At both levels there are in place, in varying forms, formal mechanisms of conciliation and arbitration for the settlement of industrial disputes between employers and employees, and provision for the making and registration of enterprise agreements. Within those systems, there may be certain protection given to some workers against discrimination, for example, to those who conscientiously object to belonging to unions, or to non-unionists, so there is often a protective element in the industrial relations legislation. Given the systems which exist for making consent awards and agreements, the parties may agree on workplace rules, subject to the constraints of the legislation. For example, some systems prohibit agreement about compulsory unionism or the closed shop so that these cannot be the subject of valid agreements. There may also be provision for minimum standards below which parties cannot agree so that the workplace rules are subject to constraints. The minimum standards, or floor of rights, may be set directly through government intervention via the legislation as, for example, annual leave and long service leave in Victoria and notice periods to terminate the employment relationship in the *Industrial Relations Act* 1988 (Cth). Alternatively, they may be set by the independent industrial relations tribunal itself as in the case of the Australian Industrial Relations Commission's power to provide for minimum floor of rights in some matters under the *Industrial Relations Reform Act* 1993 (Cth).

Other constraints on the freedom to enter into agreements or to determine the workplace rules of the parties are to be found in legislation promoting standards of occupational health and safety and legislation protecting employees from discrimination on the basis of their sex, marital status, race, pregnancy and so on. These laws which promote workplace safety and equity on the one hand, and equality of opportunity within the workplace on the other, represent standards which must be maintained by employers and which are therefore a parameter or framework within which Australian industrial relations will or can operate. Suppose employers and employees or unions in negotiating about pay agree to a very large increase in pay on the basis of performing dangerous work, but the employer continues permitting employees to do the dangerous work on the basis that they are paid handsomely for it; occupational health and safety laws in the various states of Australia will specify minimum standards of occupational health and safety or make provision for those standards which impose a duty on the employer and which the employer is not permitted to avoid by contract. There may be criminal law or penal consequences for failure to abide by those standards; in addition, or in the alternative, the common law through the law of negligence may require the maintenance of those standards and grant employees monetary compensation for any injuries which flow from such negligence. So that an agreement of the kind above may well contravene legislative health and safety standards and result in tortious and other liability to the employer.

Equal opportunity legislation means that an employer will not be able to refuse to employ, discriminate in employment or terminate the employment of a person because of certain specified prohibited reasons which are discriminatory such as race, sex and so on. This brings with it a right for individuals not to be discriminated against in this way and imposes a duty on employers not to engage in discrimination. Consequences of failure to observe such requirements of equal opportunity may result in orders of compensation and/or reinstatement. Thus, for example, it will not be open to employers and employees or unions to agree on who will be employed and who will be terminated where there are discriminatory grounds involved. Again, this represents a constraint or parameter in which industrial relations must operate.

In matters of occupational health and safety and equal opportunity there is legislation in force at state and federal levels which prescribes and maintains certain standards in these areas. However, sometimes these matters have been the subject of industrial relations disputes and can be regarded as part of the industrial relations agenda. They have been treated formally as such and relevant provisions laying down standards in these matters have been inserted into industrial awards.

This chapter explores the nature and scope of laws in Australia dealing with occupational health and safety and discrimination or equal opportunity in employment, and examines also the industrial relations aspects of these particular matters.

Workplace health and safety

Occupational health and safety is a vital aspect of the Australian workplace. Safety standards represent important conditions within the workplace and the health and safety of the workplace is important to both the employer and the wider community and, of course, to the employee himself or herself. Safety issues today will range from staffing levels essential to operate equipment or machinery, including aircraft, the nature of the equipment or machinery, including the provision of guards around machinery, safe practices within the workplace, for example, where employees are required to perform work on scaffolding or to perform work involving dangerous substances such as chemicals, or other dangers such as electricity. Contemporary problems regarding the safety and health of the workplace today concern lung diseases caused by asbestos; the effects of smoking within the workplace on the health of other employees apart from the smoker, that is, passive smoking; the problem of contracting AIDS in high risk industries, such as medical work; repetitive strain injury caused by particular work functions and processes; and cancers arising from working with various hazardous substances. Even in the late 1990s, with increased awareness about the hazards of the workplace, there are still 400 deaths per year in Australia arising from the workplace and a large number of workplace-related injuries.

Workplace safety: an industrial relations issue

It has often been said that the traditional concerns of the industrial relations tribunal and the unions themselves have not been with occupational health and safety.[1] The main concerns have tended to be about wages and conditions of work but issues of occupational health and safety have arisen in some contexts. For example, in disputes about staffing levels and hours of work for employees, health and safety considerations have often been argued by the union and taken into consideration by the Australian Commission in making decisions.[2] Some areas where the Commission has made decisions on health and safety concern the provision of protective clothing and the provision of first-aid facilities within the workplace.[3] Wage increases have also been granted on the basis of working in hot climatic conditions.[4]

Paid sick leave, too, is regarded as a standard term to be included in an award but such leave does not usually distinguish between those illnesses which are related to work and those which are not. In other words, sick leave has not generally been regarded as linked to occupational health, although its underlying rationale and reason for acceptance (within limits) may be the need to give employees time to recover from illness and thereby maintain a healthy workforce, and such burden to be borne by the employer, not the employee. The provision of paid annual leave, too, may be accepted in order to maintain a healthy contented workforce.

Safety issues, too, may arise in the context of whether the Australian Commission can deal with a claim for wages to be paid during a period of industrial action. Section 124 of the *Industrial Relations Act* 1988 precludes the Commission from dealing with wages claims during strikes and other forms of industrial action except where the Commission is satisfied that such action was reasonable, was about the employees' health and safety and arose in relation to matters within the reasonable responsibility of the employer concerned. Thus, for example, the Commission held that industrial action taken by the Australian Public Service Association fulfilled the requirements of s.124(2) so that deductions of pay in respect of the period of industrial action should be cancelled. The employees were concerned that decentralisation of word processing operations presented a danger to their health and safety because they were less able to enjoy the rest breaks which had been set out under guidelines for using screen based equipment in Australia Post.[5]

Problems for federal jurisdiction and safety issues

One of the problems perceived by the Australian Commission in relation to prescribing workplace standards of safety has been the extent to which it could or should interfere with what has traditionally been regarded as a management decision or prerogative within the realm of management. If workplace accidents are to be avoided by prescription in award by industrial tribunals, there may be some requirement to 'intrude' into decisions such as the level of staffing, the way processes and procedures are carried out within the workplace and decisions as to the operation of the enterprise. The interpretation by the High Court of s.51(35) of the Constitution and the definition of 'matters' or 'industrial matters' in the *Industrial Relations Act* 1988, and its predecessor the *Conciliation and Arbitration Act* 1904, meant that for many years awards could not contain matters which would intrude within the realm of management prerogatives. It is only more recently, in the 1980s, that the High Court has started to move away from the notion that a matter which concerns a management prerogative is not a matter pertaining to the relation of the employer and employee.[6] Even where the Court moved away from the notion that a matter which could be included in an award may overlap with a matter which was traditionally regarded as a managerial prerogative, the Court stated in *Re Cram; ex parte New South Wales Colliery Proprietors' Association*[7] that the Commission had an 'obligation ... to give due weight, in any exercise of its discretion, to the autonomy of management to decide how the business enterprise shall be efficiently conducted'.[8] A noteworthy dispute in the 1960s concerning the number of crew and pilots on DC9 aircraft came to the High Court of Australia on a jurisdictional issue. It was perceived that this High Court decision stood for the principle that 'manning' levels were outside the scope of the Commission's or specialist tribunal's jurisdiction and that such matters were not arbitrable matters.[9] It seemed, however, that the perception of this case may have been wrong and certainly today staffing levels are regarded as relating to the employer-employee relationship and therefore arbitrable matters or matters which can validly be included in awards and certified agreements.

Another way of approaching safety and accidents was to obtain monetary compensation for employees who were injured in the workplace through appropriate clauses in federal awards. An early attempt by the President of the Commonwealth Court of Conciliation and Arbitration to enable employees in the building industry to receive compensation for injuries suffered at work was declared invalid by the High Court on the ground that the President did not have jurisdiction to make such an award.[10] Four decades later the High Court upheld the validity of a clause in a log claiming payment of compensation to an employee who was injured by illness or accident which occurred in the course of employment. However, it was a majority of judges only in this case, *R v Hamilton Knight; Ex parte The Commonwealth Steamship Owners Association*,[11] who decided that the claim was a matter which pertained to the employment relationship.[12]

Standard setting and the Australian Commssion

A decision of the Australian Commission in the mid-1960s indicates the reluctance of the Commission to intervene or arbitrate upon safety matters. In the case of *Altona Petrochemical Co. Pty Ltd v Federated Storemen and Packers Union of Australia*,[13] a dispute arose over the proposed reduction in levels of staff who operated the equipment, from two operators to one. The union was concerned that the effect would be to disable the single operator from maintaining safety standards, particularly in emergencies, but the company argued that the plant was safe; that there were arrangements to deal with emergencies; and that the operators were trained in safe practices and were given training courses from time to time. There were in addition regular inspections of safety equipment. The Commission decided that the employer had 'taken all reasonable steps to ensure the safe operation of the whole establishment' and had 'made an act of judgement that there will be no diminution in the security of his plant if he reduces the manning'. The Commission also found that 'this decision upon manning was a part of the normal functions of management, and the act of judgement with regard to safety was based upon detailed consideration of the Altona plant and upon the working experience of both this company and associated organisations overseas operating in the same field'.[14]

The Commission satisfied itself about the safe procedures but also appeared to consider that these sorts of decisions were within the realm of management decisions. In permitting the new staffing levels the Commission did require that a review take place three months later. Further, the union could bring the matter at any time before the Commission if necessary, so that the Commission had formalised a method of checking on whether the new staffing levels were appropriate.

By way of contrast, in the case of *Divcon Australasia Ltd v RW Stanley*,[15] the Commission was prepared to include a detailed code in the award relating to safety of work practices which related to divers. However, the case is significant because the industry was already regulated by legislation at federal level and at state level which made provision to licensed persons to engage in exploration and to maintain certain standards in relation to safety and health. Designated Authorities were established to issue directions about safe diving practices and in Victoria this had been done. Divcon was not covered by the Victorian provision and, given the extensive directions about safe working practices which would already apply to other employers, the Commission had little difficulty in deciding that these safe practices should be contained in an award. The provisions were detailed in relation to practices to avoid drowning, decompression, carbon monoxide poisoning, electrocution and so on.

The major decision concerning occupational health and safety standards at federal level was in the case of *AMI Toyota Ltd and Others v Association of Draughting, Supervisory and Technical Employees*.[16] Six motor vehicle manufacturers in Australia and the Vehicle Builders Employees Federation had entered into an agreement about occupational health and safety. The parties sought to make it a consent award under the provisions of the then *Conciliation and Arbitration Act* 1904 (s.28). State governments (NSW, Victoria, South Australia, Western Australia and Queensland), several unions, the ACTU and the CAI all opposed the making of the consent award. The concern of the state governments was that safety had been the province of state regulation by legislation and it would not be appropriate to place, in federal awards, standards which would have the effect of overriding state provisions. One state also raised an argument about the lack of the Commission's jurisdiction.

The ACTU and the unions, however, acknowledged jurisdiction in the Commission but thought that provisions should be in federal awards only where they would be at least as beneficial as the relevant state law. The argument was that in this case the provisions were not as advantageous because, amongst other things, the penalties for contravention of the standards was higher under state legislation and there was no relevant expertise in the inspectorate, established under the conciliation and arbitration legislation for enforcement of awards, and to maintain the standards in the agreement. This was said to contrast with the expertise of the state authorities charged with the enforcement of occupational health and safety law. The CAI was in favour of occupational health and safety remaining within the purview of state responsibility.

The Commission decided that it would make the award of occupational health and safety. It is worth quoting the reasoning of the Commission:

'Occupational health and safety has always been the concern of the sovereign Parliaments of the States. Traditionally the legislation has laid down standards, promulgated, in the main, in regulations which have particularised the statutory duties which have been more broadly laid down in Acts of Parliament relating to particular industries or to industry in general. Its existence in federal awards has been minimal probably because of a presumption that the authority which constitutes the source of that legislation should also be the authority which regulates and monitors its observance. Over the years this Commission has manifested a reluctance to adopt health and safety provisions into its awards—see for example the *Furnishing Trades* case (1964) 105 CAR 605 at 608.

'On the other hand what we have called the "old-type" legislation has not, hitherto, intruded into the field of industrial disputation in any direct way. Now, in a State which contains a substantial part of the vehicle manufacturing industry, occupational health and safety legislation now has the capacity to overlap federal regulation in the fields of industrial relations and industrial law. We speak of the State of Victoria. But that is not to say that action should be taken to curtail that overlap by federal prescription. Clearly circumstances of a special nature must be present before any such action could be contemplated. It is against this background that we have examined the issues involved in this reference.

'In summary, we have concluded that the vehicle manufacturing industry is not unqualified in the present context; the interdependence of its employers, the intradependence as between establishments of individual employers and the unique production policies which prevail throughout the industry are all relevant considerations. The established mechanisms within the industry which have engendered and maintained grass roots awareness of safety at the workplace are also germane to the central issue. In addition the federal award orientation of the industry, its policies towards union membership and the common desire for federal prescription of employers and the industry union, of which all employees are eligible for membership, are vital factors which tip the balance towards an occupational health and safety award.

'Despite the fact that the legislation, which has undoubtedly generated the present application, is at present on the statute book of only one State, there are features of this industry (already discussed) which indicate that a prescription such as that contained in the proposed award should not be fragmented. If it is prescribed at all we consider that it should have general application.'[17]

This passage, quoted from the Commission's decision, indicates the concerns with which the Commission was grappling, in particular the concern that health and safety should be matters for legislation, rather than award prescription.

The Commission acknowledged that the proposed award contained as its philosophy the maintenance of occupational health and safety at the workplace under quite a different system: one in which the goal was to maintain health and safety at the workplace using procedures 'removed from those which are generated by the command to "obey or else".'[18] The provisions in the award reflected the 'Robens-type legislation' of self regulation and involvement of employee and union representatives in occupational health and safety matters[19] and the Commission stated: 'In the circumstances already discussed there is ground for confidence that in this industry an award engendered by this philosophy will work and that the general duties prescribed therein will be maintained despite the comparative complexity of prosecution and the comparative leniency of penalty in the event of breach. Standards set by legislation appear to be exceeded significantly in this industry which is also, on balance, suited to federal regulation.'[20]

The award was to be operative for twelve months, the parties were then to report back about the operation of the award. The Commission decided after hearings in *AMI Toyota v ADSTE*[21] to continue the award for a period of two more years.

The award made by the Conciliation and Arbitration Commission in 1989 reflected substantially the safety standards required under the *Occupational Health and Safety Act* 1985 (Vic), although there were some differences in terms of penalties which might flow. This decision, which was in one sense a test case of the Australian Conciliation and Arbitration Commission, indicated that the Commission was prepared to make industrial awards regarding health and safety, that it was not prepared to abdicate this award-making jurisdiction in the field of occupational health and safety to the states and that it was prepared to regulate safety at federal level, thereby providing a uniform system of safety, certainly in instances where the parties had agreed to enter into such safety agreements.

In the *AMI Toyota* case, the ACTU and some unions opposed the claim for safety standards in a federal award. This opposition was not, as we saw, based on opposition to the particular standards but to the mechanism by which those standards were to be imposed, that is, award or legislation. Sometimes, however, the employees themselves may be opposed to changes in the name of occupational health and safety. For example, the majority of employees at a workplace voted against the employer introducing health and safety policies to ban smoking at work in order to protect employees from the hazards of passive smoking. The Australian Commission made a recommendation to try to resolve the problem by consultation and agreement saying 'I have serious doubts that matters of safety, health and welfare of employees is a matter for a vote with the majority deciding the issue because if a situation is seen to be a hazard to health, welfare and safety then by law it has to be removed or the individual confronted with that hazard has to be protected from it'.[22]

The resolution of industrial health and safety matters through industrial award, however, has not been a significant jurisdiction as we have seen. This is mainly due to the prescription of safety standards at state and federal level by legislation. The legislation will be discussed below.

Safety standards by legislative prescription

Since the commencement of operation of industry in Australia, it was acknowledged that there may be a problem with the standard of safety and the health of workers in those industries. A graphic account of the conditions under which workers, often children, laboured in the mines is extracted in Table 14.1. Although this described conditions in mines in the north of France, similar conditions existed in Australian coal mines. There was an early consciousness as to safety problems faced by workers. For example, in Victoria, a campaign was launched in the late nineteenth century with the support of the local newspapers to compel employers to maintain standards of safety.[23] Early prescriptive legislation was introduced to maintain such standards and much of the legislation enacted at state level concerned safety standards in respect of the employment of women and also children, particularly in the 'sweated' industries, and was directed to particular industries.[24]

Table 14.1 Conditions in the mines late 19th century

Émile Zola's book *Germinal*, now regarded as a sociological documentary, portrays the labour-capital struggle in a coal mine in the north of France in the late 19th century. The following extract (Penguin Classics, p. 50), describes the conditions in which the miners worked.

'The four colliers had spread themselves out, one above the other, to cover the whole coal-face. Each one occupied about four metres of the seam, and there were hooked planks between them to catch the coal as it fell. The seam was so thin, hardly more than fifty centimetres through at this point, that they were flattened between roof and wall, dragging themselves along by their knees and elbows, unable to turn without grazing their shoulders. In order to get at the coal, they had to lie on one side with twisted neck, arms above their heads, and wield their short-handled picks slantways.

...

Maheu had the worst of it. At the top, the temperature went up to 35° Centigrade, air could not circulate, and he was stifled to death. In order to see, he had to hang his lamp on a nail so near the top of his head that its heat set his blood on fire. But it was the wet that really tortured him, for the rock, only a few centimetres above his face, incessantly dripped fast and heavy drops with maddening regularity always on the same spot. Try as he might to twist his neck and bend his head backwards, the drops splashed relentlessly on his face, pit-a-pat. In a quarter of an hour he was soaked through, what with his own sweat as well, and steaming like a wash-tub. On this particular morning he was swearing because a drop was determined to go in his eye. He would not stop cutting and the violent blows of his pick shook him, as he lay between the two rocks like a fly caught between the pages of a book, in danger of being flattened out.'

There was some preservation of safety standards through the development of the common law tort of negligence, where the employer is under a duty to take reasonable care in respect of the safety of the worker and could be liable in damages at common law for breach of that standard of care.[25] However, a drawback of such tortious liability and compensation through statutory workers compensation schemes was the emphasis on compensation for injuries *after* they had occurred (and to some extent on rehabilitation in the case of workers compensation schemes) rather than prevention of the accident or illness. Such prevention could be an outcome of the common law maintaining standards of reasonable care but often the standards were set too late, that is, after an incident in the workplace involving unsafe practices. A ruthless employer might also trade the risk of expenses for industrial injuries against the certainty of increased productivity and profit by continuing unsafe practices. The cost of insurance and so on of statutory compensation was probably only a minor incentive to maintain proper safety.

However, the major reforms came in the states in the 1980s with the introduction of the Robens philosophy in Australian law. A committee of enquiry into industrial health and safety had been established in the United Kingdom under the chairmanship of Lord Robens. A two-volume report on health and safety in that country was issued by the committee after extensive enquiries and submissions in relation to safety. The main findings of the report were as follows:

a existing legislation prescribing health and safety standards was specific and voluminous;
b the existing legislation did not involve employees as to workplace safety;
c the legislation had not effected a very good track record in terms of industrial accidents and workplace related deaths;
d more responsibility should be given to both employers and employees generally to maintain industrial standards and to develop guidelines within their particular workplace and industry;
e legislation to provide for general standards of occupational health and safety for employers should be enacted;
f emphasis should be given on training programmes to maintain industrial safety;
g there should be a focus on prevention, rather than compensation;
h there should be one body to deal with the maintenance of health and safety standards.[26]

This report had a major impact in Australia because most of the state governments have followed the thrust of this legislation in one guise or another. The current legislation based on this philosophy in Australia is:

Occupational Health and Safety (Commonwealth Employment) Act 1991 (Cth)
Industrial Safety, Health and Welfare Act 1977 (Tas)
Occupational Health and Safety Act 1983 (NSW)
Occupational Health and Safety Act 1985 (Vic)
Occupational Health and Safety Act 1986 (SA)
Occupational Health, Safety and Welfare Act 1984 (WA)
Workplace Health and Safety Act 1989 (Qld)
Occupational Health and Safety Act 1989 (ACT)

The state of Victoria was one of the early leaders to enact similar Robens-type legislation with the passage in 1985 of the Victorian *Occupational Health and Safety Act*. The scheme of the Victorian Act is a good illustration of the general approach and philosophy towards occupational health and safety. The legislation lays down standards which must be maintained by employers in the workplace. Section 21(1) of the Act provides: 'An employer shall provide and maintain so far as is practicable for employees a working environment that is safe and without risks to health'. The section further prescribes the duty of employers in terms of such matters as providing safe systems of work, engaging competent staff and maintaining safe practices within the workplace.[27] It also elaborates on the obligations of the employer in respect of training.[28] Any failure to adhere to such standards may result ultimately in a prosecution for an offence under the Act and in the short term could result in an order to cease operating because of any immediate risk to health and safety. In general terms, the standard which is imposed on employers in respect of workplace safety under the legislation is very close to the standard the courts developed in the law of negligence in the duty owed by employers to employees. The standard is not absolute but is one which must be maintained 'so far as is practicable'.[29]

The legislation envisages involvement of several persons apart from the employers themselves in safety matters. First, health and safety committees may be set up within the workplace to deal with and advise on occupational health and safety matters.[30] These are to comprise an equal number of employer and employee representatives and there are procedures laid down in the legislation as to how they are to operate, the frequency of meetings and so on. Secondly, there is provision for the appointment in each workplace of a health and safety representative.[31] The health and safety representative has power of inspections of the workplace and has, after mandatory consultation with the employer, the power to serve a provisional improvement notice on the employer. Once such a notice is issued, an inspector can be called to affirm or cancel the notice.[32] The purpose of these notices is to compel the employer to rectify the problem within the period of time specified in the order. The representative also has the power to order the cessation of work if the health and safety representative has a reasonable basis for believing that there is an immediate threat to health and safety of the particular employees or in the workplace. The power of health and safety representatives to halt work was a matter of some concern to employers as Table 14.2 indicates. Thirdly, inspectors (appointed by the government) are engaged to inspect workplaces and maintain health and safety standards.[33] Inspectors have the power independently of the health and safety representatives to issue prohibition notices to prohibit the employer carrying on the activity until the inspector is satisfied the problem causing the risk to health and safety has been rectified[34] and also to compel employers to maintain particular health and safety standards by issuing improvement notices.[35]

Originally, the Victorian legislation established an Occupational Health and Safety Commission, which was an independent body under the statute to oversee health and safety standards and to deal with education and training programmes. In 1992, legislative amendments to the *Occupational Health and Safety Act* disestablished the Occupational Health and Safety Commission and transferred its functions to the Department of Business and Employment. These functions are therefore now carried out under the direction of the relevant minister.[36]

The main philosophy of the legislation is that it is the responsibility of the workplace to define health and safety standards. Whilst there are general rules regarding the obligation of employers to maintain safe standards so far as is practicable, the responsibility of working out how those standards are to be maintained in a particular enterprise in an industry is now given to joint consultative groups involving employers and employees.

The ability of trade unions to be involved since the original legislation in 1985 has altered in Victoria. When the Act was enacted then, it was trade unions which could appoint health and safety representatives and via the procedure of determining designated workgroups establish health and safety representatives. See Table 14.2 for employer reaction at the time of the original proposed legislation in Victoria and the attitude to unions' involvement in health and safety matters. Legislative amendments in 1993 have effected the bypassing of trade unions to make sure that employees themselves within the workplace select such representatives without union involvement. This legislative development has moved the issue of occupational health and safety away from the responsibility of the trade unions and therefore further away from the industrial relations arena. However, the legislation frequently provides for a review mechanism, for example, in relation to whether health and safety representatives have acted reasonably in ordering a cessation of work, and this review mechanism frequently involves the relevant industrial relations tribunal—for example in Victoria, it is the Employee Relations Commission and in New South Wales it is the Industrial Commission of New South Wales.[37] Thus, there is some link between occupational health and safety and the industrial relations tribunals. Further, the Australian Commission, when settling an industrial dispute, is obliged to take into account state or territory law relating to 'safety, health and welfare of employees in relation to their employment'.[38] Although the Australian Commission cannot deal with a claim for wages in respect of industrial action, as we have seen, under s.124(2) of the *Industrial Relations Act* 1988, it can deal with a wage claim where the industrial action was due to a reasonable concern of employees about health or safety matters which are the responsibility of the employer. Hence there are express provisions acknowledging links between health and safety issues and industrial relations tribunals.

The occupational health and safety legislation is an example of a form of worker participation in the workplace in relation to defined issues. Government involvement is however not entirely excluded—there is of course the role of inspectors and, in addition, there is a role that ministers can perform in declaring codes of practice for a particular industry.[39] Codes of practice may be detailed specifications as to practical guidance on health and safety standards in the particular industry and may be taken into account in hearings in relation to offences for contravention of the legislation as evidence of the standards, although there are provisions whereby it is not always to be taken as the absolute standard.[40] Regulations made under the Act may also provide a source of obligation and a continuing government review mechanism to introduce new standards or amend standards by the making of regulations.

The legislation not only imposes obligations on the employers in respect of standards which they must maintain towards their employees, but it also ensures that employers maintain such standards in relation to independent contractors, and to persons entering the workplace, for example members of the public or other tradespersons, etc.[41] Responsibilities are also imposed on occupiers of workplace (that is persons who have the management or control of a workplace) and manufacturers and suppliers of plant.[42] In addition, there are responsibilities placed on the employees themselves in order to maintain safe practices and to take reasonable care towards their fellow employees and for their own health.[43]

One area of controversy in relation to the legislation concerned the standards which employers are under an obligation to maintain. The duty of care under the legislation is one which the employer must maintain 'so far as is practicable'.[44] In a sense, this has brought in a defence section because it is not an absolute standard of safety which must be maintained by the employer but it is one which must be maintained within the realm of possibility or perhaps foreseeability. The High Court of Australia in *Chugg v Pacific Dunlop Pty Ltd*[45] decided that the informant (that is, the person who brings a prosecution for contravention of the Act) has the burden of establishing practicability. The legislation gives some guidance as to the definition of 'practicable'. Such factors as the severity of the hazard risk in question, the state of knowledge about that hazard or risk, and any ways of and the availability and suitability of ways of removing or mitigating it, as well as the cost of removing or mitigating the risk are relevant. The problem, of course, is to translate these matters to the particular workplace. Is it relevant that there have not been any accidents at the particular workplace for several decades? What level of cost is within or outside the range of practicability? When should the hazard or risk have been known about?

Although the Robens-type philosophy envisaged self regulation, the regulation is not one without sanctions. There are provisions for enforcement and in the Victorian legislation consequences of failure to maintain appropriate standards of safety may result in prosecution for criminal offences. If employers do not comply with prohibition or improvement notices, proceedings may be instituted for prosecution for an offence.[46] The Minister has laid down the guidelines in relation to when offences will be prosecuted and there is some criticism about the level of prosecution.[47] Further, the criminal law itself may provide sanctions involving imprisonment in the law of manslaughter in particular.[48]

It can be seen therefore that the occupational health and safety legislation operates not only as a parameter within which employer and employee relations in the workplace operate but also provides a vehicle for involvement of employees in workplace decisions.

Even though there is both employer and employee involvement in the setting up and overseeing of appropriate standards within the concept of the Robens philosophy, given that there are penal and possibly criminal consequences for failure to maintain standards, it is not open to employers and employees to agree to procedures which may fall short of safety standards. In this way, the occupational health and safety legislation in Australia operates as a parameter for employer and employee relations in the workplace. It is of course open for the parties to agree on higher standards than those prescribed in the legislation and on particular matters which implement the standards laid down in the legislation.

Workplace equity: discrimination and equal opportunity

Discrimination may operate in the workplace on the basis of different treatment of persons of different sexes, on the basis of age, pregnancy, marital status, a person's religion or beliefs or sexual preference. In the workplace, the

Table 14.2 Employers' reactions to proposed safety legislation 1984, Victoria

New safety law has employers scurrying

BY PAUL ROBINSON

The State Government's radical new industrial safety legislation has sent employers scurrying to lawyers and lobbyists to block moves to increase trade union control over the workplace.

The intense employer campaign, that has lasted for up to a year, has prompted the State Liberal Party to plan a package of six amendments to the proposed legislation.

The amendments are aimed at the heart of the Occupational Health and Safety bill. They will seek to curb dramatically the proposed powers of union safety representatives to stop unsafe work practices and to ensure that representatives are elected by all employees, not appointed.

The Victorian Government and the trade union movement say that they have consulted extensively with employers about the elements of the bill. They believe they have answered employers' fears and made concessions, but have a mandate from the electorate to reduce the State's high accident and death rate in industry.

The ALP points to Department of Labor and Industry figures which show that approximately 30,000 industrial accidents occur in Victoria each year. Of those 56 people died last year, six people have already died this year, and employers have had to pay for an average of 300,000 worker's compensation claims a year.

Employers, while accepting the need for new safety legislation due to be considered by Parliament on 28 February, will fight to have safety officers elected by all employees in a workplace, not, as outlined in the bill, appointed by trade unions.

The Liberal Party will also move to reduce penalties for breaches of the new act by companies or company officials found guilty of neglect. Fines under the bill range from $5000 to $50,000.

Under the proposed new laws, trade unions can appoint any number of safety representatives who will have the power to stop work practices that are deemed to be unsafe. The work ban can last up to 24 hours by which time an inspector from the State's newly created Health and Safety Commission must investigate the stoppage.

The inspector will determine whether the work practice is safe or not, recommend changes and consider prosecutions if a company is breaching regulations. If an inspector fails to arrive within 24 hours the ban lapses.

The executive director of the Victorian Employers Federation, Mr Ian Spicer, has said that giving union safety representatives power to stop work practices for 24 hours was an open invitation for unions to use the bans for claims other than safety issues.

The State Opposition's spokesman on industrial relations, Mr Peter Block, has said, in stronger terms, that the safety representative's power would lead to "the concrete pour syndrome". "What's to stop a union like the Builders Labourers' Federation from dreaming up a safety issue half way through a concrete pour and banning the job. It's not much comfort to an employer if an inspector decides later that there was no safety issue," he said.

Mr Block said the Opposition would move to amend the legislation by removing a safety representative's power to issue temporary prohibition notices and transferring the responsibility to Government appointed inspectors.

The head of the Trades Hall Council's occupational health and safety unit, Dr John Mathews, has disagreed with the employers. He said there was ample precedent to show that workers would use the new powers responsibly and provisions in the bill existed to constrain abuse.

First, in Australia the Waterside Workers' Award has given the WWFA delegates the right to stop a job they consider unsafe for more than 15 years. This right has been used sparingly and responsibly—and it has saved lives and prevented injuries on the waterfront. Second, workers' health and safety delegates within the State Electricity Commission of Victoria have for the past year enjoyed the right to stop unsafe jobs under the Health and Safety Agreement of 1982. This too has worked well for the past year and the right has not been abused," he said.

Dr Mathews said that workers in Scandinavia had the right to stop unsafe work and "the record shows that the right has been exercised responsibly". He said workers in Australia, as distinct from delegates, have always had the common law right to stop unsafe work.

Dr Mathews said more than 500 workers had already been trained as safety representatives in preparation for the new responsibility but he conceded that there could be some over-zealous use of bans in the initial period of the new laws.

"It could be a problem, particularly in the first few months, if safety reps go to town with prohibition notices, but I think it will be a teething problem," he said.

Dr Mathews said that a provisional prohibition notice only lasted 24 hours and that inspectors would be expected to investigate bans as soon as possible. If an employer was being harrassed by a safety representative who used bans irresponsibly, the employer could appeal to the Industrial Relations Commission of Victoria to have the representative removed from office.

But employers believe that the proliferation of safety representatives and the possible over-use of prohibition notices would force the Government to employ "thousands" of inspectors to cope with demand. That would leave little time for inspectors to investigate safety at work places that did not have union labor.

Mr Spicer said: "There's no limit on how many safety reps a union can have. For example, take a large manufacturing company that employs 1500 workers in 25 different unions that are housed in six different buildings that are each divided into different divisions. Just for a start you would have 25 reps but multiply that by the six buildings and then by the number of tasks. They'd be all over the place."

> Dr Mathews scoffed at the suggestion and said that it was in the trade union movement's interest to develop an orderly and manageable safety system. He said under legislation in Britain 130,000 safety representatives had emerged since 1978. "In five years we would anticipate about 30,000 here," he said.
>
> Dr Mathews conceded that the Government would need to ensure that the commission was well staffed to cope with demand for inspections. At present inspectors from three different departments are being drawn under the authority of the commission. There are about 200 inspectors and the Government will evaluate the new safety system before deciding whether to hire more.
>
> Employers also see chaos arising from the proliferation of safety representatives in workplaces, demarcation disputes between officers and the high cost of paying for safety training.
>
> "Where now the proposed legislation gives rights to certain people in the workplace and denies it to others, it also doesn't allow any accountability for the safety representatives' action to the community, the company or those who are affected by the decision (to stop a work practice)," Mr Spicer said.
>
> "We would see those parts of the legislation as providing a privileged position to trade unionists that could well be used by them to expand their membership and power throughout industry."
>
> Mr Spicer said the Opposition would fight to have safety representatives elected by all employees at a company or workplace. He said their appointment by trade unions alone disenfranchised and discriminated against non-union labor.
>
> Dr Mathews said the argument that non-union labor would be disenfranchised and that all employees should elect safety representatives was "superficially attractive in that it appears to be democratic".
>
> He said there was no problem in a workplace where all workers were unionists. Arrangements between different unions in that workplace could be made to allow a reasonable number of safety representatives to act on behalf of all unions.
>
> "If only some of the workers are union members then what might happen if non-union or anti-union workers stand for election? A network of health and safety representatives indifferent or even hostile to the unions would be created; they might pursue policies and standards that directly conflict with policies and standards developed by the union movement as a whole. At worst they might consciously or unconsciously collaborate with the employer and frustrate union efforts to achieve genuine improve-ments in health and safety," he said.
>
> Dr Mathews said the trade union movement was the legitimate channel through which workers took collective action to improve conditions.
>
> "Unions, too, provide an effective means of ensuring that health and safety representatives remain accountable for their actions and exercise their powers responsibly. A representative who uses them irresponsibly and deprives members of wages by provoking stoppages over allegedly unsafe conditions that are not upheld by the inspectorate, will not long remain a representative," he said.

Source: The Age, Saturday 18 February 1984

discrimination may take various forms. These include refusing in the first place to employ a person of a particular sex or with certain attributes, dismissing that person on those grounds, denying that person promotion or denying that person access to other benefits of employment, for example, training. Thus, discrimination in employment may occur at the stages of hiring or firing, or during the currency of the employment relationship.

Judge-made law before the enactment of protective legislation provided no redress for individuals who felt that they had been discriminated against in the workplace. For example, a contract of employment could be terminated on the basis of a female worker's marriage or pregnancy and so long as the terms of the contract regarding termination were complied with, that is, appropriate notice was given, no reason had to be given at all by the employer; or indeed even if the real reason were given, the common law provided no protection for this form of discrimination. Indeed, in the public service in Australia it was not open for women to continue in employment once they had married. Similarly, in instances where a person was denied employment on the basis of certain characteristics, there was no redress at common law, the notion of 'the right to hire' which entailed freedom to hire whoever the employer wished being firmly entrenched. Discriminatory conduct once a person was employed in terms of denying that person access to promotion, for reasons unrelated to seniority or merit for example, could not be remedied by any allegation of breach of contract—it would be a rare contract which would have an entitlement or right to promotion where particular conditions were fulfilled!

Ironically, other forms of discrimination in the workplace were once officially sanctioned by the industrial relations tribunals. Such discrimination occurred in relation to wage rates, where from 1904 until the early 1970s, it was acknowledged that a differential rate should be paid to male and female workers. The basic wage or later as it was known the minimum wage was determined on the basis of a male worker supporting a family.[49] Lower wages were also at one stage paid to aboriginal workers.[50]

Recent decisions of the Australian Commission have promoted equality and equity in areas such as wages and maternity leave. These decisions, together with the enactment of legislation at state and federal levels which provided for equal opportunity in employment and prohibited discrimination on certain grounds, have made great strides to promoting equality and equity within the workplace but have not eliminated all such practices.

This section will address first of all matters of discrimination from the industrial relations perspective and then examine the prescriptive legislation.

Industrial awards, agreements and equity

Wages

When Higgins J decided the famous *Harvester* case in 1907,[51] the wage which he struck as a fair and reasonable wage was one for a male worker to live on based on a man supporting a wife and three children. This decision was used as the basis for the determination of minimum wages plus margins for skill and gave rise to the acceptance of the notion that there would be a differential rate for men and women. This was so regardless whether the male worker was single or married, and whether the female worker was supporting a family.[52] When a local government council in England in the 1920s attempted to pay its male and female workers the same wage rate, the Court held that the council had not acted within its powers by pursuing notions of philanthropy or feminist ambition![53] It was not until the equal pay cases of 1969 and 1972 that the then Conciliation and Arbitration Commission agreed to the adoption in principle of equal pay for work of equal value.[54]

Despite the adoption of this principle, male and female average earnings are not equal. A differential has arisen between the two because of systems of over-award payments and also because in industries where employees are predominantly female, there is a compression of wages (see Table 16.1 and discussion in chapter 16). It has been sought to argue that a 'comparable worth' principle should be adopted whereby wages of workers in predominantly female workforces should be compared to similar occupations undertaken by men. In the *Re Private Hospitals and Doctors ACT Award*, 1972,[55] the Australian Commission rejected the notion of comparable worth.

The *Industrial Relations Reform Act* 1993 (Cth), which amended the *Industrial Relations Act* 1988 (Cth) extensively, has adopted International Labour Organisation conventions and recommendations concerning equality of treatment of men and women. In doing so, there is now provision for the Industrial Relations Commission to ensure that there is equality of treatment of men and women in the area of wages. The legislation is expressed in such a way that it is anticipated that the Commission may be able to make use of the notion of comparable worth in adjudicating on such pay matters or making such orders.[56]

It was not only in the area of female wages that there was discrimination. Wages of aborigines were also treated differently—aboriginal rural workers were paid less than white employees.[57] It was not until the mid- to late 1960s with the making of the Stockmen's Award that the Commission acknowledged that there should be no differential wages between aboriginal and non-aboriginal stockmen.[58]

Parental leave

The Australian Commission made a significant contribution to the rights of women in the workplace when it awarded 52 weeks' unpaid maternity leave and in effect the right to return to the job held by the woman before taking the leave.[59] Gradually, this leave was extended to leave which could be taken on the adoption of a child, and leave which could be taken by either parent on the birth of their child (parental leave).[60] These types of leave have now been enshrined in the *Industrial Relations Act* 1988 (Cth) as amended by the *Industrial Relations Reform Act* 1993 (Cth). Parental leave is provided for in Division 5 of Part VIA which is to give effect to Australia's obligations under the ILO Family Responsibilities Convention and the Workers with Families Responsibilities Recommendation to provide for a system of unpaid parental leave and unpaid adoption leave. Many public sector employees also enjoy a period of *paid* maternity leave and it is queried whether the legislative entitlements go far enough in setting the standard as unpaid leave.[61] In addition the Commission is empowered under s.170KAA to conduct a test case to consider and make recommendations about leave to care for the immediate family.

Discrimination and dismissals

The standard term in a federal award on termination of employment was the giving of one week's notice by either employer or employee. This provision was altered by the *Termination Change and Redundancy* case[62] when the Commission adopted standard provisions which improved the job security of employees. One of these provisions related to unfair dismissal: an employer could not harshly, unjustly or unreasonably dismiss an employee. Moreover, the standard clause provided that for the purposes of the unfair dismissal clause,

> 'termination of employment shall include terminations with or without notice. Without limiting the above, except where a distinction, exclusion or preference is based on the inherent requirements of a particular position, termination on the ground of race, colour, sex, marital status, family responsibilities, pregnancy, religion, political opinion, national extraction and social origin, shall constitute a harsh, unjust, or unreasonable termination of employment.'[63]

This provision, introduced for the first time in a federal award, provided that dismissal should not be on the basis of discriminatory grounds. If dismissal took place on one of the grounds, there would be a breach of award and a fine could be imposed under s.178 of the *Industrial Relations Act* 1988 (Cth). In addition, for a period from 1988 to 1994, it was held that the unfair dismissal clause in the award was incorporated into the contract of employment so that contractual remedies, in particular, damages, could be awarded where the dismissal was unfair.[64]

The provisions arising from the *Termination Change and Redundancy* case of 1984 were included as standard provisions in most federal awards, thereby the question of discriminatory conduct in termination of employment was addressed in federal awards from that date. The *Industrial Relations Reform Act* 1993 (Cth) has enacted provisions in s.170DF(1)(f) which prescribe prohibited grounds for dismissal which include the standard grounds already itemised in the standard clauses in the *Termination Change and Redundancy* case, but add three other grounds—age, sexual preference, and physical or mental disability—for which dismissal is prohibited. If employment is terminated on any of those grounds, an employee may seek redress of reinstatement or compensation in the Industrial Relations Court of Australia.[65]

Negotiating agreements

Questions of equity arise in the context of legislation at both state and federal levels to encourage and facilitate the negotiation and registration of industrial agreements. The issue which has concerned many unions is whether workers such as women and migrants will be disadvantaged in the negotiation of such agreements. The main thrust of the concern appears to be that they are generally groups with weaker bargaining power and may be inexperienced in bargaining or not have the skills necessary to bargain effectively.[66] It remains to be seen whether these concerns are realised but a recent report commissioned by the New South Wales government into the effect of bargaining on women has disclosed disturbing results in terms of wages and other allowances which women have negotiated less favourably than their male counterparts.[67] The *Industrial Relations Reform Act* 1993 (Cth) has endeavoured to ensure that the agreements themselves are not discriminatory because the Australian Commission may refuse to certify or approve implementation of the agreement if it thinks the agreement discriminates against an employee on grounds such as sex, race and so on.[68] However, this does not seem to address the issue of less beneficial deals being negotiated because workers are, say, women or migrants.

Unlawful discrimination in the workplace under statute

The Commonwealth and all states of Australia except Tasmania, have enacted legislation which prohibits discrimination based on grounds such as race, sex, and so on. Most of the Acts are not confined to discrimination in employment but include matters such as discrimination in the provision of goods and services and in education. The legislation does however, include employment matters and performs an important function in this field. The following is the relevant legislation:

Commonwealth
Racial Discrimination Act 1975
Sex Discrimination Act 1984
Human Rights and Equal Opportunity Commission Act 1986
Disability Discrimination Act 1992

State
Anti-Discrimination Act 1977 (NSW)
Equal Opportunity Act 1984 (Vic)
Anti-Discrimination Act 1991 (Qld)
Equal Opportunity Act 1984 (SA)
Equal Opportunity Act 1984 (WA)
Discrimination Act 1991 (ACT)
Anti-Discrimination Act 1992 (NT)

The provisions vary slightly amongst the states. However, the legislation in force has certain characteristics in common. First, the legislation at state and federal levels prohibits discrimination in employment on certain specified grounds and the unlawful discrimination may include direct discrimination or indirect discrimination. Generally, discrimination is direct where it operates directly against an employee by treating that person less favourably or less beneficially than someone else in that person's position. Indirect discrimination, on the other hand, includes discrimination which is effected by imposing some condition or requirement which the person is not able to comply with but with which a substantially greater number of persons of a different race or sex etc. are able to comply. This type of discrimination may include a policy which operates unevenly between men and women so that women are less able to take the benefit of the particular policy. An example occurred in the *Australian Iron & Steel Pty Ltd v Banovic* case[69] where the redundancy policy of 'last on, first off' adopted by the employer, which on its face did not appear to be discriminatory against men or women, was held by the High Court to involve indirect discrimination because it operated unfavourably against women as most of the more recent employees had been women. The *Annual Report* of the Anti-Discrimination Board of New South Wales 1992-3 gives the example of a complaint alleging indirect discrimination: a nurse working night duties complained that her work affected her unstable insulin-dependent diabetes.[70]

Secondly, the legislation usually makes unlawful discrimination at the time of hiring a person, during the employment relationship and also when dismissing a person. Table 14.3 shows a breakdown of the nature of complaints received by the New South Wales Anti-Discrimination Board.

Thirdly, the grounds for unlawful discrimination will be specified in the legislation. These do vary amongst the jurisdictions but generally will include discrimination on the basis of sex, pregnancy, marital status, race and physical or mental impairment. Table 14.4 contains a survey of grounds of discrimin-

Table 14.3 New South Wales: employment complaints

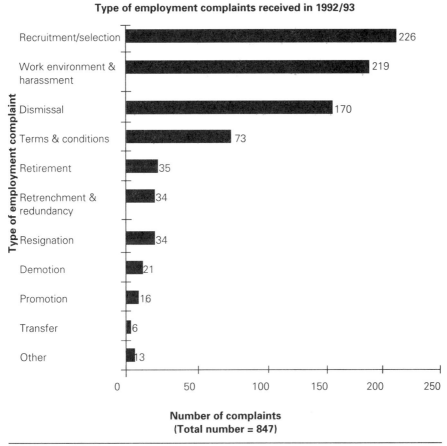

Source: Anti-Discrimination Board of NSW *Annual Report 1992-1993*, p. 22.

ation which are expressly prohibited in the legislation of the Commonwealth and the States. Some jurisdictions include such discriminating grounds as age or sexual preference. Two jurisdictions, South Australia and New South Wales, have specifically addressed the issue—in South Australia, awards and industrial agreements which impose a retiring age are void and of no effect, in New South Wales it is unlawful to impose a compulsory retirement age for employees.

Fourthly, there is established under the legislation procedures for dealing with complaints for unlawful discrimination and for bodies to deal with these. The general focus of the legislation in all jurisdictions has been to set up specialist tribunals and to appoint special commissioners to deal with matters of unlawful discrimination. These tribunals in all jurisdictions are separate and distinct from the industrial relations tribunals. Finally, remedies can be sought by the person alleging unlawful discrimination. These will usually include the remedy of monetary compensation and may also include an order for reinstatement where the person has been dismissed. There are also

Table 14.4 Grounds of discrimination prohibited in legislation

Jurisdiction	Sex	Marital Status	Pregnancy	Race	Impairment— Physical or Mental	Family Responsibilities or Parental Status	Political Opinion	Age	Compulsory Retirement Unlawful	Homosexuality or Sexual Preference
Commonwealth	•	•	•	•	•	•				
New South Wales	•	•	•	•	•				•	•
Victoria	•	•	•	•	•	•	•			
Queensland	•	•	•	•	•	•	•			(a)
South Australia	•	•	•	•	•	•	•	•	(b)	•
Western Australia	•	•	•	•	•	•	•	•		
Australian Capital Territory	•	•	•	•	•	•	•	•		•
Northern Territory	•	•	•	•	•	•	•			•

(a) "lawful sexual activity" is unlawful discriminatory ground

(b) not unlawful; but makes awards or industrial agreements with retiring age void and of no effect

Explanation: In some instances, where a discriminatory ground is not set out in the legislation, there may still occur indirect discrimination where an employer discriminates indirectly against a person by imposing a condition which a proportionally higher number of persons without the characteristics can comply. This may cover, e.g., family responsibilities in South Australia. At the time of writing Tasmania did not have discrimination legislation.

procedures for conciliating the complaint before the matter proceeds to formal hearing. Table 14.5 shows the procedure for handling complaints in New South Wales under its *Anti-Discrimination Act* 1977.

The legislation at state level sometimes overlaps with unfair dismissal legislation at state level and there will sometimes be a problem of choosing the appropriate forum by the complainant. Sometimes, too, a complaint could either be made under federal law dealing with equal opportunity or under relevant state law dealing with employment matters. In some instances the federal law may prevail ovedr the state legislation to make it inoperative, although the *Sex Discrimination Act* 1984 (Cth) requires a choice of remedy to be made under another state or federal law.[71]

These statutory requirements have not eliminated all forms or acts of discrimination in the workplace. They do, however, provide a remedy for persons who can establish that they have been discriminated against on the basis of the grounds set out in the legislation and it should be recalled that such discrimination had in effect been permitted by the common law. The statutory laws, therefore, set standards of prohibited discrimination and furnish a mechanism for redress. They also ensure that employers are aware that in matters of who they will employ, who they will promote, or to whom they will give benefits during employment, and who they will dismiss, they must act fairly and not for discriminatory reasons. These laws operate as constraints on employers and cannot be avoided even by agreement between employer and employees and union.

Sexual harassment

There is statutory protection at both state and federal level[72] against sexual harassment of workers in the workplace. There are, then, laws specifically designed to protect the health and physical safety and well-being of workers from intimidatory and unwanted sexual conduct by other employees or the employee's superior. The definitions of sexual harassment are different in the various statutory regimes. One consequence of legislating against sexual harassment to provide monetary compensation for the victims of such conduct has been the introduction by many employers of sexual harassment policies in the workplace. Such policies are designed to provide for a fair means of complaint by those alleging sexual harassment.

Affirmative action

One approach to ensuring equality of opportunity in employment is to prescribe the numbers of men and women which should be employed. In other words, the policy envisages positive discrimination in favour of otherwise disadvantaged groups. This approach has not generally been adopted by Australian legislation which has been mainly directed to prohibitions on discriminatory practices. However, at Commonwealth level, the *Affirmative Action (Equal Employment Opportunity for Women) Act* 1986 (Cth) has been enacted to promote equal opportunity for women in employment in areas covered by Commonwealth legislation, for example banking, insurance,

Table 14.5 Handling complaints of discrimination in New South Wales

How are complaints handled?

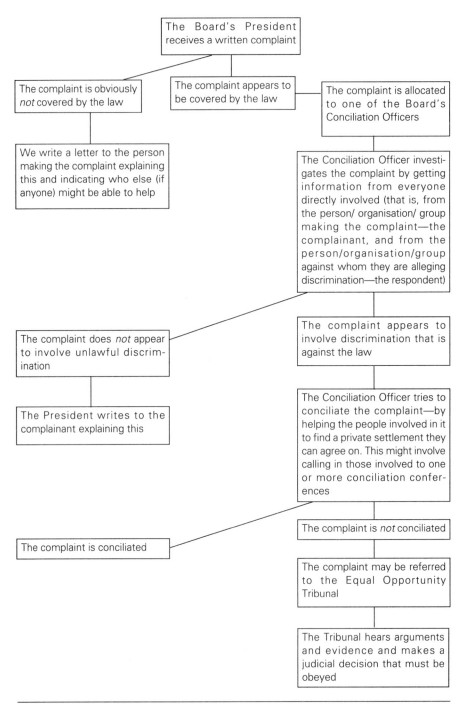

Source: Anti-Discrimination Board of NSW *Annual Report 1992-1993*, p. 14.

Table 14.6 Equal opportunity and affirmative action: ACTU policies

---

7. EQUAL EMPLOYMENT OPPORTUNITY AND AFFIRMATIVE ACTION POLICIES AND PROGRAMS INCLUDING POLICIES DESIGNED TO COMBAT SEXUAL HARASSMENT

7.1 In pursuing equal employment and affirmative action policies and programs Congress supports the following principles:

(i) That all workers are entitled to equal employment opportunity and in particular there should be no discrimination in wages and employment on the basis of sex, race, religion, disability, sexual preference, pregnancy, marital status, or family responsibilities.

(ii) That in developing equal employment policies and programs the special needs of particular groups of women will be taken into account:

(a) aboriginal women,

(b) women from non-english speaking backgrounds,

(c) low income women,

(d) women with disabilities,

(e) rural and isolated women,

(f) young women,

as well as recognising the special needs of all workers in these categories and in addition addressing the needs of all workers with family responsibilities.

(iii) That all workers have the right to work in an environment free from sexual harassment and that such activity in any workforce should not be tolerated as sexual harassment is a denial of the right to equal employment opportunity.

7.2 Congress condemns in the strongest terms the recent trends in service industries such as retail, hairdressing and hospitality to promote sales and services through the employment of topless and scantily clad staff. Such developments encourage the perpetuation of sexist attitudes towards women. Union taking action against employers who engage in such activities will receive the support of the entire trade union movement.

Source: ACTU Policies and Strategies (as adapted at the 1991 ACTU Congress, Melbourne September 9–13, 1991).

broadcasting and television, employment in connection with trade and commerce or where employers are trading (financial or foreign corporations). The legislation operates by requiring employers to develop affirmative action programs which are programs designed to make sure that appropriate action is taken to eliminate discrimination by employers against women in employment matters and to make sure that the employer takes measures to promote equal opportunity of employment for women. Contents of the affirmative action program are laid down in the legislation and the Affirmative Action Agency is established to monitor the program and to assist employers. Employers are required to report annually on the development and implementation of their affirmative action program. However the sanctions are extremely weak under this system because the only sanction for failure to report is that the employer will be named in the Commonwealth parliament. It can be seen that in Australia the approach has not been to adopt measures for affirmative action by *requiring* the employment of defined numbers in minority groups.

Even the ACTU policies in respect of discrimination and equal opportunity (see Table 14.6), whilst generally using the term 'affirmative action' and showing commitment to equal opportunity, do not go so far as prescribing such positive discrimination in the form of employment 'targets' designed to ensure employment of disadvantaged groups.

Conclusion

Important changes have been made legislatively in the area of occupational health and safety and discrimination and equal opportunity in employment. Without these legislative developments it is doubted whether there would have been significant change through the common law or through tribunal decisions in these areas. It has taken government initiative to lead the community down the path of ensuring minimum standards in relation to occupational health and safety and ensuring that there is a certain degree of equity within the workplace. However, critics would argue that there is still a long way to go in terms of satisfactory standards of workplace safety and also appropriate elimination of discrimination in employment. After all, workplace related deaths of approximately 400 per year in Australia is unacceptable. It must be remembered that the legislative prescriptions as they exist today form a framework in which the relations of employers and employees in the workplace must operate and which cannot be avoided by agreement or by consent of the parties. An employer will still be liable in respect of unlawful discrimination even if the employer enters into an agreement with the union that there should exist redundancy policies which operate unfavourably towards a certain group such as women. An employer will be liable under state occupational health and safety legislation for unsafe work practices even where employer and employees have agreed to retain the practice and receive higher wages. Thus, the workplace rules must be made within the framework of the legislative prescription.

Notes

1 See M. Quinlan (ed.), *Work and Health: the Origins, Management and Regulation of Occupational Illness*, Macmillan, Melbourne, 1993.
2 See, e.g., *Barrier Branch of the Amalgamated Miners' Association v BHP* (1916) 10 CAR 155 where work hours were reduced on account of health and safety matters.
3 See *Australian Workers' Union and Confederation of ACT Industry* (Print G6696, 6/3/87) and the *Furnishing Trades* case (1964) 105 CAR 605.
4 See *AWU Amalgamated Society of Carpenters and Joiners and Amalgamated Society of Engineers v Vestey Brothers* (1915) 9 CAR 1; see *Re Municipal Employees (WA) Award 1983* (1987) 23 IR 387, where the award was varied so that employees were not required to work in inclement weather.
5 *Australian Postal Corporation v Australian Public Service Association* (1990) 35 IR 160.
6 See chapters 10 and 12. See, e.g., *Re Cram; Ex parte New South Wales Colliery Proprietors' Association Ltd* (1987) 163 CLR 117; 72 ALR 161.

7 (1987) 72 ALR 161.
8 *ibid.*, p. 161.
9 *Australian Federation of Air Pilots v Flight Crew Officers Industrial Tribunal* (1968) 119 CLR 16. See the detailed discussion of this decision and the perceptions flowing from it in A. Brooks, *Occupational Health and Safety Law in Australia* (4th ed.), CCH Australia Ltd, 1994, pp. 895-899.
10 *R v The Commonwealth Court of Conciliation and Arbitration; the President and the Australian Builders' Labourers' Federation; Ex parte Jones* (1914) 18 CLR 224. The court largely rested its decision on the ground that a judicial power would be wrongly conferred on a Board of Reference which was to determine compensation. Griffith CJ also stated at 236: 'In my opinion the conditions of employment which the President has power in a proper case to regulate are the external conditions in which a workman will find himself when engaged in work (including, of course wages and companions) and do not include stipulations as to the liability of his employer to him in respect of matters that may happen while employed.'
11 (1952) 86 CLR 283.
12 Dixon CJ, Webb and Kitto JJ upheld the validity of the claim in respect of it being an 'industrial matter'. McTiernan and Williams JJ were in dissent and Fullagar J expressed no opinion on the matter.
13 (1965) 111 CAR 382. See also *Alcan Australia Ltd v FIA* (1987) 59 AILR (11).
14 See L. Bennett, Making Labour Law in Australia: Industrial Relations, Politics and the Law, *Law Book Co, Sydney, 1994, pp. 119-126, for a more detailed discussion.*
15 (1969) 129 CAR 751 See Bennett, *op. cit.*, pp. 124-125, who discusses the case in the context of industrial action which had taken place.
16 (1986) 17 IR 1.
17 *ibid.*, pp. 26-27.
18 *ibid.*, p. 27.
19 This philosophy of self-regulation is discussed in the next section.
20 *ibid.*, p. 27.
21 (1989) 30 IR 5.
22 *Albany International Pty Ltd v Amalgamated Footwear and Textile Workers Union* (1990) 35 IR 479.
23 See N. Gunningham, *Safeguarding the Worker*, Law Book Co., Sydney, 1984, p. 65.
24 See Gunningham, *ibid.*, pp. 65-74 for the history of factory legislation in Australia.
25 See, e.g., *Kondis v State Transport Authority* (1984) 154 CLR 672 and generally J. Fleming, *The Law of Torts* (8th ed.), Law Book Co., Sydney, 1992, chapter 24 and F. Trindade and P. Cane, The Law of Torts in Australia (2nd ed.), Oxford University Press, 1993, chapter 4.
26 See Robens, *Report of the Committee of Inquiry on Safety and Health at Work*, 1970-1972, HMSO, London, Cmnd 5034.
27 Section 21(2).
28 Section 21(2)(e).
29 The terminology differs in the various state Acts but generally the duty imposed on the employer is not absolute. See further discussion on the standard below.
30 Section 37.
31 Section 30.
32 Section 35.
33 See Part V.
34 Section 44.
35 Section 43.
36 See now s.8.
37 See *Occupational Health and Safety Act* 1985 (Vic.), ss 32 and 40(5); *Occupational Health and Safety Act* 1983 (NSW) where the Industrial Court can impose penalties for offences (Part 6).
38 *Industrial Relations Act* 1988 (Cth), s.97.

39 Section 55.
40 Section 22.
41 See ss 21 and 22.
42 Sections 23 and 24.
43 Section 25.
44 This issue was debated in the Victorian Parliament in the first attempt to enact health and safety legislation. See Creighton, Ford and Mitchell, *Labour Law: Text and Materials* (3rd ed.), 1993, Law Book Co., chapter 37.
45 (1990) 170 CLR 249.
46 See Part VII.
47 See Creighton, Ford and Mitchell, *ibid.*, chapter 40.
48 See H. Glasbeek and Rowland, 'Are Injuring and Killing at Work Crimes?' *Osgoode Hall Law Journal 17*, 1979, p. 506 and B. Fisse, *Howard's Criminal Law* (5th ed.), Law Book Co. Ltd, chapter 7.
49 See *Harvester* decision (*Ex parte HV McKay* (1907) 2 CAR 1) and R Hunter, 'Women Workers and Federal Industrial Law: From Harvester to Comparable Worth' (1988) *Australian Journal of Labour Law 1*, 1988, p. 147.
50 See further discussion below under Industrial Awards and Equity: Wages.
51 *Ex parte HV McKay* (1907) 2 CAR 1.
52 See *Fruitpickers'* case (*Rural Workers' Union v Mildura Branch of the Australian Dried Fruits Association*) (1912) 6 CAR 61 where the Arbitration Court decided that women's wages should be lower than men's wages and also that the basis for determining their wages should be different.
53 *Roberts v Hopwood* [1925] AC 578. This House of Lords decision in the UK in 1925 considered whether a local council had exceeded its power by paying male and female workers the same wage rate. Lord Atkinson stated at 594 that the council had been guided (wrongly) by 'some eccentric principles of socialist philanthropy, or by a feminist ambition to secure the equality of the sexes in the matter of wages in the world of labour'!
54 *Equal Pay Case 1969* (1969) 127 CAR 1142; *Equal Pay Case 1972* (1972) 147 CAR 172.
55 (1986) 300 CAR 185; 13 IR 108.
56 *Industrial Relations Act* 1988 (Cth) s.170BA. See also M. Pittard, 'International Labour Standards in Australia: Wages, Leave, Termination of Employment', *Australian Journal of Labour Law 7*, 1994, p. 170.
57 See *Graziers Association of New South Wales v Australian Workers Union* (1932) 31 CAR 710 and *Australian Workers' Union v Abbey* (1944) 53 CAR 212.
58 See *Re Cattle Industry (Northern Territory) Award* (1966) 113 CAR 651 and *Re Pastoral Industry Award* (1967) 121 CAR 454.
59 See *Maternity Leave* case (1979) 218 CAR 120.
60 See *Paternity Leave* case (1990) 32 AILR para 284.
61 The ILO Conventions and Recommendations provide for unpaid leave. It may have been constitutionally difficult, therefore, to have legislated for paid maternity leave.
62 (1984) 294 CAR 175; 8 IR 35.
63 *ibid.*
64 In 1988, the Federal Court in *Gregory v Philip Morris Ltd* (1988) 80 ALR 455 so held that the award term is incorporated in the contract. More recently, in *Byrne v Australian Airlines Ltd* (1994) 120 ALR 274, the Federal Court held that award terms were not implied automatically or in fact into the contract of employment so that this form of remedy now appears not to be available. At the time of writing, application for leave to appeal the decision in *Byrne's* case had been made to the High Court.
65 See further M. Pittard 'The Age of Reason: Principles of Unfair Dismissal in Australia' in McCallum, McCarry and Ronfeldt (eds), *Employment Security*, Federation Press, Sydney, 1994, chapter 2.
66 See also Women's Electoral Lobby, *Impact of Enterprise Bargaining on Women: Statement of Concerns*, April 1992; *Half Way to Equal* AGPS, 1992.
67 See L. Gale, 'Enterprise Bargaining in NSW Endangers Women's Employment

Conditions', *NTEU Frontline 1*, 1994, p. 16.
68 See ss 170MD(5) and 170ND(10).
69 (1989) 89 ALR 1.
70 The problem was solved by informal discussion with her employer resulting in an agreement that she work during the day only.
71 Section 8.
72 This statutory protection against harassment is found in the state equal opportunity legislation and in the *Sex Discrimination Act* 1984 (Cth).

Further Reading

Occupational health and safety

L. Bennett, *Making Labour Law in Australia: Industrial Relations, Politics and the Law*, Law Book Co Ltd, Sydney, 1994.

D.R. Biggins, M. Phillips and P. O'Sullivan, 'Benefits of Worker Participation in Health and Safety', *Labour and Industry 4*, March 1991, pp. 138-159.

A. Brooks, *Occupational Health and Safety Law in Australia* (4th ed.), CCH Australia Ltd, Sydney, 1994.

W.B. Creighton, 'Statutory Safety Representatives and Safety Committees: Legal and Industrial Relations Implications', *Journal of Industrial Relations 24*, September 1982, pp. 337-364.

W.B. Creighton and A. Stewart, *Labour Law: An Introduction* (2nd ed.), Federation Press, Sydney, 1994, chapter 11.

W.B. Creighton and E.J. Micallef, 'Occupational Health and Safety as an Industrial Relations Issue: The Rank-General Electric Dispute, 1981', *Journal of Industrial Relations 25*, September 1983, pp. 255-268.

I. Low, 'The Effect of Industrial Relations on Absence Attributed to Injury', *Journal of Industrial Relations 26*, December 1984, pp. 472-483.

H. Luntz, 'The Role of Compensation in Health and Safety at Work', *Journal of Industrial Relations 23*, September 1981, pp. 383-396.

M. Quinlan, 'Occupational Illness, Industrial Conflict and State Regulation: Establishing Some Linkages', in G.W. Ford, J.M. Hearn & R.D. Lansbury (eds), *Australian Labour Relations: Readings* (4th ed.), Macmillan, Melbourne, 1987, pp. 343-385.

M. Quinlan (ed.), *Work and Health: The Origins, Management and Regulation of Occupational Illness*, Macmillan, Melbourne, 1993.

R. Spillane and L. Deves, 'RSI: Pain, Pretence or Patienthood?', *Journal of Industrial Relations 29*, March 1987, pp. 41-48.

Equal employment opportunity and discrimination

L. Bennett, 'Equal Pay and Comparable Worth: Doctrine and Practice in the Commission', in B. Dabscheck, G. Griffin and J. Teicher (eds), *Contemporary Australian Industrial Relations: Readings*, Longman Cheshire, Melbourne, 1992, pp. 419-432.

W.B. Creighton and A. Stewart, *Labour Law: An Introduction* (2nd ed.), Federation Press, Sydney, 1994, chapter 10.

W.J. Kilberg, 'Equal Employment Opportunity in the United States: the Affirmative Action Concept', *Journal of Industrial Relations 17*, June 1975, pp. 148-155.

R. Kramar, 'Affirmative action: a Challenge to Australian Employers and Trade Unions', *Journal of Industrial Relations 29*, June 1987, pp. 169-189.

P.A. Riach, 'Equal Pay and Equal Opportunity', *Journal of Industrial Relations 11*, July 1969, pp. 99-110.

Questions

1. Do you think that our equal opportunity and anti-discrimination legislation goes far enough? What policy arguments are there in favour of and against introducing legislation which provides for positive discrimination in relation to otherwise disadvangaged groups? Is this a matter which could be the subject of industrial agreements between employers and union?
2. Explain the so-called policy of 'self regulation' which derived from the Robens Report. Has this been fully adopted in Australia?
3. What role do you see the Australian Industrial Relations Commission playing in respect of occupational health and safety matters given the legislation which exists at State level in respect of this matter?

15
Conciliation and Arbitration

Contents

Development of the federal system
The Australian Industrial Relations Commission: function and operation
The process of conciliation and arbitration
- conciliation vs arbitration
- conciliation
- arbitration
- compulsion and compliance
- government intervention: formal and informal
- voluntary conciliation and arbitration
- relationship between conciliation, arbitration and collective bargaining

Arbitrated awards: a critique
- 'floor' of rights
- coverage and structure
- centralism reconsidered

Introduction

The processes of conciliation and arbitration have been the dominant feature of public regulation of Australian industrial relations in the twentieth century in the federal and in most state jurisdictions. During the 1980s, the two states which relied on the conceptually different wages board regulatory system, which did not provide for compulsory arbitration, amended their legislation to move closer to the dominant arbitral pattern. In this chapter, consideration will be confined to the processes of the federal system. State processes are discussed in chapter 13.

The prevalence of compulsory conciliation and arbitration means that Australians have grown up with a process of industrial relations that is unusual by the standards of the capitalist world, but it is one which the nation as a whole has accepted with apparent equanimity. Arbitration is a familiar process to industrial relations practitioners outside Australia, but its usual form is voluntary, where both contesting parties agree that issues should be submitted to an agreed neutral third party for decision within parameters predetermined by the parties. In the Australian case, however, arbitration can be imposed by either party on the other, the third party is a public official, and the arbitrator's decision is legally enforceable. The arbitrator's discretion is not determined by the parties in dispute, but by statute and administrative rule. That discretion includes the right to withhold arbitration and to lead the parties to agreement, or to persuade them to accept voluntarily a proposed solution. Achieving agreed solutions between the parties is, of course, conciliation; the Australian tribunals use conciliation as well as arbitration to settle disputes, but inevitably, arbitration attracts greater public attention.

Where conciliation is a process which attempts to force the parties themselves to develop a solution to the issue in question, it will almost certainly involve a variety of bargaining, but the bargaining concerned is undertaken in the context of a conciliation and arbitration system, and this provides unusual characteristics. A particular feature distinguishes bargaining in this context from the more general practice in industrial relations. The right and capacity of either party to take industrial action to press its claims is a generally accepted corollary of collective bargaining, but until recently the bargaining that took place under the conciliation process in Australia saw the right to take industrial action severely constrained, if not eliminated, by legislative and policy constraints. The enactment of the *Industrial Relations Reform Act* 1993 has brought Australian law relating to strikes into conformity with International Labour Organisation standards permitting the right to strike during bargaining under certain conditions (for amplification see chapters 5 and 17).

The system of conciliation and arbitration has been the subject of constant criticism for most of the period since the 1920s, but rarely has that criticism amounted to more than suggestions that it has erred on particular matters. One of the more fundamental criticisms is the view that the system is predicated on conflicting premises. First, the basic philosophy of compulsory arbitration is that the presence of a neutral umpire, able to enforce minimum standards, renders industrial action unnecessary. At the same time, however, it is recognised that awards of the tribunal establish minimum conditions only, thus bargaining for over-award conditions ensues, entailing, inevitably, some likelihood of industrial action.[1] The only governments to attempt fundamental change were those led by Prime Ministers W.M. Hughes, who, in 1920, introduced alternative legislation in the form of the *Industrial Peace Act*, and S.M. Bruce, whose election campaign in 1929 included a promise to abolish the (then) Commonwealth Court of Conciliation and Arbitration. It is arguable that the fate of Bruce, who lost not only the election, but his own seat in parliament, has been the most effective protection that the system has had. While later analyses of the Bruce debacle suggest that other factors were critical,[2] the folklore has been that tampering with the arbitral system induced Bruce's downfall. The popular version may be incorrect, but Australian politicians have not shown much eagerness to put it to the test. It is therefore, arguable that the Australian 'system' of conciliation and arbitration owes at least as much to political timidity as it does to popular confidence and support. That argument would probably be supported by the history of legislative tinkering (see below) with the Act since its inception.

It would require a considerable degree of boldness or prescience to predict the future of the Australian arbitral system. It has come under increasing criticism since the latter part of the 1980s as the decline of Keynesian economics has been followed by a reversion to enthusiasm for versions of *laissez-faire*, neoclassical economics. It is to be noted, however, that renewed faith in the free interplay of market forces is confined to a few politicians, journalists and theoreticians, rather than being a popular groundswell. Such voices rarely form public opinion. Popular support for the Commission has never been fully tested but it may be waning. This is suggested by the results of a 1989 and a 1992 Saulwick *Age* Poll. The 1989 survey showed that fifty per cent of voters polled believed that the Commission should continue to have a central role in fixing wages compared with sixty-nine per cent in an *Age* Poll in 1981. In 1992, direct employer-worker negotiations were preferred by 49% of respondents compared with 22% who believed that the Commission should decide on wages, hours and working conditions.[3]

Perhaps the strongest defenders of conciliation and arbitration would be, in the end, employer associations and unions. It would be an exaggeration to suggest that the survival of both is entirely dependent on the continuation of conciliation and arbitration, but the status and achievement of each is very strongly influenced by this. While they are the major elements of a small industry that has developed around the conciliation and arbitration system, it has also sponsored the growth of large public service and private company bureaucracies, and large specialist legal practices. All these would prove to be powerful lobbyists should the preservation of the system ever be threatened. It needs to be remembered, however, that the fundamental purposes of the system are to serve those employers and employees who need assistance in resolving industrial disputes. The benefits which other parties and organisations draw from the system are of secondary importance.

Recent significant amendments brought by the *Industrial Relations Reform Act* 1993 support the foregoing argument. Despite the fact that the amendments promote and facilitate collective bargaining and in particular enterprise bargaining, the 'system' of conciliation and arbitration has not been dismantled. Specifically, any agreement must be related to an award of the Commission and the Commission retains a power of veto, albeit limited, in relation to applications for certification of agreements.[4]

Development of the federal system

Australian unions, with the support of protectionists, used their political power to secure arbitral systems (other than in Victoria and Tasmania which opted for wages boards), curial in form, with compulsory powers.[5] They needed such a system to ensure that they could, despite their industrial weakness, force recognition and secure concessions from the more powerful employers. As explained in chapter 12, the system began, therefore, as a Court of Conciliation and Arbitration, established by the federal parliament under the power of s.51(35) of the Australian Constitution. The strikes of 1890–91, showed disputes could cross state boundaries, and they had also shown that disputes could easily involve other workers with whom they had contact, the most obvious case being the support which waterfront employees would provide to seamen in disputes. While some of those responsible for drafting and adopting the Constitution,[6] and some of those who drafted and passed the *Conciliation and Arbitration Act* may have been aware of the significance of their decisions, it seems probable that the Act was seen by most as being designed to plug any gaps between the various state jurisdictions.

The tendency of businesses and employer associations to become national, rather than state organisations, the dominance of the federal government and bureaucracy over the states, and some federation of state union branches have all helped to shift the federal industrial relations machinery to a dominant position among the tribunals. The national focus of unionism is probably the weakest of those forces, and for most of their history, the typical national Australian union has been a federation of more or less autonomous state branches. Further, until the 1980s, the influence of the national inter-union federation, the ACTU, was also slight.

A major force pushing the federal tribunal to the fore has been the long history of High Court constitutional decisions. The effect of these over the century has been to evolve towards a situation in which the constitutional limitations on the jurisdiction are far from restrictive. As discussed in chapter 12, the High Court has ruled that a 'dispute' which the tribunal may settle is no more than the service and rejection of a claim, and, similarly, the interstate character of a dispute may be attained by way of paperwork rather than by industrial action. For many years, the term 'industrial' was a matter which inhibited the jurisdiction of the federal tribunal, for the Court had ruled that certain employed people were not employed in industry, and well-known examples were schoolteachers and firefighters,[7] thus could not be involved in industrial disputes. Similarly, it had held that certain matters were not industrial matters, and usually this meant that such issues could be determined unilaterally by managers. Following the *Social Welfare* case of 1983,[8] these restrictions have disappeared. The situation now appears to be that an industrial dispute, if it is to lie within the federal jurisdiction, should be a dispute between an employer and an employee over any aspect of the terms and conditions of employment. As this can include settlement of such issues as crew sizes, or rights to be given particular kinds of work,[9] it clearly allows the tribunal to rule on issues which are critical to the efficient management of enterprises. The legally tested jurisdiction of the federal tribunal extends much further in the 1990s than it did in the 1920s, and it is of concern to those committed to accountability in public administration that this expansion has been achieved entirely without legislation.

The original hope for conciliation and arbitration seems to have been that it would be the mechanism for producing voluntary agreement between disputing parties, probably aided by conciliation, and that it would be concerned with industrial relations at the individual workplace, rather than with some aggregation of industrial relations. It is, of course, difficult to reconcile concern with the individual workplace with the interstate requirement for federal jurisdiction, but that may indicate that the federal legislation was intended to be confined to the unusual case where no single state could establish exclusive jurisdiction. Certainly, it is probably easier to reconcile this apparent difficulty than it is to accept that there can be any operational significance to the concept of national industrial relations, the matter which has come to be the staple of the federal tribunal.

If its founders had hoped that the federal tribunal would confine itself to the microcosm of industrial relations, their hopes have been disappointed, for the tribunal is occupied for the most part with issues that go well beyond the scope of individual workplaces. These developments are discussed below and in chapter 16. What should be noted here is that there is no direct, express constitutional or legislative mandate for the tribunal to be involved in such issues as the determination of policy concerning national wages. Further, it should be noted that, on the occasions on which federal governments have sought increased powers to regulate directly wages and other conditions of employment, the voters at referendums have refused to grant those powers. In 1973 for example, the Whitlam government was defeated on two referenda which sought powers for the federal parliament to legislate over prices and incomes. The ACTU campaigned against an incomes power on the ground that it might be used by a non-Labor government to freeze wage levels. It would be idle to argue that the effective power to regulate wages has not been applied by the tribunals in the post-war years, despite the electorate's specific rejection of approval for that course.

The Australian Industrial Relations Commission: function and operation

In this section the nature and operation of the organisation within which the processes of conciliation and arbitration are conducted is explained. The *Conciliation and Arbitration Act* of 1904 had been changed many times, some suggested that by 1988, when it was replaced by the *Industrial Relations Act*, it had been amended, on average, once a year during its lifetime. The quest for bureaucratic order alone may have justified the redesign of the Act, but the government had, initially, more expansive plans than housekeeping alone.

In 1985 it commissioned an enquiry to review and recommend any necessary improvements to Australian industrial relations law and systems. The review comprised Professor K. Hancock (now Senior Deputy President Hancock of the Industrial Relations Commission), a labour economist whose special interest had been the analysis of economic outcomes of the arbitral system, as chairman, Mr G. Polites, a former employer association executive, and Mr C. Fitzgibbon, a former union official. Given that the three Committee members had a formidable knowledge of the working of the federal system of conciliation and arbitration, but little demonstrated experience of other industrial relations machinery, it was unlikely that the recommendations of this group would be for other than marginal changes.

While the Hancock Report may have been intended to provide the basis for reviews of the Act, in the event it had little impact on the *Industrial Relations Act* of 1988. Its agenda for reform was modest, Dabscheck describing it as a 'celebration of the *status quo*',[10] but even the original draft Bill of 1987 was withdrawn, and a further-diluted version passed in 1988.

The Act of 1988 certainly comprises a more compact and editorially consistent document than did its predecessor. It is difficult to identify any major thrust of the Act which differs from its predecessor. One might speculate that it establishes the institutional interests of the Commission. The original statute saw the Commission as being almost entirely passive, it would respond to matters brought to it by legitimate parties, and it would be constrained only by jurisdictional issues. The *Industrial Relations Act*, however, as explained in chapters 7 and 8, has allowed the Commission considerable scope to reorganise unionism according to its tastes. Notwithstanding parliament's lack of Constitutional power to legislate in the area, the *Industrial Relations Act* has attempted to provide some legislative support for the Commission's involvement in wage policy. It did so by borrowing language from the *Conciliation and Arbitration Act* which required the Commission to '... take into consideration the public interest and for that purpose shall have regard to the state of the national economy and the likely effects on the economy of any award ... with special reference to likely effects on the level of employment and on inflation.'[11]

The term 'public interest' lacks any precise meaning, for it cannot mean majority interest, since minorities are as much part of the public as is the majority, nor can it mean government interest, since substantial parts of the population are usually opposed to this. To act in the public interest could only mean, technically, to take some action which benefits at least part of the population and disadvantages none, and it is difficult to imagine such an act. Public interest is thus essentially a question begging phrase, a rhetorical flourish that might be suited to a political oration, but it has no place in statutes, where a Court might be called upon to impart meaning to it, and where its very imprecision could provide scope for legal action. The *Industrial Relations Act* directs the Commission that:

> 'In the performance of its functions, the Commission shall take into account the public interest, and for that purpose shall have regard to:
>
> (a) the objects of the Act; and
> (b) the state of the national economy and the likely effects on the national economy of any award or order that the Commission is considering or proposing to make, with special reference to likely effects on the level of employment and on inflation.'[12]

If the matters in paragraph (b) lack a constitutional basis, as argued above, this presumably implies that whatever meaning the Commission may choose to give the term 'public interest' the legislation can have no more than persuasive power.

The personnel charged with undertaking conciliation and arbitration comprise a group dedicated to that function, and through the 1980s, that group was about forty strong. Over the years the Commission has grown in size and in the early 1990s, its membership of Presidential members and Commissioners approaches fifty.

Those appointed to the Commission are public employees, and, unusually for the public sector, they are appointed by invitation rather than by response to public advertisement. It is not known whether recommendations for appointment come to the government from the Commission or from other sources, or whether such recommendations are solicited or not. The end result is that the Commission tends to be staffed by personnel who are knowledgeable about this particular industrial relations process, that is, conciliation and arbitration, and may not necessarily be informed about industrial relations as a whole, or expert in fields relevant to settling disputes.[13] Essentially, this method of staffing may make for a staff which is inward-looking. Any major reform to the system is unlikely, therefore, to come from within.

The method of appointment of members of the Commission follows the method of selection and appointment of judges. The judicial heritage is apparent too, in the organisation of the Commission's staff. The judge's role requires independence of thought and self-reliance, consequently teamwork and co-operative style are not attributes especially sought after for the judiciary; any unity of purpose is attained through the individual interpretations of a common legal code. That method applied to the conciliation and arbitration system at least until the *Boilermakers* case,[14] and possibly for some years after. The Commission, and before it, the Court, consisted simply of a group of judges given a unity of purpose by the Act they administered. The direction which the Commission members were given consisted of little more than the assignment of cases by the President.

The members of the Commission have been distributed over a series of industries, in the form of industry-specific panels, each under the direction of a Presidential member. The notion of 'industry' which underlies the panels is not especially precise, and this is illustrated in Table 15.1. The purpose of the panels is to permit the members of the Commission concerned to develop familiarity with the industry with which they deal, and to provide for the availability of informed substitutes for any particular panel member who may be unavailable. This method has undoubted efficiencies, but it is also possible to wonder whether the development of close knowledge of individuals and institutions in this way is a desirable trait in a quasi-judicial process. The panel system may be more likely to inhibit change and development, rather than to encourage it. It might be noted that the private arbitration which exists in North America does include a few who are permanently retained by employers and unions in various industries, plants or firms, but a more common process involves the selection of arbitrators by lot from a list provided by a voluntary association of arbitrators. In this system at least, close knowledge of the industry and its participants is not deemed necessary, but it is to be noted that the system charges arbitrators with functions a good deal more restricted than does the Australian system.

Table 15.1 Australian Industrial Relations Commission: industry panels as at 30 June 1993

- Brickmaking industry
  Cemetery operations
  Cleaning services
  Cork manufacturing industry
  Diving services
  Funeral directing
  Gardening services
  Hairdressing services
  Industries not otherwise assigned
  Painting industry
  Pest control services
  Pharmaceutical industry
  Pharmacy operations
  Salt industry

- Aluminium industry
  Catering industry
  Coal treatment industry
  Mining industry (includes on site processing)
  Northern Territory
  Northern Territory administration
  Quarrying industry
  Uranium mining (including construction)

- Business equipment industry
  Educational services
  Federal police services
  Fire fighting services
  Health and welfare services
  Library services
  Local government administration
  Water, sewerage and drainage services

- Graphic arts
  Journalism
  Photographic industry
  Printing industry
  Private transport industry
  Publishing industry
  Sanitary and garbage disposal services
  Scientific services
  Security services
  Technical services

- Building, metal and civil construction industries
  Cement and concrete products
  Electrical contracting industry
  Gypsum, plaster board and plaster of paris manufacturing industry
  Insulation materials manufacturing
  Paper products industry
  Plumbing industry

- Arts administration
  Defence support
  Electrical power industry
  Entertainment and broadcasting industry
  Horse and greyhound training industry
  Mannequins and modelling industry
  Oil and gas industry
  Tourism industry
  Travel industry

- Brush and broom making industry
  Furnishing industry
  Glass industry
  Glue and gelatine industry
  Rope, cordage and thread industry
  Rubber, plastic and cable making industry
  Saddlery, leather and canvas industry
  Timber industry
  Vehicle industry

- Commonwealth employment
  Communications industry
  Postal services
  State government administration
  Telecommunications services

- Agricultural industry
  Clothing industry
  Dry cleaning and laundry services
  Food, beverage and tobacco industry
  Grain handling industry
  Grocery products manufacture

- Airline operations
  Airport operations
  Chemical industry
  Liquor and accommodation industry
  Paint manufacturing industry
  Public transport industry

  Maritime industry
  Pet food manufacturing
  Port and harbour services
  Textile industry
  Wool industry

- Agricultural implement manufacturing
  Aircraft industry
  Brass, copper and non-ferrous metals industry
  Engine drivers and firemen
  Jewellery manufacturing
  Metal industry
  Shipbuilding industry
  Space tracking industry
  Storage services
  Watchmaking
  Wholesale and retail trade

- Banking services
  Clerical industry
  Data processing industry
  Finance and investment services
  Health insurance industry
  Insurance industry
  Market and business consultancy services
  Meat industry

Source: Adapted from President of the Australian Industrial Relations Commission *Annual Report* 1992-93, AGPS, Canberra, pp. 25-27.

Every member of each industry panel has the power to conciliate and to arbitrate the disputes referred to them by panel chairpersons. There are however, certain issues which, regardless of the industry, are deemed to be of such national importance that they must be heard by a full bench of the Commission, a specially convened group of three or more Commission members, including at least two Presidential members. The Act defines these issues, and they involve the standard hours of work in an industry, national wage cases, determining or varying minimum wages, and determining or varying annual leave and long service leave provisions.[15]

The full bench may also be convened to hear appeals against the decision of any single Commission member, or against a member's failure to make a decision. There is also, although to the lay mind its connection with the settlement of industrial disputes may seem remote, provision for the Minister for Industrial Relations to initiate such an appeal. It is possible too for either party or for the Minister to apply to have a dispute, or some aspect of it, referred to a full bench for decision. The Commission's President determines whether or not this shall be done, and is required to consult with the person hearing the dispute before deciding. The President's decision is to be based on the importance 'in the public interest' which is attached to the decision. In practice, this probably means that any decision likely to break new ground, to impinge on government policy, to apply to a community broader than those before the Commission and, perhaps any matter which is likely to draw an appeal from any party, will be referred to a full bench.

In 1994, following the passage of the *Industrial Relations Reform Act* 1993, a separate Bargaining Division of the Commission was established. Its function is to facilitate agreements primarily by the exercise of conciliation powers.[16] The Division is headed by a Vice-President and includes other members of the Commission who are assigned to it.

The process of conciliation and arbitration

Before turning to the operating processes of the tribunal, its performance in general terms in considered. The purpose of the system of conciliation and arbitration was to end the 'rude and barbarous'[17] process of the strike, and the system has not done that. It has resulted in an industrial relations performance whose strike experience is not noticeably different from those nations which have no structures or regulations designed to prevent strikes. In the years following the election of the Hawke-led ALP government, a marked decline in strikes resulted (see chapter 3), but this is to be attributed to the agreement negotiated between the ALP, the ACTU and union leaders, rather than to any efforts of the tribunal, or to a sudden appreciation by working people of the virtues of conciliation and arbitration. One may presume that all the fundamental causes of industrial disputes remain unchanged.

The Industrial Relations Commission and its predecessors have, for almost the whole of the 20th century, been charged with the substitution of other methods for the strike. For the whole of that period, the tribunal has not achieved this. There is little doubt that the majority of analysts of industrial relations would argue that to have set a goal of strike prevention was probably foolish, and unlikely to succeed without intolerable incursions into democratic freedoms, but that is the task which was set, and by which it must inevitably be judged. Commentators in Australia are oddly reluctant to accept that. Indeed, far more public criticism has been directed to labour and management where either has taken actions which culminate in work stoppages. Such discussion tends to proceed as though it is incumbent on managers to sublimate their obligation to shareholders to make profits, and on unions to sublimate their duty to protect members' interests, to the needs of the Commission. Australia, having created the 'system' to serve industry, now complains that industry does not serve the arbitral 'system'.

Conciliation vs arbitration

In undertaking its statutory duty, the Industrial Relations Commission is restricted to using conciliation and arbitration. These are distinct processes, conciliation being the means by which a third party helps those in dispute to reach agreement on the issues in contention. The role of the third party is to provide whatever help is needed to allow the protagonists to resolve the matters that have separated them. That help may involve suggested compromises, analyses, predictions of outcomes if the dispute is not settled, providing services to keep the discussions continuing or other tactics. The conciliator will not, however, make a decision and impose that on the parties. That is the function of arbitration, and this is essentially a simpler task than conciliation. The arbitrator will expect to hear argument from each party, and will then devise the best solution, and will impose that solution on the parties.

As noted above, it appears from the emphasis of the original legislation that those who introduced the system had hoped that its dominant function would be conciliation. If that had been realised, the system would have seen the development of a process whereby the unions and managers would settle their differences by agreements, and those agreements would be reached with the conciliator's assistance. The rare exceptions would be the cases which resisted conciliation and had to be arbitrated. The emergence of conciliation as the key process did not take place, although it has remained as important in the day to day operations of industrial relations. The high hopes for conciliation probably were not realised due to the taste for uniformity which the tribunal and its clients quickly developed; whether this developed out of the Australian 'talent for bureaucracy'[18] or from other sources is a matter for conjecture. The procedures adopted also had some influence, because the conciliator, at least in the early years, was also the eventual arbitrator. A party dissatisfied with an outcome supported by a conciliator probably felt that there was little or no downside risk involved in rejecting a conciliated proposal in favour of arbitration. In 1993 a preference for conciliation was reflected in the revised objects[19] of the *Industrial Relations Act* but there were no changes to the provisions dealing specifically with processes and these are now explained.

Conciliation

While the individual members of the Commission have a broad discretion as to the way they will conduct the cases before them, the legislation does require that certain steps be followed. The method, which was the only available method until the reforms of 1994, is to first ensure that a dispute exists, and that the Commission has the jurisdiction to resolve it by conciliation and arbitration. For the most part this is a fairly routine process, and involves ensuring that appropriate notification has been filed, and that the issue in dispute is clearly identified. In all but a tiny minority of cases, the parties to the dispute will have ensured that a dispute within the meaning of the Act does exist, and that the parties have satisfied the major jurisdictional requirements, mainly that the dispute has an interstate element, and that it involves an industrial matter. These jurisdictional hurdles are discussed in detail in chapter 12.

Having determined that a dispute does exist, and that the Commission has jurisdiction, the Commissioner handling the case will normally begin by seeking to conciliate. The Commissioner is selected to handle the case by a bureaucratic process. One or other of the parties will notify the Commission of the dispute, and if, as is normally the case, the dispute has arisen under an existing award, the Presidential member in charge of the panel covering the relevant industry will assign the task. In other cases, where the parties have recently had dealings with a member of the Commission, that person may be approached directly.

The conciliation process normally includes a substantial element of fact-finding. This serves not only to inform the conciliator, but it can also aid the process of dispute settling, for the statements of position by each party can reveal that the issues in dispute are less than had been assumed initially.

During conciliation, it is often the case that participants are less aggressive in stating their preferences than they have been at earlier stages. This comes about in part because they are taking positions before an independent third party who may be able to assist them, and who may, eventually, as an arbitrator, sit in judgement on their cases. It is therefore unwise to appear to be unreasonable or intransigent.

The Act gives wide discretion to conciliators in the methods they may adopt:

> Where an industrial dispute is referred for conciliation, a member of the Commission shall do everything that appears to the member to be right and proper to assist the parties to agree on terms for the prevention or settlement of the industrial dispute.[20]

Conciliators devise their own methods of proceeding, and, obviously, they adapt these to the circumstances at hand. Some may choose to dominate proceedings, to develop agenda and timetables if they prefer to work by formal means. Others may elect to work by counselling each party, by guiding them towards a preferred solution. Whatever the mode the conciliator chooses, the process will often begin with a compulsory conference called by the conciliator between the disputing parties. It is at this conference that the conciliator learns the facts and details of the dispute, and these, and the attitudes of the parties probably determine the approach the conciliator will follow. The conciliator's goal is to reduce, and eventually to eliminate the gap between the demand of one party and the offer of the other. Conciliation is the art of inducing one to offer a little more, and the other to demand a little less, and to persist in this until the two have reached agreement. It is a difficult task, requiring unusual skills, and if it is to be successful, it is essential that the conciliator has the trust and respect of the parties.

Normally, conciliation continues until the parties reach agreement, or until the conciliator is satisfied that no further progress is likely to be made. Meaningful data are not available, but observers generally believe that the majority of issues brought to the Commission are resolved at conciliation; whether the issues of most importance to the parties are resolved in this way is not known. It is, of course, to be kept in mind that usually the disputes taken to the Commission involve many separate matters, and these involve varying degrees of difficulty of solution. Conciliation involves the parties voluntarily reaching agreement. As these often seem to involve an increase in the welfare of one party at the expense of the other, it is not surprising that there are often issues which conciliation cannot resolve, and these are referred to arbitration.

If the parties reach agreement during conciliation, the Commission may give legal effect to the agreement. One form the agreement may take is a consent award,[21] so called because it arises out of the parties' consensus rather than from an arbitral decision. Another form is the certified agreement[22] which is usually couched in the phrasing of the parties rather than written by the Commission. Both these instruments have the same legal status as arbitrated awards and may either come before the Commission after conciliation or after purely private negotiations, that is, not involve any formal conciliation under the statute.

If there are other issues on which the parties to an industrial dispute cannot reach agreement, they must be submitted to arbitration.[23] Even in those cases in which the conciliator is convinced that agreement can be reached if the parties persist in negotiations, if they will not persist, the issue must go to arbitration. It would be arbitrated also if the conciliator decided that this was the best course, but in general, since the 1960s at least, Commission members have shown a decided preference for conciliation over arbitration.

This process of conciliation described above, which may be followed by arbitration, is invoked when there is an industrial dispute within the meaning of the *Industrial Relations Act* 1988. Since the reforms of 1994, there exist other circumstances in which the Commission is able to exercise powers of conciliation. Neither of these circumstances requires the existence of an industrial dispute before the Commission's conciliation powers can be invoked. First, if there is a situation likely to give rise to an interstate industrial dispute, called an 'industrial situation' in the Act, the parties may negotiate a certified agreement.[24] Secondly, where the negotiating parties are an employer, which is a constitutional corporation, its employees and any eligible union which chooses to take part, the parties may negotiate an enterprise flexibility agreement.[25] An enterprise flexibility agreement like a certified agreement, may also be the product of purely private negotiations, that is, not involving any conciliation prior to Commission approval. One company which negotiated such an agreement in 1994 is Optus Communications. An interview with the Human Resources Manager of this company appears in Table 10.11.

Parties wishing to negotiate either type of agreement may ask the Commission in its Bargaining Division to exercise its powers of conciliation in relation to the proposed agreements. Conciliation undertaken by the Bargaining Division is the same as conciliation for settlement of industrial disputes (as discussed above) but in addition the Commission can make orders that the parties must bargain in good faith.[26]

Arbitration

Once an industrial dispute goes to arbitration, the role of the third party changes from that of a person helping to reach an agreement to that of one who hears evidence and makes a judgement. The shift in process does not usually mean a change in the third party representative, that is, it is usually the conciliator who assumes the function of arbitrator. There is provision for either party to request as an arbitrator a member of the tribunal who was not involved in the conciliation process.[27] The AMIEU exercised this right during proceedings which culminated in the Mudginberri dispute[28] (see chapters 4 and 5 for discussion of this dispute). Cupper suggests that the reasons for the limited exercise of this principal party prerogative include a desire not to offend tribunal members and the blurring of the processes in practice, for example some advocacy may precede intensive negotiations.[29] The style in which different arbitrators hear evidence varies a good deal. Though some arbitrators prefer to hear argument in a rather formal and typically courtroom environment, others operate in a conference style format and the current arbitral style leans more to this less formal approach. Parties may be, and often are, represented either by a lawyer engaged for the case or an industrial officer who has legal training, and this may have an impact on the nature of proceedings. Regardless of whether the proceedings are formal or otherwise, the function of each party is to present cases to the arbitrator in the strongest possible terms. The arbitrator's judgement, or award, is then based on this evidence. Unlike the conciliation proceedings, the arbitrator is not expected to lead the parties to a mutually acceptable agreement. Technically, the arbitrator is not concerned with agreement, but rather is expected to exercise judgement as to the best solution of the dispute before him or her.[30]

Naturally enough, this process incorporates nothing designed to lead the parties to agreement, and more seriously, it includes nothing to ensure that either party will be satisfied with the award. Indeed, the process itself probably forces the parties further apart, rather than encouraging them to reach an agreed solution. This occurs because each party, in seeking a favourable judgement, naturally tries to belittle the opponent's case, whilst enhancing and embellishing its own. At the conclusion of their submissions to the arbitrator, the parties may be further apart than they were at the end of conciliation. Whatever else arbitration might be designed to do, it is not intended to achieve a meeting of minds between the opposing parties. Figure 15.1 provides a diagrammatic representation of the sequence of events and the resultant alternative tribunal instruments which are discussed below.

Figure 15.1 The process of conciliation and arbitration: federal jurisdiction

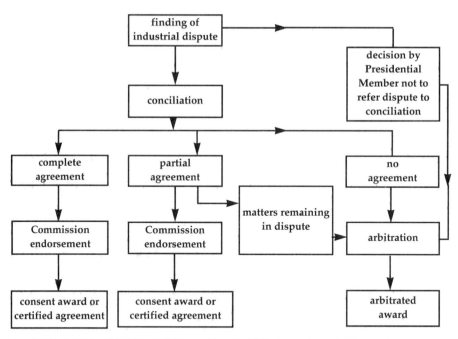

Source: Adapted from *Industrial Relations Act 1988* ss 99–104 and s.111(1)(b).

Note 1: It is possible for private negotiations to result in complete agreement. In these circumstances the parties may apply to the Commission for conversion of their agreement to either a consent award or certified agreement. In these cases there will be no (need for) conciliation (see p. 459).

Note 2: This diagram does not illustrate the conciliation process which may follow from an 'industrial situation' or which may arise in the context of negotiations/applications for enterprise flexibility agreements.

Note 3: Commission endorsement is not automatically granted (see chapter 12).

In theory, arbitration is a normative proceeding, that is, whatever decision is provided, it is in some sense correct. In practice few arbitrators would wish to ignore the reality that they must produce solutions which are at least partial responses to the needs of the parties before them. The arbitrator is required to award decisions that must be put into practice in the workplace, an atmosphere considerably removed from the orderly world of arbitral chambers. If the award is to be workable, and by inference, the Commission to be credible, it must not be insensitive to the expectations, aspirations and industrial powers of the disputing parties. In recent years, the process of arbitration has edged away from the formal, idealised process of seeking a decision that accords to normative standards. Instead, arbitrators have sought to identify the needs of each party, and to find solutions compatible with their needs, and one observer has suggested that this practice was that adopted in the early decades of conciliation and arbitration.[31]

This 'accommodative arbitration', as it has been called, is an attempt to reconcile the judgemental process of arbitration with the fact that parties do have the capacity to resist awards they perceive as not being in their interests. Arbitration is considered to be 'accommodative' when the arbitrator's decision is influenced by his or her assessment of the relative power of the parties. One example of an accommodative decision was the adoption of an Enterprise Bargaining Principle in the October 1991 *National Wage* case following trenchant criticism by the Government and the ACTU of the Commission's refusal to do so in April 1991 (see pp. 528 and 614-619). Accommodative arbitration is to be distinguished from normative or judicial arbitration, mentioned above. Isaac, paraphrasing Higgins, says this latter approach 'called for the determination of issues in the light of evidence and argument, not in accordance with the dictates of the strong. The tribunal should not be opportunist and never yield to force'.[32] Romeyn,[33] in a detailed analysis of the factors influencing arbitrators' decisions, distinguishes the characteristics of these two arbitration types and a third type 'administrative arbitration'. These characteristics are set out in Table 15.2. In questioning the applicability of judicial arbitration, Romeyn points out that supposedly objective criteria such as 'work value' in fact allow for substantial degrees of subjective judgement. 'Work value' is one example of the set of principles which the Commission has developed in arbitration. These principles relate to National Wage decisions and to other matters which come before it and some of these principles are discussed in chapters 16 and 18.

Knowledge of the nature of arbitration decisions provides one indicator of the impact of the Commission's function as rule-maker in terms of the content of workplace or substantive rules. The Commission may be any of the following: pace-setter; leveller; catalyst; or replicator of privately regulated outcomes.[34] In respect of the possible 'leveller' or uniformity impact, about which there has been much conjecture, opinion divides between attaching primary importance to the force of coercive comparisons or to the high degree of centralisation of tribunal structure. Isaac, while remaining equivocal, has suggested tribunals may have sped the flow of comparable wage increases through the system, especially in areas where union power is weak.[35]

Table 15.2 Characteristics of identified arbitration types

Arbitration type	Characteristics/Preconditions
Adjudication or Normative or Judicial arbitration	1. Parties participate in the decision-making process through the presentation of proofs and reasoned arguments aimed at achieving a decision in their favour. 2. An arbitrator who is accessible to reason arrives at and explains his decisions by the logical or analogical development of given or stated premises. 3. There exist 'principles' or 'criteria of decision' common to the dispute and capable of being rationally elaborated and applied in making the decision. The principles or criteria must be of a sufficient character and quality that proofs and argument can be rationally related to them.
Administrative arbitration	1. The parties participate as above, but the realm of judicial notice is enlarged beyond the proofs and arguments presented by the parties. 2. The arbitrator assumes a legislative mantle. His decisions are characterised by a strong element of 'social engineering', and are fashioned out of the wealth of the arbitrator's own empirical knowledge, according to his conception of a just solution.
Autonomous or Accommodative Arbitration	1. The arbitrator is reluctant to supplant the union and employer bodies as the dynamic forces in industrial relations. Consequently, judicial notice is limited to a consideration of the parties' own presentations. 2. The arbitrator's decision is devoid of articulated social engineering goals. 3. The arbitrator attempts to reach a decision by placing himself in the position of the negotiators. Regarding arbitration as an extension of negotiation, the arbitrator attempts to reach a decision which approximates the 'power' position of the parties.

Source: J. Romeyn, 'Towards a Motivational Theory of Arbitration in Australia', *Journal of Industrial Relations 22*, June 1980, p. 187.

Compulsion and compliance

A system of compulsory arbitration must either produce outcomes acceptable to its clients, or it must have the capacity to enforce unpopular, 'non-accommodative' decisions. The Australian system has seen an era in which award enforcement was tried and generally was found wanting. The two decades after 1950 saw attempts to impose sanctions on those who breached awards. The tactic applied was that awards were written or amended to contain provisions forbidding bans or limitations against award conditions, known as bans clauses, and should these be broken, injunctive relief was available to the employer.

Whether the enforcement provisions themselves were insufficiently flexible to permit their sensitive utilisation, or whether they were over-used and became a strike breaking tactic, the fact remains that, in 1969, a union official, on behalf of his organisation, refused to co-operate with this enforcement system, and was gaoled. The immediate result of this was industrial action approximating a national strike, and the union official concerned was subsequently released. The union movement as a whole set its face against these penal provisions, and resolved to support any union facing similar fines; these enforcement procedures have, in effect, been a dead letter since that time. The *Industrial Relations Act* does include provisions for enforcement,[36] and while the tolerance of the unions of the 1990s for the application of these sanctions has not been tested, it could be argued that the long period of quiescence of unionism in the 1980s and early 1990s may suggest that unions have lost the taste for struggle that they had in the 1960s. Certainly, it has been possible for a public employer to threaten, apparently with success, to invoke these sanctions.[37]

Although it is true that, by definition, a compulsory arbitration system needs an enforcement mechanism, sanctions, during the 1970s, became, effectively, unavailable, and from the mid-1980s to the early 1990s, they were apparently replaced by internal union arrangements. During the 1970s, the unions had committed themselves to such drastic responses, should sanctions be reimposed, that they were as reluctant to take the kinds of action that would commit them to those responses as the employers and arbitral authorities were to induce it. Arbitration in the 1980s and 1990s became sensitive to the needs and individual capacities of labour and management. Increasingly, arbitrators are concerned with leading the parties to a resolution of their differences rather than imposing solutions upon them. Consequently, arbitration as a process has moved closer to conciliation, and in many cases it is not easy to discern where conciliation ends and arbitration begins. To those not convinced that industrial peace resides in the self-reliance of the parties, this may seem to be progress, but conciliation is still far distant from the ideal of bipartite dispute settlement. So long as a third party remains so intimately involved in industrial relations, there remains the strong possibility that the ideas or policies of that third party can be inserted, possibly as an irritant, into industrial disputes.

Under many circumstances, tripartite dispute resolution can be more difficult than the bipartite form, simply because there is an additional client to satisfy. Even if the arbitrator and the parties were in accord as to the precise terms of settlement of a dispute, problems could still arise, as the arbitrator may be required to include additional conditions that suit neither party, or to insist on using decision-making processes that are unsatisfactory to other parties. Obviously too, there are instances in which the arbitrator's own needs will prevent the award of a decision satisfactory to the other parties, and this is common during periods in which the Commission attempts to assist in imposing a wage policy. Such outcomes are not, of course inherent in the process of arbitration itself, but they arise from the Australian practice and the constraints which arbitrators accept. In those situations in which arbitration is undertaken on a more or less casual, or consultancy, basis, as is the case in most of North America, rather than by a permanent arbitral organisation as is the Australian case, the dominant form consists of outcomes designed to meet the needs of the disputing parties alone.

Any compulsory system may require a system of enforcement, but following the 1969 affray the unions made it clear that any attempt to reimpose sanctions would result in a confrontation of such dimensions that it would probably destroy the arbitral system. From 1969 to 1975, the arbitral system learned to survive without sanctions, relying exclusively on 'accommodative arbitration'. It was not a matter of choice, for the unions of the time could probably not have been held back from taking action from which the system could not recover, and all parties were reluctant to see that conclusion.

The union defiance of the penal sanctions came in the last years of the Liberal-National Party dominance of Australian politics. In the last weeks of 1972, the Whitlam-led ALP government was elected to office and began a program of extensive reform in most areas of government. The Whitlam government showed itself to be ready to consult with the trade unions and with the ACTU, a body whose influence within trade unionism had increased considerably with the rise of Mr Bob Hawke, originally ACTU advocate, subsequently Secretary and finally President. When the Whitlam government left office late in 1975, a significant change it had helped to bring about was to leave the ACTU a considerable power in the land.

The period of the Fraser government, which succeeded Whitlam, saw the emergence of high profile conservative organisations which were anxious for employers to take the fight up to any unions which showed aggression.[38] These groups often berated the Commission for its refusal to apply penal sanctions to unions using the strike, and called frequently for various legal sanctions to be applied to strikers. The union response to these proposals, or even to the Commission's occasional resort to the first stages of the penal procedures, was to remind critics of the union movement's resolution to resist the process, and it should be noted that the period of the Fraser government saw the emergence of the ACTU as clearly the leader of the trade unions. If the resolution to resist the application of sanctions were to be implemented, it would be the ACTU which would initiate it, something that could not automatically have been assumed in 1972.

As events unfolded, it became clear that the ACTU took a technical view of its resolution of 1972. That resolution[39] was framed entirely in terms of the Commission's use of its penal powers under the *Conciliation and Arbitration Act*; it did not refer to legal sanctions of other kinds which might be applied.

When employers in the *Mudginberri* and *Dollar Sweets* cases sued under the *Trade Practices Act* and at common law respectively, (for discussion, see chapter 5) the striking unions were subject to considerable financial detriment in the form of fines for contempt of court and damages in the *Mudginberri* case and an out of court damages settlement in the *Dollar Sweets* case. While the legal process differed, the circumstances looked, to the non-technical observer, uncommonly like the events which had led to the ACTU resolution: unions had been 'fined' because members struck. The resolution did not, however, commit ACTU affiliates to support unions facing damages claims and penalties for industrial action, but only to supporting them against fines imposed under the *Conciliation and Arbitration Act*. It seems improbable that any of those supporting the 1972 resolution intended, where direct action was taken, to combat fines levied under that Act, and to tolerate those imposed under other processes, but that, apparently was the interpretation adopted.

The ACTU moved from its implacable opposition to sanctions against industrial action and by 1985 it showed that at least some sanctions were tolerable. In the first years of the Hawke-led ALP government it took the next step to become the virtual enforcer of Commission decisions. The prices and incomes accord between the ALP and ACTU involved, in its first incarnation, a guarantee that unions would not pursue wage claims, nor use the strike to support such claims, outside the Commission. In return, the ALP, in government, would support ACTU claims for indexing wages to the retail price index. By 1984, the extent of the ACTU commitment became clear. An affiliated union, the Builders Labourers Federation, refused in both Victoria and New South Wales, with the support of its national office, to refrain from using the strike to support claims for increases in wages and allowances for members. When the union was deregistered without opposition from the ACTU, neither the ACTU nor the relevant State Trades and Labour Councils attempted to impose an embargo on other unions seeking to enrol members of the deregistered union. Embargos of this kind had previously been used to protect the interests of deregistered unions, and they constituted an exercise in union solidarity that was the envy of many. The solidarity that was deployed in the Builders Labourers case was impressive, but it was directed to a novel end. Because the union would not agree to cease pursuit of increased wages and allowances, and because it would not cease backing its demands with strikes and other coercion, not only did the ACTU affiliates tolerate a remarkable range of intimidatory tactics being applied to the union by government agencies, but they consented to an arrangement which saw all BLF members in the two States enrolled in rival unions. Closed shop agreements meant that the unionists concerned had no choice about joining the new union if they wished to remain in the industry.

The ACTU provided no assistance to the non-affiliated Australian Federation of Airline Pilots in its 1989-90 dispute with the domestic airlines (see chapters 4 and 5). That is probably less remarkable than its failure to do more than formally express concern at the precedents set by the Commission in its failure to attempt to settle the dispute, and by the government in its complicity in something difficult to distinguish from strike-breaking.[40]

In the early 1990s, the situation seemed to be that while it may be imprudent for the Commission to attempt to rely on the enforcement procedures in the *Industrial Relations Act* (see chapter 5), the ACTU would enforce those awards on its behalf. However, in mid-1991, the Commission arbitrated, in the *National Wage* case, a decision which did not accord with the submissions of the ACTU and the government. As a consequence, ACTU and some union officials, like the Builders Labourers Federation and the Airline Pilots before them, claimed that they would resort to collective bargaining to achieve their goals. It cannot yet be discerned if this episode signified the end of the role of the ACTU as enforcer of awards. Whether unions would, in fact, resist the application of sanctions under the *Industrial Relations Act* is impossible to predict. The penalties prescribed are, if anything, more severe than those of the *Conciliation and Arbitration Act*, but they do provide the Commission with a good deal of discretion about their implementation. If the 1972 resolution were taken to be a rejection of the notion of applying punitive sanctions to strikers, a superficially, at least, plausible meaning, then unions have undertaken to resist. If on the other hand, the ACTU would prefer to avoid a confrontation, which the *Mudginberri* and *Dollar Sweets* cases might imply, it could be argued that the 1972 resolution refers to proceedings under the now-defunct *Conciliation and Arbitration Act*. While that is a very technical interpretation, it could be argued by those wishing to avoid a confrontation on the issue.

Government intervention: formal and informal

The parties to the industrial dispute (or their representatives) will participate in conciliation and/or arbitration proceedings before the Commission. However, there are a number of provisions in the *Industrial Relations Act* enabling the involvement or intervention of Government, in the capacity of a third party, in relation to industrial disputes. The Government, by virtue of the Ministerial power to notify a dispute,[41] may initiate tribunal involvement. Further, the Commission may permit an organisation, a person (including the Minister) or a body to be heard in the proceedings 'where the Commission is of the opinion' that such persons 'should be heard'.[42] There is then a wide discretion given to the Commission to hear interested parties, including the Minister.

The Minister, on behalf of the Commonwealth, also has a right of intervention, rather than just intervention with the Commission's permission, in certain matters. These are in matters before a full bench[43] and matters before the Commission involving public sector employment.[44] In each case, the intervention is 'in the public interest'. Written notice must be given to the Industrial Registrar. The most notable example of the Minister intervening on behalf of the Commonwealth is in the National Wage hearings before the full bench of the Commission. Indeed in such cases the extensive submissions and statistical data produced by the Commonwealth is of great utility generally, not just to the other participants in the process.

Another feature of Australian industrial relations is involvement of governments in industrial disputes on an informal basis. This participation, on the basis of convention rather than formal powers, may be on the Government's initiative or at the request of one or more of the principal parties. The involvement may be confined to an expression of views or involve direct action. In both cases, the involvement may be partisan or non-partisan. An example of partisan involvement is the statements and actions of the Hawke government during the 1989 air pilots' dispute (see Table 4.4). In a Supreme Court decision arising from this dispute, reference is made to discussions taking place involving the Prime Minister, the Minister for Industrial Relations, the Minister for Civil Aviation and representatives of the airline companies involved, during the dispute.[45] Similarly partisan intervention occurred in 1980 when the Fraser Government authorised the use of Air Force planes to transport civilian passengers during a pilots' strike. Table 15.3 provides information on a more recent example of intervention by Government. Aspects of this dispute, the 1992 APPM (Burnie) dispute, were noted in the discussion of industrial conflict in chapter 3.

Table 15.3 Government intervention: 1992 APPM (Burnie) dispute

Minister steps in on APPM dispute
BY LYNNE COSSAR
Chief Industrial Reporter

INDUSTRIAL ROUND-UP

The Federal Government has moved to head off a serious industrial dispute at Associated Pulp and Paper Mills over the company's decision to cancel all over-award payments to its employees.

The Minister for Industrial Relations, Senator Cook, yesterday asked the Industrial Relations Commission to call the parties together and mediate a settlement. So far the company has refused to meet the unions and the ACTU.

Senator Cook's unusual move signals how seriously the Government and the ACTU regard the dispute at APPM, a subsidiary of North Broken Hill Peko Ltd.

The ACTU has also asked the on-site unions at the company's eight Tasmanian plants to call off a strike planned for next Wednesday. It is believed the unions have agreed.

The ACTU does not want to bring the dispute to a head before it has a chance to talk to the company. Under the Industrial Relations Act (1988), the commission has the power to call all parties to a compulsory conference.

In a statement yesterday, Senator Cook said his request to the commission was not designed to be an intervention. "It is an action to bring the parties together and use the processes of the commission to resolve their differences," he said.

An ACTU industrial officer, Mr Bob Richardson, welcomed Senator Cook's move. He said the ACTU was keeping "a lot of potential allies" briefed on developments. He said those allies included the Waterside Workers Federation.

The unions plan to meet at the ACTU on Tuesday to devise their strategy, which may include the setting up of a fighting fund. They have been told to expect a long campaign.

A company spokesman, Mr Chris Oldfield, said Senator Cook's statement had been noted and he would wait to see what happened. But Mr Oldfield was adamant that there was nothing to discuss. "We have nothing to negotiate," he said.

The company argues that the cuts, to take effect from 2 April, are critical to the future of the company.

The dispute flared this month when the company notified its employees that it intended to cancel all over-award agreements, except a few including superannuation and special arrangements on working hours.

Over-award payments are those made by agreement over and above what the award specifies. The company is not proposing cuts in award wages and conditions. It has, however, told its employees that it will not authorise them to attend stopwork meetings organised by unions. Such attendance would be regarded as a breach of contract.

In a letter to employees this week, the Tasmanian secretary of the Construction, Forestry, Mining Employees Union, Mr Shayne Murphy, called for support.

"I ask you to defend your democratic right to meet collectively to defend the right of your organisation to represent you," the letter said. "I urge you to stand together with your fellow workers as workers have traditionally done over years gone by."

In newspaper advertisements scheduled to appear today, the company tells employees that if they withdraw their labor, they will be breaching their contract of employment.

Source: *The Age*, 21 March 1992, p. 12.

Voluntary conciliation and arbitration

If the Commission did no more than maintain and refine its formal and highly centralised structure of awards, it is unlikely it would have survived for nearly a century, even in a nation notably tolerant of bureaucratic edifices of largely symbolic function. In practice it seems that the Commission does, with the support of labour and management, operate in areas in which it lacks jurisdiction and in which it may depart considerably from its centralised and centralising principles. In the years following the Second World War, and possibly even earlier, Commission members have been engaged in industrial peace-keeping considerably more related to industrial relations realities than is the formal process described above.

As noted earlier, many disputes arise out of largely specific issues at particular workplaces, which, because they are confined to one state, do not provide jurisdiction for the Commission to intervene. The matter of managerial prerogative similarly restricts the Commission's technical power, even though there has been considerable liberalisation in this area through High Court judgements, particularly the *Social Welfare* case. In earlier times, many issues of labour-management conflict had been ruled to be outside the Commission's jurisdiction because they were judged to have been disputes over matters that were not industrial, as defined in the Act. Such disputes, which concerned, among others, issues as central to labour relations as crew sizes and allocation of duties, were held to be matters over which managers held unilateral control, a position which derived essentially from the laws of contract and property. The meaning of industrial dispute has been broadened considerably by the High Court, so that the technical and lay meanings of the term are now quite similar. Naturally there do remain areas in which the authority of managers remains intact, and the Commission entirely without jurisdiction.[46]

In practice, the lack of jurisdiction has not in the past, and still does not always prevent the Commission from hearing and settling disputes. In these situations, employers and employees who are unable to resolve disputes without assistance, or who value the assistance of the Commission, do frequently call upon its conciliatory or arbitral services. A Commission member, satisfied that his or her assistance is genuinely sought, and that the Commission's jurisdiction will not be challenged will usually agree to provide these services. The case will proceed with conciliatory or arbitral services being provided in the usual way. The outcome of the process will not be an award, or the variation of one—the outcome where there are not jurisdictional problems—but the provision of a recommendation. Because this recommended settlement is not recorded, it will not constitute persuasive authority or precedent for the adjustment of awards generally. The recommended settlement may, therefore, depart quite considerably from the structure of wages, hours and working conditions existing in awards. The new workplace rules, or in the case of a rights dispute such as a dismissal, the proposed course of action, will not be legally enforceable under the Act. It is in this unofficial, and generally unpublicised area that the Commission makes significant contributions to the preservation of industrial peace.

The discussion here has focused on the federal machinery which has been very similar, if not replicated, in the state systems, albeit comparatively recently in Victoria and Tasmania. The state systems do not experience the jurisdictional problems of the federal system hence there has been less demand for the unregulated processes of voluntary conciliation and arbitration. Notably however, in 1992 the Victorian parliament legislated[47] for voluntary conciliation and arbitration in respect of all matters other than disputed dismissals. In the latter case an aggrieved employee or a recognised association has the right to seek redress via the process of arbitration.[48] In the case of interest disputes the processes of conciliation and arbitration cannot be activated, that is the Employee Relations Commission must not convene any proceedings, unless *inter alia*, all the parties to the dispute or industrial matter consent to the Commission exercising powers under the statute and agree to accept the outcome of the proceedings.[49] The Victorian tribunal's powers with respect to process are discussed in chapter 13. This diversity means that possible outcomes range from third party recommendations, where the settlement is not recorded, to legally enforceable awards. Thus the Victorian statute endorses and regulates behaviour which is extra-jurisdictional in the federal system and it excludes, that is, makes no provision for, compulsory conciliation and arbitration.

Relationship between conciliation, arbitration and collective bargaining

One form the relationship takes is when collective bargaining occurs as the corollary of conciliation and with the possibility of unilateral resort to arbitration. Another form, used for many years, is good faith collective bargaining. After agreeing on all issues, the parties, often seeking to have the outcome of their negotiations formally established in award form, request the Commission to write a formal award incorporating the issues on which agreement has been reached. The Commission will normally prepare this 'consent award', and its distinguishing feature is that it is the outcome of agreement between the parties rather than being a solution imposed on them. In other cases, the parties may prefer to draft the complete agreement themselves and have this legitimised by the Commission, so that it has all the administrative, legal and other qualities of an award, but remains written in the language of the parties; these documents have been known as registered agreements or, in more recent times, certified agreements (see Figure 15.1, note 1).

It is not easy, especially for those accustomed to collective bargaining, to understand why the parties wish to have this award status conferred on their agreements, for the legal protection, which award status confers, is not great. In many cases this status may be sought as an indication that the bargaining process has been completed. It may also provide some reassurance to workers or employers whose understanding of industrial relations is rudimentary and who see some security in the existence of an award. In the case of government or semi-government institutions and their employees, policy reasons or statutory requirements usually demand that all work-rules be encompassed in an award. Where labour and management groups, wishing to negotiate their own workplace rules are faced with these constraints, they can do so only by using the consent award or certified agreement mechanism.

Consent awards and certified agreements can be regarded as the outcome of the marriage of collective bargaining to compulsory arbitration. It should be noted, however, that the two processes historically have had relationships of a different kind, in that unregulated bargaining supplemented arbitration. In most instances, a national or industry-wide award provided only broad guidelines. That award was supplemented at individual workplaces by collectively bargained arrangements to meet particular local needs. These local agreements covered a variety of issues, but in almost all cases they included a wage rate exceeding that provided in the award. It may be that following the 1994 reforms there will emerge a regulated variant of this traditional relationship—the award may now provide a safety net with individual enterprise agreements, subject to Commission endorsement, supplementing the award.

Another form of the relationship between arbitration and collective bargaining is one in which collective bargaining is entirely separate from, and apparently uninfluenced by, the arbitral system. The purest form of comprehensive uninhibited bargaining was in the Melbourne newspaper industry printing industry, but it is not clear whether this has survived the accord wage policy intact. It had enabled the parties to settle many thorny issues, including that of changing technology which has proven troublesome in newspaper printing in other countries. Uninhibited collective bargaining has also tended to characterise the industrial relations of isolated mining communities, but probably only Broken Hill has developed a mature and stable system. Even in Broken Hill, there have been incursions of the tribunal system, and in 1986 the NSW Industrial Commission issued an award covering mine workers. The unions rejected that award, and collective bargaining appears to have resumed there: in 1993, all mine employees are covered by an enterprise agreement which provides *inter alia* almost total labour flexibility.

Arbitrated awards: a critique

'Floor' of rights

A formal Commission hearing is normally directed to the substantive rules of the workplace, and these are usually expressed in the making of a new award, or in the variation or addition to an existing award. Awards are normally quite wide-ranging in terms of wages, hours and working conditions. Award provisions in each of these areas are binding minimum standards, and penalties may be imposed in cases of breaches of the established award minima. These standards have no intrinsic qualities rendering them especially laudable; they are merely conditions which Commission members consider should be met by every employer within their jurisdiction, and they are normally exceeded by many.

Award conditions have long formed the floor or lower end of a continuum existing in the labour market. If this floor was not provided by Commission awards, the continuum would be longer, and its bottom end, determined by the extent of the community's tolerance of low living standards, would probably be even lower. The Commission, in making its awards, expresses the minimal standards that it judges the community should accept. Many other countries also express such standards but do so through legislation rather than through their industrial relations machinery. The intermingling of industrial relations and social welfare in Australia may not be in the best interests of either, and although it would be difficult to disentangle the components of such a well-entrenched practice, it has been argued that there are compelling reasons and feasible means to do so.[50]

The award contains a schedule or structure of wage rates which are the minimum rates payable to each category of labour covered by it. In establishing this structure, the award may also set out the minimal qualifications and duties appropriate to each category of labour. Apart from wage rates, the award will also establish minimum standards in a number of other work rule areas, including hours of work, holidays, working conditions and similar issues. It has application to all persons and groups named as respondents to it, and these normally constitute the employers and employees of an industry, or some section of an industry, but a few awards apply to particular enterprises (see below), occupations, or are restricted to certain regions.

Although the award prescribes minimum conditions of employment, it usually does not cover every aspect of the employer-employee relationship. Of those not covered it is usually assumed in the first instance, that these are technically at the disposal of the employer. The extent of unfettered managerial prerogative has receded over the 1980s, but for many enterprises the change in legal status merely reflects longstanding practices that have been determined by the balance of industrial power. In the era in which employers technically held the right to dismiss employees at their discretion, there were many parts of industry in which that right could not be enforced. The security of tenure enjoyed by seamen, for example, or by miners, has been almost absolute, so long as the employees concerned retained the support of their unions. (For discussion of the current rights of employers and employees with respect to dismissal, see chapters 12 and 13.) As discussed in chapter 10, while managerial prerogative, in strict legal terms, has often seemed to be very extensive in Australia, it has been restricted a good deal in practice, and apparent reductions in its extent may often have merely brought the legal position closer to actual practice.

The Commission is prepared to assist certain groups, in an unofficial way, to reach more satisfactory outcomes than awards provide. During the period in which it administers a wage policy, Commission members do not, so far as is generally known, preside over cases involving the determination of over-award pay rates, but in 'policy off' periods, this has been a common activity. In these cases, the Commission while it does make decisions, does not do so formally, preferring to adopt some practice such as reserving its decision, or adjourning the hearing. The Commission's resolution of the dispute would then not be a decision but a recommendation made on adjournment. Either party could technically reject that recommendation, but it would do so in the realisation that it could no longer look forward to receiving the assistance and co-operation of the Commission.

The award is, in a sense, the document which provides a theoretical outline of employer-employee relations. In practice, all of its conditions may not apply in strict detail, but the award does indicate the ordering of relations applying in any plant. For example, unskilled workers will be paid less than skilled, and work outside normal hours will be paid at premium rates, but the actual rates involved may very well be different from those specified by the award.

The law of conciliation and arbitration is complex, and while it is an essential part of our industrial relations process, it must be placed in its correct perspective, for it is easy to exaggerate the influence of the law on the practice of labour relations. A parallel example may help understanding here; most commercial transactions in which people engage are subject to laws, and particularly to the law of contract. Yet salespersons who live by their ability to undertake commercial transactions are not especially skilled in the law of contract. Their particular ability is the skill to persuade clients to buy a particular item, and to buy it from them. It is only in the most exceptional of cases that the law becomes involved. The labour relations case is similar. There is a body of relevant law, but expertise in the field is not a matter of legal skills, but rather a matter of reaching agreements, and of administering those agreements.

Coverage and structure

A persistent problem is that, usually, the Commission's formal awards apply to more than one effective industrial relations decision-making unit, of which the individual workplace is typical. The corollary is, of course, that any individual workplace is likely to be covered by more than one award. The Workplace Survey found an average of 2.1 awards in the workplaces surveyed and a universal positive correlation between number of awards and number of employees per workplace: in workplaces with 5-19 employees, for example, the average number of awards was two, while in workplaces with 500 or more employees the average number of awards was ten. A factor increasing the average was the existence of a number of single issue awards, especially in the public sector.[51] (For ABS data on the major awards and the number of employees covered see Appendix, Table 15.6). Precise data on single enterprise awards is not available, but research undertaken for the Business Council of Australia in the late 1980s suggests it is unlikely that more than ten per cent of award-covered workers are covered by enterprise awards.[52] There are both constitutional and practical reasons for the broad focus of awards. As discussed in chapter 12, the Constitution requires that the dispute must satisfy interstateness before the Commission has jurisdiction. Obviously there are stratagems by which a local dispute can be provided with interstate character, but even the most technical compliance with this requirement does provide an aggregative bias to the Commission's work. Additionally, the Commission is pushed in the direction of providing broad coverage awards by practical necessity. It would simply not be physically possible for the Commission to provide separate awards for each of the multitude of industrial relations decision-making entities. It has, therefore, generally sought to deliver awards which cover entire industries, occupations or groups of workers.

The Commission's awards are centralised in more than the geographic sense, for they contain common principles which enable the Commission to eliminate or at least minimise inter-industry and inter-regional differences in wages, hours and working conditions. The Commission's view is that the wage rate payable to a labourer should not vary whether he or she works in a cannery in Shepparton or a brickyard in Perth. Its approach is that special conditions attaching to a job, or the effect of remote locations, should be compensated for by special allowances. These centralised principles, which are discussed in more detail in chapter 16, mean that it is very difficult for Commission awards to reflect the fact that, from time to time, in particular locations, industries or occupations, circumstances require some changes in wage rates. History indicates that if the award is changed to reflect these needs, there will arise a general expectation that all other awards and rates should be adjusted so that pre-existing wage and conditions relationships or 'relativities' are restored.

It may also be surmised that unions, peak union bodies and employer organisations seek to have broad coverage provided by awards. Not only does this lessen their various workloads, at least in the first instance, but also cements their hold over industrial relations. It seems intuitively obvious that within the union movement, control over the wage determination process is the key to power and influence over the union rank and file, and that the same considerations would apply with even more force to employer associations. The wide scope of industry-wide or national awards ensures that individual employers, shop stewards or localised sections of unions, will not gain access to industrial relations power. If the centralised nature of the arbitral system meets the needs of the Commission, it may also ensure that those employer and employee representatives currently central to the industrial relations process will remain so.

Centralism reconsidered

During 1990, an unusual consensus appeared to develop regarding future trends in industrial relations, but it may take some time to determine whether the unanimity is more apparent than real. The ACTU-Government negotiations on the sixth version of the Accord, finalised in February 1990, incorporated reference to enterprise level agreements. The parties agreed on various matters they would submit to the Commission including support for enterprise bargaining in the terms set out in Table 15.4. This was sought as a means of supplementing award provisions with enterprise specific wage increases based on productivity and profitability.

Table 15.4 Enterprise bargaining as proposed in Accord Mark 6

'The no extra claims commitment in Minimum Rates Awards needs to be varied to provide the opportunity for claims based on achieved increases in productivity and profitability with restructuring provided:

(a) There is no double counting.
(b) The increases shall be monitored by the parties to this agreement and the IRC to ensure consistency with the aggregate wage outcome.
(c) The unions shall where practicable negotiate with appropriate employer organisations the framework within which *enterprise bargaining* may occur.
(d) The restructured awards which include the fundamental conditions of employment shall continue to be the minimum basis of enterprise agreements.
(e) The IRC establishes appropriate principles'.

(emphasis added)

Source: Agreement between the federal Government and the ACTU, February 1990, clause 9(vi) (roneoed).

By mid-1991, the ACTU was strongly supporting what it called enterprise bargaining. The federal Opposition parties revealed a preference for replacing, either in whole or in part, the centralised wage fixing system with enterprise centred methods. The Opposition's proposals were not entirely clear, but it may be assumed that they envisaged smaller roles being played by both the ACTU and the Industrial Relations Commission. Perhaps to forestall that eventuality, the full bench (Maddern J, Keogh & Hancock DP, Connell & Oldmeadow CC) in its decision at the October 1991 *National Wage* case introduced an Enterprise Bargaining Principle (For details see Table 18.11).

It is not easy to explain the switch of the ACTU away from the centralism it had so strongly defended in preceding years, but doubtless it had become increasingly difficult for constituent unions to prevent rank and file dissatisfaction with the wage control policy from becoming apparent. It is also possible that the ACTU was motivated by concerns that the Opposition parties would form the next federal government, as opinion polls seemed to imply. It could be argued that, should the ACTU remain committed to a centralised industrial relations system when a new government took office with a policy of decentralising the system, the ACTU, in those circumstances, would have given the government a virtual free hand to determine a new and decentralised system entirely as it saw fit. On the other hand, should the ACTU have already established the outlines of a system of workplace bargaining, and have relegated the Commission to a task of determining minima, the government's task would have become one of reforming an existing decentralised system, rather than designing a new system.

The conversion of the Opposition parties, the Government, the Commission and the ACTU to the view that industrial relations is most productively and feasibly practised at the workplace, a conclusion they had resisted for many years, suggests that during 1990 and 1991, traffic on the road to Damascus must have been heavy indeed. The obstacles in the way of affirming the new faith would seem to be greatest in the case of the Commission. It is constitutionally restricted to making awards which involve disputes extending beyond any one state, a characteristic which must surely be found at few workplaces. The push for reform led to some legislative change in 1992 and culminated in the passage of the *Industrial Relations Reform Act 1993* to facilitate the making of enterprise agreements and to circumvent some of the constraints imposed by s.51(35) of the Constitution.

Conclusion

While it is possible to consider conciliation and arbitration from many standpoints, the student of industrial relations would do well to see it as a process involved in an industrial relations system, a means by which workplace rules are produced.

One must remember that the influence of the Commission waxes and wanes over time. It became central to the process by which the Hawke-led

ALP government sought to control wage increases, and did so with the aid of the ACTU, but the centrality of the Commission during that period may be a deviation from the long-term trend in Australian industrial relations. This trend seems to be that if the Commission produces outcomes that are not in accord with the bargaining strengths of the participants, the Commission will be bypassed. The alliance of the ACTU and government, with joint support for the Commission, has resulted in a period in which, at least in the mid- to late 1980s unions accepted outcomes that were probably less than the strength of some might dictate.

If it is the fact that outcomes in industrial relations are determined by power, then the dominance of the Commission will survive only as long as either the powerful can be restrained, or until power balances can be permanently altered. Unions may be restrained by either a depressed economy which reduces their bargaining power, or by political alliances with an incumbent government. History suggests that these are transitory factors. Whether fundamental power balances between labour and management can be permanently altered is a matter for speculation, but its most feasible alteration would come from some change that radically reduced or increased the coercive power of unions. That is probably not in sight. It is however these industrial relations fundamentals, the power of either union or employer to force their will on the other, which determine outcomes. Alterations to the *Industrial Relations Act* may be of secondary importance in the longer term.

The fact that an agency of the state—the Industrial Relations Commission—is used to seek outcomes in industrial relations, does not of itself establish the right of government to participate as a party to workplace rule making. The right of government to simulate the action of a principal party in workplace regulation has not been argued in Australia; government officials have simply tended to assume that the right exists. This matter is complicated by the fact that the industrial relations mechanisms have been used extensively as a mechanism for economic regulation. This side of the arbitral machinery is considered in the following chapter.

Notes

1. E.I. Sykes and H. Glasbeek, *Labour Law in Australia*, Butterworths, Melbourne, 1972, p. 549.
2. D. Carboch, *The Fall of the Bruce-Page Government*, Cheshire, Melbourne, 1964.
3. *The Age*, 5 September 1989, p. 16; *The Age* 13 July 1992, p. 3.
4. *Industrial Relations Act* 1988 s.170MC inserted by *Industrial Relations Reform Act* 1993, s. 31.
5. D. Plowman, *Holding the Line-Compulsory Arbitration and National Employer Co-ordination in Australia*, Cambridge University Press, Melbourne, 1989, chapter 1.
6. The final vote on the 'industrial power' was 22 to 19. For a discussion of the difficulties the Higgins' proposal encountered see J. Niland, *Collective Bargaining and Compulsory Arbitration in Australia*, University of New South Wales Press, Kensington, 1978, chapter 2.
7. The relevant High Court judgements are discussed in chapter 12.
8. *R v Coldham and Ors Ex parte: The Australian Social Welfare Union*, (1983) 47 ALR 225. See chapter 12 for details of this decision.
9. It is noteworthy that this has always been possible in the state tribunal systems but has occurred infrequently.

10 B. Dabscheck, *Australian Industrial Relations in the 1980s*, Oxford University Press, Melbourne, 1989, p. 88.
11 *Conciliation and Arbitration Act* 1904, s.39(2). This provision was introduced in the 1970s.
12 *Industrial Relations Act*, 1988, s.90.
13 As to qualifications for appointment see chapter 12.
14 *R v Kirby; ex parte Boilermakers' Society of Australia* (1956) 94 CLR 254.
15 *Industrial Relations Act* 1988, s.106(1).
16 *Industrial Relations Act* 1988, Part VIB, Division 5 inserted by *Industrial Relations Reform Act*, 1993, s.31.
17 H.B. Higgins, 'A New Province for Law and Order', *Harvard Law Review*, November 1915, p. 14.
18 A.F. Davies, *Australian Democracy*, Cheshire, Melbourne, 1969, p. 5.
19 *Industrial Relations Act* 1988, s.3(d) as amended by *Industrial Relations Reform Act* 1993, s.4.
20 *Industrial Relations Act* 1988, s.102(1).
21 *ibid.*, s.111(1)(b).
22 *ibid.*, s.103(1)(a) and Part VIB, Division 2 inserted by *Industrial Relations Reform Act*, 1993, s.31. In the *Conciliation and Arbitration Act* 1904 certified agreements were provided for in s.28.
23 *ibid.*, s.104(1).
24 *ibid.*, s.4 and s.170MA(2) inserted by *Industrial Relations Reform Act*, 1993, ss 26 and 31 respectively.
25 *ibid.*, Part VIB, Division 3, *ibid.*
26 For details see chapter 17.
27 *Industrial Relations Act*, 1988, s.105.
28 J. Kitay and R. Powe, 'Exploitation at $1000 per week? The Mudginberri Dispute', *Journal of Industrial Relations 29*, September 1987, p. 374.
29 L. Cupper, 'Legalism in the Australian Conciliation and Arbitration Commission: The Gradual Transition' in G.W. Ford, J.M. Hearn and R.D. Lansbury (eds), *Australian Labour Relations: Readings* (3rd ed.), Macmillian, Melbourne, 1980, pp. 413-414.
30 The statute requires the Commission to 'act according to equity, good conscience and the substantial merits of the case, without regard to technicalities and legal forms.' *Industrial Relations Act*, 1988, s.110(2)(c).
31 M. Perlman, *Judges in Industry: A Study of Labour Arbitration in Australia*, Melbourne University Press, Melbourne, 1954, cited in J. Romeyn, 'Towards a Motivational Theory of Arbitration in Australia', *Journal of Industrial Relations 22*, June 1980, p. 186.
32 J.E. Isaac, 'The Arbitration Commission: Prime Mover or Facilitator?', *Journal of Industrial Relations 31*, September 1989, p. 417.
33 Romeyn, *op. cit.*, pp. 181-195.
34 C.B. Fox, 'The Role of the State in Industrial Relations', in G.W. Ford, J.M. Hearn and R.D. Lansbury (eds), *Australian Labour Relations: Readings*, (4th ed.) Macmillan, Melbourne, 1987, p. 215.
35 J.E. Isaac, 'Economics and Industrial Relations', *Journal of Industrial Relations 24*, December 1982, p. 504.
36 *Industrial Relations Act*, 1988, ss 4, 125, and Part VIII.
37 This occurred in April 1989 when the federal Government advocated support for an application by the Civil Aviation Authority for the insertion of a bans clause in the award covering air traffic controllers who were imposing overtime bans, *The Age*, 13 April 1989, p. 5.
38 Dabscheck, 1989, *op cit.*, pp. 113-141.
39 *Consolidation of ACTU Policy Decisions 1951-1980*, undated, Industrial Printing and Publicity Co Ltd., Richmond, pp. 50-51.
40 A resolution concerning the pilots' dispute was carried at the September 1989 ACTU Congress. ACTU *Policies and Strategy Statements Adopted by the ACTU Congress September 1989*, October 1989, p. 158.

41 *Industrial Relations Act* 1988, s.99.
42 *ibid.*, s.43.
43 *ibid.*, s.44(1).
44 *ibid.*, s.44(2).
45 See *Ansett Transport Industries (Operations) Pty Ltd v Australian Federation of Air Pilots* (1989) 95 ALR 211 at 252-253.
46 For discussion see chapter 12.
47 *Employee Relations Act*, 1992 (Victoria).
48 *ibid.*, ss 38 & 92(2).
49 *ibid.*, s.92(2)(a) & (c).
50 See W.A. Howard and C. Fox, *Industrial Relations Reform*, Longman Cheshire, Melbourne, 1988, pp. 35-37.
51 R. Callus, A. Morehead, M. Cully and J. Buchanan, *Industrial Relations At Work: The Australian Workplace Industrial Relations Survey*, Commonwealth Department of Industrial Relations, AGPS, Canberra, 1991, pp. 40-41 and 241.
52 Business Council of Australia, *Enterprise-Based Bargaining Units-A Better Way of Working*, Report to the Business Council of Australia by the Employee Relations Study Commission, volume 1, July 1989, p. 50.

Further Reading

Development of the federal system

B. Brooks, 'From Higgins to Hancock: the boundaries of a new province for law and order', *Journal of Industrial Relations 27*, December 1985, pp. 472–483.

B. Dabscheck, 'A critical examination of the Hancock report', *Journal of Industrial Relations 27*, December 1985, pp. 511–528.

K. Hancock and D. Rawson, 'The Metamorphosis of Australian Industrial Relations', *British Journal of Industrial Relations 31*, December 1993, pp. 489–513.

H.B. Higgins, *A New Province for Law and Order*, Constable, London, 1922.

J. T. Ludeke, 'Is now the time for radical change?', *Journal of Industrial Relations 26*, June 1984, pp. 254–266.

J. Niland, *Collective Bargaining and Compulsory Arbitration in Australia*, New South Wales University Press, Kensington, 1978.

M. Perlman, *Judges in Industry: A Study of Labour Arbitration in Australia*, Melbourne University Press, Melbourne, 1954.

R. Reitano, 'Legislative Change in 1993', *Journal of Industrial Relations 36*, March 1994, pp. 57–73.

Report of the Committee of Review-Australian Industrial Relations Law and Systems, (Hancock Report) volume 2, AGPS, Canberra, 1985, chapter 2.

E.I. Sykes, 'Labour Arbitration in Australia', in G.W. Ford, J.M. Hearn and R.D. Lansbury (eds), *Australian Labour Relations: Readings* (3rd ed.), Macmillan, Melbourne, 1980, pp. 300–343.

The Australian Industrial Relations Commission: function and operation

S. Crawshaw, 'The Arbitration Commission's conflict of identity', *Journal of Industrial Relations 18*, December 1976, pp. 400–410.

J. Kitay and P. McCarthy, 'Justice Staples and the Politics of Australian Industrial Arbitration', *Journal of Industrial Relations 31*, September 1989, pp. 310–333.

P.L. Kleinsorge, 'Public interest as a criterion in settling labour disputes: the Australian experience,' *Journal of Industrial Relations 6*, July 1964, pp.1–22.

J.T. Ludeke, 'The Public Interest and the Australian Industrial Relations Commission', *Journal of Industrial Relations 34*, December 1992, pp. 593–604.

J.C. Moore, ' The Australian Commission — should it be preserved?', *Journal of Industrial Relations 29*, December 1987, pp. 544–547.

President of the Australian Industrial Relations Commission, *Annual Report 1992–93*, AGPS, Canberra.

Report of the Committee of Review-Australian Industrial Relations Law and Systems (Hancock Report), volume 2, AGPS, Canberra, 1985, chapter 8.

The process of conciliation and arbitration

L. Cupper, 'Legalism in the Australian Conciliation and Arbitration Commission: The Gradual Transition', in G.W. Ford, J.M. Hearn and R.D. Lansbury (eds), *Australian Labour Relations: Readings* (3rd ed.), Macmillan, Melbourne, 1980, pp. 409-441.

B. Dabscheck, 'Enterprise Bargaining: a new province for law and order?', in B. Dabscheck, G. Griffin and J. Teicher (eds), *Contemporary Australian Industrial Relations*, Longman Cheshire, Melbourne, 1992, pp. 309-323.

C.B. Fox, 'The Role of the State in Industrial Relations', in Ford, Hearn and Lansbury (eds), (3rd ed.), *op. cit.*, pp. 204-228.

K. Hancock, 'Compulsory Arbitration *versus* Collective Bargaining: Three Recent Assessments', *Journal of Industrial Relations 4*, April 1962, pp. 20-31.

W.A. Howard and C. Fox, *Industrial Relations Reform: A Policy for Australia*, Longman Cheshire, Melbourne, 1988, pp. 21-28 and 45-50.

J. E. Isaac, 'The Prospects for Collective Bargaining in Australia', *The Economic Record* , December 1958, pp. 347-361.

J.E. Isaac, 'The Co-existence of Compulsory Arbitration and Collective Bargaining', in W.A. Howard (ed.), *Perspectives on Australian Industrial Relations*, Longman Cheshire, Melbourne, 1984, pp. 126-139.

J.E. Isaac, 'The Arbitration Commission: Prime Mover or Facilitator?', *Journal of Industrial Relations 31*, September 1989, pp. 407-427.

B. Keller, 'The State as Corporate Actor in Industrial Relations Systems', in Dabscheck, Griffin and Teicher (eds), *op. cit.*, pp. 360-376.

K. M. Laffer, 'Compulsory Arbitration and Collective Bargaining' *Journal of Industrial Relations 4*, October 1962, pp. 146-151.

J. Niland, *Collective Bargaining and Compulsory Arbitration in Australia*, University of New South Wales Press, Kensington, 1978.

D.H. Plowman, 'An Uneasy Conjunction: Opting Out and the Arbitration System', *Journal of Industrial Relations 34,* June 1992, pp. 284-306.

J. Romeyn, 'Towards a Motivational Theory of Arbitration in Australia', *Journal of Industrial Relations 22*, June 1980, pp. 181-195.

Arbitrated awards: a critique

Annual Report of the President of the Australian Industrial Relations Commission, AGPS, Canberra.

Australian Bureau of Statistics, *Award Coverage Australia*, May 1990, Catalogue No. 6315.0.

R. Callus, A. Morehead, M. Cully and J. Buchanan, *Industrial Relations at Work: The Australian Workplace Industrial Relations Survey*, Commonwealth Department of Industrial Relations, AGPS, Canberra, 1991, pp. 39-42 & 195-199.

W.K. Fisher, 'Plant level relationships: the role of the tribunal,' *Journal of Industrial Relations 14*, September 1972, pp. 264-271.

Questions

Development of the federal system

1. Explain the following statement: 'The adoption of the "industrial power" provision in the *Commonwealth Constitution Act* owed a great deal to the "Great Strikes" of the early 1890s'.
2. Identify the factors which have led to the federal industrial relations tribunal assuming a dominant position among the industrial tribunals.

The Australian Industrial Relations Commission: function and operation

3. Explain how the work of the members of the Commission is allocated.
4. What is (i) the method of selection and (ii) the criteria for appointment for members of the Commission?
5. Discuss the strengths and weaknesses of the 'public interest' provisions of the *Industrial Relations Act*.
6. Identify the two major functions of the Commission and discuss the constraints on this tribunal in the successful execution of these functions. (This question should be attempted after chapter 16 has been read.)

The process of conciliation and arbitration

7. Explain the process of dispute settlement under the *Industrial Relations Act* (Commonwealth) from the creation of an industrial dispute to the handing down of an award.
8. Distinguish between conciliation and arbitration in terms of the dynamics of the processes.
9. Explain and illustrate the term 'accommodative arbitration'.
10. Most criticisms of compulsory arbitration have assumed that there was little or no scope for collective bargaining within the Australian industrial relations system. Do you agree?
11. Explain the nature of the arbitration decisions in
    i the 1967-68 metal trades work value case.
    ii the 1986 Victorian nurses' strike.
    These disputes are summarised in chapter 4.
12. Distinguish between 'voluntary' and 'compulsory' conciliation and arbitration.
13. Explain the nature of voluntary conciliation and arbitration in the federal jurisdiction in Australia and the positive features of these processes.
14. a Was the government intervention in (i) the 1992 APPM (Burnie) dispute and (ii) the 1994 waterfront dispute (see Appendix Table 15.5) formal or informal? Explain your answer.

b Identify and explain what you consider to be the advantages and disadvantages of Government intervention in industrial disputes on an informal basis.

Arbitrated awards: a critique

15 a Identify the various instruments of the Commission and provide an illustration of each.
   b What are the essential differences between each of these instruments?
16 What are the factors which encourage the broad scope of awards?
17 Distinguish 'minimum rates awards' and 'paid rates awards'.
18 Summarise the criticisms of awards discussed in this chapter. Do you consider that any of these features advantages or disadvantage
   a management, and
   b employees?

Exercise

1 Locate in the Registry of the Australian Industrial Relations Commission a copy of a recent certified agreement. Locate also an arbitrated industry award for the same or a similar industry. (See Appendix Table 15.6.)
What are the major differences between the two documents? Are the differences important, and if so, to which parties are they important? Why do you believe these differences exist? Why do you believe the two documents are or are not
   a consistent?
   b independent?
   c a reflection of relations in the workplace?

APPENDIX

Table 15.5 Government intervention: 1994 waterfront dispute

IRC may intervene in harbour dispute

BY NICHOLAS JOHNSTON, Industrial Reporter

The Federal Government will ask the Industrial Relations Commission today to intervene in the crippling waterfront dispute in Sydney after talks between the parties broke down last week.

The Minister for Transport and Industrial Relations, Mr Brereton, will seek a hearing in the commission, possibly as early as today, after negotiations between Australian Stevedores and the Maritime Union of Australia collapsed on Friday.

A spokeswoman for Mr Brereton said yesterday that he had studied a report on the dispute, by the former head of the Waterfront Industry Reform Authority, Mr Peter Evans, at the weekend. "The aim is to have the commission arbitrate on the outstanding matters between the parties," she said.

These include the sacking of 55 waterside workers in Sydney, which triggered the row. The spokeswoman said the commission's intervention would not require the Government to bring forward its new industrial laws, which Mr Brereton had threatened to do if the parties could not resolve the dispute.

The managing director of Australian Stevedores, Mr Jim Sweetensen, yesterday welcomed the Government's decision to take the dispute back to the commission.

But the union's national secretary, Mr John Coombs, said last night he was unaware of the Government's move. "Why have we been mucking around for a week if that was all that was required," he said.

The company retrenched the 55 workers at the port in Sydney two weeks ago after the breakdown of redundancy negotiations, sparking a nationwide strike that crippled ports aound the country.

Workers at all ports except Sydney returned to work after the Government intervened and asked the parties to negotiate with Mr Evans. But the union has raised the possibility of further national industrial action after the collapse of talks last week.

Dockside union jubilant as commission tells company to reinstate 55

BY NICHOLAS JOHNSTON, Industrial Reporter

The Maritime Union Australia last night claimed victory in the waterfront dispute after the federal Industrial Relations Commission ordered Australian Stevedores to reinstate 55 waterside workers sacked in Sydney.

The commission told the company to re-employ the workers at the Port of Sydney in return for an end to industrial action.

The deal followed intervention in the dispute by the federal Minister for Transport and Industrial Relations, Mr Brereton.

But the managing director of Australian Stevedores, Mr Jim Sweetensen, last night warned that the company might refuse to reinstate the 55, a move that could cause the three-week dispute to flare again.

He said the company would consider its position overnight and report to the commission in Sydney today.

"I wouldn't say it's a great victory for the union," Mr Sweetensen said. "They are still in breach of a very clear agreement that they have with us and that is still the core of this dispute."

An IRC deputy president, Mr Simon Williams, directed the company to reinstate the workers. They would be placed on leave by the company until their future employment was resolved between the parties.

The ruling followed a recommendation by the former head of the Waterfront Industry Reform Authority, Mr Peter Evans. Mr Brereton asked Mr Evans to report on the dispute after talks between the parties broke down, triggering industrial action at ports around Australia.

The union's national secretary, Mr John Coombs, last night described the IRC ruling as an "enormous victory" and said he believed that employees would return to work after stopwork meetings this morning. "The fundamental issue has been resolved—that's the reinstatement of the 55 people," he said.

The company told the commission yesterday that it did not accept the recommendations of Mr Evans's report. Appearing for Australian Stevedores, Mr Frank Parry said it had followed an agreement reached with the union over the retrenchment of workers.

The ACTU accused the company of treating the dispute with contempt and warned that the union would take national industrial action unless Mr Evans's recommendations were adopted.

Mr Evans recommended that the workers be reinstated and placed on leave until their future was decided. They could take voluntary redundancy packages, transfer to vacancies in Fremantle or find jobs with another stevedore.

The company has maintained that it must retrench workers if it is to remain competitive.

Source: *The Age,* 28 February 1994, p. 4, & *The Age,* 1 March 1994, p. 6.

Table 15.6 Major awards: Australia, May 1990

Jurisdiction	Name of Award, Determination or Collective Agreement	No. of Employees covered
AUST	Metal Industry, Part 1 (b)	185,100
NSW	Shop Employees	107,500
NSW	Clerks	85,200
VIC	Commercial Clerks	77,400
AUST	Bank Officials	76,500
AUST	Vehicle Industry, Repair Service and Retail 1983	60,000
QLD	Clerks and Switchboard Attendants	56,400
AUST	General Conditions of Service, Australian Government Employees	56,100
NSW	Club Employees	53,800
VIC	Teachers, Government Teaching Service	50,400
VIC	Hospital and Benevolent Homes	48,300
VIC	Victorian Public Service Act 1974	44,000
WA	Shop and Warehouse, Wholesale and Retail Establishment	42,800
NSW	Crown Employees Teachers, Educational Teaching Service	42,100
VIC	General Shops	35,000
QLD	Shop Assistants, General, Southern Division	34,100
AUST	Clothing Trades	34,000
AUST	Graphic Arts	33,800
VIC	Painters	33,700
QLD	Teachers	32,000
NSW	Public Hospital Nurses	31,700
QLD	Public Service	31,200
NSW	Crown Employees, Administrative and Clerical Salaries	30,100
WA	Education Act Teaching Staff	29,400
VIC	Registered Nurses	28,800
SA	Clerks	28,000
VIC	Food Shops	27,700
AUST	Administrative and Clerical Officers, APS Salaries	27,200
AUST	Transport Workers	25,200
AUST	Hotels, Resorts and Hospitality Industry	24,300
WA	Public Service Salaries Agreement	23,600
QLD	Shop Assistant, Retail Stores Southern Division	20,800
QLD	Railways	20,400
AUST	Higher Education General and Salaried Staff Interim	20,400
Aust	Australian Universities, Academic and Related Staff Salaries	20,300
VIC	Hotel, Restaurant and Boarding Houses	20,200
AUST	Textile Industry	19,400
AUST	National Building Trades Construction	18,800
AUST	Insurance Officers, Clerical Indoor Staff Consolidated	18,800
AUST	Timber Industry Consolidated	18,400
NSW	Restaurants	18,400
WA	Metal Trades General	16,800
AUST	Local Government Authority Employees VIC	16,400
AUST	Motels	16,200
AUST	Rubber, Plastic and Cable Making Industry	16,200
NSW	Local Government Salaried Officers	15,800
SA	Administrative and Clerical Officers, SA Government	15,500
NSW	Municipal and Shire Councils, Wages	15,400
SA	Teachers, Casual, Department of Education	15,200
AUST	Local Governing Authority Officers VIC	15,200

SA	Shops	15,100
AUST	APS, Senior Executive Administrative and Clerical	14,800
AUST	Vehicle Industry	14,700
QLD	Shop Assistants, North and Mackay Division	13,900
NSW	Teachers, Non-Government Schools	13,800
NSW	Hospital Employees	13,700
SA	Hospital Etc Ancillary Employees	13,300
QLD	Nurses, Public Hospitals	13,300
NSW	Cleaning Contractors	13,100
AUST	Metal Trades, Part III VIC Employees	13,000
NSW	Crown Employees, Non-Commissioned Police Officers	12,600
AUST	Railways, Traffic Permanent Way and Signalling Staff	12,500
NSW	Pharmacy	11,900
VIC	Store Packers and Sorters	11,600
VIC	Clothing and Footwear Shops	11,200
QLD	Mechanical Engineering	11,100
QLD	Local Authority, Excl Brisbane and Main Roads Etc	11,100
NSW	Private Hospital Nurses	10,900
NSW	Crown Employees, Clerical Assistants in Schools, General Division	10,800
AUST	Transport Workers, General	10,800
AUST	Railways, Salaried Officers	10,600
NSW	Hospital Employees General Administrative Staff	10,500
VIC	Law Clerks	10,400
WA	Clerks, Wholesale and Retail Establishments Agreement	10,400
NSW	Vehicle Repair Service and Retail	10,300
NSW	Crown Employees, Teachers, TAFE Teaching Service	10,200
VIC	Determination 179 Victorian Public Service Board	10,000

(a) Major awards, etc are those which affect the pay and conditions of 10 000 or more employees in the survey pay-period. Due to sampling variability the estimates shown should be regarded as broad approximations only. The estimates shown have been rounded to the nearest hundred.

(b) Includes the Metal Trades Award.

Note: In addition to the major awards shown in this table there are 8 major awards, etc. covering 10 000 or more employees in the pay period, each of which relate to a single employer. These major awards affected 148 900 employees.

Source: Australian Bureau of Statistics, *Award Coverage Australia, May 1990*, Catalogue No. 6315.0.

16

Arbitration and Economics

Contents

Equal pay
Wage determination
- basic wage and margin adjustments
- the total wage 1967
- work value inquiries
- productivity and wages: the *GMH* and Oil Industry cases
- wage indexation

The ALP-ACTU Prices and Incomes Accord
Progress of the Accords

Introduction

There can be no doubt about the purpose for which the Australian arbitral system was established; its constitutional function was to prevent and settle industrial disputes. Yet for much of its existence it has been acknowledged that its dispute settling activities, especially where these involve wage determination, have an effect on the national economy. The Commission has generally been unwilling to be drawn into a discussion of the relative weights to be given to economic and industrial relations conditions, but when forced to do so has usually pointed to its constitutional responsibility in industrial relations. The election of the Fraser government in 1975 saw a sharp increase in government expressions of concern about union power, and of intent to reduce that power. The Federal Treasury had by this time achieved the bureaucratic ascendancy to which it had long aspired, but had rarely held for long, and it elected to view the arbitral tribunals as having almost exclusively economic functions. Government and bureaucracy argued that, at the very least, the tribunals should accord the needs of economic policy primacy over those of industrial relations. The specifics of economic and industrial relations policy may have altered somewhat on the election of the Hawke-led ALP government. The wage policy expressed in the Party's 'accord' with the trade unions or, more properly, with the ACTU (see below), suggested that the priorities the government expected the Commission to accord economics and industrial relations were unchanged.

There has been a long tradition of Australian economic argument to the effect that the Commission ought to use its powers in wage determination to manipulate Australian wages in general so that certain economic policy goals could be met. Much of this argument has been made on the assumption that the industrial relations consequences of gearing wages to economic policy needs, rather than to the coercive capacities of labour and management, are of momentary or minimal interest, or perhaps of no importance at all. Wage policy generally has meant that wages should be prevented from rising in periods of inflation, on the assumption, apparently, that the inflation derives from the wage sector itself, an assumption for which it is difficult to find conclusive evidence. Further, the dominant macro-economic theory derives from monetary theory, and this suggests that cost inflation hypotheses of this kind are invalid. Monetary theorists argue that, whatever may be happening in the labour market or elsewhere, inflation will only take place if government will increase the money supply to accommodate the pressures raised, thus the direct way to restrain inflation is to restrict the money supply.

Until 1994 the Commission's capacity to influence minimum rates was restricted to those covered by its awards. Section 170AC, introduced by the *Industrial Relations Reform Act* 1993, broadens this power by permitting the Commission to make 'minimum wage orders' which would provide minimum wages for a group or class of employees specified in the order. Such an order cannot be made where a minimum wage has already been set by a federal award or by a state authority. The practical impact of this new provision, at the time of writing, remains a matter for conjecture. Although there are certain difficulties in fleeing the federal jurisdiction in favour of one of the states, these problems can be overcome by a union sufficiently determined to do so. This determination would be increased should one or more state tribunals decide not to follow the federal tribunal's lead in adopting a wage policy. State tribunals are not required to follow the Commission, and at times the states' interpretations of wage fixing principles have illustrated this. Clearly then, one problem for the Commission in implementing a wage policy is not only that it serves only about half of the total wage and salary earning population, but that its grip on even those clients is far from firm. It is to be noted also that the group of employees not subject to awards at all, the 'award-free' group is substantial and expanding, having risen from twelve per cent of the labour force in 1974 to twenty per cent in 1990.[1] This growth is largely determined by shifts in the occupational and industrial mix of the labour force, but it does suggest that many of those who can evade the tribunal network do so.

A second problem is that the technical capacity of the Commission to restrain the rate of wage increase is quite limited. Technically, the fact is that the Commission can control only minimum, and not maximum rates of pay. In practice a number of factors influence actual pay rates available in a single occupation and there will be a structure of rates applying to almost every separate wage or salary classification. There will, for example, be a minimum pay rate for a plumber and a maximum rate, and these, as well as the intervening rates, will be influenced by several factors which will include job location; tenure; working conditions; precise nature of work; industry; market position of employer; custom; nature of remainder of workforce; relative availability of plumbers, and so forth. The Commission can only directly influence the minimum rate, and if the parties agree to a rate higher than this, the Commission cannot prevent that agreement.

As has been discussed previously, the Commission did experiment, notably during the 1950s and 1960s, with an attempt to prevent over-award wage increases by a system of fines for unions striking in breach of suitably amended awards. Following the failure of this policy, compulsory arbitration, until the beginning of the indexation policy, lacked the effective sanctions which a system of compulsion presumably requires. The indexation policy, as discussed below, relied in part on the co-operation of the ACTU and its affiliates, that is, they voluntarily accepted the policy, and in part on the threat that if unions sought gains beyond those granted by the Commission the quasi-automatic indexation of wages would be stopped. In strict terms, therefore, the Commission's capacity to enforce its policy depends heavily on the willingness of unions to co-operate with that enforcement.

The whole issue of Australian wage policy flows from the wage determination processes undertaken by the Commission in preventing and settling, at least in a technical sense, industrial disputes as it is constitutionally required to do. If a dispute involves wage rates, then obviously the Commission must influence wage rates in order to settle the dispute. Although wage-related disputes may be those most often in the public eye, they do not comprise the majority of disputes and may not always be those with the most serious industrial relations implications.

While the Commission is in some sense an 'official' determinant of wages, it is probably correct to view it rather as an influence on wage rates. In general three mechanisms have operated to determine pay rates:

- The first is the award rates of the Commission, rates determined centrally, and operating normally on an industry or nation-wide basis.
- The second force is the collective agreements drawn up between employer groups or associations and relevant unions. These are normally industry-based, though they may be state-wide, or even nation-wide.
- The third mechanism is the company plant-specific agreement which often supplemented either or both the award and the industry agreements. These localised rates were determined with varying degrees of formalities, but usually involved union officials and job delegates, and were mostly the product of tight labour or skill markets.

The second and third of these influences have been eliminated or substantially modified by the indexation policy and by the Prices and Incomes Accord. The Commission's influence is exerted via its control of minimum rates in all periods free of wage policy, and in some policy-influenced periods. Beginning in the indexation period, and strengthening in the 1980s and early 1990s, the Commission attempted to incorporate over-award elements into its awards by developing what were known as 'paid rates' awards. It is intended that wage rates specified in these awards should be those received by employees, and identifying awards in this way emphasises that the wages prescribed in other than paid rates awards are not intended to be those received by employees. It is one of the more bewildering aspects of the system that it should address itself to the determination of wage rates which will not be paid, but are in fact minima.

While increases made to the minima are not reflected in exactly proportionate increases in the various above-award strata, they will have some effect. If the over-award rates do not also shift upwards, then labour would normally be expected to move into other areas. For example, the public sector is one element of the workforce mostly paid at award rates. However, while this group receives relatively low wages, it has, to date at least, enjoyed relative security of tenure, employment under less than rigorous supervision, and perhaps a slower tempo of work than other sectors. Public sector wages, being at the award level, rise by the full extent of award increases, but unless all over award rates shift by an appropriate amount, the public sector wages and non-wage conditions will have become relatively more attractive. In order to reduce this relative change, over-award rates will need to rise to restore pre-existing relativities, otherwise labour will seek to shift to the now more attractive public sector. Consequently as the award rate moves, the structure of wages rates erected on the award will also move, but the extent of this secondary shift may be proportionately greater or less than the initial movement.

It is possible therefore, to argue that historically, the Commission has influenced, but not controlled, wages. Additionally this influence is somewhat skewed, for when there are forces exerting upward pressure on wages operating in the community, the Commission cannot usually prevent these from taking effect by refusing to raise award rates. It might succeed for a time in preventing those whose pay rates are administratively or by statute tied to award rates from achieving increases, but should this persist, one would expect, particularly in a near full employment situation, that labour would leave the area concerned. In such circumstances it would be surprising if labour and management did not jointly seek to have wages adjusted.

The implication of this is that while the arbitral mechanism might superficially seem to be a feasible means of controlling wages according to some central plan, there are real limitations. Firstly, most Commission members have shown they accept that their primary responsibility is to dispute settlement rather than to economic management. Secondly, should either employer or employee seek to escape from the Commission's jurisdiction it can do so by resorting either to collective bargaining or to a more compatible state tribunal. Finally, the Commission can control only one tier of a multi-tiered wage structure. In the final analysis, it is relative bargaining power which influences the actions of labour and management, and other parties seeking to exert their influence must understand the nature and use of that power. The wage indexation and accord episodes discussed later do constitute more subtle approaches to bargaining power than has been typical of Australian wage policy.

It would be erroneous to argue that the Commission has no influence over wages, or, alternatively, that it controls them, just as it would be wrong to conclude that its influence is spread equally over all sectors of the labour market. The existence of this market and the capacity and willingness of labour and management to resort to it are major factors preventing the Commission from ever controlling wage rates.

Equal pay

The extent of the Commission's control, or lack of it, over actual wages is nowhere better illustrated than in the case of wages for women. In a decision of 1969,[2] the Commission awarded women employed under the *Metal Trades Award* equal pay with men. Given that the Commission, predictably, complicated the decision by setting out 'principles' (nine on this occasion) which must be satisfied, and insisted that each industry must be considered separately, this was no hasty rush to equality. Since 1969, however, the march towards a profession of equality for women in all areas, including pay, has continued and, since the election of the Hawke government in 1983, rhetoric on this subject has been all but torrential. The extensive reforms to the industrial relations statute, introduced in 1993 by the Keating government, included a provision, s.170 BC of the *Industrial Relations Act*, empowering the Commssion to make an order requiring an employer to pay employees equal remuneration for work of equal value. Whether this is likely to achieve more than to attest to the government's good intentions is doubtful. With the Commission already committed to equal pay, and making no distinction between men and women in its awards, it is apparent that the Commission's inability to regulate and control pay has resulted in the preservation of some at least of the old inequality. The following data were included in a paper prepared by an ACTU official.[3]

Table 16.1 Over-award payments by occupational group and gender

Occupation	Female Employees %	Female Average Over-award $	Male Average Over-award $	Ratio F/M Average Over-award %	Females Receiving Over-awards %	Males Receiving Over-awards %
Professionals	41.4	3.30	5.40	61	2.6	4.6
Para-professionals	44.3	2.40	6.00	40	5.8	6.6
Tradespersons	10.0	12.60	21.90	58	22.8	27.4
Clerks	77.3	9.70	8.40	115	15.0	12.3
Salespersons & Personal Service Workers	64.1	4.30	14.40	30	9.1	18.8
Plant & Machine Operators, & Drivers	16.3	7.40	13.50	55	20.8	24.7
Labourers & related workers	35.2	6.50	10.90	60	22.0	23.8
All occupations	41.4	6.90	13.00	53	12.7	19.3

Source: ABS, *The Labour Force, Australia*, August 1991, Catalogue No. 6203.0; ABS, *Distribution and Composition of Employee Earnings and Hours*, May 1990, Catalogue No. 6306.0 (including unpublished data).

In 1970 Sharpley[4] noted the gender based award wage differentials set out in Table 16.2. Clearly, the data in Tables 16.1 and 16.2 are not directly comparable, but one may conclude that while the gap has narrowed, the female disadvantage would appear to have shifted from the controlled segment of pay to the over-award portion which is unregulated. Doubtless most women workers will be less interested in the location of the disadvantage than the fact that it persists, and that protestation and promise has achieved less for them than they might reasonably expect.

Data published by the ACTU[5] confirm the view that the least regulated component of earnings may be the source of the greatest part of the male/female differential. It is suggested that in 1991, for non-managerial adult award wage rates, the female to male ratio was 91.7 per cent.[6] For the same group in respect of average weekly total earnings, the ratio in 1991 was 83.7 per cent,[7] while with respect to over-award payments, the 1991 ratio was 61.5 per cent.[8] Obviously there are many factors which may go to explain the persistence and source of the differential, and industry and skill concentration among females are two of them. The persistence of major differentials in the

Table 16.2 Percentage wage-differentials between female and male adult minimum legal total wages, by occupation groups: 1969

Occupation Group	Maximum Wage Differential %	Modal Wage Differential %	Minimum Wage Differential %
Professional, Technical and Related Workers	14.7	11.0	2.0
Administrative, Executive and Managerial Workers	N.A.	N.A.	N.A.
Clerical Workers	26.3	21.0	20.3
Sales Workers	23.8	23.0	18.1
Farmers, Fishermen and Related Workers	N.A.	N.A.	N.A.
Miners	N.A.	N.A.	N.A.
Workers in Transport & Communications	18.8	18.0	13.6
Craftsmen, Production Process Workers and Labourers n.e.i.	35.1	25.0	16.6
Service, Sport and Recreation Workers	28.2	22.0	9.6

N.A. Not available.

Source: J. G. Sharpley, *The Economic Consequences of Equal Pay for Women in Australia*, Unpublished M.Ec. Thesis, Monash University, Clayton, 1970, p. 219.

over-award component, which typically is largely characterised by bargaining, may suggest that increased reliance on enterprise bargaining, as forecast in the seventh version of the Accord (see below) may require particular care to ensure that the differential does not widen again. The persistence of unequal pay following the 1969 award does demonstrate, among other things, that the Commission's ability to control, rather than influence, wages is far from absolute.

Wage determination

In undertaking its wage determination function, the Commission has historically carried out two major exercises. It conducts, at regular intervals, what is known as the *National Wage* case, the periodicity of which was originally annual, but during the wage indexation episode was first quarterly, and later every six months. In the *National Wage* case, the Commission considers the entire award structure and decides whether there are factors within the economy which suggest that wages as a whole should be varied. The Commission does not have the constitutional power to initiate and to undertake such a review, so a *National Wage* case must be placed in the context of dispute settlement. Labour and management, via representative organisations, contrive a dispute, within the meaning of the Industrial Relations Act, over critical elements of the award wage structure, and the Commission hears this synthetic dispute and determines what, if any, variation in award wages is appropriate.

The *National Wage* case, under various guises, has been part of Australian life since 1907 when, in the *Harvester* case,[9] the President of the then Arbitration Court, Judge Higgins, introduced the Basic Wage. His intention was to provide a wage which served as a minimum, given the aspirations of what he termed a civilised society. The Basic Wage was intended to be sufficient to permit an unskilled labourer to rear a family in conditions other than those of abject poverty, and the context within which that judgement was made included the conviction that tariff protection should be used to ensure that employers could survive while meeting that standard.

Basic wage and margin adjustments

The Basic Wage, while itself a 'living wage', became the floor of the Australian wage structure. Arbitrators then determined amounts known as 'margins', or allowances for skills, and these were added to the Basic Wage to determine award rates for the whole range of skilled and semi-skilled workers. From this evolved a structure of relative wages whose ordering has remained largely unchanged to this day. Obviously this assessment and valuation of the skill component could not be other than a comparative process, although it was not always presented as such.

The two elements of the award wage were adjusted separately, the Basic Wage being adjusted automatically for quarterly cost-of-living changes, and also as a result of specific Basic Wage Inquiries. The criteria adopted for these inquiries certainly originally included the needs of the wage earner, but, as a result of the economic strictures of the 1930s Depression, became dominated by a concept described as 'the capacity of industry to pay'. This concept, though less than precise and occasioning considerable argument but little clarification, dominated Basic Wage adjustment for many years. It should be noted that the capacity of the economy to pay a given level of wages is not a meaningful concept unless the constraints on the Commission are fully specified. That is, if it decided that the distribution of income between wages and profits should be varied, then, assuming that the Commission could effect such a variation, the capacity to pay particular wage rates is considerably greater than if it is assumed that the income distribution should not be varied. Similarly, if the Commission sought to prevent inflation, it would be more constrained in its assessment of capacity to pay than if it did not. As there are, of course, no absolute standards by which such matters as rates of inflation or distribution of income can be judged, then capacity to pay is an empty criterion, and it will remain meaningless until these parameters are specified.

In 1953, as a result of significant inflation levels, automatic cost-of-living adjustments to the Basic Wage were abandoned. At the same time the Arbitration Court specified certain economic indicators which it would consult in future. They were: production and productivity; employment; investment;

external trade; external balances; the competitive position of secondary industry, and related trade conditions. It is doubtful that any tribunal could have used these criteria to determine an unequivocally correct wage—such a wage probably does not exist. In fact, the decisions which emerged in the wake of these principles seemed little different from those that had gone before. The judgement did, however, usher in an era in which the tribunal's Basic Wage cases seemed to be dominated by considerations of national productivity and prices, with the increases arising from these being moderated by the Commission's concern with the inflationary effects of its decisions. By 1961, the Commission had adopted the concept of national productivity increase as a major determinant of wage adjustment. Following the Basic Wage inquiry of that year the concept of a formal, annual *National Wage* case was adopted.

When the Basic Wage component of this two-part wage determination system was adjusted, this influenced the relative size of the margin for skill, for the two were not simultaneously adjusted. For example, had a particular occupation been assessed at deserving a margin amounting to twenty per cent above the Basic Wage, then each subsequent Basic Wage increase would reduce the relative value of the margin. A consequence was that irregular reviews of margins were undertaken to preserve or adjust these established wage relativities. Over time the Court, and later the Commission, adopted the practice of reviewing only one margin (usually that of the metal trades fitter), and of treating this as the benchmark from which all other margins would be adjusted, thus preserving, in a relative sense, the pre-existing hierarchy of wage rates.

The total wage 1967

The Basic Wage plus margin system facilitated a leap-frogging process whereby any adjustment in either part of the wage could be argued to have upset pre-existing wage relativities. This was one reason persuading the Commission, in 1967,[10] to abandon this system, and to opt for a wage structure which comprised consolidation of these two separate components into the Total Wage; this was then to be adjusted as a single unit. Having adopted this system the Commission found it necessary to determine a minimum wage since none, other than the now defunct Basic Wage, had existed. This minimum wage, it was thought, would provide new freedom for the Commission to improve the wage of the lowest-paid workers. Under the old system, any attempt to raise the minimum wage would have involved raising the basic wage, and this would have raised the whole wage structure, since the Basic Wage was a component of every award rate. Now, by establishing a minimum wage, the Commission was able to raise this relatively faster than was possible under the old system.

Work value inquiries

The *National Wage* case is one method by which the Commission adjusts the overall level of wages. The other has been by means of periodic work value inquiries. The *National Wage* case serves to adjust the general level of wages for price changes, to distribute productivity increases, or otherwise to manipulate the overall wage level. But it does not purport to adjust the structure of wages—to alter wage relativities, which, as noted earlier, have been strongly influenced by considerations of skill. It might be noted that the skills which the system has recognised most readily are those for which some formal training period is required, and for which some formal qualification is issued. Generally, skilled tradesmen, those who have completed a formal apprenticeship, have been awarded higher rates than those whose skills are acquired on the job. However the arbitral system has not been able to ignore the bargaining power of certain groups of unskilled workers, and the Commission has awarded wages that at least partially recognise that bargaining power.

In all countries, wage relativities tend to be inflexible as workers seek to maintain historical wage relationships. Certainly in Australia the wage system was administered in a way which built considerable rigidity into the wage structure. Increases in the basic wage tended to reduce the relative size of skill margins thereby compressing the wage structure, but these would be followed by special inquiries into margins which normally restored pre-existing relativities. The introduction of the Total Wage has altered the process to a greater extent than it has altered the end results. The Commission's practice of increasing the minimum wage faster than other award rates has affected relativities by treating both skilled workers and semi-skilled relatively worse than the minimum wage earner. Although the Commission sought to obtain greater flexibility, and especially the capacity to aid the lowest-paid, unions still attempt to retain existing relationships.

Wage determination practices adopted during the 'Accord' period, notably a process called award restructuring, have influenced wage relativities, but the extent and durability of change cannot, at the time of writing, be determined. It does seem, however, that the basic framework of relativities has remained. The wage policy of this period has left the future of work value inquiries unclear, but historically they have been the vehicle by which the Commission has attempted to change relativities. Though these irregular inquiries were rarely intended to have nation-wide impact, they almost invariably did spread through the entire economy. A work value inquiry is usually a review of wages in a particular industry or occupation, and its precise focus will depend on the unions and employers involved. The inquiry is normally undertaken in response to union claims that the value of the work done by some or all of its members has increased. The concept of work value is closely linked with another of the Commission's concepts, that of comparative wage justice. While the Commission has behaved as though these were quite separate matters, it is doubtful whether, in the last analysis, one can be distinguished from the other.[11]

There has never been a precise definition of work value, but clearly it is related to job content. The work value of a job is said to have increased when the degree of required training, skill or responsibility required increases, or when working conditions became harder or more unpleasant. In seeking to establish the extent of work value change the Commission undertakes some process akin to job evaluation, whereby jobs are analysed to determine the extent to which certain critical factors are contained in them. These factors include skill, responsibility, working conditions, effort involved and similar characteristics. The job evaluator, by examining each job, establishes a hierarchy of jobs, ranked according to the extent to which the relevant factors, appropriately weighted, are present. He then derives a wage structure to apply to this hierarchy, by comparing that of jobs under evaluation with the content of other jobs for which the wage rate is known. Thus the evaluator seeks to ensure that this wage structure is consistent with the rest of the wage structure.

Job evaluation is an apparently precise undertaking, applying to a single plant or department. Work value inquiries undertaken by the Commission do not purport to be precise and they apply on a very broad scale—to an entire industry, or an occupation or group of occupations—but it is intended that similar principles should be applied. Unions do seek, in such inquiries, to have the Commission establish a new wage structure, based on an examination of members' job content.

It is an inescapable reality that, after the Commission made its examination of a particular occupation and recommended higher wages for that group, the process would not end there. Workers in the same plant, those in similar jobs, and any others who could argue that their jobs were, or had been, related to the group in question, would seek wage adjustments to regain pre-existing relativity. They would claim that comparative wage justice demanded this, or in more familiar terms, their claim would be that the conditions which gave rise to the increase granted to the first group apply equally to them. In these circumstances, justice required that their wages be adjusted comparably.

It could be argued that if work value was the process by which traditional wage relativities were shifted, then comparative wage justice would be the process by which those relativities would be restored. However, this distinction cannot be pushed too far, for it must be remembered that the new rates evolved under the work value process are themselves derived from a comparative process as noted earlier. In other words, it compares the value of the job in question with other jobs and adjusts the wage so as to provide one that is just, by comparison with other rates.

Work value cases may, and usually do, flow through the entire wage structure, either by the comparative wage justice route, or by inducing other work value cases in areas where comparability cannot be claimed. The process of a work value inquiry is a good deal less detailed than is the job evaluation procedure. It normally involves inspections of some workplaces in which the jobs in question are being done by representatives of labour and management as well as Commission members. It is difficult to know the precise significance of the inspections, whether they do inform the Commission or whether they are merely symbolic. Certainly, however, they are integral to work value inquiries. The concepts of work value and comparative wage justice are so similar that it may well be that the purpose of the inspection is to emphasise that a particular inquiry is work value, not comparative wage justice. The major part of a work value case involves considerable argument in the Commission itself, the introduction of evidence, and of claims and counter-claims.

The Commission takes the view that work value inquiries are particularised; that they refer to less than the whole wage structure. However, over time, these inquiries touch off a succession of claims for comparative adjustments, and these eventually cover the entire wage-earning group. A typical episode was experienced between 1978 and 1981, as an $8.00 work value increase won in the transport sector seeped through the entire wage structure. It is clear that some work value inquiries will have a more pervasive impact than others, and a critical factor will certainly be the size of the group affected by the decision. In general, however, the labour market does serve to provide a loose and imperfect linkage between all wage rates. From a long term macro-economic perspective, it makes little difference whether a wage increase derives from work value, comparative wage justice, or the *National Wage* case; the same forces determine them all. In the short term, in any particular plant, the various sources of wage adjustment are quite important as it is this short-term, particular situation which has the greatest impact on labour relations.

It may be that the Commission uses the *National Wage* case to adjust the wage level in general, and seeks to vary or preserve the level of real wages. In the application of the principles of work value and of comparative wage justice, the Commission may seek instead to impose a particular structure, or logical order of wage relativities. If the Commission is to attempt to control and manipulate both wage levels and the wage structure, then perhaps it is only possible to do so through this apparently cumbersome multi-stage process. It is important to remember that in each of these operations the Commission's decisions apply only to award wages, so that the precise effects of its decisions on workers' actual earnings are simply not known.

In 1991, the federal government and the ACTU began to argue that wage determination ought to be enterprise based (see below). While the concept may lack precision, and may pose many difficulties for all parties, including the Commission, it is probable that enterprise based wage determination will include inter-enterprise or inter-plant wage differentials. While such a development would inject a welcome note of realism into the system, it must be remembered that it runs counter to the long tradition of comparative wage justice and to the expectations which that has generated. These can be overcome, of course, but it would be unwise to assume that inter-plant differentials can be introduced widely in a short time.

Productivity and wages: the GMH and Oil Industry cases

It is important to note that the Commission has sought to distribute the gains from productivity increases only for the economy as a whole. A worker at a plant which enjoyed a ten per cent productivity increase could expect from the Commission the same wage increase as a worker at a plant at which productivity had declined: both would obtain increases in accord with national movements in productivity. The Commission, through the 1960s and 1970s, heard applications based on specific company performance, and it rejected those applications. Perhaps the most celebrated of the individual productivity based cases was that led by the Vehicle Builders Federation against General Motors Holden in 1965-1966.[12] The union case was for a wage increase of $6 per week for employees at General Motors Holden in Australia.

The union argued that the profit and productivity performance of the company virtually obligated it to provide the increase. The case was presumably strengthened in some minds by the fact that as a wholly-owned subsidiary of a United States parent, General Motors Holden distributed none of its profits, which were immense by the standards of the time, to any Australians. It seemed to some that the only means by which the fruits of the company's Australian prosperity could be shared in its host country was by paying an enhanced wage to its employees.

These considerations did not appeal to the Commission. Indeed, two members of the Bench declared that to grant the union's claim 'would in our opinion amount to irresponsible promiscuity'.[13] A third member suggested that to grant the application would be to abandon the principle of comparative wage justice: 'It seems inescapable that if the Commission were to destroy the doctrine of comparative wage justice on the grounds advanced in this matter it could only create in its place a tenet of comparative wage injustice'.[14] Employees in the oil industry found their arguments similarly treated in a 1970 case.[15] Again the notion of awarding pay increases in response to specific industry or company profits and productivity was rejected. As it had done in the *GMH* case, the Commission adverted to the possibility of over-award rates being agreed privately, but the fact remained that if the unions sought to impose sanctions on the employers to force concession to their demands, the employers could call on the Commission to force the unions to desist. In those circumstances, despite the Commission's hints, the union's ability to force over-award rates was constrained.

These cases demonstrated the Commission's determination to maintain a uniformity in the national wage structure, whether justified by its principle of comparative wage justice or by the somewhat nebulous notion of national capacity to pay wage increases. The Bench did rule, in the *Oil Industry* case, that it might be possible to consider industry- or plant-specific productivity increases where the parties had agreed to this, or in those circumstances in which it had been the practice of the parties to rely on those criteria.[16] The *GMH* and *Oil Industry* cases were seen as critically important decisions at the time. The unions had carefully selected cases in which levels of profit and productivity could be shown to be well beyond the norms of industry as a whole. It was argued that as long as employers were able to make unusually high levels of profits, yet employees were not permitted to extract a higher than normal wage from them, employees were in a situation that was close to exploitative. The Commission elected to be guided by its long-standing criteria, possibly seeing no acceptable alternative, and in so doing probably encouraged the further development of over-award bargaining outside its control. The Commission, of course, through that period, elected to concern itself with attempting to restrain inflation, and its view of inflation and of industrial relations was that to have granted the wage increases sought in these cases would have begun an irresistible tide of national wage demands, and it believed these inevitably led to inflation. The doctrine of comparative wage justice provided justification for refusing to increase wages in those industries in which they were clearly affordable. To have conceded would have been, presumably, unjust to those employers who could not afford the increase. While such logic may be difficult to accept, it is a logic by which the Commission had worked for most of its existence.

Wage indexation

The Commission, after adopting the Total Wage concept in 1967, proceeded to hear *National Wage* cases annually, and, at irregular intervals, to undertake work value inquiries. Actual wage rates had, from the beginnings of the arbitral system, been influenced by forces other than award wage variations alone. Some element of collective bargaining had always been present, but was stimulated by the suspension of automatic cost-of-living adjustments in 1953, by the persistence of full employment and by the migration to Australia of foreign firms and workers accustomed to the practice. Consequently, by the late 1960s, such control as the Commission had over wages was well dissipated.

Growing public awareness of the extent of collective bargaining coincided with the early stages of a period of rapid inflation. The causes of the inflation were varied, probably the most important being the boom in export prices in 1972-1973 whilst the Australian dollar remained undervalued, and the remarkable money supply increases begun by the McMahon government in the second half of 1972. These were continued for some months in 1973 by the Whitlam government. The election of a Labor government in late 1972 in itself had a considerable impact on industrial relations, with unionists, if not their leaders, expecting much from the first government, in the experience of many of them, which did not project itself as an anti-labour force. This, as well as the inflationary climate, encouraged the union movement to seek extensive and rapid wage increases.

The simplistic nature of Australian political and economic debate led many Australians to conclude that inflation was being created by these wage increases. Others argued that if the Commission had remained central to wage determination, the wage increases, and consequently the inflation, would not have taken place. In retrospect, it seems unlikely that the Commission could have restrained wages in this period had it sought to do so. But the Labor government was sensitive to the political consequences of the growth of industrial disputes, and the perceived impotence of the Commission. Of at least equal importance was the extent of wage increases as shown by Table 16.3.

The experience of 1974, when the rate of wage increases peaked and unemployment began to increase, finally induced the government to act. In its first years the Whitlam government had not been concerned at the decline of the Commission's influence, and in fact had welcomed the growth of collective bargaining. But an awareness of the political consequences of rising unemployment and rapid wage increases induced the government to reconsider its view on the Commission. This reappraisal was helped by the fact that, despite the apparent loss of relevance of the Commission, there remained among many unionists a determination to have cost-of-living adjustments returned to award wages. This sentiment was probably less than logical in the circumstances, but was a valuable political asset in the government's emerging wage policy.

The government issued an extensive discussion paper canvassing the notion of a policy of wage indexation—that is, the adjustment of wages in

Table 16.3 Extent of wage increases, 1971 to 1975

Year	Average weekly earnings per employed male unit $	Percentage change over previous year
1971-2	93.00	—
1972-3	101.50	9.1
1973-4	118.00	16.3
1974-5	148.30	25.7

Source: Australian Bureau of Statistics, *Monthly Review of Business Statistics*, 1972-5, Reference No. 1.4.

accordance with cost-of-living increases. No doubt the government's generally favourable attitude to the concept was dictated by the politics of the matter: if the Conciliation and Arbitration Commission could somehow be restored to an apparently central role in industrial relations, this would do much to ease the public disquiet promoted by overt collective bargaining and its attendant disputes. Unions, on the other hand, might be induced to desist from the turbulent process of bargaining if they could be guaranteed some form of automatic wage adjustment. The government's early view, that collective bargaining was a superior industrial relations process, was now seen as of considerably less importance than the political advantages to be expected from a return to the apparent tranquillity of the arbitral system.

It is also fair to point out that the government did see economic advantages in a system of guaranteeing regular wage adjustment via a price index. In this matter, the government's view was that exceedingly high wage claims were being made for two reasons: to obtain compensation for past price increases, and in anticipation of future price increases. In this period of rapid inflation, unions sought to build some protection against anticipated inflation, but in so doing they were thought to be ensuring that their anticipations were fulfilled.

The Commission did not introduce its chosen form of wage indexation until 1975,[17] after the ACTU had in effect agreed that it would use its influence to discourage unions from pursuit of other wage increases once indexation was granted. Given that support, the Commission elected not to provide an automatic link between wages and the price index, but to review wage rates each quarter, and in so doing, to review the extent to which unions had observed the requirement that they should not pursue wage increases beyond indexation. If unions which had the power to force higher wages for their members used that power, the Commission would deny indexation to all. The threat to withdraw its guarantee of real wage maintenance for all award-covered employees, in the environment of 1975, gave the Commission its first effective sanction since the failure of the penal powers. As it drew on the logic of industrial relations and on the nature of Australian trade unionism, as well as the economic climate, it was a more sophisticated approach than any attempted to that time.

The Commission derived 'principles' for wage indexation, and these were essentially that there would be quarterly wage indexation hearings, and that changes in work value and increases in national productivity should be the only means of wage adjustment. It was conceded that special arrangements might have to be made to bring certain award rates closer to the market rates which relevant workers attained, but these 'catch up' adjustments, as they were called, were a matter of adjusting the award rates alone, for the actual wage adjustments had been made by over award payments. Clearly, the Commission saw the principles as a means of maintaining the real wage, of distributing the gains from productivity, but of preventing other changes in wage rates.

Until 1978, the Commission undertook quarterly inquiries to determine the appropriate wage adjustment necessitated by the price increases in the previous quarter. For each quarter in 1975, wages were increased by a rate equivalent to the increase in the Consumer Price Index. The indexation package after 1976 was subjected to increasing strain, because the Liberal Party government, which took office in late 1975, took the view that while decreases in industrial disputes and in collective bargaining were desirable, increases in money wages were not. Consequently, the government argued for rates of wage increase less than the rates of price increase, and, in 1976, the Commission began a policy of providing full indexation only to the lower end of the wage structure. For example, the indexation increase for the March quarter was three per cent for those earning up to $125 per week, and $3.80 to all higher wage earners. The effect of this was to compress wage relativities, a policy fraught with industrial relations difficulties. In the later seventies this 'plateau' indexation was displaced by partial indexation, whereby all wages were adjusted at a rate less than the rate of price increases.

These changes in indexation were supported by the government, largely on the grounds that in certain cases government policy was devised to raise prices in selected areas to achieve particular ends. The government argued that for the Commission to adjust wages so as to compensate for these policy-induced price increases would be to frustrate government policy, as well as to penalise employers, who did not obtain any compensating price increase.

The Commission in 1978 extended the periodicity of its indexation hearings from three to six-monthly intervals. A result of these changes was that the unions increasingly questioned the value of remaining party to the indexation policy. In 1978, perhaps in response to union unease, full indexation was granted, although the Commission's expressed reason was that neither employers or government representatives had made a case justifying a departure from full indexation.

The Commission concluded a long inquiry into its wage fixing principles in 1981. It undertook this, ostensibly at least, because, against a background of dissatisfaction expressed by unions employers and government, the Commission believed the indexation system to be in danger of collapse. The Commission proposed a further variation on the now half-yearly indexation hearing, one which involved splitting the adjustment due into partial payments to be made at the beginning of each six-month period, with an adjustment at the end. The approach was not fully tested, as the Commission found insufficient compliance by its clients with the requirement to refrain from collective bargaining. It therefore brought the indexation system to an end in July 1981.

As incomes policies go, the indexation policy was surprisingly long-lived, though it owed some of its longevity to the Commission's preparedness to temper strict interpretation of its policy in the interests of maintaining a necessary degree of industrial harmony. No doubt it proved a valuable lesson for those who were to fashion the Accord between the ACTU and the then-in-opposition ALP. It had shown that appropriate administration of a wage policy could induce a reduction in industrial disputes, that labour and management could be persuaded to return from collective bargaining to the fold of arbitration, and, importantly, it was possible for the Commission, with appropriate collaboration, to develop workable sanctions to enforce its rulings. The sanction, of threatening to withdraw indexation from all parties should the most powerful break the rules, is unlikely to inspire much confidence in a tight labour market, but Australia has experienced few of these since the beginning of the indexation era.

In establishing that the Commission could administer a wage policy, the indexation period did not, of course, provide any evidence regarding the desirability of this. On the other hand, in the political climate of the early 1980s, it no doubt seemed imperative to the leadership of the ALP that it should go to the electorate with a policy which appeared to promise industrial peace and relative stability of real wages. The Party's Accord with the ACTU was to furnish that policy. An extract from an analysis of the ALP position by two industrial relations journalists in *The Age* is contained in Table 16.4.

The ALP-ACTU Prices and Incomes Accord

The ALP announced its Prices and Incomes Accord with the ACTU shortly before it was elected to government in 1983. The Accord itself was a lengthy document which contained a number of quite specific undertakings.[18] In government, the ALP has found difficulty in fulfilling many of those obligations, most notably the undertaking to provide wage indexation to preserve the real value of wages. The ACTU has shown itself to be understanding of the government's problems, and has consented to many modifications to the original agreement. The Accord thus joined those industrial relations agreements which are found to be considerably more elastic than they may have originally appeared to be. An early example of these was the General Motors-United Automobile Workers agreement of 1950 in the United States. Here the union had forced a five year agreement on the reluctant company as the first stage in its campaign to win a guaranteed annual wage for members. The tightly specified wage increases included in the agreement were rapidly rendered grossly inadequate in the inflation of the Korean war period. The union was able to convince General Motors management that re-opening the contract was likely to be a more palatable alternative than seeking to enforce it. The union's justification for resiling from the contract in this way was claimed to be that the agreement was a 'living document' which had to be modified according to circumstances. The management's acquiescence was certainly to be explained in terms of its view of the cost of trying to hold the union to its contract. The 1950 Agreement was the first and last attempt by the

Table 16.4 The Accord: before the 1983 election

ELECTION '83

The Issues

M!CHAEL GORDON and
PETER STEPHENS
on industrial relations

The ALP will have to dispel fears that it will, in Mr Fraser's words, be subservient to the unions 'at every twist and turn'.

So far, the unions have been subservient to the Labor Party. On the central question of maintenance of real wages, they have made concessions which would have been unthinkable in the past and which many unions still find hard to swallow.

The prices and incomes policy rests heavily on faith and trust between all parties. It relies on strong unions accepting less than the market would bear so weak unions can get more.

The employers have, with justification, raised doubts about the ability of ACTU-affiliated unions to pull together for a common cause. The ACTU response is that over-award pay increases will be expressly outlawed by 'no extra claims' provisions.

The problem with the policy is that its outcome is uncertain. The practicalities after the planned economic summit are hazy and the policy is so badly worded in some important areas that it is open to different interpretations.

The main question facing both parties is the timing of wage increases after the pause. Because of the strong public support for the pause, the ALP has refused to commit itself to anything more definite than possible support for an extension of the pause after the economic summit.

In reality, it will face great pressure to support a wage rise in July to ease some of the pressure of 15 months of price rises that have not been compensated for by wage increases. The ever-volatile building industry could pose the greatest threat to the policy.

Source: Extract from M. Gordon and P. Stephens, 'Clear choice on approach to the unions', *The Age*, 4 March, 1983, p. 13.

United Automobile Workers to secure a long-term agreement, for subsequent contracts were usually of two and three years' duration. A further safeguard was built into the post-1950 contracts, for they all provided for quarterly cost-of-living adjustments and for company productivity adjustment.

The ALP-ACTU Accord is a living document in this tradition, and has demonstrated its vitality on six occasions, as it has undergone extensive restatement and formal renegotiation, and it has become accepted usage to refer to Accords Mark I to Mark 7.

The agreement which began life as the Prices and Incomes Accord between the ALP and ACTU became simply the Accord. In popular discussion, it acquired a status much more akin to that reserved for legislation than is usually applied to agreements between two private organisations. The signatories do represent private (that is, non-government) organisations for the ACTU reached the first agreement with the ALP rather than the government. The ALP had formed government by the time the first revision took place, but the various revisions remained, on the ALP side, with Party members who are also government Ministers, but it was not a Parliamentary matter.

The status of the Accord has grown considerably over the years, but its dimensions have become correspondingly indistinct. By the beginning of the 1990s, the Accord had altered in concept from a fairly specific agreement to become a forum for discussion and negotiation between ACTU officials and government ministers. Indeed, the *Australian Financial Review* cited a one-time Federal Treasurer, Mr P. Keating, to the effect that the Accord was 'a state of mind'.[19] The focus of accord processes was, for the most part, to reach agreement on the cases which the ACTU and government would put to the Commission at forthcoming *National Wage* cases. From inception, however, the Accord had included agreements on measures designed to inhibit the rate of price increase, to reform taxation and to maintain or improve various welfare and family assistance measures, these being, perhaps unfortunately, described as a 'social wage'.

The wages policy element of the Accord clearly required the unions to cease all over-award bargaining, and to agree to make no extra wage claims (other than in certain circumstances designed to remedy problem areas), and in general to confine all wage adjustments to *National Wage* cases. The Accord proposed, therefore, centralising wage determination and investing the Commission with greater *de facto* control of wages than it had held since the Second World War. As the process developed, the ACTU and government would make complimentary submissions to the Commission regarding wage adjustment and other industrial relations issues, and for the most part the Commission made awards consistent with those submissions.

The Accord was presented as an essential element of an overall macro-economic strategy designed to increase employment, achieve economic growth and to restrain inflation. The Commission could reject Accord-based submissions, or so it probably seemed, only if it was prepared to upset the Government's economic strategy. This appears not dissimilar to the position the Commission occupied during the Fraser years, although the government's economic policies of that period were somewhat more enigmatic, at least in their articulation.

The analogy with the Fraser years cannot be pushed too far, however, for in that period, the government accepted that, however regrettable it might be, the Commission was independent and authoritative. In 1991, the Minister for Industrial Relations, Senator Peter Cook did not see it that way. 'The Commission was a major player when it endorsed the Accord', he (Cook) says, but `it is not when it doesn't. I don't think the Commission has ever understood that. It has misjudged its wage-setting role—what was primary...' Cook says the Commission has tended (wrongly) during the Accord period to see its *National Wage* cases as the prime wage-setting mechanism. `But our view is that the primary wage-setter is the Accord......'[20] A fine disregard for statutory instruments is not usually associated with government Ministers.

It must be noted that the Accord, whatever its actual impact may be, has been of considerable political significance to the government. The Accord has been presented as the instrument that has prevented industrial disputes from becoming a major social problem, it has been suggested that it has ensured that wage increases have been moderate, and this, it has been implied, has restrained inflation. In the 1990s, it has been suggested that the Accord has been the key to major changes in workplace behaviour which are destined to lead to greatly enhanced efficiency in industry. A sober analysis would probably suggest that industrial disputes have rarely, in Australian history, constituted significant social or economic problems, although they have had considerable political fallout, so the contribution of the Accord here may have been less than it seems. The moderation of wage increases, given that inflation did not decline until the nation went into a major recession, resulted in a decline in real wages, and 'an unprecedented redistribution of national income from wages to profits'.[21] Further, it seems inherently unlikely that the solution to the less than competitive performance of many Australian industries is to be found in the behaviour of award-covered employees. None of this is intended, of course, to suggest that the Accord has not been extremely productive, in a political sense, for the government.

Progress of the Accords

The wage indexation which was a central part of the Accord did not last long. Full indexation of wages was provided for the year ended December 1983, and also in the 1984[22] case, although there were signs of a less than complete commitment to indexation. In 1985, however, the ACTU and ALP renegotiated the Accord following a large depreciation of the dollar and a worsening balance of trade. The government's attempt to obtain the agreement of the ACTU for some 'discounting' of the expected indexation was resisted initially by the then President of the ACTU, Mr Dolan, who had, unlike either his predecessor or his successor, reached his office after starting life as a rank and file unionist. Dolan's view was, it seemed, that the first duty of the ACTU was to serve the immediate interests of union members, thus he sought the full indexation agreed in the Accord. Dolan, however, perhaps because he was in the twilight of his Presidency, did not see this view prevail: 'The ACTU Executive however, encouraged by Crean and Kelty, adopted a more conciliatory approach'.[23]

Accord Mark 2 was born of this approach, and it resulted in two per cent being cut from the indexation figure to compensate for the appreciation of the dollar, and this was to be partly compensated by a future tax cut. The Accord parties also agreed to discount the claim to be made for wage adjustment based on national productivity increase, and further, that the productivity increase should be distributed in the form of employer contributions to occupational superannuation schemes.

Intrinsically desirable and long overdue as occupational superannuation may have been, its introduction is not without potential problems. As with many of the Accord outcomes, the extent of rank and file involvement in the ACTU decision to trade off wage gains for a superannuation system seems to have been minimal. In an ethical sense, the tendency to impose decisions on the rank and file is disturbing, and in practical terms, the absence of a campaign to convince unionists of the desirability of the wage—superannuation trade-off may be harmful. Should unionists not have been convinced of the worth of the shift, they may very well, in more prosperous times, apply pressure to obtain that foregone wage increase, regardless of the fact that their employers are already contributing to the superannuation funds.

The third version of the Accord was delivered by the *National Wage* case of 1987. It provided what was described as a two-tiered wage system (thereby provoking a series of witticisms referring to the lachrymose tendencies of the then Prime Minister), the tiers being an increase of $10 per week to all covered workers, and a further increase, not to exceed four per cent, would be available to workers who could negotiate suitable agreements with employers. The agreements were to incorporate productivity improvements in a number of specified areas in exchange for the four per cent wage increase. The Commission supervised the agreements which were reached in this process, which came to be known as 'award restructuring', in order to ensure that genuine productivity-enhancing changes, sufficient to justify the four per cent increase, had been agreed. There are many problems with this form of constrained productivity bargaining, especially if it is induced and supervised by third parties, and these problems, extensively discussed by Riach and Howard,[24] are detailed in chapter 18.

The fourth manifestation of the Accord is less easy to distinguish: that is, the outcome of the 1988 *National Wage* case is a matter of record, but Accord between the ACTU and ALP is less readily apparent. The two sought marginally different outcomes from the Commission which accepted neither submission. As Singleton put it 'The Accord once more had proved to be flexible'.[25]

The 1988 decision introduced the Commission's next wage fixing principle, the 'structural efficiency principle' which was to displace the existing award restructuring principle. This took the Commission into dangerous waters, for it sought to remove inhibitions on productivity that were created and protected by award structures. As those awards had been established by the Commission itself, there would seem to be considerable reason for reservation about the suitability of the Commission for the role of enhancing efficiency. To some extent, the Commission's decision was a revised and improved version of the 1987 decision, and it may prove to have been a cautious step in the direction of decentralisation, albeit closely managed, of the industrial relations process. Whether such decentralisation, under the Commission's supervision, is possible is dubious however, for the long history of flow-on of wage increases from sector to sector is difficult to overcome. The structural efficiency principle required that awards must be reformed before arbitrated increases could be paid. In practice, however, the increases were often provided in many cases after the unions gave commitment to restructure, but before that restructuring had occurred.[26]

The 1988 decision of the Commission left the Accord parties with certain unfinished business. The government had earlier proposed income tax reductions which were yet to materialise, but the partners had expressed concerns about low paid workers and there were indications that union membership disquiet about declining real wages had increased. The fifth incarnation of the Accord sought to focus on income tax reduction and social welfare payments, with wage determination being handled through refinement of the structural efficiency principle. The parties sought a wage adjustment of $30 per week, in return for a specific process of award restructuring which provided for further wage increases on implementation in certain cases.

The immediate wage increase sought was probably less than many of the favourably placed unions might have been able to achieve through collective bargaining, but it was focused mainly on those in weak bargaining positions, and receiving low wages, and for many of these, the $30 increase would have exceeded anything which bargaining power alone may have brought them. In fact, the Commission awarded an increase of between $10 and $15 per week, to be followed by a second increment within six months. It also expressed satisfaction with the progress of implementation of its structural efficiency principle, and ruled also on an ACTU application to set a pattern to be followed in award restructuring.

The ACTU proposal would have involved the Commission in establishing a framework for wages within each award. It sought quite close definition of skills, of levels and criteria for advancement, including appropriate skills and training. The proposal apparently envisaged a more detailed involvement in internal wage structures than the Commission had taken before, and would probably have involved, eventually, the Commission in national manpower policy. While it rejected the detail of this proposal, the Commission did accept the principle of simplifying the wage structure by establishing relativity ranges for key classifications, and of seeking, usually through broad-banding methods, to reduce the total numbers of classifications within awards.

The sixth incarnation of the Accord saw the parties move the Commission back to a role of earlier times. Under earlier forms of the Accord, as the unions had committed themselves to making no claims outside the Commission, the *National Wage* case had, in effect, set total wages for workers. The 1990 version of the Accord envisaged that the Commission would set a minimum wage, and that collective bargaining at the level of the enterprise would supplement that minimum. The collective bargaining was to be based on productivity improvements to ensure that any wage increase was cost neutral, and these should not exceed seven per cent. As well the parties agreed that the Commission should be asked to increase superannuation contributions paid by employers by a further three per cent of weekly wages.

For the first time, the Commission unambiguously rejected submissions by the ACTU and Government, and awarded a 2.5 per cent wage increase, rejecting the superannuation and enterprise bargaining claims. It considered the parties insufficiently mature to undertake a bargaining process, and believed that superannuation should be referred to a national conference for decision. The Commission's response provoked strident protests from ACTU officials, some unleashing vituperation that verged on the hysterical, and seemed to posit a view that the Commission had no mandate to do more than to accept the submissions of the Accord partners. Government spokesmen professed great indignation, but were generally more restrained in their criticisms.

It is difficult to understand the motives of the ACTU in seeking reliance on collective bargaining. The most likely hypothesis is that the pressures of rank and file discontent at the continuing wage restraint had become politically dangerous. As the ACTU Executive is elected by delegate conference, its members are well-insulated from the immediate wrath of the rank and file. Executive members who are also union officials may themselves enjoy fairly secure tenure, but their daily contacts are with lower level officials who are exposed to the consequences of rank and file dissatisfaction, and these can apply meaningful pressure to their union officials. There is a time lag and a diffusion before the dissatisfaction of members reaches the level of the ACTU Executive, but it may well have done so by 1991—indeed Singleton reports a group of militants at the 1988 *National Wage* case '..shouted abuse at ACTU Secretary Kelty as he attempted to put the union case.'[27] One might wish to argue that some unionists, by 1991, had begun to make clear their preference for pursuit of wage gains by individual unions, and that others wanted, in deteriorating economic circumstances, to try to win back some of the real wage increase that had been forgone.

Such hypotheses would suggest that the ACTU was motivated by a concern for its survival as the supreme trade union authority in seeking to move to enterprise bargaining. Concern with survival too, might explain why the Industrial Relations Commission rejected the submissions. It had known brushes with irrelevance in wage determination at times in the 1960s and in the 1970s as unions and employers almost routinely bypassed it in determining over-award pay. Its emergence as the key institution in wage fixing under the Labor government had been based securely on its involvement in a centralised system. While the ACTU proposals on enterprise bargaining still envisaged a role for the Commission, they were a step in the direction of deregulation of labour markets, something that eventually would leave no role for the Commission. Decentralisation of industrial relations and deregulation of the labour market were policies being discussed by many employer organisations, and by the federal Opposition parties, and it could well have seemed important to the Commission to state its official view that neither unions nor employers were yet capable of managing their own relationships.

After the 1991 decision, ACTU and union officials stated their intentions of rejecting the Commission's award, and of obtaining the $12 plus enterprise productivity agreements outside the Commission, and subsequently they claimed success in this. On the other hand, some unions which lacked immediate bargaining power appeared to find the Commission's offer of 2.5 per cent as something more favourable than the results their own bargaining efforts were likely to secure. For some low-paid workers, of course, $12 per week was a better result than a 2.5 per cent increase, and these would have supported the ACTU claim.

The outcome of this is not unambiguous. There is no doubt that some private agreements were concluded, outside the Commission, and that these incorporated some versions of the ACTU claim. It is also clear that, as passions cooled, the ACTU abandoned its apparent early opposition to unions' acceptance of the 2.5 per cent award in cases in which it would be to their benefit. The ACTU and union reaction was sufficient to induce the government to consider reviewing the role of the Commission in the process of making certified agreements under the *Industrial Relations Act*. In 1992 the statute was amended to restrict very closely the capacity of the Commission to intervene or to refuse certification. For all practical purposes, the Commission was required to register any agreement brought to it by the parties. This position has been modified somewhat by the complex provisions introduced by the *Industrial Relations Reform Act* 1993.

In the early 1990s, with the economy in severe recession, and unemployment rapidly approaching crisis levels, the attention of the government was not focused on wage levels. The main concerns of the ACTU appeared to be directed towards unemployment and it pressed the government to adopt expansionary economic policies. A seventh version of the Accord was yet to be formulated, and there was some cause to wonder if it had not gone the way of indexation, work value and comparative wage justice, all of which had seemed to dominate Australian wage determination at times.

The survival of the ALP government at the election of 1993 ensured the relevance of the seventh version of the Accord. Precisely what this document is designed to achieve is not entirely clear, and to some it may seem to represent a further step in a progression towards the entirely ceremonial. Perhaps those Australians wondering, in 1993, whether the nation could either do without entirely, or review the style and title of the office of Governor General, might have extended those same musings to the Accord— is it necessary?

The seventh version states a commitment to increasing employment, and, admirable as that sentiment may be, it is difficult to understand how unions might influence this, other than by the lobbying which one might routinely expect during a period of depression. The Accord's Stakhanovist (see p. 160) tendencies are reinforced, as it commits unions to enhancing international competitiveness and to 'improving productivity and enhancing flexibility',[28] and at the same time to maintaining low levels of inflation. Again, many economists would argue that the levels of inflation in any society are unlikely to be influenced by the actions of trade unions, that the instruments for manipulation of inflationary levels are in the hands of the government and central bank. The Accord also promises to 'continue the process of increasing equity and pay in the conditions of employment for women workers'.[29] As noted above, the first steps in the achievement of equal pay for women began in 1969, almost a quarter of a century before the date of the seventh Accord, and that has not been achieved. To promise a continuation of this attenuated process seems, in fact, to be to promise very little. Perhaps the most interesting of the nine proclaimed objects of the Accord are the four objectives covering arbitration and bargaining. These are set out in Table 16.5.

With customary caution, the ACTU has refrained from commitment to a decentralised system of collective bargaining. It has suggested in fact that where bargaining is difficult, the parties should use arbitration, but should bargain where it is easy. As noted in chapter 17, these conditions ensure that neither bargaining nor arbitration will operate to deliver optimum performance. The ACTU policy requires, apparently, that awards continue to be updated and to underlie the actual rates of pay and conditions of workers. This is a proposal to revert to the practices of the 1960s and much of the 1970s, where over-award pay, usually by agreement, supplemented award rates, a system which was to have been supplanted by the Accord and centralised wage fixing. One of the problems which centralised wage fixing was intended to overcome was the leapfrogging process by which various groups of workers sought to catch up with wage gains won by others, a process popularly believed to create inflation. While the structure of unions has changed over the 1980s and 1990s, it remains an inevitability that some workers will be leaders and some laggers in the matter of pay adjustment, and that many

> **Table 16.5** Accord Mark 7: objectives concerning arbitration and bargaining
>
> - to continue the devolution of wage fixation by encouraging bargaining at industry and workplace levels involving employees and their unions;
> - to ensure that all workers are protected by a safety net of minimum award wages and conditions and have access to arbitration;
> - to provide access to arbitrated safety net award adjustments;
> - to increase living standards over time through:
>   - increases in real wages associated with improving productivity and implementing flexibility at industry and workplace levels consistent with the objective of low inflation;
>   - further improvements in the social wage, including substantial tax cuts, child care improvements, education and training...
>
> Source: ACTU, 'Putting Jobs First: Accord Agreement 1993-1996', March 1993, D52/1993, Processed, p. 1.

unionists will then argue that unequal pay for superficially similar jobs is unjust. Whether the new structure of unionism will allow the leaders to ignore the membership's claims for equality of pay regardless of other factors is matter for speculation.

To the extent that the Commission has accepted the concept of enterprise bargaining, it has, of course, accepted the legitimacy of arguments that enterprise-specific productivity is a legitimate criterion for wage adjustment. No doubt the findings in the *Oil Industry* case, that this could be a legitimate criterion where both parties agreed, or where it had traditionally been a criterion[30] could be interpreted as consistent with this.

One outcome of the seventh Accord was the 1993 amendment to the *Industrial Relations Act* (for further discussion of this, see chapters 12 and 18). The ACTU submitted, at the National Wage hearing of October 1993, that the Commission's existing wage fixing principles should be abandoned in the new era of enterprise bargaining.[31] It is probably not surprising that the Commission again found itself unable to concede to the Accord-originated submission of the ACTU; as much as any institution, the Commission finds it difficult to surrender authority it has gained. Its decision was to adopt yet another principle, the Enterprise Bargaining Principle, and this and its outcomes are discussed further in Chapter 18. The decision in the 1993 case, and presumably its rejection of the ACTU submission, encouraged the government to introduce the 1993 amendments (effective from 30 March, 1994) to the Act, and these are reviewed in chapters 12, 17 and 18 but essentially they provided legislative support for enterprise bargaining, and made arrangements for it to co-exist within the Commission with a separate arbitral system.

These developments appear to have moved the Commission to a position from which it may have less influence on wages in general. Its major wage impact will be on award rates, and for the bargaining sector at least, the upper end of the wage spectrum will be unconstrained by the Commission. Exactly how the labour market will sort itself into bargaining and arbitration sectors is not, at the time of writing, entirely clear, nor are such issues as migration to and from these sectors.

The Commission will retain the capacity to influence minimum wages and conditions through its award network, and the influence on the award minima will necessarily have some effect on the bargaining sector. Only time will show whether the Commission will regain the capacity to administer policies of wage restraint or wage control, but it would seem likely that this will be more difficult after March 1994 than has hitherto been the case. The extent to which the Commission can alter or control the wage structure, the network of wage relationships in the market, seems to have been eroded considerably. As bargaining expertise grows at the enterprise level, it can be expected that wage differences will increasingly be influenced by localised factors which national awards have ignored. One might expect in the next decade to see factors such as internal company profitability and local labour market conditions playing a larger part in wage negotiations.

Whether this form of bargaining is compatible with large and centrally managed unions is a matter yet to be tested. The maintenance of both bargaining and arbitration streams in the revised Commission suggests that an orderly line of retreat from the rigours of bargaining, should that be thought necessary, is to be available.

These amendments to the legislation do add some specificity to the seventh Accord, specificity which was lacking at the outset. The seventh Accord is perhaps a ritualistic observance, rather than a program for action. Had there been no Federal election scheduled for 1993, it may have been judged that renewal of the Accord was no longer necessary. Perhaps the process has become too strongly associated with ACTU officials to be easily abandoned. For a post-election analysis of the seventh Accord see Table 16.6. The practice of some trading enterprises is possibly a model for the ACTU in dealing with an Accord that is growing redundant. When many businesses change their names or corporate logos, they adopt policies of gradually fading out the old and enhancing the new. The introduction of the seventh Accord was certainly a matter for less pomp and circumstance than was that of the original, and it may be that the ACTU is endowing each version with progressively less substance. Like an old soldier, it may be allowed simply to fade away, rather than be abruptly abandoned.

The Accord, which began as a private agreement, came to mean something else entirely, thus Singleton cites Mr W. Kelty, the ACTU Secretary, to the effect that 'The important thing about the Accord.... is what it produces'.[32] Such a view as Kelty's is uncomfortably close to suggesting that ends justify means, and that philosophy is probably not viable in organisations which enjoy even the levels of representative government to be found in Australian unionism.

What, after six revisions, has the Accord achieved? It has fostered a centralisation and co-ordination of unionism, giving the ACTU officials a powerful leadership role. That role, of course does not emerge from any structured or formal changes, and is dependent on the ACTU retaining the confidence of individual union officers.

The Accord has facilitated a considerable decline in real wages, and this has been resented by many. In discussion of the 1991 *National Wage* case position, Mr S. Sharkey, an official of the Building Workers Industrial Union, is cited by Mitchell[33] to the effect that 'what it does is continue the process of transferring even greater amounts of domestic product to profits'. While some may argue that the various social welfare and non-wage benefits that the

Accord delivered, and the concern with the low paid, are counter balances to these criticisms, this could be of scant interest to the workers represented by Mr Sharkey.

The fact is that unionists are not a homogenous mass, the logic of trade unionism is that they do represent discrete sets of interests. Policies which benefit one group of workers may not benefit others, and unionists expect their officials to represent the interests of members first, and those of other unionists later. This is a problem that many unions face in participating in wage control policies. Union members may accept a kinship of interests within the union, but are unlikely to extend it to the entire working class. No doubt recognition of this tendency of unionists is one of the reasons that underlies the policy of the ACTU in seeking to reorganise the Australian unions into a smaller number of very large unions in which it would be difficult for discrete sets of interests to emerge as effective pressure groups.

Only those intimately involved in the Accord processes can know, but to external observers, it does seem that the Accord negotiations have succeeded in establishing the ALP, at least when in, or on the verge of, government, as the senior partner in the union and Party relationship. The marked reduction in disputes, the increased willingness of unions to negotiate and confer, as well as the reduction in real wages, are all likely to confer political advantage on government at the cost of independent action by unions.

It is interesting to compare the ACTU approach to that expressed by Ernest Bevin in 1923, when that great unionist was responding to calls for union moderation during the term of Britain's first Labour Party government: 'There is work to do on the industrial field as well as in the political arena. While it is true that the two are to some extent part of the same effort, we must not lose sight of the fact that governments may come and go, but the workers' fight for betterment of conditions must go on all the time.'[34] Perhaps, as in so many issues, a greater prescience was shown by Marx who, according to Lozovsky '...placed the political all-class tasks of the trade unions higher than the private corporative tasks and, secondly, that the political party of the proletariat must define the economic tasks and lead the trade union organisation itself'.[35]

Has the loss of union independence and the fall in real income been balanced by other gains? This is a difficult question, for while there is no doubt there have been benefits to wage earners during the Accord period, it is not possible to determine whether there is a causal connection between those gains and the Accord. It is the habit of all politicians and bureaucrats to attribute all gains to their policies, and all losses to exogenous factors. Apologists for the Accord will see that it is directly responsible for the growth of jobs in the middle and late 1980s, but not for the enormous growth of foreign debt or the alarming growth of unemployment in the 1990s. If the Accord had any effect on inflation, it was negligible, and this was to have been its major achievement. The nature of economics is not such that one can identify precisely the effect of the Accord. It may be fair to say that it began its life in the beginning of an economic upswing, and that it persisted into a major recession. Perhaps it was the cause of one, both or neither of these economic episodes.

Table 16.6 The Accord: ten years later

Labor's industrial agenda is to be found in Accord

KENNETH DAVIDSON

Contrary to reports about the industrial relations agenda of the Prime Minister, the leopard is not changing his spots, says Kenneth Davidson.

If you believe Jeff Kennett, Paul Keating has stabbed the ACTU in the back, abandoned the Accord process, and is in the process of deregulating the Australian labor market by marginalising industry awards and the Industrial Relations Commission, which sets awards and settles disputes.

During the last weeks of the recent federal election campaign, when Mr Keating rediscovered his ALP roots in order to save himself and his Government, three differences between the two contenders for government were hammered home by Mr Keating—the GST, Medicare and industrial relations.

As Mr Keating clawed his way back from apparent defeat, there was one question at the back of the minds of both those who voted for him and those who didn't: was Mr Keating a "true believer" after all, or was he simply an economic rationalist dressed up in sheep's clothing for the duration of the election campaign?

The majority of those who supported the Labor Government for a record fifth term and those who voted for the Opposition share one thing in common: a deep seated anxiety about who and what Mr Keating is attached to and where he really stands on most issues.

How else to explain the feverish reaction to Mr Keating's speech to the Institute of Company Directors in Melbourne on Wednesday?

According to Mr Keating, "the model of industrial relations we are working towards...is a model which places primary emphasis on bargaining at the workplace level within a framework of minimum standards provided by arbitral tribunals".

This has been described as a revolutionary shift towards labor market deregulation.

Yet before the election the Accord Mark VII was announced.

The agreement said: "The Accord partners support an approach which places the primary responsibility for industrial relations at the workplace level within a framework of minimum standards provided by awards of industrial tribunals."

Mr Keating said: "It is a model under which compulsorily arbitrated awards and arbitrated wage increases would be there only as a safety net."

The Accord Mark VII said: "The provision of a permanent and reliable safety net is the essential foundation upon which industrial relations reforms should proceed... The parties consider that in future the role of industrial tribunals should be increasingly focused on safety net provisions, test case standards, conciliation and dispute settlement. In coming years the Accord partners anticipate that most of the workforce will be covered by workplace agreements."

It is clear that all of what Mr Keating said with respect to industrial relations was either lifted straight out of the Accord Mark VII document or is based on its principles.

Mr Keating also said that "over time the safety net would inevitably become simpler. We would have fewer awards with fewer clauses".

This has been interpreted to mean the safety net would become weaker. Not so.

What this means is that awards must become more coherent in that minimum rates in different industries for similar skills should be similar.

The Industrial Relations Commission is already well down this path. In a decision on the building industries brought down on 8 April the full bench said: "The establishment of constant relativities within and between minimum rates awards ...will continue to be a central issue generally as moves towards decentralisation of the wages system continue. A rational system of award relationships...is necessary to underpin those moves and provide a safety net for further decentralisation."

While big disparities exist between minimum awards in different industries for the same or similar skills, scope exists for leap-frogging wage claims which can undermine wage stability.

The changes being introduced under Accord Mark VII are evolutionary rather than revolutionary.

Accord Mark VII represents a continuation of the shift away from the highly centralised accord process which began with the 1989 [sic] national wage case.

Throughout the long history of federal arbitration there have been cycles of centralisation and decentralisation in wage fixation which, in the case of centralisation, go back at least to 1931 when the basic wage was cut 10 per cent as one of the measures associated with the premiers' plan to deal with the Great Depression. (The measures, which mainly involved cutting Government spending to balance state and federal Budgets, are hauntingly similar to the measures being taken today by state governments whose revenues have been diminished by both the recession and the Federal Government which is "solving" its structural deficit by cutting funding to the states.)

Decentralised wage fixation will not provide the boost to labor productivity its proponents hope nor, of itself, lead to greater income dispersion and inequality that its critics fear.

It is intended that the flexibility will be expressed in negotiations which will link bargaining about wages, skills and career paths in a more pointed and integrated way than is possible under a highly centralised system, rather than lead to wage dispersion as a result of cut-throat bargaining to achieve a "market clearing" wage.

And by retaining Australia's award/arbitral structure as a safety net now, it means that there is a coherent system and structure in place when, as is certain, it will be advantageous for macro-economic reasons to re-introduce the centralised system as it was most recently between 1975 and 1981 and between 1983 and 1987.

And what some of the enthusiasts for a deregulated labor market in which there is direct negotiation between employers and employees have thus far failed to realise is that such a system cannot operate without employees having the right to strike.

Centralised wage fixation, where the economy-wide wage increase is negotiated on the basis of what the economy as a whole can afford to pay, cannot function effectively where individual unions (such as the Pilots Federation) attempt to break out of the wage guidelines by using industrial muscle.

If Accord Mark VII is to be acceptable to the ACTU, individual unions and groups of workers, it will have to have the right to strike (and picket) during the negotiation period and this means that repealing 45D and E of the Trade Practices Act (which outlaw secondary boycotts) has to be on the agenda of the reform process.

Source: *The Age*, 24 April 1993, p. 13.

Conclusion

Notwithstanding the 1994 statutory changes which increase the difficulty the Commission would have in imposing a wage policy, it may be that a substantial attitudinal change would be required before one could be confident that it will not again be used to pursue such a policy. The Commission has not shown itself to be especially good at this, but the main political parties have elected to place their respective attitudes to industrial relations and trade unionism at the centre of political debate, and the Commission affords them an effective public forum in which they may display their ideological positions.

The Accord, like indexation before it, has probably shown that the Commission can maintain a wage policy for what, by international standards, are long periods, but this is due more to the inherent lack of self-reliance in the Australian unions than to any other factor. What it has not demonstrated is that restraining wages is an effective way of resolving Australian economic problems. It is yet to be seen whether the success of the Accord in reducing real wages has sown the seeds for further industrial relations and economic problems.

In other times and other places, unions have shown themselves to have long memories, and in a future boom, Australian unions, not shackled by the bonds of loyalty to the party in government, may set about regaining the loss of wages. Such a campaign would involve disputes and stoppages, and, if successful, would unleash fears of inflation as wages rose.

Notes

1 ABS, *Award Coverage Australia*, May 1990, Catalogue No. 6315.0.
2 *Equal Pay Case 1969*, (1969) 127 CAR 1159.
3 J. George, 'Issues for Women in Enterprise Bargaining', Paper presented to Australian Services Union Women's Conference, 24 July, 1992, p. 9.
4 J.G. Sharpley, *The Economic Consequences of Equal Pay for Women in Australia*, Unpublished M.Ec. Thesis, Monash University, Clayton, 1970, p. 219.

5. ACTU, *Advances in Equal Pay Under the Accord*, D11/93, February, 1993.
6. *ibid.*, p. 11.
7. *ibid.*, p. 9.
8. *ibid.*
9. *Ex parte H. V. McKay*, (1907), 2 CAR 1.
10. Australian Conciliation and Arbitration Commission, *National Wage cases*, (1967) 118 CAR 655.
11. J.R. Kerr, 'Work Value', *Journal of Industrial Relations 6*, March 1964, pp.1–19.
12. *The Vehicle Builders Employees Federation of Australia and others v General Motors-Holden Pty. Ltd.*, (1965), 115 CAR 931–968.
13. *ibid.*, at 948.
14. *ibid.*, at 968.
15. *Electrical Trades Union of Australia and others v. Altona Petrochemical Company Pty Ltd and others*, (1970), 134 CAR 159.
16. *ibid.*, at 166.
17. For discussion of the policy, see J.P. Nieuwenhuysen, 'The Wage Indexation Experiment', in W.A. Howard (ed.), *Perspectives on Australian Industrial Relations: Essays in Honour of Kingsley Laffer*, Longman Cheshire, Melbourne, 1984, pp. 149–164.
18. *Statement of Accord between the Australian Labor Party and the Australian Council of Trade Unions Regarding Economic Policy*, February 1983. Some of these undertakings are identified in chapter 4.
19. *Australian Financial Review*, 29 June 1989.
20. *The Age*, 6 May 1991, p. 13.
21. W.F. Mitchell, 'Wage Policy and Wage Determination in 1990', *Journal of Industrial Relations 33*, March 1991, p. 111.
22. A. Petridis, 'Wage Policy and Wage Determination in 1985', *Journal of Industrial Relations 28*, March 1986, p. 125.
23. G. Singleton, *The Accord and the Australian Labour Movement*, Melbourne University Press, Melbourne, 1990, p. 163.
24. P.A. Riach and W.A. Howard, *Productivity Agreements and Australian Wage Determination*, Wiley, Sydney, 1973.
25. Singleton, *op. cit.*, p. 173.
26. See J. Sloan and M. Wooden, 'The Structural Efficiency Principle in Action-Management Views', *Australian Bulletin of Labour 16*, September 1990, pp. 199–223.
27. Singleton, *op. cit.*, p. 172.
28. See the ACTU document, '*Putting Jobs First*', *Accord Agreement, 1993-1996*, March 1993 D52/1993, Processed, p. 1.
29. *ibid.*
30. *Electrical Trades Union of Australia and others v Altona Petrochemical Company Pty Ltd and others*, (1970), 134 CAR 159 at 166.
31. Australian Industrial Relations Commission, *Review of Wage Fixing Principles*, October 1993, 50 IR 285 at 289.
32. Singleton, *op. cit.*, p. 166.
33. Mitchell, *op. cit.*, p. 116.
34. Cited in E.M. Kassalow, 'The Development of Western Labor Movements: Some Comparative Considerations', in R.A. Lester (ed.), *Labor: Readings on Major Issues*, Random House, New York, 1965, p. 81.
35. A. Lozovsky, *Marx and the Trade Unions*, cited in W.E.J. McCarthy (ed.), *Trade Unions*, Penguin, Harmondsworth, 1972, p. 57.

Further Reading

Equal Pay

ACTU, *Advances in Equal Pay Under the Accord*, D11/93, February 1993.

L. Bennett, 'Equal pay and comparable worth and the Australian Conciliation and Arbitration Commission', *Journal of Industrial Relations 30*, December 1988, pp. 533–545.

D. Brereton, 'Gender differences in overtime', *Journal of Industrial Relations 32*, September 1990, pp. 370–385.
B.J. Chapman and C. Mulvey, 'An Analysis of the Origins of Sex Differences in Australian Wages', *Journal of Industrial Relations 28*, December 1986, pp. 504–520.
P.A. Riach, 'Equal pay and equal opportunity', *Journal of Industrial Relations 11*, July 1969, pp. 99–110.
C. Short, 'Equal pay—what happened?' *Journal of Industrial Relations 28*, September 1989, pp. 315–335.
M. Thornton, '(Un)equal pay for work of equal value', *Journal of Industrial Relations 23*, December 1981, pp. 466–481.

Wage determination

In considering the matter of wage policy, it should be kept in mind that until 1983 the Australian currency exchange rate was fixed. In the current world of floating exchange rates, wage policy has different implications, and must be justified on different grounds to those used earlier. The issue is complicated, but as a first approximation it might be said that the object of wage policy under fixed exchange rates is to defend the national balance of payments. Under a floating exchange rate, the object is directed more to the distribution of national income between wages and profits. At the time of writing, very little had been written to justify the restriction of wages under the flexible exchange rates. The references on wage policy should therefore be read bearing in mind that they refer to an economic regime which has fundamentally altered.

S. Brittan and P. Lilley (eds), *The Delusion of Incomes Policy*, Temple Smith, London, 1977.
R. Gregory, 'Wages Policy and Unemployment in Australia', *Economica*, November 1986 (supplement).
R.J. Hawke, 'The Growth of the Court's Authority' in J.R. Niland and J.E. Isaac (eds), *Australian Labour Economics: Readings* (new ed.), Sun Books, Melbourne, 1975, pp. 16–48.
J.R. Kerr, 'Work Value', *Journal of Industrial Relations 6*, March 1964, pp. 1–19.
K. Laffer, Some Critical Elements in Incomes Policies, *Journal of Industrial Relations 14*, June 1972, pp. 113–124.
J.P. Nieuwenhuysen, 'The Indexation Experiment', in W.A. Howard (ed.) *Perspectives on Australian Industrial Relations: Essays in Honour of Kingsley Laffer*, Longman Cheshire, Melbourne 1984, pp. 149–164.
J. Niland, *Wage Fixing in Australia*, Allen & Unwin, Sydney, 1986.
C. Provis, 'Comparative Wage Justice', *Journal of Industrial Relations 28*, March 1986, pp. 24–39.
E. Russell, 'Wages Policy in Australia', in J.R. Niland and J.E. Isaac (eds) *Australian Labour Economics: Readings*, (New Edition), Sun Books, Melbourne, 1975, pp. 283–312.
J. Staples, 'Uniformity and Diversity in Industrial Relations', *Journal of Industrial Relations 22*, September 1980, pp. 353–362.
M. Watts and W. Mitchell, 'Australian Wage Inflation: Real Wage, Resistance, Hysteresis and Incomes Policy 1968(3)-1987 (3)', Research Paper 88-3, Discipline of Economics, Flinders University of South Australia, 1988.

The Accords

ACTU, *'Putting Jobs First': Accord Agreement 1993–1996*, March 1993, D52/1993, Processed (Accord Mark 7).

Agreement between the Federal Government and the ACTU, 21 February, 1990, Roneoed (Accord Mark 6).

B. Dabscheck, *Australian Industrial Relations in the 1980s*, Oxford University Press, Melbourne, 1989.

P. Lewis and D. Spiers, 'Six Years of the Accord: an Assessment', *Journal of Industrial Relations 32*, March 1990, pp. 53-68.

G. Singleton, *The Accord and the Australian Labour Movement*, Melbourne University Press, Melbourne, 1990.

Statement of Accord by the Australian Labor Party and the Australian Council of Trade Unions Regarding Economic Policy, February, 1993, Roneoed (Accord Mark I).

Questions

Equal pay

1   If equal pay for women was awarded in 1969, why is it necessary for unions and other groups to continue to seek this in the 1990s?

Wage determination

2   Explain the differences between 'work value' and 'comparative wage justice'.
3   Did the Arbitration Commission have its major effect in determining wages, or in influencing their levels? Explain how these two effects arise?
4   How would you justify a policy of centralised industrial relations, including wage determination?
5   How would you justify a policy of decentralised industrial relations, including wage determination?
6   Compare the judgement in the *Total Wage* case of 1967 with Nieuwenhuysen's account of the Wage Indexation Policy and with the original Statement of Accord between the ACTU and the ALP. What are their common factors, and what are their main differences?

The ALP-ACTU Prices and Incomes Accord

7   What is the Prices and Incomes Accord? How does its seventh version differ from its first?
8   Which group is the major beneficiary of the accords, and what is the nature of those benefits?

Exercises

1   Carefully examine each of the Statements of Accord between the ACTU and the ALP.
    a   Identify the objectives sought in each of the statements, and decide the extent to which those objectives have been achieved. You will need to justify your identification of objectives by reference to the documents, and your evaluation of success by external criteria.
    b   To the extent that the objectives of the Accord have changed over the years, identify the changes and suggest reasons for them.

17

Collective Bargaining

Contents

Nature of collective bargaining
- distinguishing features
- government involvement
- necessary conditions
- bargaining power

The technique of collective bargaining
The negotiation process: a behavioural approach
Collective bargaining in Australia
- hybrid processes
- distinguishing characteristics
- collective bargaining and public policy
- union purpose and collective bargaining
- grievance procedures
- bargaining and arbitration: consequences of co-existence
- recent developments: the Industrial Relations Reform Act 1993

Introduction

During most of Australia's industrial relations history, workplace rules, including wages and conditions of employment, have been determined, at least in part, by some form of collective bargaining. Since the beginnings of the arbitral systems, in the late nineteenth and early twentieth centuries, collective bargaining has been adapted to coexistence with compulsory arbitration. The amalgam of the two processes has meant that neither arbitration nor collective bargaining has operated in even a crude approximation to the ideal sense. While each process should offer precision and certainty of outcome, in the Australian long-term experience, neither has been able to do so. A party dissatisfied with the outcome of arbitration will seek to try again by resort to bargaining. One result is that neither labour nor management has become committed in any way to the use of either process, neither will forego an opportunity to obtain a short-term benefit, even though that may involve damaging either one of the industrial relations processes.

Nature of collective bargaining

The process by which workplace rules are developed in most industrial democracies is that of collective bargaining. In addition it is not unusual to find that various forms of conciliation and arbitration are available to labour and management. In some instances they are provided by the state, in other cases the parties pay for these services. While some industrialised nations offer support or protection for a particular industrial relations process, the Australian practice of insisting on compulsory arbitration of disputes is unusual, if not for its compulsion, then at least for its injection of a third party, the arbitral tribunal, into the process.

Distinguishing features

Collective bargaining is a process derived from the familiar business practices of purchase and sale, practices that are bipartite under normal circumstances. Typically, prices are negotiated between buyer and seller, and haggling over prices is the method of negotiation; buyers will threaten to withdraw from the process, and sellers will sometimes offer to vary the quantity or quality of their product to accommodate to lower prices. Any haggling process contains elements of bluff, threat and compromise, and collective bargaining contains all of these, but it has unique features as well.

The factor which serves most obviously to set apart collective bargaining from commercial activity is the commodity in exchange. Managements seek to purchase labour, and they normally negotiate with unions, the representatives of the various owners of labour. However, employers cannot purchase labour itself, they must negotiate to hire people, who in turn will supply their labour. Collective bargaining then is an arrangement to hire people, and this is sufficient to ensure that the transaction will be characterised by emotion, value judgements and a variety of ethical arguments, all of which add a dimension lacking in negotiations concerning the price of machines or raw material. While this human relations aspect is one distinguishing feature of collective bargaining, there is another, perhaps of even greater analytical significance, which sets it apart from the normal run of commercial transactions. Collective bargaining over the terms and conditions of employment of labour is not a one-shot operation, as are most sales. In any particular bargaining episode, the parties involved are in fact bound to deal with each other in perpetuity, rather than being free to seek other buyers and sellers in subsequent transactions. It is an exceptional case in which an employer, failing to reach agreement with a union, would wish to seek an entirely new workforce, and it would be even more unusual if the union concerned did not try to prevent the employer doing this. In realistic terms, there are no short-run alternatives for either employer or employees; they must continue their pre-existing relationship, thus, every episode of collective bargaining is viewed by the parties as being but one link in a continuing chain of negotiations. In these circumstances, the actions of the bargainers may be considerably conditioned by an awareness that the immediate rewards of the fullest exploitation of an opponent's current vulnerability must be balanced against its longer-run effects.

Yet another feature distinguishing collective bargaining from the normal commercial case is that labour invariably participates through its agent, the union, and management not infrequently does so via employer associations, consultants or counsel. It needs to be borne in mind that the inclusion of any of these agents does result in the bargaining process being required to satisfy sets of interests additional to those of the labour and management directly involved. One of the more sagacious comments in the industrial relations literature was Arthur M. Ross' remark that: 'It is the beginning of wisdom in the study of industrial relations to understand that the union, as an organisation, is not identical with its members, as individuals'.[1] That comment might reasonably be extended to point to the lack of identity between employer associations and individual employers.

Government involvement

Collective bargaining, as discussed above, includes the specific oddities of incorporating a human relations attitude, of being a serial process and of normally involving bargaining agents on behalf of at least one of the parties. In addition to these aspects, analysis of collective bargaining is not normally thought to be complete without reference to government's relationship to the process. While the form of government involvement in collective bargaining varies between countries, the situation for most nations is that governments have concerned themselves only with procedural rules. These are rules which govern the processes and practices which the bargainers may adopt, but which do not influence the subjects upon which they reach agreement. An analogous situation applies to the law of contract: it specifies the procedures which must be followed if a commercial contract is to be legally binding, but these rules of process have no bearing on the substance of the contract. It is not the usual practice for there to be any government control, other than the provision of the general commercial code, over the issues on which the parties choose to negotiate, on the substantive rules, as these are called.

In practice, it is obvious that attempts of government in general to interfere in industrial relations processes are the product of political and social custom, as well as of the preferences of particular governments. Some processes of industrial relations may be inherently compatible with such external interference, but collective bargaining is not. That is to say, a government wishing to influence outcomes before an arbitral tribunal can arrange to put its views to the tribunal, but collective bargaining, being an employer-employee relationship, does not automatically facilitate this. Governments may, of course, regulate collective bargaining, but do so by means other than direct participation in the bargaining process.

Necessary conditions

Niland has identified some of the unique elements or necessary conditions of collective bargaining:[2]

- The first element is that conflict resolution is sought primarily through direct negotiation between the parties. Arbitrated outcomes are precluded unless both principal parties voluntarily agree to involve a third party and accept the arbitrator's decision. This may arise from the law or from the internalised preferences of the principal parties.
- The second element is substantial uncertainty at the commencement of bargaining as to the final outcome.
- The third element is good faith, the parties have a philosophical commitment to direct negotiation as the appropriate process for dispute resolution.
- The fourth element is that the parties themselves decide how they will resolve any impasse, which includes the right to strike and the right to lock-out, at least until such time as their continued disagreement over settlement terms threatens public health and safety.
- The fifth element is that the parties participate from reasonably even power bases. Power is defined as the ability to determine unilaterally the terms and conditions of work.

Niland notes that even in countries where collective bargaining is the dominant process and underwritten by public regulation these five elements or conditions may not be met in every instance. This highlights the importance of distinguishing between the process viewed from a theoretical or idealised standpoint and its operation in any particular industrial relations system. In addition to the necessary conditions, Niland identifies desirable elements which enhance the prospect of genuine resolution. They include the appropriate resources and skills in negotiation practice and the involvement of third party neutrals. Two other features usually associated with collective bargaining where the process is the subject of public regulation are:

1. a clear distinction between interest and rights disputes: the agreement exhausts the negotiable issues for the duration of the agreement; and
2. there are formal procedures for determining bargaining units.

Bargaining power

Collective bargaining is a process which operates within, indeed arises from, a power relationship. The power implicit in the right to strike and in the right not to employ labour gives rise to collective bargaining. One model of bargaining power is that developed by Chamberlain and Kuhn.[3] They define bargaining power as the ability to secure another's agreement on one's own terms. The bargaining power of the union at any time is the employer's willingness to agree to union terms. The employer's willingness in turn depends on their assessment of the cost of disagreeing with union demands, relative to the cost of agreeing with them. Thus the cost to each party of disagreeing or agreeing with the other is central to the bargaining power concept. Union bargaining power at any time may be expressed as:

$$\text{Bargaining power UNION} = \frac{\text{Employer estimate of cost of disagreeing with union demands}}{\text{Employer estimate of cost of agreeing with union demands}}$$

So if the employer assesses the cost to the enterprise of disagreeing is high, relative to the cost of agreeing, the union's bargaining power is enhanced. This would be so for example if a strike was very costly to an enterprise and the union's settlement terms were relatively inexpensive.

The employer's bargaining power may be similarly expressed:

$$\text{Bargaining power EMPLOYER} = \frac{\text{Union estimate of cost of disagreeing with employer offer}}{\text{Union estimate of cost of agreeing with employer offer}}$$

To assess *relative* bargaining power both equations must be known. The party with the lower ratio has greater bargaining power. In other words, union bargaining power is greater than the employer's if the difference to the employer between the cost of disagreement and agreement on union terms is proportionally greater than the difference to the union between the cost of disagreement and agreement on the employer's terms. In practice of course neither party knows the other party's estimates of the cost to that other party of disagreeing or agreeing. It is part of the skill of negotiators to maximise the volume and accuracy of this information. The gathering of intelligence both from within the bargaining forum and from other sources is an important means of establishing what is in the mind of the opposing party and its constituency. It is also part of the negotiators' skill to make it difficult for the opposition to make correct estimates of their true position, hence bluffing is a common tactic used to influence the other party's assessment in a favourable way. On the other hand, if negotiators assess the other party is making an unjustifiably optimistic or unrealistic assessment then a direct disclosure of the factual position may be appropriate. The changes in information which result from these tactics and exchanges cause assessments of costs to change and therefore relative bargaining power may also change.

This definition of bargaining power means if agreement is reached it must be on terms which represent for each party a cost of agreement equal to, or less than, a cost of disagreement. It means also if disagreement persists it will be due to terms (the demand or the offer) which for at least one of the parties represents a cost of disagreement equal to, or less than, a cost of agreement.

The purpose of coercive pressure, such as a strike, is to raise the other party's costs of disagreeing with your demands relative to the costs of agreeing with them and thereby increasing the likelihood of settlement on your terms. Such action is designed to inflict economic or political harm on the other party. A strike may result from a union initiative or from an employer decision to 'take a strike'. The latter involves the employer holding firm with an offer the employer knows will not be acceptable to the union. A strike is costly to both parties and shrewd negotiators will resort to it or allow it to occur, as the case may be, only when they assess it will pay dividends and only when less costly methods will not produce the desired result. In Australia, these alternative methods include negotiation, conciliation, arbitration as well as less costly forms of direct action. The capacity to strike, or to take a strike, is not an unlimited resource. An appreciation of its scarcity should lead the parties to use the resource wisely.

Bargaining power may be altered by changing either the cost to the other party of disagreement with one's own terms or the cost to the other party of agreement with one's own terms. Thus from the union perspective, bargaining power can be increased by increasing the cost to the employer of disagreeing with union demands or reducing the cost to the employer of agreeing with the union's demands. Chamberlain and Kuhn qualify this conclusion by noting either party may not always be able to change one determinant independently of changing the other determinant. If a union reduced its wage demand for example, this would reduce the cost to the employer of agreeing. The reduced demand could, however, simultaneously alter the resolve of the union membership to take coercive action in pursuit of the lower increase. It may become a goal not worth striking for. In the event the employer made such an assessment of likely union behaviour, the employer's costs of disagreeing would be reduced. The union's bargaining power would depend on the employer's revised estimates and, on balance, may be reduced rather than increased. This also demonstrates that bargaining power varies with demands, that is bargaining power is relative to what is being bargained for.

The notion of 'cost' adopted by Chamberlain and Kuhn is broad. They use the term in the sense of a disadvantage and thereby include monetary and non-monetary costs. Because of the diverse matters which may constitute a cost it is not possible to reduce all costs to a common denominator, that is, to dollars. Chamberlain and Kuhn conclude that this 'very incommensurability of certain issues makes possible the changing of minds that might be unpersuaded if all significant issues could be reduced by an economic calculus to a numerical balance or imbalance'.[4] They point out that if decisions are to be made and action taken then some sort of balance must be struck and that this will occur through the exploratory process of bargaining. Table 17.1 draws on the Chamberlain and Kuhn discussion and lists some factors affecting costs of

Table 17.1 Factors affecting bargaining power

- Nature and size of union claim
- Union capacity and inclination to strike
- Union density
- Availability of alternative employment
- Ideology of union and employer representatives
- Nature of employer product(s) and product market conditions
- Labour market conditions
- Historical relationship between the parties
- Substitutability of employee skills
- Public opinion
- Government ideology and opinion
- Inter-union and inter-employer relationships and support
- Size of union and employer strike funds
- Laws relating to industrial action
- Negotiation skills of employer and union negotiators

Source: Adapted from N.W. Chamberlain and J.W. Kuhn, *Collective Bargaining*, (3rd ed.), McGraw-Hill, New York, 1986, chapter 6.

disagreeing and agreeing. The list includes non-monetary as well as monetary factors or variables and the former will in turn affect monetary or economic calculations. Some of these factors are also discussed below when the technique of collective bargaining is considered.

As suggested above, bargaining power changes over time. It is not an inherent attribute of the parties nor a constant available for use in each dispute. In fact it will change during the course of a dispute, for example if and when a bargaining process commences and the parties eventually move a little way from their respective preferred positions. In other words, as some shift occurs in demands and offers, so estimates of relative costs of disagreeing and agreeing alter. As already explained, those estimates will alter dramatically when coercive action begins. Bargaining power is influenced by (objective) environmental factors such as the state of the labour market, characteristics of the industry or occupation and public opinion, as well as internal factors such as the extent of hegemony within union or employer ranks, and the skills of their respective negotiators. The estimates of costs will vary with the influences bearing upon the individuals doing the estimating and Chamberlain and Kuhn note that the political structure of the enterprise and the union is relevant here. This concept of bargaining power takes into account the total situation: the strike capacity or resistance capacity of the parties and the economic, political and social circumstances to the extent these affect the cost of agreement or disagreement. The concept can also be applied to situations involving joint decisions of more than two parties.[5]

Table 17.2 contains quotations from both principal parties and third parties during the 1986 Victorian nurses' strike. This dispute occurred in an environment in which industrial tribunal processes and tribunal wages policy were pre-eminent. Nonetheless, it was a trial of strength strike in the tradition of systems of public regulation of industrial relations based on collective bargaining. In such systems, where strikes over interest disputes have legitimacy, relative bargaining power is recognised as critical in determining outcomes.

Table 17.2 Bargaining power: the 1986 nurses' strike

Despite our best efforts and those of the volunteers and remaining nursing staff, we are very concerned patient needs are not being met. The situation is deteriorating daily.

> Resident Medical Officers
> Prince Henry's Hospital
> *The Age*, 14 November 1986, p. 3

It is not our reading of the situation... They are likely to inflame the situation. We want people to just grind their teeth and keep on keeping on.

> Dr John Mathew
> AMA President
> *The Age*, 14 November 1986, p. 3 &
> *The Australian*, 14 November 1986, p. 2

Things are unmanageable. You can't run hospitals without nurses. There are sick people with threatening conditions unable to get into hospitals.

> Donald Macleish
> President, Royal Australasian
> College of Surgeons, *The Age*
> 19 November 1986, p. 1

We will win. We haven't been out here for 20 days to lose...

> RN, St. Vincent's Hospital
> Picket Line, 19 November 1986

For years we've been the dedicated little girls who did the dirty jobs and did what they were told...

> RN, Cabrini Hospital
> Picket Line, 21 November 1986
> *Transcript* video: *Running Out of Patience*
> Producers: Serena Everill and Chris Brown

RANF demands that if the ACTU decides to make submissions to the Victorian IRC, such submissions be confined to total support for RANF (Vic Branch) and its members' claims. As the ACTU proposal seriously disadvantages claims in Victoria and other States and Territories, it is rejected completely.

> Resolution, RANF secretaries
> and industrial officers, 23 November, 1986

...The ACTU President, Simon Crean, strongly criticised the RANF leadership, saying it had not been sensible when it rejected ACTU peace proposals last weekend... 'It's a proposal that can work and it has been adopted by the HEF' he said.

> *The Sun*, 27 November, 1986, p. 3

Our claim stands fully consistent with the principles adopted by the ACTU and... we will stand ready, willing and available to take instructions from the ACTU and the VTHC in respect of any amendments that might be required in respect of our claim.

> HEF submission
> Industrial Relations Commission
> of Victoria, cases 156 & 190/1986
> *Transcript*, 28 November, 1986 p. 8

The horrendous, heartless nurses' strike in Victorian reached an even more critical state yesterday with more than 20 hospitals about to run out of clean linen because of escalation of picket line action by the nurses' union. The Victorian government should have no compunction in breaking these picket lines and doing for the patients the duty that the nurses have shirked. This strike does not any longer have the support of the ACTU. It has been criticised by Mr Crean. The nurses should go back to work immediately and continue talks with the government before even more serious damage is done to the patients and to their own professional honour.

The Weekend Australian
Editorial
29-30 November 1986, p. 16

The Treasurer, Mr Jolly, yesterday denied that the government could have made the same response and ended the dispute weeks ago. He said it was only after the ACTU had made its submission to the commission that it had helped them 'identify a number of key problems'.

The Age, 6 December, 1986, p. 1

...Mr. White said last night the Government wanted to thank medical staff, state enrolled nurses, volunteers and registered nurses who remained on the job for their 'tremendous efforts' in keeping the hospital system running. Meanwhile ALP President Gerry Hand yesterday called off a special ALP administrative committee meeting that had been scheduled for tomorrow to discuss the nurses' dispute. But Mr. Hand said the Government should have agreed much earlier in the dispute to direct negotiations with the RANF.

The Sun
20 December 1986, p. 3

There were probably only two winners. One was the ACTU, which, through the skilful intervention of its secretary, Bill Kelty, not only helped to settle the dispute, but confirmed its status as the power-broker in Australian industrial affairs...The other winner was the Australian industrial community which for years has regarded Victorian arbitration and labour relations as the worst in the land. Their assessment was confirmed.

Peter Stephens
The Age, 22 December 1986, p. 4

No other group of workers in this country has won against those odds, in the face of the range of forces that were arrayed against nurses in this dispute.

Michael O'Grady
RANF Industrial Officer 1986-1988
Interview, November 1989

Trades Hall was a disgrace. There were people bleeding on the picket line. Not literally I mean but they were being mentally destroyed and other unions couldn't stand up and be counted. I was ashamed. While this continues unions are not dying from the outside, they are dying from the inside.

Daniel Gillespie, HEF Shop Steward
Western General Hospital
Interview, August 1991

Source: C. Fox, *Enough is Enough: The 1986 Victorian Nurses' Strike*, Australian Studies in Health Service Administration No. 73, School of Health Services Management, University of New South Wales, 1991.

The technique of collective bargaining

Where the traditional highly-systematised world of American collective bargaining survives, each new episode in the process begins automatically when the existing contract expires. In Australia, in the absence of wage policy, a new round of bargaining may be triggered by a variety of occurrences, the most common being a shift in the employment conditions of a comparable group of workers, but a variety of other events can have this effect. An increase in the vulnerability of the employer, a sudden increase in living costs, a rise in the employer's profitability, or a shortage of labour may all stimulate fresh demands.

In the most formal circumstances, the process will begin with the union serving the relevant management with a written series of demands—or log of claims. The management might indicate that it requires time to consider its response, and occasionally the first item negotiated is the length of time that will be acceptable to each side before a response is made. The management response to the initial demand is the first step in a bargaining process which will culminate in an agreement.

Managerial responses to union demands may vary from a truculent assertion that all the demands are impossible, to the more conciliatory response that some common ground can certainly be found. Among sophisticated parties, both demand and response are conditioned by the perception of relative power, by pressures exerted by principals, and by expectations about the future. It is only among the inexperienced or the ingenuous that anger or other emotions dictate demand or response. This is not to suggest that emotions are absent from the bargaining of sophisticates, it is rather that they are used to influence outcomes in deliberate and rational ways.

The nature of collective bargaining requires that the initial demand and offer establish the boundaries of differences between the parties. The ensuing bargaining process is intended to close the gap between offer and demand, each party going some way towards the other's position. A union will reduce its demands in the expectation that this will in turn encourage management concessions. The nature of bargaining is that each party moves a little away from its initial, most preferred position, each doing so in the hope of inducing its adversary to move toward that preferred position. This is a form of bartering, with, for example, a union offering to refrain from strikes and bans in the future in return for management raising its wage offer now. Agreement is of course reached when demand and offer coincide.

This view of the process suggests that, whatever may be a union's genuine goals, it does well to serve wider-ranging claims, pitched at a level beyond its actual aspirations. If the union does this, it has the capacity to concede a good deal before eroding any of its actual needs. Similarly, management's initial response to the union log will be to offer considerably less than it is really prepared to concede, a tactic which employers occasionally reinforce by serving counter-logs on unions. Clearly, these tactics are to a large extent self-cancelling, with the reduction of inflated demands being exchanged for the increase of deflated offers.

It is most unlikely that agreement can be reached without each party having given some ground which originally it felt important to retain. This phase of bargaining, occurring after the tactical elements of demand and offer are concluded, is the stage at which the real forces of the process are revealed. In this zone of hard bargaining neither party concedes on any point simply because the other has offered a concession which needs to be matched. Bargaining over the central elements of the agreement takes place against a background of the threat of economic coercion. While collective bargaining can be depicted as a process of reasoned persuasion, obviously management responds to the union claims in the first instance only because the union does have the capacity eventually to impose costs if its demands are not met. Similarly, the union responds to management pressures because costs can be inflicted on the union and its members in the same way.

The costs in question are, ultimately, the costs of a work stoppage, either a strike or lock-out. This results, of course, in a loss of wages for employees, and a loss of production and revenue for employers. Unless labour and management do have recourse to the work stoppage it is unlikely that bargaining would be fruitful, for there would be no reason for a party, believing it would be disadvantaged by making a particular concession, to do so. In fact, in the absence of this coercive power, it is unlikely that bargaining would even commence. To indicate however that the freedom to strike, to lock-out, or to induce the strike, are essential to collective bargaining, is not to indicate that such rights will be exercised.

The implications of work stoppages are easy to exaggerate or misinterpret, and it should be remembered that they are non-existent only in the most repressive societies. Unions in a capitalist economy will insist on their right to strike, just as employers will insist on their right not to employ labour. It is the simultaneous existence of these union and employer rights which gives rise to collective bargaining, for when the two parties each have power, they are all but certain to insist on dealing with each other on the basis of that power. In the application of industrial power, unions and employers mirror business behaviour in general, that is, they accept conditions that are to their detriment only in situations in which they lack the power or resources to resist.

Because the fundamental determinant of bargaining outcomes is vulnerability to the effects of the strike, each party must resort to strategies designed to reduce its own vulnerability and to increase that of its opponent. The matter of timing is critical in industries in which there are seasonal peaks and troughs, and many Australians will recall that the brewing industry saw strikes become an annual ritual, as summer and the holiday season approached. The unions concerned were acutely conscious that as this was the season in which sales peaks were achieved, the employers were most anxious to avoid production interruptions.

It is frequently possible for employers and unions to adopt tactics which reduce the impact of the work stoppage upon themselves. In some industries employers can build up inventories so that sales and revenue flows may be continued while the strike persists. This enables the employer to withstand the strike without financial penalty, whilst striking employees of course receive no wages. However this may be a two-edged sword, if inventories can only be built up by plants working extra hours, thus providing employees with increased overtime earnings and so increasing their financial ability to withstand a long strike. Employers may adopt other devices including subcontracting, out-ordering, or revenue-pooling with unaffected employers to minimise the strike's impact. Obviously, the employer's ability to call on the support of fellow employers in such ways is limited, for the inter-employer relationship is primarily one of rivalry rather than fraternity.

For employees, the cost of work stoppages is mainly in the form of lost wages. Unions in many countries seek to hedge against these costs by building strike funds, that is, by establishing a fund to tide members over periods when wages are not paid. This strike pay is normally a good deal less than the weekly wage, but does allow members to hold out longer than they would otherwise be able to do. Australian unions do not normally accumulate strike funds, preferring to rely on collections during the strike. As it is unusual for all members, or even most of them, to be on strike at one time, Australian unions usually levy their employed members for weekly donations to help support their fellow members on strike. At times other unions will come to the aid of striking workers with financial donations.

It is not unusual for other unions to refuse to deal with the employers of any union members on strike. They have refused to make deliveries; to handle goods produced by the struck employer; to supply goods or services to that employer and, under the threat of strike, have placed pressure on that employer's major customer or supplier to prevent their dealing with him or her. In Australia in 1977, in an attempt to reduce the union movement's resort to these tactics, the federal government amended the *Trade Practices Act* to remove the exemption from secondary boycotts which unions had formerly enjoyed. The consequence was that unions supporting striking workers by direct or indirect pressure on employers not directly involved could be liable to severe penalties. Since the passage of the *Industrial Relations Reform Act* 1993 the statute law relating to union secondary boycott activity is contained in the *Industrial Relations Act* (see chapter 5 for details).

Unions have been unhappy with these provisions, but have been unable to secure their repeal or substantial revision. Very few employers have shown much enthusiasm for applying these provisions, but where they have been used, as they were in the *Mudginberri* case,[6] the outcomes have not provided much comfort to unions. It may be that in the future, some of the unions which have relied on the assistance of industrial pressure from other workers will have to consider accumulating strike funds to allow them to maintain pressure on employers for long periods. There is, however, no current indication that such funds are being built up, despite ACTU advocacy of the need for this.[7]

These various employer and employee tactics are aimed at extending their periods of endurance of the work stoppage, and can do no more than postpone the day on which costs will become intolerable. No matter how large the employer's inventory may be, therefore, or how large the union's strike fund, a compromise must eventually be sought as the cost of the stoppage begins to outweigh any possible benefit to be derived from it.

Collective bargaining strengths and, consequently, relevant tactics, are often determined by the industry's characteristics. There are some industries in which a strike has very little influence on the performance in the long run of the employer. For example, in the case of mining operations, a strike merely extends the time required to deplete the resource, and thus usually has a negligible effect on profit. Consequently, effective use of the strike in this industry is often possible only when the employer is contractually required to meet delivery targets. At the other extreme are those industries in which revenues foregone during the work stoppage can never be fully recovered. It is an old adage that one cannot sell yesterday's newspaper; thus, a work stoppage in the newspaper industry will create a permanent loss of revenue.

Until a government/employer alliance virtually destroyed their union in 1989, the domestic airline pilots had shrewdly exploited their employers' vulnerability to strikes. Airlines were unable to regain foregone sales and, rather than allowing their expensive equipment to remain idle for long periods, management usually conceded to the pilots' demands. Defeat of the pilots in the 1989 airlines dispute certainly conferred a political advantage on the ACTU and the government, which were then keen to protect the wage restrictions imposed on wage and salary earners through the Accord, but only time will show whether it has inflicted a harmful blow on unions in general.

Collective bargaining clearly involves considerable skill, and bargaining power must be supplemented by the ability to exploit that power. It is widely believed that, in the United States, the experienced and capable people who undertake highly-developed forms of collective bargaining, are fully aware, even before they begin negotiations, of the settlement position that will finally be reached, and that they can predict accurately each step along the way. Notwithstanding their mutual knowledge, the parties meticulously bargain out each point, not to satisfy some ritual, but to make certain that nothing is conceded unnecessarily, that all possible gains are made, and that any unanticipated weakness on the opponent's part is fully exploited. There are real skills to negotiation, and although skilful bargaining will not overcome a party's industrial weakness, it can reduce the extent of exploitation of these weaknesses. It is also possible that the concerns of some employers were that the mutual understandings enjoyed by industrial relations executives and union officials could lead to a neglect of the best interests of management, that the predictions of the parties would become self-fulfilling prophesies. Concerns of this kind may have encouraged some managements, when the economic and political climates were appropriate, to adopt human resource strategies which are a good deal less accommodative to unionism.

The foregoing discussion suggests that collective bargaining, as a rule-making process, does not necessarily favour either labour or management. Rather, it implies that those who have the most bargaining power, and the greatest skill in using it, are likely to be the successful parties. Bargaining power is a difficult concept with which to grapple, and is not be confused with size or wealth. Many large and wealthy organisations are also powerful in the industrial relations sense, but this is by no means an inevitable correlation.

The Shop Distributive and Allied Employees Association, for example, has for many years been one of the largest Australian unions, but it has typically been less able to coerce employers than have been smaller unions such as the Seamens Union of Australia or the Waterside Workers' Federation. Industrial relations power is a dynamic concept, and the relative powers of unions and employers can, in response to changing environmental variables, shift quite markedly over time. A union with strong influence over some employers in an industry will not necessarily have the same degree of power over all of them. Surprisingly, within a specific industry, it is often the management in a precarious financial position which exercises the most power, for its resistance is stiffened by knowledge that while a strike may possibly ruin the company, conceding to the union's demands will certainly do so. Under these conditions the union may then view the cause as not worth winning.

The negotiation process: a behavioural approach

An influential conceptual framework for analysing the negotiation process is that developed by Walton and McKersie in the United States in the 1960s. They take as given the goals and structures of the principal parties and focus on the rule-making process regarding it not in deterministic terms but as 'a goal-directed activity involving a set of actions which are capable of intelligent planning and skilful implementation'.[8]

The authors distinguish four related activities or sub-processes each with its own function:

1 distributive or share bargaining;
2 integrative or problem-solving bargaining;
3 attitudinal structuring; and
4 intra-organisational bargaining.

Together these 'hypothetical constructs' cover all the behaviours observed in negotiations. Each sub-process has its own set of tactics which are developed in detail by Walton and McKersie. The tactics are not considered here but the sub-processes are explained and illuminated with illustrations from the disputes discussed in chapters 3 or 4.

'Distributive bargaining', the dominant activity in the employer-employee relationship, refers to 'the complex system of activities instrumental to the attainment of one party's goals when they are in basic conflict with those of the other party'.[9] The function of this sub-process is to resolve pure conflicts of interest. The subject matter, termed 'issues' by Walton and McKersie, is areas of common concern in which the objectives of the two parties are assumed to be in conflict.[10] The term 'fixed sum game' and the phrase 'I win, you lose' are used to describe the result of this sub-process which divides the limited and contested resources between the parties. An example of distributive bargaining, the sharing of a finite quality of assets between employer and employee, is the bargaining which occurred during the Broken Hill strike of 1919-1920 (see chapter 4). The decentralised and unregulated bargaining relating to over-award wages in the metal and engineering industry in the 1960s would also meet the definition of distributive bargaining (see *Metal Trades Work Value* case, chapter 4).

'Integrative bargaining' refers to the system of activities instrumental to the attainment of objectives which are not in fundamental conflict with those of the other party and which therefore can be integrated to some degree.[11] It is also known as problem-solving or co-operative bargaining. This sub-process has a different negotiating emphasis because the function is to find interests which are either complementary or common and to solve problems confronting both parties.[12] The settlement is one in which both parties benefit; gains are made by one party which do not equate with losses for the other party. The result is reflected in the term 'variable sum game' or the phrase 'I win, you win'. In this sub-process the parties will not necessarily see the problem in identical terms but each will be bargaining toward a similar end: the reduction of a harmful situation. An example of integrative bargaining, at least in terms of the intent of the policy makers, is the bargaining occurring in the context of federal tribunal wages policy from 1987 to 1993. The 'problem' was identified as low productivity and inefficient work operations and the solution, reflected in the tribunal's policy framework, covered the prospect of both changes in work practices and work organisation and of benefits to employees in the form of increased wages and improved career paths. (This policy is discussed in detail in chapter 18.) A case in the health sector provides another example of the sub-process of integrative bargaining: the 1985-1986 negotiations between the Cain Labor government in Victoria and the Nursing Federation in what became known as the nurses' career structure case. The integrative component of the negotiations, which concerned wide-ranging union claims, related to overcoming a shortage of specific groups of nurses in metropolitan teaching hospitals:

1 registered nurses in high technology, critical care areas such as intensive care units, coronary care units and operating theatres; and
2 charge nurses.

There was a high level of co-operation between the negotiating teams in relation to this problem. The government wished to structure the new award to maximise pay increases for these targeted groups to improve recruitment and retention. Although the Nursing Federation was seeking higher wage rates, at all levels, than the government was offering, on ordinal ranking, that is, which classifications should receive the greatest gains, the parties were at one.[13] (See chapter 4 for a discussion of the subsequent dispute.)

Walton and McKersie suggest that typically any set of negotiations includes many items which can be pursued by some combination of distributive and integrative bargaining. Both these sub-processes are joint decision-making processes relating to economic issues and the rights and obligations of the parties. They are the 'generally recognised content' of industrial relations negotiations.[14]

The third sub-process, attitudinal structuring, concentrates on the function of negotiation to influence relationships between the parties. The subject matter of this sub-process is 'desired relationship patterns'. In contrast to the two sub-processes identified above, it is a 'socio-emotional inter-personal process designed to change attitudes and relationships'.[15] Walton and McKersie use this category to refer to activities associated with the development of the qualitative relationship between the parties. This may range from collusion to direct aggression. The writers recognise that the existing relationship pattern is influenced by many more enduring forces, such as the technical and economic contexts, but they suggest the negotiators can and do take advantage of the interaction inherent in negotiations to produce changes in attitude. There are no examples of this activity available from the disputes discussed in chapters 3 and 4, that is of comments made within the negotiating forums. The nurses' strike however provides examples of public comments outside the negotiating forums which, while not meeting the strict definition, do approximate to this sub-process. Statements may be designed to produce a positive attitude change, for example strengthening the opponents' position within the opponents' organisation or conferring status on the opponent. A negative attitude change may be the objective and one tactic here would be to weaken an opponents' position in their own organisation. The following statement from an individual speaking from the employer position seems designed to have such a negative effect. At an early stage of the nurses' strike a Ministerial adviser 'questioned the union leader's motives, suggesting they might be trying to bring the government down because of another political agenda. He said if the government gave in to the nurses' militant industrial tactics outside the arbitration system, it would be ringing its own death-knell and the nurses should cease their action to allow proceedings to continue before the tribunal: This is their only option unless they are determined to cause more suffering and even deaths in pursuit of political objectives'.[16]

The focus of the attitudinal structuring sub-process is behaviour at the bargaining table and this will in part define the spirit of the relationship and impact on behaviour during the operation of the agreement. Walton and McKersie also point out that these activities, relating to attitudes and feelings may impact on the substantive settlement.[17]

The fourth sub-process, 'intra-organisational bargaining', is the system of activities which bring the expectations of each constituency into alignment with those of their negotiators.[18] The function of these activities is to achieve consensus within each of the parties to the negotiations. The activities are therefore those undertaken by the negotiators within their own organisations to establish priorities, reconcile diverse, and perhaps competing interests and justify the settlement. In the 1992 APPM (Burnie) dispute[19] there were a number of unions involved and negotiations were led by the ACTU President Martin Ferguson in collaboration with full-time officials from those unions. At one stage the chief union negotiator announced that a settlement had been reached. These terms were rejected by a mass meeting of unionists in Burnie. The subsequent negotiations included local union representatives and after some revision of the terms of the agreement it was endorsed by the rank and file members. It is unlikely that such an event would occur in intra-organisational bargaining among the unions at Broken Hill where the union negotiators also work the mines thereby minimising the risks of differing priorities and expectations between the negotiators and their principals. It has been suggested that the union log of claims in the Broken Hill strike of 1919-1920 contained an item, the abolition of contract mining, which was strongly opposed by the then radical leadership but which generated little opposition from the rank and file. Significantly, this item in the log was not achieved in a settlement which saw most of the union claims realised.[20]

The nurses' career structure case of 1985-1986 provides an example of the neglect of the sub-process of intra-organisational bargaining with dramatic adverse consequences. In the case of the union, membership involvement in the formulation of the claim and during the protracted negotiations was minimal, confined to inconsequential, limited participation in formulating benchmark job descriptions. Further, some information provided by the Federation to the membership was misleading, intentionally or not. The leadership did not seek membership ratification of the negotiated elements of the new award. One reason may have been that the closing stages of the negotiations coincided with an election for the key position of Secretary. The challenger, Irene Bolger, was successful and she campaigned on the basis of opposition to the new award structure then being negotiated. Thus the union electoral process was the means of re-aligning membership and leadership objectives in relation to wages and award structure. The employer, the Health Department of Victoria, similarly neglected intra-organisational bargaining. The Department provided little information to management on the new award prior to concluding negotiations and did not counter misleading aspects of the union material. The sole consultation with managers at the 'coal-face' was an eleventh-hour meeting with a small group of line managers (directors of nursing) from teaching hospitals. This selective consultation reflected government priorities. The final draft of the new negotiated award structure received no testing with the employer 'constituency' that is hospital management, not even a 'table top' test. Further, there was no *ex ante* guide to implementation. The net result of the bipartite neglect was a four month battle over the implementation of an award structure which was not only badly crafted but which lacked support among the principals who had to live with the unacceptable product every working day.[21]

Each of the above four sub-processes had been discussed by other writers prior to Walton and McKersie's work. Part of their distinctive contribution was to provide a synthesis of all elements of the negotiation together with a comprehensive treatment of the internal dynamics of each sub-process.[22]

Collective bargaining in Australia

The process of making workplace rules by collective bargaining is widespread in Australia, for there are few workplaces in which the process is entirely absent. It is very difficult to identify features common to every set of negotiations, for each may be unique in its rituals and practices. On the other hand, as discussed above, there are factors that are essential to the operation of all collective bargaining, and consideration of these aids understanding of the Australian situation.

Hybrid processes

The collective bargaining practised in Australia has usually differed in a number of ways from the theoretical model discussed above. Niland[23] identifies forms of direct negotiation used frequently in Australia which breach at least one of the necessary conditions of collective bargaining: administrative negotiation, strategic negotiation and referred negotiation. 'Administrative negotiation involves the parties meeting to resolve terms and conditions that are already foregone conclusions by virtue of tribunal decisions made in the broader industrial environment.' This process fails to meet the necessary condition of uncertainty regarding substantive outcomes. Niland states that the strong commitment to comparative wage justice and flow-ons generally has made administrative negotiation the main variety of direct negotiation. An example is the negotiation which followed the 1981 Metal Industry Agreement. The increases determined in negotiations between the Metal Trades Industry Association and the then AMWU and other unions covered by the *Metal Industry Award* flowed to most awards within eighteen months and in most cases by negotiation rather than arbitration. The Metal Industry increases of $25 per week plus a further $14 per week six months later became in other industries a foregone conclusion, with uncertainty in outcomes confined to operative date. This occurred during a period when no formal tribunal policy concerning wage fixation was operative although a deputy president of the federal tribunal presided over the Metal Industry negotiations, acting as a conciliator.

Strategic negotiation occurs when one or both parties fully expect the matter to finalise in compulsory arbitration, but see some benefit in negotiating the issues in the early stages. This process fails to meet the necessary condition of good faith, a philosophical commitment to the bargaining process. Niland explains that in this form of negotiation, the parties 'go through the motions'. This form of negotiation may result from a legal obligation to participate in a conciliation phase. It may also be sought by principal parties:

1 to avoid (anticipated) criticism from a tribunal that the parties made no genuine attempt to resolve the dispute themselves;
2 as a means of prolonging the *status quo*; or
3 as a tactic to maximise knowledge and understanding of the other party's case in preparation for the advocacy phase.

An example of strategic negotiation is the negotiations on wages for nurses which preceded a lengthy tribunal hearing in Victoria in 1985 and 1986. Escalating industrial action generated a wages offer from the major employer, the Victorian government, but the union, the then Royal Australian Nursing Federation, had already lodged a claim with the tribunal and held a belief that the process of arbitration would provide an advance on any government offer.[24]

'Referred negotiation occurs when an arbitrator suspends his or her handling of a case by instructing the parties to attempt a negotiated settlement.' This is one option available to conciliators under federal legislation; it provides *inter alia* that tribunal members may arrange 'for the parties or their representatives to confer among themselves at conferences at which the member is not present'.[25] This process fails to meet the necessary condition of the parties themselves shaping any third party involvement, because it is the arbitrator who determines the nature of his or her involvement and the stage at which negotiation will occur. These hybrid processes illustrate what is a pervasive feature of industrial relations in Australia, the co-existence of bargaining and arbitration. The consequences of this co-existence are discussed in a later section.

Distinguishing characteristics

The appropriate place to begin examining collective bargaining might be with the question of the identities of the bargainers, and this is one problem of the Australian practice. It is especially apparent in the case of unions that the identities of the decision makers are often obscure. In a technical sense, a union mass meeting makes a final decision on whether or not to accept a proposed collective agreement. The meeting is normally addressed by the union official who has undertaken the negotiations, and he or she typically recommends that provisions should be accepted or rejected. While it is part of the skill of an experienced union officer to be able to anticipate the reactions of members, and thus the officials' recommendations are rarely rejected, mass meetings do sometimes refuse to ratify draft agreements. Such a refusal poses some difficulty for union negotiators for, as elected officers, they incur a considerable political risk by advocating their electorate's acceptance of an unpopular course; but if they do not achieve ratification of the proposals concerned, their credibility will suffer with the employer officials with whom they deal. As the business enterprise always does contain a party with ultimate authority, and is not constrained by democratic procedures, employers sometimes become impatient with union officials who cannot give a binding acceptance or rejection of a proposal. Employer representatives in these cases often want to deal with a higher authority, and will not accept that the ultimate authority is the mass meeting.

After 1983, when the ACTU/ALP Accord began to dominate industrial relations, the identification of key union decision-makers became even more difficult. ACTU officials gained very considerable influence, and this came close to control, over individual union officials. It is difficult to understand how mass meetings of unionists could be persuaded to accept the Accord-based tribunal outcomes which reduced their real wages. One must hypothesise that either ACTU and union officials possess the power to induce working people to undertake mass self-sacrifice, or, alternatively, that mass meetings were not asked to endorse such decisions. It also appears that while ACTU officials were careful to make it clear that they could not speak on behalf of any union, they were, in fact, able to influence all of them. Whether key decision-making power has passed to the ACTU, and whether its increased influence is permanent, are questions which can only be answered in the future. The employer now seeking to identify the critical decision-making force in unions has no clearer direction in 1990 than he or she had in 1970. It is clear only that there are several influential forces.

Imprecise identification of negotiating power arises from sources other than the nature of union government. In a great many Australian cases, multi-union plants are involved in bargaining, and unions participate on a coalition basis. Where this occurs, one union official will speak on behalf of a number of unions, although the arguments mounted, offers accepted and concessions given will normally have been approved by the representatives of other unions involved. Coalition bargaining of this kind involves three main areas of danger, and the first is simply that although the union officials concerned may reach agreement on the acceptability of proposals, their consensus may not be reflected among their members. This is a more complicated version of the problems faced by individual union officials in dealing with their own members. The second problem that coalition bargaining can entail is that the union representatives may not have given a sufficiently precise delegation of authority to their spokesperson who may begin dealing with issues for which some of his colleagues are not prepared. The third major problem of multi-union bargaining is that the concessions which unions are forced to make may have a differentiated effect on members of various unions, and as the bargaining unfolds, one group may find it is either disadvantaged, or that its bargaining power has been unexpectedly enhanced. In these circumstances, the coalition may crumble as one party holds out to secure its own, rather than the group's advantage. Whether multi-union bargaining is undertaken by shop stewards, by a committee of union officials or by a union peak council (such as a Trades and Labour Council or the ACTU), the same risks of disintegration of the coalition are involved. For over sixty years, the Barrier Industrial Council, the peak body of Broken Hill's unions, had demonstrated, in dealing with the local mining industry, an impregnable solidarity. The three mining unions were led by the Council President at bargaining sessions, with any differences they had being resolved elsewhere. However, in 1986, even this rock of solidarity was broken as the miners' union, allying itself with its national Federation rather than the local body, refused to accept the Accord-based agreement signed by the other unions. Those aware of the history of the Barrier Industrial Council might want to conclude that if this monument to solidarity has shattered, no bargaining coalition can be free of the risk of disintegration.

While coalition bargaining may seem to economise on the time spent in negotiation, this may be illusory, at least so far as union officials are concerned. The employer may need to undertake the process only once, although it may be long drawn out compared with a single union negotiation. Each union however is forced to present the argument to its own membership at separate meetings, but before reaching that stage, there will certainly be a difficult and involved process of inter-union bargaining to determine a common strategy. While coalition bargaining has many attractions, it can be a difficult process.

Multi-union bargaining is probably not the norm for Australian industry, negotiation between an employer and one of the several unions represented at his or her plant is as frequent. The series of agreements reached by several unions in one plant are unlikely to be unrelated to each other, even though they are achieved through independent processes. The separate agreements are achieved with the one employer whose needs, for the most part, may not vary between unions. Where separate agreements are made, they will contain many identical provisions, concessions granted will be of the same order, and pre-existing relativities of wage rates and other rules will normally be maintained. The incidence of individual or multi-union bargaining at particular sites may be a product of many factors; often a major reason is that every union involved cannot make representatives available at the same time. In other cases, inter-union rivalry may be involved, it may be customary to use individual or group union bargaining, or it may be that unions perceive that their power to extract concessions is enhanced by one or other method.

On occasions unions encounter a series of problems which arise from the diffusion of managerial authority. Even though there is an ultimate authority in a business enterprise, union negotiators do not always find access to that authority easy and, of course, where unions deal with groups of employers in industry-wide agreements, the ultimate authority may be as difficult to identify as it is in the unions. The union negotiators seek, as do managers, to deal only with principals, those who have the authority to concede particular issues. Most employers restrict fairly closely the authority of their bargaining representatives, but, within an individual firm, if a union is persistent in its bargaining demands, this can usually secure access to the executive with authority sufficient to provide the necessary concession. In industry-wide, or multi-firm bargaining, there can be real difficulties for unions seeking to identify the location of bargaining authority. Employers typically participate in multi-firm bargaining through a negotiating committee made up of the relevant industrial relations managers, and chaired by the representative of the largest firm. Since it is unlikely that each firm involved will empower its representative to the same extent, it may be impossible for the committee as a whole to provide the concessions demanded of it. In such cases the negotiating committee becomes a sounding board for top managements who retain for themselves the capacity to make compromises and concessions. Unions, needless to say, find this experience irritating, and relations with the negotiating committees are often poor. As a consequence, industry-wide agreements are often little more than a series of general understandings, which then are buttressed by local agreements setting out precise rules relevant to each of the workplaces concerned.

From the foregoing discussion, it will be apparent that collective bargaining is practised on differing scales throughout industry. There is a degree of ambivalence about this aspect which suggests that Australian collective bargaining is far less orderly and predictable than the highly-structured models in countries such as Canada, Germany and the United States. This requires an initial process whereby an appropriate bargaining unit is selected, and that bargaining unit will remain until formal procedures are undertaken to have it redefined. The appropriate bargaining unit is selected after negotiations between labour, management and a specialised government agency which may make a final determination. Once identified, the bargaining unit can be presumed likely to remain unaltered for a considerable period.

A major source of instability in Australian collective bargaining is that there are no accepted processes for determining a bargaining unit, nor is there any certainty that once a particular group of employers and employees is covered by a single agreement, an agreement of the same scope will be repeated. Just as there are no formal processes required to adopt such a unit, there are none required to abandon it either. This instability in a most fundamental aspect of collective bargaining makes it all but impossible to plan industrial relations policies and to develop the accommodative relationships between negotiators which are essential if satisfactory outcomes are to be achieved.

If imprecision regarding the bargaining unit is one area in which the general structure of Australian collective bargaining has been unsatisfactory, another problem which has plagued Australian collective bargaining is the imprecision of the duration of the agreement. This was rarely specified, and the consequent uncertainty of duration of agreements robbed the parties of a major benefit of collective bargaining: the known period of precisely defined rights and obligations and the consequent ability to plan carefully for future negotiations. The federal *Industrial Relations Act* now requires, in the case of certified agreements for example, that 'the agreement specifies the period of operation of the agreement'.[26] The Victorian *Employee Relations Act* provides that, 'Every industrial agreement shall be in a form approved by the registrar and for a term to be specified therein not exceeding three years from the making of the agreement'.[27] While these represent an attempt to deal with a major problem of Australian collective bargaining, only experience will determine whether they have succeeded in providing a precise duration to collective agreements. It is possible to be pessimistic about this issue, for the very strong forces of comparative wage justice, or flow-on, have accustomed the parties to expect almost instantaneous wage adjustment on the movement of a key wage rate, regardless of any agreement that might exist.

If indexation of wages for cost-of-living changes were to return permanently to industrial relations, this would offer some hope that the federal provisions concerning agreements may be effective. In earlier years, very few collective agreements provided for cost-of-living adjustments of any form. A result was that, in periods of inflation, the rates specified in agreements very quickly became inappropriate, and this could be remedied only by re-negotiating the agreement. One might expect the next generation of agreements will provide for adjustment in accordance with *National Wage* cases, or similar criteria. The *National Wage* case decision of October 1991[28] for example did, in setting out conditions for approval of enterprise agreements, provide for such adjustments to be made.

Australian collective agreements are often silent on large areas of the labour-management relationship. This can place collective bargaining under considerable strain, as labour and management often take action with respect to these 'uncovered areas', each arguing that it is not in breach of any agreement. While there is no universally agreed solution to problems that stem from this kind of imprecision, imprecise rules alone do not make processes unworkable. Mature collective bargaining relationships in which the parties are determined to maintain a workable environment, do evolve techniques which permit satisfactory solutions to the problem of non-regulated areas. The simplest of these is that a disadvantaged party should accept the situation for the short-term future, but resolve to ensure that the matter is raised when the parties re-negotiate these agreements. Another relatively common practice is for the parties to refer any disputes on uncovered items to some form of private arbitration. Other parties develop techniques of continuous bargaining. Arrangements of this kind are of course the outcome of the determination of the parties to ensure that their agreement operates efficiently, a characteristic not typical of the Australian experience. The more usual process in Australia has been to apply strikes and work bans, and possibly eventually to resort to the conciliation procedures of the Commission.

Collective bargaining and public policy

Because collective bargaining is essentially bipartite, exclusion of government from the process is almost axiomatic, but in Australia it does not sit easily with the preferences of governments or public expectations. While collective bargaining has a long and respectable history in Australia, its presence has not permeated the public awareness as has the more common arbitral process. The arbitral proceedings are widely reported, possibly because they are readily accessible to journalists, and they have acquired a status of correctness, and convey an aura of probity that is, quite wrongly, denied collective bargaining. It is scarcely surprising, therefore, that when the Industrial Relations Commission determined in the October 1991 *National Wage* case, to approve enterprise bargaining, it did not indicate its intention of vacating the field. The Commission would evaluate agreements before approving them, to ensure they did not conflict with the Commission's principles for wage determination. This decision so constrained the parties that the process was effectively tripartite, and resembled genuine collective bargaining only in the style that was adopted.

As noted in chapter 15, in earlier times, there was also some connection between the form of collective bargaining then practised and the (then) Conciliation and Arbitration Commission. The parties were free to reach collective agreements, and could, if they wished to do so, have their agreements registered by the Commission, or they could, subject to a few conditions, have them converted into consent awards. The parties may have had many motives for doing this, but unions often did so since an incorporation of provisions into an award was a cheap and easy means of spreading their effect to a wider group of workers, and at worst would provide a more powerful precedent than an unregistered agreement. This provision created only a formal connection between bargaining and arbitration, for the two processes were kept quite distinct, and it was entirely feasible for one award to incorporate some provisions reached by each process.

Initially, the *Industrial Relations Act* 1988 provided, in the then s.115, for a greater degree of Commission involvement in the certification of agreements reached without the assistance of the Commission than for its predecessor the Conciliation and Arbitration Commission. Amendments in 1992, apparently influenced by Government and ACTU dissatisfaction with the Commission's *National Wage* case decision in April 1991, reduced the tribunal's control somewhat. The October 1991 and October 1993 *National Wage* case provisions, in the form of the Enterprise Bargaining Principle and the Enterprise Awards Principle respectively, required even more input from the Commission although traditionally the Principles have been more susceptible to rapid change than the legislation. Neither the Commission nor the government's legislation has indicated the presence of any enthusiasm for unfettered collective bargaining: they may, it is true, find the process of bargaining to be preferred to that of arbitration, but each is reluctant to permit the parties unconstrained pursuit of their own goals. This remains the case following the passage of the *Industrial Relations Reform Act* 1993 (see below).

Union purpose and collective bargaining

The arbitral process can inhibit the development of collective bargaining in indirect ways, and one of them is in its influence on the structure of unions. While those who are determined to maximise possible benefits from collective bargaining could probably achieve this with any form of union structure, the fact is that Australian unions were formed and shaped under the influence of the various arbitral statutes, and in particular the *Conciliation and Arbitration Act* (largely by ss 132, 142 and 158 of that Act). The resultant forms of unions owed more to the needs of the arbitral system, and to various long forgotten political constraints, than they did to bargaining logic, and they owe nothing at all to employee choice or aspiration. While union structure is unlikely to be a critical factor in the development of collective bargaining, it is to be kept in mind that, as it has developed in response to an arbitration system, it may not be entirely conducive to collective bargaining.

The structure of unionism may be a less enduring inhibition to the development of collective bargaining than is the motivation, or essential purpose of unionism. Successful bargaining unions focus on optimising the working conditions of their current dues-paying membership. Because their function is to extract benefits from employers, they can afford no excursions into areas in which employers cannot provide the concessions required.

The case was argued by Marx, and perhaps more directly by Lenin,[29] that the economic problems with which workers struggled, could not be resolved by other than political means, and consequently unions should abandon the pursuit of benefit through extracting concessions from employers, but they should involve themselves in the broader issues of political reform. Lenin's argument, and it depends heavily on acceptance of Marxist economics, has never been fully accepted by the majority of Australian union leaders, but all of them have accepted the view that the concerns of unions must extend beyond the boundaries of the workplace. Many of them have seen concentration on wages, hours and working conditions as being too narrow, and the ACTU/ALP Prices and Incomes Accord reflects that view.

The great theorist of capitalist trade unionism was Selig Perlman who argued[30] that the essential purpose of unionism, and its appeal to working people, was that it should concern itself exclusively with their job needs alone. He noted, however, that unions were frequently influenced by those whose concerns went much further than this, and he would have included the political revolutionaries, of whom Lenin approved, as well as other social reformers. Unions which took action outside the realm of wages, hours and working conditions, Perlman regarded as being in the grip of those he described as 'intellectuals', who sought to divert unions from their natural tasks. The wide range of concerns addressed by every Australian union, from international affairs to civil liberties, would suggest to Perlman that the power and resources of unions were being misdirected. Important as these issues might be, they are not the outputs which workers require from unions, and they are not concessions which the coercive strength of unions can wring from employers.

If the Leninist doctrines have not convinced Australian union leaders to eschew the struggle for economic benefits for members, neither have they been convinced by the Perlman approach, that those benefits are the sole business of unions. The Australian unions are as deeply involved in political processes as they are in industrial relations, and the support of the ACTU for a policy which steadily reduced real wages through the 1980s is testament to that. This is not, of course, to argue that the policy was right or wrong, merely that it is directed to a broader area than gaining concessions from employers in the narrow areas of wages, hours and working conditions, and perhaps directed to the concerns of a wider group than dues-paying union members.

The question is whether this approach of Australian unions is appropriate to collective bargaining. Is it likely that unions which will refrain from applying industrial relations pressure to support a political party will be effective and reliable in collective bargaining? Might not such unions be equally likely to apply pressure and disruptive tactics to disadvantage another political party? Collective bargaining will only operate effectively where the process is directed to gaining benefits that are within the control of the bargaining parties, and it could not be argued that Australian unions have restricted themselves to such matters. In order to make a successful transition to collective bargaining, their fundamental character would need to change from their current concern with broad social issues as well as members' welfare, to a narrower concern with the benefits to members which each of their employers can give them.

Unions are unlikely to undergo major shifts of character of this kind. Whether a union, at inception, chooses to follow a narrow path, adapting to the world of business and providing service to members alone by extracting concessions from employers, or whether it concerns itself with a broader notion of welfare, seeking social and political reform to benefit the working class, or the whole of humanity, once it has selected that path, it is unlikely to change. The organisation will build, as all institutions do, processes and methods which secure its survival as an institution, and this creates, automatically, defences against challenge to its policy directions. The staff, the alliances and affiliations formed, as well as the established practices of the union will all point in the direction of maintaining the course that has been followed. This is a tendency which characterises most organisations in the non-profit sector, where the absence of the commercial ethic allows organisational interests to dominate those of owners or members. To shift the general direction of union philosophy in the short or medium term would require a revolutionary change, and that is improbable. The implication of this is that if Australian unions are based on philosophies, resources, alliances and institutions which are less compatible with the needs of collective bargaining than are more business-oriented approaches, then it is less than likely that they will change.

An alteration to the Industrial Relations Commission's policy, that is the wage fixing principles, or even a change to the *Industrial Relations Act*, would be a stimulus insufficiently powerful to overcome the personnel and processes of the unions. This is not to say that the motivation of Australian unions is such that they are not compatible with collective bargaining. It is rather to suggest that they will not, in the foreseeable future, change so that collective bargaining will be their central concern, the process which they will nurture and accept as their major purpose. If unions cannot make that commitment to collective bargaining, it is not likely that the process will be more successful in the future than it has been in the past.

Collective bargaining is not a process which is intrinsically favourable to either labour or management, but it ensures that the stronger party usually fares better than the weak. As industrial power balances shift between labour and management, their attitudes towards collective bargaining may shift too. At the beginning of the twentieth century, for example, Australian employers opposed the introduction of compulsory arbitration because it neutralised their superior bargaining power, but in the 1960s, they supported it because they sensed that unions enjoyed a bargaining advantage. While parties may often wish to dress their tactical preferences in protestations of principle, the fact is that every party's preferences towards any industrial relations process will be based on the advantages they believe that process will bring to them, thus preferences will switch as power balances alter.

It follows that a government policy to support compulsory arbitration or collective bargaining will necessarily advantage one of the participants in the short term. Generally, compulsory arbitration confers some advantage on the weaker, and bargaining allows the stronger to exploit its power. A government seeking to be neutral in industrial relations may adopt either of these processes, and be fully aware that in the short term, one party will be assisted by the chosen policy. Should the government choose to support collective bargaining, its neutrality, in the medium to longer term, would be secured by ensuring that it placed no obstacles in the way of the waxing and waning of the industrial relations power of either party. As much of the law and practice of arbitration has imposed such barriers—the basis of judicial arbitration is to render relative power irrelevant—it would be unwise to attempt to force bargaining to operate under laws designed to facilitate conciliation and arbitration.

It is apparent that the workers' right to strike is integral to collective bargaining, just as is the employer's right to induce strikes or to lock out workers. Recognition of the right to strike carries no implication about the frequency of strikes: it is not axiomatic that once the right to strike is recognised it will be exercised frequently. It might be expected, however, that more extensive collective bargaining in Australia would encourage the use of forms of strikes different from those usually experienced. As the collective bargaining process involves work stoppages as instruments of coercive pressure, it is likely that the typical length of stoppages would be greater than is the current experience. If the highly systematic and regularised form of American, Canadian, German or Japanese collective bargaining were adopted, strikes would be considerably more predictable than they are at present, for they would be applied only at the time of contract re-negotiation.

In countries in which collective bargaining is the norm, the strike is an important union resource. It is the pressure applied to force concessions from managers and in a sense represents the working capital of the bargaining union. A union, if prudently led, will be concerned to use this working capital only where it brings worthwhile returns. In practice, as explained in chapter 3, Australian workers and their unions have often used the strike as a protest, a demonstration, or for symbolic purposes. In contrast, a union committed to the pragmatic course of collective bargaining would eschew these purposes, since every day of strike motivated by these concerns is one less day of strike available to wrest concessions from management. Probable effects on strikes as a result of a general shift to collective bargaining would include an increase in their duration, a lessening of their frequency, and an improvement in strike forecasting.

Grievance procedures

There is considerable international evidence that collective bargaining moderates, even eliminates, the tendency, still apparent in Australia, of striking first and negotiating later. The area in which this is most pronounced, and in which it might prove most intractable, is in the matter of administering the established collective agreement. The fact that an agreement has been made does not eliminate the possibility of subsequent disagreement over interpretation, correct application of the agreement, facts in particular cases, or over issues not expressly covered by the agreement. The existence of these potential areas of disagreement requires some procedure for their resolution, otherwise they will only be resolved by a trial of strength, a remedy which negates the very purpose of the agreement. Most collective bargaining countries have developed grievance processing techniques with varying degrees of formality and complexity. In the United States there has evolved an elaborate technique of grievance processing, where attempts are made at varying hierarchical levels within the firm and union to agree on solution to these immediate problems. The process is one where, failing agreement, the matter is referred to progressively higher levels of authority. The critical factor in its success is that those referring the matter to the next level are viewed by both labour and management as making public their failure in a critical area of responsibility. The successful supervisor or union official is one who resolves these issues, and so avoids having to refer them to the next level, and who succeeds in resolving them in favour of his or her own side, for a referral up the line is an admission of failure.

The inclusion of similar disputes procedures in Australian awards and agreements is not uncommon. The Workplace Survey found that a formal grievance or dispute settlement procedure existed in 49 per cent of 2004 workplaces surveyed (all with 20 or more employees). The incidence of formal procedures was significantly higher in the public sector (79 per cent of workplaces) than in the private sector (40 per cent). Organisational structure was also a significant factor in incidence of procedures: 55 per cent of workplaces that were part of a large organisation had formal procedures while only 26 per cent of single workplaces did so. The incidence of formal procedures by industry and by number of employees per workplace is set out in Table 17.3.

Table 17.3 Incidence of formal grievance/dispute settlement procedures by industry and employment size (AWIRS)

Industry	Per cent of workplaces
Mining	52
Manufacturing	44
Electricity, Gas & Water	70
Construction	51
Wholesale & Retail Trade	35
Transport & Storage	57
Communication	82
Finance, Property & Business Services	41
Public Administration	78
Community Services	64
Recreation, Personal & Other Services	32

Employment size	Per cent of workplaces
20-49	39
50-99	50
100-199	60
200-499	76
500 or more	86
All Workplaces (N=2004)	49

Source: R. Callus, A. Morehead, M. Cully and J. Buchanan, *Industrial Relations at Work—the Australian Workplace Industrial Relations Survey*, Commonwealth Department of Industrial Relations, AGPS, Canberra, 1991, p. 312.

In each workplace the manager with the most day to day responsibility for workplace industrial relations was interviewed. Thus, except in the case of small workplaces, the responses are from functional specialists rather than line managers. The reasons identified by these respondents for introducing a formal grievance/dispute settlement procedure are set out by industry in Table 17.4. They illustrate the influence of industrial tribunals on workplaces, in this case on particular procedural rules. The managers were asked which of the statements in the table best explained why the grievance procedure was introduced.

The most frequently cited reason for introducing such procedures, an award requirement, reflects the promotion of grievance procedures by

Table 17.4 Reasons for introducing a formal grievance or dispute settlement procedure by industry (AWIRS)

	Required By Award %	Agreement Between Management and Unions at Workplace %	Agreement Between Management and Unions Eslewhere %	Initiative of Workplace Management %	Initiative of Management at a Higher Level Beyond Workplace %	Weighted Number of Workplaces '00s
All Workplaces (20 or more employees)	34	13	16	14	21	148
Industry						
Mining	(21)	(21)	(18)	(26)	(14)	(2)
Manufacturing	49	29	3	13	7	29
Electricity, Gas & Water	23	12	31	12	22	4
Construction	56	13	18	5	7	7
Wholesale & Retail Trade	31	6	14	21	28	19
Transport & Storage	20	23	13	20	23	7
Communication	31	6	37	2	23	6
Finance, Property & Business Services	31	8	5	25	31	13
Public Administration	40	13	15	16	17	11
Community Services	25	7	27	14	27	41
Recreation, Personal & Other Services	37	13	21	5	25	8

Unweighted N = 1148

( ) Relatively few respondents (20 to 50) so estimate may differ substantially from the true value.

Source: R. Callus, A. Morehead, M. Cully and J. Buchanan, *Industrial Relations at Work—the Australian Workplace Industrial Relations Survey*, Commonwealth Department of Industrial Relations, AGPS, Canberra, 1991, p. 313.

industrial tribunals since the March 1987 national wage decision. Inclusion of grievance procedures in awards became a widespread 'concession' by unions in return for arbitrated wage increases in the period 1987-1989. An increasing incidence of grievance procedures from this source may result from the inclusion in the 1988 *Industrial Relations Act* of a requirement for certified agreements to include a grievance procedure. It is also possible that the category 'Agreement between Management and Unions Elsewhere' has included tribunal influence exercised during the course of conciliation.

The survey estimates revealed a high incidence (forty per cent) of non-use or very limited use of grievance procedures, as shown in Table 17.5.

Table 17.5 Frequency of grievance procedure use by industry (AWIRS)

	All the Time	Most of the Time	Some of the Time	Rarely	Never	Weighted Number of Workplaces
	%	%	%	%	%	'00s
All Workplaces (20 or more employees)	16	27	18	29	11	150
Industry						
Mining	(19)	(29)	(23)	(28)	(0)	(2)
Manufacturing	14	29	21	26	10	29
Electricity, Gas & Water	22	22	21	25	10	4
Construction	16	32	19	26	7	7
Wholesale & Retail Trade	20	26	18	21	15	19
Transport & Storage	15	29	35	17	4	7
Communication	(19)	(47)	(19)	(9)	(6)	(6)
Finance, Property & Business Services	11	30	25	29	5	14
Public Administration	18	25	18	30	9	11
Community Services	16	22	13	36	13	42
Recreation, Personal & Other Services	17	24	4	42	13	8

Unweighted N = 1158

Source: R. Callus, A. Morehead, M. Cully and J. Buchanan, *Industrial Relations at Work—the Australian Workplace Industrial Relations Survey*, Commonwealth Department of Industrial Relations, AGPS, Canberra, 1991, p. 312.

The estimates in Table 17.5 are based on management responses to the question: 'How often do you think the grievance procedure is actually used to deal with grievances?' The authors of the Survey Report state that effective operation of procedures requires either the commitment of local managers or, in some cases, the application and insistence of employees and the unions. They also note that of the 63 per cent of workplaces that indicated the procedure was used, 37 per cent said it had not been used in the previous year despite the fact that grievances occurred at most workplaces. The Report concluded that the low level of regular use suggests grievances may be dealt with effectively by informal methods.[31]

Managers were also asked: 'In the last year which issue has the grievance handling procedure most often been used for?' In 26 per cent of workplaces the procedure was most often used for disciplinary issues, that is an employee, and perhaps union, response to management action. The Survey found that 73 per cent of workplaces had a formal disciplinary procedure with 85 per cent of employees in the survey population being covered by these arrangements.[32] The 'personality conflict' category was the issue for which grievance procedures were most frequently used in 19 per cent of workplaces (31 per cent in wholesale and retail trade and 33 per cent in community services). It may be that this 'issue' includes conflict over various aspects of job control. This was discussed in chapter 3 as one of the enduring causes of industrial conflict.

A caveat attaching to these responses, which is recognised in the Survey Report, is that specialist managers may be unaware of grievances successfully resolved at a lower level in the line and that their observations are based on issues which reach a higher level in the grievance procedure. However no information was sought in the Survey about the level, or stage, at which grievances were resolved or the associated matter of the extent of reliance on industrial tribunals for final resolution. Anecdotal evidence suggests that a considerable problem in Australia has been in having the parties use the processes in seeking a genuine dispute resolution. Casual observation reveals that in Australian industrial relations, the indicator of failure may not be the referral of the matter to the next hierarchical level, but of conceding anything at all. Since the typical disputes procedure in Australian awards culminates in a referral to the Commission, the effect is generally to rush through the intervening steps so as to have the matter taken to arbitration. It is here, before the arbitrator, that concessions are made, and one can only assume that concessions and compromises made in the presence of a Commission member are thought not to carry the stigma of concessions made elsewhere.

Obviously disputes procedures will not work unless there is a genuine desire by both parties to use them positively. The effectiveness of the procedures cannot be improved by altering their structural features, but only by the participant's genuine attempts to resolve differences as smoothly as possible. If every issue is taken through all the steps of the disputes procedure, it can only be concluded that at least one party is not prepared to let the mechanism function effectively. The successful American experience, for example, has been that the overwhelming majority of grievances is resolved at the first or second step of the process.

Australian disputes procedures, and by inference, collective bargaining, will only be viable if unions and management accept their joint responsibility to make every step in the process effective, and only if each side attempts to make the resolution of industrial disputes an integral part of the duties of all its representatives. A very important aspect of grievance handling is that both parties must recognise that disputes are only resolved by each giving some ground, and are exacerbated by a stubborn refusal to concede anything. This often mutual intransigence explains why Australian disputes procedures are so rarely effective and become no more than a circuitous route to arbitration. The parties regard it as weak or wrong to concede anything, and will only give ground when ordered to do so by an arbitrator. In short, in such cases the disputes procedures do not function because the parties will not allow them to.

Bargaining and arbitration: consequences of co-existence

The general failure of disputes procedures to provide genuine alternatives to arbitration is but one reflection of an overall problem besetting Australian collective bargaining. This arises from the fact that there is relief from the rigours and realities of bargaining. A party can refuse to adhere to the terms of a bargained agreement and suffer no consequences of that behaviour, for it can resort to the arbitral machinery for future settlements. In an industrial society in which there is no alternative to collective bargaining, the agreement must be observed simply because there is no other means of making workplace rules. The parties who rely solely on collective bargaining are forced to develop an appropriate bargaining relationship, and to protect that relationship by ensuring it is not exposed to excessive pressures. If either party breaks an agreement merely to satisfy immediate ends, the resultant strain will usually destroy that relationship. Because, in most countries, there is no alternative process to collective bargaining, that destructive behaviour is avoided.

In periods of coexistence of Australian arbitral and bargaining processes neither has functioned in an ideal or even adequate manner. The fact is that a party dissatisfied with results from either process would usually seek to use the alternative, and no force could compel the parties to consider themselves bound by the agreements reached in either venue. This ensured that a party which felt it had the industrial strength to improve its position would not be bound by an adverse arbitral decision, and one which believed it had fared badly at collective bargaining would seek to better this result via arbitration. Australia has seen cases in which some satisfactory amalgam of the two processes emerged. These are, however, developments which owe their existence very largely to the personal qualities of those parties involved, and must therefore be seen as ephemeral.

The fundamental problem of coexistence of arbitration and collective bargaining remains notwithstanding the 1993 changes to legislation which are designed to facilitate enterprise and workplace bargaining (see below). It is a dubious proposition that, if either party, dissatisfied with a bargained outcome, was determined to have resort to the arbitral services of the Commission, it could not achieve this. The past experience has been that the coexistence of the two processes has increased the numbers of failures to abide by the results of either. In those countries in which collective bargaining has worked well, some part of its success lies in the fact that it is the only means of dispute resolution available. In such situations, union leaders convince members that to fail to honour their current contract will cause future negotiations to be difficult and protracted; indeed, it may lead to a complete breakdown of relations. An argument of this kind has rarely been accepted by Australian unionists, for they believe that arbitration is always available to them. If relations between management and union were hostile and uncompromising, the Commission has nevertheless issued an award, and an award could be used to replace the broken agreement. The Australian unionists are not accustomed to the dominance of either arbitration or collective bargaining, but are prepared to resort to either should it offer short-term advantages. While it may be true that compulsory arbitration has often depended on a supplementary process of collective bargaining to give it relevance, it is also true that collective bargaining cannot mature as a determinate process so long as it is possible for the parties to escape from it by resorting to arbitration.

Where it exists, the intermingling of arbitration and bargaining makes for confusion in the analysis of Australian industrial relations and creates considerable difficulty in predicting outcomes. Many observers apparently do not understand the extent to which the two processes coexist, and public policy is frequently directed to creating an industrial relations environment dominated by a single process. Yet external endeavours to remove either bargaining or arbitration from the industrial relations practice are unlikely to meet with much success. The parties develop institutions and expectations which revolve around resort to this mixed system, and to change it would first require that the institutions and expectations were changed. Should a different process emerge, it is unlikely to grow out of public policy; rather, it would evolve because existing processes were not meeting the needs of labour and management.

This mixture of processes is also confusing to both observer and student, although it may be clear to the parties involved. After all, they have established the processes by which they operate and presumably can agree on nothing more suitable to their needs. If rule making processes suit those who are directly involved in them, it matters little whether they conform to any particular logical or analytical method.

Australian problems with collective bargaining are the result of an immature local system, rather than being inherent in the process itself, and that immaturity is in very large part the outcome of the simultaneous existence of the arbitral and bargaining systems. While the arbitral procedures remain accessible to parties who have been reckless, impatient or stubborn in bargaining, then maturity will evade those who do not seek to acquire it. That satisfactory and sophisticated bargaining is not beyond the capacities of Australian employers and employees is nowhere better illustrated than in the Melbourne newspaper printing agreements. Employers and printing employees in this industry, used only collective bargaining, and it would appear to have served them well. In a sector of industry characterised by quite rapid and considerable technological change and a consequent decrease in labour requirements, the parties negotiated mutually satisfactory arrangements to cope with this, and did so with a minimum of disturbance.

The experience of the Accord years has distracted attention from the fact that the long-term experience is that the Australian conciliation and arbitration processes cannot exist without a supplementary process of collective bargaining. The Accord saw the coercive capacity of Australian unions effectively neutralised, but such a situation is likely to be a temporary expedient, and it is remarkable that the process endured as it did. Arbitration could stand alone only for as long as unions could be dissuaded from challenging its awards, and in opening the way for some form of collective bargaining in October 1991, the Commission accepted that a mixture of bargaining and arbitration would ensue. While it is common to depict the processes of collective bargaining and compulsory arbitration as competing alternatives, and indeed they are incompatible to the extent that their coexistence prevents either from delivering optimum performance, Australia's experience is that, within limits, one process is supportive of the other.

The Australian processes developed mainly because generations of Australian arbitrators, union leaders and employers have learned to adapt their immediate objectives and policies to the institutional environment in which they exist. The parties have also learned to adapt their interpretation of externally set policies, those of government, employer councils or union peak organisations, to the limits set by this institutional framework. The framework is not immutable, but it changes slowly, and if collective bargaining is to replace arbitration, the institutions concerned would ensure that the change was accomplished via a gradual drift from one process to another, rather than by a sharp discernible shift. This slow progression would allow the satisfaction or restatement of personal and institutional needs and goals in the relatively long interim period. Legislative changes introduced in 1993 provide explicitly for the coexistence of collective bargaining and arbitration. The provisions specific to collective bargaining are now considered.

Recent developments: the Industrial Relations Reform Act 1993

As explained in chapters 12 and 15, this complex legislation secures the award system as a 'safety net' while promoting enterprise and workplace bargaining through a newly-established Bargaining Division of the Commission. Thus the bargaining takes place in the context of a pre-existing federal award which continues to apply except to the extent that it is inconsistent with any of the provisions of an agreement. The agreement may take one of two forms, a certified agreement or an enterprise flexibility agreement. The latter is distinguished in particular by the fact that it can only apply to a single enterprise which must be a corporation and that there is no requirement that a registered union be a party to the agreement.

The legislation was introduced by the Keating government in October 1993 following protracted negotiations between the government and the ACTU in relation to the enterprise flexibility agreement provisions. After its unexpected election victory in March 1993, the government had made a strong commitment to encouraging increased use of the certified agreement provisions and this included their application to areas of employment where unions were inactive or absent. Introducing the Bill, the Minister for Industrial Relations said:

> 'This legislation marks the culmination of the government's break with the past—our move as a nation from a centralised to a decentralised industrial relations system, to a system based primarily on bargaining at the workplace, with much less reliance on arbitration at the apex'.[33]

In this chapter a number of distinguishing characteristics of the process of collective bargaining have been identified. In some cases they have been presented as features of a model divorced from any particular system (see p. 546). In other cases the characteristics are identified as features of systems which have highly-structured legal frameworks for collective bargaining (see for example pp. 586–588). The position in the Australian federal jurisdiction in 1994 is now considered in terms of those features.

One pre-condition for obtaining Commission endorsement of an agreement is the existence of an award and the features of this instrument were discussed in chapters 12 and 15. The result is that machinery for collective bargaining is interwoven with machinery for compulsory arbitration. This is illustrated in one of the new objects of the long-standing part of the statute dealing with dispute prevention and settlement. This object is to ensure that:

> 'the Commission's functions and powers in relation to making and varying awards are performed and exercised in a way that both:
> (i) gives employees prompt access to fair and enforceable minimum wages and conditions of employment, so far as they do not already have them; and
> (ii) encourages the prevention and settlement of industrial disputes by the making of agreements under Part VIB'.[34]

This integration of bargaining and compulsory arbitration is not a characteristic of the collective bargaining model or of any legal frameworks in countries where there is state support for collective bargaining. In the first *National Wage* case decision since the operation of the legislation, the Commission arbitrated three $8 per week increases available over a minimum period of 18 months from September 1994. Unions will be required to apply to the Commission for these increases, and workers eligible for the increases will be those who have genuinely tried to negotiate enterprise agreements but have not been able to reach agreement with their employers.[35] One possible consequence here will be to devalue the collective bargaining forum by the continued provision of an alternative forum for wage increases.

More generally, while it appears that the operations of the new Bargaining Division preclude the use of arbitration, it is not clear whether the Commission could refuse to intercede where bargaining encounters difficulty. Regardless of the intentions of the Commission it seems unlikely that it could withstand pressures that might be applied to make its arbitral services available in the event of failure of the conciliation process.

A feature of the collective bargaining model which is endorsed by the legislation concerns the concept of good faith bargaining. The legislation imposes a duty on the parties to bargain in good faith. The principal object of the Act includes:

> providing a framework of rights and responsibilities for the parties involved in industrial relations which encourages fair and effective bargaining and ensures that those parties abide by agreements between them.[36]

More specifically, in relation to the negotiation of agreements, the Commission is empowered to make orders 'ensuring that the parties negotiating an agreement under this Part do so in good faith'.[37] It may also make orders for other reasons, for example promoting the efficient conduct of negotiations.[38] The legislation identifies specific aspects of the conduct of the parties which the Commission must consider in deciding what order, if any, to make in relation to, *inter alia*, good faith bargaining. These aspects of conduct, which are not exhaustive, are set out in Table 17.6.

Thus the legislation, which is centred on the procedural aspects of negotiations, does not provide any comprehensive definition of good faith bargaining. The parties will, of course, be able to make use of the new

Table 17.6 'Good faith' bargaining: conduct to be considered by the Commission

'(3) In deciding what orders (if any) to make, the Commission:

(a) must consider the conduct of each of the parties to the negotiations, in particular, whether the party concerned has:

   (i)   agreed to meet at reasonable times proposed by another party; or
   (ii) attended meetings that the party had agreed to attend; or
   (iii) complied with negotiating procedures agreed to by the parties; or
   (iv) capriciously added or withdrawn items for negotiation; or
   (v)   disclosed relevant information as appropriate for the purposes of the negotiations; or
   (vi) refused or failed to negotiate with one or more of the parties; or
   (vii) in or in connection with the negotiations, contravened section 170RB by refusing or failing to negotiate with a person who is entitled under that section to represent an employee; and

(b) may consider:

   (i) proposed conduct of any of the parties (including proposed conduct of a kind referred to in paragraph (a)); and
   (ii) any other relevant matter.'

Note: Section 170RB concerns union representation in relation to enterprise flexibility agreements.
Source: *Industrial Relations Act* 1988, s.170QK(3).

Industrial Relations Court (see chapter 12) to seek clarification of the concept. It may be that the American and Canadian experience and example will provide a source for the development of principles relating to good faith bargaining.

A second feature of the legislation relevant to the conventional features of collective bargaining concerns the right to strike or lock-out that is, to apply coercive pressure to influence the outcome of the negotiations. There is provision for the parties, in specified circumstances, to take legal industrial action in support of their negotiating position.[39] This limited right to industrial action, 'protected action' as it is termed, is established via a sanction-free bargaining period and does not apply to the negotiation of enterprise flexibility agreements. A corollary here is the drawing of a distinction between the bargaining phase and the period when the agreement is in force when industrial action is prohibited. There are a number of other limitations on this right to strike. An application must be made to the Commission for access to the bargaining period and one condition precedent to sanction-free industrial action is that an attempt has been made to reach agreement by negotiation.[40] The legislation, in distinguishing between the bargaining period when new workplace rules are negotiated and the period of the operation of the agreement, moves towards a clear distinction between interest disputes and rights disputes. It parallels a common feature of collective bargaining regulation in other countries by requiring agreements to include grievance procedures to deal with disputes relating to matters arising under the agreement, that is, rights diputes.[41] However, the legislation does enable the agreement to be varied during its operation, albeit provided the substantive issues and the procedures for such variation are spelt out in the agreement.[42] Significantly such discipline does not apply to the relevant awards, any term of which may be varied at any time.

In countries where collective bargaining is established and supported by public regulation, the powers of third parties to intervene in the bargaining process are usually confined to circumstances where the exercise of coercive power threatens public health, safety or welfare. The position in the federal jurisdiction in Australia in 1994 is that the Commission may suspend or terminate the bargaining period if it is satisfied that the industrial action is threatening:

i to endanger the life, the personal safety or health, or the welfare of the population or of part of it; or
ii to cause significant damage to the Australian economy or an important part of it.[43]

The legislation is silent on the matter of the processes for determining a bargaining unit so these remain a matter for private negotiation. Bargaining units are implicit in the specification of parties which may apply for Commission certification or approval of agreements. The term bargaining unit however, does not appear in the legislation. Finally, the contents of agreements are subject to tribunal scrutiny and ratification before they can be legally enforceable under the statute. The aspects requiring scrutiny and the tribunal powers are detailed in chapter 12. Some of these requirements are no greater than the boundaries set by legislatures in countries with established regulation of collective bargaining, for example a prohibition on provisions which discriminate on grounds such as gender and race.[44] Other requirements in the *Industrial Relations Act* distinguish the Australian case yet again by affording the tribunal considerable discretion on the 'public interest' ground.[45]

Conclusion

Collective bargaining has always been present in Australian industrial relations. It was, in the nineteenth century, the first workplace rule making process adopted, and though displaced from primacy by the arbitral machinery, it has never been entirely absent. Until 1993 collective bargaining had received no legislative or government support but even the current support is qualified given the specific commitments to arbitration. Thus if the processes of arbitration and bargaining have been thought to be incompatible, this may be due to government support for one rather than the other. There have been considerable public misgivings concerning collective bargaining, and often these are based on an assumption that more collective bargaining necessarily implies an increase in strike action. However, experience elsewhere suggests that these fears have been exaggerated. Whether the Australian mix of arbitration and collective bargaining is now in its final equilibrium form, or whether it is in transition to some different mix of the two processes, is a question that can only be answered a generation from now.

Collective bargaining developed in Australia because labour and management jointly found the process to satisfy their interests. They have used the process despite a climate which has been generally discouraging. This suggests that the process has powerful attractions to many of those who practise labour relations, and, ultimately, it is the wishes of these participants which must carry the day. If we recall that the function of an industrial relations system is to evolve rules which govern workplaces, it becomes apparent that the crucial factor is the extent to which these rules provide satisfaction, not the process by which they are derived.

Notes

1. A.M. Ross, *Trade Union Wage Policy*, University of California Press, Berkeley, 1956.
2. J. Niland, 'The Case for More Collective Bargaining in Australia', *Journal of Industrial Relations 18,* December 1976, p. 367.
3. N.W. Chamberlain and J.W. Kuhn, *Collective Bargaining* (3rd ed.), McGraw-Hill, New York, 1986, pp. 176–198.
4. ibid., p. 178.
5. ibid., pp. 178–179
6. *Australasian Meat Industry Employees Union v Mudginberri Station Pty Ltd.*, (1985) 61 ALR 417.
7. ACTU, *Future Strategies for the Trade Union Movement*, 1987, pp. 19 & 29.
8. R.E. Walton and R.B. McKersie, *A Behavioral Theory of Labor Negotiations*, McGraw-Hill, New York, 1965, p. 2.
9. ibid., p. 4.
10. ibid., p. 5.
11. ibid.
12. ibid., p. 4.
13. C. Fox, 'Antecedents of the 1986 Victorian Nurses' Strike', *Journal of Industrial Relations 32*, December 1990, pp. 472–473.
14. Walton and McKersie, *op. cit.*, p. 5.
15. ibid.
16. *The Age*, 10 November 1986, p. 1.
17. Walton and Mckersie, *op. cit.*, p. 3.
18. ibid., p. 5.
19. For an account of this dispute see H. Thompson, 'The APPM Dispute The Dinosaur and Turtles the ACTU', *The Economic and Labour Relations Review 3*, December 1992, pp. 148–164.
20. W.A. Howard, *Barrier Bulwark: The Life and Times of Shorty O'Neil*, Willry Pty Ltd, 1990, chapter 3.
21. Fox, 1990, *op. cit.*, p. 484.
22. Walton and McKersie, *op. cit.*, p. 8.
23. Niland ,1976, *op cit.*, pp. 367–368.
24. For an account of the events surrounding these negotiations see C. Fox, *Industrial Relations in Nursing Victoria 1982 to 1985.* Australian Studies in Health Service Administration, No. 68, School of Health Services Management, University of New South Wales, 1989, chapters 4 and 5.
25. *Industrial Relations Act*, 1988, s.102(2)(b).
26. *Industrial Relations Act* 1988 s.170MC(1)(h) inserted by the *Industrial Relations Reform Act* 1993, s.31.
27. Section 11(1).
28. Australian Industrial Relations Commission, *National Wage* case, October 1991, 39 IR 127 at 141.
29. V.I. Lenin, *What Is To Be Done?*, International Publishers, New York, 1929.

30 S. Perlman, *A Theory of the Labor Movement*, Augustus Kelley, New York, 1949 (1st ed. 1928).
31 R. Callus, A. Morehead, M. Cully and J. Buchanan, *Industrial Relations At Work-The Australian Workplace Industrial Relations Survey*, Commonwealth Department of Industrial Relations, AGPS, Canberra, 1991, p. 132
32 *ibid.*, p. 129.
33 Australia, House of Representatives, *Debates*, Weekly Hansard, No. 10 1993, 28 October 1993, p. 2778.
34 *Industrial Relations Act* 1988, s.88A(e) inserted by *Industrial Relations Reform Act* 1993, s.7.
35 *Australian Financial Review*, 22 September 1994, p. 10.
36 *ibid.*, s.3(c) as amended by *Industrial Relations Reform Act* 1993, s.4.
37 *ibid.*, s.170QK(2)(a) inserted by *Industrial Relations Reform Act* 1993, s.31.
38 *ibid.*, s.170QK(2)(b).
39 *ibid.*, ss 170PA-170PO.
40 *ibid.*, s.170PI.
41 *ibid.*, s.170MC(1)(c).
42 *ibid.*, s.170ME.
43 *ibid.*, s.170PO(1)(b).
44 *ibid.*, s.170MD(5).
45 See, for example, *ibid.*, ss 170MC(2)(b) and 170MD(1)(b).

Further Reading

Nature of collective bargaining

N.W. Chamberlain and J.W. Kuhn, *Collective Bargaining* (3rd ed.), McGraw-Hill, New York, 1986, chapters 5 and 6.

T. L. Leap and D. W. Grigsby, 'A Conceptualisation of Collective Bargaining Power', *Industrial and Labor Relations Review 39*, January 1986, pp. 202–213.

J. Pen, 'A General Theory of the Bargaining Process', *American Economic Review*, 1952, vol. 42, no. 1, pp. 24–42.

G. G. Somers, 'Bargaining Power and Industrial Relations Theory', in G. G. Somers (ed.) *Essays in Industrial Relations Theory*, Iowa State University Press, Ames Iowa, 1969, pp. 39–53.

The technique of collective bargaining

S. B. Bacharach and E. J. Lawler, 'Power and Tactics in Bargaining', *Industrial and Labor Relations Review 34*, January 1981, pp. 219–233.

T.A. Kochan, *Collective Bargaining and Industrial Relations: From Theory to Policy and Practice*, Irwin, Homewood, 1980.

The negotiation process

Chamberlain and Kuhn, *op. cit.*, chapter 3.

W.J. Holdsworth, *Advocacy and Negotiation in Industrial Relations* (3rd ed.), Law Book Co., Sydney, 1987.

R. Walton and R.B. McKersie, *A Behavioral Theory of Labor Negotiations*, McGraw-Hill, New York, 1965.

Collective bargaining in Australia

R. Callus, A. Morehead, M. Cully & J. Buchanan, *Industrial Relations At Work-The Australian Workplace Industrial Relations Survey*, Commonwealth Department of Industrial Relations, AGPS, Canberra, 1991.

F.T. De Vyver, 'The Melbourne Building Industry Agreement', *Journal of Industrial Relations 1*, April 1959, pp. 7–19.

F.T. De Vyver, 'The Melbourne Building Industry Agreement: A Re-examination', *Journal of Industrial Relations 12*, July 1970, pp. 166–181.

R.C. McCallum and G.F. Smith, 'Opting Out from Within: Industrial Agreements Under the Conciliation and Arbitration Act 1904', *Journal of Industrial Relations 28*, March 1986, pp. 57–85.

J. Niland, 'The Case for More Collective Bargaining in Australia', *Journal of Industrial Relations 18*, December 1976, pp. 365–390.

G.F. Smith and R.C. McCallum, 'A Legal Framework for the Establishment of Institutional Collective Bargaining in Australia', *Journal of Industrial Relations 26*, March 1984, pp. 3–24.

Questions

1 Explain the Chamberlain-Kuhn model of bargaining power.
2 What were the most important variables increasing
   a union bargaining power and
   b employer bargaining power in the 1919-20 Broken Hill strike (see chapter 4 for a summary of the dispute).
3 Explain the analytical framework developed by Walton and McKersie for the study of the negotiation process.
4 Discuss the distinguishing features of collective bargaining as it has been traditionally practised in Australia during the twentieth century.
5 Explain how the processes of conciliation and arbitration and collective bargaining interact within the Australian industrial relations system.
6 Define each of the following and indicate in what respect it breaches the necessary conditions for collective bargaining:
   'administrative negotiation'
   'referred negotiation'
   'strategic negotiation'.
7 Critically evaluate the following statement:

   'Australian problems with collective bargaining are the result of an immature system rather than being inherent in the process itself, and that immaturity is in very large part the outcome of the simultaneous existence of the arbitral and bargaining 'systems'.

Exercises

1 Identify the variable(s) relevant to costs of disagreeing or costs of agreeing in each of the quotations which appear in Table 17.2 and explain the probable influence on bargaining power in each case.
2 It is sometimes argued that collective bargaining can be fully effective only if there is no alternative process available. One of the objects of the federal legislation and Commission policy between 1987 and 1994 has been to enhance collective bargaining.
   i   Examine the above proposition concerning collective bargaining.
   ii   Has the legislation in fact denied bargaining parties resort to the process of arbitration?

18

Enterprise Bargaining: Origins, Techniques, and Applications

Contents

Enterprise bargaining and productivity
Origins of enterprise bargaining: a conventional model
- productivty bargaining: distinguishing characteristics
- necessary conditions

Productivity bargaining at enterprise level: case studies
- Fawley: the 1960 agreements
- Fawley: the 1960s to the 1980s

Enterprise bargaining in Australia
- early attempts
- wages policy and the evolution to enterprise bargaining
- the conventional model and the Australian case distinguished

Introduction

This chapter considers the origins, applications and techniques of enterprise bargaining, a process which has prominence in Australian industrial relations in the early 1990s. The origins and evolution of this process, operating within a public policy linking wage fixation to notions of productivity and efficiency, is examined in detail. The public policy was based on the continuing assumption that the industrial relations system should accept a substantial measure of the responsibility if not for delivering the nation from economic crisis then at least for correcting adverse trends in macro-economic indicators. In addition to a critical examination of public policy in Australia and its impact on practice, there is a detailed summary of two case studies of productivity bargaining at an enterprise in Great Britain which initially was heralded as the exemplar. The case studies are included for their valuable insights into the operational problems at the enterprise level. They show, incidentally, that productivity bargaining has a long history and has been used by management without public policy inducement. The chapter draws on material contained in chapters 6 and 9 (motives and behaviour of actors) and much of the discussion of public policy processes and bargaining power builds on material (especially relating to processes and to wage policy) contained in chapters 15, 16 and 17. The material in this chapter therefore serves to integrate some of the material that has necessarily been treated somewhat artificially through discussion in discrete sections.

Enterprise bargaining and productivity

Enterprise bargaining has no necessary connection with productivity and efficiency. It is a process, which may be individual or collective, conducted at a particular level—the enterprise (however defined). Enterprise bargaining may be subject to public or private regulation or be conducted on an *ad hoc* basis, that is, unregulated. The process may be associated with different bargaining structures and the product of the process, enterprise agreements, may exist as a supplement or complement to existing awards and certified agreements (in Australian terminology) or be a complete substitute for these. The bargaining agenda, or substantive issues for bargaining, may be unlimited or may contain mandatory and prohibited matters. In the case of wages these may be adjusted for one or more criteria including prices, changes in work value and productivity just as with wages determined by other processes, for example arbitration. In the Australian case it is the bargaining agenda determined by public policy that has created an identity between bargaining at enterprise level and bargaining over wages and productivity. Since the late 1980s, Australian industrial relations has been dominated by notions of 'productivity' and 'efficiency' and 1991 saw the emergence of a public policy framework linking these concepts to enterprise bargaining.

Productivity bargaining is a special case of collective bargaining. In terms of the Walton and McKersie typology of negotiation sub-processes summarised in chapter 17, it is a form of integrative bargaining. The next section abstracts from the Australian case and considers the distinguishing characteristics of this process, and industrial relations theory suggests that the enterprise is typically the appropriate level for its conduct. The motives for management and unions engaging in the process and the necessary conditions for its effectiveness, especially from the perspective of management, are also considered.

Origins of enterprise bargaining: a conventional model

Productivity bargaining: distinguishing characteristics

The following discussion draws on a detailed study of productivity bargaining by Riach and Howard.[1] They identify the special features which British experience with productivity bargaining in the 1960s suggested were necessary for successful productivity bargaining. They also identify the difficulties and dangers which may result if a productivity bargaining programme is not carefully planned from the outset. Riach and Howard define a productivity agreement as follows:

> 'A productivity agreement between labour and management is one whereby labour makes an essential contribution, via carefully specified changes in methods and practices of work, to an increase in the overall efficiency in the resource utilisation of the enterprise and in return is compensated by some material benefit such as increased leisure or weekly pay. ... The essence of such agreements is the exchange—the provision of improved employee benefits in return for labour's co-operation in improving the efficiency of operations—but the precise way whereby labour makes its contribution to efficiency is via the acceptance of changed working practices.'[2]

The form of the material benefit may depend on the kind of variation in work practice: if employees were merely relinquishing some restrictive practice the compensation may be a lump sum bonus; if the variation involved on-going work that was more responsible or more arduous then a continuing benefit may be appropriate. Riach and Howard cite the case of London's Lambeth Council dustmen who agreed to forego their totting rights in return for a lump sum payment of £500. In other words, because the change in work practices involved the cessation of an inefficient practice, the appropriate compensation was deemed to be a single payment. An example illustrating improved resource utilisation occurred in British Rail in the late 1960s: workshop staff agreed to undertake work at weekends resulting in capital savings by enabling off-peak locomotive maintenance and thus a smaller fleet.

Productivity bargaining is a process to be engaged in at discrete and probably irregular intervals. It is not a process for establishing a permanent link between productivity and wages but rather involves a specific exchange at a point of time. Thus a productivity agreement is to be distinguished from piece-work systems which aim to stimulate greater effort by gearing pay directly to labour output. Similarly, productivity bargaining is not a technique to produce a regular linkage between pay and some output or productivity indicator.[3]

One issue to consider is the circumstances under which productivity bargaining might be chosen. As noted, it is a form of integrative bargaining which means that the approach to negotiation is in terms of a problem or issue to be solved. In the case where the problem is inefficient work practices, productivity bargaining is one of a number of possible responses. The origins of inefficient work practices and the possible responses to this problem have been discussed by Flanders.[4] He observes that where this problem exists it is likely to be one which has developed over a long period by work groups or perhaps by unions. In some cases the practices may be formalised in agreements or awards. In other cases they will exist in a *de facto* form as custom and practice workplace rules. Where they have developed over a long period they will be entrenched, as part of the workplace culture. The practices will probably have developed as a defensive mechanism, as a protection against lack of security in employment. As Flanders says, the restrictive practices which employees believe to be necessary and justified are determined by 'what they have to protect themselves against'.[5] Inefficient work practices may also be caused by sloppy or weak management, particularly where work methods, crew sizes and the like are not adjusted to suit new equipment or products.

A matter related to the choice of productivity bargaining to deal with restrictive work practices, is the identification of primary responsibility for initiating action to deal with the problem. This is related in turn to one's view concerning the purpose of trade unions. If, for example, the concept of responsible unionism (see chapter 4) is endorsed, then unions will be seen as having at least equal responsibility to do something about the problem. If, on the other hand, the primary responsibility of trade unions is considered to be the welfare of dues-paying members then responsibility for overcoming the problem of inefficiency will be seen to rest with management. This view regards a commitment to efficiency as a primary function of management. As defined by Chamberlain, Cullen and Lewin in chapter 9, the function of management is to organise the use of human and material resources to produce the best results with an economy of effort. From this perspective, if management ignores grossly inefficient work practices then management is guilty of professional incompetence.[6]

However, as Flanders points out, even if management accepts this responsibility restrictive practices are not something that can be removed overnight, at least not without running the risk of incurring major costs as a consequence. Those costs may take the form of rigid attitudes and a withdrawal of co-operation on the part of the workforce affected. A number of methods are available to management. One is simply to attempt to change behaviour through persuasion; to persuade workers that it is in their interests or the interests of the company and probably also those of the nation, to shed inefficient work practices. This action is consonant with the unitary frame of reference discussed in chapter 9. Nonetheless, it is not necessarily inconsistent with a pluralist frame of reference to the extent that it is seen by management as one part of a strategy which will probably also require other methods. Another method is consultation. Management may assess it will be able to introduce changes in work practices through a process of joint consultation, that is, management retains the power to decide but consults with work groups or unions. In certain circumstances this may be assessed as sufficient to gain acceptance of change. The third method available to management is productivity bargaining, that is negotiation to buy out inefficient work practices. This is an appropriate process in circumstances where management lacks the power to impose change unilaterally. In the case of job-conscious unions, productivity bargaining may be an acceptable process when benefits cannot be obtained any other way. From the perspective of such unions, 'the most telling argument in favour of productivity bargaining is the lack of a practical alternative'.[7] It offers the possibility of improvement for workers when bargaining power is so limited that further benefits could not be obtained without making concessions, when bargaining power has been exploited to the full. If it had not been, it would be logical to pursue a strategy of obtaining the benefits and reducing or eliminating the concessions. Job-conscious unions and work groups in the Perlman mould are interested in employment security and they will become interested in efficiency if they perceive that this is necessary for employment security.

Necessary conditions

Riach and Howard[8] set out a number of necessary conditions for the effectiveness of productivity bargaining. Their discussion draws on British experience with the use of this process including the Fawley case which is detailed below.

- First, the detailed negotiations should be conducted at a level where there is a homogeneous set of work practices. This could be at industry, enterprise or plant level. Thus if employers identified a problem common to the industry because of a homogeneous technology, negotiations could be conducted at an industry level. Riach and Howard cite British examples of such negotiations in the case of cement manufacturing and glass container manufacturing where changes in manning levels and rosters were negotiated at industry level. The authors point out that if it was decided that detailed negotiations should be at enterprise level this would not preclude negotiation of an industry framework agreement, or enterprise framework agreement in the case of plant negotiations, establishing some basic ground rules and setting minimum rates so that negotiations would be about total earnings.
- Secondly, and perhaps most importantly, there should be painstaking, thorough preparation by management before negotiations commence. The process is one of mutual benefit. From a management perspective, the potential savings have to be established because it is the potential savings that will be the subject of negotiation, specifically how much of these will be conceded to the employees. Thus management will need to undertake a systematic review of current production methods and working practices,

cost them, identify the desired changes and then cost the savings. This requirement means that it is crucial that management can control the timing of the exercise. There are probable intangible benefits for management arising from a detailed survey of working methods. These include greater knowledge and understanding of overall operations and more effective managerial control of work activity. The scope of managerial involvement in negotiations and the subject matter of negotiations means that a wider group than has been previously involved 'will gain an understanding of the inter-relationship between technical, financial and industrial relations decisions'.[9]

- Thirdly, the scope of negotiations ideally should be comprehensive with respect to both personnel and work practices. Unless this occurs the productivity agreement may disturb the pattern of relativities and generate pressure for flow-on to other employees within the plant, enterprise or industry as the case may be.
- Fourthly, the negotiating team for each party needs to have a close understanding of the subject matter of the bargaining, the work processes and practices. In the case of management this will mean the involvement of line managers from an early stage, as well as industrial relations/ personnel management specialists. The participation of first-level line managers will be important because they will possess the technical knowledge of the nature and conditions of labour utilisation and also because they will have responsibility for implementation of any agreement. It may well be that senior management does not understand the detailed nature of the work or the pace of the work. First-line managers on the other hand will need to be made aware of the new managerial objectives being attempted and trained to cope with this. An important point made by Flanders is that true productivity bargaining is a consequence of management as innovator. In the case of the union(s) the negotiating team should comprise, or at least include, those representatives with the power to deliver the changes in work practices which management seeks. Thus, as with management, the union representatives should be those with the greatest knowledge of the work practices and the greatest responsibility for implementation of any agreement. A task for management will be to assess the level within the union which power resides in relation to the issues to be negotiated.
- Fifthly, the complete agreement and co-operation of the work groups concerned is critical to success. These are the people who have the control over work practices. They must believe that a proposed agreement is a good settlement for them, and so as a pre condition they must be regularly informed and consulted about the progress of negotiations. It also follows that union representatives should only make concessions which the employees are ready to accept.
- Sixthly, there must be agreement to changes before the money is paid or other benefit(s) granted. In other words, there needs to be a control mechanism to ensure co-operation is forthcoming, that payment is made only as productivity increases or as changes in working practices take place.

- Seventhly, there must be acceptance by management that this type of bargaining may require disclosure of hitherto undisclosed details about enterprise costs and operations. One of the skills identified in the discussion of collective bargaining in chapter 17 was the ability to persuade the opposing party of the merits of one's case; it would be a gullible union negotiating team which accepted at face value management claims of the costs of particular working practices.
- Finally, productivity bargaining should be quarantined from compulsory arbitration. The latter process is not an appropriate means for resolving conflict over the issues in dispute here. Compulsory arbitration involves an imposed solution by outsiders. Riach and Howard argue this will not be effective for two reasons.
    a First, as mentioned above, a critical factor in success is full co-operation at the shop floor level in adopting methods of work that have previously been refused. Changes in working methods which labour has refused to concede to management authority are not likely to be conceded to an external third party.
    b Secondly, the third party is unlikely to possess the necessary detailed local knowledge. The issue is control, and control can only be determined by negotiation. Riach and Howard also point out that if management is genuine in its acceptance of responsibility it would not wish to abdicate to a third party. Management may have to compromise but it will prefer to retain some measure of control and move forward slowly pursuing a long-term strategy.

The issue of flow-on of the terms of a productivity agreement is discussed by Riach and Howard. If a plant, enterprise or even an industry has concluded an agreement, the terms of that agreement do not indicate anything about the capacity of other plants, enterprises or industries to conclude similar agreements. The internal logic of a productivity agreement is that it creates its own capacity to pay for increased benefits at constant or lower labour cost per unit of output. Flow-on of similar outcomes to dissimilar situations could occur if other employers conceded without demanding equivalent concessions.

Riach and Howard note how productivity bargaining became devalued and debased in Britain in the mid-1960s when the Wilson Labor government introduced a prices and incomes policy and made a productivity agreement one of the few grounds for wage increases outside the norm. This led to a mushrooming of bogus productivity agreements between unions and those employers willing to grant further pay rises. The productivity agreement became a ritual and a contrivance, although for the government it became a convenient safety valve in the face of potential industrial unrest and political embarrassment.[10] A later section of this chapter will detail the operation of productivity bargaining in Australia during the period 1987–1993 in the context of a wages policy being managed by the federal and state industrial tribunals.

The productivity agreements concluded at the Esso oil refinery in England in 1960 were initially heralded as the exemplar of the process. The following sections draw on the Flanders study of the initial agreements and a subsequent study by Ahlstrand of productivity bargaining at the refinery from the 1960s to the 1980s.

Productivity bargaining at enterprise level: case studies

Fawley: the 1960 agreements (Flanders)

The best-known example of productivity bargaining was that conducted at the Esso Petroleum U.K. Ltd. oil refinery at Fawley near Southhampton in the late 1950s, resulting in an initial set of agreements in July 1960. Prior to the Ahlstrand study, Fawley was associated with the purest form of productivity bargaining and was pointed to as the exemplary case. The negotiations leading to the celebrated Blue Book agreements, whose application extended over two years, were documented and analysed by Flanders[11] with management and union consent. Esso is the oldest affiliate of the American-based Exxon Corporation, formerly known as Standard Oil of New Jersey. At the time of the first productivity negotiations, the refinery employed a workforce of about 3500 comprising 2500 wage employees and 1000 salaried employees. The refinery management concluded the agreements with the local representatives of eight unions. Flanders identifies a number of factors precipitating 'the growth of managerial initiative in labour relations'[12] at the refinery. Thus a link was established between productivity bargaining and the notion of management strategy (see chapter 9). The reform process began with external pressure from the parent company for the Esso board and its managerial hierarchy to achieve economies in the use of manpower, and the origin of this pressure was economic factors related to certain market and technological conditions of the industry. Further, although the industry has a high capital:labour cost ratio, labour costs at Fawley were calculated to represent more than half the total costs which were subject to some degree of direct control by management and they compared unfavourably with capital:labour cost ratios in very similar refineries. Management at the refinery faced a range of restrictive work practices including:

1. high levels of institutionalised overtime;
2. inter-craft job demarcations;
3. unproductive employment of craftsmen's mates; and
4. union restrictions on supervision and promotion procedures.

Management was advantaged by the fact that it was operating in an environment with new plant coming into operation. Flanders emphasises that the pressures on management created a situation which demanded an appropriate response but did not pre-determine the nature of the response, in detail or in principle. The management response had to be shaped within the refinery and Flanders believes that the pre-eminent force determining this was the conviction held about the responsibilities of management. He points out that there was nothing very original about the ideas behind the proposals for change presented to the unions in 1959 and which came to be known as the Blue Book. Thus, 'Most of the arguments against systematic overtime, for instance, were familiar enough. What was lacking was enough people with a sufficiently strong conviction that it should be got rid of. Once that deficiency was made good, the intellectual exercise of devising ways and means presented no overwhelming difficulties.'[13] The change in managerial attitudes and beliefs was given some impetus by the effect of national rivalry within an international organisation, in particular the desire to match achievements of refineries in the United States. The identification of areas of inefficiency at Fawley began in mid-1957. The pivotal figure of the movement for reform within management however was the Assistant Refinery Manager whose objective was a more responsible management, a management at all levels fully conscious of the scope of its responsibilities and willing to accept them. One of the first actions was the engagement of a consultant who acted as a catalyst for changes in managerial attitudes and beliefs and whose report led initially to a reorganisation of management late in 1958.[14]

The consultant advocated the need for a low overtime—high wage policy. This was a decided break with prevailing thought and practice which had been to approximate the wages of other employers in the local community and to regard overtime as inevitable for running a refinery, both for technical reasons and to satisfy the workers. The consultant identified the 'pernicious economic and social effects of overtime'[15] which in 1959 was averaging between fifteen and twenty-five per cent of total hours worked. He argued that overtime need not exceed one per cent on day work and that the refinery could be maintained with a maintenance and construction labour force of 800 (it was then 1200) to be achieved through attrition; there would be no redundancies. A number of radical measures concerning work practices were proposed to achieve these objectives together with a wage rise, partly in basic rates and partly in benefits, sufficient to compensate the employees for the amount of money they would have earned if overtime had remained at twenty per cent per annum.[16]

A significant feature of the reform was that formal union-management negotiations were preceded by formal and subsequent informal consultations between management and employees and shop stewards between November 1958 and December 1959. These were designed to: air the arguments for change; dispel any exaggerated fears that the proposed changes might otherwise have aroused and give management greater confidence in advancing the proposals for change. There was also consultation with local and national union officials and presentations by management to the Esso Board. Flanders refers to an impression of 'an infectious spread of intellectual activity on all sides which compelled a re-thinking of past attitudes'.[17] One definite effect was that when the 88-page Blue Book was presented to the unions there were few people on the refinery who did not know what to expect. The extensive pre-negotiation consultation achieved considerable union support for the company's general approach although the unions had made no commitments on specific proposals.[18]

The formal union-management negotiations were intensive, occurring over five months (February to May 1960). Management maintained the traditional practice of negotiating separately with the Transport and General Workers' Union (TGWU), the sole representative of non-craft employees, and the Southhampton Craft Union Committee (CUC) representing the various skilled trades on the refinery covered by seven craft unions.[19] The only departures from the traditional negotiating structure were six 'joint' negotiating meetings, at different stages in the bargaining process, in which TGWU delegates 'sat in' at the management-CUC meetings. The union negotiators were full-time officials and referred to as union delegates: district or trade group secretaries in the case of the TGWU and a district officer from each craft union in the case of the CUC. The members of the eight unions on-site were represented by a total of seventy-two shop stewards. They had a crucial role in negotiations, complementary to that of the union delegates. The latter decided the principles of the agreements: the issues of general concern to the union nationally and locally, while the shop stewards worked out most of the detail. This was an appropriate demarcation given their greater knowledge of refinery conditions and their closer relationship to the membership. This was especially apparent in the negotiations relating to inter-craft flexibility which entailed time-consuming discussion in working parties.[20]

Management prioritised its proposals for change and assessed the anticipated degree of union resistance for each proposal. The greatest resistance was expected from the craft unions and probably specifically in relation to: 'the training of selected mates to be craftsmen; the administrative supervision of all craftsmen by area supervisors; and the optional withdrawal of line supervisors from union membership'.[21] Management assessed that all other proposed changes affecting the craftsmen would involve hard bargaining with the possibility of compromise. The greatest resistance from the TGWU was anticipated to the proposal for redeployment of craftsmens' mates; there were possible national implications given these jobs were a source of employment for thousands of TGWU members.

A spontaneous teamwork was evident among managers, attributed by Flanders to the personality of the Refinery Manager. Senior management met frequently during negotiations to review and discuss the arguments for alternative courses of action in a free, 'almost Socratic' style. This proved invaluable given the intricate nature of the negotiations which demanded a greater calculation of risks and weighing of reasons than required by distributive bargaining (see chapter 17) and which benefited from the pooling of knowledge and judgement.[22]

Flanders identified three stages in the negotiation process:

1 focus on clearing the ground for compromise, dispelling misunderstandings about the Blue Book, resolving attitudes within and among the unions, narrowing where necessary possible areas of agreement;
2 management and unions became fully conscious of their mutual readiness to reach an agreement and decided how to compromise on its main provisions; and
3 the hardening of specific group resistances among the employees to particular items in the impending agreements, thereby delaying their conclusion.[23]

The dynamics of the negotiations will not be detailed here but they included many of the features discussed in chapter 17. The proposal to upgrade craftsmens' mates proved to be a complicated and strongly contested issue, primarily because all but one of the craft unions had unemployed members in the district. Management had established that these employees were working for about forty per cent of the hours for which they were employed. Their existence was a reflection of the status of tradesmen. As noted above, negotiations to settle the details of inter-craft flexibility between individual unions were conducted via a series of working parties comprising senior shop stewards of the relevant unions and appropriate line managers. This activity was marred by the failure of CUC delegates to inform their membership, including the shop stewards, of the progress of (top-level) negotiations. One outcome of the resultant union intra-organisational bargaining was a demand for an interim wage rise and a forty-hour week which, fortuitously for management, created pressure on the union delegates to resolve the outstanding differences.[24]

Generally inter-craft flexibility was an area of strong resistance. Management estimated that more than two-thirds of the Blue Book's propositions were agreed. A year later the senior craft stewards' estimate was about one-half. Flanders suggested the probable actual outcome was somewhere between.[25]

The CUC negotiations were chaired by the ETU delegate. Both he and the union's senior shop steward were avowed and long-standing members of the Communist Party. Flanders explains their constructive attitude to negotiations by the proposition that trade unions, whatever their leaders' politics, tend to react to industrial disputes or problems strictly in terms of their industrial interests. In this case, the ETU members had the least to lose and the most to gain from the Blue Book given that the union did not have unemployed members in the district and electricians had done little overtime. Strong resistance to the training of process workers to take over minor maintenance work came from the Plumbing Trades Union because of the low craft content of much of the work of the pipefitters. The delegate eventually accepted some verbal reassurances from management.[26] Even stronger resistance to inter-craft flexibility came from the welders (members of three unions) due to a number of factors: their high levels of overtime which meant less than full compensation from the rise in basic rates; uncertainty as to their craft status with wide variations in the degree of skill and technical competence required; the fact that welding skills formed part of the training of other craftsmen. The welders succeeded in having the clause on welding flexibility confined to a trivial concession, showing that occupational groups among the trades were strong enough to prevent work practice change being forced upon them.[27] This was not the case for discontented groups within the TGWU.

The TGWU negotiators signed the productivity agreement despite a narrow vote against it by members of the union's Day Branch: members of the Shift Branch voted overwhelmingly in favour of acceptance. The most discontented groups within the TGWU—craftsmen's mates and tank and mechanical cleaners—were however a decided minority of the union's total refinery membership. The major reason for the craftsmen's mates' opposition appears to have been personal insecurity. For the cleaners it was the threat to their separate group identities entailed in a proposed consolidation of pay grades from eighteen to four to include a new occupational group of 'cleaner-labourers', later renamed 'maintenance operators'. The wiping out of status distinctions and the abolition of washing time and special payments, compounded their disaffection.

This opposition illustrated the independent authority of the work group, based on similarity of occupation function and status, and its elected leader, the shop steward. This informal structure is intermediary between the union and the workers as individuals. According to Flanders, the lesson for management was that in collective bargaining management must:

1 reach agreement with the unions as unions; and
2 secure the co-operation of the appropriate work groups to make the agreement work and this usually requires the support of their shop stewards.

In the Fawley case, early neglect of the work group, for example the Day Branch of the TGWU, was costly and despite the agreement, the grievances of this group left a heritage of bitterness manifest when the agreements were implemented.[28]

Flanders attributed the 'comparatively successful outcome' of the negotiations to a combination of:

1 the attractiveness of the offer which, although it included substantial increases in ordinary time rates, was *de facto* predominantly in the form of a shorter working week;
2 the pre-negotiation discussions on the ideas behind the Blue Book which contributed significantly to a changing of the ideas of many of the employee representatives on issues of principle, for example of established beliefs about what a good trade unionist should stand for; and
3 the 'no redundancy' pledge.[29]

The main features of the 1960 agreements are set out in Table 18.1.

Fawley: the 1960s to the 1980s (Ahlstrand)

Ahlstrand's research explores the evolution of management's industrial relations strategy at Fawley from 1960 to 1985. The 1960 agreements were the first of twenty-one productivity agreements negotiated over the twenty-five years covered by the case study. Ahlstrand's evaluation and analysis uses the analytical framework of three alternative approaches to management industrial relations strategy: rational, political and symbolic. The distinguishing features of these three approaches are set out in Table 9.1 (see chapter 9). Some of the major findings from this study follow.

The case study data reveal quite significant failure at the rational level i.e. the level of stated objectives. Ahlstrand finds a significant creep back to pre-existing work practices with each successive agreement experiencing a similar fate and little adaptive learning by management.[30] Ahlstrand concludes that his longitudinal study provides no foundation for the Marxian scholars' forebodings that a 'full effort' strategy would transform British workers into 'exploited efficiency automatons'. Rather, from a Marxist perspective, the failure of management strategy at Fawley could be interpreted as a major victory of labour over capital.[31]

Table 18.1 Main features of the 1960 Fawley productivity agreements: the 'craft' Blue Book and the 'TGWU' Blue Book

Management concessions
- increase in standard hourly rate of pay of the order of 40 per cent phased in from May 1960 to August 1962 to correspond with the targets for overtime reduction.
- introduction of 40 hour week in place of the previous 42 hour or $42\frac{1}{2}$ hour week.
- no redundancies.
- no benefit to one craft at the expense of another and no change among the existing balance of crafts.

Union concessions
- relaxation of demarcation practices within and between departments: inter-craft flexibility; transfer of minor maintenance work from craftsmen to process workers; craftsmen undertaking some slinging work.
- elimination of occupation of craftsmen's mates; 280 craftsmen's mates to be upgraded to craftsmen or redeployed as scaffolder-slingers, brush and spray-gun operators or cleaner-labourers.
- greater freedom for management in its use of supervision, for example line supervisors from one craft to be able to give administrative orders to other crafts.
- elimination of special payments, for example heat and dirt money.
- elimination of points rating scheme used for wage fixation and the consolidation of 22 pay rates to 5 main shift grades and 2 day grades.
- introduction of system of 'substitute' working on the process side; substitutes were to be highly flexible trained operators who could move from one unit to another.
- a management right to introduce temporary two- or three-shift systems to meet emergencies.
- alteration of working time arrangements through elimination of unproductive time allowances such as walking time, washing time and set tea-breaks.

Source: Adapted from A. Flanders, *The Fawley Productivity Agreements*, Faber, London, 1964, and B. Ahlstrand, *The quest for productivity: A case study of Fawley after Flanders*, Cambridge University Press, Cambridge, 1990.

The 'creep back' to old practices in most areas accelerated after the final wage increase was paid in August 1962. Ahlstrand believes that management turned to productivity bargaining again in 1968 primarily because it failed to achieve the Blue Book objectives, although this decision was less autonomous than the original management initiative because of the inducement effect of incomes policy in the late 1960s.[32] Management abandoned its 'high-wage and high-productivity' based strategy and returned to its traditional 'low-wage and low-productivity' practice. The creep back on overtime levels varied in terms of both quantum and timing between departments and occupations. In the maintenance crafts, overtime reached 10.5 per cent of the normal weekly hours in 1966, fell to 6 per cent in 1967 and crept back invidiously from 1968. In 1969, overtime levels for pipefitters and boilermakers exceeded 20 per cent. The pattern was similar for non-craft maintenance workers: an upward trend from 1962 to 1965, a decline in 1967 and a further rise thereafter. Overtime levels in the process department remained consistently high: 1966—15 per cent; 1967—17 per cent; 1968—16.5 per cent. Variations in staffing levels during this time had no effect on the high overtime levels. Ahlstrand rejects the explanations offered by the

National Board for Prices and Incomes: in the case of the maintenance department the cause was held to be structural contingencies, an unpredictable rise in fires and breakdowns; in the case of the process department, it was allegedly caused by reduced manning levels arising under a voluntary redundancy programme. He considers a more likely explanation for the return to high overtime levels to be problems of management control and worker and trade union pressure. For example, management never overcame the resistance by boilermakers and welders to working temporary shifts which had been designed to facilitate the completion of urgent maintenance work and help reduce overtime. Further, interviews with shop stewards revealed worker perception that overtime payments were seen as the means to compensate for the lean results of bargaining from 1962 to 1968, for the loss of value of the Blue Book base rate. Finally, some supervisors used the granting of overtime as a means of obtaining worker co-operation, including co-operation on other aspects of the agreement. Ahlstrand also found that contractor labour appeared to be used as a kind of substitute for overtime working. A pre-condition for overtime reduction had been greater functional flexibility (see Table 18.6), thus the failure to sustain a reduction in overtime suggested a failure of other provisions in the 1960 agreements.[33]

The Blue Book objective in relation to craftsmen's mates was achieved however. The withdrawal of 274 mates resulted in a net increase of 65 craftsmen. The remainder were redeployed although, for some, redeployment was a change of name rather than substance; they still assisted craftsmen while no longer classified as craftsmen's mates and they comprised the majority of those who left on the voluntary redundancy programme.[34] The most pessimistic picture was provided by the job flexibility provisions. Flanders' early assessment was not particularly favourable and Ahlstrand's case study reveals considerably greater failure. There were three types of job flexibility provisions:

1 inter-craft;
2 intra TGWU (both operating process shift workers and day non-craft maintenance workers); and
3 between the craft unions and the TGWU.

Ahlstrand identifies three reasons for the general demise of the flexibility provisions by the end of the 1960s:

- First, there was a proliferation of rules, an outcome precisely the opposite of that intended. This resulted from the codification of past restrictive practices prior to the buy-out negotiations and the clear, detailed specification of new working practices. The codification of past custom and practice rules emphasised them, gave them a 'stamp of approval' thereby making them more difficult to overcome. The new working practices were either so well defined they became new restrictive practices or did not allow for all operating contingencies, generating constant shop floor debates concerning how a demarcation relaxation was to operate. This was fuelled by a dramatic increase in worker awareness of demarcation. According to one manager 'it was calculated that for every demarcation relaxation gained, three rules were developed relating to the changed work practice'.[35] The problems highlighted a fundamental mismatch: 'flexible working defies the notion of control through rule'.[36] A significant finding was that before the agreements, informal or 'goodwill' flexibility operated, dependent directly on the supervisor-crew relationship. It was not merely granted on a contractual basis but was linked to a more complex set of workplace relations and associated directly with the nature and quality of supervisor-worker relationships.

- Secondly, the flexibility provisions failed because of management's indifference to training requirements. Implementation of the flexibility provisions required a vast technical training of workers and Ahlstrand attributes much of the failure to management's inability to organise this. The under-resourced training department retained its low status and 'This was a classic situation where the designers of a change programme were the 'power brokers' in an organisation, while the implementors were a relatively powerless group'.[37]
- Thirdly, agreement provisions were undermined by changes in technology and operating methods. At shop steward insistence, flexibility provisions became redundant with even minor changes in operating methods, and managers regarded the negotiations necessary to achieve re-application as prohibitive.

From the 'worker reward' perspective, the 1960s saw an erosion of wage differentials for Fawley workers in terms of the local labour market following their initial elevation with the agreements' implementation. This led to an informal re-negotiation of the agreements with the creep back of old working practices. Ahlstrand notes that Marxian scholars interpreted the relative wage loss as evidence of loss of shop floor control. He offers a possible alternative interpretation: management's abandonment of a high wages strategy may have been a reflection of the power of workers to devalue the content of the Blue Book agreement from the outset. He interprets the introduction of a voluntary redundancy scheme in 1964 as a failure of management's manpower planning: the need to reduce manpower was in direct conflict with management's need to win the high levels of commitment and consent necessary to achieve other aspects of the agreements.[38]

In economic terms, Ahlstrand found a break-even position with the productivity improvement between 1960 and 1966, due principally to manpower reductions via voluntary redundancy rather than through the productivity bargaining process. The Fawley management did not improve its relative position within the Exxon league efficiency table.[39] In institutional terms, productivity bargaining did not appear to be directed at the creation of a new 'higher' order pluralism as Flanders had hoped or presumed. Flanders had conceded problems arising from greater formality in industrial relations, governed by more explicit and less flexible rules. He recorded more conflict-prone relations due to the augmented role of shop stewards in negotiations and the workers' capacity to turn the new rules back on management by observing the letter thereof and reasserting the significance of their own role.[40] Flanders believed nonetheless that the greater turbulence would be counter-balanced by positive aspects of increased worker participation and by what he regarded as management's democratic behaviour. Ahlstrand finds however that management behaviour did not appear to fit the classical pluralist model and was more closely aligned with a unitarist ideology. He concludes that the management motive for introducing the Blue Book was to restore unilateral management control. Further, when management realised it had been unsuccessful, that there was an unintended new era of joint-control it was not welcomed by management. In cultural terms, Ahlstrand detects evidence of a growing worker hostility to the Blue Book. Flanders had considered that a long-term justification for the reforms was to be found in the objective of changing attitudes towards change. Ahlstrand draws on union correspondence and newsletters indicting the Blue Book to conclude that it had created a climate of resistance to change.[41]

Ahlstrand uses the political approach to management strategy (see chapter 9) to explain strategy failure at a rational level during each of four discrete phases of the bargaining process: design; negotiation; implementation; and day-to-day operation.[42] Some examples of the political forces at work are provided in Table 18.2.

Finally, the symbolic approach (see chapter 9) is used to explain the perpetuation of the agreements, year after year, despite their failure in terms of the rational perspective. Ahlstrand identifies three functions which gave logic and predictability to these management activities and initiatives. The first symbolic function of productivity bargaining was as a symbol for the manage-

Table 18.2 Management strategy: the influence of political factors

Design phase
- Designers of the agreements were isolated from those who were to implement the agreements. The former group was confined to senior managers and senior stewards.
- Involvement of supervisors and local stewards was largely token and input from workers on the shop-floor was non-existent. These key people were deprived of any sense of ownership and this contributed to the low level of commitment to the process at the shop-floor level where commitment was critical.

Implementation phase
- There was the problem of 'managerial fatigue', a product of the lengthy and demanding design and negotiation phases. In the agreements the crucial training tasks were allocated to the implementation phase and this was when the interest and energy of senior managers in the process began to wane.
- There was a marked status and power difference between the designers and implementors of the agreements. The former were the senior managers, regarded as the 'power brokers' in the organisation. The latter, comprising primarily first-line supervisors and the training department, were of much lower status, lacking in both power and resources. The implementation of change, being a 'politically charged' activity, involving for example the break up of coalitions and 'cherished' job demarcations, was however more suited to the 'power brokers'.

Source: Adapted from B. Ahlstrand, *The quest for productivity: A case study of Fawley after Flanders*, Cambridge University Press, Cambridge, 1990, pp. 197–199, 203–204.

ment of uncertainty and crisis.[43] Thus, when managers were faced with continually poor standings compared with other Exxon refineries in relation to labour productivity or a long-term decline in demand for refined oil, they repeatedly turned to productivity bargaining. The process was institutionalised as a ritualistic 'way out' of a crisis. Ahlstrand finds the Blue Book had become enshrined as a myth within the organisation. Managers repeatedly referred to the Blue Book era which was a 'glorious past' when Fawley enjoyed celebrity status and could do no wrong. Significantly it was found that the design, negotiation and implementation rituals of the process remained very similar over the twenty-five years even though the shape and form of the bargaining varied. Ahlstrand observes that the fundamental principle of the process was never questioned by managers who would criticise particular aspects. He assessed that it 'existed as a sacred totem, ... that could be touched up with paint, adjusted slightly—but never taken down, never totally dismissed or rejected'.[44] Further testimony to the ritualistic status was the importance attached to the colour coding and packaging of the agreements which provided the link with the past.

The second symbolic function was concerned with the management of impressions. The process was used to project desirable impressions of efficiency and achievement simultaneously to various target groups: Exxon company board; United Kingdom board; the government; its employees; the public. Management at all levels participated in a charade of 'good news reporting', concealing the absence of substantial progress in practice. The false propaganda cycle was in the interests of senior and junior management and the unions. For senior managers, it disguised the inability to manage the productivity problems, thereby reducing pressure from the United Kingdom and parent company boards. Ahlstrand explains that management used the rhetoric of productivity bargaining to conceal the harsh reality; claims and exhortations concerning involvement in productivity bargaining assumed a greater importance than the results themselves. For lower levels of management there was logic in providing their superiors with news they wanted to hear. For the unions the incentive to offer positive assessments of the process was the likelihood that management would be more receptive to future union claims.[45]

The third symbolic function was the careerist function. The design and negotiation, but not the implementation, of productivity agreements became a vehicle for the career advancement of managers, both within the organisation and outside it. This was true for both line managers and personnel managers. Managers involved in the agreements were viewed favourably by senior management and such involvement became accepted as a 'rite of passage'—'a set of activities or an 'ordeal' which accords to the initiate either a formal or informal stamp of approval'.[46]

Two factors made a productivity agreement an ideal career tool:

1 a performance appraisal system which encouraged managers to exceed the limits of formal job descriptions to initiate high profile projects;
2 a two to three year career cycle system in which high performance was rewarded with promotion.

The sufficient condition for promotion was participation in the glamour design and negotiation phases of the process, devaluing the implementation phase and leaving incoming managers to make agreements work, agreements in respect of which they felt no sense of ownership.[47] The high turnover of management stood in contrast to continuity on the worker side and was successfully exploited by the unions at the day-to-day operation level. The careerist symbolic function was also exploited by the unions when it placed a premium on managers' ability to reach agreement, making them vulnerable to union demands.[48] In terms of the Chamberlain-Kuhn model of bargaining power discussed in chapter 17, it increased management's cost of disagreeing with union demands which, in this special case context, would probably be demands to maintain the *status quo*.

Enterprise bargaining in Australia

Early attempts

The prominent public policy of the late 1980s, directed to improving productivity within a framework of federal government advocacy and industrial tribunal policy, has tended to obscure the fact that examples of management use of productivity bargaining existed in the 1960s and 1970s. They include an agreement between the Commonwealth Department of the Navy and a number of unions at the Naval Dockyards in Sydney and an agreement between the Associated Steamship Company and the Seamen's Union in 1969.[49] An example of an unsuccessful attempt to negotiate a productivity agreement was that made by the management of Petroleum Refineries Australia at an oil refinery at Altona, Victoria between 1969 and 1970. A case study by Riach and Howard[50] of this unsuccessful exercise is now summarised. In addition to illustrating the requirements for productivity bargaining discussed above, the case study illuminates aspects of union behaviour considered in chapter 6 and the process of collective bargaining considered in chapter 17.

The unsuccessful negotiations at the Altona refinery occurred in the context of local (plant) negotiation of exceptions to the general conditions of an oil industry agreement. The agreement was determined periodically by a process of good faith collective bargaining between an employer negotiating committee, the Oil Industry Industrial Committee, comprising representatives of each employer in the industry and a coalition of unions in the industry. The refinery was one of the oldest in Australia and the technical context for the industry was one of significant change over the three preceding decades reflected mainly in increasing capital intensity. As equipment changed, so did employee duties and the extent of job content change was therefore greatest in the oldest plants. Given that working practices are largely the product of custom, this increased the significance and difficulty of work practice issues at this plant compared with newer refineries. There was a multi-union workforce at the plant. The production workers were represented by the then Federated Storemen and Packers' Union (now part of the National Union of Workers). This group included

1 the more skilled refinery operators who operated the refinery production machinery and possessed relatively high-order refinery specific, and therefore mainly non-transferable, skills; and
2 a smaller group of employees concerned with the more traditional kind of storemen's duties.

The maintenance workers were organised by unions representing traditional crafts; those with the largest numerical representation being the then Amalgamated Engineering Union (now part of the Automotive, Metals and Engineering Union) and the then Federated Ironworkers' Association (now part of the Federation of Industrial, Manufacturing and Engineering Employees). The practice of the Altona plant was for separate negotiations to be undertaken between management and each of the several unions represented, except in the case of the metal trades unions which negotiated with management as a group.

During the period 1960 to 1971 management, in response to the major problem of job demarcation, had reduced the number of craft classifications at the plant from twenty-six to thirteen. Demarcation disputes continued and in the mid-1960s there was an abortive attempt by management to negotiate a job flexibility arrangement. In 1969 a new industrial relations manager was appointed whose philosophy included the idea that managerial concessions granted to labour ought to be matched at least roughly by concessions granted to management by labour.

The opportunity for management to move on work practice issues arose when the refinery operators pressed management for severance of their award conditions from those awarded storemen and packers in the oil industry as a whole. This group of workers, a minority among the unions' members in the industry, believed award provisions tended to reflect the needs of the less skilled majority and to neglect their own. Their claim was for separate coverage under the award and an increased relative wage. The management response was a counter-offer, essentially accepting the operators' proposal, subject to operator agreement to undertake a wide range of tasks some of which involved job flexibility between operators and maintenance craftsmen. The Storemen and Packers' Union response was understandably negative: the prospective benefits for what was a small proportion of its membership were presumably outweighed by the prospective interunion friction on work practice flexibility. Notwithstanding this response, the management now held the initiative and proceeded to attempt job rationalisation on a broad scale. The management objectives were

1 job flexibility within the maintenance group and
2 limited extension of operators' duties into the maintenance craftsmen's area of job control.

Management expected the operators to be enthusiastic supporters of the flexibility proposals and the tradesmen to be antagonistic, given that maintenance of explicit and clear-cut job jurisdiction is the whole basis of craft union tactics. Management decided that, given the restructuring of production workers' duties necessarily involved negotiation with the maintenance group, negotiations to rationalise the tradesmen's duties should be initiated simultaneously with negotiations affecting the operators. Management presented a two-stage proposal to the tradesmen. The first stage involved their surrendering fringe areas of their jobs to the operators. The second-stage involved in-principle recognition by the tradesmen that there were prime crafts common to more than one trade and that all trades sharing that particular skill should agree to work flexibility within the defined limits of that skill. The practical result would be the definition of various tasks as common to a particular range of skill groups, rather than being individual skill group specific. The management exchange for these non-pecuniary disadvantages was a cash offer in the form of a flexibility allowance, added to existing allowances and computed in cash terms. Management envisaged offering the tradesmen the entire savings in labour costs. In determining the upper limit of the offer management followed the procedure identified above as one of the necessary conditions for effective productivity bargaining. Management made a simulated calculation of the saving of labour hours which would result from the introduction of the proposed flexibility scheme. These savings were converted into cash terms and averaged over the entire refinery workforce; the annual average amount saved per employee would then represent the maximum annual increase per employee which could be financed from the new arrangements, if management were not to leave itself worse off as a result of making the changes.

The offer to the operators was based on two factors. The first was additional compensation for the operators' acceptance of a wider range of duties, a simple case of productivity bargaining. The second (implicit) element in the offer was based on the more typical context of distributive bargaining. It reflected management's implied recognition of the special skills and bargaining power of this group when it conceded their *sui generis* treatment within the award. The management offer however did not distinguish the productivity and bargaining power elements of the increase.

A crucial element in management negotiating tactics was the use of direct communication with the workforce to ensure the entire workforce was aware of the precise management proposals; this was a departure from past practice of relying on unions to communicate management proposals to their memberships. The overt rationale for this was entirely one of providing information. Riach and Howard point out that the direct appeal to the workforce was also designed to combat in advance any arguments the unions might put against the proposals. Management attached considerable importance to the communications program, placing heavy reliance on it to provide a basis for bargaining with employees. It was not intended to undercut the authority of the unions to negotiate on behalf of their members and management did undertake discussion with the officials of the various unions involved simultaneously with its communications program. Riach and Howard note that it was not clear however whether management would have been prepared, if the opportunity had arisen, to have negotiated an agreement with local shop stewards acting in defiance of union wishes. They also question two aspects of management tactics. The first was the almost simultaneous approach to both the unions and the union members in its employ. They argue that it would be more conducive to successful negotiations if the case was put to the union(s) initially and the communication program designed in the light of the union reaction. The second aspect was that the whole approach may have been too streamlined, attempting to achieve too much in too short a space of time. The writers acknowledge that a complete knowledge of the pressures and relationships is necessary to judge the appropriateness of a strategy but they observe that successful agreements have typically been negotiated over very long periods, sometimes taking several years to complete. The first-generation Fawley agreements for example, took three years to finalise if the initial management planning and reorganisation and the extensive and comprehensive consultation processes are regarded as part of the process (see above pp. 590-591).

Management was satisfied its proposals had the support of all work groups but this was not sufficient to achieve a productivity agreement. Separate negotiations with all unions represented at the plant, other than the AEU, resulted in agreement and the agreement of all unions was required for implementation. AEU officials had never expressed enthusiasm for the scheme and no formal offer was ever submitted to this union. Management was unable to submit an offer to the organiser called in to assist the tradesmen. Although the union members and presumably the union officials, were fully aware of the proposals under discussion, the contents were never considered and were certainly never the subject of negotiation. Riach and Howard cite British experience which supported the desirability of involving unions in the preparatory processes well before the negotiation stage and certainly before the presentation of formal proposals. As noted above, this was a feature of the first Fawley agreements. They suggest this prescription would seem to have offered more fruitful possibilities than the course actually taken. Negotiations ceased early in 1970 without the support of the AEU having been gained. The union's tactics seemed to be to postpone a decision on the issues involved for as long as possible, presumably to diminish rank and file enthusiasm for the scheme. Management had no counter to these tactics but was certain its proposals were entirely acceptable to all the tradesmen. However, the union had apparently convinced its members that the appropriate position was to resist the flexibility proposals to prevent dilution of craft skills and to maintain employment opportunities for members.

The negotiating structure adopted at Altona contrasts with that used at the Fawley refinery—a multi-union team acting jointly for all craft unions. Riach and Howard suggest the latter seems to promise better results simply because if difficult compromises have to be made between unions, it is likely to be more conducive to good industrial relations if such compromises are made by the unions alone.

Riach and Howard point to the irony of subsequent concessions obtained by management at Altona without compensation. They included some inter-craft flexibility and extension of some limited degree of tradesmen's work to non-tradesmen employed in the maintenance section. There was also a concession obtained through management coercion at negligible cost and for which management had been prepared to concede more in the comprehensive flexibility proposal. The restrictive practice was that tradesmen were driven to distant parts of the refinery rather than drive themselves. The coercive pressure was the contracting out of a substantial portion of skilled work on a new and distant section of the refinery. The company offered to substitute the tradesmen if they agreed to drive themselves. The tradesmen accepted the offer on the company's undertaking to meet the costs of the drivers' licences for the tradesmen concerned. The authors suggest the lesson here seemed to be that unions would be wise to assess the possibility of their being able to withstand subsequent employer pressure before refusing a productivity bargaining offer.

Riach and Howard provide an analysis of the practices of the AEU to aid understanding of what they term its 'enigmatic rejection' of the flexibility plan. The reasons were seen as important, given the strategic significance of the union in many Australian plants. This also holds true now more than twenty years later. The first factor is the union's explicit concern with job security and job opportunities, reflected in a statement by the then Victorian secretary of the AEU, John Halfpenny:

> 'It might appear as though the Trade Unions' influence on maintenance programs and techniques is somewhat of a negative influence as they are attempting to cling to old customs and practices. However, in the society in which we live, this is the only positive way in which unions can preserve job security and extend job opportunities. That is an extremely important matter for any Trade Union and its members. It should also be remembered that, on the other hand, employer attempts to introduce into engineering maintenance programs flexibility between trades, rationalisation of labour, and the like, has a very negative effect on job security and job opportunities.'[51]

Riach and Howard comment that the rights of the union and its duty to its members in this area are fundamental to unionism but that a large proportion of productivity bargaining is concerned with the identification and provision of mutually acceptable substitutes for the employee's need for stability in work processes and management's need for change. The authors note that a generalised working principle of the AEU was willingness to accept wage differentials for similar jobs between enterprises, a principle which does not preclude pressure for equalisation. They believe that precise identification of the union's interest is difficult in the productivity bargaining context. They note the union's devotion to the principles of craft unionism notwithstanding its self-image of industrial unionism. The former involves the tactic of defending a series of strong points rather than pursuing industrial objectives on a broad front (see chapter 7). However, Riach and Howard conclude that the union is undoubtedly aware of the dangers inherent in relying entirely on an uncompromising control of currently-vital skills and that it seems unlikely that this multi-craft union's distaste for job flexibility will prove to be permanent. Noting that the merger of the AEU with the Boilermakers' and Blacksmiths' Society and the Sheetmetal Workers' Union in January 1973 provided the combined union (the Amalgamated Metal Workers' Union) with control of a wide range of skills, they predict that this will probably induce the union to engage in flexibility-related productivity bargaining, at least where this involves inter-craft flexibility on an intra-union basis.

Another relevant factor identified is the philosophy of the union leadership and its practice in the matter of decision making. This aspect approximates the 'union values' area of strategic choice in Gardner's union strategy model (see chapter 6). The union operated on the principle that local issues should be determined by the local rank and file. Any changes in individual working conditions (including wage adjustments) were therefore necessarily ratified by a mass meeting of the particular workforce directly affected. This principle held in this case and the rank and file rejection of management proposals simply reflected the fact that in the last analysis they decided to accept the advice of the union. In terms of Gardner's typology, the concept of 'autonomous action' was applicable.

The final factor Riach and Howard raise in analysing the union's behaviour is bargaining power. They suggest that AMWU action here may have been based on its assessment of bargaining power, that is, an assessment that it had not yet reached a point at this refinery where its members could obtain further concessions only by granting concessions to management. In that event, they suggest the appropriate union action would be to attempt to obtain the offered renumeration increase without any concessions or, in more practical terms, to seek to reduce union concessions rather than to attempt to raise management offers for the same set of concessions.

In the late 1980s, the then Metals and Engineering Workers' Union (the product of other unions amalgamating with the AMWU), embraced productivity bargaining. Responding to further adverse changes in its environment, the union became party to comprehensive changes in the pattern-setting *Metal Industry Award*. These changes in turn became a basis for the development and revision of federal tribunal policy concerning productivity bargaining. This policy is now considered.

Wages policy and the evolution to enterprise bargaining

During the period 1987 to 1993 productivity bargaining was pervasive in Australian industrial relations. It was induced by federal tribunal wages policy and spread through the adoption of this policy by all state tribunals. The key features of this policy of evolutionary change, including the environmental context and the objectives, are considered below. This will be followed by an analysis of the differences between bargaining undertaken in the context of tribunal policy and the conventional model of productivity bargaining reflected in the Riach and Howard discussion and the Fawley case studies.

Wages policy and productivity bargaining 1978-1983

The term 'productivity bargaining' was first used by the federal tribunal in the late 1970s. The Commission's comments at that time came to be regarded as guidelines for a form of productivity bargaining, limited and controlled by the Commission, to take place within the centralised wage determination system[52] which sought to control all wage movements. The Commission's guarded approval allowed, between 1978 and 1981, a so-called form of productivity bargaining to be the mechanism for spreading a reduction in standard hours of work through industry, in apparent accord with the Commission's guidelines on wage adjustment. In April 1981 the tribunal changed its mind on the acceptability of the productivity bargaining it had previously approved. It said the issue was whether productivity bargaining could co-exist in a centralised system against the background of a general campaign for shorter working hours. It held it could not because the following combination of factors no longer obtained:

1. productivity bargaining exercises not being part of a campaign for shorter hours generally but were based on a rationalisation of working standards within the particular establishment;
2. productivity bargaining exercises being treated as exceptions to the general rule that productivity distribution must be on a national basis;
3. no protracted strike action being involved;
4. each establishment being able to be examined separately with conclusions being drawn on cost savings independently of averaging with other establishments; and
5. the exercises took as long as the investigation required.[53]

In these comments the tribunal was identifying a number of the essential qualities of productivity bargaining discussed above. These pronouncements became irrelevant three months later when the Commission abandoned its attempt to control wages and reverted to its constitutionally defined function of dispute prevention and settlement (see chapters 12 and 16). The Commission resumed the role of economic regulator in September 1983, identifying the grounds on which wage adjustment would be approved and productivity bargaining was specifically excluded (see Table 18.3).

One of the notable casualties of the Commission's 1983 policy was a proposal emanating from a review team in Australia Post. Its report proposed eliminating a number of restrictive practices, designed to help the organisation's transition to viable commercial status. The report was not acted upon because the tribunal policy precluded negotiations about wages and other changes essential to employee acceptance of the proposed reforms.[54]

Table 18.3 Federal tribunal exclusion of productivity bargaining, 1983

5. STANDARD HOURS
(a) In dealing with agreements and unopposed claims for a reduction in standard hours to 38 per week, the cost impact of the shorter week should be minimised. Accordingly, the Commission should satisfy itself that as much as possible of the required cost offset is achieved by changes in work practices.
Opposed claims should be rejected
(b) Claims for reduction in standard weekly hours below 38, even with full cost offsets, should not be allowed.
(c) 'The Commission should not approve or award improvements in pay or other conditions on the basis of productivity bargaining. These improvements should only be allowed on the basis of the appropriate Principles.'
    (emphasis added)

Source: Australian Conciliation and Arbitration Commission, *National Wage* case, September 1983, 291 CAR 3 at 53.

A policy reversal

By March 1987, the wheel had turned sufficiently for the Commission's policy to have been reviewed again. The pursuit of productivity changes at the micro level had become its priority. This version of the policy included the objectives of:

1. close monitoring of changes in labour costs;
2. provision of opportunities to increase efficiency and productivity at the enterprise level; and
3. protection for lower paid workers.[55]

While it is easy and tempting to ridicule, in retrospect, the meanderings of the Commission on this issue, it does need to be kept in mind that the political wisdom of the time sought to place wages and other labour costs in a central role in policies designed to overcome the economic vicissitudes of the period.

Between 1987 and 1993, the Commission's wage policy sought to establish a link between wage increases and improvements in efficiency and productivity. The Commission, therefore, was concerned with both elements of the contract of employment: the reward for work and the work itself. It had, for much of its history, been primarily concerned with only the matter of reward. During this period there were some changes in the objectives of federal tribunal policy. Table 18.4 shows that the diverse objectives of March 1987 had narrowed to the objective of enterprise competitiveness by October 1991. In the October 1993 decision there was no comparable statement concerning objectives although the Commission said that the objectives of recent years should continue to be pursued. The discussion here is confined to the objectives relating to productivity and efficiency. The evolution of the policy followed closely developments already occurring in the metal and engineering industry.

The Commission's new policy invited comparison with the British wage policy of the 1960s, whereby wage increases outside the norm would only be sanctioned if they resulted from a productivity agreement. It was noted above that the effect of this policy was to induce bogus productivity agreements whereby managerial concessions to union pressure were disguised so as to apparently accord with the policy. The Australian policy had a considerable similarity to that which failed in Britain.

Restructuring and Efficiency Principle, March 1987

The tribunal decision of March 1987 reflected a consensus position among the major parties. These were the ACTU, BCA, the then CAI and the federal government. The consensus was that the adverse state of the economy required the indexation-based system of wage fixation to be abandoned and a shift in the focus of wage fixation to encouraging efficiency in industry. The reasons for decision nonetheless reflected the continuing concern of the parties with macro-economic indicators and with problems in the manufacturing sector, this being the only sector of the economy to receive specific attention. They also referred to a deterioration in the economic situation including further rises in the national debt and the cost of servicing it, high interest rates, a discouraging level of private investment and an uncomfortably large increase in the Consumer Price Index. The Commission did note

Table 18.4 Federal tribunal policy objectives March 1987 to October 1991

March 1987

The principles have been developed in the context of general agreement as to the need for restraint and sustained efforts on the part of all concerned—employers, employees and their unions, governments and tribunals—to address the serious economic problems facing Australia. In particular, the package has been introduced to ensure in the current economic circumstances that changes in labour costs are closely monitored; opportunities are provided to increase efficiency and productivity at the industry and enterprise level; and protection is accorded to lower paid workers.

National Wage case (1987) 17 IR 65 at 98

August 1988

These principles have been developed with the aim of providing, for their period of operation, a clear framework under which all concerned—employers, workers and their unions, governments and tribunals—can co-operate to ensure that labour costs are monitored; that measures to meet the competitive requirements of industry and to provide workers with access to more varied, fulfilling and better paid jobs are positively examined; and that lower paid workers are protected.

National Wage case (1988) 25 IR 170 at 177–178

August 1989

These principles have been developed with the aim of providing, for their period of operation, a clear framework under which all concerned—employers, workers and their unions, governments and tribunals—can co-operate to ensure that labour costs are monitored; that measures to meet the competitive requirements of industry and to provide workers with access to more varied, fulfilling and better paid jobs are positively examined; and that lower paid workers are protected.

National Wage case (1989) 30 IR 81 at 100

April 1991

These principles have been developed with the aim of providing, for their period of operation, a clear framework under which all concerned—employers, workers and their unions, governments and tribunals—can co-operate to ensure that labour costs are monitored; that measures to meet the competitive requirements of industry and to provide workers with access to more varied, fulfilling and better paid jobs are positively examined and implemented; and that lower paid workers are protected.

National Wage case (1991) 36 IR 120 at 179–180

October 1991

These principles have been developed with the aim of providing, for their period of operation, a framework under which all concerned—employers, workers and their unions, governments and tribunals—can co-operate to ensure that measures to meet the competitive requirements of enterprises are positively examined and implemented in the interests of management, workers and, ultimately, Australian society.

National Wage case (1991) 39 IR 127 at 139

that the bulk of the increase in this index came from the depreciation of the exchange rate and from public sector charges and taxes but concluded:

> 'The prevailing uncertainty and lack of confidence in the economy which underlines the economic circumstances briefly outlined must be allayed to halt further decline and to turn the economy around. In this connection, what happens to labour costs is of critical importance.'[56]

The ACTU concern with the state of the economy and its support for a wage fixation system which was both flexible and capable of maintaining restraint on wages reflected the 'responsible' character of unionism. This concern was categorised by the ACTU as one element of 'strategic unionism'. It also reflected elements of 'bargained corporatism' (see chapter 6). The ACTU submission said it was essential:

> ' ... that wage fixing arrangements recognise and accommodate industry efforts to improve productivity and efficiency at the enterprise level in order to improve our productive base and our competitive performance.'[57]

The other element of corporatism present in submissions was the support for a relationship of co-operation and consultation between labour and management in bringing about the changes necessary to achieve the above objectives.

The tribunal's reasons for decision reflected the preoccupation of the parties in industrial relations with efficiency in the manufacturing sector and included extracts from an Australian Manufacturing Council publication explaining the organisational, technological, attitudinal and marketing weaknesses of the sector and the fact that strategies for improvement would have impact only in the medium to longer term.[58] The tripartite Council was illustrative of the ideology of the Accord: the emphasis on consensus and a central role for the state in the management of the economy.

In March 1987 an automatic and universal wage rise of $10 was arbitrated, together with an additional conditional wage increase of up to four per cent of total wage or salary costs. This was known as the 'four per cent second-tier' and could be achieved under a number of Principles but in most cases attention was focused on the Restructuring and Efficiency Principle. Enterprise bargaining was central to this Principle which provided for increases in pay rates or improvement in conditions of employment as a result of measures to improve efficiency. In terms of the concept of exchange central to productivity bargaining, the employee benefit was a maximum pay rise of four per cent, with changes in conditions of employment being marginalised and the employer benefit was to be reflected in any combination of the changes listed in Table 18.5. This bargaining agenda, framed by arbitration, included mandatory and discretionary issues and, by implication, covered award and non-award matters.

The Commission's view was that the objectives of the Principle would be achieved primarily at the enterprise level and that national guideline agreements may assist the proper processing of enterprise based exercises.[59] It stipulated three general conditions to apply in relation to pay increases:

1. there should be no expectation that all employees' remuneration would be adjusted when the work of only some employees had been affected;
2. it would be inappropriate and contrary to the spirit as well as the objectives of the principle, if increases in remuneration were paid before a restructuring exercise was implemented;
3. it should be clear the principle is not intended to operate on the assumption that there must be a return to the employees of benefits commensurate with the value of the changes to the employer.[60]

Table 18.5 Restructuring and Efficiency Principle, March 1987

(a) Increases in rates of pay or improvements in conditions of employment may be justified as a result of measures implemented to improve efficiency in both the public and private sectors.
   (i) Changes to work practices and changes to management practices must be accepted as an integral part of an exercise conducted in accordance with this principle.
   (ii) Other initiatives may include action to reduce demarcation barriers, advance multi-skilling, training and re-training, and broad-banding.
   (iii) Changes to working patterns may be necessary.
(b) This principle shall be subject to the second-tier ceiling.
(c) Any changes in the nature of the work, skill and responsibility required or the conditions under which the work is performed taken into account in assessing an increase under this principle shall not be taken into account in any claim under the work value changes principle.

Source: Australian Conciliation and Arbitration Commission, *National Wage* case, March 1987, 17 IR 65 at 99-100.

There was arguably a divorcing of responsibility and control in the operation of this policy. The Commission said the responsibility for the successful application of the principle must be borne both by management and the workforce.[61] However these parties had little if any input concerning the formulation of this policy which was a product of the pre-eminence of top levels of hierarchical organisations. Further, they had no control over the duration of the policy. The policy can be characterised in Flanders' terms (see chapter 2) as comprising:

1 a set of procedural rules;
2 a predetermined substantive rule (a wage maximum); and
3 a defined range of negotiable substantive issues.

Most significantly, the parties assigned responsibility by the Commission could nonetheless be overruled by it. The process of compulsory arbitration was available and even where agreement was reached the tribunal would ' ... examine agreements and applications for consent awards to ensure that such agreements are justified on their merits'.[62]

In many cases the bargaining structure which existed for an award may not have been appropriate in dealing with the Restructuring and Efficiency Principle. The negotiable issues, both mandatory and discretionary, included work and management practices not covered by an award and there may well have been many variations in these practices between the industries and/or enterprises covered by the award. In such circumstances, the parties would have needed to establish subsidiary bargaining structures if they were to meet one necessary condition for effective productivity bargaining: a homogeneous set of work practices. This occurred in many cases in the metal and engineering industry.

In August 1988, the Commission held that the usefulness of the Restructuring and Efficiency Principle had been exhausted. The full bench (Maddern P, Keogh and Hancock DP, Sweeney and Lear CC) said that in the Commission's experience many of the parties made positive efforts but some were inadequate for the task. The best had derived benefits which produced immediate efficiency and productivity improvements and also laid the foundation for future improvement. The ambiguous rationale for discontinuing the principle was that: 'Because of the general approach adopted to its application, some parties have exhausted the usefulness of the Principle and it would seem impractical to expect others, who have not yet been capable of applying the principle successfully, to repeat the process'.[63]

No audit was conducted of the operation of the Principle by the tribunal although the department of state, the Department of Industrial Relations, published a report on its operation.[64] There are some published independent studies concerning this phase of the policy. A study which reported positive outcomes at an early stage was that by Rimmer and Zappala.[65] They examined twelve second-tier agreements: metal trades, building trades; federal public service (administrative and clerical), retail (Victoria), Commonwealth Bank, clothing trades, teachers (NSW), textile industry, nurses (NSW), Australia Post and Graphic Arts. The agreements were at industry level except for the metal trades, which involved extensive workplace agreements, and graphic arts, which involved some workplace agreements. The authors considered changes in terms of five main forms of internal labour market flexibility. These are set out in Table 18.6.

The authors offer the following conclusions concerning the sample of agreements:

1 The greatest changes occurred in the areas of internal numerical flexibility and functional flexibility;
2 The dominant approach, bargaining, was more valuable than either unilateral managerial action or arbitration;
3 The 'second-tier' agreements went beyond 'give back' or 'trade off' approaches, producing genuine attitudinal change in the form of genuine employee commitment to efficiency and competitiveness;
4 Differing conditions between industries and enterprises meant the scope for productivity bargaining was similarly diverse. This would lead to equity problems should there be further restructuring and efficiency negotiations; and
5 The main implication was that existing industrial relations institutions could facilitate considerable gains in labour market flexibility provided appropriate policies were adopted. Major change to these institutions was not needed to achieve labour market flexibility.[66]

Rimmer and Zappala note that the labour market changes 'coincided with major programs to overhaul certain employers and industries'.[67] In these cases it may have been environmental variables, other than industrial tribunal policy, which precipitated the labour market reforms. These areas and the possible determining environmental variables were: Commonwealth Bank (privatisation); metal trades (industry decline); clothing and textiles (tariff reduction); Australia Post (increased competition). The researchers' optimistic early assessment is not unlike Flanders' reaction to the initial agreements at Fawley. In the light of Ahlstrand's findings concerning management's inability to sustain changes, there would be value in follow up studies in the Australian cases to assess the extent of change over time.

> **Table 18.6** Internal labour market flexibility criteria
>
> **External numerical flexibility**—A firm's ability to adjust its level of labour inputs (by increasing or reducing its workforce) to meet changes in demand. Practices which facilitate short-term adjustments to the numbers of employeees include short–term contracts and greater use of casual and part–time workers. 'Distancing' strategies such as use of sub–contract workers and franchise arrangements transfer changes in labour demand beyond the firm's own employees who may be reduced to a small stable and skilled 'core' workforce.
>
> **Internal numerical flexibility**—A firm's ability to adjust the quantity and timing of labour input such as the number of working hours and the timing of work without modifying the number of employees. This includes flexible arrangements for overtime work and shift work and adjustments to annual leave and rostered days off to meet production demands. These devices permit more intensive use of expensive capital equipment and allow fluctuations in demand to be met without engaging or dismissing labour.
>
> **Functional flexibility**—An employer's capacity to move labour to different tasks within the workplace. This will depend on the range of tasks workers can perform which depends on the range of skills they possess. The more 'multi-skilled' the employees, the greater the capacity of the employer to handle bottlenecks or slackness in production by moving labour rather than hiring or firing. This form of flexibility depends heavily on reduced demarcation barriers and improved training facilities.
>
> **Wage flexibility**—Conventionally this has taken the form of remuneration systems which link earnings to individual or group output (piecework or bonus schemes). Other variables which could be used to adjust wages are profitability and value–added within decentralised cost centres. Time–wage relativities are another area where flexibility may be sought in order to provide an incentive normally lacking in the absence of piecework or profit sharing systems. These various schemes may have a dual objective: (1) to provide an incentive for workers and (2) to establish a nexus between the product and labour markets.
>
> **Procedural flexibility**—Establishing within the firm a machinery for consultation or negotiation concerning the above aspects of internal labour market flexibility. The agenda for such procedures may be widespread (as with a general disputes procedure) or confined to a single issue (such as technological change); the machinery may be fixed or temporary and its powers may be weak (consultation) or strong (decision making). Such procedures reflect commitment to joint adminstration of labour market flexibility at workplace level. Alternative approaches are unilateral management decision making or external regulation e.g. by industrial tribunals.
>
> Source: Adapted from M. Rimmer and J. Zappala, 'Labour Market Flexibility and the Second Tier', *Australian Bulletin of Labour 14*, September 1988, pp. 567–568.

Structural Efficiency Principle, August 1988

In August 1988 the Commission introduced what it termed a new wage system which sought to build on the steps already taken to encourage greater productivity and efficiency stating: 'Attention must be now directed toward the more fundamental institutionalised elements that operate to reduce the potential for increased productivity and efficiency'.[68] It provided two wage increases, a maximum of three per cent and a uniform $10, the latter to be awarded no earlier than six months after the operative date of the first increase and operative dates themselves were a negotiable issue. The wage increases were to be paid in accordance with a new principle Structural Efficiency, which came to be widely known as award restructuring. The *quid pro quo* for this benefit was far less stringent than that applied under the previous policy for it was procedural only, there being no requirement to demonstrate progress on substantive issues: the union(s) party to an award had to agree formally to co-operate positively in a fundamental review of the award with a view to implementing measures to improve the efficiency of industry and provide workers with access to more varied, fulfilling and better paid jobs (see Table 18.4). The latter objective was new and could be characterised as 'career path' development and might involve both the restructuring of jobs and award classifications. In terms of the 'exchange' characteristic of productivity bargaining, it represented another potential benefit for employees in addition to the immediate benefit of wage increases. The negotiable issues to be considered in the award review showed considerable overlap with those specified in March 1987 and were to include the issues which appear in Table 18.7.

Review of progress, May 1989

In the first half of 1989 the full bench (Maddern P, Ludeke, Keogh, Peterson DP, Johnson, Nolan, Laing CC) reviewed the progress of award restructuring. Submissions indicated uneven progress with inter-industry and inter-enterprise variation. Where progress was slow, it was attributed to disagreement over the agenda or a lack of preparedness to consider change. The Commission concluded that the principle framed in 1988 was satisfactory, although progress was minimal in the majority of areas.[69] It said the success of the principle would be measured by the extent to which changes made at award level were implemented at plant and enterprise level.[70] The Commission also endorsed in principle the pursuit of a set of appropriate (equitable) wage relativities between all federal awards based on generic skill levels.[71]

Table 18.7 Structural Efficiency Principle, August 1988

Increases in wages and salaries or improvements in conditions allowable under the *National Wage* Case decision of 12 August 1988 shall be justified if the union(s) party to an award formally agree(s) to co-operate positively in a fundamental review of that award with a view to implementing measures to improve the efficiency of industry and provide workers with access to more varied, fulfilling and better paid jobs. The measures to be considered should include but not be limited to:

- establishing skill-related career paths which provide an incentive for workers to continue to participate in skill formation;
- eliminating impediments to multi-skilling and broadening the range of tasks which a worker may be required to perform;
- creating appropriate relativities between different categories of workers within the award and at enterprise level;
- ensuring that working patterns and arrangements enhance flexibility and the efficiency of the industry;
- including properly fixed minimum rates for classifications in awards, related appropriately to one another, with any amounts in excess of these properly fixed minimum rates being expressed as supplementary payments;
- updating and/or rationalising the list of respondents to awards;
- addressing any cases where award provisions discriminate against sections of the workforce.

Source: Australian Conciliation and Arbitration Commission, *National Wage* case, August 1988, 25 IR 170 at 179.

The process of award restructuring now had two potentially conflicting objectives:

1 award modernisation (eliminating impediments to efficiency and improving productivity); and
2 ensuring stability between awards.

The latter objective was designed to eliminate irregularities in the award wage system including inequities within and between awards and employer initiated variations from award relativities, which presumably meant over-award rates. These were held to be responsible for industrial disruption, unwarranted 'flow-on' settlements and leap-frogging. This had handicapped the Commission in its attempts to achieve the objects of the Act and led to economically unsustainable general wage increases with adverse effects on the state of the economy.[72]

These two objectives of the tribunal policy placed the productivity bargaining component at odds with the purposes and requirements of productivity bargaining discussed above. The level of negotiations under the Structural Efficiency Principle was a significant issue in the review proceedings. The Commission said that the level of negotiations would vary according to the nature of individual awards and the respondents thereto. However the Principle was directed primarily to changing award structures which inhibited measures to improve efficiency in individual establishments. This meant employer associations should ensure their members' needs for award changes became negotiable issues.[73]

Structural Efficiency Principle, August 1989

As is evident in Table 18.4 there was no change in tribunal policy objectives in the August 1989 national wage decision but there was some strengthening of the requirement concerning evidence of substantive change and a clarification of negotiable issues. As in August 1988, two pay increases were awarded with a minimum of six months between them and with three alternative weekly increases—$10, $12.50 and the higher of $15 or three per cent—depending on an employee's existing wage level. The key difference in terms of the 'work' component of the exchange was that the Commission now required that the parties were 'implementing measures'[74] to achieve the objectives of August 1988. The 1988 decision could be seen as providing compensation to employees for their agreement (or their union's agreement) to award reviews, while in 1989 they were to be rewarded for having done so. From the Commission's comments it appears that the most common proposed changes concerned broad-banding and multi-skilling and here the Commission endorsed the trialling of new classification structures, before award changes were made, as was occurring in an agreement between the MTIA and the federation of metal trades unions. The Commission wisely advocated allowing sufficient time for both immediate training needs and on the job experience, if required, before finalising implementation of the new award structure.[75] The tribunal also made the bargaining agenda explicit in relation to changes in working patterns and arrangements (see Table 18.8). This was in response to confusion concerning the prerequisites for obtaining

Table 18.8 Possible changes to working patterns and arrangements identified by the Australian Industrial Relations Commission, August 1989

- averaging penalty rates and expressing them as flat amounts;
- compensating overtime with time off;
- flexibility in the arrangement of hours of work, for example:
  - wider daily span of ordinary hours
  - shift work, including 12 hour shifts
  - ordinary hours to be worked on any day of the week
  - job sharing;
- introducing greater flexibility in the taking of annual leave by agreement between employer and employee;
- rationalising the taking of annual leave to maximise production;
- reviewing the incidence of, and terms and conditions for, part-time employment and casual employment;
- reducing options for payments of wages other than by electronic funds transfer;
- extending options as to the period for which wages must be paid to include fortnightly and monthly payment;
- changes in manning consistent with improved work methods and the application of new technology and changes in award provisions which restrict the right of employers to manage their own business unless they are seeking from the employees something which is unjust or unreasonable;
- reviewing sick leave provisions with the aim of avoiding misuse; and
- developing appropriate consultative procedures to deal with the day to day matters of concern to employers and workers.

Source: Australian Industrial Relations Commission, *National Wage* case, August 1989, 30 IR 81 at 91–92.

the wage increase and claims by employers that unions were seeking to restrict the negotiable issues. The Commission advised that proposals for such changes should not be approached in a negative cost-cutting manner and be introduced by agreement, that is bargaining rather than arbitration, as far as possible.[76]

Structural Efficiency Principle, April 1991

In April 1991, a full bench (Maddern P, Keogh and Hancock DP, Connell and Oldmeadow CC) awarded a 2.5 per cent pay rise subject to more explicit and detailed progress on implementation of award restructuring than was required for previous wage increases. The conditions justifying wage increases are set out in Table 18.9. They covered both award and non-award matters, both procedural and substantive issues with some requirements directed to the parties to the award (usually employer associations and national unions) and others directed to the management of enterprises. The decision illustrated the volatility of tribunal policy and the consequential complexity of the regulation of industrial relations practice in Australia.

Rejection of enterprise bargaining, April 1991

In the above decision the hybrid form of productivity bargaining entailed in the Structural Efficiency Principle took second place to the matter of enterprise bargaining. This process became a centre of controversy when the Commission declined to adopt an enterprise bargaining principle despite its advocacy by the ACTU, the federal government and all major employer

Table 18.9 Structural Efficiency Principle, April 1991

Consistent with the ongoing implementation of the structural efficiency principle determined in the *National Wage* Case decision of 7 August 1989, any party to a minimum rates award or a paid rates award seeking the increases in wages or salaries allowable under the *National Wage* Case decision of 16 April is required to satisfy the Commission:

(a) that the parties to the award have examined or are examining both award and non-award matters to test whether work classfications and basic work patterns and arrangements are appropriate — the examination to include specific consideration of:
   (i) the contract of employment including the employment of casual, part-time, temporary, fixed term and seasonal employees,
   (ii) the arrangement of working hours,
   (iii) the scope and incidence of the award;

(b) that facilitative provisions have been inserted in relevant clauses of the award;

(c) that the award requires enterprises to establish a consultative mechanism and procedures appropriate to their size, structure and needs for consultation and negotiation on matters affecting their efficiency and productivity;

(d) that the award, in order to ensure increased efficiency and productivity at the enterprise level, while not limiting the rights of either an employer or union to arbitration, provides a process whereby consideration can be given to changes in award provisions; any agreement reached under this process would have to be formally ratified by the Commission and any disputed areas should be subject to conciliation and/or arbitration;

(e) that there is a provision in the award to the effect that an employer may direct an employee to carry out such duties as are within the limits of the employee's skill, competence and training;

(f) that the parties to the award have implemented, substantially, the structural efficiency principle determined in the 7 August 1989 *National Wage* Case decision and have applied or are applying consequential award reforms to the workplace; and

(g) that the parties to the award have commenced the minimum rates adjustment process or are prepared to commence it, in the acceptable near future.

Source: Australian Industrial Relations Commission, *National Wage* case, April 1991, 36 IR 120 at 180–181.

associations except the MTIA (see Table 15.4 for ACTU-government position). At face value the term 'enterprise bargaining' refers to a particular process, bargaining, conducted at a particular level, the enterprise. It could operate with any substantive issue agenda, relate to collective and/or individual bargaining and could either co-exist with, or be completely independent of, processes of conciliation and arbitration. The workplace rules arising from enterprise bargaining could supplement, complement or replace those arising from other processes including conciliation and arbitration.

The submissions to the federal tribunal in 1990–1991 advocating enterprise bargaining varied in their views concerning these aspects. This diversity, the significant areas of disagreement on the detail of such a principle, the potential for excessive (large) wage outcomes (increases) and the incompleteness of the award reform process as well as its application at enterprise level, led the full bench to refuse to endorse any new form of enterprise bargaining. The tribunal did not exclude its subsequent adoption but rather suggested the need for careful attention to unresolved issues and further debate.[77] The response of the ACTU and government to the rejection of what was an important element of their 1990 Accord is discussed in chapter 16 where it is pointed out that collective bargaining, including such bargaining at an enterprise level, has been a perennial, though unheralded and subsidiary, feature of industrial relations in Australia. The enterprise bargaining of earlier times can be distinguished from that being contemplated here in that it was not subject to any form of public regulation. The best known example of the older form was that undertaken by unions party to the then *Metal Trades Award* during the 1960s in relation to wages. It is well-known in part because of the federal tribunal's unsuccessful attempt to eliminate such bargaining (see *Metal Trades Work Value* case (1967-1968) chapter 4).

For the purposes of the focus of this chapter, the process of productivity bargaining, the most pertinent aspects of the full bench's lengthy reasons for decision are the observations on the effectiveness of the Structural Efficiency Principle. The tribunal's assessment was unfavourable and the significance of this may have been swamped by the strength of the reaction to the enterprise bargaining component of the decision. The 'substantial progress' which the Commission found had been made in some areas amounted to a framework for change at enterprise level in the form of an award clause usually titled 'award modernisation' or 'enterprise flexibility'. This was essentially a procedural rule, sometimes with constraints on decision-making autonomy for employees at enterprise or workplace level, as illustrated by the example in Table 18.10. The 'substantial progress' meant only the removal of some impediments to implementation of award changes at enterprise level. Other areas were found to have shown little progress, either in terms of an appropriate framework at enterprise level or in any other respect. The Commission envisaged a clear sequence: award change followed by change at workplace level. The full bench expressed grave concern with the limited substantive agenda, the fact that the emphasis had been on classification restructuring, training and associated issues. It stressed the need for proper examination of other equally important measures to increase efficiency and productivity. The bench observed that substantial award changes had not been accompanied by any real impact at enterprise level and:

> 'This is inconsistent with the structural efficiency principle. It was not, and is not, contemplated that award change alone could achieve the purpose of the principle: that change must be applied as necessary at the workplace level in order to achieve real gain. This is true of award changes to classification structures and associated training issues; it is equally true for other award changes bearing on work requirements, patterns and arrangements'.[78]

The Commission also expressed grave concern about the lack of progress in relation to its second major objective established in the 1989 review: the realignment of award relativities to remove award system irregularities.

The Commission's reservations concerning the Structural Efficiency Principle were applicable to the award cited in Table 18.10. Although the major union, the Australian Nursing Federation, floated the idea of invoking this provision in the field, it was not used and it was superseded *de facto* by

> **Table 18.10** Award modernisation
>
> **Enterprise Agreement (Public Sector)**
>
> (i) It is open to Health Department Agencies covered by this part to reach agreement at the level of individual Agencies to provide for more flexible working arrangements.
>
>   (1) Such Enterprise Agreements may involve a variation in the application of award provisions in order to meet the requirements of individual enterprises and their employees. Agreements may be negotiated and consequential Award variations processed in accordance with the provisions of paragraph 36 (b) (ii).
>
> (ii) The union is prepared to discuss all matters raised by employers and employees within an agency. Enterprise Agreements may be concluded, subject to the following conditions:
>
>   (1) the employees must genuinely agree;
>
>   (2) no employees will lose income as a result of the change i.e. no negative offsets;
>
>   (3) any agreement must be approved by the union and the Health Department of Victoria. Where enterprise level agreements are considering matters requiring any award variation, the Federation and the Health Department of Victoria must be invited to participate;
>
>   (4) the union shall not withhold such approval unreasonably;
>
>   (5) agreements involving variations to the Award Standards shall come into effect upon approval of the Australian Industrial Relations Commission and shall be referred to in a schedule to this part after such approval.
>
> Source: *Nurses (Victorian Health Services) Award* 1992, Part B, clause 36.

the Enterprise Bargaining Principle (see below). It is possible of course for improvements in productivity to be effected through means other than tribunal policy, or award provisions which flow from that policy, and this has been true of the health services industry. A positive view of the impact of the Structural Efficiency Principle is held by the Metal Trades Industry Association. The Association has praised the Commission's policy frameworks regarding them as 'absolutely vital in achieving change'. In presenting the Association's submission to the Review of Wage Fixing Principles in August 1993, the Director of Industrial Relations said:

> 'In my considered opinion, having been deeply involved at a senior level in MTIA's policy formulation at the time and having participated in all discussions and negotiations with the ACTU and metal trades unions, through the period 1987 to 1991 in relation to award restructuring, the parties to the Metal Industry Award would not have achieved the structural efficiency changes which have become part of that award, in the absence of wage fixing principles and without the assistance of the Commission.'[79]

The praise did not end there. The MTIA view was that the fact that the enterprise awards negotiated under the industry framework agreement were subject to the scrutiny and approval of the Commission was the key to 'ensuring a consistent high quality of outcomes and it assisted in maintaining the overall integrity of the enterprise bargaining process.'[80]

Case studies of award restructuring commissioned by the federal government have reported encouraging results. An example is the findings of 27 case studies (14 from manufacturing, 2 government departments, 6 government business enterprises and 5 private sector service organisations) undertaken by the National Key Centre in Industrial Relations at Monash University. Their overview report distinguishes three types of outcome. Award restructuring:

1 has led (directly or indirectly) to workplace reform and can therefore be deemed a success;
2 has not led to workplace reform, and may be considered as failure; and
3 has not induced workplace reform, but this has taken place anyway. In this circumstance, award restructuring may be considered irrelevant.[81]

One specific finding of this research was that the vast majority of manufacturing and public sector cases had secured an enterprise agreement to facilitate workplace reform and were actively engaged in implementation. It was concluded that, given that the case studies typically dealt with events up to May 1991, award restructuring in these areas had been as successful as could be reasonably expected.[82]

Enterprise Bargaining Principle, October 1991

In the October 1991 *National Wage* case, the full bench (Maddern P, Keogh & Hancock DP, Connell & Oldmeadow CC) maintained the Structural Efficiency Principle but abandoned control over aggregate wage outcomes. It also established an Enterprise Bargaining Principle which incorporated the efficiency/productivity objective operative since 1987. An important difference however was that the tribunal reduced its control by refusing to arbitrate, that is restricting itself to a conciliation role and placing no upper limit on wage increases. It also absolved itself from responsibility for the outcome of enterprise bargaining by placing primary responsibility for achieving successful results from the process on the direct parties.[83] Limited control was maintained to the extent of stipulating certain procedural and substantive requirements in the new Principle (see Table 18.11).

The major substantive requirements for enterprise agreements were:

1 to meet the structural efficiency principle requirements established in April 1991;
2 to be consistent with the continuing implementation of this principle at enterprise level, with any wage increases being based on the actual implementation of efficiency measures designed to effect real gains in productivity; and
3 not to involve a reduction in ordinary time earnings or departures from Commission standards of hours of work, annual leave with pay or long service leave with pay.[84]

The October 1991 decision retained an arbitration function in relation to claims for the 2.5 per cent increase awarded in April and special case claims. The decision as a whole provided a clear example of accommodative arbitration: the tribunal responded to the pressure for enterprise bargaining despite the fact that its concerns, expressed in the April decision, had not been allayed.[85]

Table 18.11 Enterprise Bargaining Principle, October 1991

The Commission is prepared to approve, pursuant to section 112 or section 115 of the Act, enterprise bargaining agreements made between parties bound by minimum rates or paid rates awards, subject ot the following requirements:
(a) the parties satisfy the Commission that they have met the structural efficiency principle requirements prescribed in the April 1991 *National Wage* case decision;
(b) the agreement is consistent with the continuing implementation at enterprise-level of the structural efficiency principle and any wage increases contained therein are based on the actual implementation of efficiency measures designed to effect real gains in productivity;
(c) the parties demonstrate that they have considered a broad agenda in the development of their enterprise agreement;
(d) the agreement has been negotiated through a single bargaining unit in an enterprise or section of an enterprise. In the case of a single bargaining unit in a section of the enterprise, the parties must demonstrate that the section is discrete; its being treated separately from other sections of the enterprise must not restrict the implementation of the structural efficiency principle and enterprise bargaining in that establishment, or other sections of the enterprise;
(e) where the agreement operates in conjunction with an award or awards, it details the wage increases involved for each classification and all efficiency measures agreed. Alternatively, where an agreement replaces an existing award or awards, it must express the enterprise bargain wage increase as a separate amount from the standard rates of pay and state all efficiency measures agreed;
(f) the agreement provides no further wage or salary increase for its life, except when consistent with a *National Wage* case decision;
(g) the agreement does not involve a reduction in ordinary time earnings or departures from Commission standards of hours of work, annual leave with pay or long service leave with pay;
(h) the agreement:
 (i) is for a fixed term; and
 (ii) will not continue in force after its expiry date, unless renewed;
(i) the operative date of any wage increase for which an agreement provides is no earlier than the date of approval or certification of the agreement; and
(j) where parties to an enterprise agreement reached through negotiations with a single bargaining unit include employees covered by a State award, an agreement covering those employees is submitted to the relevant State tribunal for approval.
At the time of expiration of an agreement it is the responsbility of the parties to seek its renewal or replacement.

Source: Australian Industrial Relations Commission, *National Wage* case, October 1991, 39 IR 127 at 140–141.

Certified agreements legislation, July 1992

In July 1992 the federal government legislated new certified agreement provisions.[86] These changes in procedural rules further reduced third party control and promoted the progressive shift in the centre of gravity of industrial relations rule making to enterprise and workplace level. The legislation was a response by the Keating government to the conflict with the Commission arising from the April 1991 *National Wage* case. There was no change of substance to the consent award provisions (see chapters 12 and 15 for a discussion of the different tribunal instruments). This meant the Keating government had not responded to the concern expressed by the Commission in October 1991 namely, the existence of two sections in the legislation with different requirements for processing negotiated settlements.[87] In other words, two methods and two sets of rules for processing enterprise agreements remained, one for certified agreements and one for consent awards. Significantly, enterprise agreements involving a single business, part of such a business or a single workplace, were not to be subject to the public interest test in the *Industrial Relations Act*, 1988. Furthermore, any application for a certified agreement was not required to meet a key test established in the Enterprise Bargaining Principle, namely, that any wage increases in the agreement were based on the actual implementation of efficiency measures designed to effect real gains in productivity (see Table 18.11). The Commission was required to certify an agreement if it was satisfied that:

1. it did not disadvantage employees in relation to their terms and conditions of employment;
2. included procedures for preventing and settling disputes about matters arising under the agreement;
3. unions party to the agreement had consulted with their members covered by the agreement; and
4. there was a specified period of operation.[88]

This was, on the face of it, an easier path to a legally enforceable agreement than the alternative which involved the Enterprise Awards Principle (see below) followed by a consent award and which contained an efficiency-productivity test.

The Minister for Industrial Relations, Senator Cook, said the objective of the new provisions was 'to facilitate workplace bargaining agreements that boost productivity and improve the living standards of workers. There is now consensus in Australia on the need to focus industrial relations more directly on the enterprise and workplace.'[89] The government was concerned with the limited use which had been made of the existing certified agreement provisions and sought to make them less restrictive, that is, reduced discretion for the tribunal to refuse to certify an agreement. The relaxation of barriers to certification, in conjunction with a promotion of certified agreements by specifying encouragement of their use as an explicit object in the legislation, was intended to make enterprise ('single business') or workplace agreements available as 'a real alternative to the mainstream award system and not reserved for exceptional circumstances'.[90] This Labor government legislation may have, at least so far as certified agreements are concerned, restored the *status quo ante* of the 1960s. At that time the Commission's practice was to register, or certify, the agreements resulting from collective bargaining virtually on application. Exceptional cases were those in which certification was refused.[91]

By April 1993, there were approximately 800 enterprise agreements covering about one third of the workforce under federal awards.[92] Just under half of these, about 350, were negotiated for enterprises in the metal and engineering industry. The industry's major employer association, MTIA, considered that the 'initial foray into enterprise bargaining' undertaken through an industry framework agreement produced excellent results for both employers and employees.[93] This was not sustained however. During 1993 the metal trades unions (AMEU; FIMEE; CFMEU; EPU; NUW and ALHMWU) commenced a company by company campaign for a six per cent wage increase. MTIA has argued that the unions' perception of the increase appears to be that it is payable simply on the basis of allowing the reform process, commenced under the 1991-1992 enterprise bargaining round, to continue to be implemented.[94] This highlights a point made more than once by the Commission, namely, that success depends on the principal parties' responses to its policy. It also suggests a flaw in the policy itself, that is, the continuous nature of the process of productivity bargaining under tribunal policy since 1987. This feature is a point of departure from the conventional model of productivity bargaining. A number of other distinctions between the policy and the model are considered later in this chapter.

By October 1993, the number of enterprise agreements had increased to about 1200, with a little more than half of these being processed as certified agreements under the 1992 legislative amendments.

Enterprise Awards Principle, October 1993

Following a review of wage fixing principles which commenced in June 1993, the full bench (Maddern, J, Moore, VP, Keogh, Marsh, SDP, Harrison, DP, Cox and Smith, CC), in a decision on 25 October 1993,[95] introduced an Enterprise Awards Principle (see Table 18.12) to replace the Enterprise Bargaining Principle.

The key differences between the Enterprise Bargaining Principle and the Enterprise Awards Principle are set out in Table 18.13. The first difference is a consequence of the 1992 legislation discussed above. Although the new Principle remained a vehicle for processing the successful outcomes of enterprise bargaining based on productivity, it incorporated technical features associated with the traditional award system. In its reasons for decision, the full bench was critical of the legislated certified agreement provisions, arguing they had the potential to undermine the separation of the award system and enterprise bargaining outcomes which the Commission had sought to establish. Specifically, the Commission had recognised the risk to an award framework of equitable minimum standards, which it had been advocating since 1989, if the disparate outcomes of enterprise bargaining were to feed back into the award system.[96] This aspect is discussed in chapter 16.

For the purposes of the subject focus of this chapter, one significant issue arising from the 1993 decision is the two sets of rules for dealing with enterprise bargaining in the federal legal and public policy framework explained above. Another significant issue is the 're-introduction' of arbitration, albeit as a final resort. The Commission observed that the number of agreements was minimal given the number of companies bound by awards. It concluded that it should be prepared to arbitrate in enterprise bargaining disputes for two reasons:

1 the fact that conciliation had failed to achieve agreement on some or all issues in some enterprise bargaining disputes. This often meant shelving worthwhile efficiency improvements, with consequential loss of extra income to the principal parties and longer term reduction in competitiveness. In other words, the availability of arbitration would enable more improvements in efficiency and productivity; and
2 on past experience, the availability of arbitration of itself should enhance the prospects of success in conciliation.[97]

Table 18.12 Enterprise Awards Principle, October 1993

A. A consent award may be made to reflect an enterprise agreement between parties bound by an award, subject to the following:

(a) the proposed award is consistent with the continuing implementation at enterprise level of the structural efficiency principle (i.e. ensuring existing structures are relevant to modern competitive requirements of industry and are in the best interests of both employers and employees), including the consideration of a broad agenda;

(b) any wage rates contained in the proposed award (apart from rates that might be approved on the basis of other principles) which exceed the appropriate rates set in accordance with the minimum rates adjustment principle, or prescribed in an existing paid rates award, must be based on the actual implementation of efficiency measures designed to effect real gains in productivity;

(c) the agreement has been negotiated through a single bargaining unit in an enterprise or section of an enterprise. In the case of a single bargaining unit in a section of an enterprise, the parties must demonstrate that the section is discrete: its being treated separately from other sections of the enterprise must not restrict the implementation of the structural efficiency principle and enterprise bargaining in that establishment, or other sections of the enterprise;

(d) where the proposed award will operate in conjunction with another award or other awards, it details the wage increases involved for each classification;

(e) where the proposed award is not to operate in conjunction with another award, then the award should specify the classification in the relevant minimum rates award on which the actual rate prescribed for the key classification in the new award is calculated. It should also contain a procedure for renegotiation of the award at the expiry of its term;

(f) the proposed award does not result in a reduction in ordinary time earnings, or departures from parental leave and termination change and redundancy standards, determined in test case proceedings and Commission standards of hours of work, annual leave with pay or long service leave with pay;

(g) where parties to an enterprise agreement reached through negotiations with a single bargaining unit include employees within a State jurisdiction an agreement covering those employees is submitted for approval through the processes provided under that jurisdiction.

B. Consistent with provisions of the Act, the Commission will in relation to enterprise bargaining assist the parties to an industrial dispute in relation to any part of the dispute arising at an enterprise level. The Commission will initially do so by conciliation and, as a final resort, shall do so by arbitration.

In any arbitration, the Commission will have particular regard to the need for continued implementation at enterprise level of the structural efficiency principle and any wage increases awarded through arbitration (apart from increases that might be approved on the basis of other principles) must be based on the actual implementation of efficiency increases designed to effect real gains in productivity.

Any arbitrated award or award variation is to be consistent with the application of paragraphs (d), (e) and (f) of Part A of this principle.

Source: Australian Industrial Relations Commission, *Review of Wage Fixing Principles*, October 1993, 50 IR 285 at 319–320.

Table 18.13 Differences between Enterprise Bargaining Principle (October 1991) and Enterprise Awards Principle (October 1993)

Enterprise Bargaining Principle	Enterprise Awards Principle
(1) uses either consent award or certified agreement provisions for processing	(1) uses only consent award provisions for processing
(2) proscribes substantive rules which • reduce ordinary time earnings; • depart from Commission standards of hours of work, annual leave with pay or long service leave with pay	(2) proscribes substantive rules which • reduce ordinary time earnings; • depart from parental leave and termination, change and redundancy standards, determined in test case proceedings, and Commission standards of hours of work, annual leave with pay or long service leave with pay
(3) provides for a fixed term agreement	(3) makes no reference to the term of a consent award
(4) prohibits any wage increase during the life of the agreement other than an increase consistent with a *National Wage* case decision	(4) contains no prohibition on further wage increases
(5) precludes the use of arbitration, that is, conciliation is the only process available from the Commission [this was not in the Principle but in the text of the decision]	(5) provides for the exercise of arbitration powers as a final resort

Source: Adapted from Australian Industrial Relations Commission, *National Wage* case October 1991, 39 IR 127 at 141 and *Review of Wage Fixing Principles*, October 1993, 50 IR 285 at 319–320.

The final matter of relevance to enterprise bargaining and productivity was the Commission's statement that, because enterprise awards were singularly based on the needs of a particular enterprise, the terms of any enterprise award would not be taken into account by the tribunal in any other enterprise award matter.[98] The 1993 tribunal policy was overshadowed and probably marginalised by the legislative reforms of 1993.

Industrial Relations Reform Act 1993

The promotion of enterprise and workplace bargaining has been heralded as a central aspect of this statute, which contains complex and extensive changes to federal industrial relations regulation operative, in most cases, from 30 March 1994. While the legislation does include the goal of 'efficiency' this co-exists with other objects relating to social equity, including obligations on the Commission to protect the interests of certain employees for example, persons whose first language is not English.

There is now explicit reference to workplace and enterprise agreements in the objects of the *Industrial Relations Act* 1988. The first-cited means for achieving the principal object of providing a framework for dispute prevention and settlement which promotes the economic prosperity and welfare of the people of Australia is:

> encouraging and facilitating the making of agreements, between the parties involved in industrial relations, to determine matters pertaining to the relationship between employers and employees, particularly at the workplace or enterprise level.[99]

The only reference to efficiency (and by implication to productivity) in the objects of the legislation in 1994 is in Part VI—Dispute Prevention and Settlement. There are no such references in the new Part VIB entitled 'Promoting Bargaining and Facilitating Agreements'. One object of Part VI is to ensure that:

> awards are suited to the efficient performance of work according to the needs of particular industries and enterprises, while employees' interests are also properly taken in account.[100]

Another relevant provision linked to efficiency and the specific needs of the enterprise or workplace, encourages enterprise flexibility provisions in awards:

> So far as the Commission considers appropriate, an award must establish a process for agreements to be negotiated, at the enterprise or workplace level, about how the award (as it applies to the enterprise or workplace concerned) should be varied so as to make the enterprise or workplace operate more efficiently according to its particular needs.[101]

This is similar to the policy provision in the Structural Efficiency Principle which required enterprise flexibility clauses in awards (see Table 18.9).

The conventional model and the Australian case distinguished

A number of differences between the productivity bargaining occurring in Australia from 1987 to 1993 and the characteristics identified as necessary for this process to be effective, are now considered. In this discussion the Australian practice will be referred to as 'tribunal policy' to distinguish these practices from the features of the productivity bargaining model.

Productivity bargaining casts management in the role of innovator and accepting primary responsibility for efficiency. Under tribunal policy, the initiative has come from union and employer peak councils and the formal direction from the tribunal in its National Wage decisions. It is not a management initiative. With productivity bargaining, the focus of concern about efficiency is typically the enterprise or the individual workplace. In the tribunal policy the focus of concern has been the national economy, until 1991, supplemented by concern with problems and deficiencies in the manufacturing sector.

With productivity bargaining, management must identify the unsatisfactory work practices it wishes to change or eliminate and establish the potential savings which will become the subject of negotiations. The tribunal policy reverses this process. The tribunal specifies the rewards and negotiations then focuses on the changes to be made in work practices. Thus under the Restructuring and Efficiency Principle the Commission specified a maximum benefit of four per cent of total wage costs together with a very non-specific 'improvement in conditions' benefit. Management was then required to identify work or management practices it wished to change (these issues were mandatory) and, if it wished, various other changes which were discretionary. This was subject initially to union acceptance of the changes and failing that, to arbitration. Not surprisingly, this reversal of process and its application at an aggregated level failed to attract the union commitment identified earlier as essential for effectiveness. The union view was illustrated in a comment from Victorian Trades Hall Council secretary John Halfpenny who said 'The four per cent is an entitlement based on the trade union movement's commitment to the wages system'.[102] With conventional productivity bargaining, management identifies the workplace specific problems, identifies the savings and negotiates the buy-out price. Under the tribunal policy until October 1991, the price was identified first and it was usually uniform, then negotiation, or possibly arbitration, occurred in relation to inefficiencies, the parameters of which were set by the tribunal.

Productivity bargaining is probably a lengthy process but it is not a continuous one. It is a process to be undertaken at discrete intervals. Further, it will not be appropriate to all industrial situations and cannot, under any feasible circumstances, be envisaged as the sole means of determining changes in all wages.[103] The tribunal policy had the effect of creating continuous bargaining or arbitration over productivity/efficiency from March 1987 to October 1991 and beyond. This was not unqualified or predictable continuity however because the procedural rules changed on a number of occasions. For some of this period, wage rises under this process (Principle) were the sole source of wage rises although at all times the policy contained a special case category (variously titled) which created the opportunity for the parties to circumvent the constraints of the policy. This appears to have been used more often to accommodate areas of political or market power within the ACTU constituency than to facilitate management initiatives in the Fawley mould.

The responsibilities assumed by management under productivity bargaining require that management should control the timing of the exercise. In the case of the tribunal policy until 1991, the time period available for the exercise was to a large degree determined by the tribunal. In fact the tribunal dictated the timing; it determined when a particular Principle began and ended and there was inevitable uncertainty concerning the latter. Thus in introducing a hybrid form of productivity bargaining in March 1987, the Commission could only say the new Principles would operate until the next review of Principles was completed and that this would commence in May 1988. The modified rules were introduced in August 1988. The essential point here is that an external party was controlling the timing without regard for the stage of negotiations reached by particular parties; for any who may have been in the midst of complex negotiations, the ground may have been cut from under their feet. This was because once a particular Principle was 'discarded' by the tribunal it was immediately drastically devalued, especially by the unions.

Understandably, the unions' energies would be directed to a quick solution so that attention could be redirected to obtaining the wage rise available under the new set of procedural rules. There is anecdotal evidence that when each 'new' set of Principles was introduced, initial meetings between unions and employers were consumed with trying to work out the meaning of the fine print of the tribunal decision. This demonstrated dramatically where control lay. This feature may not have been applicable to negotiations in the metal trades which to some degree have determined the tribunal policy. Also, some parties may have had inside or advance knowledge of prospective changes if they were close to the elites who presented submissions and dealt directly with the tribunals. Generally however the frequent adjustments of policy may have thwarted progress in particular cases.

The causes and nature of inefficiencies can be expected to vary between workplaces. If productivity bargaining is to be effective there should be no limit, at least at the outset, on the substantive issues subject to negotiation. This does not, of course, imply that unions will necessarily concede on all issues. The tribunal policy set the parameters for negotiation and these were restrictive/prescriptive in 1987 and 1988, but in 1989 the tribunal did broaden the substantive issue agenda and emphasised that the parties should not be restricted to the specified issues.

Effective productivity bargaining requires agreement to changes before the money or other benefit is paid. In other words, a control mechanism is necessary to ensure co-operation is forthcoming. One of the conditions stipulated under the Restructuring and Efficiency Principle satisfied this requirement: money was not to be paid before a 'restructuring exercise' was implemented. There were, however, instances where the tribunals contravened their own condition, that is, granted a wage increase before concessions on work practices or other changes were made. This could be due to one or more of the following: management uncommitted to the process; management disenfranchised in the process; weak or sloppy management; union possessing greater relative bargaining power; accommodative arbitration by the tribunal. An example of apparent non-compliance with the tribunal requirement in the federal jurisdiction involved railway employees, members of the ARU and the Public Transport Corporation[109] (see Table 18.14).

An example in a state jurisdiction concerned the health services industry in Victoria. The unions bargained with the employer—the Health Department Victoria—as a coalition. The four per cent increase was awarded to all employees covered by about ten awards and no operational concessions on work practices at workplace level were made by the unions, either at the time the agreement was reached in October 1987 or during its period of operation. Over a twelve month period following the signing of the agreement, managements in about 160 public hospitals were required to participate in a time-consuming exercise to identify inefficient work practices and management practices. The workplace working party structures for these deliberations were determined externally and workplace union representatives were given paid 'leave' to work full-time identifying inefficient work practices. This all took place after employees had received the four per cent pay rise. In October 1988, Health Department Victoria, which had negotiated the agreement and managed the implementation, returned to the Victorian Commission to argue that the work practice review process had failed and should be abandoned. The employer representatives submitted that the cost of the implementation exercise was greater than the benefits it was producing. In addition to the direct administrative costs there were indirect costs resulting from what was

Table 18.14 Restructuring and Efficiency Principle: a case of non-compliance?

Rail workers win 4pc rise before trade-offs

BY JOHN MASANAUSKAS
Transport Reporter

An Arbitration commissioner yesterday awarded two rail unions the four per cent, second-tier wage increase despite only partial agreement by transport authorities and the unions on required trade-offs under national wage guidelines.

Mr Frank Neyland, who decided to arbitrate after three months of frustrating negotiations between the parties, said he found it incredible that the Australian Railways Union and the Amalgamated Metal Workers Union could not agree on trade-offs totalling four per cent of wage costs.

But Mr Neyland declined to blame either the unions or the Government for the dispute. "It is not appropriate that I attempt to apportion blame for a totally unsatisfactory state of affairs which resulted in the travelling public of Victoria and those users of freight services suffering massive inconvenience over the last few months' and it is an endeavor to avoid any further disruption that the commission is taking the action it is today," he said.

As part of his decision, Mr Neyland appointed a former arbitration commissioner, Mr Alan Vosti, to liaise with the parties in a bid to find the remaining cost offsets for the increase.

Negotiations between management and the two unions resulted in little more than three-quarters of the $10.7 million in offsets needed. And this was despite management's decision to lower its earlier demand of $12 million in trade-offs.

Transport Department officials are believed to be shocked by the commissioner's decision to award the full four per cent. A source said management was now likely to "stretch" the agreed offsets, leading to the loss of up to 300 railway jobs.

A spokesman for the Transport Minister, Mr Roper, said the authorities were considering an appeal against the decision. He said it would be made clear to the unions that the wage increase could not add four per cent to the budget.

The state secretary of the ARU, Mr Joe Sibberas, described the decision as a victory, saying that it was the first second-tier case which had been arbitrated by the commission.

"From day one we said that all rail workers asked for was treatment in accordance with the community standards set and observed by hundreds of employer and employee groups across the country," he said.

Mr Sibberas said the ARU had not accepted any job cuts in the second-tier negotiations and he did not rule out further industrial action in the remaining discussions to find the required offsets.

Mr Sibberas savors victory in his Unity Hall office before a mural depicting 75 years of the union's state branch.

Source: The Age, 27 October 1987. p. 10.

perceived to be an interference with, and inhibition of, normal management decision making.[105] In this instance employer, that is government, willingness to concede a pay rise without a *quid pro quo* may have reflected its desire to avoid industrial action at all costs. A few months earlier the government had been involved in a fifty day strike with nurses (see chapter 4) and any further overt industrial conflict could have damaged the credibility of a government elected on a platform of reducing such conflict, especially in the areas of teaching and health services.

In circumstances where management has initiated, and is committed to, a process of productivity bargaining it is to be expected that management will document the results in detail. It was noted above that the Commission appeared to rely on impressionistic and anecdotal evidence concerning the effectiveness of the Restructuring and Efficiency Principle. It certainly did not conduct any audit, even for a sample of workplaces or awards. Reilly, in a critique of the process, identifies a number of complex issues which were ignored, including the need for monitoring programs to provide 'before and after' benchmarks against which the introduced productivity measures could be evaluated and the interrelationship between input and output, that is the extent to which reduction in the cost of an input will affect long term productivity.[106] Any evaluation of the process would also need to:

1 eliminate those changes which merely codified practices that were already in operation;
2 identify any dead letter provisions removed from awards, that is, which appeared to involve the elimination of an inefficiency but in practice involved no changes; and
3 assess the extent of adherence to the new rules.

If productivity bargaining was operating in accord with the pre-conditions discussed above, the success or otherwise of the exercise would be known precisely. Further, as Reilly recognises in her analysis of productivity offsets used to achieve second-tier increases for workers covered by federal and Queensland awards, the durability of the changes is an important factor for consideration. She points out that unless the factors which produced such inefficient work practices as excessive washing time, unofficial 'smokos' (*sic*) and additional tea breaks were dealt with, their removal, although recorded in a formal agreement, would be of limited durability.[107]

It is clear that the continuity and complexity of issues involving the work component of the contract of employment make them incompatible with third party control. The inappropriateness of compulsory arbitration in the context of productivity bargaining was explained above. During the period 1987 to 1991 the use of compulsory arbitration was an ever-present option: at any time during negotiations either the union or the employer could unilaterally seek arbitration. Indeed the Commission said it would arbitrate if agreement could not be reached,[108] which was simply an articulation of its statutory obligation. As explained in chapter 15, tribunal members do have the discretion to continue to encourage parties to seek agreement. However any principal party may claim that negotiation is exhausted and the arbitration process must then be invoked.

The internal logic of a productivity agreement is that it creates its own capacity to pay at the plant, firm or industry level. Under the tribunal policy, the tribunal defines capacity to pay in terms of the national economy although it does not necessarily set the allowable increase in labour costs at the level reflecting that assessment. The tribunal adjusts that figure by industrial relations considerations. This may be characterised as its statutory obligation to prevent and settle disputes and, if institutional objectives are taken into account, by its assessment of the relative power of its various groups of clients and their inclination to continue to use the tribunals. It has been argued that the Commission policy from 1987 to 1991 was internally contradictory on the matter of capacity to pay: while the upper limit on the rewards was to be consistent with some concept of national capacity adjusted for assessments of bargaining power, the changes in work practices were required to be consistent with the needs and requirements of the industry or enterprise.[109]

The period 1990-1991 was one of declining tribunal control in the face of the preference of most of the major parties for a greater measure of autonomy, particularly in respect of wage outcomes. This change reflected in the October 1991 decision, unintentionally, moved Australian practice potentially closer to the productivity bargaining model discussed above. First, employers had greater discretion in determining the nature and quantum of benefits to be offered in return for union concessions. Secondly, the decision precluded access to arbitration where increases beyond the April 1991 2.5 per cent were being sought and there was no special case to be argued. Thus, one of the necessary conditions for effective productivity bargaining would now be present namely, the absence of compulsory arbitration. The prevalence of uniform wage increases in the enterprise agreements approved during 1992 suggests either that employers chose not to adopt the approach of the Fawley management in the first generation productivity agreements or that the pressure of coercive comparisons proved too great for employers to resist. The removal of arbitration avoided unacceptable imposed solutions in terms of third party control. This did not of course ensure a commitment to the provisions of the agreement by those employees with control over the work practices and arrangements in question or by those managers with responsibility for implementation. This is something which cannot be ascertained from an examination of the agreement itself and probably not by the Commission when it considers whether to approve agreements. It requires a longitudinal empirical investigation of the kind undertaken by Ahlstrand.

The Commission maintained the suspension of arbitration in relation to enterprise bargaining until October 1993. The rationale for restoring arbitration, that this would facilitate conciliation and that past failures of conciliation had prevented settlements which would have increased both incomes and competitiveness, is a view directly at odds with the conventional model. The latter argues for the absence of compulsory arbitration on the basis that imposed solutions are incompatible with full co-operation at the shop floor level and that the third party is unlikely to possess the necessary detailed local knowledge. The issue is control and this can only be determined by negotiation.

By the end of 1993 the Commission was continuing with a hybrid form of productivity bargaining under a new Enterprise Awards Principle. This co-existed with an alternative legislated mechanism for making enterprise agreements enforceable under the statute which had no (third party) test regarding productivity outcomes. The latter could be seen however as implicitly consistent with the 'management as innovator' and 'managerial responsibility' characteristics of the conventional model. This feature remains following the 1993 amendments. The Minister for Industrial Relations explained that the 1992 changes were designed to lift productivity performance and reflected 'the Government's expectation that the parties will increasingly seek to have their own arrangements accepted and given effect in the Federal system'.[110] If these changes had the capacity to improve outcomes in a relation to an objective which had been a policy priority since 1987 then, in terms of the rational approach, it is difficult to understand why they were not introduced earlier. It may be that the political and symbolic approaches, used by Ahlstrand in relation to management strategy, could usefully be applied here to explain tribunal and government strategy.

Conclusion

The public policy framework for enterprise bargaining developed in the federal jurisdiction in the early 1990s consists of industrial tribunal policy and legislation. The marketing or promotion of enterprise bargaining in the popular press perhaps unintentionally, presented it as a new, if not revolutionary, feature of industrial relations in this country. The distinction between form and substance was explained by the federal tribunal in April 1991:

> 'Enterprise bargaining' is the means proposed to effect a change of focus. The term may be relatively new in Australian industrial relations. The substance is not. Forms of enterprise bargaining are familiar to anyone with a practical knowledge of the formal and informal processes of industrial relations as they have operated over many years. In its simplest form, enterprise bargaining explains much of the growth of over-award payments which has occurred since the 1940s. These over-award payments have generally reflected 'market' rather than efficiency and productivity considerations. ... The tribunals have, over many years, facilitated enterprise bargaining by registering or certifying agreements, making enterprise awards by consent and conciliating in disputes about over-award payments and other non-award matters. A very high proportion of paid rates awards are the outcome of bargaining. ... In more recent years, this Commission and its predecessor have tried to encourage a form of enterprise bargaining which is not of the simplistic kind typified by the over-award campaigns of the past. That is, they have fostered the approach that any benefits conceded by employers should be in return for improved efficiency. Productivity bargaining for the 38-hour week was one example; offsets for superannuation benefits another. Only patchy success attended these efforts. Enterprise bargaining was central to the restructuring and efficiency principle, introduced in 1987. It was discontinued by the August 1988 *National Wage* case decision'.[111]

Thus forms of enterprise bargaining have operated for many decades in Australia. The most distinctive feature of the 1990s is that enterprise bargaining is subject to public regulation and is being strongly promoted by government, in some states as well as at the federal level.

This chapter has sought to explain the origins of the process of enterprise bargaining which came to dominate Australian industrial relations in the early 1990s. The historical approach, complemented by the conventional model framework, places the current developments in context and provides one benchmark for assessment and explanation of outcomes. A number of potential weaknesses of the Australian public policy have been emphasised. However there are positive outcomes and success stories—the metal and engineering industry, at least until 1993, is one such example. In the services sector, the much heralded 1992 enterprise agreement at a greenfields site between ITT Sheraton Hotels group, the ACTU and the Liquor, Hospitality and Miscellaneous Workers' Union is another notable example.[112] A less optimistic picture is provided by developments in the metal trades sector during 1993 and perhaps by the September 1994 *National Wage* case decision. Those taking a longer range view of Australian industrial relations practice and regulation and those adopting a pluralist or radical frame of reference will not be surprised by these developments. Similarly, the management experience at Fawley testifies to the reality of a perennial struggle for control. Nonetheless the language of the unitary frame of reference remains pervasive at the level of public policy, at the company level and, at times, in the ACTU literature. Longitudinal studies, incorporating the recent distinctive phase of Australian industrial relations, will be important in evaluating the relative durability and the practical impact of the competing ideologies.

Notes

1 P.A. Riach and W.A. Howard, *Productivity Agreements and Australian Wage Determination*, Wiley, Sydney, 1973.
2 *ibid.*, p. 1.
3 *ibid.*
4 A. Flanders, *The Fawley Productivity Agreements*, Faber, London, 1964, pp. 221–256.
5 *ibid.*, p. 235.
6 *ibid.*
7 *ibid.*, p. 245.
8 Riach and Howard, *op cit.*, chapter 2.
9 *ibid.*, pp. 2–3.
10 Riach and Howard, *op. cit.*, pp. 5–8.
11 Flanders, *op. cit.*
12 *ibid.*, p. 100.
13 *ibid.*, p. 101.
14 *ibid.*, pp. 69–70 & 73.
15 *ibid.*, p. 80.
16 *ibid.*, pp. 80 & 88.
17 *ibid.*, p. 98.
18 *ibid.*
19 The unions in descending order of size of refinery membership were: Amalgamated Engineering Union; Plumbing Trades Union; Electrical Trades Union; Boilermakers Society; Amalgamated Society of Woodworkers; Amalgamated Union of Building Trade Workers; National Society of Printers.
20 Flanders, *op cit.*, pp. 140–141.
21 *ibid.*, p. 104.
22 *ibid.*, p. 132.
23 *ibid.*, pp. 105–106.
24 *ibid.*, pp. 109–111.
25 *ibid.*, p. 118.
26 *ibid.*
27 *ibid.*, pp. 124 & 127.
28 *ibid.*, pp. 139–140.

29 *ibid.*, pp. 133–136.
30 B.W. Ahlstrand, *The quest for productivity: A case study of Fawley after Flanders*, Cambridge University Press, Cambridge, 1990, p. 6.
31 *ibid.*, pp. 5–6.
32 *ibid.*, p. 115.
33 *ibid.*, pp. 93–96.
34 *ibid.*, p. 97.
35 *ibid.*, p. 100.
36 *ibid.*, p. 193.
37 *ibid.*, p. 101.
38 *ibid.*, pp. 98–106.
39 *ibid.*, p. 109.
40 Flanders (1964) *op. cit.*, pp. 201 & 266–267.
41 Ahlstrand, *op. cit.*, pp. 113–114.
42 *ibid.*, p. 197.
43 *ibid.*, p. 213.
44 *ibid.*, p. 216.
45 *ibid.*, pp. 217–219.
46 *ibid.*, p. 222.
47 *ibid.*, pp. 226–227.
48 *ibid.*, pp. 227–228.
49 For a case study of the latter agreement see Riach and Howard, *op. cit.*, pp. 139–149.
50 *ibid.*, pp. 156–171.
51 J. Halfpenny, *Trade Unions and Maintenance Engineering—Some Observations*, 19 March 1971, p. 2 (roneoed).
52 Australian Conciliation and Arbitration Commission, *Inquiry Into Wage Fixing Principles*, April 1981, 254 CAR 341 at 361.
53 *ibid.*, at 362–363.
54 Australian Conciliation and Arbitration Commission, Australian Postal Commission/PSOA Award 1986 (and others), *Decision*, 28 August, 1987, Print G9043, p. 2. Noted in (1987) 29 AILR 396.
55 Australian Conciliation and Arbitration Commission, *National Wage* case, March 1987, 17 IR 65 at 98.
56 *ibid.*, at 72.
57 *ibid.*, at 78.
58 *ibid.*, at 77–78.
58 *ibid.*, at 79.
60 *ibid.*, at 80.
61 *ibid.*, at 79.
62 *ibid.*, at 75.
63 Australian Conciliation and Arbitration Commission, *National Wage* case, August 1988, 25 IR 170 at 174.
64 Department of Industrial Relations, *Report on the Operation of the Restructuring and Efficiency Principle*, AGPS, Canberra, April 1990.
65 M. Rimmer and J. Zappala, 'Labour Market Flexibility and the Second Tier', *Australian Bulletin of Labour 14*, June 1988, pp. 564–591.
66 *ibid.*, pp. 588–589.
67 *ibid.*, p. 580.
68 Australian Conciliation and Arbitration Commission, *National Wage* case 1988, 25 IR 170 at 174.
69 Australian Industrial Relations Commission, *National Wage* case February 1989 Review, 27 IR 196 at 197.
70 *ibid.*, at 199.
71 *ibid.*, at 201.
72 *ibid.*, at 200–201.
73 *ibid.*, at 198.

74 Australian Industrial Relations Commission, *National Wage* case, August 1989, 30 IR 81 at 102.
75 *ibid.*, at 90.
76 *ibid.*, at 92.
77 Australian Industrial Relations Commission, *National Wage* case, April 1991, 36 IR 120 at 158. For list of areas of disagreement see 144–145.
78 *ibid.*, at 142.
79 Submission by Metal Trades Industry Association of Australia, *Review of Wage Fixing Principles*, August 1993, p. 22.
80 *ibid.*, p. 24.
81 R. Curtain, R. Gough and M. Rimmer, *Progress at the Workplace, Workplace Reform and Award Restructuring—An Overview*, National Key Centre in Industrial Relations, Monash University, 1992, p. 1.
82 *ibid.*, pp. 3 & 7.
83 Australian Industrial Relations Commission, *National Wage* case, October 1991, 39 IR 127 at 131.
84 *ibid.*, at 141.
85 *ibid.*, at 130.
86 *Industrial Relations Act* 1988, Division 3A-Certified Agreements as amended by *Industrial Relations Legislation Amendment Act* 1992, s.8.
87 Australian Industrial Relations Commission, *National Wage* case October 1991, 39 IR 127 at 131.
88 *Industrial Relations Act*, 1988, s.134E.
89 Senator Cook, Second Reading Speech, Industrial Relations Legislation Amendment Bill, 1992, *Parliamentary Debates*, Senate, Weekly Hansard, No. 6 1992, p. 2519.
90 *ibid.*
91 See, for example, F.T. DeVyver, 'The Melbourne Building Industry Agreement', *Journal of Industrial Relations 1*, April 1959, pp. 7–19.
92 Speech by the Prime Minister, The Hon. P.J. Keating MP, to the Institute of Directors Luncheon, Melbourne, 21 April 1993.
93 Submission by Metal Trades Industry Association of Australia, *Review of Wage Fixing Principles*, August 1993, p. 23.
94 *ibid.*, p. 33.
95 Australian Industrial Relations Commission, *Review of Wage Fixing Principles*, October 1993, 50 IR 285.
96 *ibid.*, at 299.
97 *ibid.*, at 303.
98 *ibid.*, at 306.
99 *Industrial Relations Act* 1988, s.3(a) as amended by *Industrial Relations Reform Act* 1993, s.4.
100 *ibid.*, s.88A, inserted by s.7.
101 *ibid.*, s.113A inserted by s.15.
102 J. McKenna, 'Wages warfare warning to Govt.', *The Herald*, 2 February 1988, p. 3.
103 Riach and Howard, *op. cit.*, p. 96.
104 Australian Conciliation and Arbitration Commission, *Locomotive Operating Grades (State Transport Authority, Victoria) Award* 1987, Print G9410, 9 October 1987.
105 Industrial Relations Commission of Victoria, re The Health Industry, Victoria, Public Sector, *Statement*, 10 October 1988, pp. 1-2.
106 S. Reilly, 'An Analysis of the Factors Influencing the Second Tier and Its Evolution', *Australian Bulletin of Labour 15*, June 1989, p. 216.
107 *ibid.*, p. 218.
108 Australian Conciliation and Arbitration Commission, *National Wage* case, March 1987, 17 IR 65 at 75 & 79.
109 A. Petridis, 'Wages Policy and Wage Determination in 1987', *Journal of Industrial Relations 30*, March 1988, p. 157.

110 Cook, *op. cit.*, p. 2520.
111 Australian Industrial Relations Commission, *National Wage* case, April 1991, 36 IR 120 at 154–155.
112 For details of the agreement see A. Masterton, 'Sheraton Leads Way for Hospitality', *Workplace*, Summer 1992-93, pp. 8-11.

Further Reading

Origins of enterprise bargaining: a conventional model

A. Flanders, *The Fawley Productivity Agreements*, Faber, London, 1964.

P. Riach and W. Howard, *Productivity Agreements and Australian Wage Determination*, Wiley, Sydney, 1973.

Productivity bargaining at enterprise level: case studies

B. Ahlstrand, *The quest for productivity: a case study of Fawley after Flanders*, Cambridge University Press, Cambridge, 1990.

A. Flanders, *The Fawley Productivity Agreements*, Faber, London, 1964.

Enterprise bargaining in Australia

Australian Conciliation and Arbitration Commission, *National Wage* case, March 1987, 17 IR 65.

Australian Conciliation and Arbitration Commission, *National Wage* case, August 1988, 25 IR 170.

Australian Industrial Relations Commission, *National Wage* case, February 1989 Review, May 1989, 27 IR 196.

Australian Industrial Relations Commission, *National Wage* case, August 1989, *Reasons for Decision*, 30 IR 81.

Australian Industrial Relations Commission, *National Wage* case, April 1991, *Reasons for Decision*, 36 IR 120.

Australian Industrial Relations Commission, *National Wage* case, October 1991, *Reasons for Decision*, 39 IR 127.

Australian Industrial Relations Commission, *Review of Wage Fixing Principles*, October 1993, 50 IR 285.

N. Blain, 'Enterprise Bargaining: an Overview', *Economic and Labour Relations Review 4*, June 1993, pp. 77–97.

M. Bray, 'Award Restructuring and Workplace Reform in New South Wales Road Freight Transport', *Journal of Industrial Relations 34*, June 1992, pp. 199–220.

R. Curtain, R. Gough and M. Rimmer, *Workplace Reform and Award Restructuring: An Overview*, National Key Centre in Industrial Relations, Monash University, 1992.

R. Curtain and J. Mathews, 'Two Models of Award Restructuring in Australia', *Labour & Industry 3*, March 1990, pp. 58–75.

B. Dabscheck, 'Enterprise bargaining: a new province for law and order?' in B. Dabscheck, G. Griffin and J. Teicher (eds), *Contemporary Australian Industrial Relations: Readings*, Longman Cheshire, Melbourne, 1992, pp. 309–323.

Department of Industrial Relations, *Operation of the Restructuring and Efficiency Principle*, AGPS, Canberra, April 1990.

Department of Industrial Relations, *Federal Agreements Ratified under the October 1991 Enterprise Bargaining Principle*, 11 June 1992.

Department of Industrial Relations, *Workplace bargaining: the first 1000 agreements*, AGPS, Canberra, August 1993.

S. Frenkel and M. Shaw, 'No Tears for the Second Tier: Productivity Bargaining in the Australian Metal Industry', *Australian Bulletin of Labour 15*, March 1989, pp. 90–114.

W.A. Howard and P. Riach, 'Productivity Bargaining in the Public Sector', *Public Administration 30*, June 1971, pp. 117–134.

J.T. Ludeke, 'Enterprise Bargaining and its Consequences', *The Australian Law Journal 66*, August 1992, pp. 509–521.

T. MacDonald and M. Rimmer, 'Award Structure and the Second Tier', *Australian Bulletin of Labour 14*, June 1988, pp. 469–491.

D. Plowman, 'Award Restructuring: Possibilities and Portents', *Economic and Labour Relations Review 1*, June 1990, pp. 15–40.

B. Probert, 'Award Restructuring and Clerical Work: Skills, Training and Careers in a Feminized Occupation', *Journal of Industrial Relations 34*, September 1992, pp. 436–454.

S. Reilly, 'An Analysis of the Factors Influencing the Second Tier and its Evolution', *Australian Bulletin of Labour 15*, June 1989, pp. 200–222.

M. Rimmer and J. Zappala, 'Labour Market Flexibility and the Second Tier,' *Australian Bulletin of Labour 14*, September 1988, pp. 564–591.

J. Sloan and M. Wooden, 'The Structural Efficiency Principle in Action-Management Views', *Australian Bulletin of Labour 16*, September 1990, pp. 199–223.

M. Wooden & J Sloan, 'Award Restructuring: Factors Associated with its Progress and Success', *Labour & Industry 3*, June/October 1990, pp. 215–234.

Questions

Origins of enterprise bargaining: a conventional model

1. Define a productivity agreement.
2. List the major requirements for effective productivity bargaining identified by Riach and Howard.
3. Distinguish between collective bargaining, enterprise bargaining and productivity bargaining.

Productivity bargaining at enterprise level: case studies

4. Explain the reasons for the failure of management strategy at the rational level as developed by Ahlstrand in his case study of productivity bargaining at the Esso oil refinery at Fawley from the 1960s to the 1980s.
5. Explain the application of the symbolic approach to management industrial relations strategy in Ahlstrand's study.

6 Given the findings of Ahlstrand's research, do you consider there are any requirements for effective productivity bargaining additional to the requirements discussed by Riach and Howard?
7 Categorise the changes involved in the first generation Fawley productivity agreements in terms of the labor market flexibility criteria detailed in Table 18.6.

Enterprise bargaining in Australia

8 What were the reasons for the lack of success in the productivity bargaining attempted at the Altona plant of Petroleum Refineries of Australia in 1969?
9 Identify what you consider to be the most significant differences between the bargaining over productivity in the context of industrial tribunal policy between 1987 and 1993 and the requirements for effective productivity bargaining identified by Riach and Howard.
10 Explain the following statement indicating whether you agree or disagree:

'The major problem with productivity bargaining as practised in Australia is that industrial tribunals are invariably involved and this prevents the process being successful.'

11 Comment on employer and industrial tribunal behaviour in the application of the Restructuring and Efficiency Principle to the Victorian public health sector in 1987-88.
12 Assume you are the employee relations manager of a manufacturing company covered by federal awards. The new chief executive, who has just arrived from the United States, says he has heard it is difficult for managers to manage in employee relations in Australia because of the continuous changes in the industrial relations public policy framework. He asks you to explain what has occurred since 1987 and whether you agree with what he has heard. What will you tell him?
13 Does the *Industrial Relations Act* 1988, as amended by the *Industrial Relations Reform Act* 1993 provide any barriers to the successful conduct of productivity bargaining at an enterprise level?

Exercises

1 (a) Select a federal or state award and identify the changes attributable to the implementation of tribunal policy directed towards improving efficiency and productivity during the period 1987 to 1993.
   (b) Select one or more workplaces covered by the award you have selected and identify the impact of the award changes on any aspect of the workplace rules in terms of the goals of efficiency and productivity.
2 Select an agreement certified under s.170MC or an enterprise flexibility agreement approved under s.170NC of the *Industrial Relations Act* 1988 and evaluate the provisions in terms of the efficiency-productivity ethos of Australian industrial relations in the early 1990s.
3 Collate the assessments of tribunal wages policy relating to the productivity/efficiency objective provided by the Commission in its *National Wage* case decisions between 1988 and 1993. Prepare a summary of the tribunal's view of the success of this element of its policy.
4 Examine the publications concerned with evaluating the Restructuring and Efficiency Principle and the Structural Efficiency Principle and categorise the types of research undertaken.
5 Select any three articles from those examined for Exercise 4, summarise the conclusions and compare each of them with the assessment made by the tribunal.

Index

Aboriginal rural workers 460
absenteeism 50, 64–70
Accord see Prices and Incomes Accord
affirmative action 227, 465–468
Affirmative Action (Equal Employment Opportunity for Women) Act 1986 (Cth) 465
Administrative and Clerical Officers Association 218
agreements
 certified 115, 385, 386–387, 390, 475, 485, 495, 532, 563, 564, 570, 583, 619–621
 collective 8, 48, 206, 265, 334, 426, 430, 513, 563
 defined 385–388
 employment 430–433, 475
 enforcement 388
 enterprise 329, 336, 344, 372, 414, 415, 417, 618, 620, 623
  flexibility 115, 372, 387–388, 390, 485, 575, 595–596, 600, 603, 610
  productivity 532, 584, 587, 588, 593–594, 599
 industrial 107, 115, 149, 329, 332, 461, 513, 610
 negotiating 461, 475, 485, 486–487, 590–593, 620
 state 426–429
 union-employer 204
 union-government 53, 158
 union-management 149–150, 513
 and unions 428–429, 461
 workplace 420, 427–428, 620, 623
agricultural workers, unionisation 17
Ahlstrand, B. 3, 255, 256, 257, 258, 262, 263, 269, 288, 588, 593–599, 610, 629
air pilots' dispute (1989) 37, 90–92, 93, 99, 100, 103, 104, 116, 117, 146–147, 155, 158, 371, 390, 491, 492, 554
Amalgamated Engineering Union 83, 151, 179, 183, 334, 600, 602
Amalgamated Metal Workers' Union 83, 146, 157, 179, 183, 291, 603
Amalgamated Metal Workers' and Ship-wrights' Union 185
Ambulance Employees' Association of Victoria 188

Amoco 47
Anti-Discrimination Act 1977 (NSW) 462, 465
Anti-Discrimination Act 1992 (NT) 462
Anti-Discrimination Act 1991 (Qld) 462
Anti-Discrimination Board of New South Wales 462–463, 466
Annual Leave Payments Act 1992 (Vic) 430
Ansett Airlines v Australian Federation of Airline Pilots 100, 103, 104, 117
Ansett Transport Industries 90
arbitration
 'accommodative' 487
 and ambit 383
 and awards 2, 151, 334, 376–383, 433–434, 488, 489, 511
 and bargaining 573–575
 compulsory 139, 206, 325, 331, 340, 350, 370, 373, 411, 474, 476, 488–492, 489, 490, 495, 512, 567, 574, 576, 588, 628
 defined 474
 and employer associations 475
 and enterprise bargaining 475, 573, 629
 and management prerogatives 305–399, 379
 process 23, 142, 384–385, 474, 482–483, 485–488
 system 132, 139–140, 150–152, 206, 369, 382, 474–475, 482–496, 511, 524, 628–629
 tribunals 16, 31, 139–140, 141, 142, 151, 511
 types 487, 488
 and unions 475
 and wage determination 511, 513
 voluntary 474, 493–495
 see also bargaining; conciliation
Argentina 19
Armstrong, P. 258
Associated Pulp and Paper Mills (APPM) dispute 38, 39, 50, 54, 492–493, 557
Associated Steamship Company 599
Australasian Meat Industry Employees Union (AMIEU) 83, 85, 86, 108, 110–112, 113, 485
Australia Reconstructed 189
Australian Airlines 90
Australian Building Construction Employees 158

Australian Bureau of Statistics 50–51, 52, 53, 54, 172–176, 194
Australian Chamber of Commerce and Industry 227–228, 331, 342, 343, 350
Survey 298–301
Australian Chamber of Manufactures 343, 348, 350
Australian Conciliation and Arbitration Commission 81, 82, 332
Australian Council of Trade Unions (ACTU) 50, 56, 150, 152, 153, 154, 183, 211, 225, 476, 487, 492, 554, 557, 606, 608
ALP relationship 155, 161, 219, 482, 490, 491, 525,
526–538, 560, 575
creation 182
and enterprise bargaining 500, 521, 534
policy 156, 179, 185–190, 224, 226, 467, 468, 500, 533, 536
on union mergers 184–185
Australian Federation of Air Pilots 37, 90, 91, 92, 100, 146–147, 151, 155, 158, 159, 491, 554
Australian Health Survey 66
Australian Industrial Relations Commission 69, 101, 114, 116
and awards 496–497, 498, 511, 604–631
AMI Toyota Ltd and Others v Association of Draughting, Supervisory and Technical Employees 449–451
Altona Petro chemical Co. Pty Ltd v Federated Storemen and Packers Union of Australia 448
appointments 374–375, 479
Bargaining Division 481–482, 485, 575, 576
Divcon Australasia Ltd v RW Stanley 449
and enterprise bargaining 385, 487, 499-500, 521, 528, 534, 614-619
equal pay 514-516
function and operation 374, 477–482, 500–501, 511, 514
GMH case 521–522
Harvester Case 391, 459, 517
and *Industrial Relations Act* 114, 478–479, 576
jurisdiction 374, 376, 390, 477, 483, 487, 494, 496–497, 498, 514
legal procedure 384–385
and managerial prerogative 307, 494
National Wage case 83, 90, 159, 307, 333, 369, 390–391, 487, 516–517, 518, 521, 528, 529, 530, 535, 563, 564, 576, 614–619, 631
occupational health and safety 447, 448–451
Oil Industry case 522, 534
policy 170, 629
popular support 475
power 113, 115, 191, 376–383, 445, 485, 491, 494, 511

principles 487, 498, 534, 567
Re Private Hospitals and Doctors ACT Award 459
on registration of organisations 191, 219
Termination, Change and Redundancy case 292, 388, 460
and unions 191, 192, 478
and wage determination 170, 210–211, 511, 512–514, 516–526, 528, 530–532, 534–535, 538, 604–631
Australian Industrial Relations Court 114, 116, 177, 375
see also Industrial Relations Court of Australia
Australian Labor Party (ALP)
ACTU relationship 155, 219, 482, 490, 491, 525, 526–538, 560, 575
Industrial Groups 143, 217
policy 152, 153, 158, 159, 491, 511, 526, 620
union relationship 16, 18, 139, 145, 152, 157–159, 161, 183, 203, 210–212, 217, 482, 490, 491, 511, 523, 536
Australian Manufacturing Council 153
Australian Nursing Federation 40, 86, 142, 146, 149, 150, 152, 157, 221, 222, 393, 556, 558, 559, 616
Australian Tramway and Motor Omnibus Employees' Union 50
Australian Workers' Union 151, 182
Australian Workplace Industrial Relations Survey (AWIRS) 59–60, 66, 67, 69, 149, 255, 300, 301, 340, 341, 347, 356, 357, 498, 568–572
Automotive, Metals and Engineering Union 83, 600
award restructuring 56, 86, 170, 189, 296, 300–301, 336, 519, 612, 613, 618
awards
ambit 383
arbitrated 496–500
'award-free' group 512
breach 115–116, 117, 488, 512
cancellation 116
and collective bargaining 389–390
common rule and Mutual insurance 130, 299, 300, 330, 381–382
conditions 388–389, 474, 496
consent 332, 449, 495, 620
defined 385
enforcement 388, 426, 434–435, 488–489, 491
enterprise 498, 621–623
federal 369, 374, 380, 385, 461, 475, 575, 620
interpretation 335, 374
and non-unionists 383
'paid rates' 513
state 412, 426–429, 433–435

tribunal 332, 474
see also arbitration; industrial; wages

Babbage principle 26, 27
Bain, G.S. 172
bans clauses 82, 115, 289, 488
bargaining
    conciliation and arbitration 474, 533, 534, 573–575
    distributive 555
    integrative 555–556, 583, 585
    inter-organisational 555, 557–558
    multi-employer 330, 332, 333
    power 546–550
    see also coalition; collective; enterprise; productivity; unions; wage; workplace
Barrier Industrial Council 147, 151, 182, 223, 561
Batstone, E. *et al* 258
Bevin, Ernest 536
BHP 284–287, 292, 312
BLF Deregulation Act 220
Boilermakers' and Blacksmiths' Society 183, 603
Boland, R. 336–339, 340
Bolger, Irene 142, 558
Bramble, T. 287–292, 311, 312, 313
Braverman, H. 25–28, 31, 240, 241, 242, 260
Bray, M. 28, 150
Brewster, C. 258
Broken Hill strike (1919-20) 76–81, 93, 555
Brookfield, Percival 78, 79–80
Brooks, G.W. 208
Brown, W. 258
Bruce, S.M. 475
Bruce-Page government 216
Buckley, K.D. 150
Builders Labourers' Federation 17, 40, 57, 117, 142, 144, 157, 158, 159, 219, 220, 491
Building Workers Industrial Union 103, 157, 535
Business Council of Australia 228, 280, 281, 343, 344, 349, 351, 357, 606

Cain government 556
Cameron, Clyde 218, 219, 222–223
capitalism 25, 26, 27, 42, 145
capitalist industry 144
Chamberlain N.W. 238–240, 546, 547, 548, 585, 599
Chandler, A. 259
change
    employee opposition 42, 45, 299
    environmental variables 53, 288
    and industrial relations 29, 30, 42, 160, 250–251, 298–301, 474–475, 533
    and technology 45, 307, 379
Chifley government 217

civil conspiracy 105–106, 108
civil liberty groups
    and unions 214
coalition bargaining 180, 329–333
Coleman, J.R. 209, 213, 214, 353
collective agreements 8, 48, 206, 265, 334, 389–340, 426, 430, 513, 563
collective bargaining
    and arbitration 139, 389, 573–575
    Australia 47, 151, 543, 558–578
    and Australian Federation of Air Pilots 155, 158, 491
    and awards 389–390
    bargaining power 18, 81, 130, 134, 141–142, 159, 289, 546–550, 561–564
    Britain 23
    characteristics 560–564, 575
    conciliation and arbitration 139, 389–390, 474, 475, 495–496, 514, 523, 524, 533, 564, 574, 576
    Conciliation and Arbitration Act 389
    elements 545
    employer associations 18, 172, 329–333, 334, 544
    features 543–544
    good faith 495, 545, 559, 577
    government involvement 152, 411, 426, 545–545
    grievance procedures 568–572
    industrial democracy 265
    Industrial Relations Reform Act 1993 (Cth) 575–578
    legislation 152, 389–390, 411, 426, 575–578
    nature 543–550
    processes
        hybrid 558–560
        negotiation 81, 98, 545, 551, 555–558, 559, 575
    and public policy 564–565
    and right to strike 98
    technique 551–555
    uninhibited 496
    and unions 18, 132, 139, 141–142, 151, 152, 155, 172, 206, 210, 250, 251, 289, 565–568, 130, 566, 573
    United States 23, 29, 249, 251, 253, 254
Commons, John R. 127, 130
Communist Party of Australia 142, 143, 182, 217
conciliation
    and arbitration system 98, 139, 370, 373, 374, 375, 474–475, 476–477, 478–479, 482, 524
    collective bargaining 139, 389–390, 474, 475, 495–496, 514, 523, 524, 533, 564, 574, 576
    compulsory 139, 474, 476, 495
    defined 474

and employer associations 475
and enterprise bargaining 475, 495–496,
    514, 523, 524, 533, 629
legal procedures 384–385
process 98, 142, 306, 314, 332, 369, 370,
    373–374, 433–434, 474, 482–496
and unions 475
versus arbitration 482–483
voluntary 493–495
Conciliation and Arbitration Act 1904 (Cth)
amendments 16, 215, 374, 477
and collective bargaining 389
first enacted 373, 389
and formation of unions 565
and industrial disputes 140, 378, 474
and management prerogatives 447
penal provisions 50, 490, 492
and registered organisations 141, 216, 219,
    325, 423
restraining orders 82
and union amalgamation 225
and union government 215
and union protection 140, 141
Conciliation and Arbitration Commission 374
Confectionery Workers' Union of Australia
    426
Confederation of Australian Industry 307,
    327, 328, 331, 357, 606
conflict
and employer associations 354–358
resolution 24, 101, 107, 113, 494, 545
theories 25, 133
see also control; industrial conflict; power
Constitutional power 369–373, 387, 476, 478
Construction, Forestry, Mining and Energy
    Union 221, 222
Consumer Price Index 525, 606
contract of service 6
contract of services 6
contractors, independent 6, 371
contracts see employment contracts
control
and conflict 43–44, 54, 96–118
of labour process 26, 43, 240–242, 260
managerial 43, 44, 54, 251, 268, 305–309
and the right to strike 99, 107, 118
of workers by employees 7, 27, 28, 43–44,
    572
Cook, Peter 191, 226, 528, 620
corporatism 133, 152, 154
bargained 134, 135–136, 161, 608
pure 134, 161
Court of Conciliation and Arbitration 98,
    370, 373, 374, 375, 476
Crawford, B. 66, 67, 68
Crouch, C. 38, 133, 134, 135
Cullen, D.E. 238–240, 585
Cupper, L. 310, 485

Dabscheck, B. 478
damages claims 490
Davis, E.M. 311–312
Deery, S. 301
deregulation of labour relations 107, 411
Disability Discrimination Act 1992 (Cth) 384,
    462
disciplinary action 44, 46
discrimination 445–446, 456–460
legislation 334, 461–468
Discrimination Act 1991 (ACT) 462
disputes
demarcation 54, 180, 183, 191, 192–193,
    224, 225, 600
grievance 413
interest 47, 334, 494, 545
inter-union 54, 150, 156, 180, 189, 193, 216,
    224, 286, 294, 423–426
rights 334, 335, 370, 386, 413, 494, 545
see also industrial disputes
Dollar Sweets case 490
Duffy, N.F. 143, 258, 259
Dunlop, J. T. 14–22, 24, 28, 29, 30, 42, 43, 53,
    125, 133, 242, 250, 259, 292
Dynavac Charitable Trust 310

Economic Planning Advisory Council 153
economic policy 152, 153, 158, 159, 189, 511
economics
and industrial relations 17–18, 475, 51
neo-classical 3, 4, 475
employee
and control 305–9, 572
dismissal 104, 306, 336, 372, 379, 388–389,
    420–422, 435, 460–461, 494, 497
government 153
grievances 45, 46, 48, 216, 413, 68–72
redundancy 256, 462, 468
relations 2, 3–4
security 43, 54, 307, 460, 497, 586, 603
see also employer; management;
    redundancy; unfair dismissal
Employee Contracts Act 1991 (NZ) 429
Employee Relations Act 1992 (Vic) 56, 103,
    107,115, 116, 350, 390, 411, 420, 426,
    429–438, 563
Employee Relations Commission 429,
    433–437, 494–495
Employee Relations Study Commission 280,
    281, 282, 344
employer
authority 44
and control 7, 26, 27, 28, 42, 43
degree of control 7
employee relations 2–3, 4, 6–8, 9, 15, 24,
    41, 42, 43, 46–47, 101, 147, 148, 243–249,
    251, 255–256, 266, 280–282, 296–298, 305,
    379, 497, 555

independent contractor relations 6–8, 371, 380
and labour power 26, 43, 243, 266
peak councils 331, 332, 334, 341, 342, 344, 345, 351
see also management
employer associations
  Australia 324–326, 327–329, 331–333, 335–340, 342–344, 347–351, 353–358
  collective bargaining 329–333, 334, 544
  conciliation and arbitration 475
  functions 329–344
  ideology 326–329, 341
  and industrial relations 16, 260, 322
  internal government 350, 351–358
  media and public relations 343–344
  membership and structure 344–351, 354, 476
  organising principles 347–348
  origins and development 323–326
  and political parties 341, 342, 350
  registration 349–351, 358, 391, 436–437
  relations with state 340–343
  specialised services 333–340
employers' representatives 15–16
employment
  and unions 4, 148–150, 204–205, 281–282, 379, 468
  non-union 253, 379, 382–383
employment contracts 6–8, 9, 37, 38, 40, 43, 56, 83, 85, 139, 282, 301
enterprise
  agreements 329, 336, 344, 372, 414, 415, 417, 618, 620, 623
  flexibility 372, 387–388, 390, 485, 575, 595–596, 600, 603, 610
  productivity 532, 584, 587, 588, 593–594, 599
  awards 498, 621–623
Enterprise Awards Principle 620, 621–623, 629
enterprise bargaining
  and the Accord 499
  and ACTU 500, 521, 534
  and awards 332–3
  and arbitration 475, 570, 629
  Australia 599–631
  Australian Industrial Relations Commission 385, 487, 499–500, 521, 528, 534, 614–619
  certified agreements 385, 475, 583, 619–621
  and conciliation 475, 495–496, 514, 523, 524, 533, 629
  and corporations power 372
  defined 630
  and federal government 385, 426, 521, 573, 583, 619–621, 630
  Industrial Relations Reform Act 1993 (Cth) 475, 623–624

origins 584–588
and productivity 583–584
and productivity bargaining 583, 584–599, 604–605
rejection 487, 583, 614–618
Restructuring and Efficiency Principle 606–611
and strikes 107, 289
Structural Efficiency Principle 611–617
and union amalgamation 224
wages policy 604–624
Enterprise Bargaining Principle 487, 500, 528, 534, 564, 618–619, 620, 621, 623
equal opportunity 446, 456–459, 465, 468
Equal Opportunity Act 1984 (SA) 462
Equal Opportunity Act 1984 (Vic) 462
Equal Opportunity Act 1984 (WA) 462
equal pay for equal work 372, 459–460, 514–516
Essential Services Act 1958 (Vic) 437
Essential Services legislation 117
Esso oil refinery 288
Esso Petroleum U.K. Ltd 589–599

family leave *see* parental leave
Fawley (1960 agreements) 589–599
Federal Court of Australia
  and Australian Industrial Relations Commission 113, 114
  and Australian Industrial Relations Court 114, 116, 375
  Bailey v Krantz 425
  Byrne v Australian Airlines Ltd 38
  Frizziero v Rice 426
  Georgevski v Bostik (Australia) Ltd 389
  Gregory v Philip Morris Ltd 388
  Mudginberri dispute (1985) 83–86, 93, 108, 110–112, 113, 485, 490, 492, 553
  Sharpe v Goodhew 425
Federal Court of Australia Act 1976 (Cth) 375
Federated Clerks' Union 157, 218
Federated Confectioners Association 103
Federated Engine Drivers and Firemen's Association 180
Federated Ironworkers' Association 40, 157, 218, 286, 600
Federated Storemen and Packers' Union 216, 218, 355, 600
Federation of Industrial, Manufacturing and Engineering Employees 600
Fells, R.E. 143, 258, 259
fines 50, 85, 102, 115, 117, 289, 388, 461, 489, 490, 512
Fisher, C. 181, 182, 184, 185, 193
Fitzgibbon, C. 478
Flanders, Allan 23–24, 31, 256, 262, 263, 331, 585, 588, 589–599, 609
Food Preservers' Union 157, 188

Ford, G.W. 291
Fox, A. 31, 41, 243, 244, 245, 258, 281, 327
Fox, C. 86
Fraser government 218, 223, 490, 492, 511, 525
Future Strategies for the Trade Union Movement 185

Gahan, P. 301
Gallagher, Norm 142
Gardner, M. 131, 132, 133, 136, 150, 151, 156–157, 182, 286, 299, 604
General Motors Holden 521–522
Gilmore, P. 166–167, 309
Gladstone, A. 322, 330–331, 333, 334, 340, 341, 343, 344
Goodman, G. 258
Gospel, H. 259, 260
government
    and employer associations 342–343, 344
    behaviour 30
    and collective bargaining 544–545
    and enterprise bargaining 385, 426, 521, 573, 583, 619–621, 630
    intervention 492
    policy 152, 153, 158, 159, 342, 372, 478, 523–524, 525, 532, 534, 567, 630
    powers 477, 478
    role 16
    and unions 19, 19–20, 22, 50, 53, 117, 132, 134–135, 139, 153, 154, 157–159, 183, 190–3, 206, 210, 215–230, 251, 482, 490, 523, 554
    reform 490
grievance procedures 334, 335, 413, 568–572

Hagan, J. 150, 182
Halfpenny, John 603, 625
Hancock Report 477–478
Hamersley Iron Pty Ltd 292, 293–296
Harbison, F.H. 42, 43
Hawke, Bob 490
Hawke government 224, 225, 482, 491, 492, 501, 511, 514
Hayman, R. 43
health and safety issues 76, 77, 334, 343, 379
    see also occupational health and safety
Health Services Union of Australia 37
Higgins, Henry Bourne 140, 370, 373
High Court
    Aberdeen case 381
    Australian Iron & Steel Pty Ltd v Banovic case 462
    Australian Social Welfare Union case 377, 378, 476, 494
    Re Bain; Ex parte Cadbury Schweppes 383
    Beaudesert Shire Council v Smith 106
    Boilermakers' case 374, 479
    Chugg v Pacific Dunlop Pty Ltd 456
    constitutional decisions 476
    Re Cram; ex parte New South Wales Colliery Proprietors' Association 448
    Downey v Trans Waste Pty Ltd 435
    Re Finance Sector Union case 382
    and industrial disputes 375–383, 389, 476
    Jumbunna Coal Mine No Liability v Victorian Coal Miners' Association 376, 377, 392
    re Lee; Ex parte Harper 378
    Municipalities case 377
    Professional Engineers' case 377
    R v Gough; Ex parte BP Refinery Pty Ltd 381
    R v Hamilton Knight; Ex parte The Commonwealth Steamship Owners' Association 448
    State Public Service Federation case 378, 383
    State School Teachers case 377
    Whybrow's case 382
hours of work 15, 55, 56, 76, 130, 289, 356, 475, 497
Howard, W.A. 67, 76, 145, 584, 586, 588, 599, 601, 602, 603, 604
Hughes government 475
human resource management 2, 30, 41, 250, 269, 283, 296–298, 304, 485
Human Rights and Equal Opportunity Commission Act 1986 (Cth) 462
Hutson, J. 81
Hyman, R. 43, 44, 45, 46, 126, 127, 259

ICI Australia 282–284
ideology 19–21, 23, 132, 133–134, 139, 242–245
income distribution 41, 54, 517
industrial
    awards 6, 115, 380
    capitalism 26
    democracy 263, 265–267, 268, 270
    progress 25
industrial action 37, 46–50, 59, 60, 61, 65, 96–118, 153, 282, 437–438, 474
    see also strikes; industrial conflict
Industrial and Employee Relations Act 1994 (SA) 411, 415, 421, 425
industrial conflict
    and absenteeism 64–70
    causes 40–44, 55, 64, 572
    and distribution of revenues 90, 555
    employer-employee 24, 25, 38, 244, 494, 555, 572
    functions 62–64
    and governments 64, 117, 493–495
    and industrial relations 70, 244
    methods for resolving 90, 113, 482
    and political issues 49–50, 85–86
    manifestations 37–40, 46
    measures 50–62

and unions 44–46, 85–86, 90, 113
see also industrial action; conflict; strikes;
  unions
Industrial Court 49, 50, 374
industrial disputes
  defined 376–383, 494
  government intervention 492–493, 554
  interstate 371, 374, 379, 380–381, 387, 390,
    476, 477, 483, 485, 498
  legal procedures 336, 340, 384–385, 413
  negotiation 334, 555–560, 585, 586–587,
    475, 590–593
  resolution 139, 475, 512
    Commonwealth 369–370, 373–374,
      376–383, 390, 438–439, 476, 482–496,
      497
    state 369, 370, 380, 382, 411–440
  see also Associated Pulp and Paper Mills
    (APPM) dispute; air pilot's dispute;
    demarcation disputes;
    disputes; High Court; Mudginberri
    dispute; strikes; unions
Industrial Peace Act 1920 (Cth) 475
industrial relations
  alternative approaches 23–31, 256–259,
    573
  analysis 4, 10, 30–31, 251–252
  Australia 23, 31, 100, 101–102, 104, 106,
    107, 303–305, 474–475, 479, 492, 501, 543,
    573, 574, 578, 583, 630–631
  balances 17
  Britain 23, 100, 101–102, 241, 256–258, 262,
    312, 589–599
  Canada 48, 562, 568
  defined 2
  deregulation 107, 411, 429–438
  development 9
  and economic strategies 15
  floor of rights 372, 445, 496–498, 517
  institutions 9
  law 6, 7, 16, 97–99, 101–107, 369–374, 477
  legal framework 288, 292, 304, 358, 371,
    376, 411–440, 445, 475, 476, 478, 583
  methodology 130–131
  New Deal legislation 20, 251
  New South Wales 411–414, 421, 421, 423,
    428, 455, 462, 463, 465, 466
  New Zealand 370
  pluralist approach 31, 43, 54, 243–245, 246,
    278, 280, 327, 347, 586
  policy 327–329, 583
  process 23, 28, 113, 393, 477, 545, 551,
    555–560
  Queensland 282, 417–418, 421, 422, 462
  radical approach 31, 278
  reform 280–281, 344, 478, 496, 514, 532
  regulation 342, 371, 373–374, 390, 411–440,
    482
  South Australia 415–416, 421, 423, 425,
    426, 462, 463
  Tasmania 416–417, 422, 426
  theories 14, 24, 28, 31, 125, 250–252,
    263–270
  and unions 2, 4, 125, 153, 180, 183,
    191–192, 250, 251, 278–282, 512, 566
  United States 20, 23, 29, 31, 48, 241,
    249–252, 254, 303–305, 312, 346, 479,
    526–527, 554, 562, 568
  unitary approach 41, 243, 244, 245, 246,
    278, 279, 280, 281, 282, 314, 347, 585
  Victoria 421, 422, 423, 426, 428, 429–438,
    453–455, 462, 494–495
  Western Australia 418–420, 423, 426,
    427–428, 462
  workplace safety 446–447
  see also change; economics; management;
    society
Industrial Relations Amendment Act 1993 (WA)
  420
Industrial Relations Amendment Act (No.2)
  1992 438
Industrial Relations Amendment Bill 226
Industrial Relations Act 1988 (Cth)
  and the Accord 534
  amendments 374, 379, 380, 501
  and arbitration 374, 375, 384
  bans clause 115
  breach of contract 101, 103
  certified agreements 385, 388, 532, 563,
    564, 570
  and conciliation 384, 484, 485
  equal pay for equal work 514
  employment termination 445
  enforcement procedures 388, 489, 491
  enterprise agreements 388, 623
  equality 459
  federal/state law inconsistency 439
  and government intervention 492
  and Hancock Report 478
  health and safety 447
  industrial action 47, 101, 103, 107, 115, 447
  industrial disputes 378, 415, 439
  industrial torts 107
  operative 374, 477
  public servants 373
  secondary boycotts 47, 99, 108, 114, 371,
    553
  statutory offences 117
  territories power 373
  and Trade Practices Act 113, 114
  strikes 98
  unfair dismissal 461
  union
    amalgamation 191, 225
    corporate status 101, 391, 422
    deregistration 116

elections 220, 375
employee representation 304
finance 220
government 219
objects 146, 191
registration 228, 391, 422
Industrial Relations Act 1991 (NSW) 115, 411, 413, 414, 421, 429
Industrial Relations Act 1990 (Qld) 107, 411, 417, 421
Industrial Relations Act 1972 (SA) 107, 421, 425
Industrial Relations Act 1984 (Tas) 411, 416, 422
Industrial Relations Act 1979 (Vic) 429, 430, 433, 435
Industrial Relations Act 1979 (WA) 411, 418, 420, 422, 423, 427
Industrial Relations Commission *see* Australian Industrial Relations Commission
Industrial Relations Commission of New South Wales 413–414
Industrial Relations Commission of South Australia 415
Industrial Relations Court of Australia 375, 379, 380, 388
see also Australian Industrial Relations Court
Industrial Relations Court of South Australia 416
Industrial Relations Reform Act 1993 (Cth) 47, 101, 107, 108, 114, 117, 192, 228, 372, 374, 386, 387, 420, 445, 459, 461, 474, 475, 481, 500, 511, 532, 575–578, 623–624
Industrial Relations Reform Act 1994 (Qld) 418
industrial relations system
   actors 14, 15–16, 250–251
   centralised 499–500, 523
   components 14
   environmental contexts 16–19, 23
   ideology 19–21, 23, 242–245
   theory 249, 251–252
   web of rules 15, 16, 18, 21–22, 23, 24
Industrial Relations Systems 14, 28
Industrial Safety, Health and Welfare Act 1977 (Tas) 453
industrial tribunals 44, 49, 50, 93, 139–140, 209, 210, 240, 260, 314, 446
   and employer associations 325, 332, 333, 351
   federal 47, 81, 85, 151, 153, 170, 181, 290, 305, 306, 369, 438–439, 476, 477, 512, 630
   policy 53, 56, 152, 630
   processes 548
   state 306, 369, 420–422, 438–439, 512, 514
   see also wages
Industrial Workers of the World 182

industrialisation 5
industrialism 6, 9
inflation 15, 22, 511, 523, 524, 533
International Labour Office 52
International Labour Organisation 225, 228, 372, 421, 459, 460, 474
International Typographical Union 128, 150
International Workers of the World (IWW) 20
intimidation 104–105
Isaac, J.E. 487

jobs see employment
jurisdiction
   Australian Industrial Relations Commission 374, 376, 390, 477, 483, 487, 494, 496–497, 498, 514
   federal 152, 199, 332, 379, 388, 411–422, 374, 375, 379, 447–448, 201, 342, 464, 474, 476, 479, 483, 486, 494, 511, 575, 630
   state 152, 332, 463, 464, 474, 476, 494, 512
Just-In-Time 290, 291

Katz, H.C. 3, 20, 28–31, 249–254, 259, 260, 261, 262, 269, 278, 283, 292, 304, 312
Keating government 224, 344, 514, 575
Kelty, Bill 185, 224, 535
Kennett government 50
Kerr, C. 37, 42, 43
Kitay, J. 83, 85
Kochan, T. 2, 3, 20, 28–31, 249–254, 259, 260, 261, 262, 269, 278, 283, 292, 293, 304, 312
Korpi, W. 136
Kuhn, J.W. 546, 547, 548, 599

Labor and Monopoly Capital 25
Labor governments 19, 194
labour
   division 26–27
   and management 3, 25, 238–242, 260, 288, 289, 305, 494
   power 25, 26, 42, 43, 240–241, 289
   process 25–26, 27, 42, 240–242, 285, 299
   relations 2, 6
   subcontracting 240–241, 260
   see also employer, management
labour electoral leagues 139
labour movement
   Australian 142, 143, 152, 182
   defined by Perlman 127–129
Laidely, Leon 47
Lane, William 139
Lansbury, R.D. 166–167, 309, 311–312
Latham v Singleton 104
Latrobe Valley strike (1977) 156
law
   common 6, 8, 91, 93, 98, 99, 100, 107, 118, 388, 465, 490

of contract 98, 100, 389, 494
  and the right to strike 97–99, 118
  tort 98, 99, 108, 437
    causing loss by unlawful means 106
    civil conspiracy 105–106
    and contractual relations 102–103
    interference with trade 104
    intimidation 104–105
    justification 106
    liability 101–102, 393
    merits of the dispute 107
  see also industrial relations, law
law, federal labour 16, 98, 99, 101, 118
  Constitutional power 369–371, 387, 476, 478
  corporations power 371–372, 387–388
  defence power 372
  external affairs power 372
  'incidentals' power 373
  institutions 374–376, 496–498
  public service 372–373
  regulating industrial relations 373–374, 474
  Territories power 373
  trade and commerce power 371
  see also agreements; arbitration; Australian Industrial Relations Commission; awards; conciliation; High Court
Lee, M. 57
legislation 99, 306, 329, 334, 342, 344, 347, 350
  and collective bargaining 152, 389–390, 411, 426, 575–578
  discrimination 334, 461–468
  Essential Services 117
  federal 132, 139, 141, 152, 219, 369, 372, 373, 374, 390, 438–439, 445, 449, 461–468, 474–475, 476, 478, 534, 535, 620, 630
  and industrial action 117, 139, 282, 474
  New Deal 20, 251
  and safety standards 451–456
  secondary boycott 108
  state 152, 282, 369, 411–440, 445, 449, 461–468, 476, 494
  trade practices 113
  and union government 219
  and union recognition 139, 141
  and union regulation 86, 130, 132, 139–142, 150, 153, 161, 181, 183, 190–193, 211, 215–230, 250–251, 282, 288, 304, 373, 478, 482
  see also Industrial Relations Acts
Lenin, Vladimir 126, 127, 565, 566
Levine, S. 189
Lewin, D. 31, 238–240, 249, 253–254, 585
Liberal-National government 183, 184, 342, 490, 525
liberalism 134–135
Lindblom, C. 131

Littler, C. 28, 258
lock-outs 37, 38–39, 40, 46, 50, 545
Lozovsky, A. 126, 536
Lumley, R 310–311

McCallum, R. 222
McDonald, D. 305
McKersie, R.B. 3, 20, 28–31, 249–254, 259, 269, 278, 283, 292, 304 312, 555, 556, 557, 558, 583
McMahon government 523
management
  attitudes 246
  behaviour 24, 31, 246, 254, 268, 285
  capitalist 241
  and collective bargaining 593
  collectivism 246–248, 281, 282–287, 285, 314, 327, 329, 347
  and employee participation 263–269, 270, 282, 290, 305–312
  functions 238–245, 585
  goals 30–31
  ideologies 242–245, 278–282
  individualism 246–248, 281, 282–287, 285, 292, 314, 327
  and industrial relations 30, 31, 238, 244, 249–263, 278–303, 312–314, 569–572, 599–604
  internal hierarchies 260, 288, 294
  joint consultation processes 311–312, 313, 586
  and labour 3, 26, 27, 29, 30, 238, 246, 260–263, 285, 288, 289
  legitimacy 44
  negotiation 585–586, 590–593, 599–604
  objectives 238, 292
  practices 246
  prerogatives 238–240, 244, 248, 285, 305–309, 379, 494, 497
  and productivity bargaining 586–599
  strategies 238, 248, 249–259, 269–270, 285, 287–292, 597
  structures 246, 259–263, 301–303
  style 245–249, 282–287, 292
  three-tier framework 250, 251–252, 269, 270, 283, 292
  two-tier employment relationship 292
  union relations 3, 28–30, 31, 149–150, 204, 206, 214, 239, 243, 246, 253–254, 281–282, 288–292, 311–312, 313, 551–552, 585–586, 590, 599–604
  see also employer; workplace
managerial control 43, 44, 54, 251, 268, 305–9
managerial policy 250
  analysis 2, 248
  and employees 30, 246, 248
manufacturing industry policy 153
market environment 18

Martin, R.M. 49, 50, 85, 225
Marx, Karl 24, 31, 42, 125, 126, 127, 144, 160, 536, 565
Marxist
   analysis 28
   approach to conflict 42, 43, 54
   and exploitation 43
maternity leave 460
Mayo, Elton 41
Meat and Allied Trades Federation of Australia 83, 85
Menzies government 217
metal and engineering industry 287–292, 335–340
Metals and Engineering Workers' Union (MEWU) 146, 147–148, 155–156, 167–168, 179, 604
Metal Industry Award 81, 289, 335, 336, 390, 391, 514, 559, 604, 616
Metal Trades Employer Association 81
Metal Trades Federation of Unions 340
Metal Trade Industry Association 83, 329, 336, 337–339, 356, 559, 621
Metal Trades Work Value Case (1967-1968) 81–83, 84, 93, 356, 382, 555, 559, 614
Michels, R. 127, 209, 210
Miners' Federation 147, 157, 182
Minimum Conditions of Employment Act 1993 (WA) 411, 420, 427, 428
Mining industry 292–296
Mintzberg, H. 288
Mitchel, W.F. 535
Monk, Albert 224
'*Moyle v Doyle* problem' 423–425, 437
Mt. Newman Mining Ltd 292, 293
Mudginberri dispute (1985) 83–86, 93, 108, 110–112, 113, 485, 490, 492, 553
Murray, R. 286
Myers, C.A. 42, 43

National Civic Council 143
National Farmers Federation 83, 85, 342, 351
National Labour Consultative Council 342
National Union of Workers 193, 600
National Wage case *see* Australian Industrial Relations Commission; wages
negotiation
   agreements 461, 475, 485, 486–487, 590–593, 620
   and collective bargaining 390, 545, 551, 555–558, 559, 575
   and industrial disputes 334, 390, 475, 555–560, 585, 586–587
   union-management 585–586, 590–593
   and women 461
New South Wales Industrial Court 414
Niland, J. 278, 545, 558, 559

Nurses (Victorian Health Services) award 1992 380, 398–409, 617
nurses' strike *see* Victorian nurses' strike

occupational health and safety 343, 445, 446–456, 468
   see also health and safety issues
Occupational Health and Safety Act 1989 (ACT) 453
Occupational Health and Safety (Commonwealth Employment) Act 1991 (Cth) 453
Occupational Health and Safety Act 1983 (NSW) 453
Occupational Health and Safety Act 1986 (SA) 453
Occupational Health and Safety Act 1985 (Vic) 451, 453, 454
Occupational Health, Safety and Welfare Act 1984 (WA) 453
Oil Industry Industrial Committee 332, 347, 599
oligarchy 127, 209, 353
One Big Union 142, 181, 182
O'Neil W.S. (Shorty) 223
Optus Communications 296–298, 485
O'Shea, 'Clarrie' 50

Palmer, G. 134
parental leave 69, 372, 430, 460
Parsons, Talcott 14, 15
Pateman, C. 266
Peko Wallsend 292, 293
Perlman, Selig 29, 127–129, 136, 143, 144, 150, 160, 565–566, 586
Petroleum Refiners Australia 599
picketing 38, 39, 83, 85, 86, 110, 114
Pilkington 44
Plowman, D. 322, 325, 347, 348, 349, 351
political system 18
Polites, G. 478
Powe, R. 83, 85
power
   context 18, 53, 161, 194, 292, 305, 358
   and conflict 43, 54, 244, 545
   power 25, 26, 42, 43, 240–241, 289
   see also bargaining; employer; labour
Price, R. 172
Prices and Incomes Accord 53, 56, 152–153, 154, 159, 491, 499, 511, 513, 516, 519, 526–538, 554, 560, 561, 565, 574
Prices Surveillance Authority 153
production
   capitalist method 26, 27
   and control 44
   and labour 27
   losses 66
   methods 17, 54, 180, 288, 292, 586

productivity agreement 532, 584, 587, 588, 593–594, 598, 599
productivity bargaining 91, 245, 256, 258, 532, 583
  characteristics 584–586
  conditions 586–588
  and enterprise bargaining 589–599
  model 621, 624–630
  and unions 603–604
  wages policy 604–605, 621, 624–630
productivity
  and enterprise bargaining 583–584
  and wages 521–523
profit-sharing schemes 42
public policy (environment) 307, 314
public servants, federal 49, 372–373
Public Service Act 1992 (Cth) 373
Purcell, J. 3, 245, 246, 247, 248, 255, 256, 258, 269, 281, 282, 283, 285, 286, 292, 311, 327

Qantas 311–312, 313
Queensland Industrial Relations Commission 417–419
Quinlan, M. 284–287, 312

Racial Discrimination Act 1975 (Cth) 372, 384, 462
Rawson, D. 140, 143, 145, 153, 155, 175, 218
redundancy 256, 462, 468
referendums 477
Reilly, S. 628
Restructuring and Efficiency Principle 56, 290, 606–611, 625, 626, 627, 628
Riach, P.A. 584, 586, 588, 599, 601, 602, 603, 604
Richardo, David 25
Richbell, S. 258
Rimmer, M. 150, 610
Robe River Iron Associates 292, 293
Robens, Lord 453
Romeyn, J. 487, 488
Ross, Arthur 29, 544
Royal Commissions
  Alleged Payments to Maritime Unions 218
  Trade Unions and Employer Associations (Britain) 256

sanctions 50, 99, 102, 113, 114, 115–117, 289, 393, 488–489, 490, 491–492, 512, 522, 524, 526
Seamen's Union 144, 188, 599
secondary boycotts 46–47, 54, 83, 85, 86, 99, 108–115, 156, 344, 371, 553
security, employee 42, 43, 54, 307, 460, 497, 586, 603

Sex Discrimination Act 1984 (Cth) 372, 384, 462, 465
sexual harassment 465, 467
Sharpley, J.G. 515, 516
shearers
  strike (1891) 37, 139, 156
Shearers Union 139
  unionisation of Australian 17
Sheldon, P. 150
Shister, J. 170, 171, 172, 175, 194
Singleton, G. 153, 535
small business survey 298–301
Smith, G. 90, 91, 92
social sub-systems 14–15
social welfare policy 153
society and industrial relations 5, 6, 17, 23, 44, 133–134, 143–146, 161
South East Queensland Electricity Board (SEQEB) 282
Spence, W.G. 139
stand-downs 116, 183
statutory offences 117
staffing levels 43, 260, 379
State Electricity Commission of Victoria (SECV) 50
steel industry 284–287
stop-work meetings 48, 53, 58, 91
Strauss, G. 252, 269
strikes 37, 38–39, 44, 47–48, 138–140, 156, 214, 355, 370, 476, 482
  Britain 129
  Broken Hill (1919-1920) 76–81, 93, 555
  causes 54–55, 482
  costs 64–70, 86, 93, 547, 552, 553
  duration 53
  employee involvement 52, 97, 98, 100, 102, 105, 107, 118
  incidence 52
  Latrobe Valley (1977) 156
  legal sanctions against 50, 289, 488–489, 490–492, 512
  method of settlement 58, 370
  pay 553
  political 49–50, 54, 56, 81, 85, 97, 144
  right to strike 50, 82, 97–99, 100, 107, 118, 474, 545, 546, 567–568
  shearers (1891) 37, 139, 156
  statistics
    Australian 50–58, 61, 86, 87, 89, 90–91, 482
    international comparisons 60–62, 63
  'trial of strength' 47, 76, 92, 139, 548
  trend of causes 56
  Victorian nurses' 40, 86–90, 93, 152, 157, 548, 549–550, 556, 557, 558, 559, 628
  working days lost 52, 54, 55, 56–57, 61, 63, 65, 82

see also fines; industrial action; industrial disputes; Victorian nurses' strike
Structural Efficiency Principle 48, 56, 91, 611–617
Summers, C. 207
superannuation 56
supervisors *see* worker, supervisor relations
Swain, P. 292–296, 312, 313, 314

Tasmanian Industrial Commission 416, 417
taxation, income 153
Taylor, F.W. 241, 242
Taylor, V. 28
Teachers Federation of Victoria 48
technological
   change 45
   development 16–17
Teicher, J. 265–267
Telecom 311–312, 313
Thurley, K. and Wood, S. 259, 285
Timperley, S.T. 256
tort *see* law, tort
Total Quality Control 290
Trade Practices Act 1974 (Cth) 47, 83, 98, 99, 108–115, 114, 371, 490, 553
trade unions *see* unions
Transport Workers' Union 193, 218, 423–425
tribunals 3, 16, 31, 40, 44, 48, 49, 50, 56, 81, 139–140, 141, 142, 334
   and economic policy 511
   unlawful discrimination 463
   see also arbitration; industrial
Turner, D. 278

unfair dismissal 336, 372, 379, 388–389, 420–422, 435, 460–461, 465
union
   action 133
   amalgamations 146, 161, 179–180, 181–193, 183–195, 199–201, 215, 224–230, 536
   autonomy 155
   behaviour 3, 29, 45, 46, 48, 131, 133, 156, 161, 180, 194, 292, 604
   contemporary 157–160
   internal 142
   conciliation and arbitration 475, 488–489, 512, 522, 536, 554
   coverage 191, 193
   democracy 154, 203–230
   density 170, 172–176, 187, 194, 340, 536
   deregistration 116–117, 216, 393, 491
   elections 209, 213, 218–219, 220, 221–224, 375
   goals 30, 31, 130, 133, 137, 205, 212, 551
   growth 170–172
   ideology 132–133, 142, 143, 181, 182
   leadership 135, 136–137, 154, 170, 172, 205–215, 230, 604
   membership 2, 4, 28–29, 128, 133, 134, 137, 138, 145–150, 155, 161, 171, 172–176, 177, 188–189, 192, 193, 204–210, 214, 216, 226, 228–230, 375, 604
   objectives 4, 135, 142–150, 157, 161
   officials 40–41, 45, 117, 142, 143, 144, 204, 205, 213, 282
   operation 3
   peak councils 156, 170, 182
   purpose and development 125–131
   rationalisation 189–190, 193, 219, 224–230
   recognition 139, 141
   registration 141, 150, 177, 191, 192, 219, 220, 228, 373, 391–393, 436–437
   dual 422–426
   secret ballots 217–218, 438
   security 149–150
   shop stewards 204, 286
   staff appointments 229
   strategies 131–136, 150–157, 161, 182, 187, 189, 604
   wealth 220
   see also Australian Labor Party; *Conciliation and Arbitration Act* 1904; *Industrial Relations Act* 1988; legislation; management
unionism
   Australia 44, 137–160, 159, 160, 161, 177, 179, 181–195, 194, 306, 476, 478, 489, 554, 565–568
   Britain 44, 46, 126, 127, 129, 137, 138, 139, 177, 206
   Canada 128, 137, 282
   closed shop 128, 148, 149, 345, 491
   compulsory 148, 149, 204, 379
   creation 5, 137–141, 160
   decline 170, 172–176, 187, 194, 249, 250
   enterprise 23
   Federal Republic of Germany 23, 127, 129, 189, 207
   Japan 189
   Soviet Union 127, 159–160
   theories 125–136, 160, 170
   United States 20, 28–29, 127, 128, 129, 137, 139, 206, 207, 215, 216, 221, 229, 250, 303
unions
   craft 132, 150, 177, 179, 180, 182, 183, 191
   bargaining power of unions 130, 140, 142, 150–151, 155, 171, 180, 206, 290, 501, 511, 514, 524, 536, 546–558, 560–564, 599–604
   and employers 132, 140–141, 151, 204, 281–282, 468
   enterprise 179, 183, 191
   exclusive representation rights 86, 150, 191, 192, 251

freedom of speech 216
general 177, 179, 180
industrial 177–179, 180, 181–182, 183–189, 191, 194
and industrial conflict 44–46, 54, 85–86, 90, 93, 101, 102–103, 104, 108–115, 282, 488–489
inter-union
  alliances 133, 476
  co-operation 156–157
  disputes 54, 150, 156, 180, 189, 193, 216, 224, 286, 294, 423–426
internal government 154, 203, 204, 206, 215–230
legal status 101, 139, 141, 373, 391, 393, 422–426, 437
legislative regulation 86, 130, 132, 139–142, 150, 153, 161, 181, 183, 190–193, 211, 215–230, 250–251, 282, 288, 304, 373, 478, 482
and policy implementation 131–132
political involvement 132, 139, 142–144, 145, 153–154, 158–159, 161, 182, 203, 210, 212, 491, 501, 536, 565, 566
in the workplace 4, 19, 20, 145, 149–150, 180, 204–205, 224–225, 281–282, 286, 289, 292, 304, 306, 311, 468, 522, 533, 565, 588, 603
see also employment; government; industrial relations; management; wage levels
United Mineworkers' Union 216–217, 221

Vaughan, E.J. 263–265, 268, 270, 309
Vehicle Builders Federation 521
Victorian Coal Miners' Association 376
Victorian Employers' Chamber of Commerce and Industry 328, 342, 344, 348, 354
Victorian Employers' Federation 343
Victorian Industrial Relations Commission 48, 429, 439
Victorian nurses' strike 40, 86–90, 93, 152, 157, 548, 549–550, 556, 557, 558, 559, 628
Viner, Ian 183
Vital Industries Act 1992 (Vic) 117, 137
Volard, S. 66, 67, 68

wage
  bargaining 29, 130, 151, 289, 499–500, 514
  basic 151, 517–518
  cases 41, 83, 90, 159, 307, 459, 516–517
  comparative 522
  fixing 91, 153, 329, 390, 475, 500, 534, 606, 617
  indexation 491, 512, 513, 514, 523–526, 606
  levels 4, 153, 477, 499, 518–519, 521
  and living costs 41, 53, 210, 517, 523
  maintenance 153
  margin adjustments 517–518
  national wage 159, 307, 331, 333, 369, 390–391, 477, 487, 491, 492, 500, 516–517, 518, 521, 522, 523, 528, 534, 563, 564, 570, 624
  policy 22, 48, 53, 91, 153, 158, 211, 478, 511–514, 518, 519, 523–524, 526, 535, 536, 538
    and enterprise bargaining 604–624
    federal tribunal 53, 81, 156, 170, 306, 548, 556, 604–611
    and productivity bargaining 604–605, 621, 624–630
  rates 81–82, 497, 498–499, 511–514, 517, 518, 523
  Total Wage 518, 519, 523
  work value 487, 518–521
  see also arbitration; Australian Industrial Relations Commission; Metal Trades Work Value case; Prices and Incomes Accord
Wage Fixing Principles 617
wages
  and the Accord 156, 158, 491, 499–500
  award 81–82, 516–517, 521, 523, 535
  equal 372, 459–460, 514–516
  flow-on 588, 613
  minimum 372, 391, 459, 474, 496, 511, 512, 513, 519
  over-award payments 389, 474, 497, 512, 513, 515, 516, 522
  and productivity 521–523
  share 41–42
Walker, K.F. 23, 28, 31
Walton, R.E. 555, 556, 557, 558, 583
Wang, K.K. 266
Waterside Workers' Federation 144, 156, 157, 188
Webb, Beatrice and Sidney 130–131
White, K. 286
Whitlam government 219, 477, 490, 523
Wielgosz, J.B. 220
Willis, Ralph 191
Windmuller, J.P. 322, 323, 326, 327, 344, 345, 346, 352, 353
women
  affirmative action 465–468
  agreement negotiation 461
  discrimination against 459–460, 461, 462, 464, 465–468
  maternity leave 460
  union representation 146, 227, 228
  wages 459–460, 514–516
work
  bans 48, 50, 91
  conditions 15, 130, 145, 475

days lost 52, 54, 55, 56–57, 61, 63, 65, 82
hours 15, 55, 56, 76, 130, 289, 356, 475, 497
patterns 613–614
practices 44, 584–586, 588, 600, 624, 626, 628
workcare 343
worker
  behaviour 24, 41
  control 26, 27, 28, 43, 44
  participation 266–267
  subordination 43
  supervisor relations 4, 15, 41, 251
workers'
  compensation 6
  representatives 16
Workers Industrial Union of Australia 142, 147, 182
working class 9, 143, 144, 160, 171
workplace
  activities 4
  agreements 420, 427–428, 620, 623
  bargaining 290, 427, 500, 568–572, 573, 575
  culture 24
  discrimination 461–468
  equity 456–459, 461, 468
  government 15, 23, 31
  labour–management co-operation 249
  problems 4
  rules 14, 15, 16, 18, 19, 20, 21–22, 23, 24, 28, 31, 62, 64, 69, 145, 147, 151, 224, 251, 286, 293, 299, 445, 487, 494, 495, 496, 500, 501, 543, 558, 577, 578, 585
  safety standards 451–456, 468
  survey 59–60, 66, 67, 69, 149, 225, 301–303
  see also unions
Workplace Agreements Act 1993 (WA) 411, 420, 426
Workplace Health and Safety Act 1989 (Qld) 453

Zappala, G. 149, 610